W9-CUE-384

FOUR EASY STEPS TO
WINNING WORD COMBINATIONS:

Alphabetize the letters you want to make into a word.

Count the letters and turn to the appropriate world-length section in this dictionary.

Match your alphabetized letters against an alphabetized sequence in the dictionary. Under the matching sequence you will find the word or words that may be spelled with your letters.

If there is at least one "S" among your letters, there is another step you can take to check for possible word combinations. Simply eliminate one "S" and then look up this shorter letter combination. If the words you find listed are nouns or verbs which take a simple "S" ending, they will be valid solutions for your letter combination. For all other endings, such as "ES, IES, ED," etc., this step is unnecessary, as these combinations are listed under their own alphabetized sequence of letters.

With the over 50,000 two-to-twelve-letter words included in this book, you'll be able to get out of tough spots, make sure every turn counts, leave no puzzle unfinished, and become a number-one word game champion. So pick your letters and team up with

BRUCE WETTERAU is a writer and former newspaper reporter. As a member of The Hudson Group, a cooperative organization of authors, he plays an active role in developing reference book projects.

Recommended SIGNET Books

☐ **THE SIGNET CROSSWORD PUZZLE BOOK #1 edited by Charles Preston.** Take on the fun-filled challenge of these 62 brand-new word teasers created by 16 of the nation's top puzzle experts. From current events to ancient lore, there are clues and quips to test everyone's knowledge.
(#W9079—$1.50)

☐ **THE SIGNET CROSSWORD PUZZLE BOOK #2 edited by Charles Preston.** Great new word challenges to test your puzzling powers! From cooking to geography, you'll find a vast array of subjects to tackle and mysteries to solve.
(#W9174—$1.50)

☐ **NEW AMERICAN CROSSWORD PUZZLE DICTIONARY edited by Albert H. Morehead and Loy Morehead.** An indispensable aid for the crossword puzzle solver—concentrates on the unusual word, the word most likely to appear in puzzles. The most comprehensive, easy-to-use dictionary of its kind.
(#E9152—$2.25)

☐ **THE NEW AMERICAN WEBSTER HANDY COLLEGE DICTIONARY edited by Albert and Loy Morehead.** An easy-to-use dictionary, with more than 100,000 clear definitions of useful words; illustrated.
(#W8790—$1.50)

☐ **THE NEW AMERICAN ROGET'S COLLEGE THESAURUS IN DICTIONARY FORM edited by Albert Morehead.** Newly revised and expanded. In alphabetical order, this thesaurus includes the latest colloquialisms and foreign words and phrases as well as synonyms and antonyms which are normally featured in this indispensable reference tool.
(#J9335—$1.95)

Buy them at your local bookstore or use this convenient coupon for ordering.

THE NEW AMERICAN LIBRARY, INC.,
P.O. Box 999, Bergenfield, New Jersey 07621

Please send me the SIGNET BOOKS I have checked above. I am enclosing
$_____ (please add 50¢ to this order to cover postage and handling).
Send check or money order—no cash or C.O.D.'s. Prices and numbers are subject to change without notice.

Name_____

Address_____

City_____ State_____ Zip Code_____

Allow 4-6 weeks for delivery.
This offer is subject to withdrawal without notice.

THE WORD GAME WINNING DICTIONARY

BY BRUCE WETTERAU

A HUDSON GROUP BOOK

A SIGNET BOOK
NEW AMERICAN LIBRARY
TIMES MIRROR

NAL Books are available at quantity discounts when used to promote products or services. For information please write to Premium Marketing Division, The New American Library, Inc., 1633 Broadway, New York, New York 10019.

Copyright © 1980 by Bruce Wetterau

All rights reserved

Library of Congress Catalog Card Number: 79-90460

SIGNET TRADEMARK REG. U.S. PAT. OFF. AND FOREIGN COUNTRIES
REGISTERED TRADEMARK—MARCA REGISTRADA
HECHO EN CHICAGO, U.S.A.

SIGNET, SIGNET CLASSICS, MENTOR, PLUME, MERIDIAN
AND NAL BOOKS
are published by The New American Library, Inc.,
1633 Broadway, New York, New York 10019

First Printing, May, 1979

1   2   3   4   5   6   7   8   9

PRINTED IN THE UNITED STATES OF AMERICA

CONTENTS

ACKNOWLEDGMENTS

I would like to thank the free-lancers who helped bring this book along so quickly from a promising idea to an accomplished fact. In compiling and checking the basic word list Donna Bevona, Frank Brady, Lilian Brady, Joan Cohen, Ray Hand, Jr., and Ruth Van Liew proved to be invaluable. Mary Egner, as able a typist as can be found, keyboarded the basic word list single-handedly. Finally, I want to thank all my good friends at The Hudson Group, especially Gorton Carruth and Gene Hawes, for the advice and encouragement they gave during every phase of producing this book.

Bruce Wetterau

INTRODUCTION

The *Word Game Winning Dictionary* turns jumbled letters into the words you need to win any scrambled-letter puzzle or game. It doesn't matter how you get the letters themselves: they can appear on game tiles, letter cubes, special game cards, a printed puzzle, a contest entry blank, or a scrap of paper. Nor does it matter whether you want the game letters to spell one word or as many as possible. Whenever making words from jumbled letters is part of the puzzle or game, this dictionary will help find the answer words.

Just decide which letters are to be made into a word and look them up as described in the front of this book. In a few seconds this dictionary can tell you if the letters form an everyday word such as house or car, or an exotic word such as paxwax, qoph, or crwth. The dictionary can even help you decide which letters to make into a word. It makes finding words that easy.

Without this dictionary, however, unscrambling letters is a completely different matter. It does require skill and a good vocabulary, but there is easily as much drudgery and outright guesswork involved. Whenever you don't happen to see a word in the letters right away, or when a word of a special length or spelling is needed, you have no choice but to use trial and error methods to find it.

Every word game player knows how tedious this process can be. The player always starts out energetically enough. First he picks a short combination, such as TION, EAD, TH, or ARY, from the letters to be made into a word. Next he tries adding the remaining letters to the short combination. He tries them in front of it, in back of it, and in every imaginable order around it until all the possibilities have been exhausted. Then, his enthusiasm only beginning to dampen, he picks another short combination and repeats the process. Again, and again, and again.

This slow, laborious procedure was once the only way to find a word among jumbled letters. If game rules imposed no time limit, a player might try hundreds of combinations until he either found the word or gave up in frustration. And after one or even a hundred attempts, there was no way to tell whether the next try would produce a word or not. In fact, a player could never be certain the letters actually spelled a word until he found one.

The *Word Game Winning Dictionary* eliminates the aggravation and uncertainty. Now there is no need to spend more than a few minutes at juggling letters back and forth. If you cannot find a word quickly on your own, look up the letters in this dictionary and get the answer word without any further trouble. And because this dictionary is so comprehensive it automatically identifies "dead-end" letters, those insidious combinations of letters that will never form a word. If you cannot find a set of letters in this dictionary, then it is unlikely the letters will spell a word you can use in play.

This reliability makes the *Word Game Winning Dictionary* the most important reference for scrambled-letter puzzles and games that you can own. You can use it during play to get the answers you need, when you need them, or as a learning tool to build your vocabulary and word-forming skills. Either way this valuable resource, jam-packed with over 50,000 answer words, is sure to help you win your favorite scrambled-letter puzzles and games.

Here are just some of the ways you can take advantage of this versatile solving dictionary:

—Get out of tough spots. Use it as a last resort to finish off the really stubborn words in scrambled-letter puzzles. Or avoid losing your turn in a game by using it to find a word in a difficult set of letters.

—Improve your score. Many word games assign point values to the letters that make up a word. This dictionary can help you form thousands of words with letters that have high point values.

—Find the combination of letters you need to form a word. Suppose you have drawn eight random game letters, AADEILRS. Together they do not form a word and you decide to make a six-letter word instead (you can usually make a six-letter word from eight random letters). Start by looking up *the first three* letters (AAD) in the Six-Letter Section. Just a few entries begin with AAD, and it is unlikely one will use three of your leftover letters, EILRS. But eliminate the first A and you find hundreds of entries beginning with ADE. Scan them to find one that uses three of your leftover letters. Here ADEILR matches an entry. Remember, look for the common three-letter combination first. It always saves you time and guesswork!

—Find all words the letters spell. When the object is to make not one word but as many as possible from the game

letters, this dictionary helps find words you missed. Use it systematically to check every possible combination of letters or selectively to eliminate "dead-end" combinations.

—Find handy "special" words. In your spare time, look up and memorize especially useful words that have odd spellings or letters with high point values. Or, after the game is over, find out how you could have played a difficult set of letters.

—Find anagrams. Whenever more than one word is listed under an alphabetized sequence of letters in this dictionary, the two (or more) words are anagrams of each other. To find the anagram of a word, simply alphabetize the letters of the word and look them up. If only the word itself is listed, the word has no anagrams. But whenever additional words are listed, each is an anagram.

You will undoubtedly discover other ways to use this dictionary, but one thing is important to remember. In games where several players are involved, all players must agree to allow the dictionary in play. Though game rules do not restrict or even mention the use of a *solving* dictionary, the time to discuss it is before the game begins—not in the middle of play. Then you and your friends can make your own rules on how it will be used. You may want to consult it freely to play a high-powered, high-scoring game. Or perhaps you will refer to it on a restricted basis, with fixed handicap (such as 4 points off the score) for each word formed. Of course, where puzzles and games are designed for one player, the decision to use this dictionary is yours alone.

Though the solving system in the *Word Game Winning Dictionary* greatly simplifies the task of unscrambling letters, it is also important because it gives access to thousands upon thousands of words. Not even the best word game players have vocabularies that equal the 50,000-plus words this dictionary puts at your disposal. Whether you desperately need a word to get out of a tough spot or just want a word to boost your score, you are sure to find one among the 50,000 that serves your purpose.

The dictionary is so comprehensive that you will find words of every description ranging from aardvark, the strange animal usually found at the beginning of alphabets, to zythum, the name for ancient Egyptian beer. There are everyday words such as he, has, gone, fishing; slang expressions such as boonies, bonkers, boffo, and bummer; and contemporary words such as sitcom, skyjacker, stagflation, superstar, and swinger.

In addition there are thousands of esoteric, archaic, and obscure words that will liven up any word game. As you begin to use this dictionary more frequently, you will come across such words as: dhow, an Arabian sailing vessel; estoile, an heraldic star with six wavy points; facula, an unusually bright spot on the sun's surface; fanam, a gold coin of India; funambulist, a tightrope walker; ghat, a mountain pass; and gorget, a piece of armor for the throat.

You will soon discover that this rich diversity of words is both amusing and valuable in play. Because any of the words might turn out to be the one your scrambled letters spell, every word in the dictionary is potentially important. Thus, an oddly spelled, esoteric word may have just the letters you need to get out of a tight spot. You may need a word with two X's, such as paxwax and exlex, or a word with a Q but no U, such as qintar and qoph. Or perhaps it will be one of the rare words with no vowels, such as crwth and shh!

But do not be fooled by strange looking words. Every word in this dictionary, from the most common slang expression to the most obscure noun, is a legitimate English word and can be found in an unabridged dictionary. Though you will have to consult *Webster's Third New International* to verify some of the really obscure words, most can be found in an abridged, collegiate dictionary.

Furthermore, this dictionary contains only those words that are usually eligible in scrambled-letter games. This means you can play any word you can find, because only common nouns and their plurals, verb forms, and various adverbial and adjectival forms have been included. Proper nouns, abbreviations, contractions, hyphenated forms, and foreign words, which are not part of the English language, do not appear in this dictionary because they are generally not acceptable.

One last point. The fact that this dictionary finds only eligible words need not discourage all "challenges," where they are part of a game. For these games players routinely pick one standard English dictionary to settle challenges over the validity of words. If you use a heavily abridged, mass-market paperback dictionary, and allow in play only those words that appear in it, you can keep alive the possibility of a successful challenge. Anytime you find an unfamiliar or obscure word in the *Word Game Winning Dictionary,* you will have to guess whether or not it appears in the "challenge" dictionary (many will not). For these words you must then decide to play it and risk a challenge or try to form a new word using different letters.

2-LETTER WORDS

AB	**BO**	te	xi
ba	bo	**EW**	**JO**
AD	**BU**	we	jo
ad	bu	**EX**	**LO**
AE	**BY**	ex	lo
ea	by	**EY**	**MO**
AF	**CE**	ye	mo
fa	ce	**FI**	om
AH	**DE**	if	**MU**
ah	de	**FO**	mu
ha	**DI**	of	um
AI	id	**GO**	**MY**
ai	**DO**	go	my
AK	do	**HI**	**NO**
ka	od	hi	no
AL	**EE**	**HO**	on
la	ee	ho	**NU**
AM	**EF**	oh	nu
am	ef	**HS**	**OR**
ma	**EH**	sh	or
AN	eh	**IK**	**OS**
an	he	ki	os
na	**EI**	**IL**	so
AP	ei	li	**OT**
pa	**EL**	**IM**	to
AR	el	mi	**OW**
ar	**EM**	**IN**	ow
AS	em	in	**OX**
as	me	**IO**	ox
AT	**EN**	io	**OY**
at	en	**IP**	oy
ta	ne	pi	yo
AW	**EO**	**IR**	**PU**
aw	oe	ri	up
AX	**EP**	**IS**	**SU**
ax	pe	is	us
AY	**ER**	si	**TU**
ay	er	**IT**	ut
ya	re	it	**UX**
BE	**ET**	ti	xu
be	et	**IX**	

3-LETTER WORDS

AAB	cad	dap	fag	gay	**AKS**	tam	pay
aba	**ACE**	pad	**AFK**	**AHH**	ask	**AMW**	pya
baa	ace	**ADR**	kaf	hah	**AKT**	maw	yap
AAG	**ACL**	rad	**AFN**	**AHM**	kat	**AMX**	**APZ**
aga	lac	**ADS**	fan	ham	**AKU**	max	zap
AAH	**ACM**	sad	**AFO**	**AHP**	auk	**AMY**	**AQT**
aha	cam	**ADT**	oaf	hap	**AKW**	may	qat
AAL	mac	tad	**AFR**	pah	awk	yam	**AQU**
ala	**ACN**	**ADW**	arf	**AHR**	**AKY**	**ANP**	qua
AAM	can	wad	far	rah	kay	nap	**ART**
ama	**ACO**	**ADY**	**AFT**	**AHS**	yak	pan	art
AAN	oca	day	aft	ash	**ALL**	**ANR**	rat
ana	**ACP**	**ADZ**	fat	has	all	ran	tar
ABB	cap	adz	**AFX**	sha	**ALM**	nar	**ARW**
abb	**ACR**	**AEG**	fax	**AHT**	lam	**ANT**	raw
ABC	arc	age	**AFY**	hat	mal	ant	war
cab	car	**AEH**	fay	**AHU**	**ALP**	nat	**ARY**
ABD	**ACS**	hae	**AGG**	ahu	alp	tan	ray
bad	sac	**AEK**	gag	**AHW**	lap	**ANV**	rya
dab	**ACT**	ake	**AGH**	haw	pal	van	yar
ABG	act	kea	hag	**AHY**	**ALR**	**ANW**	**ASS**
bag	cat	**AEL**	**AGJ**	hay	lar	awn	ass
gab	**ACV**	ale	jag	yah	**ALS**	wan	**AST**
ABH	vac	lea	**AGL**	**AIL**	sal	**ANY**	sat
bah	**ACW**	**AEM**	gal	ail	**ALT**	any	**ASW**
ABJ	caw	mae	lag	**AIM**	alt	nay	saw
jab	**ACY**	**AEN**	**AGM**	aim	lat	**AOR**	was
ABK	cay	ean	gam	**AIN**	**ALU**	oar	**ASX**
kab	**ADD**	nae	mag	ani	ula	**AOT**	sax
ABL	add	**AEP**	**AGN**	**AIR**	**ALV**	oat	**ASY**
alb	dad	ape	gan	air	lav	**AOV**	say
bal	**ADF**	pea	nag	**AIS**	**ALW**	ova	**ATT**
lab	fad	**AER**	**AGO**	ais	awl	**AOZ**	tat
ABM	**ADG**	are	ago	**AIV**	law	zoa	**ATU**
bam	dag	ear	goa	via	**ALX**	**APP**	uta
ABN	gad	era	**AGP**	**AJM**	lax	pap	**ATV**
ban	**ADH**	**AES**	gap	jam	**ALY**	**APR**	tav
nab	dah	sea	**AGR**	**AJR**	lay	par	vat
ABO	had	**AET**	gar	jar	**AMM**	rap	**ATW**
abo	**ADI**	ate	rag	raj	mam	**APS**	taw
boa	aid	eat	**AGS**	**AJT**	**AMN**	asp	wat
ABP	**ADK**	eta	gas	taj	man	pas	**ATX**
bap	dak	tae	sag	**AJW**	**AMO**	sap	tax
ABR	**ADL**	tea	**AGT**	jaw	moa	spa	**AWW**
bar	lad	**AEU**	gat	**AJY**	**AMP**	**APT**	waw
bra	**ADM**	eau	tag	jay	amp	apt	**AWX**
rab	dam	**AEV**	**AGU**	**AKL**	map	pat	wax
ABT	mad	ave	gau	alk	**AMR**	tap	**AWY**
bat	**ADN**	**AEW**	**AGV**	**AKO**	arm	**APW**	way
tab	and	awe	vag	koa	mar	paw	yaw
ABY	dan	**AEY**	**AGW**	oak	ram	wap	**AXZ**
aby	**ADO**	aye	gaw	oka	**AMT**	**APX**	zax
bay	ado	yea	wag	**AKR**	amt	pax	**BBE**
ACD	**ADP**	**AFG**	**AGY**	ark	mat	**APY**	

ebb	rib	**CEP**	**DEG**	jod	**EEW**	**EHO**	**ELW**
BBI	**BIS**	cep	deg	**DLO**	ewe	hoe	lew
bib	bis	**CET**	**DEI**	dol	wee	**EHP**	**ELX**
BBO	sib	tec	die	old	**EEY**	hep	lex
bob	**BIT**	**CEU**	**DEL**	**DMO**	eye	**EHR**	**ELY**
BBU	bit	cue	eld	dom	**EEZ**	her	ley
bub	**BJO**	ecu	led	mod	zee	**EHS**	lye
BCO	job	**CGO**	**DEN**	**DMU**	**EFF**	she	**EMN**
cob	**BKO**	cog	den	mud	eff	**EHT**	men
BCU	kob	**CHI**	end	**DNO**	**EFI**	eth	**EMR**
cub	**BLO**	chi	**DEO**	don	fie	the	rem
BDE	lob	hic	doe	nod	**EFK**	**EHU**	**EMT**
bed	**BMO**	**CHO**	ode	**DNU**	kef	hue	met
BDI	mob	cho	**DER**	dun	**EFL**	**EHW**	**EMU**
bid	**BMU**	**CIP**	red	**DOP**	elf	hew	emu
BDU	bum	pic	**DET**	pod	**EFN**	**EHX**	**EMW**
bud	**BNO**	**CIS**	ted	**DOR**	fen	hex	mew
dub	bon	sic	**DEU**	dor	nef	**EHY**	**ENO**
BEE	nob	**CIT**	due	rod	**EFO**	hey	eon
bee	**BNU**	cit	**DEV**	**DOS**	foe	**EIL**	one
BEG	bun	tic	dev	sod	**EFR**	lei	**ENP**
beg	nub	**CIY**	**DEW**	**DOT**	erf	lie	nep
BEL	**BNY**	icy	dew	dot	ref	**EIP**	pen
bel	ynb	**CLO**	wed	tod	**EFT**	epi	**ENS**
BEN	**BOO**	col	**DEX**	**DOU**	eft	pie	sen
ben	boo	**CMU**	dex	duo	fet	**EIR**	**ENT**
neb	**BOP**	cum	**DEY**	udo	**EFU**	ire	net
BET	bop	**CNO**	dey	**DOW**	feu	**EIT**	ten
bet	**BOR**	con	dye	dow	**EFW**	tie	**ENW**
BEW	orb	**COO**	**DEZ**	**DOY**	few	**EIV**	new
web	rob	coo	zed	yod	**EFY**	vie	wen
BEY	**BOS**	**COP**	**DFI**	**DRU**	fey	**EJO**	**ENY**
bey	sob	cop	fid	urd	**EFZ**	joe	yen
bye	**BOT**	**COR**	**DGI**	**DRY**	fez	**EJT**	**EOP**
BFI	bot	cor	dig	dry	**EGG**	jet	ope
fib	**BOW**	roc	gid	**DSU**	egg	**EKL**	**EOR**
BFO	bow	**COS**	**DGO**	sud	**EGK**	elk	ore
fob	**BOX**	cos	dog	**DUX**	keg	lek	roe
BFU	box	**COT**	god	dux	**EGL**	**EKN**	**EOT**
fub	**BOY**	cot	**DGU**	**EEF**	gel	ken	toe
BGI	boy	**COW**	dug	fee	leg	**EKO**	**EOV**
big	**BPU**	cow	**DHI**	**EEG**	**EGM**	oke	voe
gib	pub	**COX**	hid	gee	gem	**EKP**	**EOW**
BGO	**BRU**	cox	**DHO**	**EEJ**	**EGN**	kep	owe
bog	rub	**COY**	hod	jee	eng	**EKT**	woe
gob	**BSU**	coy	**DHU**	**EEK**	gen	ket	**EPP**
BGU	bus	**COZ**	hud	eke	**EGO**	**EKU**	pep
bug	sub	coz	**DIK**	**EEL**	ego	uke	**EPR**
BHO	**BTU**	**CPU**	kid	eel	**EGP**	**EKX**	per
hob	but	cup	**DIL**	lee	peg	kex	rep
BHU	tub	**CRU**	lid	**EEN**	**EGR**	**EKY**	**EPT**
hub	**BUY**	cur	**DIM**	nee	erg	key	pet
BIJ	buy	**CRY**	dim	**EEP**	ger	**ELL**	**EPW**
jib	**CDO**	cry	mid	pee	**EGT**	ell	pew
BIL	cod	**CTU**	**DIN**	**EER**	get	**ELM**	**EPY**
lib	doc	cut	din	ere	teg	elm	yep
BIM	**CDU**	**DDI**	**DIP**	ree	**EGY**	**ELS**	**ERR**
mib	cud	did	dip	**EES**	gey	sel	err
BIN	**CEE**	**DDO**	**DIR**	see	**EHI**	**ELT**	**ERS**
bin	cee	odd	rid	**EET**	hie	let	ers
nib	**CEI**	**DDU**	**DIT**	tee	**EHM**	**ELU**	res
BIO	ice	dud	dit	**EEV**	hem	leu	**ERT**
bio	**CEO**	**DEF**	tid	eve	**EHN**	**ELV**	ret
BIR	coe	fed	**DJO**	vee	hen	lev	**ERU**

rue	fun	gun	who	mix	**JOW**	**MPU**	row
ure	**FOO**	**GOO**	**HOY**	**INN**	jow	ump	**ORY**
ERV	foo	goo	hoy	inn	**JOY**	**MRU**	ory
rev	**FOP**	**GOR**	**HPT**	**INO**	joy	rum	**OST**
ERX	fop	gor	pht	ion	**JNU**	**MSU**	sot
rex	**FOR**	**GOT**	**HPU**	**INP**	jun	sum	**OSU**
ERY	for	got	hup	nip	**JSU**	**MUX**	sou
rye	fro	tog	**HSY**	pin	jus	mux	**OSW**
ESS	**FOT**	**GOY**	shy	**INR**	**JTU**	**NNU**	sow
ess	oft	goy	**HTU**	rin	jut	nun	**OSX**
EST	**FOU**	**GPU**	hut	**INS**	**KOP**	**NOR**	sox
set	fou	pug	**HTY**	sin	kop	nor	**OSY**
ESU	**FOX**	**GPY**	thy	**INT**	**KOR**	**NOS**	soy
sue	fox	gyp	**HWY**	nit	kor	son	**OTT**
use	**FOY**	**GRU**	why	tin	**KOS**	**NOT**	tot
ESW	foy	rug	**IJN**	**INW**	kos	not	**OTU**
sew	**FRU**	**GTU**	jin	win	**KOW**	ton	out
ESX	fur	gut	**IJU**	**INX**	wok	**NOV**	**OTW**
sex	urf	tug	uji	nix	**KST**	von	two
ESY	**FRY**	**GUV**	**IKL**	**IOP**	tsk	**NOW**	tow
yes	fry	vug	ilk	poi	**KSY**	now	**OTY**
ETV	**GGI**	**GUY**	**IKN**	**IPP**	sky	own	toy
vet	gig	guy	ink	pip	**KUU**	won	**OUY**
ETW	**GHO**	**HHS**	kin	**IPR**	uku	**NOY**	you
tew	hog	shh	**IKP**	rip	**LOO**	yon	**OVW**
wet	**GHU**	**HHU**	kip	**IPS**	loo	**NPU**	vow
ETY	hug	huh	**IKR**	sip	**LOP**	pun	**OWW**
tye	ugh	**HIM**	irk	**IPT**	lop	**NRU**	wow
yet	**GIJ**	him	**IKS**	pit	**LOS**	nur	**OWY**
EVX	jig	**HIN**	ski	**IPX**	sol	run	yow
vex	**GIM**	hin	**IKT**	pix	**LOT**	urn	**OXY**
EWY	mig	**HIP**	kit	**IPY**	lot	**NSU**	oxy
wey	**GIN**	hip	**ILL**	yip	**LOW**	sun	**PPU**
wye	gin	phi	ill	**IPZ**	low	**NSY**	pup
yew	**GIP**	**HIS**	**ILM**	zip	owl	sny	**PRY**
FFO	gip	his	mil	**IRS**	**LOX**	**NTU**	pry
off	pig	ish	**ILN**	sir	lox	nut	**PSU**
FGI	**GIR**	**HIT**	lin	**IRT**	**LPU**	tun	pus
fig	rig	hit	nil	rit	pul	**OOT**	sup
FGO	**GIT**	**HIU**	**ILO**	**ISS**	**LPY**	too	**PSY**
fog	tig	hui	oil	sis	ply	**OOW**	spy
FGU	**GIW**	**HKO**	**ILP**	**IST**	**LSY**	woo	**PTU**
fug	wig	hok	lip	ist	sly	**OOZ**	put
FHO	**GIZ**	**HMO**	**ILS**	its	**LUU**	zoo	tup
foh	zig	mho	lis	sit	ulu	**OPP**	**PXY**
FIK	**GJO**	ohm	**ILT**	**ISV**	**LUX**	pop	pyx
kif	jog	**HMU**	til	vis	lux	**OPR**	**RTU**
FIL	**GJU**	hum	**IMM**	**ISW**	**MMO**	pro	rut
fil	jug	**HNO**	mim	wis	mom	**OPS**	**RTY**
FIN	**GLO**	hon	**IMN**	**ISX**	**MMU**	sop	try
fin	log	**HOO**	nim	six	mum	**OPT**	**STY**
FIR	**GLU**	hoo	**IMP**	**ITT**	**MNO**	pot	sty
fir	lug	oho	imp	tit	mon	top	**TTU**
FIT	**GMU**	**HOP**	**IMR**	**ITU**	**MOO**	**OPX**	tut
fit	gum	hop	mir	tui	moo	pox	**TUU**
FIX	mug	**HOR**	rim	**ITW**	**MOP**	**ORT**	utu
fix	**GMY**	rho	**IMS**	wit	mop	ort	**TUX**
FLU	gym	**HOT**	ism	**IVY**	**MOT**	rot	tux
flu	**GNO**	hot	sim	ivy	mot	tor	
FLY	nog	tho	**IMV**	**JOT**	tom	**ORU**	
fly	**GNU**	**HOW**	vim	jot	**MOW**	our	
FNU	gnu	how	**IMX**		mow	**ORW**	

4-LETTER WORDS

AABB	raga	anta	**ABDW**	bhat	bawn	face
abba	**AAGS**	**AANZ**	bawd	**ABIL**	**ABOR**	**ACEG**
baba	saga	azan	**ABEK**	bail	boar	cage
AABC	**AAHM**	**AAPP**	bake	**ABIM**	bora	**ACEH**
caba	amah	papa	beak	iamb	**ABOT**	ache
AABH	**AAHR**	**AAPR**	**ABEL**	**ABIN**	boat	each
haba	haar	para	able	bain	**ABOX**	**ACEK**
AABL	**AAHY**	**AAPT**	bale	bani	abox	cake
alba	ayah	tapa	blae	**ABIR**	**ABOZ**	**ACEL**
AACC	**AAIR**	**AAQU**	**ABEM**	abri	boza	alec
acca	aria	aqua	beam	**ABIS**	**ABPU**	lace
AACM	**AAJR**	**AARU**	bema	basi	bapu	**ACEM**
caam	ajar	aura	**ABEN**	bias	**ABRT**	acme
AACP	raja	**AARV**	bane	**ABIT**	brat	came
capa	**AAJV**	vara	bean	bait	**ABRW**	mace
paca	java	**AAWY**	**ABER**	**ABIW**	braw	**ACEN**
AACR	**AAKK**	away	bare	biwa	**ABRY**	acne
arca	kaka	**ABBE**	bear	**ABJM**	bray	cane
AACS	**AAKN**	abbe	brae	jamb	**ABSS**	**ACEP**
casa	kana	babe	**ABES**	**ABJU**	bass	cape
AACT	**AAKR**	**ABBL**	base	juba	**ABST**	pace
acta	arak	blab	besa	**ABKL**	bast	**ACER**
AACV	**AAKV**	**ABBR**	**ABET**	balk	stab	acre
cava	kava	barb	abet	**ABKN**	**ABSW**	care
AACZ	**AALM**	**ABBU**	bate	bank	swab	race
caza	alma	babu	beat	**ABKR**	**ABTU**	**ACES**
AADR	lama	**ABBY**	beta	bark	abut	case
raad	mala	baby	**ABEU**	**ABKS**	tuba	**ACET**
AADT	**AALN**	**ABCH**	beau	bask	**ABTZ**	cate
data	alan	bach	**ABEY**	**ABKU**	batz	tace
AAEL	anal	**ABCK**	abye	baku	**ACCE**	**ACEV**
alae	**AALR**	back	**ABFR**	**ABLL**	ceca	cave
AAER	alar	**ABCN**	barf	ball	**ACCK**	**ACFL**
area	**AALS**	banc	**ABFT**	**ABLM**	cack	calf
AAFH	alas	**ABCR**	baft	balm	**ACCO**	**ACFT**
haaf	**AALU**	crab	**ABGI**	lamb	coca	fact
AAFJ	aula	**ABCS**	biga	**ABLS**	**ACDE**	**ACGL**
faja	**AALV**	scab	**ABGM**	slab	aced	clag
AAFL	aval	**ABDE**	gamb	**ABLT**	cade	**ACGR**
alfa	lava	abed	**ABGN**	blat	dace	crag
AAFR	**AAMM**	bade	bang	**ABLW**	**ACDI**	**ACGS**
afar	mama	bead	**ABGR**	bawl	acid	scag
AAGG	**AAMN**	**ABDL**	brag	**ABLY**	cadi	**ACHK**
gaga	aman	bald	garb	ably	caid	hack
AAGL	mana	**ABDN**	grab	**ABMO**	**ACDL**	**ACHM**
alga	**AAMY**	band	**ABGY**	ambo	clad	cham
gala	maya	**ABDO**	gaby	**ABMR**	**ACDO**	mach
AAGM	**AANN**	doab	**ABHL**	barm	coda	**ACHP**
agma	anna	**ABDR**	blah	**ABNO**	**ACDR**	chap
maga	**AANR**	bard	**ABHS**	bona	card	**ACHR**
AAGN	arna	brad	bash	**ABNR**	scad	arch
anga	**AANS**	drab	**ABHT**	barn	**ACEF**	char
AAGR	ansa	**ABDU**	baht	bran	cafe	**ACHS**
agar	**AANT**	daub	bath	**ABNW**		cash

ACHT	cram	**ADEG**	**ADHJ**	maud	atef	jean
chat	marc	aged	hadj	**ADNR**	fate	**AEJP**
tach	**ACMS**	egad	**ADHK**	darn	feat	jape
ACHW	scam	gade	dhak	nard	**AEFZ**	**AEJY**
chaw	**ACMY**	**ADEH**	**ADHN**	rand	faze	yaje
ACIL	cyma	hade	dhan	**ADNS**	**AEGG**	**AEKL**
laic	**ACNR**	head	hand	sand	gage	kale
ACIM	carn	**ADEI**	**ADHR**	**ADNU**	**AEGL**	lake
mica	narc	aide	hard	duan	gale	leak
ACIN	**ACNS**	idea	**ADHS**	**ADNW**	**AEGM**	**AEKM**
inca	scan	**ADEJ**	dash	dawn	game	kame
ACIP	**ACNT**	jade	shad	wand	mage	make
pica	cant	**ADEL**	**ADIK**	**ADOR**	**AEGN**	**AEKP**
ACIS	**ACNY**	dale	kadi	ador	gena	peak
asci	cany	deal	**ADIL**	orad	**AEGP**	**AEKR**
ACJK	**ACOP**	lade	dial	road	gape	rake
jack	capo	lead	laid	**ADOS**	page	**AEKS**
ACKL	**ACOR**	**ADEM**	**ADIM**	soda	peag	sake
calk	cora	dame	amid	**ADOT**	**AEGR**	**AEKT**
lack	orca	made	maid	toad	ager	take
ACKP	**ACOT**	mead	**ADIP**	**ADPR**	gear	teak
pack	coat	**ADEN**	paid	pard	gare	**AEKW**
ACKR	taco	dean	**ADIQ**	prad	rage	wake
cark	**ACOX**	**ADEO**	qadi	**ADQU**	**AEGS**	weak
rack	coax	odea	qaid	quad	sage	weka
ACKS	coxa	**ADEP**	**ADIR**	**ADRS**	**AEGT**	**AELL**
cask	**ACPR**	aped	arid	sard	gate	leal
sack	carp	**ADER**	raid	**ADRT**	**AEGU**	**AELM**
ACKT	crap	dare	**ADIS**	dart	ague	alme
tack	**ACPT**	dear	dais	drat	**AEGV**	lame
ACKU	pact	read	said	**ADRU**	gave	male
cauk	**ACRS**	**ADET**	**ADIT**	dura	vega	meal
ACLL	scar	date	adit	**ADRW**	**AEGW**	**AELN**
call	**ACRT**	**ADEV**	**ADIV**	draw	wage	elan
ACLM	cart	deva	avid	ward	**AEGZ**	lane
calm	**ACRW**	**ADEW**	diva	**ADRY**	gaze	lean
clam	craw	awed	**ADIW**	dray	**AEHJ**	**AELO**
ACLN	**ACRY**	wade	wadi	yard	haje	aloe
clan	racy	**ADEX**	**ADKN**	**ADTW**	**AEHK**	olea
ACLO	**ACRZ**	axed	dank	dawt	hake	**AELP**
alco	czar	**ADEZ**	**ADKR**	**ADVY**	**AEHL**	leap
coal	**ACSS**	daze	dark	davy	hale	pale
cola	cass	**ADFF**	**ADLN**	**AEEG**	heal	peal
loca	**ACST**	daff	land	agee	**AEHM**	plea
ACLP	cast	**ADFO**	**ADLO**	**AEEL**	ahem	**AELR**
clap	scat	fado	load	alee	hame	earl
ACLR	**ACSU**	**ADFR**	**ADLR**	**AEES**	**AEHP**	lear
carl	acus	fard	lard	ease	heap	rale
ACLT	**ACTT**	**ADFT**	**ADLU**	**AEFK**	**AEHR**	real
talc	tact	daft	auld	fake	hare	**AELS**
ACLU	**ACVY**	**ADFU**	dual	**AEFL**	hear	sale
caul	cavy	faud	laud	feal	**AEHT**	seal
ACLW	**ADDE**	**ADGI**	udal	flea	hate	**AELT**
claw	dead	gadi	**ADLY**	leaf	heat	late
ACLX	**ADDO**	**ADGL**	lady	**AEFM**	**AEHV**	leat
calx	dado	glad	**ADMN**	fame	have	tael
ACLY	**ADDU**	**ADGO**	damn	fane	**AEHY**	tale
clay	daud	dago	mand	**AEFN**	yeah	teal
lacy	duad	goad	**ADMP**	fane	**AEHZ**	tela
ACMO	**ADDY**	**ADGR**	damp	**AEFR**	haze	**AELV**
coma	dyad	drag	**ADMR**	fare	**AEJK**	lave
ACMP	**ADEF**	grad	dram	fear	jake	leva
camp	deaf	**ADGU**	**ADMU**	**AEFS**	**AEJN**	vale
ACMR	fade	gaud	duma	safe	jane	veal

AELW	apse	**AFFW**	fora	gamp	hail	whoa
wale	**AEPT**	waff	**AFOS**	**AGMR**	hila	**AHOX**
weal	pate	**AFGL**	sofa	gram	**AHIM**	hoax
AELX	peat	flag	**AFOY**	**AGMU**	hami	**AHOY**
axle	tape	**AFGN**	ofay	gaum	**AHIN**	ahoy
AELZ	**AEPV**	fang	**AFPR**	**AGMY**	hain	**AHPR**
laze	pave	**AFGR**	frap	gamy	**AHIR**	harp
zeal	**AEPX**	frag	**AFRT**	**AGNO**	hair	**AHPS**
AEMN	apex	**AFHL**	fart	agon	**AHJJ**	hasp
amen	**AERR**	half	frat	gaon	hajj	**AHPT**
mane	rare	**AFHS**	raft	**AGNP**	**AHJO**	path
mean	rear	fash	**AFRY**	pang	hoja	**AHRS**
name	**AERS**	**AFHT**	fray	**AGNR**	**AHKL**	rash
AEMR	arse	haft	**AFRZ**	garn	lakh	**AHRT**
mare	rase	**AFIK**	zarf	gnar	**AHKN**	hart
ream	sear	faik	**AFST**	rang	ankh	rath
AEMS	sera	kaif	fast	**AGNS**	hank	**AHSS**
mesa	**AERT**	**AFIL**	**AFTU**	sang	khan	sash
same	rate	alif	faut	snag	**AHKP**	**AHST**
seam	tare	fail	tufa	**AGNT**	kaph	hast
AEMT	tear	fila	**AFTW**	gant	**AHKR**	tash
mate	**AERU**	**AFIN**	waft	gnat	hark	**AHSW**
meat	urea	fain	**AGGN**	tang	**AHKW**	shaw
meta	**AERV**	naif	gang	**AGNU**	hawk	wash
tame	aver	**AFIR**	**AGGO**	guan	**AHLL**	**AHSY**
team	rave	fair	agog	guna	hall	ashy
AEMX	**AERW**	**AFIT**	**AGHI**	**AGNV**	**AHLM**	shay
exam	ware	fiat	hagi	vang	halm	**AHTT**
AEMZ	wear	**AFIW**	**AGHN**	**AGNW**	**AHLO**	that
maze	**AERY**	waif	hang	gnaw	halo	**AHTW**
AENO	aery	**AFKL**	**AGHS**	**AGNY**	**AHLR**	thaw
aeon	eyra	flak	gash	yang	harl	what
eoan	yare	**AFLL**	shag	**AGOS**	**AHLS**	**AHYZ**
AENP	year	fall	**AGHT**	sago	lash	hazy
nape	**AERZ**	**AFLM**	ghat	**AGOT**	**AHLT**	**AIIL**
neap	raze	flam	**AGIN**	goat	halt	ilia
pane	**AEST**	**AFLN**	gain	toga	lath	**AIIX**
pean	east	flan	**AGIO**	**AGOY**	**AHLU**	ixia
AENR	sate	**AFLO**	agio	yoga	haul	**AIJL**
earn	seat	foal	**AGIT**	**AGPS**	hula	jail
near	seta	loaf	gait	gasp	**AHLY**	**AIKK**
AENS	**AESV**	**AFLP**	**AGIV**	**AGQU**	hyla	kaki
sane	save	flap	vagi	quag	**AHMR**	**AIKL**
AENT	vase	**AFLS**	**AGKN**	**AGRU**	harm	kail
ante	**AESX**	fals	kang	gaur	**AHMS**	**AIKM**
neat	axes	**AFLT**	**AGKO**	ruga	mash	kami
AENV	seax	flat	kago	**AGRY**	sham	maki
nave	**AESY**	**AFLW**	**AGKU**	gray	**AHMT**	**AIKN**
vane	easy	flaw	kagu	**AGST**	math	akin
vena	eyas	**AFLX**	**AGKW**	gast	**AHMW**	**AIKP**
AENW	**AETT**	falx	gawk	stag	wham	pika
anew	teat	flax	**AGLL**	**AGSW**	**AHNT**	**AIKR**
wane	**AETZ**	**AFLY**	gall	swag	hant	raki
wean	zeta	flay	**AGLO**	**AGUY**	than	**AIKS**
AENY	**AEUV**	**AFMO**	goal	yuga	**AHNW**	saki
yean	uvea	foam	**AGLS**	**AHHS**	hwan	**AIKV**
AENZ	**AEUX**	**AFMR**	slag	hash	**AHOP**	kiva
naze	eaux	farm	**AGLT**	**AHHT**	opah	**AILM**
AEPR	**AEVW**	**AFNU**	galt	hath	**AHOR**	alim
pare	wave	faun	**AGLU**	**AHIJ**	hoar	mail
pear	**AFFG**	**AFNW**	gula	haji	hora	**AILN**
rape	gaff	fawn	**AGMO**	**AHIK**	**AHOT**	anil
reap	**AFFR**	**AFOR**	ogam	haik	oath	lain
AEPS	raff	faro	**AGMP**	**AHIL**	**AHOW**	nail

AILP
pail
pila
AILR
aril
lair
liar
lira
rail
rial
AILS
sail
AILT
alit
lati
tail
tali
AILV
vail
vial
AILW
wail
AILX
axil
AIMM
imam
maim
AIMN
main
mina
AIMR
amir
rami
AIMT
mita
AIMX
maxi
AINP
nipa
pain
pian
AINR
rain
rani
AINS
nasi
sain
AINT
anti
tain
AINV
vain
vina
AINW
wain
AINY
ayin
AIOT
iota
tiao
AIPR
pair
AIQZ
qazi

AIRS
sari
AIRV
vair
AIRY
airy
AIRZ
izar
AISV
visa
AISX
axis
AITW
wait
AITX
taxi
AIVV
viva
AJKU
jauk
AJLR
jarl
AJMS
jasm
AJNN
jann
AJOT
jato
jota
AJPU
jaup
AJRU
jura
AJSZ
jasz
AJZZ
jazz
AKLN
lank
AKLO
kola
AKLR
lark
AKLS
lask
AKLT
talk
AKLW
walk
AKLY
laky
AKMO
amok
AKMR
mark
AKMS
mask
AKNO
kaon
koan
AKNP
knap
AKNR
knar

nark
rank
AKNS
sank
AKNT
tank
yank
AKOR
okra
AKOS
soak
AKOY
kayo
oaky
okay
AKPR
park
AKRS
sark
AKRT
kart
AKST
skat
task
AKSU
skua
AKSW
skaw
AKTY
kyat
ALLL
lall
ALLM
mall
ALLO
olla
ALLP
pall
ALLT
tall
ALLW
wall
ALLY
ally
ALMM
malm
ALMO
loam
loma
mola
ALMP
lamp
palm
ALMR
marl
ALMS
alms
slam
ALMT
malt
ALMU
alum
maul

ALMY
amyl
ALNO
loan
ALNP
plan
ALNT
lant
ALNU
luna
ulna
ALNW
lawn
ALNX
lanx
ALOP
opal
ALOR
oral
ALOS
also
ALOT
alto
lota
tola
ALOV
oval
ALOW
alow
ALPP
palp
ALPS
slap
ALPT
plat
ALPW
pawl
ALPY
paly
play
ALRY
ryal
ALSS
lass
ALST
last
salt
slat
ALSW
slaw
ALSY
slay
ALUU
luau
ulua
ALWY
waly
yawl
ALYZ
lazy
AMMO
ammo
AMNO
moan

noma
AMNU
maun
AMNY
many
myna
AMOR
amor
mora
roam
AMOS
soma
AMOT
atom
moat
AMOX
moxa
AMOY
mayo
AMPR
pram
ramp
AMPS
samp
AMPT
tamp
AMPU
puma
AMPV
vamp
AMRT
mart
tram
AMRU
mura
AMRW
warm
AMRY
army
AMSS
mass
AMST
mast
AMSW
swam
AMTY
maty
AMYZ
azym
mazy
ANNO
anon
nona
ANOR
roan
ANOS
naos
ANOT
nota
ANOV
nova
ANOX
axon
oxan

ANOZ
zona
AMNU
snap
span
ANPT
pant
ANPW
pawn
ANRT
rant
ANRW
warn
ANRY
nary
yarn
ANSS
sans
ANST
nast
ANSU
ansu
anus
ANSW
sawn
swan
ANTU
aunt
tuna
ANTW
want
ANUY
yuan
ANVY
navy
ANWY
wany
yawn
ANYZ
zany
AOPR
proa
AOPS
soap
AOPT
atop
AORR
roar
AORS
soar
sora
AORT
rota
taro
AOSS
ossa
AOST
oast
stoa
AOTU
auto
AOVW
avow
APPU

pupa
APRR
parr
APRS
rasp
spar
APRT
part
rapt
tarp
trap
APRW
warp
wrap
APRY
pray
APSS
pass
APST
past
spat
APSU
upas
APSW
swap
wasp
APSY
spay
APTY
paty
APUY
yaup
AQUY
quay
ARST
sart
star
tsar
ARSU
sura
ARTT
tart
ARTW
wart
ARTY
arty
atry
tray
ARVY
vary
ARWY
awry
wary
ARZZ
razz
ASSS
sass
ASST
tass
ASTV
vast
ASTW
swat
wast

ASTY stay
ASWY sway
ATTU taut
ATTW watt
AVWY wavy
AWXY waxy
BBBI bibb
BBEL bleb
BBII bibi
BBLO blob
BBLU bulb
BBMO bomb
BBOO boob
BBOR brob
BBOU bubo
BCEI bice
BCEK beck
BCEU cube
BCHU chub
BCIR crib
BCKU buck
BCLO bloc
BCLU club
BCMO comb
BCRU curb
BDEI bide
BDEL bled
BDEN bend
BDEO bode
BDER bred
BDET debt
BDIN bind

BDIR bird, drib
BDIS dibs
BDLO bold
BDMU dumb
BDNO bond
BDOR brod
BDOY body
BDRU drub
BEEF beef, feeb
BEEN been
BEEP beep
BEER beer, bree
BEES bese
BEET beet, bete
BEGI gibe
BEGR berg
BEGY gybe
BEHR herb
BEHT beth
BEIJ jibe
BEIK bike, kibe
BEIL bile
BEIN bein, bine
BEIR bier
BEIS bise
BEIT bite
BEIX ibex
BEIZ bize
BEJU jube

BEKR kerb
BELL bell
BELO bole, lobe
BELP pleb
BELT belt
BELU blue, lube
BELW blew
BEMR berm
BENO bone, ebon
BENT bent
BEOO oboe
BEOR bore, robe
BEOX obex
BEOY obey
BERR brer
BERU rube
BERV verb
BERW brew
BERY byre
BEST best
BESY byes
BETU tube
BETY byte
BEUZ zebu
BEVY bevy
BFFI biff
BFFU buff
BFLU flub
BFOR forb
BGIL glib

BGIN bing
BGIR brig
BGLO glob
BGNU bung
BGOY bogy, goby
BGRU burg, grub
BHIK bikh
BHLU buhl
BHOO hobo
BHOS bosh
BHOT both
BHSU bush
BIIS ibis
BIKL bilk
BIKS bisk
BILL bill
BILM limb
BILO boil
BILP blip
BILR birl
BIMN nimb
BIMR brim
BINS nibs
BINY inby
BIOT obit
BIRR birr
BIRT brit
BITT bitt
BKLU bulk
BKNO knob
BKNU bunk

BKOO book, kobo
BKOS bosk
BKSU busk
BLLO boll
BLLU bull
BLOO bolo, bool, lobo, obol
BLOS slob
BLOT blot, bolt
BLOU boul
BLOW blow, bowl
BLRU blur, burl
BLSU slub
BMNU numb
BMOO boom
BMOT tomb
BMOU umbo
BMOW womb
BMPU bump
BNOO boon
BNOR born
BNOS snob
BNOY bony
BNRU burn
BNSU snub
BNTU bunt
BOOR boor, broo
BOOT boot
BOOZ bozo

BORS sorb
BORT bort
BORW brow
BORY orby
BOSS boss
BOST bots, stob
BOTT bott
BOTU bout
BOTY toby
BOUY buoy
BOXY boxy
BPRU burp
BRRU burr
BRTU brut
BRUY bury, ruby
BSSU buss
BSTU bust, stub
BSUY busy
BTTU butt
BUZZ buzz
CCHI chic
CCKO cock
CCOO coco
CCOR croc
CDEE cede
CDEI dice, iced
CDEK deck
CDEO code, coed
CDEU cued, duce

CDHI chid
CDIK dick
CDIO odic
CDIS disc
CDKO dock
CDKU duck
CDLO clod, cold
CDOR cord
CDRU crud, curd
CDSU scud
CDTU duct
CEEH eche
CEEP cepe
CEER cere
CEET cete
CEFH chef
CEFI fice
CEFK feck
CEFL clef
CEGK geck
CEHK heck
CEHL lech
CEHO echo
CEHT echt, etch
CEHW chew
CEHX chex
CEHZ chez
CEIL ceil, lice
CEIM mice
CEIN nice

CEIP
epic
pice
CEIR
eric
rice
CEIS
sice
CEIT
cite
CEIV
vice
CEKK
keck
CEKN
neck
CEKO
coke
CEKP
peck
CEKR
reck
CEKU
cuke
CELL
cell
CELM
clem
CELO
cole
CELT
celt
CELU
clue
luce
CELW
clew
CEMO
come
CEMY
cyme
CENO
cone
once
CENR
cern
CENT
cent
CEOP
cope
CEOR
cero
core
CEOT
cote
CEOV
cove
CEPU
puce
CERU
cure
ecru
CERW
crew

CESS
cess
CEST
sect
CESY
scye
syce
CETU
cute
CETY
cyte
CFFU
cuff
CFIO
coif
fico
foci
CFIS
fisc
CFLO
floc
CFOO
coof
CFOR
corf
CFRU
curf
CGHU
chug
CGKU
guck
CGLO
clog
CGSU
scug
CHIK
hick
CHIN
chin
inch
CHIP
chip
CHIR
rich
CHIT
chit
itch
CHIU
huic
CHKO
hock
CHLO
loch
CHMU
chum
much
CHOP
chop
CHOS
cosh
CHOU
chou
ouch
CHSU
such

CIKK
kick
CIKL
lick
CIKN
nick
CIKP
pick
CIKR
rick
CIKS
sick
CIKT
tick
CIKW
wick
CIKY
icky
CILO
coil
loci
CILP
clip
CINO
cion
coin
icon
CINU
unci
CINZ
zinc
CIOR
coir
CIOT
otic
CIRU
uric
CIST
cist
CITY
city
CJKO
jock
CKLO
lock
CKLU
luck
CKMO
mock
CKMU
muck
CKNO
conk
nock
CKOO
cook
CKOP
pock
CKOR
cork
rock
CKOS
sock
CKPU

puck
CKRU
ruck
CKSU
cusk
suck
CKTU
tuck
CLLO
coll
CLLU
cull
CLMU
culm
CLOO
cool
loco
CLOT
clot
colt
CLOW
cowl
CLOY
cloy
CLRU
curl
CLTU
cult
CMOO
coom
CMOP
comp
CMOR
corm
CMSU
scum
CNOO
coon
CNOR
corn
CNOU
unco
CNOY
cony
CNSY
sync
COOP
coop
poco
COOT
coot
COPR
crop
COPS
scop
COPU
coup
COPY
copy
CORW
crow
COST
cost
scot

COSW
scow
COSY
cosy
COYZ
cozy
CPSU
cusp
scup
CRRU
curr
CRSU
crus
CRTU
curt
CRUX
crux
CSSU
cuss
CSTU
scut
CSTY
cyst
DDEE
deed
DDEI
died
DDEU
dude
DDEY
dyed
eddy
DDIO
dido
DDOO
dodo
DDRU
rudd
DDSU
sudd
DEEF
feed
DEEG
edge
geed
DEEH
heed
DEEI
eide
idle
DEEJ
jeed
DEEK
eked
DEEL
dele
DEEM
deem
deme
meed
DEEN
dene
need
DEEP
deep

peed
DEER
deer
dree
reed
DEES
seed
DEET
teed
DEEW
weed
DEEY
eyed
DEFL
delf
DEFN
fend
DEFT
deft
DEFU
feud
DEFY
defy
DEGL
geld
DEGO
doge
DEGY
edgy
DEHI
hide
hied
DEHL
held
DEHO
hoed
DEHR
herd
DEHS
shed
DEHU
hued
DEIK
dike
DEIL
deil
deli
lied
DEIM
dime
idem
DEIN
dine
nide
DEIP
pied
DEIR
dire
ride
DEIS
ides
side

DEIT
diet
edit
tide
tied
DEIV
dive
vied
DEIW
wide
DEKS
desk
DEKU
duke
DEKY
dyke
DELL
dell
DELM
meld
DELN
lend
DELO
dole
lode
DELS
sled
DELU
duel
DELV
veld
DELW
lewd
weld
DEMN
mend
DEMO
demo
dome
mode
DEMY
demy
DENO
done
node
DENP
pend
DENR
rend
DENS
send
DENT
dent
tend
DENU
dune
nude
unde
DENV
vend
DENW
wend
DENY
deny

dyne
DEOP
dope
oped
DEOR
doer
redo
rode
DEOS
does
dose
DEOT
dote
toed
DEOV
dove
DEOW
owed
DEOZ
doze
DEPS
sped
DEPU
dupe
DERU
dure
rude
rued
DERW
drew
DERY
dyer
DESS
dess
DESU
sued
used
DETU
duet
DEWY
dewy
DFFO
doff
DFFU
duff
DFIN
find
DFIO
fido
DFLO
fold
DFNO
fond
DFNU
fund
DFOO
food
DFOR
ford
DFRY
fyrd
DGIL
gild
DGIN
ding
DGIR
gird
grid
DGLO
gold
DGNO
dong
DGNU
dung
DGOO
good
DGOY
dogy
DGRU
drug
DHIN
hind
DHLO
hold
DHOO
hood
DHOS
shod
DHOW
dhow
DHTU
thud
DIIM
midi
DIIN
nidi
DIIS
sidi
DIKN
dink
kind
DIKR
dirk
DIKS
disk
skid
DILL
dill
DILM
mild
DILO
idol
loid
DILR
dirl
DILS
slid
DILW
wild
DILY
idly
idyl
DIMN
mind
DINO
doni
nodi
DINP
pind
DINR
rind
DINT
dint
DINW
wind
DIOT
doit
DIOV
void
DIPR
drip
DIQU
quid
DIRT
dirt
DISS
diss
DITY
tidy
DJOO
dojo
DJOU
judo
DKNU
dunk
DKSU
dusk
DKUU
kudu
DLLO
doll
DLLU
dull
DLMO
mold
DLOP
plod
DLOR
lord
DLOS
sold
DLOT
dolt
told
DLOU
loud
DLOW
dowl
wold
DLUY
duly
DMOO
doom
mood
DMOR
dorm
DMPU
dump
DMRU
drum
DNOP
pond
DNOU
undo
DNOW
down
DNOY
yond
DNRY
rynd
DNWY
wynd
DOOR
door
odor
ordo
rood
DOOW
wood
DOPR
dorp
drop
prod
DOQU
quod
DORT
dort
trod
DORU
dour
duro
DORW
word
DORY
dory
DOSS
doss
DOTY
tody
DOXY
doxy
DOYZ
dozy
DPSU
spud
DRSU
surd
DRTU
turd
DSSU
suds
DSTU
dust
stud
DTUY
duty
EEEP
epee
EEFK
keef
EEFL
feel
flee
EEFM
feme
EEFR
fere
free
reef
EEFT
feet
fete
EEGH
ghee
EEGK
geek
EEGL
glee
EEGN
gene
EEGO
ogee
EEGR
gree
EEHL
heel
EEHM
heme
EEHR
here
EEHT
thee
EEJP
jeep
EEJR
jeer
EEJT
jete
EEJZ
jeez
EEKK
keek
EEKL
keel
leek
EEKM
meek
EEKN
keen
knee
EEKP
keep
peek
EEKR
reek
EEKS
seek
skee
EEKT
keet
EEKW
week
EELP
peel
EELR
leer
reel
EELS
else
seel
EELT
leet
tele
EELW
weel
EEMR
mere
EEMS
seem
seme
EEMT
meet
mete
teem
EEMU
emeu
EENP
neep
peen
EENR
erne
esne
EENS
seen
EENT
teen
EENV
neve
even
EEPP
peep
EEPR
peer
EEPS
seep
EEPV
veep
EEPW
weep
EERS
seer
sere
EERT
rete
tree
EERV
ever
veer
EERW
ewer
were
EERY
eery
eyre
EESS
esse
EFFI
fief
fife
EFHT
heft
EFIK
fike
kief
EFIL
file
lief
life
EFIN
fine
neif
EFIR
fire
rife
EFIV
five
EFIW
wife
EFKR
kerf
EFKY
fyke
EFLL
fell
EFLO
floe
EFLP
pelf
EFLS
self
EFLT
felt
flet
left
EFLU
flue
fuel
EFLW
flew
EFLX
flex
EFMU
fume
EFNR
fern
EFOR
fore
froe
EFRS
serf
EFRT
fret
reft
EFRU
feru
ufer
EFSS
fess
EFSU
fuse
EFTW
weft
EFUZ
fuze
EGGL
gleg
EGGY
yegg

EGHU huge
EGIS egis, gies
EGIT tige
EGIV give
EGKS skeg
EGLL gell
EGLN glen
EGLO loge, ogle
EGLT gelt
EGLU glue
EGLY gyle
EGMR germ
EGMU geum
EGNO gone
EGNS gens
EGNT gent
EGOR ergo, goer, gore, ogre
EGOS goes, sego
EGRS gres
EGRU grue, urge
EGRW grew
EGRX grex
EGRY grey, gyre
EGST gest
EGUZ guze
EGVY gyve
EHHT heth
EHIK hike

EHIR heir, hire
EHIV hive
EHKU huke
EHLL hell
EHLM helm
EHLO hole
EHLP help
EHLR herl
EHLY hyle
EHMO home
EHMP hemp
EHMR herm
EHMS mesh
EHMT them
EHNO hone
EHNR hern
EHNS nesh
EHNT hent, then
EHNW hewn, when
EHOP hope
EHOR hero, hoer
EHOS hose, shoe
EHOV hove
EHPW phew
EHPY hype
EHRS hers, resh
EHST hest
EHSW shew
EHTT teth

EHTW thew, whet
EHTY hyte
EHWW whew
EHWY whey
EIJV jive
EIKL like
EIKM mike
EIKN kine
EIKP kepi, pike
EIKR keir, kier
EIKS sike
EIKT kite, tike
EILM lime, mile
EILN lien, line
EILP pile, plie
EILR lire, riel, rile
EILS isle
EILT lite, tile
EILU lieu
EILV evil, live, veil, vile
EILW wile
EILX ilex
EIMM mime
EIMN mien, mine
EIMR emir, mire, riem, rime
EIMS mise
EIMT emit, item, mite, time
EINN nine
EINP pine
EINR rein
EINS sine
EINT tine
EINV nevi, vein, vine
EINW wine
EINY yeni
EINZ zein
EIPP pipe
EIPR peri, pier, ripe
EIPS pise, sipe
EIPW wipe
EIPY yipe
EIRS reis, rise, sire
EIRT iter, rite, tier, tire
EIRV rive
EIRW weir, wire
EIST site
EISV vise
EISW wise

EISZ size
EITU etui
EITW wite
EITX exit
EITY yeti
EIVW view, wive
EJKO joke
EJKR jerk
EJKU juke
EJLL jell
EJLO jole
EJOS joes
EJOY joey
EJPU jupe
EJSS jess
EJST jest
EJTU jute
EKLL kell
EKLP kelp
EKLT kelt
EKLY kyle, yelk
EKMO moke
EKMP kemp
EKMR merk
EKNO keno
EKNR kern
EKNT kent
EKNU nuke
EKNW knew
EKOP poke
EKOS soke

EKOT keto
EKOW woke
EKOY yoke
EKPR perk
EKPS skep
EKPT kept
EKPU puke
EKRT trek
EKRY yerk
EKSW skew
EKTY kyte, tyke
ELLM mell
ELLP pell
ELLS sell
ELLT tell
ELLV vell
ELLW well
ELLY yell
ELMO mole
ELMR merl
ELMT melt
ELMU mule
ELMW mewl
ELMY elmy
ELNO enol, leno, lone
ELNS lens
ELNT lent
ELNU lune
ELOO oleo
ELOP lope, olpe, pole

ELOR lore, orle, role
ELOS lose, sloe, sole
ELOV levo, love, vole
ELPT pelt, plet
ELPU pule
ELPY pyle, yelp
ELRU lure, rule
ELRY lyre, rely
ELSS less
ELST lest
ELSU lues, slue
ELSW slew
ELSY lyse
ELTU lute, tule
ELTW welt
ELUX luxe
ELUY yule
ELVY levy
EMMO memo, mome
EMNO meno, nome, omen
EMNU menu
EMOP mope, poem, pome
EMOR

more
omer
EMOS
some
EMOT
mote
tome
EMOV
move
EMOW
meow
EMRT
term
EMSS
mess
EMST
stem
EMSU
muse
EMSW
smew
EMTU
mute
ENNO
neon
none
ENOP
nope
open
peon
pone
ENOS
noes
nose
ENOT
note
tone
ENOV
oven
ENOW
enow
ENOX
exon
ENOZ
zone
ENPT
pent
ENRT
rent
tern
ENRU
rune
ENRW
wren
ENSS
ness
ENST
nest
sent
ENSW
sewn
ENTT
tent
ENTU

tune
ENTV
vent
went
newt
sept
next
tyne
ENVY
envy
EOOZ
ooze
EOPP
pepo
pope
EOPR
pore
rope
EOPS
epos
peso
pose
EOPT
poet
pote
tope
EOPX
expo
EORS
rose
sore
EORT
rote
tore
EORU
roue
EORV
over
rove
EORW
wore
EORY
oyer
yore
EORZ
zero
EOSY
oyes
EOTT
tote
EOTV
veto
vote
EOVW
wove
EOYZ
oyez
EPPR
prep
repp
EPRT
pert

EPRU
pure
EPRY
prey
pyre
EPST
pest
step
EPSU
spue
EPSW
spew
EPSY
espy
EPTW
wept
EPTY
type
ERRU
ruer
ERST
erst
rest
ERSU
ruse
sure
user
ERTT
tret
ERTU
true
ERTV
vert
ERTY
trey
ERVY
very
ESSS
sess
ESTT
stet
test
ESTU
suet
ESTV
vest
ESTW
stew
west
ESTX
sext
ESTZ
zest
ESXY
sexy
ETTX
text
FFGU
guff
FFHU
huff
FFIM
miff

FFIR
riff
FFIT
tiff
FFIY
iffy
FFLU
luff
FFMU
muff
FFOT
toff
FFPU
puff
FFRU
ruff
FFTU
tuff
FGIR
frig
FGIT
gift
FGLO
flog
golf
FGLU
gulf
FGOO
goof
FGOR
frog
FGOY
fogy
FGRU
frug
FHIS
fish
FHOO
hoof
FIKN
fink
FIKR
firk
FILL
fill
FILM
film
FILO
foil
FILP
flip
FILS
fils
FILT
flit
FILX
flix
FIMR
firm
FINR
firn
FIRT
frit

rift
FIRZ
friz
FIST
fist
sift
FITT
tift
FITX
fixt
FIZZ
fizz
FKLO
folk
FKNU
funk
FKOR
fork
FLLU
full
FLOO
fool
FLOP
flop
FLOT
flot
loft
FLOU
foul
FLOW
flow
fowl
wolf
FLRU
furl
FLUX
flux
FMOR
form
from
FMUY
fumy
FNOS
fons
FNOT
font
FOOR
roof
FOOT
foot
FOOW
woof
FOPR
prof
FOPU
pouf
FORT
fort
FORU
four
FORW
frow
FOSS
foss

FOST
soft
FOTT
toft
FOXY
foxy
FOYZ
fozy
FRRU
furr
FRSU
surf
FRTU
turf
FRUY
fury
FSSU
fuss
FSTU
fust
FTTU
tuft
FUZZ
fuzz
GGIM
migg
GGIR
grig
GGNO
nogg
GGOO
gogo
GGOR
grog
GHHI
high
GHIN
nigh
GHIS
sigh
GHIT
thig
GHIW
whig
GHNO
hong
GHNU
hung
GHOS
gosh
shog
GHPU
pugh
GHSU
gush
GHTU
thug
GIKN
gink
king
GILL
gill
GILM

glim
GILN
ling
GILR
girl
GILT
gilt
GILU
iglu
GIMP
gimp
GIMR
grim
GINP
ping
GINR
grin
ring
GINS
sign
sing
GINT
ting
GINW
wing
GINZ
zing
GIOR
giro
GIOY
yogi
GIPR
grip
prig
GIRT
girt
grit
trig
GIRY
gyri
GIST
gist
GISW
swig
GITW
twig
GKNU
gunk
GKOO
gook
GKOW
gowk
GLLU
gull
GLMU
glum
GLNO
long
GLNU
lung
GLOO
gool
logo
GLOP

glop	hush	howk	**HORT**	**IKLN**	limp	**IMRT**
GLOS	**HIKS**	**HKSU**	thro	kiln	**ILMS**	trim
slog	kish	husk	**HORU**	link	slim	**IMRY**
GLOW	**HIKT**	**HLLU**	hour	**IKLO**	**ILMT**	miry
glow	kith	hull	**HOST**	kilo	milt	rimy
GLOY	**HILL**	**HLMO**	host	**IKLS**	**ILMY**	**IMSS**
logy	hill	holm	shot	silk	limy	miss
GLPU	**HILT**	**HLOP**	tosh	**IKLT**	**ILNN**	**IMST**
gulp	hilt	holp	**HOSW**	kilt	linn	mist
plug	**HIMS**	**HLOT**	show	**IKMN**	**ILNO**	**IMSW**
GLSU	shim	holt	**HOTU**	mink	lion	swim
slug	**HIMW**	loth	thou	**IKMS**	loin	**IMTT**
GLTU	whim	**HLOW**	**HPSU**	skim	noil	mitt
glut	**HINS**	howl	push	**IKNO**	**ILNT**	**IMTX**
GLUY	hisn	**HLOY**	**HRSU**	kino	lint	mixt
ugly	shin	holy	rush	**IKNP**	**ILNY**	**INOR**
GMOS	sinh	**HLRU**	**HRTU**	pink	inly	iron
smog	**HINT**	hurl	hurt	**IKNR**	liny	**INOT**
GMRU	hint	**HLSU**	ruth	rink	**ILOO**	into
grum	thin	lush	thru	**IKNS**	olio	**INOW**
GMSU	**HIOT**	**HMNY**	**HSSU**	sink	**ILOR**	wino
smug	thio	hymn	huss	skin	roil	**INOY**
GNOO	**HIPS**	**HMOR**	**HSTU**	**IKNT**	**ILOS**	yoni
goon	pish	mohr	shut	knit	silo	**INPR**
GNOS	ship	**HMOT**	thus	tink	soil	pirn
song	**HIPT**	moth	tush	**IKNW**	**ILOT**	**INPS**
GNOT	pith	**HMOW**	**HUZZ**	wink	toil	snip
tong	**HIPW**	whom	huzz	**IKNY**	**ILOV**	spin
GNOW	whip	**HMOY**	**IIKW**	inky	viol	**INPT**
gown	**HIRW**	homy	kiwi	**IKPS**	**ILOY**	pint
GNOY	whir	**HMPU**	**IIMN**	skip	oily	**INPY**
gony	**HISS**	hump	mini	**IKRS**	**ILPS**	piny
GNPU	hiss	**HMSU**	**IIMP**	kris	lisp	**INRU**
pung	**HIST**	mush	impi	risk	slip	ruin
GNRU	hist	**HMTY**	**IINS**	**IKSS**	**ILPU**	**INTT**
rung	shit	myth	nisi	kiss	puli	tint
GNSU	sith	**HNOR**	**IIPT**	**IKST**	**ILPY**	**INTU**
snug	this	horn	tipi	kist	pily	unit
sung	**HISV**	**HNOS**	**IIRS**	skit	**ILRT**	**INTW**
GOOR	shiv	nosh	iris	**ILLL**	tirl	twin
goor	**HISW**	**HNSU**	**IISW**	lill	**ILST**	**INTY**
GOPR	wish	shun	iwis	**ILLM**	list	tiny
prog	**HITW**	**HNTU**	**IITT**	mill	silt	**INVY**
GOPY	whit	hunt	titi	**ILLN**	slit	viny
pogy	with	**HOOP**	**IJKN**	nill	**ILTT**	**INWY**
GORS	**HIWZ**	hoop	jink	**ILLP**	tilt	winy
gros	whiz	**HOOS**	**IJLL**	pill	**ILTW**	**IOPT**
GORT	**HJNO**	shoo	jill	**ILLR**	wilt	topi
grot	john	**HOOT**	**IJLT**	rill	**ILWY**	**IORS**
GORW	**HJOS**	hoot	jilt	**ILLS**	wily	sori
grow	josh	toho	**IJNN**	sill	**IMNT**	**IORT**
GORY	**HKLO**	**HOPQ**	jinn	**ILLT**	mint	riot
gory	kohl	qoph	**IJNO**	lilt	**IMNX**	tiro
gyro	**HKLU**	**HOPS**	join	till	minx	tori
orgy	hulk	posh	**IJNX**	**ILLW**	**IMOT**	trio
GOTU	**HKNO**	shop	jinx	will	omit	**IORZ**
gout	honk	soph	**IKKN**	**ILLY**	**IMPP**	zori
GRTU	**HKNU**	**HOPT**	kink	lily	pimp	**IPPY**
gurt	hunk	phot	**IKKR**	**ILMN**	**IMPR**	pipy
GRUU	**HKOO**	**HOPW**	kirk	limn	prim	**IPQU**
guru	hook	whop	**IKLL**	**ILMO**	**IMPS**	quip
GSTU	**HKOP**	**HOPY**	kill	moil	simp	**IPRT**
gust	koph	hypo	**IKLM**	limo	**IMPW**	trip
HHSU	**HKOW**		milk	**ILMP**	wimp	**IPRX**

prix
IPSS
piss
IPST
spit
IPSV
spiv
IPSW
wisp
IPTY
pity
IPXY
pixy
IQTU
quit
IQUZ
quiz
IRRY
yirr
IRST
stir
IRTW
writ
IRTZ
ritz
IRWY
wiry
ISST
sist
ISTU
suit
ISYZ
sizy
ISZZ
sizz
ITTW
twit
JJUU
juju
JKNU
junk
JLOT
jolt
JLOW
jowl
JMPU
jump
JNTU
junt
JOSS
joss
JRUY
jury
JSTU
just
KKOO
kook
KLOO
look
KLOY
yolk
KLPU
pulk
KLRU
lurk
KLSU
sulk
KMNO
monk
KMRU
murk
KMSU
musk
KNOO
nook
KNOP
knop
KNOT
knot
KNOW
know
KNPU
punk
KNRU
knur
KNSU
sunk
KOOR
rook
KOOT
koto
took
KOPR
pork
KOPY
poky
KORW
work
KORY
roky
KRSU
rusk
KRSY
skyr
KSTU
tusk
LLLO
loll
LLLU
lull
LLMO
moll
LLMU
mull
LLNU
null
LLOP
poll
LLOR
roll
LLOT
toll
LLPU
pull
LLUU
lulu
LMOO
loom
mool
LMOT
molt
LMOY
moly
LMPU
lump
plum
LMSU
slum
LNOO
loon
LNOR
lorn
LNOY
only
LNRU
nurl
LNTU
lunt
LNUY
luny
LNXY
lynx
LOOP
loop
polo
pool
LOOS
solo
LOOT
loot
tool
LOOW
wool
LOPP
plop
LOPS
slop
LOPT
plot
LOPW
plow
LOPY
ploy
LORT
rotl
LORY
lory
LOSS
loss
LOST
lost
LOSU
soul
LOSW
slow
LOTU
lout
tolu
LOTV
volt
LOWY
yowl
LPPU
pulp
LPRU
purl
LPSU
plus
LRSU
slur
LSTU
lust
slut
MNOO
mono
moon
MNOR
morn
norm
MNOS
mons
MNOU
muon
MNOW
mown
MOOR
moor
room
MOOT
moot
MOOZ
zoom
MOPP
pomp
MOPR
prom
romp
MORT
mort
MORW
worm
MOSS
moss
MOST
most
MOSU
sumo
MOUV
ovum
MPPU
pump
MPRU
rump
MPSU
sump
MPTU
tump
MSSU
muss
MSTU
must
smut
stum
MSUW
swum
MTTU
mutt
NNOO
noon
NNOU
noun
NNSU
sunn
NOOP
poon
NOOS
soon
NOOT
onto
toon
NOOW
woon
NOOZ
zoon
NOPR
porn
NOPS
pons
NOPU
upon
NOPY
pony
NORS
sorn
NORT
torn
NORW
worn
NOST
snot
NOSU
nous
onus
NOSW
snow
sown
NOSY
nosy
NOTU
nout
unto
NOTW
nowt
town
wont
NOTY
tony
NOWY
nowy
NOXY
onyx
NPSU
spun
NPTU
punt
NPUY
puny
NRTU
runt
turn
NSTU
stun
OOPP
poop
OOPR
poor
roop
OOPS
oops
OORT
root
roto
OOST
soot
OOTT
toot
OOYZ
oozy
OPPR
prop
OPRT
port
OPRU
pour
OPRW
prow
OPRX
prox
OPRY
ropy
OPST
post
spot
stop
OPSU
opus
soup
OPSY
posy
OPTU
pout
OPTY
typo
ORRT
torr
ORSS
ross
ORST
sort
ORSU
sour
ORSY
rosy
ORTT
tort
trot
ORTU
rout
tour
ORTW
trow
ORTY
ryot
troy
tyro
ORUX
roux
ORUY
your
ORXY
oryx
OSSS
soss
OSST
toss
OSSU
sous
OSTT
stot
tost
OSTU
oust
OSTW
stow
OTTU
tout
PPTY
typp
PRRU
purr
PRSU
spur
PRSY
spry
PSSU
puss
PTTU
putt
RSTU
rust
RSUU
urus
RTUY
yurt
SSUU
usus
STXY
xyst
TTUU
tutu

5-LETTER WORDS

AAAABC
abaca
AAACM
caama
AAAGM
agama
AABBK
kabab
AABCI
abaci
AABCK
aback
AABCL
cabal
AABCN
banca
AABCR
carab
AABEM
abeam
AABES
abase
AABET
abate
batea
AABFT
abaft
AABGM
gamba
AABHM
bamah
AABHS
abash
AABIL
labia
AABJR
bajra
AABKN
banka
AABKR
abkar
AABLN
banal
AABLR
labra
AABLS
balas
balsa
basal
AABLT
tabla
AABMM
mamba
AABMS

samba
AABNW
bwana
nawab
AABRS
sabra
AABRT
rabat
AABRZ
braza
zabra
AABST
basta
batta
AABTU
bauta
AACCO
cacao
AACCY
yacca
AACDH
dacha
AACEP
apace
AACER
arcae
areca
AACEV
cavae
cavea
AACFF
caffa
AACFT
facta
AACGR
carga
AACHJ
chaja
AACIP
caapi
AACIR
acari
AACKL
alack
AACLL
calla
AACLN
canal
AACLS
scala
AACLV
caval
AACMS

camas
AACMW
macaw
AACOR
caroa
AACPT
pacta
AACRS
sacra
AACRT
carat
AACSU
causa
vacua
AADDX
aaddx
AADEG
adage
AADEH
ahead
AADFR
farad
AADIN
naiad
AADLS
salad
AADLU
duala
AADMM
madam
AADMN
adman
AADMR
drama
madar
AADNP
panda
AADNV
vanda
AADPT
adapt
AADRR
radar
AADRW
award
AADTY
adyta
AAEGL
algae
galea
AAEGP
agape
AAEGT

agate
AAEGV
agave
AAEGZ
agaze
AAEKL
akela
AAEKP
apeak
AAEKW
awake
AAELP
palea
AAELU
aulae
AAEMZ
amaze
AAENP
apnea
paean
AAENR
anear
arena
AAENS
ansae
AAENT
antae
AAEQU
aquae
AAERT
reata
AAERU
aurae
AAERW
aware
AAFIT
tafia
AAFLN
fanal
AAFLT
fatal
AAFMN
fanam
AAFNU
fauna
AAGIM
amiga
AAGIN
again
AAGIS
saiga
AAGIT
taiga
AAGLL

algal
AAGLN
lagan
AAGLV
vagal
AAGLX
galax
AAGMM
gamma
magma
AAGNP
pagan
panga
AAGOR
agora
AAGSU
guasa
AAGTY
agaty
AAGUV
guava
AAHJR
rajah
AAHKS
kasha
AAHLM
almah
hamal
AAHLO
aloha
AAHLP
alpha
AAHLV
halva
AAHMZ
hamza
AAHNZ
hazan
AAHPS
pasha
AAHSW
awash
AAIJV
ajiva
AAIKK
kaiak
AAILM
lamia
AAILN
liana
AAILS
alias
AAILV
avail

AAILX
axial
AAIMN
amain
anima
mania
AAIMR
maria
AAIMZ
zamia
AAINP
apian
AAINV
avian
AAIRT
atria
riata
tiara
AAIRV
varia
AAISS
assai
AAITW
await
AAJLP
jalap
AAJNN
jnana
AAJNP
japan
AAJNW
jawan
AAJOT
atajo
AAKKY
kayak
AAKLM
kalam
AAKLO
koala
AAKLR
kraal
AAKMR
karma
krama
AAKNT
tanka
AAKPP
kappa
AAKPR
parka
AAKRT
karat
AALLM

llama
AALLP
palla
AALLU
alula
AALLV
valla
AALLY
allay
AALMO
alamo
AALMP
palma
AALMR
alarm
malar
AALMT
talma
AALNN
annal
AALNS
nasal
AALNT
natal
AALNU
lauan
AALNV
naval
AALPP
papal
AALPS
salpa
AALPY
playa
AALPZ
plaza
AALRT
altar
AALRU
aural
AALRV
laura
larva
AALRY
alary
AALRZ
lazar
AALST
atlas
AAMMM
mamma
AAMNN
manna
AAMNT

atman
manta
AAMNX
axman
AAMOR
aroma
AAMPP
pampa
AAMRZ
mazar
AAMSS
amass
AAMTX
matax
AANPV
pavan
AANRS
saran
AANRT
antra
AANRV
varna
AANSS
sansa
AANSU
sauna
AAORT
aorta
AAPPW
papaw
AAPRT
apart
AAPST
pasta
AARRS
arras
AARRY
array
AARTT
attar
AASSY
assay
AASTV
avast
AATXY
ataxy
AATZZ
tazza
ABBCO
cabob
ABBCY
cabby
ABBEK
kebab
ABBEY
abbey
ABBGY
gabby
ABBIR
rabbi
ABBKO
kabob
ABBLU
babul

ABBNO
nabob
ABBOT
abbot
ABBTY
tabby
ABCEH
beach
ABCEI
ceiba
ABCEL
cable
ABCER
acerb
brace
caber
ABCHR
brach
ABCHT
batch
ABCIN
cabin
ABCIO
cobia
ABCIR
baric
ABCIS
basic
ABCKL
black
ABCLN
blanc
ABCLO
bocal
ABCNO
bacon
banco
ABCNU
bucan
ABCOR
carbo
carob
cobra
ABCOT
cabot
ABCRT
bract
ABCSU
scuba
ABDEG
badge
begad
ABDEI
abide
ABDEK
baked
ABDEL
baled
ABDEO
adobe
abode
ABDER
ardeb

bared
beard
bread
debar
ABDES
based
ABDET
bated
ABDEY
bayed
beady
ABDIR
braid
rabid
ABDIT
tabid
ABDLN
bland
ABDLO
dobla
ABDLU
blaud
ABDLY
badly
baldy
ABDNR
brand
ABDNY
bandy
ABDOR
board
broad
dobra
ABDUY
dauby
ABDWY
bawdy
ABEEL
abele
ABEFL
fable
ABEGI
bigae
ABEGL
bagel
gable
ABEGN
began
ABEGR
barge
ABEGT
begat
ABEHK
bekah
ABEHO
bohea
obeah
ABEHT
bathe
ABEIZ
baize
ABEJM
jambe
ABEJN

bejan
ABEKL
blake
bleak
ABEKR
baker
brake
break
ABELL
label
ABELM
amble
blame
melba
ABELR
abler
blare
blear
ABELS
blase
sable
ABELT
bleat
table
ABELY
belay
ABELZ
blaze
ABEMR
amber
bream
ABEMY
beamy
embay
maybe
ABEOV
above
ABERR
barer
barre
ABERS
baser
saber
sabre
ABERV
brave
ABERZ
braze
zebra
ABESS
bases
ABEST
baste
beast
tabes
ABESU
abuse
ABETT
betta
ABETU
beaut
ABFFR
barff
ABGGY

baggy
ABGHN
bhang
ABGUZ
abzug
ABHIM
bimah
ABHIS
sahib
ABHIT
habit
ABHMO
abmho
abohm
ABHOR
abhor
ABHRS
brash
shrab
ABHTU
bahut
ABIIL
alibi
ABIIM
iambi
ABIIT
tibia
ABIKL
kibla
ABIKT
batik
ABILN
binal
blain
ABILO
aboil
ABILQ
qibla
ABILR
brail
libra
ABILS
basil
ABILY
baily
bialy
ABIMR
abrim
ABIMT
ambit
ABINR
bairn
brain
ABINS
basin
sabin
ABINU
nubia
ABINV
bavin
ABIOT
biota
ABIRR
briar

ABIRS
baris
ABISS
basis
ABJNO
banjo
ABJOT
jabot
ABKLN
blank
ABKLY
balky
ABKNO
koban
ABKRU
burka
ABKRY
barky
braky
ABLLU
bulla
ABLLY
bally
ABLMU
album
ABLMY
balmy
ABLNU
balun
ABLOR
boral
labor
lobar
ABLOS
bolas
ABLOT
bloat
ABLOY
boyla
ABLRW
brawl
ABLST
blast
ABLTU
tubal
ABLWY
bylaw
ABMMO
mambo
ABMOS
sambo
ABMRU
rumba
umbra
ABMRY
ambry
barmy
ABMSY
abysm
ABNNS
banns
ABNOO
aboon
ABNOR

baron
ABNOT
baton
ABNOZ
bonza
ABNRU
buran
urban
ABNRW
brawn
ABOOT
taboo
ABORR
arbor
ABORT
abort
tabor
ABORV
bravo
ABORX
borax
ABORY
boyar
ABOSS
basso
ABOST
basto
boast
sabot
ABOTU
about
ABOUY
bayou
ABQSU
squab
ABRRY
barry
ABRSS
brass
ABRSU
bursa
ABRXY
braxy
ABSSY
abyss
ABSTU
tsuba
ABTTU
tabut
ABTTY
batty
ABUZZ
abuzz
ABWYY
byway
ACCDY
cycad
ACCEH
cache
ACCEL
cecal
ACCHK
chack
ACCHO
accho

coach
ACCHT
catch
ACCIM
acmic
ACCIO
icaco
ACCIR
circa
ACCIT
cacti
ACCKL
clack
ACCKO
acock
ACCKR
crack
ACCOO
cocoa
ACCOP
capoc
ACCOS
casco
ACCOT
coact
ACCOU
couac
ACCUY
yucca
ACDDY
caddy
ACDEF
faced
ACDEG
cadge
caged
ACDEH
ached
ACDEK
caked
ACDEL
decal
laced
ACDEM
maced
ACDEN
caned
dance
ACDEP
caped
paced
ACDER
acred
arced
cadre
cared
cedar
raced
ACDES
cased
ACDET
acted
cadet
ACDEV

caved
ACDEY
decay
ACDHR
chard
ACDIN
canid
ACDIR
acrid
caird
carid
daric
ACDIS
cadis
ACDIT
dicta
ACDIY
acidy
ACDLS
scald
ACDLU
cauld
ducal
ACDNY
candy
ACDOR
cardo
ACDOT
octad
ACDTU
ducat
ACEEP
peace
ACEES
cease
ACEFH
chafe
ACEFL
fecal
ACEFR
facer
farce
ACEFT
facet
ACEGL
glace
ACEGR
grace
ACEGY
cagey
ACEHK
hacek
ACEHL
chela
leach
ACEHN
hance
ACEHP
chape
cheap
peach
ACEHR
chare
reach

ACEHS
chase
ACEHT
cheat
tache
teach
theca
ACEIL
ileac
ACEIM
amice
ACEIR
ceria
ACEIV
cavie
ACEKR
crake
creak
ACELL
cella
ACELM
camel
ACELN
canel
clean
lance
ACELP
caple
place
ACELR
clear
ACELS
scale
ACELT
cleat
eclat
ACELV
calve
cavel
clave
ACEMO
cameo
ACEMR
crame
cream
macer
ACENO
canoe
ocean
ACENP
pecan
ACENR
caner
crane
crena
nacre
ACENS
scena
ACENT
enact
ACEOR
ocrea
ACEOX
coxae

ACEPR
caper
crape
pacer
recap
ACEPS
scape
space
ACEPT
epact
ACERR
racer
ACERS
carse
caser
ceras
serac
ACERT
caret
carte
cater
crate
react
recta
trace
ACERV
carve
crave
ACERZ
craze
ACEST
caste
ACESU
cause
sauce
ACETT
tacet
ACETU
acute
ACETX
exact
ACFFH
chaff
ACFIR
farci
firca
ACFKL
flack
ACFLO
focal
ACFNR
franc
ACFNY
fancy
ACFOT
facto
ACFRS
scarf
ACFRT
craft
ACFRU
furca
ACGHT

gatch
ACGIM
gamic
magic
ACGIN
acing
ACGIR
cigar
ACGLN
clang
ACGNO
conga
ACGOR
cargo
ACGRS
scrag
ACHHT
hatch
ACHIN
chain
china
ACHIO
chiao
ACHIR
chair
ACHIT
aitch
ACHKL
chalk
ACHKS
shack
ACHKW
whack
ACHKY
hacky
ACHLO
loach
ACHLR
larch
ACHLS
clash
ACHLT
latch
ACHMO
macho
mocha
ACHMP
champ
ACHMR
charm
march
ACHMS
chasm
ACHMT
match
ACHNR
ranch
ACHNT
chant
natch
ACHNU
nucha
ACHOO
achoo

ACHOP
poach
ACHOR
orach
roach
ACHOS
chaos
ACHOV
havoc
ACHPR
parch
ACHPT
patch
ACHRS
crash
ACHRT
chart
ACHRY
chary
ACHSW
schwa
ACHTW
watch
ACHTY
yacht
ACIIL
cilia
iliac
ACIIN
acini
iniac
ACILL
lilac
ACILM
claim
malic
ACILN
calin
ACILP
plica
ACILS
aclis
ACILT
cital
tical
ACILU
aulic
ACILV
cavil
clavi
ACILX
calix
ACIMN
manic
ACINP
panic
ACINR
cairn
ACINT
antic
ACINU
uncia
ACIOR
coria

ACIOT
coati
ACIOZ
azoic
ACIPR
carpi
ACIPS
aspic
spica
ACIRU
auric
curia
ACIRV
vicar
ACITT
attic
tacit
ACITV
vatic
ACJKY
jacky
ACJNO
cajon
ACKKN
knack
ACKKY
kyack
ACKLN
clank
ACKLO
cloak
ACKLS
slack
ACKLU
caulk
ACKMS
smack
ACKMU
amuck
ACKNR
crank
ACKNS
snack
ACKOR
croak
ACKQU
quack
ACKRT
track
ACKRW
wrack
ACKST
stack
ACKTY
tacky
ACKWY
wacky
ACLLO
local
ACLLS
scall
ACLMO
comal
ACLMP

clamp	**ACNOT**	haded	gamed	raked	sedan	**ADEWX**
ACLOP	acton	**ADDEI**	madge	**ADEKS**	**ADENV**	waxed
copal	canto	aided	**ADEGP**	asked	naved	**ADEWY**
ACLOR	cotan	gaped	paged	**ADEKW**	dewan	yawed
carol	**ACNOW**	jaded	waked	**ADELL**	waned	**ADFFR**
claro	cowan	**ADDEL**	**ADEGR**	ladle	**ADEOR**	draff
coral	**ACNOX**	addle	grade	lamed	oared	**ADFFY**
ACLOT	caxon	dedal	raged	**ADELM**	oread	daffy
calot	**ACNOY**	laded	**ADEGS**	lamed	**ADEOZ**	**ADFLU**
ACLOV	cyano	**ADDER**	degas	medal	adoze	fauld
vocal	**ACNRY**	adder	**ADEGT**	**ADELN**	**ADEPR**	**ADFRT**
ACLOX	carny	dared	gated	eland	drape	draft
coxal	**ACNST**	dread	**ADEGW**	laden	padre	**ADFRU**
ACLOZ	scant	**ADDET**	waged	lande	pared	fraud
colza	**ACOPP**	dated	**ADEGZ**	**ADELP**	raped	**ADFRW**
ACLPS	coppa	**ADDEW**	gazed	paled	**ADEPS**	dwarf
clasp	**ACOPR**	waded	**ADEHJ**	pedal	spade	**ADGIL**
scalp	copra	**ADDEZ**	jehad	plead	**ADEPT**	algid
ACLPT	**ACORT**	dazed	**ADEHK**	**ADELR**	adept	**ADGIU**
clapt	actor	**ADDGI**	kheda	alder	taped	guida
ACLPU	**ACOST**	gaddi	**ADEHL**	lader	**ADEPV**	**ADGLN**
culpa	ascot	gadid	haled	**ADELS**	paved	gland
ACLRT	coast	**ADDGJ**	**ADEHR**	slade	**ADEPW**	**ADGMO**
clart	costa	adjag	heard	**ADELT**	pawed	dogma
ACLRW	**ACOTT**	**ADDHO**	**ADEHS**	dealt	**ADEPY**	**ADGNO**
crawl	cotta	haddo	sadhe	delta	payed	donga
ACLRY	**ACPRS**	**ADDIM**	shade	lated	**ADERS**	gonad
acryl	scarp	madid	**ADEHT**	**ADELV**	rased	**ADGNR**
clary	scrap	**ADDNY**	death	deval	**ADERT**	grand
ACLSS	**ACPSU**	dandy	hated	laved	rated	**ADGRU**
class	scaup	**ADDPY**	**ADEHW**	**ADELW**	tared	guard
ACLSY	**ACPTU**	paddy	hawed	dwale	trade	**ADGUY**
scaly	caput	**ADDRY**	**ADEHX**	waled	tread	gaudy
ACLXY	**ACRRU**	dryad	hexad	weald	**ADERV**	**ADHIJ**
calyx	crura	**ADDWY**	**ADEHY**	**ADELX**	raved	hadji
ACMMO	**ACRRY**	waddy	hayed	axled	**ADERW**	**ADHIK**
comma	carry	**ADEEM**	heady	**ADELY**	wader	khadi
ACMOP	**ACRSS**	edema	**ADEHZ**	delay	wared	**ADHIP**
campo	crass	**ADEER**	hazed	layed	**ADERY**	aphid
ACMOR	**ACRSU**	eared	**ADEIL**	leady	deary	**ADHLO**
carom	arcus	**ADEES**	ailed	**ADELZ**	deray	ahold
ACMPR	**ACRSY**	aedes	ideal	lazed	rayed	**ADHNY**
cramp	scary	eased	**ADEIM**	**ADEMN**	ready	handy
ACMPS	**ACRTT**	**ADEEV**	aimed	admen	**ADERZ**	**ADHOR**
scamp	tract	evade	amide	amend	razed	hoard
ACMPY	**ACRYZ**	**ADEFG**	media	maned	**ADEST**	**ADHRS**
campy	crazy	fadge	**ADEIR**	menad	sated	shard
ACMRS	**ACSSU**	**ADEFK**	aired	named	stead	**AHDRY**
scram	ascus	faked	irade	**ADEMR**	**ADESV**	hardy
ACMSU	**ACSTU**	**ADEFM**	**ADEIS**	armed	saved	hydra
camus	scuta	famed	aside	derma	**ADESW**	**ADHST**
sumac	**ACSTY**	**ADEFR**	**ADEIU**	dream	sawed	hadst
ACMUV	styca	fared	adieu	**ADEMT**	**ADESZ**	**ADHSU**
cavum	**ACSUY**	**ADEFS**	**ADEIZ**	mated	adzes	sadhu
ACNNO	saucy	safed	azide	tamed	**ADETW**	**ADHSY**
ancon	**ACTTY**	**ADEFT**	**ADEJP**	**ADEMZ**	tawed	dashy
canon	catty	fated	japed	mazed	**ADETX**	shady
ACNNY	**ADDDE**	**ADEFZ**	**ADEJW**	**ADENO**	taxed	**ADIIR**
canny	added	fazed	jawed	anode	**ADEVW**	radii
ACNOP	**ADDDY**	**ADEGG**	**ADEKN**	**ADENP**	waved	**ADIJT**
capon	daddy	gaged	knead	paned	**ADENR**	djati
ACNOR	**ADDEF**	**ADEGL**	naked	**ADENR**	redan	**ADILL**
acorn	faded	glade	**ADEKR**	redan	**ADENS**	**ADILL**
narco	**ADDEH**	**ADEGM**	drake	**ADENS**		dalli

ADILN	skald	**ADOPT**	**AEESV**	gerah	auger	**AEHNT**
nidal	**ADKNR**	adopt	eaves	**AEGIL**	rugae	neath
ADILO	drank	**ADORR**	evase	agile	**AEGRV**	thane
dolia	**ADKOV**	ardor	**AEEVW**	**AEGIM**	grave	**AEHNV**
ADILP	vodka	**ADORS**	weave	image	**AEGRW**	haven
plaid	**ADKRY**	dorsa	**AEFFG**	**AEGIN**	wager	**AEHNY**
ADILR	darky	**ADOTY**	gaffe	gaine	**AEGRY**	hyena
laird	**ADLLY**	toady	**AEFGN**	**AEGIS**	gayer	**AEHPS**
liard	dally	today	ganef	aegis	yager	phase
ADILT	**ADLMO**	**ADQSU**	**AEFHS**	**AEGLL**	**AEGRZ**	shape
tidal	dolma	squad	sheaf	legal	graze	**AEHRS**
ADILV	modal	**ADRSW**	**AEFIR**	**AEGLM**	**AEGSS**	share
valid	**ADLMU**	sward	afire	gleam	gases	shear
ADILY	almud	**ADRTY**	feria	**AEGLN**	**AEGST**	**AEHRT**
daily	**ADLMY**	tardy	**AEFKL**	angel	stage	earth
ADIMT	madly	**AEEFZ**	flake	angle	hater	hater
admit	**ADLNO**	feaze	**AEFKN**	glean	**AEGSU**	heart
ADIMX	nodal	**AEEGL**	kenaf	**AEGLP**	usage	rathe
admix	**ADLOT**	eagle	**AEFKR**	plage	**AEGUV**	**AEHRZ**
ADINO	dotal	**AEEGR**	faker	**AEGLR**	vague	hazer
danio	**ADLOU**	agree	freak	glare	**AEGUZ**	**AEHSS**
ADINR	aloud	eager	**AEFLL**	lager	gauze	ashes
dinar	**ADLRU**	**AEEHV**	fella	large	**AEHHP**	**AEHST**
drain	dural	heave	**AEFLM**	regal	ephah	haste
nadir	**ADLRW**	**AEEIR**	flame	**AEGLT**	**AEHHT**	**AEHSV**
ADINV	drawl	aerie	fleam	aglet	heath	shave
divan	**ADLRY**	**AEELS**	**AEFLR**	**AEGLU**	**AEHIR**	**AEHSW**
viand	lardy	easel	feral	gulae	hiera	hawse
ADIOR	**ADLSY**	lease	flare	**AEGLV**	**AEHKS**	**AEHTT**
doria	sadly	**AEELT**	**AEFLS**	gavel	shake	theta
radio	**ADLTU**	elate	false	glave	**AEHLM**	**AEHTW**
ADIOS	adult	telae	**AEFLT**	**AEGLZ**	hemal	wheat
adios	**ADMNO**	**AEELV**	fetal	glaze	**AEHLP**	**AEHVY**
ADIOU	monad	leave	**AEFLY**	**AEGMM**	aleph	heavy
audio	nomad	**AEEMN**	leafy	gemma	**AEHLR**	**AEIKL**
ADIOV	**ADMNU**	enema	**AEFMR**	**AEGMN**	haler	alike
avoid	maund	**AEEMR**	frame	mange	**AEHLS**	**AEILN**
ADIPR	**ADMSU**	ameer	**AEFNR**	**AEGMO**	leash	alien
pardi	adsum	**AEENR**	frena	omega	selah	aline
rapid	**ADMTU**	ranee	**AEFOR**	**AEGMR**	shale	anile
ADIPS	datum	**AEENT**	afore	gamer	**AEHLT**	liane
sapid	**ADNNO**	eaten	**AEFOV**	marge	lathe	**AEILR**
ADIPV	donna	enate	fovea	**AEGNO**	**AEHLU**	ariel
vapid	**ADNNU**	**AEENV**	**AEFRS**	genoa	lehua	**AEILS**
ADIRT	nandu	venae	safer	**AEGNR**	**AEHLV**	aisle
triad	**ADNOR**	**AEEPS**	**AEFRT**	anger	halve	**AEILT**
ADIRX	adorn	pease	after	range	**AEHLW**	telia
radix	radon	**AEEPT**	**AEFRW**	**AEGNT**	whale	**AEILV**
ADIRY	**ADNOX**	etape	wafer	agent	wheal	alive
dairy	donax	**AEEPY**	**AEFRY**	**AEGNV**	**AEHLZ**	alvei
diary	**ADNPY**	payee	faery	vegan	hazel	**AEILX**
ADIRZ	pandy	**AEERS**	**AEFRZ**	**AEGPR**	**AEHMN**	axile
izard	**ADNRW**	easer	fraze	gaper	maneh	**AEIMN**
ADIST	drawn	erase	**AEFST**	grape	**AEHMO**	amine
staid	**ADNRY**	**AEERT**	feast	pager	mahoe	anime
tsadi	randy	arete	**AEGGI**	**AEGRS**	**AEHMR**	minae
ADISY	**ADNST**	eater	aggie	sager	harem	**AEIMZ**
daisy	stand	**AEERV**	**AEGGN**	**AEGRT**	herma	maize
sayid	**ADNSY**	reave	gange	grate	**AEHMS**	**AEINN**
ADITU	sandy	**AEERZ**	**AEGGR**	great	shame	inane
audit	**ADNTU**	razee	agger	targe	**AEHNN**	**AEINS**
ADITV	daunt	**AEEST**	**AEGGU**	terga	henna	anise
davit	**ADOPS**	setae	gauge	**AEGRU**	**AEHNS**	**AEINT**
ADKLS	spado	tease	**AEGHR**	argue	ashen	entia

tenia	quake	**AELOR**	exalt	paeon	parse	extra
tinea	**AEKRR**	orale	latex	**AENOT**	presa	taxer
AEINV	raker	**AELOV**	**AELUV**	atone	spare	**AERTY**
naevi	**AEKRS**	laevo	value	oaten	spear	teary
naive	eskar	**AELPP**	**AELVV**	**AENOV**	pater	**AERUZ**
AEINX	saker	appel	valve	novae	peart	azure
xenia	**AEKRT**	apple	**AELVY**	**AENOZ**	prate	**AERVV**
AEINZ	taker	pepla	leavy	zonae	taper	varve
azine	**AEKRW**	**AELPR**	**AEMNS**	**AENPP**	**AEPRU**	**AERVW**
AEIPS	wreak	paler	manes	nappe	pareu	waver
sepia	**AEKRZ**	parle	manse	**AENPS**	**AEPRV**	**AERWX**
AEIRS	karez	pearl	mensa	aspen	parve	waxer
arise	**AEKST**	**AELPS**	senam	sneap	paver	**AERWY**
raise	skate	lapse	**AEMNT**	**AENPT**	**AEPRY**	weary
serai	stake	salep	meant	paten	payer	**AESST**
AEIRT	steak	sepal	menat	**AENQU**	repay	asset
irate	**AEKSU**	spale	**AEMNV**	quean	**AEPSS**	tasse
retia	ukase	**AELPT**	maven	**AENRR**	passe	**AESSY**
AEIRU	**AEKSW**	leapt	**AEMNX**	reran	**AEPST**	essay
aurei	askew	lepta	axmen	**AENRS**	paste	**AESTT**
AEIRZ	**AEKTW**	pelta	**AEMNY**	nares	septa	state
zaire	tweak	petal	meany	saner	spate	taste
AEIVW	**AELLP**	plate	yamen	snare	**AEPSU**	testa
waive	lapel	pleat	**AEMOR**	**AENRV**	pause	**AESTU**
AEJLO	**AELLY**	**AELQU**	morae	raven	**AEPTU**	saute
jaleo	alley	equal	**AEMRS**	**AENRY**	taupe	**AESTV**
AEJPR	**AELMM**	**AELRS**	maser	yearn	**AEPTY**	stave
japer	lemma	lares	smear	**AENSS**	peaty	**AESTW**
AEJPS	**AELMN**	laser	**AEMRT**	sensa	**AEPVY**	sweat
jaspe	leman	**AELRT**	armet	**AENST**	peavy	waste
AEJST	**AELMO**	alert	tamer	nates	**AERRR**	**AESTX**
tajes	amole	alter	**AEMRZ**	**AENSV**	rarer	taxes
AEJSY	**AELMP**	later	mazer	avens	**AERRT**	texas
jasey	ample	ratel	**AEMSS**	**AENTT**	rater	**AESTY**
AEKLN	maple	taler	masse	natte	terra	yeast
ankle	**AELMR**	**AELRU**	**AEMST**	**AENTY**	**AERRW**	**AESUV**
AEKLR	lamer	alure	satem	yenta	rawer	suave
laker	realm	**AELRV**	steam	**AENWX**	**AERRY**	**AESWX**
AEKLS	**AELMS**	laver	**AEMSU**	waxen	rayer	waxes
slake	mesal	ravel	amuse	**AENWY**	yarer	**AETZZ**
AEKLY	**AELMT**	velar	**AEMSY**	waney	**AERSS**	tazze
leaky	metal	**AELRX**	seamy	**AENZZ**	arses	**AFFGR**
AEKMR	**AELMU**	relax	**AEMSZ**	zanze	**AERST**	graff
maker	ulema	**AELRY**	smaze	**AEOPR**	aster	**AFFIX**
AEKNO	**AELMY**	early	**AEMTT**	opera	stare	affix
oaken	mealy	layer	matte	**AEOPS**	**AERSV**	**AFFLO**
AEKNS	**AELNO**	relay	**AEMTY**	paseo	saver	offal
skean	alone	**AELSS**	etyma	**AEORS**	**AERSW**	**AFFLU**
snake	**AELNP**	salse	matey	arose	swear	luffa
sneak	panel	**AELST**	meaty	**AEORT**	**AERSY**	**AFFQU**
AEKNT	penal	least	**AEMUV**	orate	sayer	quaff
taken	plane	setal	mauve	**AEOSS**	**AERTT**	**AFFST**
AEKNV	**AELNR**	slate	**AEMYZ**	oases	atter	staff
knave	learn	stale	azyme	**AEOST**	tater	**AFFTY**
AEKNW	renal	steal	**AENNP**	stoae	tetra	taffy
waken	**AELNT**	tesla	panne	**AEOTV**	treat	**AFGHU**
AEKOW	leant	**AELSV**	penna	ovate	**AERTV**	faugh
awoke	**AELNU**	salve	**AENNS**	**AEOTZ**	avert	**AFGLU**
AEKPS	ulnae	slave	senna	azote	trave	fugal
spake	**AELNV**	**AELSW**	**AENNT**	**AEPPR**	**AERTW**	**AFGOT**
speak	navel	swale	anent	paper	tawer	fagot
AEKPY	**AELNX**	**AELTV**	**AENNX**	**AEPPU**	water	**AFGRT**
peaky	nexal	valet	annex	pupae	**AERTX**	graft
AEKQU		**AELTX**	**AENOP**	**AEPRS**		**AFHIN**

hanif	**AFLTU**	**AGHST**	slang	tangy	**AHKOO**	azoth
AFHIT	fault	ghast	**AGLOP**	**AGORT**	hooka	**AHPPY**
faith	**AFLTY**	**AGHTU**	galop	argot	**AHKOS**	happy
AFHIZ	fatly	aught	**AGLOR**	groat	shako	**AHPRS**
hafiz	**AFLUW**	**AGIKN**	algor	groat	**AHKRS**	sharp
AFHLS	awful	kiang	argol	gavot	shark	**AHPRY**
flash	**AFLWY**	**AGILN**	goral	**AGPRS**	**AHKSY**	harpy
AFHRW	flawy	align	largo	grasp	shaky	**AHPSS**
wharf	**AFLXY**	liang	**AGLOT**	sprag	**AHLLO**	shaps
AFHST	flaxy	ligan	gloat	**AGPRY**	hallo	**AHPST**
shaft	**AFMOR**	ligna	**AGLOW**	grapy	**AHLLS**	staph
AFIKL	foram	linga	aglow	**AGRSS**	shall	**AHPSW**
kalif	**AFMOY**	**AGILR**	**AGLRY**	grass	**AHLMU**	pshaw
AFIKR	foamy	argil	glary	**AGRSU**	haulm	**AHQSU**
fakir	**AFNNO**	glair	**AGLSS**	sugar	**AHLNU**	quash
fraik	fanon	grail	glass	**AGRUU**	uhlan	**AHRRY**
AFILL	**AFNNY**	**AGILS**	**AGLYY**	augur	**AHLOR**	harry
flail	fanny	sigla	gayly	**AGRVY**	horal	**AHRST**
AFILN	**AFNSU**	**AGILY**	**AGMMY**	gravy	**AHLOS**	trash
final	snafu	gaily	gammy	**AGSSU**	shoal	**AHRSU**
AFILO	**AFOOT**	**AGIMN**	**AGMNO**	gauss	**AHLOT**	surah
folia	afoot	gamin	mango	**AGSSY**	loath	**AHRTW**
AFILP	**AFORV**	**AGIMO**	among	gassy	lotah	thraw
pilaf	favor	amigo	**AGMNY**	**AGSTY**	**AHLPS**	wrath
AFILR	**AFORY**	imago	mangy	stagy	plash	**AHRTY**
filar	foray	**AGIMS**	**AGMSU**	**AGSUV**	**AHLPY**	rhyta
flair	**AFOSS**	agism	sagum	vagus	haply	**AHRXY**
frail	fossa	sigma	sigma	**AGTTU**	phyla	hyrax
AFINR	**AFOST**	**AGINO**	gamut	gutta	**AHLSS**	**AHSST**
infra	fatso	gonia	**AGMUY**	**AGUYZ**	slash	stash
AFINT	**AFRTU**	**AGINP**	gaumy	gauzy	**AHLST**	**AHSSW**
faint	furta	aping	**AGNOR**	**AHHPY**	shalt	swash
AFIQR	**AFRTY**	**AGINR**	argon	hypha	**AHLSW**	**AHSTW**
faqir	rafty	grain	grano	**AHHRS**	shawl	swath
AFIRR	**AFSUV**	grani	groan	harsh	**AHLTY**	**AHSTY**
friar	favus	**AGINT**	organ	**AHIJJ**	lathy	hasty
AFIRT	**AFTTY**	giant	**AGNOT**	hajji	**AHMMY**	**AHSWY**
afrit	fatty	**AGINW**	tango	**AHIKK**	hammy	washy
AFIRY	**AGGIN**	awing	tonga	khaki	**AHMNU**	**AHTTU**
fairy	aging	wigan	**AGNOU**	**AHIKM**	hanum	tuath
AFKLN	**AGGJY**	**AGINX**	guano	hakim	human	**AHTUY**
flank	jaggy	axing	**AGNOW**	**AHIKU**	**AHMNY**	thuya
AFKLS	**AGHHU**	**AGIRT**	gowan	haiku	mynah	**AIJKN**
flask	haugh	tragi	wagon	**AHILP**	**AHMRS**	kanji
AFKLY	**AGHIL**	**AGIRV**	**AGNOY**	phial	marsh	**AIKMU**
flaky	laigh	virga	agony	**AHILY**	**AHMSS**	umiak
AFKNR	**AGHIN**	**AGJLU**	**AGNPS**	haily	smash	**AIKOP**
frank	anigh	jugal	spang	**AHIMR**	**AHMSU**	okapi
AFKRT	**AGHLU**	**AGKWY**	**AGNRT**	ihram	hamus	**AIKRT**
kraft	laugh	gawky	grant	**AHIPS**	**AHMSW**	krait
AFLMY	**AGHMO**	**AGLLY**	**AGNRY**	apish	shawm	**AIKRU**
flamy	ogham	gally	angry	spahi	**AHMSY**	kauri
AFLOO	**AGHNO**	**AGLMO**	**AGNRY**	**AHIRY**	mashy	**AILLV**
aloof	hogan	gloam	rangy	hairy	**AHNST**	villa
AFLOR	**AGHNS**	**AGLMU**	**AGNST**	**AHIST**	snath	**AILMR**
flora	gnash	algum	stang	saith	**AHNTU**	armil
AFLOT	**AGHNW**	almug	**AGNSU**	**AHJTU**	haunt	marli
aloft	whang	glaum	agnus	thuja	**AHOOW**	**AILMS**
float	**AGHOY**	**AGLNO**	**AGNSW**	**AHKNS**	wahoo	salmi
flota	hoagy	along	swang	shank	**AHORY**	**AILNP**
AFLOU	**AGHPR**	**AGLNR**	**AGNTU**	**AHKNT**	hoary	lapin
afoul	graph	gnarl	gaunt	thank	**AHOST**	plain
AFLSU	**AGHRT**	**AGLNS**	**AGNTW**	**AHKNY**	shoat	**AILNS**
sulfa	garth	glans	twang	hanky	**AHOTZ**	slain

snail	mavis	**AIPSV**	**AKMOU**	allot	**ALNOX**	**ALSTY**
AILNV	**AIMSW**	pavis	oakum	atoll	noxal	salty
anvil	swami	**APIZZ**	**AKKNU**	**ALLOW**	**ALNOZ**	slaty
nival	**AIMTY**	pizza	kanun	allow	zonal	**ALSUU**
AILNW	amity	**AIQSU**	**AKNOR**	**ALLOY**	**ALNPT**	usual
inlaw	**AINNO**	quasi	krona	alloy	plant	**ALSVY**
AILNY	anion	**AIRRS**	**AKNPR**	loyal	**ALNRS**	sylva
inlay	**AINNP**	arris	prank	**ALLPS**	snarl	**ALTUV**
AILOV	pinna	**AIRSS**	**AKNPS**	spall	**ALNRU**	vault
viola	**AINOP**	arsis	spank	**ALLRY**	lunar	**ALTWZ**
AILPP	piano	**AIRST**	**AKNPU**	rally	**ALNST**	waltz
palpi	**AINOR**	astir	punka	**ALLST**	slant	**ALUUV**
pipal	noria	sitar	**AKNRS**	stall	**ALNUY**	uvula
AILPS	**AINPS**	stair	snark	**ALLSY**	yulan	**ALUVV**
lapis	spina	stria	**AKNST**	sally	**ALNWY**	vulva
AILPT	**AINPT**	**AIRSZ**	stank	**ALLTY**	lawny	**AMMMO**
plait	inapt	sizar	**AKNSU**	tally	wanly	momma
AILPU	paint	**AIRTT**	ankus	**ALLXY**	**ALNXY**	**AMMMY**
pilau	**AINRS**	trait	**AKNSW**	laxly	xylan	mammy
AILQU	naris	**AIRVX**	swank	**ALMMU**	**ALOPR**	**AMMOY**
quail	**AINRT**	varix	**AKNSY**	malum	parol	myoma
AILRT	riant	**AISTV**	snaky	**ALMNU**	polar	**AMMRS**
trail	train	vista	**AKOOP**	manul	**ALORS**	smarm
trial	**AINRY**	**AISTW**	oopak	**ALMNY**	solar	**AMMSU**
AILRV	rainy	waist	**AKOOR**	manly	**ALORV**	summa
rival	**AINRZ**	**AISTX**	karoo	**ALMOO**	valor	**AMMTY**
viral	nazir	taxis	**AKOOZ**	moola	volar	tammy
AILRY	**AINSS**	**AITTV**	kazoo	**ALMOR**	**ALORY**	**AMNNU**
riyal	sasin	vitta	**AKOPP**	molar	royal	unman
AILSS	**AINST**	**AJLRU**	koppa	moral	**ALOSS**	**AMNOR**
sisal	saint	jural	**AKOPY**	romal	lasso	manor
AILSV	satin	**AJMOR**	yapok	**ALMOY**	**ALOSV**	norma
silva	stain	major	**AKOTY**	loamy	salvo	**AMNOS**
AILTT	**AINSV**	**AJNOY**	tokay	**ALMPS**	**ALOTT**	mason
atilt	savin	yojan	**AKPRS**	psalm	total	**AMNOT**
AILTV	**AINSW**	**AJNTU**	spark	**ALMPU**	**ALOVV**	toman
vital	swain	jaunt	**AKPTU**	pluma	volva	**AMNOW**
AILTY	**AINTT**	junta	kaput	**ALMPY**	**ALPPU**	woman
laity	taint	**AJRTU**	**AKPWY**	amply	pupal	**AMNRU**
AIMMX	titan	jurat	pawky	palmy	**ALPPY**	unarm
maxim	**AINTW**	**AJYZZ**	**AKQRU**	**ALMQU**	apply	**AMNSU**
AIMNR	twain	jazzy	quark	qualm	**ALPRY**	manus
minar	witan	**AKKLU**	**AKQUY**	**ALMRU**	pyral	**AMORR**
AIMNT	**AINUX**	kulak	quaky	larum	**ALPST**	armor
matin	auxin	**AKKOP**	**AKRST**	mural	splat	**AMORT**
AIMNV	**AINYZ**	kapok	karst	**ALMRY**	**ALPSY**	amort
mavin	zayin	**AKKPU**	stark	marly	palsy	**AMORU**
AIMNZ	**AIOPT**	pukka	**AKRTU**	**ALMST**	splay	amour
nazim	patio	**AKLNP**	kurta	smalt	**ALPTY**	**AMORY**
AIMOX	**AIORT**	plank	**AKRUY**	**ALMTY**	aptly	mayor
axiom	ratio	**AKLNY**	kaury	malty	patly	moray
AIMPR	**AIOSS**	lanky	**AKSSV**	**ALNNU**	platy	**AMOST**
prima	oasis	**AKLOP**	kvass	annul	typal	stoma
AIMRS	**AIOST**	pokal	**ALLLY**	**ALNOP**	**ALQRU**	**AMOTY**
simar	stoai	polka	allyl	nopal	quarl	atomy
AIMRT	**AIOSV**	**AKLOS**	**ALLMO**	**ALNOR**	**ALRRU**	**AMOTZ**
amrit	aviso	skoal	molal	loran	rural	matzo
AIMRZ	**AIPRT**	**AKLST**	**ALLMS**	**ALNOS**	**ALRTU**	**AMPRT**
mirza	atrip	stalk	small	salon	ultra	tramp
AIMSS	tapir	**AKLTU**	**ALLNO**	solan	**ALRTW**	**AMPSS**
amiss	**AIPSS**	taluk	llano	**ALNOT**	trawl	spasm
AIMST	apsis	**AKLTY**	**ALLOS**	notal	**ALSTU**	**AMPST**
tamis	**AIPST**	talky	salol	talon	sault	stamp
AIMSV	tapis		**ALLOT**	tonal	talus	**AMPSW**

swamp
AMQSU
squam
AMRRU
murra
AMRRY
marry
AMRST
smart
AMRSU
ramus
AMRSW
swarm
AMRUU
aurum
AMSSY
massy
AMSTU
matsu
AMSWY
swamy
ANNNY
nanny
ANNOY
annoy
ANOPR
apron
ANOPY
yapon
ANORS
arson
saron
sonar
ANORT
orant
ANORW
rowan
ANORY
rayon
ANOTT
tanto
ANOTY
atony
ANOUY
noyau
ANOWY
noway
ANPPY
nappy
ANPRW
prawn
ANPSW
spawn
ANPSY
pansy
ANPTU
unapt
ANPTY
panty
ANQTU
quant
ANSSU
nasus
ANSTY

nasty
tansy
ANTTU
taunt
ANTTY
natty
ANTUV
vaunt
ANTWY
tawny
ANVVY
navvy
AOPRS
sapor
AOPRT
aport
AOPRV
vapor
AOPSY
soapy
AOPTZ
topaz
AOQTU
quota
AORRW
arrow
AORRZ
razor
zorra
AORSS
saros
AORST
roast
AORSV
savor
AORSW
sowar
AORTT
tarot
AORTY
otary
AORVY
ovary
AOSTT
stoat
toast
AOSVY
savoy
APPSY
sappy
APRRY
parry
APRST
sprat
strap
APRSU
supra
APRSY
raspy
APRTW
wrapt
APRTY
party

APSTU
sputa
stupa
APSTY
pasty
patsy
APSWY
waspy
APTTY
patty
AQRTU
quart
AQSSU
quass
AQSTU
squat
AQSUW
squaw
ARRSU
surra
ARRTY
tarry
ARSST
trass
ARSTT
start
ARSTU
sutra
ARSTW
straw
ARSTY
swart
satyr
stray
ARSUV
varus
ARSUY
saury
ARTTY
ratty
ARTWY
warty
ASSSY
sassy
ASTTY
tasty
ASTVY
vasty
ASVVY
savvy
ATTTY
tatty
BBBOY
bobby
BBCUY
cubby
BBDEE
ebbed
BBDOY
dobby
BBEIR
bribe
BBEKO
kebob

BBEMO
bombe
BBEOP
bebop
BBEWY
webby
BBHOY
hobby
BBHUY
hubby
BBILO
bilbo
BBILU
bulbi
BBIMO
bimbo
BBLOY
lobby
BBLRU
blurb
BBNOY
nobby
BBNUY
nubby
BBOOY
booby
BBSUY
busby
BBTUY
tubby
BCCIO
bocci
BCCIU
cubic
BCDEU
cubed
BCEEH
beech
BCEER
rebec
BCEEX
xebec
BCEEZ
zebec
BCEHL
belch
BCEHN
bench
BCEKL
bleck
BCELO
coble
BCEMO
combe
BCENO
bonce
BCENU
bunce
BCHIR
birch
BCHIT
bitch
BCHNU
bunch

BCHOT
botch
BCIKR
brick
BCILM
climb
BCIOR
boric
BCIPU
pubic
BCITU
cubit
BCKLO
block
BCKOR
brock
BCKOU
bucko
BCLMO
clomb
BCMOO
combo
BCMRU
crumb
BCNOU
bunco
BCRSU
scrub
BDDEI
bided
BDDEO
boded
BDDIY
biddy
BDDUY
buddy
BDEEL
bleed
BDEEM
embed
BDEER
breed
BDEEY
debye
BDEGI
gibed
BDEGU
budge
debug
BDEIJ
jibed
BDEIK
biked
BDEIL
bield
BDEIM
bedim
imbed
BDEIO
dobie
BDEIP
biped
BDEIR
bride

BDEIT
bidet
debit
BDELN
blend
BDELO
bodle
lobed
BDELU
blued
BDEMO
demob
BDEMU
bemud
BDENO
boden
boned
BDENY
bendy
BDEOO
booed
BDEOR
bored
orbed
robed
BDEOW
bowed
BDEOX
boxed
BDERY
derby
BDESU
bused
BDETU
debut
tubed
BDFII
bifid
BDIIR
bidri
BDILN
blind
BDILU
build
BDIOV
bovid
BDLNO
blond
BDLOO
blood
BDNOU
bound
BDOOR
brood
BDOTU
doubt
BEEFY
beefy
BEEGI
beige
BEEGL
glebe
BEEGR
gerbe

grebe
BEEGT
beget
BEEIL
belie
BEELL
belle
BEELN
nebel
BEELP
bleep
plebe
BEELR
rebel
BEELT
betel
BEELV
bevel
BEELZ
bezel
BEEMR
ember
BEENN
benne
BEEOS
obese
BEERT
beret
BEERV
bever
breve
BEERY
beery
BEEST
beset
BEFGO
befog
BEFIR
brief
fiber
BEFIT
befit
BEGIL
bilge
BEGIN
begin
being
binge
BEGIO
bogie
BEGLO
globe
BEGLU
bugle
bulge
BEGMU
begum
begnu
begun
BEGOT
begot
BEGOY
bogey
BEHRT

berth
BEHRY
herby
BEIJR
jiber
BEILL
libel
BEILO
obeli
BEIMU
imbue
BEINR
brine
BEIRR
brier
BEIRS
birse
brise
BEIRT
biter
tribe
BEISV
vibes
BEITZ
zibet
BEJNY
benjy
BEKLO
bloke
BEKOR
berok
broke
BEKRU
burke
BELLY
belly
BELMU
umbel
BELNO
noble
BELNT
blent
BELOO
obole
BELOR
roble
BELOU
boule
BELOW
below
bowel
elbow
BELRU
bluer
ruble
BELRY
beryl
BELSS
bless
BELST
blest
BELTU
bluet
BEMOR

omber
ombre
BEMOS
besom
BEMOW
embow
BEMRU
brume
umber
BEMSU
sebum
BENNY
benny
BENOR
boner
BENOY
ebony
BENOZ
bonze
BEOOZ
booze
BEOPR
probe
BEORR
borer
BEORS
sober
BEORV
bevor
BEORW
bower
BEORX
boxer
BEORY
boyer
BEOST
besot
BEOSU
bouse
BEPSU
pubes
BERRY
berry
BERSU
burse
rebus
BERTT
brett
BERTU
brute
rebut
tuber
BERUX
exurb
BERUY
buyer
BESSU
buses
BETTU
butte
BFFLU
bluff
BFFOO
boffo

BFFOU
buffo
BFFUY
buffy
BFORY
forby
BGGUY
buggy
BGHIT
bight
BGHOU
bough
BGHRU
burgh
BGHTU
bught
BGILY
bigly
bilgy
BGINO
bingo
BGINR
bring
BGIOT
bigot
BGLUY
bulgy
BGMOU
gumbo
BGMUY
gumby
BGNOO
bongo
BGNOU
bungo
BGORU
bourg
BGOSU
bogus
BHIRT
birth
BHLSU
blush
BHMOR
rhomb
BHMRU
rhumb
BHMTU
thumb
BHOOT
booth
BHORT
broth
throb
BHRSU
brush
shrub
BHSUY
bushy
BIILR
libri
BIIMN
nimbi
BIINX

bixin
BIIOR
oribi
BIIRR
birri
BIJOU
bijou
BIKLN
blink
BIKNR
brink
BIKRS
brisk
BILLY
billy
BILMO
limbo
BILMP
blimp
BILOO
oboli
BILOR
broil
BILSS
bliss
BILSY
sibyl
BILTU
built
BILTZ
blitz
BIMOZ
zombi
BINOR
robin
BINOS
bison
BINRU
bruin
burin
BINRY
briny
BIORT
orbit
BIPSU
pubis
BIQSU
squib
BIRTU
bruit
BISSY
byssi
BJMOU
jumbo
BKLUY
bulky
BKNOU
bunko
BKOOR
brook
BKOSY
bosky
BKRSU
brusk

BLLUY
bully
BLMOO
bloom
BLMPU
plumb
BLNOW
blown
BLNOY
nobly
BLNTU
blunt
BLOOY
looby
BLOSU
bolus
BLOWY
blowy
BLRSU
slurb
BLRTU
blurt
BLRUY
burly
BLTUY
butyl
BMOOR
bromo
broom
BMOOS
bosom
BMOUX
buxom
BMPUY
bumpy
BNNOY
bonny
BNNUY
bunny
BNOOR
boron
BNORU
bourn
BNORW
brown
BNOSU
bonus
bosun
BNRTU
brunt
burnt
BOORT
robot
BOOST
boost
BOOTY
booty
BOOWX
oxbow
BORRU
burro
BOSSY
bossy
BOTUY

outby
BRSTU
burst
BUYZZ
buzzy
CCCIO
cocci
CCEHK
check
CCEIR
ceric
CCELY
cycle
CCEMU
cecum
CCEOS
secco
CCESU
cusec
CCHHI
chich
CCHIK
chick
CCHIN
cinch
CCHIO
chico
CCHKO
chock
CCHKU
chuck
CCHLU
culch
CCHNO
conch
CCHOU
couch
CCHRU
curch
CCHTU
cutch
CCIIV
civic
CCIKL
click
CCIKR
crick
CCILO
colic
CCIMO
comic
CCINO
conic
CCINY
cynic
CCIOS
cisco
CCKLO
clock
CCKLU
cluck
CCKOR
crock
CCKOY

cocky
CCORU
occur
CDDEE
ceded
CDDEI
diced
CDDEO
coded
CDDUY
cuddy
CDEEH
eched
CDEEI
deice
CDEER
cedre
creed
CDEEU
deuce
educe
CDEHI
chide
CDEIM
medic
CDEIR
cider
cried
riced
CDEIT
cited
edict
CDEIY
dicey
CDEKO
coked
CDELO
dolce
CDELU
clued
dulce
CDENO
coned
CDENS
scend
CDENU
dunce
CDEOO
cooed
CDEOP
coped
CDEOR
cored
credo
decor
CDEOU
douce
CDEOV
coved
CDEOX
codex
CDEOY
coyed
decoy

CDERU
crude
cured
CDERY
decry
CDETU
educt
CDHIL
child
CDHIT
ditch
CDHOR
chord
CDHTU
dutch
CDHUY
duchy
CDIIO
iodic
CDIIS
disci
CDIKY
dicky
CDILU
lucid
CDIMU
mucid
CDIOT
dicot
CDIPU
pudic
CDISU
scudi
CDKUY
ducky
CDLOS
scold
CDLOU
cloud
could
CDNOO
condo
CDORS
scrod
CDORW
crowd
CDOSU
scudo
CEEEM
emcee
CEEFN
fence
CEEFS
feces
CEEHK
cheek
keech
CEEHL
leech
CEEHN
hence
CEEHP
cheep
CEEHR
cheer
CEEIN
niece
CEEIP
piece
CEEIZ
ecize
CEEJT
eject
CEEKL
cleek
CEEKR
creek
CEELR
creel
CEELT
elect
CEELX
excel
CEEMR
creme
CEENP
pence
CEENS
cense
scene
CEEOO
cooee
CEEPR
creep
crepe
CEERS
scree
CEERT
erect
terce
CEESY
sycee
CEFHI
chief
fiche
CEFHT
fetch
CEFIT
fecit
CEFKL
fleck
CEFLT
cleft
CEFOR
force
CEGKO
gecko
CEGNO
conge
CEHIM
chime
hemic
CEHIN
chine
niche
CEHIT
ethic
CEHIV
chive
CEHKN
kench
CEHKO
choke
CEHKT
ketch
CEHLT
letch
CEHLY
chyle
CEHMY
chyme
CEHNT
tench
CEHNW
wench
CEHOP
epoch
CEHOR
chore
ocher
ochre
CEHOS
chose
CEHPR
perch
CEHRT
chert
retch
CEHRU
ruche
CEHSS
chess
CEHST
chest
CEHTU
chute
CEHTV
vetch
CEHTY
techy
CEHVY
chevy
CEHWY
chewy
CEIIR
icier
CEIJU
juice
CEIKL
cleik
CEIKR
icker
CEILM
clime
melic
CEILN
cline
CEILO
oleic
CEILR
relic
CEILS
slice
CEILT
telic
CEILV
velic
CEIMN
mince
CEIMR
crime
merci
CEIMS
mesic
CEIMT
metic
CEIMX
cimex
CEINR
nicer
CEINS
since
CEINW
wince
CEIOV
voice
CEIPR
price
CEIPS
spice
CEIRR
crier
ricer
CEIRS
cries
CEIRT
trice
CEIRU
curie
CEIRX
xeric
CEIRY
ricey
CEIST
cesti
CEITU
cutie
CEITV
civet
evict
CEITW
twice
CEKLR
clerk
CEKPS
speck
CELLO
cello
CELNO
clone
CELNU
uncle
CELOP
ploce
CELOR
ceorl
CELOS
close
socle
CELOU
coule
CELOV
clove
CELOZ
cloze
CELPU
cupel
CELRU
cruel
lucre
ulcer
CELSU
luces
CELTU
culet
CELTY
cetyl
CELUX
culex
CEMOR
comer
CEMOT
comet
comte
CEMRY
mercy
CENNO
nonce
CENOR
crone
CENOS
censo
CENOT
cento
conte
CENOU
ounce
CENOV
coven
CENOY
coney
CENOZ
cozen
CENST
scent
CEOOR
cooer
CEOOY
cooey
CEOPS
copse
scope
CEOPU
coupe
CEOQU
coque
CEORR
corer
crore
CEORS
corse
score
CEORT
recto
CEORV
cover
CEORW
cower
CEORY
coyer
CEORZ
croze
CEOST
estoc
CEOTT
octet
CEOTV
covet
CEOVY
covey
CEPRT
crept
CEPSS
specs
CERRU
recur
CERSS
cress
CERST
crest
CERSU
cruse
curse
CERSW
screw
CERTU
cruet
curet
cuter
eruct
truce
CERUV
curve
CESTU
scute
CETUY
cutey
CFFHU
chuff
CFFIL
cliff
CFFLO
cloff
CFFOS
scoff
CFFSU
scuff
CFHIL
filch
CFHIN
finch
CFHIT
fitch
CFHIU
fichu
CFIKL
flick
CFINU
funic
CFKLO
flock
CFKOR
frock
CFLOO
cloof
CFMOY
comfy
CFORT
croft
CFOSU
focus
CFRSU
scurf
CFSUU
fucus
CGHLU
gulch
CGHOT
gotch
CGHOU
cough
CGIIN
icing
CGILN
cling
CGILO
logic
CGINU
cuing
CGIOR
corgi
CGLNU
clung
CGLOO
colog
CGNOO
congo
CGORS
scrog
CHHIT
hitch
CHHIW
which
CHHNU
hunch
CHHOO
hooch
CHHTU
hutch
CHIIL
chili
lichi
CHIKN
chink
CHIKR
chirk

CHIKT thick
CHILL chill
CHILM milch
CHILT licht
CHILZ zilch
CHIMO ohmic
CHIMP chimp
CHIMR chirm
CHIMU humic
CHINO chino
CHINP pinch
CHINW winch
CHIOR chiro, choir, ichor
CHIPR chirp
CHIPT pitch
CHIRR chirr
CHIST stitch
CHITW witch
CHITY itchy
CHKNU chunk
CHKOS shock
CHKOY choky
CHKSU shuck
CHLMU mulch
CHLNU lunch
CHLNY lynch
CHLOR chlor, chlor
CHLOS closh
CHLOT cloth
CHLRU churl, lurch
CHMNU munch
CHMOO mooch
CHMOP chomp
CHMOS schmo
CHMOU mouch
CHMPU chump
CHNNU nunch
CHNOT notch
CHNPU punch
CHNRU churn
CHOOP pooch
CHOPR porch
CHOPU pouch
CHORT torch
CHOSU hocus
CHOTU couth, touch
CHOUV vouch
CHPSY psych
CHRRU churr
CHRSU crush
CHRTW crwth
CHSUY cushy
CIILT licit
CIILV civil
CIILY icily
CIIMM mimic
CIINO ionic
CIINR ricin
CIINV vinic
CIIOR cirio
CIIPP cippi
CIIRR cirri
CIJUY juicy
CIKLN clink
CIKLS slick
CIKMY micky
CIKNS snick
CIKPR prick
CIKPY picky
CIKQU quick
CIKRT trick
CIKST stick
CILNO colin
CILOU oculi
CILOW wilco
CILPT clipt
CILPU picul
CILRY lyric
CILTY lytic
CILXY cylix
CIMNU cumin
CIMOR micro
CIMOS osmic
CIMPR crimp
CIMRS scrim
CIMSU music
CINOS scion, sonic
CINOT tonic
CINRU incur, runic
CINSU incus
CINTT tinct
CINTU cutin, tunic
CIOPT optic, picot, topic
CIORR roric
CIORT toric
CIORU curio
CIOST stoic
CIOTX toxic
CIPRS crisp, scrip
CIPSY spicy
CISTU cutis, ictus
CJKOO jocko
CJNOU junco
CKKNO knock
CKLNU clunk
CKLPU pluck
CKLUY lucky
CKMOS smock
CKMUY mucky
CKOOR crook
CKOOY cooky
CKORY corky, rocky
CKOST stock
CKRTU truck
CKSTU stuck
CLLOY colly
CLLSU scull
CLLUY cully
CLMOP clomp
CLMPU clump
CLMTU mulct
CLNOO colon
CLNOW clown
CLOOP cloop
CLOOR color
CLOOT cloot
CLOOY cooly
CLORW crowl
CLOSU locus
CLOSW scowl
CLOTU clout
CLOYY coyly
CLPSU sculp
CLRUY curly
CMOOP compo
CMOPT compt
CMORU mucor
CMPRU crump
CMRSU scrum
CMSUU mucus
CNOOR croon
CNOOT conto
CNORS scorn
CNORU cornu
CNORW crown
CNORY corny, crony
CNOTU count
CNOTY cyton
CNSUU uncus
CNTUU uncut
COOPS scoop
COOPT coopt
COORT troco
COOST scoot
COPPY coppy
COPRS corps
COPRU croup
COPSY copsy
COPUY coypu
CORSS cross
CORSU scour
CORSW scrow
CORTU court
CORWY cowry
COSTU scout
CPRTY crypt
CPTUU cutup
CRRUY curry
CRSTU crust, curst
CRUVY curvy
DDEEG edged
DDEEL deled
DDEEN endec
DDEER dreed
DDEEW dewed
DDEGO dodge
DDEIK diked
DDEIL idled
DDEIN dined
DDEIO diode
DDEIR dried, redid
DDEIS sided
DDEIT tided
DDEIV dived
DDEKY dyked
DDELO doled
DDEMO domed
DDENY neddy
DDEOP doped
DDEOS dosed
DDEOT doted
DDEOV doved
DDEOW dowed
DDEOZ dozed
DDEPU duped
DDERU dured, udder
DDETY teddy
DDGIY giddy
DDGOY dodgy
DDIKO kiddo
DDIKY kiddy
DDIMY middy
DDINU undid
DDIRU druid
DDLOY oddly
DDMUY muddy
DDNOY noddy
DDOTY toddy
DDOWY dowdy
DDRUY ruddy
DEEFR defer, freed
DEEFT feted
DEEGG egged
DEEGH hedge
DEEGK kedge
DEEGL

glede	suede	gelid	ephod	denim	sired	yodle
gleed	**DEESW**	glide	hoped	mined	**DEIRT**	**DELPU**
ledge	sewed	**DEGIM**	**DEHOR**	**DEIMR**	tired	duple
DEEGO	**DEESX**	midge	horde	dimer	tried	puled
geode	desex	**DEGIN**	**DEHOS**	mired	**DEIRV**	**DELRU**
DEEGR	sexed	deign	hosed	rimed	diver	lured
edger	**DEESY**	nidge	shoed	**DEIMS**	drive	ruled
greed	seedy	**DEGIO**	**DEHPT**	deism	rived	**DELSU**
DEEGS	**DEETU**	dogie	depth	**DEIMT**	**DEIRW**	dulse
sedge	etude	geoid	**DEHPY**	demit	weird	slued
DEEGW	**DEETW**	**DEGIR**	hyped	mited	wider	**DELSY**
wedge	tewed	dirge	**DEHRS**	timed	wired	lysed
DEEHR	tweed	gride	sherd	**DEIMX**	**DEIST**	**DELTU**
heder	**DEEUX**	ridge	shred	mixed	deist	luted
DEEHW	exude	**DEGIU**	**DEIIM**	**DEINN**	sited	**DELTV**
hewed	**DEEVX**	guide	imide	inned	**DEISV**	veldt
DEEHX	vexed	**DEGJU**	**DEIIV**	**DEINP**	vised	**DELTW**
hexed	**DEEWY**	judge	ivied	piend	**DEISW**	dwelt
DEEIL	weedy	**DEGLO**	**DEIJR**	pined	wised	**DELUX**
edile	**DEFFI**	lodge	jerid	**DEINR**	**DEISW**	luxed
elide	fifed	ogled	**DEIJV**	diner	wised	**DEMNO**
DEEIR	**DEFFO**	**DEGLU**	jived	**DEINS**	**DEISZ**	demon
eider	offed	glued	**DEIKL**	snide	sized	**DEMOO**
DEEKN	**DEFGI**	**DEGLY**	liked	**DEINT**	**DEITW**	mooed
kneed	fidge	ledgy	**DEIKN**	teind	wited	**DEMOP**
DEEKY	**DEFGO**	**DEGNU**	inked	**DEINU**	**DEITY**	moped
keyed	defog	nudge	**DEIKP**	indue	deity	**DEMOS**
DEELR	**DEFGU**	**DEGOR**	piked	nudie	**DEIVW**	demos
elder	fudge	gored	**DEIKR**	**DEINW**	wived	**DEMOU**
DEELU	**DEFIK**	**DEGOT**	irked	dwine	**DEJKO**	odeum
elude	fiked	godet	**DEIKS**	widen	joked	**DEMOV**
DEELV	**DEFIL**	**DEGOY**	skied	wined	**DEJKU**	moved
delve	felid	dogey	**DEIKT**	**DEINX**	juked	**DEMOW**
devel	field	**DEGRS**	kited	index	**DEJOW**	mowed
DEEMN	filed	dregs	**DEILM**	nixed	jowed	**DEMRU**
emend	flied	**DEGRU**	limed	**DEINZ**	**DEKNO**	demur
DEEMT	**DEFIN**	urged	**DEILN**	dizen	kendo	**DEMSU**
meted	fiend	**DEGSY**	lined	**DEIOS**	**DEKOP**	mused
DEEMW	fined	sedgy	**DEILO**	eidos	poked	sedum
mewed	**DEFIR**	**DEGUY**	oiled	**DEIOV**	**DEKOY**	**DEMTU**
DEENS	fired	guyed	oldie	video	yoked	muted
dense	fried	**DEGVY**	**DEILP**	**DEIOX**	**DEKPU**	**DEMUX**
DEENU	**DEFIT**	gyved	piled	oxide	puked	muxed
endue	fetid	**DEGWY**	plied	**DEIPP**	**DELLW**	**DENNO**
DEENY	**DEFIX**	wedgy	**DEILR**	piped	dwell	donne
needy	fixed	**DEHIK**	idler	**DEIPR**	**DELMO**	**DENOR**
DEEOP	**DEFIY**	hiked	riled	pride	model	drone
epode	deify	**DEHIR**	**DEILS**	pried	**DELNO**	ronde
DEEOR	edify	hider	sidle	riped	loden	**DENOS**
erode	**DEFLT**	hired	slide	**DEIPS**	olden	nosed
DEEOX	delft	**DEHIS**	**DEILT**	siped	**DELOO**	sonde
exode	**DEFLU**	shied	tilde	spied	looed	**DENOT**
DEEPS	flued	**DEHIV**	tiled	**DEIPT**	**DELOP**	noted
speed	**DEFMR**	hived	**DEILV**	tepid	loped	toned
DEERR	fremd	**DEHLO**	devil	**DEIPW**	poled	**DENOW**
erred	**DEFMU**	dhole	lived	wiped	**DELOR**	endow
DEERT	fumed	holed	**DEILW**	**DEIQU**	older	nowed
deter	**DEFNU**	**DEHMO**	wield	equid	**DELOV**	owned
treed	unfed	homed	wiled	**DEIRR**	loved	**DENOY**
DEERY	**DEFSU**	**DEHNO**	**DEILY**	direr	**DELOW**	doyen
reedy	fused	honed	yield	drier	dowel	**DENOZ**
DEEST	**DEFUZ**	**DEHNS**	**DEIMM**	rider	lowed	dozen
steed	fuzed	shend	mimed	**DEIRS**	**DELOY**	zoned
DEESU	**DEGIL**	**DEHOP**	**DEIMN**	dries	yodel	**DENPS**

spend	vowed	**DGLOY**	solid	moldy	rowdy	**EEGLM**
DENPU	**DEPRU**	godly	**DILOT**	**DLOOR**	wordy	gemel
upend	drupe	**DGNUY**	doilt	dolor	**DOTTY**	**EEGLR**
DENRT	duper	dungy	**DILOY**	drool	dotty	leger
trend	perdu	**DGOOY**	doily	**DLOOS**	**DRSTU**	**EEGLS**
DENRU	prude	goody	**DILRU**	soldo	durst	leges
under	pured	**DGORU**	lurid	**DLOOY**	**DRUXY**	**EEGLT**
DENTU	**DEPTY**	gourd	**DIMOS**	dooly	druxy	gleet
tuned	typed	**DGPUY**	misdo	**DLORW**	**DSSUY**	**EEGLY**
DENUU	**DERRU**	pudgy	**DIMOU**	world	sudsy	elegy
undue	ruder	**DGRUY**	odium	**DLOUW**	**DSTUY**	**EEGMR**
DENUW	**DERRY**	gurdy	**DIMST**	would	dusty	merge
unwed	derry	**DHIMU**	midst	**DLRYY**	study	**EEGNR**
DEOOR	dryer	humid	**DIMTU**	dryly		genre
rodeo	**DERSS**	**DHIOT**	tumid	**DMMUY**	**EEEFZ**	green
DEOOW	dress	dhoti	**DINOR**	dummy	feeze	**EEGNT**
wooed	**DERSU**	**DHIOY**	nidor	**DMNOO**	**EEEGS**	genet
DEOOZ	druse	hyoid	**DINSU**	mondo	geese	**EEGNV**
oozed	**DERTU**	**DHIRT**	nidus	**DMNOU**	**EEEHT**	venge
DEOPR	detur	third	**DINWY**	mound	tehee	**EEGNW**
doper	trued	**DHITW**	windy	**DMOOY**	**EEEIR**	ngwee
pored	**DERUZ**	width	**DIOOV**	moody	eerie	**EEGRS**
roped	druze	**DHNOO**	ovoid	**DMPUY**	**EEEKV**	serge
DEOPS	**DETUV**	hondo	**DIOOZ**	dumpy	keeve	**EEGRT**
posed	duvet	**DHNOU**	zooid	**DNOOR**	**EEELM**	egret
DEOPT	**DFILU**	hound	**DIORT**	donor	melee	**EEGRV**
depot	fluid	**DHORY**	droit	rondo	**EEELV**	verge
poted	**DFINU**	hydro	**DIOTT**	**DNOOS**	levee	**EEGST**
toped	fundi	**DHOWY**	ditto	snood	**EEEMR**	egest
DEOPX	**DFIOR**	howdy	**DIOTV**	**DNOPU**	emeer	geest
podex	fiord	**DIILP**	divot	pound	**EEEPT**	**EEGSU**
DEOPY	**DFIRT**	lipid	**DIOWW**	**DNORU**	tepee	segue
dopey	drift	**DIILV**	widow	round	**EEEPV**	**EEHLV**
DEORR	**DFJOR**	livid	**DIPPY**	**DNORW**	peeve	helve
order	fjord	**DIIMO**	dippy	drown	**EEEPW**	**EEHLW**
DEORS	**DFLOO**	idiom	**DIPRT**	**DNOSU**	pewee	wheel
dorse	flood	modii	dript	nodus	**EEERV**	**EEHMT**
rosed	**DFNOR**	**DIIMT**	**DIQSU**	sound	reeve	theme
DEORT	frond	dimit	squid	**DNOSY**	**EEFLR**	**EEHNS**
doter	**DFNOU**	timid	**DIRTY**	synod	fleer	sheen
roted	fondu	**DIINR**	dirty	**DNOTU**	**EEFLT**	**EEHPS**
trode	found	indri	**DITTY**	donut	fleet	sheep
DEORU	**DFOOR**	**DIINT**	ditty	**DNOUW**	**EEFMM**	**EEHRS**
uredo	fordo	nitid	**DIVVY**	wound	femme	heres
DEORV	**DGGOY**	**DIIOT**	divvy	**DNOWY**	**EEFRR**	sheer
drove	doggy	idiot	**DIYZZ**	downy	freer	**EEHRT**
roved	**DGHOU**	**DIITX**	dizzy	**DOOPR**	refer	ether
DEORW	dough	dixit	**DKNRU**	droop	**EEFRV**	there
dower	**DGIIR**	**DIIVV**	drunk	**DOOST**	fever	three
rowed	rigid	vivid	**DKORU**	stood	**EEFRW**	**EEHRW**
DEOSU	**DGIIT**	**DIKNR**	drouk	**DOOTU**	fewer	hewer
douse	digit	drink	**DKOSU**	outdo	**EEFSS**	where
DEOSW	**DGILU**	**DIKNY**	kudos	**DOOWY**	fesse	**EEHRX**
dowse	guild	dinky	**DKSUY**	woody	**EEFSU**	hexer
sowed	**DGINO**	**DILLR**	dusky	**DOPRU**	fusee	**EEHST**
DEOTT	dingo	drill	**DLLOR**	proud	**EEFUZ**	sheet
toted	doing	**DILLY**	droll	**DORSS**	fuzee	these
DEOTV	**DGINR**	dilly	**DLLOY**	dross	**EEGIL**	**EEHTT**
voted	grind	idyll	dolly	**DORSW**	liege	teeth
DEOTW	**DGINY**	**DILMY**	**DLLUY**	sword	**EEGIN**	**EEILM**
towed	dingy	dimly	dully	**DORTY**	genie	elemi
DEOTY	**DGIRY**	**DILNY**	**DLMOU**	dorty	**EEGIS**	**EEILT**
toyed	dying	lindy	mould	**DORWY**	siege	elite
DEOVW	ridgy	**DILOS**	**DLMOY**	dowry	**EEGKL**	
					gleek	

EEILV
lieve
EEILX
exile
EEINS
seine
EEINX
exine
EEIPS
peise
EEIRT
retie
EEISV
sieve
EEISZ
seize
EEITV
evite
EEJLW
jewel
EEJSS
jesse
EEJSU
sujee
EEKLN
kneel
EEKLS
skeel
sleek
EEKLV
kevel
EEKOP
pekoe
EEKOV
evoke
EEKRS
esker
EEKRY
reeky
EEKST
skeet
EEKSX
kexes
EELLV
level
EELMR
merle
EELNO
leone
EELNS
lenes
EELNV
nevel
EELNW
newel
EELOP
elope
EELPR
leper
repel
EELPS
sleep
speel
EELPX

expel
EELRV
elver
lever
revel
EELRY
leery
EELST
sleet
steel
stele
EELSV
elves
EELTU
elute
EELTX
telex
EELXX
exlex
EEMMR
emmer
EEMMT
emmet
EEMNS
mesne
semen
EEMNU
neume
EEMNY
enemy
EEMOT
emote
EEMRS
merse
EEMRT
meter
metre
retem
EEMRX
remex
EEMRY
emery
EEMST
temse
EENPR
preen
EENPS
penes
EENQU
queen
EENRS
sneer
EENRT
enter
EENRV
nerve
never
EENRW
newer
renew
EENSS
sense
EENST
tense

EENSU
ensue
EENSV
seven
EENTT
tenet
EENTV
event
EENTY
teeny
EENUV
venue
EEOPT
topee
EEORS
erose
EEOXY
oxeye
EEPRS
perse
prese
speer
spree
EEPRT
peter
EEPRU
puree
rupee
EEPRY
peery
EEPSI
steep
EEPSW
sweep
EEPSY
seepy
EEPWY
weepy
EEQRU
queer
EEQSU
eques
EEQUU
queue
EERST
ester
reset
steer
stere
terse
EERSU
reuse
EERSV
serve
sever
verse
EERSW
sewer
EERTV
evert
revet
EERTW
rewet
EERTX

exert
EERUV
revue
EERVV
verve
EERVY
every
veery
ewery
EESSX
sexes
EESSY
yeses
EESTW
sweet
weest
EETTW
tweet
EFFFO
feoff
EFFIR
fifer
EFFOR
offer
EFGIN
feign
EFGIR
grief
EFGOR
forge
gofer
EFGOY
fogey
EFGUU
fugue
EFHIT
thief
EFHLS
flesh
shelf
EFHRS
fresh
EFHTT
theft
EFHTY
hefty
EFIKN
knife
EFILN
elfin
EFILR
filer
flier
lifer
rifle
EFILS
flies
EFILT
filet
flite
EFIMR
fermi
EFIMT

metif
EFINR
finer
infer
EFINT
feint
EFIRR
frier
EFIRS
fries
frise
serif
EFIRV
fiver
EFIRX
fixer
EFIRY
fiery
reify
EFIST
feist
EFISX
fixes
EFKLU
fluke
EFLLY
felly
EFLMU
flume
EFLNO
felon
EFLOR
forel
EFLRY
ferly
flyer
EFLTU
flute
EFLTY
felty
lefty
EFMRU
femur
EFNNY
fenny
EFNOT
often
EFNRY
ferny
EFORT
fetor
forte
EFORY
foyer
EFORZ
froze
EFOSS
fosse
EFOSX
foxes
EFRRY
ferry
fryer
EFRUZ

furze
EFSTU
fetus
EGGIU
gigue
guige
EGGLY
leggy
EGGOR
gorge
EGGOU
gouge
EGGRU
gurge
EGHHI
heigh
EGHIN
hinge
neigh
EGHIT
eight
EGHIW
weigh
EGHLY
hyleg
EGHNT
thegn
EGHRU
huger
EGIIN
genii
EGIKN
eking
EGIKR
grike
EGILM
gimel
EGILN
ingle
EGILT
gilet
legit
EGILU
guile
EGIMR
grime
EGINR
reign
EGINS
segni
sengi
singe
EGINT
tinge
EGINV
given
EGINY
eying
EGIOV
ogive
EGIPR
gripe
EGIRS
grise

EGIRT
tiger
EGIRV
giver
EGISU
guise
EGJRU
juger
EGLMO
golem
EGLNO
longe
EGLNU
lunge
EGLOR
ogler
EGLOV
glove
EGLOY
elogy
EGLOZ
gloze
EGLRU
gluer
gruel
EGLSU
gules
EGLUY
gluey
EGMMY
gemmy
EGMNO
gnome
EGMOT
gemot
EGMRU
grume
EGNOP
pengo
EGNOR
genro
goner
EGNOS
segno
EGNSU
genus
negus
EGNTY
genty
EGOOS
goose
EGOOY
gooey
EGOPR
grope
EGOPY
pogey
EGORR
roger
EGORS
gorse
EGORT
ergot
EGORU

rogue	hello	**EHOPR**	**EIKNZ**	slipe	**EIMST**	veiny
rouge	**EHLLS**	ephor	zinke	spiel	metis	**EINWZ**
EGORV	shell	hoper	**EIKPR**	spile	smite	wizen
grove	**EHLOS**	**EHOPU**	piker	**EILRT**	stime	**EIOPS**
EGOSS	shole	ouphe	**EIKPS**	liter	**EINNP**	poise
gesso	**EHLOT**	**EHORS**	spike	litre	penni	**EIORS**
EGOTU	hotel	horse	**EIKRT**	tiler	**EINNR**	osier
togue	thole	shoer	kiter	**EILRV**	inner	**EIORV**
EGOTY	**EHLOV**	shore	**EIKSS**	ervil	renin	vireo
goety	hovel	**EHORT**	skies	liver	**EINNU**	**EIOWZ**
EGOUV	**EHLOW**	other	**EIKST**	livre	ennui	zowie
vogue	whole	throe	skite	viler	**EINNV**	**EIPPR**
EGPRU	holey	**EHORV**	**EIKSV**	**EILSS**	venin	piper
purge	**EHLPW**	hover	skive	lisse	**EINOP**	**EIPQU**
getup	whelp	**EHORW**	**EILLR**	**EILST**	opine	equip
EGRSU	**EHLPY**	whore	iller	islet	**EINOR**	pique
surge	phyle	**EHOST**	rille	istle	irone	**EIPRR**
EGSSU	**EHLSW**	ethos	**EILLS**	stile	**EINOS**	prier
guess	welsh	shote	lisle	**EILSU**	eosin	riper
EGSTU	**EHLTY**	those	**EILMN**	ileus	noise	**EIPRS**
guest	ethyl	**EHOSU**	limen	**EILSV**	**EINOV**	pries
EHHST	**EHLXY**	house	**EILMP**	lives	ovine	spire
sheth	hexyl	**EHOSV**	impel	slive	**EINPR**	**EIPRT**
EHIKS	**EHMNY**	shove	**EILMR**	**EILSW**	ripen	tripe
sheik	hymen	**EHOSW**	miler	lewis	**EINPS**	**EIPRV**
EHIKT	**EHMOR**	whose	**EILMS**	**EILSX**	penis	viper
kithe	homer	**EHPRY**	limes	lexis	snipe	**EIPRW**
EHILT	**EHMOY**	hyper	slime	**EILTT**	spine	wiper
lithe	homey	**EHRSU**	smile	title	**EINPT**	**EIPRZ**
EHILW	**EHMPY**	usher	**EILMU**	**EILTU**	inept	prize
while	hempy	**EHRSW**	ileum	utile	**EINPY**	**EIPSS**
EHILX	**EHMRT**	shrew	**EILMY**	**EILTX**	piney	spies
helix	therm	**EHRSY**	limey	ixtle	**EINRS**	**EIPST**
EHINS	**EHMRU**	shyer	**EILNN**	**EIMMO**	resin	spite
shine	rheum	**EHRTW**	linen	mimeo	rinse	stipe
EHINT	**EHMRY**	threw	**EILNO**	**EIMMR**	risen	**EIPSW**
thine	rhyme	**EHRTZ**	eloin	mimer	serin	swipe
EHINW	**EHMSY**	hertz	olein	**EIMNR**	siren	**EIPTT**
whine	meshy	**EHTWY**	**EILNR**	miner	**EINRT**	petit
EHIRR	**EHMTU**	thewy	liner	**EIMNV**	inert	**EIPTY**
hirer	humet	**EIILP**	**EILNS**	vimen	inter	piety
EHIRS	**EHMTY**	pilei	lenis	**EIMOR**	niter	**EIPXY**
shire	thyme	**EIIMN**	**EILNT**	moire	trine	pyxie
EHIRT	**EHNOP**	imine	inlet	**EIMOV**	**EINRU**	**EIQRU**
their	pheon	**EIINX**	**EILNV**	movie	inure	quire
EHIRV	phone	nixie	levin	**EIMOX**	urine	**EIQTU**
hiver	**EHNOR**	**EIIPX**	liven	moxie	**EINRV**	quiet
EHISS	heron	pixie	**EILOO**	**EIMPR**	riven	quite
shies	**EHNOS**	**EIISV**	looie	prime	**EINST**	**EIRRS**
EHIST	hosen	ivies	**EILOR**	**EIMPT**	inset	riser
heist	shone	**EIKLN**	oiler	tempi	stein	**EIRRV**
EHISV	**EHNOY**	inkle	oriel	**EIMRS**	**EINSW**	river
shive	honey	liken	**EILOT**	miser	sinew	**EIRRW**
EHITT	**EHNPR**	**EIKLR**	toile	**EIMRT**	swine	wrier
tithe	phren	liker	**EILOU**	merit	**EINSX**	**EIRRY**
EHITW	**EHNRY**	**EIKLV**	louie	miter	nixes	eyrir
white	henry	kevil	**EILOV**	remit	**EINTU**	**EIRST**
withe	**EHNSW**	**EIKNO**	olive	timer	unite	tries
EHKLW	shewn	eikon	voile	**EIMRX**	untie	**EIRSW**
whelk	**EHNTT**	**EIKNR**	**EILPR**	mixer	**EINTW**	wiser
EHKOY	tenth	inker	peril	remix	twine	**EIRTT**
hokey	**EHOOY**	**EIKNS**	plier	**EIMSS**	**EINVX**	titer
EHLLO	hooey	skein	**EILPS**	seism	vixen	titre
			plies	semis	**EINVY**	trite

EIRTV rivet
EIRTW write
EISST sties
EISSU issue
EISTU suite
EISTX exist, sixte
EJKOP kopje
EJKOR joker
EJKRY jerky
EJLLY jelly
EJLOU joule
EJLPU julep
EJLRU jurel
EJMMY jemmy
EJNNY jenny
EJNOY enjoy
EJRRY jerry
EJTTY jetty
EKLLN knell
EKLLY kelly
EKLNT knelt
EKLOY yokel
EKLPS skelp
EKLPY kelpy
EKMOS smoke
EKNOR krone
EKNOT token
EKNOW woken
EKOPR poker
EKOPS spoke
EKOSS sekos
EKOST stoke
EKPRY perky
EKPSY pesky
EKQRU querk
EKRRY kerry
EKSYY skyey
ELLMO molle
ELLMS smell
ELLNS snell
ELLOS losel
ELLPS spell
ELLQU quell
ELLSW swell
ELLTU tulle
ELLTY telly
ELMNO lemon, melon
ELMNU lumen
ELMOR morel
ELMOT motel
ELMOU oleum
ELMPU plume
ELMRU lemur
ELMST smelt
ELMSU mulse
ELMUV velum
ELMUY muley
ELMXY xylem
ELNOT lento, olent
ELNOV novel
ELNOW nowel
ELNWY newly
ELOOS loose
ELOPR loper
ELOPS slope
ELORS loser
ELORV lover
ELORW lower, rowel
ELOSS loess
ELOST stole
ELOSU louse
ELOSV solve
ELOTV volet
ELOTW owlet, towel
ELOTX extol
ELOUV ovule
ELOUZ ouzel
ELOVW vowel
ELPRY reply
ELPST slept, spelt
ELPSU pulse
ELPTU letup
ELRRU ruler
ELRSY slyer
ELSTY style
ELSUX luxes
ELTUX exult
ELTWY wetly
EMNNO nomen
EMNNU numen
EMNOR enorm
EMNOS meson
EMNOT monte
EMNOV venom
EMNOW women
EMNOY money
EMNRU rumen
EMNUX nexum
EMOOS moose
EMOPR proem
EMOPT tempo
EMOPY myope
EMORR ormer
EMORS mores
EMORT metro
EMORV mover, vomer
EMORW mower
EMOST smote
EMOSU mouse
EMOSY mosey
EMOTT motet
EMOZZ mezzo
EMPRS sperm
EMPSU spume
EMPTT tempt
EMPTY empty
EMRRU murre
EMRRY merry
EMRSU serum
EMRUX murex
EMSSY messy
EMSUV sevum
EMSUX muxes
ENNOT tenon, tonne
ENNOX xenon
ENNPY penny
ENOOS noose
ENOOZ ozone
ENOPR prone
ENOPY peony
ENORS senor
ENORT noter, tenor, toner
ENORW owner, rowen
ENOST onset, seton, steno, stone
ENOSY nosey
ENOVW woven
ENOVY envoy
ENPRU prune
ENPST spent
ENQRU quern
ENRRU rerun
ENRST nerts, stern
ENRSU nurse
ENRTU tuner
ENRTY entry
ENRVY nervy
ENSUV nevus
ENSUX nexus
ENSWY newsy
ENTTY netty
EOORW wooer
EOOSY sooey
EOPPT epopt
EOPRR repro
EOPRS prose, spore
EOPRT toper, trope
EOPRV prove
EOPRW power
EOPSS posse
EOPST estop, stope
EOPSY poesy, sepoy
EOPXY epoxy
EOQRU roque
EOQTU quote, toque
EORRR error
EORRS sorer
EORRV rover
EORST roset, store, torse
EORSU rouse
EORSV servo, verso
EORSW serow, sower, swore, worse
EORTT otter, torte, toter
EORTU outer, outre, route
EORTV overt, trove, voter
EORTW tower, wrote
EORTX oxter
EORXX xerox
EOSSU souse
EOSTU touse
EOSTV stove
EOSTX sexto
EPPPY peppy
EPPRU upper
EPRRU purer
EPRRY perry
EPRSS press
EPRST prest, strep
EPRSU purse, sprue, super
EPRTU erupt
EPRTW twerp
EPRUY purey
EPRXY prexy
EPSTU setup, stupe, upset
EPSTW swept
EPTTY petty
EQRUY query
EQSTU quest
EQTUU tuque
ERRSU surer
ERRTU truer
ERRTY retry, terry
ERSST tress
ERSTV verst

ERSTW	**FGOOY**	**FIRST**	**FRRUY**	tough	tying	**GNRUW**
strew	goofy	first	furry	**GHRSU**	**GINVY**	wrung
trews	**FHILT**	**FIRTU**	**FRSUY**	shrug	vying	**GNSTU**
wrest	filth	fruit	surfy	**GHSUY**	**GINYZ**	stung
ERTTU	**FHIRT**	**FISTW**	**FRTUY**	gushy	zingy	**GNSUW**
utter	firth	swift	turfy	**GIILS**	**GIORR**	swung
ESTTY	frith	**FIYZZ**	**FRUYZ**	sigil	rigor	**GOORS**
testy	**FHIST**	fizzy	furzy	**GIILV**	**GIORT**	sorgo
ESTYZ	shift	**FKLNU**	**FSSUY**	vigil	trigo	**GOOTU**
zesty	**FHISY**	flunk	fussy	**GIINP**	**GIORV**	outgo
FFFLU	fishy	**FKLOO**	**FSTUY**	piing	vigor	**GOPRU**
fluff	**FHLSU**	kloof	fusty	**GIJNO**	**GIPRS**	group
FFGIR	flush	**FKLUY**	**FTTUY**	jingo	sprig	**GOPRY**
griff	**FHORS**	fluky	tufty	**GILLR**	**GIRST**	porgy
FFGRU	frosh	**FKNUY**	**FUYZZ**	grill	grist	**GORSS**
gruff	**FHORT**	funky	fuzzy	**GILNO**	**GJMUU**	gross
FFHIT	forth	**FLLOY**	**GGINO**	lingo	jugum	**GORSZ**
fifth	froth	folly	going	**GILNS**	**GKLNO**	grosz
FFHIW	**FIIIN**	**FLLUY**	**GGIOT**	sling	klong	**GORTU**
whiff	finii	fully	gigot	**GILNT**	**GLLOY**	grout
FFHUY	**FIINS**	**FLNOW**	**GGIPY**	glint	golly	**GORVY**
huffy	finis	flown	piggy	**GILNU**	**GLLUY**	grovy
FFIJY	**FIINX**	**FLOOR**	**GGMUY**	lungi	gully	**GOSTU**
jiffy	infix	floor	muggy	**GILNY**	**GLMOO**	gusto
FFIKS	**FIKRS**	**FLORU**	**GGOSY**	lying	gloom	**GOSTY**
skiff	frisk	flour	soggy	**GILOO**	**GLMOU**	stogy
FFINS	**FILLR**	fluor	**GHHIT**	igloo	mogul	**GOTUY**
sniff	frill	**FLORY**	hight	**GILPU**	**GLNSU**	gouty
FFIST	**FILLY**	flory	thigh	pugil	slung	guyot
stiff	filly	**FLOSS**	**GHILT**	**GILTU**	**GLORW**	**GPRSU**
FFITY	**FILMU**	floss	light	guilt	growl	sprug
fifty	filum	**FLOTU**	**GHIMT**	**GIMOS**	**GLORY**	**GPSYY**
FFLPU	**FILMY**	flout	might	gismo	glory	gypsy
pluff	filmy	**FLOTY**	**GHINT**	**GIMOY**	**GLOSS**	**GRRUY**
FFLSU	**FILNT**	lofty	night	goyim	gloss	gurry
sluff	flint	**FLTUY**	thing	**GIMOZ**	**GLOST**	**GRSUY**
FFNSU	**FILOO**	fluty	**GHINY**	gizmo	glost	gyrus
snuff	folio	fluyt	hying	**GIMPY**	**GMMUY**	**GSTUY**
FFPUY	**FILRT**	**FMORU**	**GHIOS**	gimpy	gummy	gusty
puffy	flirt	forum	shogi	**GIMRY**	**GMNOO**	**HHISW**
FFSTU	**FILSU**	**FMPRU**	**GHIRT**	grimy	mongo	whish
stuff	fusil	frump	girth	**GINOP**	**GMNOU**	**HHMPU**
FGGIY	**FILTY**	**FNNUY**	right	gipon	mungo	humph
figgy	fitly	funny	**GHIST**	oping	**GMOOR**	**HHSSU**
FGGOY	**FIMOT**	**FNORS**	sight	**GINOR**	groom	shush
foggy	motif	frons	**GHITT**	groin	**GMPRU**	**HIIRS**
FGHIT	**FIMTU**	**FNORT**	tight	**GINOT**	grump	rishi
fight	mufti	front	**GHITW**	ingot	**GMPYY**	**HIJOS**
FGILN	**FINNY**	**FNORW**	wight	**GINOW**	pygmy	shoji
fling	finny	frown	**GHLOU**	owing	**GNNUY**	**HIKNS**
FGINU	**FINSU**	**FNOTU**	ghoul	**GINPU**	gunny	knish
fungi	funis	fount	lough	pungi	**GNOPR**	**HIKNT**
FGIRT	**FINTU**	**FOOPR**	**GHLPY**	**GINRU**	prong	think
grift	unfit	proof	glyph	ruing	**GNORW**	**HIKOS**
FGLNO	**FINTY**	**FOOPS**	**GHNOT**	**GINRW**	grown	shiko
flong	nifty	spoof	thong	wring	wrong	**HIKRS**
FGLNU	**FINUX**	**FORRU**	**GHORU**	**GINST**	**GNORY**	shirk
flung	unfix	furor	rough	sting	gyron	**HIKSW**
FGNOO	**FINUY**	**FORST**	**GHOST**	**GINSU**	**GNOUY**	whisk
gonof	unify	frost	ghost	suing	young	**HILLS**
FGNOU	**FIOST**	**FORTY**	**GHOSU**	using	**GNPUY**	shill
fungo	foist	forty	sough	**GINSW**	pungy	**HILLT**
FGOOR	**FIRRY**	**FOSTY**	**GHOTU**	swing	**GNRTU**	thill
forgo	firry	softy	ought	**GINTY**	grunt	**HILLY**

hilly
HILMU
hilum
HILOT
litho
HILRT
thirl
HILRW
whirl
HILTT
tilth
HIMRT
mirth
HIMST
smith
HIMTY
thymi
HINNT
ninth
HINNY
hinny
HINOR
rhino
HINSY
shiny
HINWY
whiny
HIOPP
hippo
HIORU
houri
HIOST
hoist
HIPPY
hippy
HIPTW
whipt
HIPTY
pithy
HIRRS
shirr
HIRST
shirt
HISSW
swish
HISTX
sixth
HITWY
withy
HIWZZ
whizz
HKKOU
hokku
HKLUY
hulky
HKMOU
hokum
HKNOY
honky
HKNUY
hunky
HKOOS
shook
HKOOY

hooky
HKSUY
husky
HLLOO
hollo
HLLOU
hullo
HLLOY
holly
HLMPY
lymph
HLOOY
hooly
HLOPX
phlox
HLORW
whorl
HLOSS
slosh
HLOST
sloth
HLOTY
hotly
HLPSU
plush
HLPSY
sylph
HLRUY
hurly
HLSSU
slush
HLSYY
shyly
HMNOT
month
HMNPY
nymph
HMOOP
oomph
HMOPR
morph
HMORU
humor
HMOTU
mouth
HMOTY
mothy
HMPTU
thump
HMPUY
humpy
HMRRY
myrrh
HMRTU
thrum
HMSUU
humus
HMSUY
mushy
HNOOR
honor
HNOOW
nohow

HNOPY
phony
HNORS
shorn
HNORT
north
HNORY
horny
HNOSW
shown
HNOSY
hyson
HNSTU
shunt
HOOPT
photo
HOOPW
whoop
HOORT
ortho
thoro
HOOST
shoot
sooth
HOOTT
tooth
HOPRT
thorp
HOPSS
sposh
HOQTU
quoth
HORST
horst
short
HORSY
horsy
HORTT
troth
HORTW
throw
whort
worth
HOSTU
shout
south
HOSWY
showy
HOTUY
youth
HPSUY
pushy
HRRUY
hurry
HRSTU
hurst
HRSUY
rushy
HRTTU
truth
HSSUY
hussy
HUYZZ

huzzy
IIJNN
jinni
IIKLM
kilim
IILMT
limit
IILMU
ilium
IILNN
linin
IIMMN
minim
IIMMT
immit
IIMMX
immix
IIMST
mitis
IINNO
inion
IIORT
torii
IIPPT
pipit
IIRVZ
vizir
IISTV
visit
IJKMU
mujik
IJMMY
jimmy
IJNOT
joint
IJOST
joist
IKKNS
skink
IKKNY
kinky
IKKOS
kiosk
IKLLR
krill
IKLLS
skill
IKLMY
milky
IKLNP
plink
IKLNS
slink
IKLNY
linky
IKLPU
pulik
IKLRS
skirl
IKLSY
silky
IKLXY
kylix
IKMPS

skimp
IKMRS
smirk
IKNPR
prink
IKNPY
pinky
IKNST
stink
IKNYZ
zinky
IKPSY
spiky
IKQRU
quirk
IKRRS
skirr
IKRST
skirt
IKRSY
risky
IKSTU
kusti
IKTTY
kitty
ILLPS
spill
ILLQU
quill
ILLRT
trill
ILLST
still
ILLSW
swill
ILLSY
silly
ILLTW
twill
ILMPU
pilum
ILMPY
imply
ILMSY
slimy
ILNNO
linon
ILNSU
linus
ILNSY
lysin
ILNTU
until
ILNTY
linty
ILNVY
vinyl
ILOPS
polis
ILOPT
pilot
ILOPU
poilu

ILOPX
oxlip
ILORS
loris
ILORY
roily
ILORZ
zoril
ILOSU
louis
ILPPU
pupil
ILPST
spilt
split
ILPSU
pilus
ILPTU
tulip
ILQTU
quilt
ILRSW
swirl
ILRTW
twirl
ILSSY
lysis
ILSTT
stilt
ILSTY
silty
IMNOR
minor
IMNSU
minus
IMNTY
minty
IMOPR
primo
IMOPU
opium
IMOST
moist
IMOSZ
zoism
IMOTV
vomit
IMPPR
primp
IMPRS
prism
IMSSY
missy
IMSTU
tuism
IMSTY
misty
INNNO
ninon
INNNY
ninny
INNOO
onion
INNOP

pinon
INNOU
union
INNPU
unpin
INNRU
inrun
inurn
INNTY
tinny
INOPT
pinto
point
INOQU
quoin
INORS
rosin
INORT
intro
INORY
irony
INOSY
noisy
INOSZ
sozin
INOTX
toxin
INPPU
pinup
INPPY
nippy
INPRT
print
INPSY
snipy
INPTU
input
INPUZ
unzip
INQTU
quint
INSSU
nisus
sinus
INSTT
stint
INSTU
suint
INTTY
nitty
INTUW
unwit
INTUY
unity
IOPRR
prior
IOPRS
sirop
IOPST
posit
IOPSU
pious
IOPTV

pivot
IOQTU quoit
IORRS orris
IORST torsi
IORSV visor
IORVY ivory
IORVZ vizor
IOSTZ zoist
IPPYZ zippy
IPQUU quipu
IPRST sprit strip
IPRSU prius
IPRSY spiry
IPRVY privy
IPSTY tipsy
IPSTZ spitz
IPSWY wispy
IPSXY pyxis
IQRTU quirt
IRSTW wrist
IRSUV virus
IRTUV virtu
IRTYZ ritzy
ISSSY sissy
ISSTU situs
ISTTW twist
ISTXY sixty xysti
ITTTU tutti
ITTTY titty
ITTWY witty

ITYZZ tizzy
JLLOY jolly
JLOTY jolty
JLOWY jowly
JMORU jorum
JMPUY jumpy
JNOPU jupon
JNOTU junto
JORRU juror
JOSTU joust
JTTUY jutty
KKLSU skulk
KKNSU skunk
KKOOY kooky
KLLNO knoll
KLLSU skull
KLNPU plunk
KLNRU knurl
KLNSU slunk
KLOYY yolky
KLSUY sulky
KLTUZ klutz
KMOSY smoky
KMRUY murky
KMSUY musky
KNNOW known
KNOOR kroon
KNOOY nooky
KNORU korun
KNOTU knout
KNOWY

wonky
KNPSU spunk
KNPUY punky
KNRTU trunk
KNSTU stunk
KOOPS spook
KOORY rooky
KOOST stook
KOOSZ zooks
KOOTW kotow
KOPRY porky
KORST stork torsk
LLLOY lolly
LLMOY molly
LLORT troll
LLOWY lowly
LLOXY xylol
LLRTU trull
LLSTU stull
LLSUY sully
LLSYY slyly
LMOOT molto
LMOST smolt
LMPPU plump
LMPSU slump
LMPUY lumpy
LNNOY nylon
LNOOY loony
LNOPY pylon
LOOOV ovolo
LOOPR

orlop
LOOPS sloop spool
LOOST sotol stool
LOOTT lotto
LOPPU poulp
LOPPY loppy polyp
LOPRW prowl
LOPTU poult
LORRY lorry
LOSSU solus
LOSTU lotus
LOSUY lousy
LOTYZ zloty
LPPUY pulpy
LPRSU slurp
LPSUU lupus
LRRUY lurry
LRSUY surly
LRTUY truly
LRWYY wryly
LSTUY lusty
LSUUX luxus
MMMOY mommy
MMMUY mummy
MMPSU mumps
MMRUY rummy
MMTUY tummy
MMUYY yummy
MNOOR moron
MNOOY

moony
MNORU mourn
MNOTU mount notum
MNPSU numps
MOOPR promo
MOORR morro
MOORT motor
MOORY moory roomy
MOOSS mosso
MOOTT motto
MOPPY moppy
MOPST stomp
MORRU rumor
MORST storm
MORTU tumor
MORWY wormy
MOSSY mossy
MOSUY mousy
MPRTU trump
MPSTU stump
MPSUY spumy
MRSTU strum
MSSUY mussy
MSTUY musty
MSTYY stymy
NNOSY sonny
NNRUY runny
NNSUY sunny
NOOPR porno
NOOPS snoop

spoon
NOOST snoot
NOOSW swoon
NOOTY toyon
NOPTU punto
NORST snort
NORSW sworn
NOSTU snout
NOSTY stony
NOSWY snowy
NPRSU spurn
NPSUU sunup
NPTUY punty
NRTUY runty
NSTTU stunt
NTTUY nutty
OOPPZ zoppo
OOPRS sopor spoor
OOPRT troop
OOPST stoop
OOPSW swoop
OORST roost stoor torso
OORTY rooty
OOSTY sooty
OOWYZ woozy
OPPPY poppy
OPPSY soppy
OPRST sport strop
OPRSY

prosy
OPRXY proxy
OPSTT stopt
OPSTU spout stoup
OPSUY soupy
OPTTY potty
ORRSY sorry
ORRWY worry
ORSSU sorus
ORSTU stour torus
ORSTW worst
ORSTY story
ORTTU trout tutor
OSSST stoss
OSTTU stout
PPPUY puppy
PRSTU spurt
PRSUU usurp
PRSUY pursy syrup
PSSUY pussy
PTTUY putty
RSSTU truss
RSTTU strut trust
RSTTY tryst
RSTUW wurst
RSTUY rusty
RSUUY usury
RTTUY rutty

6-LETTER WORDS

AAABCL
cabala
AAABCN
cabana
AAABCS
casaba
AAABKL
kabala
AAABLR
labara
AAABLT
atabal
balata
AAABRZ
bazaar
AAACCI
acacia
AAACDN
canada
AAACJN
jacana
AAACLP
alpaca
AAACMR
maraca
AAACMT
camata
AAACNR
arcana
AAACPT
pataca
AAADMR
armada
AAAELZ
azalea
AAAGNN
nagana
AAAITX
ataxia
AAAILL
alalia
AAAKLM
kamala
AAALMS
salaam
AAALNV
analav
AAAMNT
ataman
AAAMRS
asrama
samara

AAAMRT
tamara
AAAPPY
papaya
AAARTV
avatar
AABBBO
baobab
AABBCY
abbacy
AABBET
abbate
AABCIM
cambia
AABCMN
cabman
AABCMT
tambac
AABCRS
scarab
AABCSU
abacus
AABDER
abrade
AABDES
abased
AABDET
abated
AABDEU
aubade
AABDGO
dagoba
AABDLL
ballad
AABDLM
lambda
AABDMN
badman
AABDOR
aboard
AABDRT
tabard
AABDRY
bayard
AABEGM
ambage
AABELR
arable
AABELZ
ablaze
AABEMO
amoeba
AABEMT

bemata
AABERT
trabea
AABERZ
zareba
AABETU
bateau
AABFIR
bifara
AABFKR
rabfak
AABGGS
gasbag
AABGMN
bagman
AABHSW
bashaw
AABIKR
abkari
AABILL
labial
AABILU
abulia
AABINN
banian
AABINZ
banzai
AABIST
abatis
AABLLM
ballam
AABLMS
balsam
AABLOR
aboral
AABLOV
lavabo
AABLST
basalt
AABLTU
ablaut
AABMNR
barman
AABMNT
bantam
AABMOY
bayamo
AABMRS
sambar
AABNNY
banyan
AABORR

arroba
AABORT
rabato
AABRTY
baryta
AABRWY
barway
AABTTW
abwatt
AACCDI
cicada
AACCHM
chacma
AACCKR
carack
AACCLO
cloaca
AACCLP
calpac
AACCLR
calcar
AACCMO
macaco
AACCNN
cancan
AACDDU
caudad
AACDEF
facade
AACDER
arcade
AACDIR
acarid
cardia
AACDLU
caudal
AACDMP
madcap
AACDNR
canard
AACEFL
faecal
AACEFR
carafe
AACEHP
apache
AACEHT
chaeta
AACELN
anlace
AACELP
palace
AACEMR
camera

AACENP
canape
AACENR
arcane
AACENT
catena
AACERT
cerata
AACETU
acuate
AACETV
cavate
caveat
vacate
AACETX
exacta
AACFIL
facial
AACFIS
fascia
AACFLU
facula
faucal
AACFNT
caftan
AACFRS
fracas
AACGGM
cagmag
AACGIL
caliga
AACHKR
charka
AACHLS
calash
AACHMR
chamar
AACHNS
ashcan
AACHSW
cashaw
AACHTT
attach
AACILL
laical
AACILM
calami
camail
AACILP
apical
AACILR
racial
AACIMN
caiman

maniac
AACINR
carina
crania
AACIPS
capias
AACIPT
capita
AACIRV
caviar
AACISS
cassia
AACITV
atavic
AACITX
ataxic
AACJKL
jackal
AACJOU
acajou
AACKMN
ackman
AACKRR
arrack
AACKTT
attack
AACLMU
macula
AACLNR
carnal
AACLNU
lacuna
AACLOX
coaxal
AACLPR
carpal
AACLRS
lascar
rascal
sacral
scalar
AACLSU
casual
casula
causal
AACLTU
actual
AACMNR
carman
AACMNY
cayman
AACNPT
catnap
AACNRT

cantar
AACNRY
canary
AACNST
sancta
AACNSV
canvas
AACNTV
vacant
AACPPY
papacy
AACRST
castra
AACRSU
acarus
AACRTV
cravat
AADDOU
aoudad
AADEGL
gelada
AADEGM
damage
AADEGN
agenda
AADEKW
awaked
AADELM
melada
AADELT
alated
AADEMM
madame
AADEMN
anadem
AADEMZ
amazed
AADENR
raaden
AADEPR
parade
AADFIR
afraid
AADGIO
adagio
AADGMN
gadman
AADGNO
dogana
AADGOP
pagoda
AADHIL
dahlia
AADHMR
dharma
AADHNR
dharna
AADHRZ
hazard
AADILR
radial
AADILS
dalasi
AADIMN

maidan
AADINR
radian
AADIST
stadia
AADKMS
damask
AADLMW
wadmal
AADLMY
malady
AADLNS
sandal
AADLNU
landau
AADLOP
apodal
AADLOR
adoral
AADMMN
madman
AADMNY
dayman
AADMOU
amadou
AADMRS
madras
AADMRU
maraud
AADMRZ
mazard
AADNRS
nasard
AADPYY
payday
AADQRU
quadra
AADRTU
datura
AADRTY
datary
AAEEGL
galeae
AAEEGT
eatage
AAEELP
paleae
AAEERT
aerate
AAEFLM
aflame
AAEFNU
faunae
AAEGGR
garage
AAEGLM
agleam
AAEGLN
galena
lagena
AAEGLR
aglare
laager
AAEGLV

lavage
AAEGMN
manage
AAEGMR
megara
AAEGNT
agnate
AAEGOR
agorae
AAEGPR
parage
AAEGRV
ravage
AAEGSV
savage
AAEHLM
haemal
AAEHMT
hamate
AAEHNY
hyaena
AAEHPT
apheta
AAEILM
lamiae
AAEILR
aerial
realia
AAEILX
alexia
AAEIMN
anemia
AAEITV
aviate
AAEKNW
awaken
AAEKRT
karate
AAELLP
paella
AAELLU
alulae
AAELMT
malate
tamale
AAELNN
anneal
AAELNT
lanate
AAELOR
areola
AAELPP
appeal
AAELPS
salpae
AAELPT
palate
AAELRV
larvae
AAEMMM
mammae
AAEMNS
seaman
AAENNZ

zenana
AAENPV
pavane
AAENST
ansate
AAENSU
nausea
AAEORT
aortae
AAEPPR
appear
AAEPRS
sarape
AAERRT
errata
AAERTU
aurate
AAERWX
earwax
AAESTV
savate
AAESWY
seaway
AAFFIR
affair
raffia
AAFFIT
taffia
AAFFRY
affray
AAFINR
farina
AAFIRS
safari
AAFKNT
kaftan
AAFLLL
fallal
AAFLNU
faunal
AAFLOT
afloat
AAGGMN
gagman
AAGGQU
quagga
AAGGRS
saggar
AAGGRT
tagrag
AAGHJN
ganjah
AAGHMR
graham
AAGHNR
hangar
AAGHST
aghast
AAGILR
argali
AAGILV
gavial
AAGINN
angina

AAGINU
iguana
AAGINV
vagina
AAGJRU
jaguar
AAGLLP
plagal
AAGLNO
analog
AAGLNR
raglan
AAGLST
stalag
AAGLXY
galaxy
AAGMNR
ragman
AAGMNZ
zamang
AAGMRY
margay
AAGNOR
angora
organa
AAGNPR
parang
AAGNRY
angary
AAGNST
satang
AAGPPR
grappa
AAGRVY
vagary
AAHHLL
hallah
AAHHLV
halvah
AAHHPT
aphtha
AAHILY
aliyah
AAHIPR
pariah
AAHKKN
khakan
AAHKNU
kahuna
AAHLLO
halloa
AAHLLP
pallah
AAHLMT
maltha
AAHLRS
ashlar
AAHLRT
hartal
AAHMNS
shaman
AAHMPY
mayhap
AAHMRS

ashram
AAHMST
asthma
AAHMTZ
matzah
AAHPPR
paraph
AAHPST
spatha
AAHPTY
apathy
AAHRSS
harass
AAHSSY
sashay
AAIKLL
alkali
AAIKLM
kalmia
AAILLP
pallia
AAILLX
axilla
AAILMN
animal
lamina
AAILMP
impala
AAILMS
salami
AAILNR
narial
AAILNS
salina
AAILRT
atrial
lariat
latria
AAILSS
assail
AAILSV
saliva
salvia
AAIMMS
miasma
AAIMMX
maxima
AAIMNR
airman
marina
AAIMRT
amrita
AAINNT
naiant
AAINOP
anopia
AAINPT
patina
pinata
AAINRT
antiar
AAINRU
anuria
AAINTT

attain

AAIOPR aporia
AAIORR oraria
AAIPRT patria
AAIPRY apiary
AAIPZZ piazza
AAIRST arista, tarsia
AAIRVY aviary
AAIRWY airway
AAIRZZ razzia
AAJMNP jampan
AAJRSW swaraj
AAKKLP kalpak
AAKKMR markka
AAKKOP kakapo
AAKLTU taluka
AALLPP appall
AALLRV larval
AALLVV valval
AALMMM mammal
AALMNP napalm
AALMNU alumna, manual
AALMNW lawman
AALMNY layman
AALMOR amoral
AALMPR palmar
AALMPS lampas, plasma
AALNNU annual
AALNPR planar
AALNPT planta
AALNRW narwal

AALNST aslant
AALNTU anlaut
AALOPR apolar
AALOPY payola
AALOVW avowal
AALPRT pratal
AALPRY parlay
AALPSU pausal
AALRST tarsal
AALRSY salary
AALSSV vassal
AALSWY always
AALWYY waylay
AAMMUZ mazuma
AAMNOZ amazon
AAMNPS sampan
AAMNRT mantra
AAMNTU mantua
AAMOPR paramo
AAMOST somata
AAMRSW aswarm
AAMRTU trauma
AANNTT natant
AANOST sonata
AANPPU papuan
AANPRT tarpan
AANPRY panary
AANQTU quanta
AANRRT arrant
AANRTT rattan, tartan
AANSTV savant
AANSTZ

stanza

AANTUV avaunt
AANWYY anyway
AAORRU aurora
AAOTTV ottava
AAPPWW pawpaw
AAPRST satrap
AAPWXX paxwax
AAQRSU quasar
AARRTT tartar
AARSTT strata
AARSTY astray
ABBBEL babble
ABBCDE cabbed
ABBCOT bobcat
ABBCRY crabby
ABBCSY scabby
ABBDDE dabbed
ABBDEG gabbed
ABBDEI babied
ABBDEJ jabbed
ABBDEL dabble
ABBDEN nabbed
ABBDER barbed, dabber
ABBDET tabbed, tebbad
ABBEEW bawbee
ABBEGL gabble
ABBEGR gabber
ABBEIS babies
ABBEJR jabber
ABBELR rabble
ABBELU

bauble

ABBEOR earbob
ABBERR barber
ABBERT barbet, rabbet
ABBESS abbess
ABBFLY flabby
ABBGOR gabbro
ABBHJU jubbah
ABBHSY shabby
ABBIRT rabbit
ABBLRU bulbar
ABBLSY slabby
ABBMOO bamboo
ABBNOO baboon
ABBORS absorb
ABBRTU barbut
ABCCLU buccal
ABCDEK backed
ABCDEL cabled
ABCDER braced
ABCDIR bardic
ABCDTU abduct
ABCEEM became
ABCEGU cubage
ABCEHL bleach
ABCEHR breach
ABCEHY beachy
ABCEIR caribe
ABCEJT abject
ABCEKR backer
ABCEKT backet
ABCELL becall

ABCELM becalm
ABCELT cablet
ABCEMN cabmen
ABCEMR camber
ABCENO beacon
ABCERR bracer
ABCFIR fabric
ABCFNO confab
ABCHLN blanch
ABCHNR branch
ABCHOR broach
ABCIIM iambic
ABCIMO cambio
ABCKPU backup
ABCKRU buckra
ABCLMY cymbal
ABCLOT cobalt
ABCMOP mobcap
ABCMOR crambo
ABCMOT combat
ABCNOR carbon, corban
ABCORX boxcar
ABCORY carboy
ABDDEE beaded
ABDDEG badged
ABDDEI abided
ABDDEL bladed
ABDDEN banded
ABDDER barded
ABDDEU daubed
ABDEEH behead
ABDEEK

beaked

ABDEEL beadle
ABDEEM beamed
ABDEEN beaned
ABDEER beader
ABDEES debase, seabed
ABDEET debate
ABDEFL fabled
ABDEGG bagged
ABDEGL gabled
ABDEGN banged
ABDEGO bodega
ABDEGR badger, barged, garbed
ABDEHS bashed
ABDEHT bathed
ABDEIL bailed, bidale
ABDEIS biased
ABDEIT baited
ABDEKN banked
ABDEKR barked, braked, debark
ABDEKS basked
ABDELL balled
ABDELM ambled, bedlam
ABDELO albedo
ABDELR balder, blared
ABDELT tabled
ABDELZ blazed
ABDEMM

bammed	beanie	habile	**ABELMR**	butane	bagnio
ABDEMN	**ABEEKR**	**ABEHKL**	marble	**ABENTZ**	gabion
badmen	beaker	keblah	ramble	bezant	**ABGINR**
ABDENN	**ABEEKT**	**ABEHLR**	**ABELMW**	**ABEORT**	baring
banned	betake	herbal	wamble	borate	**ABGINS**
ABDENP	**ABEELN**	**ABEHRT**	**ABELNU**	**ABEORZ**	basing
bedpan	baleen	bather	nebula	bezoar	**ABGINT**
ABDENR	enable	bertha	unable	**ABEOTV**	bating
barned	**ABEEMN**	breath	**ABELOR**	bovate	**ABGINY**
ABDEOT	bemean	**ABEIIL**	boreal	**ABEPTU**	baying
boated	**ABEEMR**	bailie	**ABELOT**	upbeat	**ABGKNO**
ABDERR	beamer	**ABEIIT**	boatel	**ABEQRU**	kobang
barred	**ABEENT**	tibiae	lobate	barque	**ABGLLO**
ABDERS	beaten	**ABEILL**	oblate	**ABEQSU**	global
serdab	**ABEEOR**	alible	**ABELRR**	basque	**ABGLMO**
ABDERU	aerobe	labile	barrel	**ABERRT**	gambol
dauber	**ABEERR**	liable	**ABELRT**	barret	**ABGNOR**
ABDERV	bearer	**ABEILT**	balter	barter	barong
adverb	**ABEERT**	albeit	labret	**ABERRV**	brogan
braved	beater	**ABEILV**	**ABELRV**	braver	**ABGSTU**
ABDERY	berate	viable	blaver	**ABERST**	sagbut
brayed	rebate	**ABEILW**	verbal	barest	**ABHIKL**
ABDERZ	**ABEERV**	bewail	**ABELRW**	breast	kiblah
brazed	beaver	**ABEILY**	warble	**ABERSU**	**ABHIKT**
ABDEST	**ABEERW**	bailey	**ABELRY**	abuser	bhakti
basted	beware	**ABEINT**	barely	bursae	**ABHIMR**
ABDESU	**ABEFFL**	binate	barley	**ABERTT**	mihrab
abused	baffle	**ABEIRS**	bleary	batter	**ABHINS**
ABDETT	**ABEFHL**	braise	**ABELRZ**	**ABERTY**	banish
batted	behalf	rabies	blazer	betray	**ABHIOP**
ABDFOR	**ABEFLL**	**ABEIRT**	**ABELST**	**ABERUU**	phobia
forbad	befall	baiter	ablest	bureau	**ABHMOT**
ABDGNO	**ABEFLM**	barite	stable	**ABESST**	bamoth
bandog	flambe	terbia	**ABELSU**	basest	**ABHMRU**
ABDILR	**ABEFLR**	**ABEIRZ**	suable	basset	rhumba
bridal	fabler	braize	usable	**ABETTU**	**ABHMSU**
ribald	**ABEFMR**	**ABEISS**	**ABELSY**	battue	ambush
ABDINR	ferbam	biases	basely	**ABETUY**	**ABHORR**
riband	**ABEGGR**	**ABEJOR**	**ABELTT**	beauty	harbor
ABDINT	bagger	jerboa	battle	**ABFGLU**	**ABHOST**
bandit	beggar	**ABEJRU**	tablet	bagful	bathos
ABDIRS	**ABEGIS**	abjure	**ABEMNO**	**ABFILU**	**ABHOTX**
disbar	gabies	**ABEJTU**	bemoan	fibula	hatbox
ABDLLY	**ADEGLM**	jubate	**ABEMNR**	**ABFISY**	**ABHRSY**
baldly	gamble	**ABEKMN**	barmen	basify	brashy
ABDNOU	**ABEGLN**	embank	**ABEMRU**	**ABFLRY**	**ABIILL**
abound	bangle	**ABEKMR**	umbrae	barfly	bailli
ABDNRY	**ABEGLR**	embark	**ABENNR**	**ABGGIT**	**ABIILT**
brandy	garble	**ABEKNR**	banner	baggit	tibial
ABDORS	**ABEGLT**	banker	**ABENRR**	**ABGGNO**	**ABIJRU**
adsorb	gablet	**ABEKRR**	barren	gobang	jabiru
ABDRRU	**ABEGLU**	barker	**ABENRT**	**ABGHTU**	**ABIKKU**
durbar	beluga	**ABEKRY**	banter	hagbut	kabuki
ABDRSU	**ABEGMN**	bakery	**ABENRU**	**ABGIKN**	**ABIKMO**
absurd	bagmen	**ABEKST**	urbane	baking	akimbo
ABDRWY	**ABEGNR**	basket	**ABENRY**	**ABGILM**	**ABIKMR**
bawdry	banger	**ABELLR**	barney	gimbal	imbark
ABEEGL	**ABEGOR**	baller	**ABENRZ**	**ABGILN**	**ABILMM**
beagle	borage	**ABELLT**	brazen	baling	imbalm
ABEEGR	**ABEGOZ**	ballet	**ABENST**	**ABGIMT**	**ABILMT**
barege	gazebo	**ABELLU**	absent	gambit	timbal
ABEEHV	**ABEGRR**	bullae	**ABENTT**	**ABGIMY**	**ABILMU**
behave	barger	**ABELMM**	batten	bigamy	labium
ABEEIN	**ABEHIL**	embalm	**ABENTU**	**ABGINO**	**ABILNO**

albino	**ABLRWY**	acetic	**ACCSUU**	**ACDELL**	**ACDERT**
ABILNS	byrlaw	**ACCEKL**	caucus	called	carted
ablins	**ABMNOW**	cackle	**ACDDEE**	**ACDELM**	crated
ABILRT	bowman	**ACCELN**	decade	calmed	redact
tribal	**ABMNSU**	cancel	**ACDDEG**	macled	traced
ABILRU	busman	**ACCELR**	cadged	**ACDELN**	**ACDERV**
burial	**ABMNTU**	cercal	**ACDDEI**	candle	carved
ABILRZ	tubman	**ACCELS**	caddie	lanced	craved
brazil	**ABMOTW**	calces	**ACDDEL**	**ACDELO**	**ACDERZ**
ABILTU	wombat	**ACCENR**	caddle	coaled	crazed
bliaut	**ABMRTU**	cancer	**ACDDEN**	**ACDELP**	**ACDESS**
ABIMMR	tambur	**ACCENT**	danced	placed	cassed
mimbar	**ABNNRY**	accent	**ACDDER**	**ACDELR**	**ACDESU**
ABIMRU	branny	**ACCEPT**	carded	cardel	caused
barium	**ABNORY**	accept	**ACDDEU**	cradle	sauced
ABIMSU	barony	**ACCERS**	adduce	**ACDELS**	**ACDETT**
iambus	baryon	scarce	**ACDDIN**	scaled	catted
ABINOS	**ABNOTY**	**ACCERU**	candid	**ACDELT**	**ACDEUX**
bonsai	botany	accrue	**ACDDIS**	talced	caudex
ABINOT	**ABNRTU**	**ACCESS**	caddis	**ACDELU**	**ACDHMR**
obtain	turban	access	**ACDDIT**	candle	drachm
ABINRS	**ABNRUU**	**ACCESU**	addict	cedula	**ACDILP**
risban	auburn	accuse	**ACDDIY**	**ACDELV**	placid
ABINRY	**ABNRUY**	**ACCGNO**	dyadic	calved	**ACDILS**
binary	anbury	cognac	**ACDEEF**	**ACDELW**	discal
brainy	**ABNRWY**	**ACCHLT**	deface	clawed	**ACDINR**
ABIORR	brawny	clatch	**ACDEEP**	**ACDELY**	rancid
barrio	**ABNTYZ**	**ACCHNO**	peaced	clayed	**ACDIOT**
ABIORS	byzant	concha	**ACDEER**	**ACDEMP**	dacoit
isobar	**ABORRW**	**ACCHNY**	decare	camped	**ACDIOZ**
ABIRRY	barrow	chancy	**ACDEES**	decamp	zodiac
briary	**ABORTU**	**ACCHOU**	ceased	**ACDENN**	**ACDIST**
ABIRSU	rubato	cachou	**ACDEFH**	canned	dicast
airbus	tabour	**ACCHRT**	chafed	**ACDENO**	**ACDLNU**
ABKNRS	**ABPRTU**	cratch	**ACDEGR**	canoed	unclad
branks	abrupt	**ACCHTY**	graced	deacon	**ACDLTY**
ABLLOT	**ABRRSU**	catchy	**ACDEHK**	**ACDENR**	dactyl
ballot	bursar	**ACCILO**	hacked	craned	**ACDNOR**
ABLLOW	**ABRSSY**	calico	**ACDEHR**	dancer	candor
ballow	brassy	**ACCILT**	arched	nacred	**ACDORW**
ABLLSY	**ABSUWY**	lactic	**ACDEHS**	**ACDENS**	coward
ballsy	subway	**ACCINY**	cashed	ascend	**ACDORX**
ABLMOO	**ACCCIL**	cyanic	chased	**ACDENT**	cordax
abloom	calcic	**ACCIPR**	**ACDEHT**	cadent	**ACEEFF**
ABLMOP	**ACCDEE**	capric	detach	canted	efface
aplomb	accede	**ACCIRT**	**ACDEIV**	decant	**ACEEFN**
ABLMRU	**ACCDEH**	arctic	advice	**ACDEOT**	enface
brumal	cached	**ACCITT**	**ACDEJK**	coated	**ACEEFS**
labrum	**ACCDEL**	tactic	jacked	**ACDEOX**	faeces
lumbar	calced	tictac	**ACDEJT**	coaxed	**ACEEFT**
ABLMRY	**ACCDII**	**ACCKRY**	adject	**ACDEPP**	facete
marbly	acidic	cracky	**ACDEKL**	capped	**ACEEGN**
ABLNOZ	**ACCDOR**	**ACCLSY**	lacked	**ACDEPR**	encage
blazon	accord	cyclas	**ACDEKP**	carped	**ACEEHK**
ABLOST	**ACCEHN**	**ACCNOO**	packed	craped	hackee
oblast	chance	cacoon	**ACDEKR**	redcap	**ACEEHL**
ABLOTV	**ACCEHT**	**ACCOSS**	carked	**ACDEPS**	chelae
abvolt	cachet	saccos	racked	scaped	**ACEEHT**
ABLPRU	**ACCEIL**	**ACCOST**	**ACDEKS**	spaced	thecae
burlap	celiac	accost	sacked	**ACDERR**	**ACEEIP**
ABLRSU	**ACCEIP**	**ACCRUY**	**ACDEKT**	carder	apiece
bursal	icecap	curacy	tacked	**ACDERS**	**ACEEJT**
ABLRTU	ipecac	**ACCSTU**	**ACDEKU**	sacred	ejecta
brutal	**ACCEIT**	cactus	cauked	scared	**ACEELL**

cellae	change	chasse	nacket	**ACELRS**	**ACENRY**
ACEELR	**ACEGHR**	cashes	**ACEKPR**	scaler	carney
cereal	charge	**ACEHST**	packer	sclera	**ACENST**
ACEELV	**ACEGHU**	catches	**ACEKPT**	**ACELRT**	ascent
cleave	gauche	chaste	packet	carlet	secant
ACEEMN	**ACEGIR**	sachet	**ACEKRS**	cartel	stance
menace	cagier	scathe	sacker	claret	**ACENSU**
ACEEMR	**ACEGLN**	**ACEHSW**	screak	rectal	usance
amerce	glance	cashew	**ACEKRT**	**ACELRV**	**ACEOPT**
raceme	**ACEGLY**	**ACEILM**	racket	calver	capote
ACEEMT	legacy	malice	**ACEKRY**	carvel	**ACEORS**
mecate	**ACEGNY**	**ACEILN**	creaky	**ACELST**	coarse
ACEEMZ	agency	ancile	**ACEKST**	castle	**ACEORX**
eczema	**ACEGOS**	**ACEILP**	casket	**ACELSU**	coaxer
ACEENR	socage	epical	**ACELLO**	clause	**ACEOST**
careen	**ACEHHT**	plicae	locale	**ACELSV**	costae
carene	chetah	**ACEILR**	**ACELLR**	calves	**ACEOSX**
ACEENS	**ACEHIK**	eclair	caller	claves	coaxes
encase	hackie	lacier	cellar	**ACELSX**	**ACEOTV**
scenae	**ACEHIL**	**ACEIMN**	recall	calxes	avocet
seance	heliac	anemic	**ACELMR**	**ACELTT**	octave
ACEENT	**ACEHIR**	cinema	calmer	cattle	**ACEPPR**
cetane	cahier	iceman	marcel	**ACELTY**	capper
tenace	**ACEHIS**	**ACEINN**	**ACELMS**	acetyl	**ACEPRR**
ACEEPS	chaise	canine	mascle	**ACELYY**	carper
escape	**ACEHKL**	**ACEINR**	mescal	clayey	**ACEPRS**
ACEERR	hackle	carnie	**ACELMT**	**ACEMNP**	escarp
career	**ACEHKR**	**ACEINS**	camlet	encamp	parsec
ACEERS	hacker	casein	**ACELNN**	**ACEMNR**	scrape
crease	**ACEHLP**	incase	cannel	carmen	spacer
ACEERT	chapel	**ACEINT**	**ACELNR**	**ACEMNU**	**ACEPRT**
cerate	pleach	enatic	lancer	acumen	carpet
create	**ACEHLS**	**ACEINU**	**ACELNS**	**ACEMOP**	**ACEPRU**
ecarte	laches	unciae	lances	pomace	apercu
ACEERZ	**ACEHLT**	**ACEIPS**	**ACELNT**	**ACEMOT**	**ACEPST**
cereza	chalet	apices	cantle	comate	aspect
ACEFFT	**ACEHLY**	spicae	cental	**ACEMPR**	**ACEPTU**
affect	leachy	**ACEIQU**	lancet	camper	teacup
ACEFIL	**ACEHMN**	caique	**ACELNU**	**ACEMRS**	**ACEQSU**
facile	manche	**ACEIRR**	cuneal	scream	casque
ACEFIN	**ACEHMS**	racier	launce	**ACEMRY**	**ACERRT**
fiance	sachem	**ACEIRS**	unlace	creamy	carter
inface	schema	caries	**ACELOR**	**ACEMTU**	crater
ACEFIR	**ACEHNU**	**ACEIRU**	coaler	acetum	tracer
fiacre	nuchae	curiae	oracle	**ACENNU**	**ACERRU**
ACEFIS	**ACEHOR**	**ACEISV**	**ACELOS**	nuance	curare
facies	chorea	cavies	solace	**ACENOR**	**ACERRV**
ACEFLS	**ACEHPR**	**ACEITV**	**ACELOT**	cornea	carver
falces	eparch	active	locate	**ACENOT**	**ACERSS**
ACEFLU	preach	**ACEIVV**	**ACELOV**	octane	caress
fecula	**ACEHPT**	vivace	alcove	**ACENPR**	crases
ACEFRU	hepcat	**ACEJKT**	coeval	prance	**ACERST**
furcae	**ACEHPY**	jacket	**ACELPR**	**ACENRS**	caster
ACEFSS	peachy	**ACEJLO**	carpel	casern	recast
fasces	**ACEHQU**	cajole	parcel	**ACENRT**	**ACERSU**
ACEFST	queach	**ACEKLM**	placer	canter	causer
fascet	**ACEHRR**	mackle	**ACELPT**	centra	cesura
ACEFSU	archer	**ACEKLT**	placet	nectar	saucer
fauces	**ACEHRS**	tackle	**ACELPU**	recant	**ACERSY**
ACEFSY	eschar	**ACEKLY**	culpae	trance	creasy
casefy	search	lackey	**ACELQU**	**ACENRV**	**ACERTU**
ACEFTU	**ACEHRX**	**ACEKNR**	claque	carven	curate
faucet	exarch	canker	**ACELRR**	cavern	**ACESTT**
ACEGHN	**ACEHSS**	**ACEKNT**	carrel	craven	stacte

ACESUY	caping	chroma	tincal	ACIOSV	claspt
cayuse	pacing	ACHNOR	ACILNU	ovisac	crural
ACFFHY	ACGINR	anchor	uncial	ACIPRY	ACLRRU
chaffy	arcing	archon	ACILOR	piracy	ACLRSW
ACFFLS	caring	rancho	caroli	ACIPTY	scrawl
sclaff	racing	ACHNOS	lorica	atypic	ACLRWY
ACFGIN	ACGINS	sancho	ACILOS	ACIQTU	crawly
facing	casing	ACHNPU	social	acquit	ACLSSY
ACFHLN	ACGINT	paunch	ACILRT	ACIRRU	classy
flanch	acting	ACHNST	citral	curari	ACLSTU
ACFHRT	ACGINV	snatch	ACILRU	ACIRSS	cutlas
fratch	caving	stanch	curial	crasis	ACLSUV
ACFILS	ACGIRT	ACHNTU	ACILSV	ACISSS	clavus
fiscal	tragic	nautch	clavis	cassis	ACMNOR
ACFIOS	ACGNOR	ACHNTY	ACIMNO	ACISTT	macron
fiasco	garcon	chanty	camion	static	ACMNOS
ACFIPY	ACGORU	ACHOOT	manioc	ACITUY	mascon
pacify	cougar	cahoot	ACIMNT	acuity	socman
ACFLNO	ACGTTU	ACHOPR	mantic	ACITVY	ACMNSU
falcon	catgut	carhop	ACIMOS	cavity	mancus
flacon	ACHHNU	ACHORR	mosaic	ACKLTY	ACMOST
ACFLNU	haunch	charro	ACIMOT	talcky	mascot
canful	ACHHTT	ACHOUV	atomic	ACKMOU	ACMOTT
ACFLPU	thatch	avouch	ACIMPS	coakum	tomcat
capful	ACHIIS	ACHPTY	scampi	ACKNPU	ACMPRY
ACFLRU	ischia	patchy	ACIMPT	unpack	crampy
fulcra	ACHIJK	ACHRRY	impact	ACKNRY	ACMPSU
ACFMTU	hijack	charry	ACIMRS	cranky	campus
factum	ACHILO	ACHRST	racism	ACKORY	ACMPTU
ACFORT	lochia	starch	ACIMST	croaky	pactum
factor	ACHILP	ACHSTU	mastic	ACKPSY	ACMRSU
ACFRTY	caliph	cushat	ACINNT	skycap	sacrum
crafty	ACHILR	ACHSTW	tannic	ACLLMY	ACMSTU
ACGGIN	archil	swatch	ACINOS	calmly	muscat
caging	ACHINR	ACHSUW	casino	ACLLOR	ACMUUV
ACGGLY	inarch	cushaw	ACINOT	collar	vacuum
claggy	ACHINT	ACHTTY	action	ACLLOW	ACNNNO
ACGGRY	canthi	chatty	atonic	callow	cannon
craggy	ACHIPS	ACIILS	cation	ACLLSU	ACNNOT
ACGHIN	phasic	silica	ACINOV	callus	cannot
aching	ACHIPT	ACIILT	incavo	ACLMMY	canton
ACGHLU	pathic	italic	ACINPR	clammy	ACNNOY
chagul	ACHISU	ACIINN	caprin	ACLMOP	canyon
ACGHOU	chiaus	niacin	ACINPT	copalm	ACNNRY
gaucho	ACHKLY	ACIIRT	catnip	ACLMOR	cranny
ACGHTU	chalky	iatric	ACINRU	clamor	ACNOOR
caught	hackly	ACIKMR	uranic	ACLMTU	corona
ACGIKN	ACHKTW	karmic	ACINST	talcum	racoon
caking	thwack	ACIKNT	incast	ACLNUY	ACNOPY
ACGILL	ACHKWY	catkin	nastic	lunacy	canopy
gallic	whacky	ACIKPX	ACINSU	ACLOPU	ACNORR
ACGILN	ACHLLO	pickax	acinus	copula	rancor
lacing	cholla	ACILLS	ACINTT	cupola	ACNORT
ACGILR	ACHLNP	scilla	intact	ACLORR	cantor
garlic	planch	ACILMX	ACINUV	corral	carton
ACGILS	ACHLNU	climax	vicuna	ACLORT	contra
glacis	launch	ACILNO	ACIOPR	crotal	ACNORU
ACGILY	nuchal	oilcan	picaro	ACLORU	cornua
cagily	ACHLOR	ACILNP	ACIORS	ocular	ACNORY
ACGIMN	choral	caplin	scoria	ACLORY	crayon
macing	lorcha	ACILNR	ACIORT	calory	ACNOSZ
ACGINN	ACHLRY	carlin	aortic	ACLOST	scazon
caning	archly	crinal	ACIOST	costal	ACNOTT
ACGINP	ACHMOR	ACILNT	scotia	ACLPST	octant

ACNOTU	fadged	ADDEOR	ADEEKP	sedate	ADEGGG
toucan	ADDEGG	adored	peaked	teased	gagged
ACNSTU	dagged	deodar	ADEELN	ADEFFG	ADEGGH
cantus	ADDEGO	ADDEOS	leaden	gaffed	hagged
ACNSTY	goaded	dadoes	leaned	ADEFGG	ADEGGJ
scanty	ADDEGR	ADDEPP	ADEELP	fagged	jagged
ACOOTV	graded	dapped	leaped	ADEFGN	ADEGGL
octavo	ADDEGU	ADDEPR	pealed	fanged	daggle
ACOPRT	gauded	draped	ADEELR	ADEFHR	ADEGGM
captor	ADDEHK	padder	dealer	fardeh	magged
cartop	keddah	ADDEPS	leader	ADEFHS	ADEGGN
ACORRT	ADDEHN	spaded	leared	fashed	ganged
carrot	handed	ADDERS	ADEELS	ADEFHT	nagged
ACORRW	ADDEHS	sadder	leased	hafted	ADEGGR
carrow	dashed	darted	sealed	ADEFIK	dagger
ACORSS	shaded	traded	ADEELT	faiked	ragged
across	ADDEII	ADDERW	delate	ADEFIL	ADEGGS
ACORST	dialed	warded	elated	afield	sagged
castor	laddie	ADDERY	ADEELV	failed	ADEGGT
scrota	ADDEIM	drayed	leaved	ADEFIR	gadget
ACORSU	diadem	yarded	ADEEMN	faired	tagged
soucar	ADDEIR	ADDGIN	demean	ADEFKL	ADEGGU
ACORTV	raided	adding	ADEEMR	defalk	gauged
cavort	ADDELL	ADDGOO	reamed	flaked	ADEGGW
ACORTX	ladled	ogdoad	remade	ADEFLM	wagged
oxcart	ADDELM	ADDIMY	ADEEMS	flamed	ADEGHI
ACORYZ	maddle	midday	seamed	ADEFLO	hidage
coryza	ADDELN	ADDORT	ADEEMT	foaled	ADEGHN
ACPPRY	dandle	dotard	teamed	loafed	hanged
crappy	landed	ADEEFL	ADEENN	ADEFLR	ADEGHS
ACPRSU	ADDELO	leafed	ennead	flared	gashed
caprus	loaded	ADEEFM	ADEENP	ADEFLS	ADEGIM
ACPSTU	ADDELP	defame	neaped	falsed	imaged
catsup	paddle	ADEEFN	ADEENR	ADEFLU	ADEGIN
upcast	ADDELR	deafen	earned	feudal	gained
ACRRSY	ladder	ADEEFR	endear	ADEFLW	ADEGKW
scarry	larded	feared	neared	flawed	gawked
ACRSTU	raddle	deafer	ADEENT	ADEFLY	ADEGLL
crusta	ADDELS	ADEEFT	anteed	deafly	galled
ADDDEG	saddle	defeat	ADEENW	flayed	ADEGLN
gadded	ADDELU	ADEEGR	weaned	ADEFMO	angled
ADDDEL	lauded	agreed	ADEENY	foamed	dangle
addled	ADDELW	dragee	yeaned	ADEFMR	ADEGLR
ADDDEM	dawdle	geared	ADEEPR	farmed	glared
madded	waddle	ADEEHL	reaped	framed	ADEGLY
ADDDEN	ADDELY	healed	ADEEPS	ADEFNN	agedly
addend	deadly	ADEEHP	pesade	fanned	ADEGLZ
ADDDEP	ADDEMM	heaped	ADEEPT	ADEFNW	glazed
padded	dammed	ADEEHR	pedate	fawned	ADEGMM
ADDDEW	ADDEMN	adhere	ADEERR	ADEFRT	gammed
wadded	damned	header	dearer	dafter	ADEGMN
ADDDOO	madden	ADEEHT	reader	farted	gadmen
doodad	ADDEMR	heated	reared	rafted	ADEGMU
ADDEEH	madder	ADEEHV	reread	ADEFRY	gaumed
headed	ADDENR	heaved	ADEERS	defray	ADEGNR
ADDEEL	dander	ADEEIL	erased	frayed	danger
leaded	darned	aedile	reseda	ADEFRZ	gander
ADDEEN	ADDENS	ADEEIT	seared	frazed	garden
deaden	dedans	ideate	ADEERV	ADEFST	ranged
ADDEEV	sadden	ADEEJY	reaved	fasted	ADEGNT
evaded	sanded	deejay	ADEERX	ADEFTT	tanged
ADDEFF	ADDENW	ADEEKL	exedra	fatted	ADEGNU
daffed	dawned	leaked	ADEEST	ADEFTW	augend
ADDEFG			seated	wafted	

unaged	**ADEHLW**	**ADEILP**	adieux	walled	yawled
ADEGNW	whaled	aliped	**ADEIVW**	**ADELMM**	**ADELZZ**
gnawed	**ADEHMM**	**ADEILR**	waived	lammed	dazzle
ADEGOS	hammed	derail	**ADEJMM**	**ADELMO**	**ADEMMN**
dagoes	**ADEHMR**	railed	jammed	loamed	madmen
dosage	harmed	relaid	**ADEJPU**	**ADELMP**	**ADEMMR**
seadog	**ADEHMS**	**ADEILS**	jauped	palmed	rammed
ADEGOT	mashed	aisled	**ADEJRR**	**ADELMR**	**ADEMNN**
dotage	shamed	deasil	jarred	dermal	manned
ADEGPP	**ADEHNR**	ladies	**ADEJZZ**	marled	**ADEMNO**
gapped	hander	sailed	jazzed	medlar	daemon
ADEGPS	harden	**ADEILT**	**ADEKKY**	**ADELMS**	moaned
gasped	**ADEHOX**	detail	yakked	damsel	**ADEMNP**
ADEGRR	hoaxed	dilate	**ADEKLR**	**ADELMT**	dampen
grader	**ADEHPP**	tailed	darkle	malted	**ADEMNR**
regard	happed	**ADEILU**	larked	**ADELMU**	remand
ADEGRT	**ADEHPR**	audile	**ADEKLS**	mauled	**ADEMNS**
grated	harped	**ADEILV**	slaked	**ADELNO**	desman
targed	**ADEHPS**	vailed	**ADEKLT**	loaned	**ADEMNT**
ADEGRU	hasped	**ADEILW**	talked	**ADELNP**	tandem
argued	phased	wailed	**ADEKLW**	planed	**ADEMNY**
ADEGRV	shaped	**ADEIMM**	walked	**ADELNR**	daymen
graved	**ADEHPT**	maimed	**ADEKMR**	darnel	**ADEMOP**
ADEGRY	heptad	**ADEIMN**	marked	lander	pomade
grayed	pathed	maiden	**ADEKMS**	**ADELNS**	**ADEMOR**
ADEGRZ	**ADEHRR**	median	masked	sendal	radome
grazed	harder	**ADEIMR**	**ADEKNR**	**ADELNT**	roamed
ADEGSS	**ADEHRS**	admire	danker	dental	**ADEMOW**
gassed	dasher	**ADEINP**	darken	**ADELOR**	meadow
ADEGST	shared	pained	ranked	loader	**ADEMPP**
staged	**ADEHRT**	**ADEINR**	**ADEKNS**	ordeal	mapped
ADEHHS	dearth	rained	snaked	reload	**ADEMPR**
hashed	hatred	**ADEINT**	**ADEKNT**	**ADELPP**	damper
ADEHIL	thread	detain	tanked	dapple	ramped
hailed	**ADEHRY**	**ADEINV**	**ADEKNY**	lapped	**ADEMPT**
halide	hydrae	invade	yanked	**ADELPR**	tamped
ADEHIR	**ADEHSS**	**ADEIOR**	**ADEKOS**	parled	**ADEMPV**
haired	dashes	roadie	soaked	**ADELPS**	vamped
ADEHJS	sashed	**ADEIPR**	**ADEKOY**	lapsed	**ADEMRR**
hadjes	**ADEHST**	diaper	kayoed	**ADELPT**	marred
ADEHKA	hasted	paired	**ADEKPR**	plated	**ADEMRT**
hanked	**ADEHSV**	repaid	parked	**ADELPW**	dreamt
ADEHKR	shaved	**ADEIRR**	**ADEKQU**	dewlap	**ADEMRW**
harked	**ADEHSW**	raider	quaked	**ADELPY**	warmed
ADEHKW	washed	**ADEIRS**	**ADEKRR**	played	**ADEMRY**
hawked	**ADEHTT**	raised	darker	**ADELRR**	dreamy
ADEHLN	hatted	**ADEIRT**	**ADEKRY**	larder	**ADEMSS**
handle	**ADEHTW**	tirade	darkey	**ADELRT**	massed
ADEHLC	thawed	**ADEIRU**	**ADEKST**	dartle	**ADEMST**
haloed	**ADEHYY**	rideau	skated	**ADELRY**	masted
ADEHLR	heyday	varied	stated	dearly	**ADEMSU**
harled	**ADEIJL**	**ADEIRV**	tasked	**ADELST**	amused
herald	jailed	varied	**ADELLL**	lasted	medusa
ADEHLS	**ADEILL**	**ADEISV**	lalled	salted	**ADEMTT**
lashed	allied	advise	**ADELLM**	slated	matted
shaled	**ADEILM**	davies	malled	staled	**ADENNP**
ADEHLT	mailed	visaed	**ADELLP**	**ADELSV**	panned
daleth	medial	**ADEITV**	palled	salved	**ADENNT**
halted	**ADEILN**	dative	**ADELLS**	slaved	tanned
lathed	alined	**ADEITW**	dalles	**ADELUV**	**ADENNU**
ADEHLU	denial	dawtie	**ADELLU**	valued	duenna
hauled	nailed	waited	allude	**ADELVV**	**ADENNW**
ADEHLV	**ADEILO**	**ADEITX**	aludel	valved	wanned
halved	eidola	taxied	**ADELLW**	**ADELWY**	**ADENOT**

atoned	**ADEPPP**	**ADERZZ**	howdah	**ADIMOT**	adjust
donate	papped	razzed	**ADHIJS**	diatom	**ADKLNY**
ADENOY	**ADEPPR**	**ADESSS**	jadish	**ADIMOY**	dankly
noyade	dapper	sassed	**ADHILO**	daimyo	**ADKLRY**
ADENPP	rapped	**ADESTT**	haloid	**ADIMRS**	darkly
append	**ADEPPS**	stated	**ADHIMR**	disarm	**ADLINN**
napped	sapped	tasted	dirham	**ADIMRU**	inland
ADENPR	**ADEPPT**	**ADESTV**	**ADHINS**	radium	**ADLLOR**
pander	tapped	staved	sandhi	**ADIMRY**	dollar
ADENPT	**ADEPPW**	**ADESTW**	**ADHIOR**	myriad	**ADLMNO**
panted	wapped	wasted	hairdo	**ADIMSS**	almond
pedant	**ADEPPY**	**ADESTY**	**ADHIRS**	sadism	**ADLMPY**
pentad	yapped	stayed	radish	**ADIMST**	damply
ADENPW	**ADEPPZ**	steady	**ADHIRY**	amidst	**ADLNOR**
pawned	zapped	**ADESWY**	hydria	**ADIMSY**	lardon
ADENPX	**ADEPRR**	swayed	**ADHLRY**	dismay	**ADLNOT**
expand	draper	**ADETTT**	hardly	**ADIMWY**	dalton
ADENRR	parred	tatted	**ADHMNO**	midway	**ADLNOU**
errand	**ADEPRS**	**ADETTV**	hodman	**ADINNN**	unload
ADENRS	parsed	vatted	**ADHNNU**	nandin	**ADLNPU**
sander	rasped	**ADFFOR**	unhand	**ADINNO**	upland
snared	spader	afford	**ADHORY**	nanoid	**ADLNRU**
ADENRT	spared	**ADFGIN**	hydroa	**ADINOR**	lurdan
ardent	spread	fading	**ADHOSW**	inroad	**ADLORS**
ranted	**ADEPRT**	**ADFGLY**	shadow	ordain	dorsal
ADENRU	depart	gadfly	**ADHPRU**	**ADINOT**	**ADLOSS**
neurad	parted	**ADFIRT**	purdah	dation	dossal
unread	petard	adrift	**ADIIKO**	**ADINOX**	**ADLOSW**
ADENRW	prated	**ADFLNU**	aikido	diaxon	dowlas
wander	**ADEPRW**	fundal	**ADIILN**	**ADINPT**	**ADMNOR**
warden	warped	**ADFLTY**	inlaid	pandit	random
warned	**ADEPRY**	daftly	**ADIILR**	**ADINPU**	**ADMNOS**
ADENRY	prayed	**ADFRTY**	iridal	unpaid	damson
denary	**ADEPSS**	drafty	**ADIIMO**	**ADINRW**	**ADMNOY**
yarned	passed	**ADGHIN**	daimio	inward	dynamo
ADENRZ	**ADEPST**	hading	**ADIIMR**	**ADINSU**	**ADMNUY**
zander	pasted	**ADGIIN**	midair	unsaid	maundy
ADENSU	**ADEPSU**	aiding	**ADIIMS**	**ADINTY**	**ADMORR**
sundae	paused	**ADGIJN**	idiasm	dainty	ramrod
ADENTT	**ADEPSY**	jading	**ADIJMS**	**ADIORT**	**ADMORU**
attend	spayed	**ADGILN**	masjid	adroit	maduro
ADENTV	**ADEPTT**	lading	**ADIJNO**	**ADIPRS**	**ADMTUY**
advent	patted	**ADGIMY**	adjoin	sparid	adytum
ADENTW	**ADEPTU**	digamy	**ADIKMO**	**ADIPSX**	**ADNNOU**
wanted	update	**ADGINO**	mikado	spadix	adnoun
ADENWY	**ADEQUY**	ganoid	**ADIKNP**	**ADIRRS**	**ADNOPR**
yawned	quayed	**ADGINR**	kidnap	sirdar	pardon
ADEOOR	**ADERRT**	daring	**ADIKOT**	**ADIRSU**	**ADNORU**
roadeo	darter	gradin	dakoit	radius	around
ADEOPS	retard	**ADGINT**	**ADILLP**	**ADIRVZ**	**ADNORW**
soaped	tarred	dating	pallid	vizard	onward
ADEORR	trader	**ADGINW**	**ADILMS**	**ADIRWZ**	**ADNRST**
adorer	**ADERRW**	wading	dismal	wizard	strand
roared	drawer	**ADGINZ**	**ADILMY**	**ADIRZZ**	**ADNRTU**
ADEORS	reward	dazing	milady	izzard	tundra
soared	warder	**ADGIRV**	**ADILNS**	**ADISST**	**ADNSTY**
ADEORT	warred	gravid	island	sadist	dynast
orated	**ADERRY**	**ADGLLY**	**ADILRZ**	**ADISYY**	**ADOPRY**
ADEOSV	dreary	gladly	lizard	sayyid	parody
vadose	**ADERST**	**ADGNOR**	**ADILST**	**ADJKOU**	**ADORTW**
ADEOTZ	stared	dragon	distal	judoka	toward
azoted	**ADERTT**	**ADGRSU**	**ADIMNO**	**ADJNOR**	**ADPRUW**
ADEOVW	ratted	gradus	daimon	jordan	upward
avowed	tetrad	**ADHHOW**	domain	**ADJSTU**	

ADRTWY	**AEEHLR**	leaper	rappee	**AEFHRT**	**AEFNST**
tawdry	healer	repeal	**AEEPRR**	father	fasten
AEEETX	**AEEHLX**	**AEELPS**	reaper	**AEFHSS**	nefast
exeate	exhale	asleep	**AEEPRS**	fashes	**AEFNSU**
AEEFIR	**AEEHMR**	elapse	serape	**AEFILL**	unsafe
faerie	hermae	please	**AEEPRT**	faille	**AEFNTT**
feriae	**AEEHMU**	**AEELPT**	repeat	**AEFILN**	fatten
AEEFLM	heaume	peltae	**AEEPRV**	finale	**AEFOSS**
female	**AEEHNP**	**AEELRS**	repave	**AEFILR**	fossae
AEEFOV	peahen	leaser	**AEEPST**	ferial	**AEFOSV**
foveae	**AEEHNT**	resale	peseta	**AEFILS**	favose
AEEFRR	ethane	sealer	**AEEPSW**	falsie	**AEFPPR**
fearer	**AEEHNV**	**AEELRT**	pesewa	**AEFIMN**	frappe
AEEFRT	heaven	earlet	**AEEPSX**	famine	**AEFRRT**
afreet	**AEEHNX**	elater	apexes	**AEFIRR**	rafter
AEEGGN	hexane	relate	**AEEPTT**	fairer	**AEFRRY**
engage	**AEEHRR**	**AEELRV**	pattee	**AEFIRS**	rarefy
AEEGLL	hearer	leaver	**AEEPVY**	fraise	**AEFRRZ**
allege	**AEEHRS**	reveal	peavey	**AEFIRY**	frazer
AEEGLP	haeres	**AEELST**	**AEEQRU**	aerify	**AEFRST**
pelage	hearse	teasel	quaere	**AEFIST**	faster
AEEGLR	**AEEHRT**	**AEELSV**	**AEEQTU**	fiesta	strafe
regale	heater	leaves	equate	**AEFITX**	**AEFRTT**
AEEGLT	hereat	sleave	**AEERRS**	fixate	fatter
eaglet	reheat	**AEELSW**	eraser	**AEFJNT**	**AEFRWY**
legate	**AEEHRV**	weasel	**AEERRT**	fanjet	wafery
telega	heaver	**AEELTT**	tearer	**AEFKRY**	**AEFSST**
AEEGLU	**AEEHSV**	alette	**AEERRW**	freaky	safest
league	sheave	**AEELTV**	wearer	**AEFLLN**	**AEFSTU**
AEEGMM	**AEEINT**	velate	**AEERST**	fallen	estufa
gemmae	teniae	**AEELTZ**	teaser	**AEFLLR**	**AEFSTY**
AEEGMN	**AEEIRS**	teazel	**AEERSV**	faller	safety
manege	easier	teazle	averse	**AEFLMN**	**AEFSUU**
menage	**AEEJVY**	**AEELWY**	**AEERTY**	flamen	fuseau
AEEGMR	jayvee	leeway	eatery	**AEFLNX**	**AEGGGL**
meager	**AEEKLR**	**AEEMNR**	**AEERVW**	flaxen	gaggle
AEEGMT	leaker	enarme	weaver	**AEFLOR**	**AEGGHL**
gamete	**AEEKMR**	meaner	**AEESSW**	loafer	haggle
metage	remake	rename	seesaw	**AEFLRS**	**AEGGJR**
AEEGNR	**AEEKNW**	**AEEMNS**	**AEESTT**	falser	jagger
enrage	weaken	mensae	estate	**AEFLRT**	**AEGGLN**
genera	**AEEKRT**	seamen	testae	falter	naggle
AEEGNS	retake	**AEEMNX**	**AEEMNX**	**AEFLRU**	**AEGGLR**
sagene	**AEEKRU**	examen		earful	gargle
senega	eureka	**AEEMPR**	**AEFFGL**	**AEFLST**	lagger
AEEGNT	**AEEKRW**	ampere	gaffle	festal	raggle
negate	weaker	**AEEMRR**	**AEFFGR**	**AEFLSY**	**AEGGLW**
AEEGNV	**AEELLL**	reamer	gaffer	safely	waggle
avenge	allele	**AEEMSS**	**AEFFHT**	**AEFLTY**	**AEGGNR**
geneva	**AEELLM**	sesame	haffet	fealty	ganger
AEEGOP	mallee	**AEENNP**	**AEFFIP**	featly	grange
apogee	**AEELMN**	pennae	piaffe	**AEFMNN**	nagger
AEEGOT	enamel	**AEENNT**	**AEFFLR**	fenman	**AEGGNU**
goatee	**AEELMP**	neaten	raffle	**AEFMNO**	gangue
AEEGRS	empale	**AEENRR**	**AEFFLW**	foeman	**AEGGRT**
grease	**AEELNR**	nearer	waffle	**AEFMOR**	garget
AEEGRV	leaner	**AEENRT**	**AEFFLY**	femora	tagger
greave	**AEELNT**	neater	yaffle	**AEFMRR**	**AEGGWW**
AEEGST	lateen	**AEENST**	**AEFGLN**	farmer	gewgaw
egesta	**AEELNV**	sateen	flange	framer	**AEGHIR**
AEEGSW	leaven	senate	**AEFGOR**	**AEFNNR**	hegari
sewage	**AEELOR**	**AEENUV**	forage	fanner	**AEGHIS**
AEEHHW	areole	avenue	**AEFHLL**	**AEFNRW**	geisha
heehaw	**AEELPR**	**AEEPPR**	fellah	fawner	**AEGHIW**
			AEFHRS		
			afresh		

aweigh	**AEGJRU**	gannet	**AEGTYY**	**AEHLOS**	shaper
AEGHLN	jugera	**AEGNOR**	gayety	haloes	**AEHPRT**
hangle	**AEGJTU**	onager	**AEHHLT**	**AEHLOT**	teraph
AEGHMO	jugate	orange	health	loathe	threap
homage	**AEGKST**	**AEGNOS**	**AEHHPY**	**AEHLPY**	**AEHPSW**
ohmage	gasket	agones	hyphae	phylae	peshwa
AEGHNR	**AEGLLT**	**AEGNRR**	**AEHHRS**	**AEHLRS**	**AEHRRS**
hanger	gallet	garner	rehash	lasher	rasher
AEGHRT	**AEGLLY**	ranger	**AEHHRT**	**AEHLRT**	sharer
gather	galley	**AEGNRS**	hearth	halter	**AEHRRT**
AEGHSS	**AEGLMN**	serang	**AEHHSS**	lather	rather
gashes	legman	**AEGNRT**	hashes	thaler	**AEHRSS**
AEGILM	mangle	argent	**AEHHST**	**AEHLRU**	rashes
milage	**AEGLMY**	garnet	sheath	hauler	**AEHRSV**
AEGILN	gamely	**AEGNRV**	**AEHHTY**	**AEHLRW**	shaver
genial	**AEGLNR**	graven	heathy	whaler	**AEHRSW**
linage	angler	**AEGNRW**	**AEHIJR**	**AEHLSS**	hawser
AEGILO	regnal	gnawer	hejira	hassle	washer
goalie	**AEGLNT**	**AEGORT**	**AEHIKS**	lashes	**AEHRTT**
AEGILS	tangle	orgeat	sakieh	**AEHLST**	hatter
silage	**AEGLNU**	**AEGOTT**	**AEHILM**	halest	threat
AEGILT	lagune	togate	hiemal	haslet	**AEHRTV**
ligate	**AEGLNW**	**AEGOTU**	**AEHILN**	**AEHLTW**	thrave
AEGILV	wangle	outage	inhale	wealth	**AEHRTW**
glaive	**AEGLOR**	**AEGOTW**	**AEHILP**	**AEHLTY**	wreath
AEGIMN	galore	towage	phiale	hyetal	**AEHRTY**
enigma	**AEGLOT**	**AEGOVY**	**AEHILR**	**AEHMMR**	earthy
AEGIMP	legato	voyage	hailer	hammer	hearty
magpie	**AEGLPU**	**AEGPRS**	**AEHILT**	**AEHMMY**	**AEHSSS**
AEGIMR	plague	sparge	halite	mayhem	sashes
gamier	**AEGLRR**	**AEGPRT**	**AEHILW**	**AEHMNT**	**AEHSSW**
maigre	larger	parget	awhile	anthem	washes
mirage	**AEGLRT**	**AEGRRT**	**AEHIMM**	hetman	**AEHSTW**
AEGIMS	tergal	garret	maihem	**AEHMNU**	swathe
ageism	**AEGLRU**	garter	**AEHIMR**	humane	**AEIIRR**
AEGINR	regula	grater	hermai	**AEHMPR**	airier
earing	**AEGLRV**	**AEGRRU**	**AEHIMS**	hamper	**AEIJLR**
gainer	glaver	arguer	mashie	**AEHMRR**	jailer
regain	gravel	**AEGRRV**	**AEHINR**	harmer	**AEIKLT**
regina	**AEGLSY**	graver	hernia	**AEHMRS**	talkie
AEGINS	sagely	**AEGRRY**	**AEHIRS**	masher	**AEIKNT**
easing	**AEGMMR**	grayer	ashier	**AEHMSS**	intake
AEGINT	gammer	**AEGRRZ**	**AEHIRZ**	mashes	**AEIKRS**
eating	**AEGMMS**	grazer	hazier	**AEHNPP**	kaiser
ingate	smegma	**AEGRSS**	**AEHISV**	happen	**AEILLM**
AEGINU	**AEGMNR**	gasser	shavie	**AEHNRT**	mallei
guinea	german	**AEGRST**	**AEHKMS**	anther	**AEILLN**
AEGIPP	manger	stager	samekh	thenar	lineal
pipage	**AEGMNT**	**AEGRSU**	**AEHKNR**	**AEHNST**	**AEILLS**
AEGIRT	magnet	sauger	hanker	hasten	allies
gaiter	**AEGMNY**	**AEGRSY**	harken	**AEHNSV**	**AEILLT**
triage	mangey	greasy	**AEHKNS**	shaven	taille
AEGIRV	**AEGMRU**	**AEGRTT**	shaken	**AEHORS**	telial
rivage	maugre	target	**AEHKRS**	ashore	**AEILMN**
AEGIRW	murage	**AEGRTY**	kasher	hoarse	menial
earwig	**AEGMST**	gyrate	shaker	**AEHORX**	**AEILMP**
AEGIST	gamest	**AEGRUV**	**AEHKRW**	hoaxer	impale
ageist	**AEGMUY**	vaguer	hawker	**AEHOSX**	**AEILMR**
AEGISV	maguey	**AEGSST**	**AEHLLT**	hoaxes	mailer
visage	**AEGMUZ**	sagest	lethal	**AEHPRR**	**AEILMS**
AEGITY	zeugma	**AEGSTY**	**AEHLMT**	harper	mesial
gaiety	**AEGNNO**	stagey	hamlet	**AEHPRS**	samiel
AEGJLN	nonage	**AEGTTU**	**AEHLNS**	phrase	**AEILNP**
jangle	**AEGNNT**	guttae	hansel	seraph	alpine

pineal	narine	**AEIRVW**	trepak	**AELMRU**	rappel
AEILNR	**AEINNS**	waiver	**AEKQRU**	mauler	**AELPPT**
linear	insane	wavier	quaker	**AELMRV**	lappet
nailer	sienna	**AEIRWX**	**AEKQSU**	marvel	**AELPPU**
AEILNS	**AEINNT**	waxier	squeak	**AELMST**	papule
saline	innate	**AEISST**	**AEKRST**	lamest	**AELPQU**
AEILNT	**AEINPR**	siesta	skater	samlet	plaque
entail	rapine	tassie	strake	**AELMSY**	**AELPRR**
tenail	**AEINPS**	**AEISSZ**	streak	measly	parrel
tineal	spinae	assize	**AEKWYY**	**AELMTU**	**AELPRT**
AEILNV	**AEINRS**	**AEISTV**	keyway	amulet	palter
alevin	arisen	sative	**AELLLY**	muleta	plater
venial	arsine	**AEISTX**	leally	**AELMTY**	**AELPRU**
AEILNX	**AEINRT**	taxies	**AELLMT**	tamely	epural
xenial	ratine	**AEITTV**	mallet	**AELNNR**	pleura
AEILPS	retain	vittae	**AELLMY**	lanner	**AELPRY**
espial	retina	**AEITTX**	lamely	**AELNOR**	parley
AEILRR	**AEINRV**	taxite	**AELLPT**	loaner	pearly
railer	ravine	**AEJMMR**	pallet	**AELNOS**	player
AEILRS	**AEINRW**	jammer	**AELLPY**	lanose	replay
sailer	wanier	**AEJMRT**	palely	**AELNPT**	**AELPSS**
serial	**AEINRZ**	ramjet	**AELLRT**	planet	passel
AEILRT	zanier	**AEJMST**	taller	platen	**AELPST**
iteral	**AEINSS**	jetsam	**AELLRU**	**AELNRT**	palest
retail	sanies	**AEJNST**	allure	altern	pastel
AEILRZ	**AEINST**	sejant	laurel	antler	septal
lazier	satine	**AEJPRS**	**AELLRY**	learnt	staple
AEILSS	**AEINSV**	jasper	really	rental	**AELQSU**
lassie	navies	**AEJPRY**	**AELLST**	**AELNRU**	squeal
AEILSV	**AEINSZ**	japery	sallet	neural	**AELRRY**
valise	zanies	**AEJRVY**	**AELLTW**	ulnare	rarely
AEILSY	**AEINTU**	jarvey	wallet	unreal	**AELRST**
easily	auntie	**AEKKNR**	**AELLTY**	**AELNRV**	laster
AEILUV	**AEINTV**	kraken	lately	nerval	salter
eluvia	native	**AEKLNR**	lealty	vernal	slater
AEIMMT	**AEIOPT**	rankle	**AELLVY**	**AELNRY**	staler
tammie	opiate	**AEKLNT**	valley	nearly	**AELRSU**
AEIMNO	**AEIORS**	anklet	**AELMMR**	**AELNSY**	saurel
anomie	ariose	**AEKLRS**	rammel	sanely	**AELRSV**
AEIMNP	**AEIPRR**	slaker	**AELMNS**	**AELNTT**	salver
pieman	rapier	**AEKLRT**	mensal	latent	serval
AEIMNR	repair	talker	**AELMNT**	latten	slaver
airmen	**AEIPRS**	**AEKLRW**	lament	talent	**AELRSY**
marine	aspire	walker	mantel	**AELNTU**	slayer
remain	paries	**AEKLTU**	mantle	lunate	**AELRTT**
AEIMNT	praise	auklet	mental	**AELNTV**	latter
inmate	**AEIPRT**	**AEKLWY**	**AELMNW**	levant	rattle
AEIMRS	pirate	weakly	lawmen	**AELNTY**	**AELRTV**
armies	**AEIRRS**	**AEKMRR**	**AELMNY**	neatly	travel
AEIMRT	sierra	marker	laymen	**AELOPR**	varlet
imaret	**AEIRRV**	remark	meanly	parole	**AELRTY**
AEIMRU	arrive	**AEKMRS**	namely	**AELOPS**	elytra
uremia	**AEIRRW**	masker	**AELMOR**	aslope	realty
AEIMRZ	warier	**AEKMRT**	morale	**AELOPT**	**AELRWY**
mazier	**AEIRST**	market	**AELMPR**	pelota	lawyer
AEIMST	satire	**AEKNRR**	ampler	**AELOPX**	**AELRYY**
maties	striae	ranker	palmer	poleax	yarely
samite	**AEIRSV**	**AEKNRT**	**AELMPS**	**AELOST**	yearly
AEINNO	varies	tanker	sample	osteal	**AELSST**
eonian	**AEIRTT**	**AEKNSY**	**AELMPU**	**AELOSV**	tassel
AEINNP	attire	sneaky	ampule	loaves	**AELSTT**
nanpie	ratite	**AEKORS**	plumae	**AELOTZ**	latest
pennia	**AEIRTW**	soaker	**AELMRT**	zealot	**AELSTU**
AEINNR	waiter	**AEKPRT**	armlet	**AELPPR**	salute

setula	**AEMPRV**	patent	**AEPPRT**	**AERSTY**	**AFGINZ**
AELSTV	revamp	patten	**AEPPRU**	estray	fazing
vestal	**AEMQRU**	**AENPTU**	**AEPPRU**	yarest	**AFGISY**
alveus	marque	peanut	pauper	**AERSTZ**	gasify
AELSUX	**AEMQSU**	**AENRRS**	**AEPPRY**	ersatz	**AFGLNO**
sexual	masque	snarer	papery	**AERSUU**	flagon
AELSVY	**AEMRRU**	**AENRRT**	prepay	aureus	fungal
sylvae	armure	errant	yapper	uraeus	**AFGLRU**
AELSYZ	**AEMRRW**	**AENRRW**	**AEPPTT**	**AERSUV**	frugal
sleazy	warmer	warren	tappet	suaver	**AFGOTU**
AELTTT	**AEMRST**	**AENRSS**	**AEPPTU**	**AERSWY**	fugato
tattle	master	sarsen	pupate	sawyer	**AFHIKL**
AELTTW	stream	**AENRST**	**AEPRRS**	**AERTTT**	khalif
wattle	**AEMRSY**	astern	rasper	tatter	**AFHIMS**
AELTUX	smeary	sterna	sparer	**AERTTY**	famish
luxate	**AEMRTT**	**AENRSW**	**AEPRRU**	treaty	**AFHIOS**
AELUUV	matter	answer	parure	**AERTUU**	oafish
uvulae	**AEMRTU**	**AENRSY**	**AEPRRW**	auteur	**AFHLOO**
AELUVV	mature	senary	prewar	**AERTWY**	loofah
vulvae	**AEMSSU**	**AENRTT**	**AEPRRY**	tawery	**AFHLSY**
AEMMNR	assume	natter	prayer	watery	flashy
merman	**AEMSTT**	**AENRTU**	**AEPRSS**	**AERVWY**	**AFHMOT**
AEMMRR	tamest	nature	passer	wavery	fathom
rammer	**AEMSTY**	**AENRTV**	sparse	**AESSSS**	**AFHORS**
AEMMRY	steamy	tavern	**AEPRST**	assess	shofar
yammer	**AEMSYZ**	**AENRTW**	paster	**AESSTT**	**AFIILL**
AEMMST	zymase	wanter	repast	tasset	filial
stemma	**AEMTTU**	**AENRWY**	**AEPRTT**	**AESSTY**	**AFIILN**
AEMMSU	mutate	yawner	patter	sayest	finial
summae	**AENNOV**	**AENSST**	**AEPRTY**	**AESTTT**	**AFIKNU**
AEMMTU	novena	assent	petary	attest	funkia
maumet	anyone	sanest	**AEPSSS**	**AESTTU**	**AFILLN**
AEMNNP	**AENNOY**	**AENSSU**	passes	astute	infall
penman	tanner	anuses	**AEPSST**	**AESTWY**	**AFILMU**
AEMNNR	**AENNRW**	**AENSTU**	stapes	sweaty	famuli
manner	wanner	nasute	**AEQRSU**	**AESTYY**	**AFILMY**
AEMNNT	**AENNTT**	unseat	square	yeasty	family
manent	tenant	**AENSUV**	**AEQRTU**	**AETUXY**	**AFILNU**
AEMNOR	**AENOPW**	naevus	quatre	eutaxy	infula
enamor	weapon	**AENSUY**	**AEQRUV**	**AFFGUW**	**AFILRY**
normae	**AENORS**	uneasy	quaver	guffaw	fairly
AEMNOY	reason	**AENTTU**	**AEQSUY**	**AFFIKR**	**AFILSY**
yeoman	senora	attune	queasy	kaffir	salify
AEMNPU	**AENORT**	tauten	**AEQUYZ**	**AFFIMR**	**AFIMNR**
pneuma	atoner	**AENTTX**	queazy	affirm	firman
AEMNRT	ornate	extant	**AERRST**	**AFFIRT**	**AFIMNY**
marten	**AENOSS**	**AEOPPS**	arrest	tariff	infamy
rament	season	appose	rarest	**AFFLOY**	**AFIMRY**
AEMNRU	**AENOTT**	**AEOPQU**	raster	layoff	ramify
manure	notate	opaque	**AERRTT**	**AFFLUX**	**AFIMSS**
AEMNST	**AENPPR**	**AEOPST**	ratter	afflux	massif
mantes	napper	postea	**AERRTY**	**AFFOPY**	**AFINNT**
stamen	**AENPRT**	**AEOPTT**	artery	payoff	infant
AEMNTU	arpent	teapot	**AERSST**	**AFGGLY**	**AFINRU**
untame	enrapt	**AEOPTY**	assert	flaggy	unfair
AEMORR	entrap	teapoy	**AERSSU**	**AFGIKN**	**AFINSU**
remora	parent	**AEORSU**	assure	faking	fusain
roamer	trepan	arouse	**AERSTT**	**AFGIMN**	**AFIQRU**
AEMPPR	**AENPRY**	**AEORTT**	taster	faming	faquir
pamper	napery	rotate	**AERSTV**	**AFGINR**	**AFIRRY**
pampre	**AENPRZ**	**AEPPRR**	starve	faring	friary
AEMPRT	panzer	rapper	**AERSTW**	**AFGINS**	**AFIRTY**
tamper	**AENPTT**	sapper	rawest	safing	ratify
			waster		

AFIRUY	gaming	nilgai	**AGIMNZ**	giaour	**AGMOYZ**
aurify	**AGGINP**	**AGIIMN**	mazing	**AGIORV**	zygoma
AFJLRY	gaping	aiming	**AGIMST**	virago	**AGMPRS**
jarfly	paging	**AGIINR**	stigma	**AGIOTU**	gramps
AFLLOR	**AGGINR**	airing	**AGIMWW**	agouti	**AGNNRY**
floral	raging	**AGIJNP**	wigwam	**AGIRST**	granny
AFLLOW	**AGGINT**	japing	**AGINNP**	gratis	**AGNORS**
fallow	gating	**AGIJNW**	paning	**AGIRTU**	sarong
AFLLPU	**AGGINW**	jawing	**AGINNV**	guitar	**AGNOST**
lapful	waging	**AGIJSW**	naving	**AGJLMO**	sontag
AFLLTY	**AGGINZ**	jigsaw	**AGINNW**	logjam	**AGNOTU**
flatly	gazing	**AGIKMN**	awning	**AGJLNY**	nougat
AFLLUW	**AGGIWW**	making	waning	jangly	**AGNPRS**
lawful	wigwag	**AGIKNR**	**AGINOR**	**AGJNOR**	sprang
AFLMNU	**AGGIZZ**	raking	oaring	jargon	**AGNRTY**
manful	zigzag	**AGIKNS**	origan	**AGLLNO**	gantry
AFLMNY	**AGGKNY**	asking	**AGINPR**	gallon	**AGOPRU**
flyman	knaggy	gaskin	paring	**AGLLOP**	gopura
AFLMOR	**AGGLNY**	**AGIKNT**	raping	gallop	**AGORSY**
formal	gangly	taking	**AGINPT**	**AGLLSU**	argosy
AFLMRU	**AGGMOT**	**AGIKNW**	taping	gallus	**AGORTU**
armful	maggot	waking	**AGINPV**	**AGLMNO**	ragout
fulmar	**AGGNRU**	**AGILLU**	paving	logman	**AGOTTU**
AFLMYY	nuggar	ligula	**AGINPW**	**AGLNNO**	tautog
mayfly	**AGGNSY**	**AGILMM**	pawing	longan	**AGRSSY**
AFLNOT	snaggy	gimmal	**AGINPY**	**AGLNNU**	grassy
fontal	**AGGQUY**	**AGILMN**	paying	lungan	**AGRSTU**
AFLNPU	quaggy	laming	**AGINRS**	**AGLNOO**	tragus
panful	**AGHIJR**	lingam	rasing	lagoon	**AGRSUY**
AFLNTU	jaghir	malign	**AGINRT**	**AGLNOS**	sugary
flaunt	**AGHIKU**	**AGILMP**	rating	slogan	**AGRUUY**
AFLORV	kiaugh	magilp	taring	**AGLNOU**	augury
flavor	**AGHILN**	**AGILNP**	**AGINRV**	lanugo	**AGSTUU**
AFLOTU	haling	paling	raving	**AGLNRU**	august
flauto	**AGHILT**	**AGILNS**	**AGINRW**	langur	**AHHILS**
AFLRTU	alight	signal	waring	**AGLNSY**	hilsah
artful	**AGHINT**	**AGILNU**	**AGINRY**	slangy	**AHHKOO**
AFLSTU	hating	lingua	grainy	**AGLNTY**	hookah
flatus	**AGHINV**	**AGILNV**	raying	tangly	**AHHLPY**
AFLSWY	having	laving	**AGINRZ**	**AGLNUU**	hyphal
sawfly	**AGHINW**	**AGILNW**	razing	ungual	**AHHOOR**
AFLTUY	hawing	lawing	**AGINSS**	ungula	hoorah
faulty	**AGHINY**	waling	assign	**AGLOOT**	**AHHRRU**
AFMORT	haying	**AGILNY**	**AGINST**	galoot	hurrah
format	**AGHINZ**	gainly	sating	**AGLOSS**	**AHHRST**
AFMOSU	hazing	laying	**AGINSV**	glossa	thrash
famous	**AGHIRS**	**AGILNZ**	saving	**AGLOWY**	**AHHUZZ**
AFNORT	garish	lazing	**AGINSW**	logway	huzzah
afront	**AGHIRT**	**AGILOR**	sawing	**AGLRUV**	**AHIILT**
AFNRYZ	aright	gloria	**AGINSY**	vulgar	lithia
franzy	**AGHISU**	**AGILOT**	saying	**AGLRUY**	**AHIKRS**
AFORRW	aguish	galiot	**AGINTW**	raguly	rakish
farrow	**AGHLOS**	**AGILOV**	tawing	**AGLRYY**	shikar
AFRSTU	galosh	ogival	**AGINTX**	grayly	**AHILLO**
frusta	**AGHNTU**	**AGILRY**	taxing	**AGLSSY**	hilloa
AGGGIN	naught	glairy	**AGINVW**	glassy	**AHILLP**
gaging	**AGHOQU**	**AGIMNN**	waving	**AGMMNO**	phalli
AGGHIS	quahog	naming	**AGINWW**	gammon	**AHILLZ**
haggis	**AGHRRY**	**AGIMNR**	wawing	**AGMMNU**	zillah
AGGHSY	gharry	arming	**AGINWX**	magnum	**AHILMU**
shaggy	**AGHTTU**	margin	waxing	**AGMNNU**	hamuli
AGGILO	taught	**AGIMNT**	**AGINWY**	gunman	**AHILNR**
loggia	**AGIILN**	mating	yawing	**AGMORS**	rhinal
AGGIMN	ailing	taming	**AGIORU**	orgasm	**AHILNU**

inhaul
AHILPS
palish
AHILRW
awhirl
AHILST
latish
AHILSV
lavish
AHILTW
withal
AHIMOR
mohair
AHIMPS
mishap
AHIMRS
marish
AHINPT
hatpin
AHINST
shanti
AHINSV
vanish
AHIPRS
parish
AHIPRU
rupiah
AHIPSS
aspish
AHIRRS
sirrah
AHIRSV
ravish
AHIRTW
wraith
AHISTU
haitus
AHKNPU
punkah
AHKNRS
shrank
AHLLMU
mullah
AHLLNU
nullah
AHLLOO
halloo
holloa
AHLLOU
hulloa
AHLLOW
hallow
AHLLRT
thrall
AHLLUX
hallux
AHLMNY
hymnal
AHLMOS
shalom
AHLOOP
hoopla
AHLORT
harlot

AHLOSY
shoaly
AHLPSS
splash
AHLRSY
rashly
AHMMSY
shammy
AHMMWY
whammy
AHMNOS
hansom
AHMNPY
nympha
AHMORZ
mahzor
AHMOSY
shamoy
AHMOTU
mahout
AHMOWY
haymow
AHMRSY
marshy
AHMRTW
warmth
AHMSSU
shamus
AHNOPR
orphan
AHNORS
shoran
AHNOWY
anyhow
AHNRTW
thrawn
AHNSTY
shanty
AHOORY
hooray
AHOPPS
sappho
AHOPRS
pharos
AHOPST
pathos
potash
AHOQTU
quotha
AHORRW
harrow
AHORRY
horary
AHORTT
throat
AHORTU
author
AHORTX
thorax
AHPRSY
sharpy
AHQSSU
squash
AHQSUY

quashy
AHRRUY
hurray
AHRSSU
hussar
AHRSTW
swarth
AHRSTY
trashy
AHRTTW
thwart
AHRTWY
wrathy
AIILMN
limina
AIILRY
airily
AIIMNS
simian
AIIMNT
intima
AIIMNV
vimina
AIIMPR
impair
AIINNZ
zinnia
AIINRS
raisin
AIINST
isatin
AIINSX
sixain
AIIRTV
trivia
AIJLOV
jovial
AIKLMN
malkin
AIKLMS
miskal
AIKLNO
kaolin
AIKLPS
kalpis
AIKMOO
oomiak
AIKMST
kismat
AIKNNN
nankin
AIKNNP
napkin
AIKOPT
katipo
AIKORT
troika
AIKRSS
krasis
AILLPR
pillar
AILLUZ
lazuli
AILLYZ

lazily
AILMNO
oilman
AILMNR
marlin
AILMNS
maslin
AILMNU
alumni
lumina
AILMNY
mainly
AILMOP
lipoma
AILMPR
primal
AILMRT
mitral
AILMSS
missal
AILMSX
smilax
AILMSY
mislay
AILMTU
ultima
AILNNU
annuli
AILNOT
talion
AILNPS
spinal
AILNPT
plaint
pliant
AILNPU
paulin
AILNRT
trinal
AILNRU
urinal
AILNST
instal
AILNSV
silvan
AILNTY
litany
AILNVY
vainly
AILNYZ
zanily
AILORS
sailor
AILORT
rialto
tailor
AILOTX
oxtail
AILPRS
spiral
AILPST
pastil
AILRTU
ritual

AILRWY
warily
AILSUV
visual
AILTXY
laxity
AIMMOS
mimosa
AIMNNO
amnion
AIMNNS
nanism
AIMNNT
tinman
AIMNNU
numina
AIMNPT
pitman
AIMNPY
paynim
AIMNRT
martin
AIMNST
mantis
AIMNSU
animus
AIMNTU
manitu
AIMOPT
optima
AIMOPY
myopia
AIMPRT
armpit
impart
AIMPSS
passim
AIMRTU
atrium
AIMRTX
matrix
AIMSTX
mastix
AINNNT
tannin
AINNOT
anoint
nation
AINNOW
wanion
AINORT
ration
AINPRS
sprain
AINPST
ptisan
AINPSV
spavin
AINPTY
painty
AINQRT
qintar
AINQTU

quaint
AINRST
instar
santir
strain
AINRTU
nutria
AINSTT
tanist
AINSTY
sanity
satiny
AINTVY
vanity
AIOORS
airoso
AIOPST
patois
AIORSV
savior
AIORTV
viator
AIOSYZ
zoysia
AIPPRY
papyri
AIPPST
papist
AIPRSV
parvis
AIPRSW
ripsaw
AIPRSX
praxis
AIPRTY
parity
AIPZZZ
pizazz
AIRRTY
rarity
AIRSST
sistra
AIRSTT
artist
strait
AISSST
assist
stasis
AITTWX
atwixt
AJLOPY
jalopy
AJNRTU
jurant
AJNTUY
jaunty
AKLLNY
lankly
AKLNOX
klaxon
AKLNRY
rankly
AKLSTY
stalky

AKMNSU
unmask
AKMPRU
markup
AKNORU
koruna
AKNRTZ
krantz
AKNSWY
swanky
AKOPUY
yakopu
AKORSS
kaross
AKQSUW
squawk
AKRTTU
kuttar
AKSWYY
skyway
ALLMOS
slalom
ALLMOT
maltol
ALLMOW
mallow
ALLMUV
vallum
ALLOPR
pallor
ALLORY
orally
ALLOSW
sallow
ALLOTW
tallow
ALLOWW
wallow
ALLPRU
plural
ALLQSU
squall
ALLSTY
lastly
ALMMUY
amylum
ALMNOR
normal
ALMNOS
salmon
ALMNTU
lantum
ALMORT
mortal
ALMORU
morula
ALMOST
almost
smalto
ALMRWY
warmly
ALMSUY
asylum
ALMTUU
mutual
umlaut
ALNNOU
nounal
ALNOOS
saloon
ALNOOZ
zoonal
ALNOPR
prolan
ALNOTV
volant
ALNRXY
larynx
ALNSTU
sultan
ALNSVY
sylvan
ALNTUW
walnut
ALOOPS
saloop
ALOPPR
poplar
ALOPRR
parlor
ALOPRT
patrol
portal
ALOPST
postal
ALOQTU
loquat
ALORST
torsal
ALORSV
salvor
ALOTUW
outlaw
ALOTUY
layout
outlay
ALPPSU
palpus
ALPRRU
larrup
ALPRSU
pulsar
ALPRSW
sprawl
ALPRTY
paltry
partly
ALPRUW
pulwar
ALPSSU
lapsus
ALRSTU
lustra
ALRSTY
stylar
ALRSUW
walrus
ALRTTY
tartly
ALRUUV
uvular
ALSSTU
saltus
tussal
ALSTVY
vastly
ALTTUY
tautly
ALTUVY
vaulty
AMMMNO
mammon
AMMORT
marmot
AMMPUW
wampum
AMMRSY
smarmy
AMNNOR
norman
AMNNOY
anonym
AMNOOR
maroon
AMNOPT
tampon
AMNORR
marron
AMNORS
ransom
AMNORT
matron
AMNOTU
amount
AMNPTY
tympan
AMNRTU
antrum
AMNTTU
mutant
AMNTUU
autumn
AMOOTT
tomato
AMOPPY
maypop
AMORRT
mortar
AMORRW
marrow
AMORRY
armory
AMORSS
morass
AMORSU
ramous
AMPSWY
swampy
AMRRTY
martyr
AMRSTU
struma
AMRSTY
smarty
ANNOOX
xoanon
ANNOST
santon
sonant
ANNOTW
wanton
ANNPSU
sannup
ANNTTU
nutant
ANOORT
ratoon
ANOPRS
parson
ANOPRT
patron
tarpon
ANOPUY
yaupon
ANORRW
narrow
ANORTT
attorn
ANORTY
notary
ANORYZ
zonary
ANOSXY
saxony
ANOUXY
noyaux
ANPPSY
snappy
ANPRTY
pantry
ANRTTU
truant
ANRTTY
tyrant
ANRUWY
runway
ANSTXY
syntax
ANSYZZ
snazzy
AOOPTT
potato
AOORRT
orator
AOORRY
arroyo
AOOTTT
tattoo
AOPRRT
parrot
AOPRRU
uproar
AOPRST
pastor
AOPRVY
vapory
AOQRTU
quarto
AORRST
rostra
AORRSY
rosary
AORRTY
rotary
AORRWY
yarrow
AORSST
assort
AORSTT
stator
AORSTX
storax
AORSUU
aurous
AORSUV
savour
AORSVY
savory
AORTVY
votary
APPPSU
pappus
APRSTY
pastry
APSSSU
passus
AQRRUY
quarry
AQRTUZ
quartz
ARRSTY
starry
ARSSST
strass
ARSSTU
tarsus
ARSTUX
surtax
ARSTWY
strawy
ASSTTU
status
BBBDEI
bibbed
BBBDEO
bobbed
BBBEIR
bibber
BBBELO
bobble
BBBELU
bubble
BBBELY
blebby
BBBEOR
bobber
BBBHUU
hubbub
BBBINO
bobbin
BBBLUY
bubbly
BBCDEU
cubbed
BBCELO
cobble
BBCEOW
cobweb
BBCHUY
chubby
BBCLUY
clubby
BBDDEU
dubbed
BBDEEW
webbed
BBDEFI
fibbed
BBDEFO
fobbed
BBDEGI
gibbed
BBDEGO
gobbed
BBDEGU
bedbug
BBDEIJ
jibbed
BBDEIL
dibble
BBDEIN
nibbed
BBDEIR
bribed
ribbed
BBDEJO
jobbed
BBDELO
lobbed
BBDELU
bulbed
BBDEMO
bombed
mobbed
BBDENO
nobbed
BBDENU
nubbed
BBDEOR
dobber
robbed
BBDEOS
sobbed
BBDEOU
buboed
BBDERU
rubbed
BBDESU
subbed
subdeb
BBDETU
tubbed
BBDIKU

dibbuk	hubbly	**BCEHOR**	**BCIINU**	**BDEELL**	nimbed
BBDINO	**BBHNOO**	broche	incubi	belled	**BDEIMU**
dobbin	hobnob	**BCEHOU**	**BCIIOT**	blende	imbued
BBDINU	**BBILLU**	bouche	biotic	**BDEINN**	**BDEINN**
dubbin	bulbil	**BCEHRU**	**BCIKNO**	**BDEELT**	binned
BBEELP	**BBILSU**	cherub	kincob	belted	**BDEINR**
pebble	biblus	**BCEIIS**	**BCIKRY**	**BDEENO**	binder
BBEFIR	**BBINNU**	ibices	bricky	debone	inbred
fibber	nubbin	**BCEIKR**	**BCILPU**	**BDEENR**	**BDEIOR**
BBEGIN	**BBINOR**	bicker	public	bender	boride
ebbing	ribbon	**BCEILR**	**BCILRU**	**BDEEOY**	**BDEIOS**
BBEGIR	robbin	crible	lubric	obeyed	bodies
gibber	**BBKNOY**	**BCEILY**	**BCIMOR**	**BDEERW**	**BDEIRS**
BBEGIT	knobby	beylic	bromic	brewed	debris
gibbet	**BBLLUU**	**BCEIOR**	**BCIRRU**	**BDEETT**	**BDEIRU**
BBEGLO	bulbul	corbie	rubric	betted	buried
gobble	**BBLNUY**	**BCEIOX**	**BCISTU**	**BDEFFU**	rubied
BBEGNU	nubbly	icebox	bustic	buffed	**BDEIRV**
bebung	**BBLOWY**	**BCEIPS**	**BCKLOY**	**BDEGGO**	verbid
BBEGOT	wobbly	biceps	blocky	bogged	**BDEISU**
gobbet	**BBLRUY**	**BCEIRS**	**BCMORY**	**BDEGGU**	busied
BBEHLO	rubbly	scribe	corymb	bugged	**BDEKLU**
hobble	**BBLSUU**	**BCEIST**	**BCMRUY**	**BDEGIL**	bulked
BBEHLU	bulbus	bisect	crumby	bilged	**BDEKNU**
hubble	**BBNNOO**	**BCEJOT**	**BCNOOR**	**BDEGIR**	bunked
BBEIIM	bonbon	object	bronco	bridge	debunk
imbibe	**BBNOSY**	**BCEKLU**	**BCNOTU**	**BDEGIU**	**BDEKOO**
BBEIJR	snobby	buckle	cobnut	budgie	booked
jibber	**BBNSUY**	**BCEKNO**	**BCNOUY**	**BDEGLO**	**BDEKRU**
BBEIKL	snubby	beckon	bouncy	globed	burked
kibble	**BBORTU**	**BCEKRU**	**BCOOWY**	**BDEGLU**	**BDELLU**
BBEILN	burbot	bucker	cowboy	bugled	bulled
nibble	**BBOSUY**	**BCEKTU**	**BDDDEE**	**BDEGNU**	**BDELNO**
BBEILR	busboy	bucket	bedded	bunged	blonde
libber	**BBRSUU**	**BCELOR**	**BDDDEU**	**BDEGTU**	**BDELNU**
BBEIRR	suburb	corbel	budded	budget	bundle
briber	**BBSTUY**	**BCELOU**	**BDDEGU**	**BDEHIN**	**BDELOO**
BBEJOR	stubby	boucle	budged	behind	boodle
jobber	**BCCEIO**	**BCEMOR**	**BDDEIN**	**BDEHLO**	**BDELOR**
BBELMU	boccie	comber	bidden	behold	bolder
bumble	**BCDEEK**	**BCEMRU**	**BDDEIO**	**BDEHOT**	bordel
BBELNO	bedeck	cumber	bodied	hotbed	**BDELOT**
nobble	**BCDEIO**	**BCENOU**	**BDDEIR**	**BDEHSU**	bolted
BBELNU	bodice	bounce	bidder	bushed	**BDELOU**
nubble	**BCDEKU**	**BCEOTT**	**BDDELU**	**BDEIIM**	double
BBELOW	bucked	obtect	buddle	ibidem	**BDELOW**
wobble	**BCDEMO**	**BCGINU**	**BDDENO**	**BDEIIR**	bowled
BBELRU	combed	cubing	bonded	birdie	**BDELRU**
burble	**BCDEOU**	**BCGORY**	**BDDERU**	**BDEIKL**	burled
lubber	obduce	cyborg	redbud	bilked	**BDEMMU**
rubble	**BCDERU**	**BCHIIR**	**BDEEEF**	**BDEILL**	bummed
BBEMNU	curbed	bichir	beefed	billed	**BDEMNU**
benumb	**BCDIOU**	**BCHLOT**	**BDEEGG**	**BDEILM**	numbed
BBEORR	cuboid	blotch	begged	limbed	**BDEMOO**
robber	**BCEEHR**	**BCHNRU**	**BDEEHL**	**BDEILN**	boomed
BBEOSU	breech	brunch	beheld	bindle	**BDEMOY**
buboes	**BCEEHY**	**BCHNUY**	**BDEEIL**	**BDEILO**	embody
BBERRU	beechy	bunchy	belied	boiled	**BDEMPU**
rubber	**BCEEKT**	**BCHOOR**	debile	bolide	bumped
BBGINO	becket	brooch	edible	**BDEILR**	**BDEMRU**
gibbon	**BCEEMO**	**BCHOTY**	**BDEEIS**	birled	dumber
BBGRUY	become	botchy	beside	bridle	**BDENNU**
grubby	**BCEHLN**	**BCIILM**	**BDEEIT**	**BDEIMN**	unbend
BBHLUY	blench	limbic	betide	**BDEIMN**	**BDENOY**

beyond	**BDLMUY**	ibexes	**BEGILT**	**BEILMR**	**BEJJUU**
BDENRU	dumbly	**BEEKRU**	giblet	limber	jujube
burden	**BDLNOO**	rebuke	**BEGINN**	**BEILMW**	**BEJLMU**
burned	doblon	**BEELMM**	benign	wimble	jumble
BDENTU	**BDLOOY**	emblem	**BEGINO**	**BEILMY**	**BEKMOS**
bunted	bloody	**BEELNS**	biogen	blimey	embosk
BDEOOT	**BDLOUY**	bensel	**BEGIOS**	**BEILNR**	**BEKNOR**
booted	doubly	**BEELNU**	bogies	berlin	broken
BDEOOZ	**BDNOOY**	nebule	**BEGIOU**	**BEILNU**	**BEKNRU**
boozed	nobody	**BEELRT**	bougie	nubile	bunker
BDEOPP	**BDNOTU**	treble	**BEGLNO**	**BEILOR**	**BEKOOT**
bopped	obtund	**BEELRU**	belong	boiler	betook
BDEOPR	**BDOORY**	brulee	**BEGLNU**	**BEILOS**	**BEKORR**
probed	broody	**BEEMMR**	bungle	besoil	broker
BDEORR	**BDORWY**	member	**BEGLOT**	**BEILRT**	**BELLOU**
border	byword	**BEEMRU**	goblet	riblet	lobule
BDEORT	**BEEEFL**	embrue	**BEGLRU**	**BEIMOZ**	**BELLOW**
debtor	feeble	**BEEMSU**	bugler	zombie	bellow
BDEOSS	**BEEEHP**	bemuse	bulger	**BEIMRT**	**BELLTU**
bossed	ephebe	**BEEOOT**	burgle	timber	bullet
BDEOSU	**BEEEKL**	bootee	**BEGNOY**	timbre	**BELLUY**
boused	kelebe	**BEEORY**	bygone	**BEIMRU**	bluely
BDEOUY	**BEEELT**	obeyer	**BEGOOR**	imbrue	**BELMMU**
bouyed	beetle	**BEERRV**	goober	**BEIMRX**	mumble
BDERRU	**BEEEMS**	reverb	**BEGOPX**	imbrex	**BELMOY**
burred	beseem	**BEERRW**	pegbox	**BEINOR**	emboly
BDESSU	**BEEEPR**	brewer	**BEGORU**	bonier	**BELMRU**
bussed	beeper	**BEERTT**	brogue	**BEINOV**	lumber
BDESUU	**BEEERZ**	better	**BEGOTU**	bovine	rumble
subdue	breeze	**BEERTV**	bouget	**BEINOZ**	**BELMTU**
BDETTU	**BEEESV**	brevet	**BEGRRU**	bizone	tumble
butted	beeves	**BEERYZ**	burger	**BEINRS**	**BELNOZ**
BDFILO	**BEEFIL**	breezy	**BEHILT**	nebris	benzol
bifold	belief	**BEFFOU**	blithe	**BEINRY**	**BELNYZ**
BDFIOR	**BEEFLL**	bouffe	**BEHLMU**	byrnie	benzyl
forbid	befell	**BEFFRU**	humble	**BEINTT**	**BELOOR**
BDGIIN	**BEEFLY**	buffer	**BEHLSU**	bitten	bolero
biding	feebly	rebuff	bushel	**BEIORX**	**BELOPU**
BDGINO	**BEEFOR**	**BEFFTU**	**BEHMOR**	boxier	pueblo
boding	before	buffet	hombre	**BEIOST**	**BELORT**
BDHIRY	**BEEFRT**	**BEFILM**	**BEHNOR**	sobeit	bolter
hybrid	bereft	fimble	brehon	tobies	**BELORU**
BDIILO	**BEEGNO**	**BEFILO**	**BEHOOS**	**BEIQSU**	rouble
libido	begone	foible	hoboes	bisque	**BELORW**
BDIITT	**BEEGRU**	**BEFLMU**	**BEHORT**	**BEIRRU**	blower
tidbit	burgee	fumble	bother	burier	bowler
BDIKNO	**BEEHLT**	**BEFLOU**	**BEHSSU**	**BEIRRY**	**BELOSU**
bodkin	bethel	befoul	bushes	briery	blouse
BDILOY	**BEEHOP**	**BEFLRY**	**BEIISS**	**BEIRST**	obelus
bodily	phoebe	belfry	ibises	bestir	**BELOTT**
BDIMOR	**BEEHRY**	**BEFSUU**	**BEIKLY**	bister	bottle
morbid	hereby	subfeu	beylik	**BEIRSU**	**BELOWZ**
BDINNO	**BEEHST**	**BEGGII**	**BEIKOO**	bruise	blowze
inbond	behest	biggie	bookie	buries	**BELRTU**
BDINOU	**BEEIMR**	**BEGGIR**	**BEIKSS**	busier	butler
boudin	bemire	bigger	bekiss	rubies	**BELRUY**
BDIOTU	bireme	**BEGGLO**	**BEILLT**	**BEIRSW**	burley
outbid	**BEEIMT**	boggle	billet	brewis	**BELSTU**
BDIRTU	betime	**BEGGRU**	**BEILMN**	**BEIRTT**	bluest
turbid	**BEEIST**	bugger	nimble	bitter	bustle
BDKLOO	betise	**BEGILO**	**BEILMO**	**BEISSU**	sublet
kobold	**BEEISV**	oblige	bemoil	busies	subtle
BDLLOY	bevies	**BEGILR**	emboli	**BEITUY**	**BEMMRU**
boldly	**BEEISX**	gerbil	mobile	ubiety	bummer

BEMNOT	**BEPRSU**	**BGINOR**	**BILLRS**	**BMOORY**	**CCEIIL**
entomb	superb	boring	brills	broomy	cilice
BEMNOW	**BERSTU**	orbing	**BILMNY**	**BMOOSY**	icicle
bowmen	buster	robing	nimbly	bosomy	**CCEILR**
BEMNRU	**BERTTU**	**BGINOW**	**BILMSU**	**BMOOTT**	circle
number	butter	bowing	limbus	bottom	cleric
BEMNSU	**BERUZZ**	**BGINOX**	**BILRTY**	**BMOOTY**	**CCEILY**
busmen	buzzer	boxing	trilby	tomboy	cicely
BEMNTU	**BESSSU**	**BGINSU**	**BILSUY**	**BNNORU**	**CCEINS**
tubmen	busses	busing	busily	unborn	scenic
BEMOOR	**BESSTU**	**BGINTU**	**BIMNSU**	**BNORSU**	**CCEIPT**
boomer	subset	tubing	nimbus	suborn	pectic
BEMORS	**BFFIIN**	**BGINUY**	**BIMSTU**	**BNORTU**	**CCEKLO**
somber	biffin	buying	submit	burton	cockle
BEMORY	**BFFORU**	**BGLNOO**	**BINNOR**	**BNOSUW**	**CCEKOP**
embryo	ruboff	oblong	inborn	sunbow	copeck
BEMOSS	**BFGOOW**	**BGLRUU**	**BINNOU**	**BNOTTU**	**CCEKOR**
emboss	fogbow	bulgur	bunion	button	cocker
BEMPRU	**BFIILR**	**BGOORU**	**BINOOT**	**BNOTUY**	**CCEKOT**
bumper	fibril	burgoo	bonito	bounty	cocket
BENNOT	**BFIINR**	**BGOTUU**	**BINORY**	**BOORRW**	**CCENOS**
bonnet	fibrin	bugout	briony	borrow	sconce
BENNTU	**BFIMOR**	**BHIKOS**	**BIOORZ**	**BOOWWW**	**CCEORS**
unbent	biform	kibosh	borzoi	bowwow	soccer
BENORR	**BFINOW**	**BHILSU**	**BIOOST**	**BORRUW**	**CCEORS**
reborn	bowfin	bluish	oboist	burrow	soccer
BENORZ	**BFIRUY**	**BHIOPS**	**BIOPSY**	**BORSTU**	**CCERSU**
bonzer	rubify	bishop	biopsy	robust	cruces
bronze	**BFLOTY**	**BHIOSY**	**BIORST**	**BORTTU**	**CCFILO**
BENRRU	botfly	boyish	bistro	turbot	flocci
burner	**BFLOUX**	**BHIRSU**	**BIOSTU**	**BSSSUY**	**CCHHII**
BENRTU	boxful	hubris	subito	byssus	chichi
brunet	**BGGIIN**	**BHLMUY**	**BIRRSU**	**CCCILY**	**CCHHIN**
burnet	biggin	humbly	birrus	cyclic	chinch
BEOORZ	**BGGIIW**	**BHLSUY**	**BIRTTU**	**CCCOSU**	**CCHHRU**
rebozo	bigwig	blushy	turbit	coccus	church
BEOPST	**BGHILT**	**BHOOOO**	**BKMNUU**	**CCCOXY**	**CCHILN**
bespot	blight	boohoo	bunkum	coccyx	clinch
BEORRS	**BGHIRT**	**BHOOTX**	**BLMOOY**	**CCDEKO**	**CCHIOR**
resorb	bright	hotbox	bloomy	cocked	choric
BEORST	**BGHMUU**	**BHORTY**	**BLMOSY**	**CCDELY**	**CCHIPU**
sorbet	humbug	brothy	symbol	cycled	hiccup
strobe	**BGHORU**	**BHRSUY**	**BLMRUY**	**CCDEOT**	**CCHLTU**
BEORSU	brough	brushy	rumbly	decoct	clutch
bourse	**BGHOTU**	**BIIIKN**	**BLOOSU**	**CCEEHR**	cultch
BEORSW	bought	bikini	obolus	creche	**CCHNRU**
browse	**BGIIJN**	**BIIKTZ**	**BLOOTT**	**CCEEOR**	crunch
BEORTT	jibing	kibitz	blotto	coerce	**CCHORS**
bettor	**BGIIKN**	**BIIMOS**	**BLOOWY**	**CCEHIL**	scorch
BEORTV	biking	obiism	lowboy	chicle	**CCHORT**
obvert	**BGIINT**	**BIITTT**	**BLOPUW**	cliche	crotch
BEORWY	biting	titbit	blowup	**CCEHIM**	**CCHORU**
bowery	**BGILLY**	**BIKLNY**	**BLOSUY**	chemic	crouch
bowyer	glibly	blinky	blousy	**CCEHIO**	**CCHOST**
BEOSSS	**BGILNO**	**BIKMNU**	**BLOSWY**	choice	scotch
obsess	globin	bumkin	blowsy	echoic	**CCHRTU**
BEOSST	goblin	**BIKNSU**	**BLOTTY**	**CCEHIT**	crutch
bosset	**BGILNU**	buskin	blotty	hectic	**CCHSTU**
BEOSTT	bluing	**BILLNO**	**BLOWYZ**	**CCEHKY**	scutch
obtest	**BGINNO**	billon	blowzy	checky	**CCIILN**
BEOSTU	boning	**BILLOW**	**BLRRUY**	**CCEHLN**	clinic
obtuse	**BGINOO**	billow	blurry	clench	**CCIINO**
BEOSTW	booing	**BILLOX**	**BLSTUY**	**CCEHLO**	iconic
bestow		bollix	subtly	cloche	**CCIINP**
					picnic
					CCIIRT

citric	CDDRUY	reduce	ticked	CDEKSU	CDERSY
critic	cruddy	CDEERW	CDEIKW	sucked	descry
CCILNO	CDEEEM	crewed	wicked	CDEKTU	CDERUV
clonic	emceed	CDEESU	CDEIKY	tucked	curved
CCIMOS	CDEEER	seduce	dickey	CDELLO	CDERUY
cosmic	decree	CDEETT	CDEILO	colled	decury
CCIOTT	recede	detect	coiled	CDELLU	CDESSU
tictoc	CDEEES	CDEFFU	docile	culled	cussed
CCIPRU	secede	cuffed	CDEILS	CDELNO	CDFIOY
cupric	CDEEEX	CDEFII	sliced	cloned	codify
CCIRSU	exceed	deific	CDEILT	CDELOO	CDGIIN
circus	CDEEFN	CDEFNU	delict	cooled	dicing
CCISTY	fenced	fecund	CDEIMN	CDELOR	CDGINO
cystic	CDEEFT	CDEFOR	minced	colder	coding
CCKOOU	defect	forced	CDEIMO	CDELOS	CDHIOR
cuckoo	CDEEHL	CDEGGO	medico	closed	orchid
CCKORY	leched	cogged	CDEINO	CDELOW	CDHIRY
crocky	CDEEHO	CDEGIN	coined	cowled	hydric
CCLOTU	echoed	ceding	CDEINR	CDELOY	CDIIIR
occult	CDEEHT	CDEGLU	cinder	cloyed	iridic
CCNOOO	etched	cudgel	crined	CDELRU	CDIINT
cocoon	CDEEHW	CDEGOR	CDEINU	curdle	indict
CCNORU	chewed	codger	induce	curled	CDIIOY
concur	CDEEIL	CDEHIL	CDEINW	CDELTU	idiocy
CCOOOR	ceiled	chield	winced	dulcet	CDIISV
rococo	decile	CDEHIM	CDEIOP	CEDMOP	viscid
CCOPUY	CDEEIP	chimed	copied	comped	CDIMOO
occupy	pieced	CDEHIN	CDEIOS	CDEMOY	comoid
CCORSU	CDEEIR	inched	esodic	comedy	CDIMTU
crocus	deicer	niched	CDEIOV	CDENOR	dictum
succor	CDEEIT	CDEHIR	voiced	corned	CDINOO
CCOSTU	deceit	herdic	CDEIOX	CDENOS	conoid
stucco	CDEEIV	CDEHIT	exodic	second	CDINOY
CDDDEO	device	itched	CDEIPR	CDENOT	cynoid
codded	CDEEIX	CDEHKO	priced	docent	CDINSY
CDDEEI	excide	choked	CDEIPS	CDENSU	syndic
decide	CDEEIZ	hocked	spiced	secund	CDINTU
deiced	ecized	CDEHNR	CDEIPT	CDEOOP	induct
CDDEEK	CDEEJT	drench	depict	cooped	CDIPSU
decked	deject	CDEHOS	CDEIRT	CDEOPP	cuspid
CDDEEO	CDEEKK	coshed	credit	copped	CDISSU
decode	kecked	CDEHOU	direct	CDEOPU	discus
CDDEEU	CDEEKL	douche	triced	couped	CDJNOU
deduce	deckle	CDEHTU	CDEIRV	CDEORR	jocund
deuced	CDEEKN	chuted	cervid	corder	CDLLOY
educed	necked	CDEIIR	CDEKLO	record	coldly
CDDEHI	CDEEKP	dicier	locked	CDEORS	CDLOUY
chided	pecked	CDEIIT	CDEKMO	scored	cloudy
CDDEKO	CDEEKR	citied	mocked	CDEORW	CDMNOO
docked	recked	CDEIJU	CDEKMU	crowed	condom
CDDEKU	CDEELL	juiced	mucked	CDEORZ	CDNOOR
ducked	celled	CDEIKK	CDEKNO	crozed	condor
CDDELO	CDEELW	kicked	nocked	CDEOSU	CDNOOR
coddle	clewed	CDEIKL	CDEKOO	escudo	cordon
CDDELU	CDEENO	licked	cooked	CDEOSW	CDOORT
cuddle	encode	CDEIKN	CDEKOR	scowed	doctor
CDDEOR	CDEENS	nicked	corked	CDEPPU	CDOORY
corded	censed	CDEIKP	rocked	cupped	corody
CDDERU	CDEENT	picked	CDEKOS	CDEPSU	CEEEFL
curded	cedent	CDEIKR	socked	cusped	fleece
CDDETU	decent	dicker	CDEKOT	CDERRU	CEEEHS
deduct	CDEERS	CDEIKS	docket	cruder	cheese
CDDLOY	screed	sicked	CDEKRU	CDERSU	CEEERS
cloddy	CDEERU	CDEIKT	rucked	cursed	creese

CEEFFO
coffee
CEEFFT
effect
CEEFHL
fleche
CEEFIR
fierce
CEEFLY
fleecy
CEEFNN
fennec
CEEFNR
fencer
CEEFSU
fescue
CEEGIR
griece
CEEGNO
congee
CEEHIL
lichee
CEEHIS
seiche
CEEHKL
heckle
CEEHKY
cheeky
CEEHLN
elench
CEEHLR
lecher
CEEHLS
lesche
CEEHMS
scheme
CEEHNT
thence
CEEHNW
whence
CEEHOR
cohere
echoer
CEEHOS
echoes
CEEHPS
speech
CEEHQU
cheque
CEEHRU
euchre
CEEHRW
chewer
CEEHRY
cheery
CEEHST
etches
CEEHSW
eschew
CEEHSY
cheesy
CEEIMN
icemen
CEEIMR
eremic
CEEIMT
emetic
CEEINT
entice
CEEINV
evince
CEEIPR
piecer
pierce
recipe
CEEIPS
specie
CEEIRS
cerise
CEEIRT
recite
tierce
CEEISS
ecesis
CEEISX
excise
CEEITX
excite
CEEJRT
reject
CEEKKL
keckle
CEEKNR
necker
CEELMO
cleome
CEELNR
crenel
CEELOR
creole
CEELOU
coulee
CEELOV
veloce
CEELRT
tercel
CEELRV
clever
CEELRW
crewel
CEELRY
celery
CEELST
select
CEEMNT
cement
CEEMRR
mercer
CEEMRT
cermet
CEENOR
encore
CEENOT
cenote
CEENPT
pecten
CEENRS
screen
secern
CEENRT
center
centre
recent
tenrec
CEEORV
corvee
CEEPRY
creepy
CEEPTX
except
expect
CEEPTY
ectype
CEEPUY
eyecup
CEERRT
tercer
CEERSS
cesser
recess
CEERST
certes
secret
CEERSU
cereus
ceruse
recuse
rescue
secure
CEERTT
tercet
CEESSX
excess
CEESUX
excuse
CEFFIO
office
CEFFLO
coffle
CEFFOR
coffer
CEFHIT
fetich
fitche
CEFHLT
fletch
CEFIKL
fickle
CEFINT
infect
CEFIOS
ficoes
CEFIRR
ferric
CEFNOR
confer
CEFORR
forcer
CEFORS
fresco
CEFRUW
curfew
CEGHIN
eching
CEGHLU
cleugh
CEGINO
coigne
CEGINR
cringe
CEGIOT
goetic
CEGIST
gestic
CEGLRY
clergy
CEGNOR
conger
CEGNOT
cogent
CEGNTY
cygnet
CEGORR
grocer
CEHIKY
hickey
CEHILN
lichen
CEHILS
chisel
CEHINR
enrich
CEHINS
chinse
inches
CEHINT
ethnic
CEHIOR
coheir
heroic
CEHIPR
cipher
CEHIQU
quiche
CEHIRR
richer
CEHIRS
riches
CEHIRT
cither
thrice •
CEHIST
itches
CEHITT
thetic
CEHKLU
huckle
CEHKNU
kuchen
CEHKOR
choker
CEHKOT
hocket
CEHKOY
chokey
hockey
CEHKST
sketch
CEHKTV
kvetch
CEHLOR
choler
CEHLOT
clothe
CEHMNS
mensch
CEHMOR
chrome
CEHMOT
cometh
CEHNOS
chosen
CEHNQU
quench
CEHNRT
trench
CEHNRW
wrench
CEHNST
stench
CEHNUU
eunuch
CEHOOS
choose
CEHORS
cosher
CEHORT
hector
rochet
rotche
tocher
troche
CEHOSU
chouse
CEHOTU
touche
CEHPRU
cherup
CEHPRY
cypher
CEHRRY
cherry
CEHRTW
wretch
CEHSTY
chesty
scythe
CEHTTY
tetchy
CEIIKR
ickier
CEIILT
elicit
CEIILX
exilic
CEIINR
irenic
CEIINS
incise
CEIINT
incite
CEIIST
cities
iciest
CEIISV
civies
CEIJNT
inject
CEIJRU
juicer
CEIKKR
kicker
CEIKLM
mickle
CEIKLN
nickel
CEIKLP
pickle
CEIKLR
licker
CEIKLS
sickle
CEIKLT
tickle
CEIKNR
nicker
CEIKNS
sicken
CEIKOO
cookie
CEIKPR
picker
CEIKPT
picket
CEIKRS
sicker
CEIKRT
ticker
CEIKRW
wicker
CEIKRY
rickey
CEIKTT
ticket
CEIKTW
wicket
CEILLO
collie
CEILNP
pencil
CEILNT
client
lentic
CEILNU
nuclei
CEILNY
nicely
CEILOO
coolie
CEILOP
police
CEILOR
recoil
CEILPS

splice	**CEIORR**	**CEKOPT**	cupule	copter	cutest
CEILPV	corrie	pocket	**CELRRU**	**CEOPRU**	**CESTUY**
pelvic	**CEIORS**	**CEKORR**	curler	couper	cutesy
CEILPY	cosier	corker	**CELRTU**	recoup	**CFFHUY**
clypei	**CEIORT**	rocker	cutler	**CEOQTU**	chuffy
CEILQU	erotic	**CEKORT**	**CELRUU**	coquet	**CFFILY**
clique	**CEIORV**	rocket	curule	**CEORRS**	cliffy
CEILRS	voicer	**CEKOST**	**CELRUV**	scorer	**CFFINO**
slicer	**CEIORW**	socket	culver	**CEORRT**	coffin
CEILRT	cowrie	**CEKPRU**	**CELRUW**	rector	**CFFOTU**
relict	**CEIORZ**	pucker	curlew	**CEORSS**	cutoff
CEILSU	cozier	**CEKRSU**	**CELTTU**	crosse	**CFFRSU**
sluice	**CEIOSS**	sucker	cutlet	**CEORST**	scruff
CEILSV	cosies	**CEKTTU**	cuttle	corset	**CFGINU**
clevis	**CEIOST**	tucket	**CELTUY**	coster	fungic
CEILTU	oecist	**CELLOT**	cutely	escort	**CFHILN**
luetic	**CEIOTX**	collet	**CEMMRU**	scoter	flinch
CEIMNO	exotic	**CELLTU**	cummer	sector	**CFIIST**
income	**CEIPPT**	cullet	**CEMNOO**	**CEORSU**	fistic
CEIMNR	peptic	**CELMNU**	oncome	cerous	**CFIITY**
mincer	**CEIPRR**	culmen	**CEMNTU**	course	citify
CEIMPU	pricer	**CELMOP**	centum	source	**CFILOR**
pumice	**CEIPRS**	compel	**CEMOOS**	**CEORSV**	frolic
CEIMRT	precis	**CELMOY**	comose	corves	**CFIMOR**
metric	**CEIPST**	comely	**CEMRTU**	**CEORSW**	formic
CEIMRU	septic	**CELMSU**	rectum	escrow	**CFIMOT**
cerium	**CEIQRU**	muscle	**CENNOR**	**CEORTT**	comfit
CEIMSU	cirque	**CELMUY**	conner	cotter	**CFISTU**
cesium	**CEIRSS**	lyceum	**CENNOX**	**CEORTU**	fustic
miscue	crises	**CELNOR**	connex	couter	**CFLPUU**
CEINOS	**CEIRST**	cornel	**CENNRU**	**CEORTV**	cupful
cosine	steric	**CELNOV**	cunner	covert	**CFRSUY**
oscine	**CEIRSU**	cloven	**CENOPR**	vector	scurfy
CEINOT	cruise	**CELNRU**	crepon	**CEORTX**	**CGGLOY**
noetic	**CEIRTU**	lucern	**CENOPU**	cortex	cloggy
notice	uretic	**CELNTU**	pounce	**CEOSST**	**CGHHOU**
CEINOV	**CEIRVX**	lucent	**CENORR**	cosset	chough
novice	cervix	**CELOOR**	corner	**CEOSSU**	**CGHILT**
CEINPR	**CEISSU**	cooler	**CENORS**	scouse	glitch
prince	cuisse	**CELOOT**	censor	**CEOSTY**	**CGHLOU**
CEINPT	**CEISSY**	ocelot	**CENORT**	coyest	clough
incept	cyesis	**CELOPU**	cornet	**CEPPRU**	**CGHORU**
pectin	**CEJKOY**	couple	**CENORU**	cupper	grouch
CEINQU	jockey	**CELORS**	rounce	**CEPRSU**	**CGIINO**
cinque	**CEJNOU**	closer	**CENOVX**	spruce	congii
quince	jounce	cresol	convex	**CEPSTU**	**CGIINR**
CEINRT	**CEJOOS**	**CELORT**	**CENOVY**	pectus	ricing
cretin	jocose	colter	convey	**CERSTU**	**CGIINT**
CEINST	**CEKKOP**	lector	**CENSSU**	rectus	citing
incest	kopeck	**CELORU**	census	**CERSUX**	**CGIKNO**
insect	**CEKLOR**	colure	**CENSTY**	cruxes	coking
nicest	locker	**CELORV**	encyst	**CERSWY**	**CGILNU**
CEINSU	**CEKLOT**	clover	**CEOOPR**	screwy	cluing
incuse	locket	**CELOST**	cooper	**CERTTU**	**CGILNY**
CEINTY	**CEKLRU**	closet	**CEOORT**	cutter	clingy
nicety	ruckle	**CELOSU**	cooter	**CERTUV**	**CGIMNO**
CEIOOT	**CEKLSU**	coleus	**CEOOTY**	curvet	coming
cootie	suckle	**CELOSX**	coyote	**CESSSU**	**CGINNO**
CEIOPR	**CEKMOR**	scolex	oocyte	cusses	coning
copier	mocker	**CELOTT**	**CEOPPR**	**CESSTU**	**CGINOO**
CEIOPS	**CEKNOR**	cottle	copper	cestus	cooing
copies	reckon	**CELPTY**	**CEOPRS**	**CESSUX**	**CGINOP**
CEIOPT	**CEKOOR**	yclept	corpse	excuss	coping
poetic	cooker	**CELPUU**	**CEOPRT**	**CESTTU**	

CGINOR	chirpy	**CIIMTV**	**CIMRUU**	column	**COOORZ**
coring	**CHIPSY**	victim	curium	**CLMOPY**	corozo
CGINOV	physic	**CIINOR**	**CIMSTY**	comply	**COOPRS**
coving	**CHIQTU**	ironic	mystic	**CLMPUY**	scroop
CGINOY	quitch	**CIINRT**	**CINNOU**	clumpy	**COOPWX**
coying	**CHISST**	citrin	nuncio	**CLMSUY**	cowpox
CGINRU	schist	nitric	**CINORT**	clumsy	**COPPRY**
curing	**CHISTT**	**CIIRSS**	citron	**CLNOOY**	croppy
CGINRY	stitch	crisis	**CINORZ**	colony	**COPRSU**
crying	**CHISTW**	**CIIRTV**	zircon	**CLNOSU**	corpus
CGLLOY	switch	vitric	**CINOST**	clonus	**COPRUY**
glycol	**CHISYZ**	**CIKLSY**	tocsin	consul	croupy
CGLNOU	schizy	sickly	**CINOSU**	**CLNRUU**	**CORRSU**
unclog	**CHITTW**	**CIKOSY**	cousin	uncurl	cursor
CGNOOU	twitch	yoicks	**CIOOPT**	**CLOORU**	**CORTUY**
congou	**CHKNUY**	**CIKPPU**	octopi	colour	outcry
CHHNOO	chunky	pickup	**CIOORT**	**CLOORY**	**COSSTU**
honcho	**CHLOOS**	**CIKRST**	octroi	colory	custos
CHHOOT	school	strick	**CIOPRS**	**CLOSTU**	**COTTUU**
hootch	**CHLORS**	**CIKRTY**	psoric	locust	cutout
CHIILT	schorl	tricky	**CIOPRT**	**CLOSTY**	**CRRSUY**
litchi	**CHLOSU**	**CIKSTY**	tropic	costly	scurry •
lithic	slouch	sticky	**CIORTT**	**CLOSUU**	**CRSTUY**
CHIINT	**CHMMUY**	**CILLSU**	tricot	oculus	crusty
chitin	chummy	cullis	**CIORTV**	**CLOTTY**	curtsy
CHIKNY	**CHMOOR**	**CILNOO**	victor	clotty	**CRSUVY**
chinky	chromo	coloni	**CIOSTU**	**CLPSTU**	scurvy
CHIKRS	**CHMOOS**	nicolo	coitus	sculpt	**DDDEEE**
kirsch	smooch	**CILNOU**	**CIPPSU**	**CLSTUU**	deeded
CHIKST	**CHMOSU**	uncoil	cippus	cultus	**DDDEEI**
kitsch	smouch	**CILNTU**	**CIPRST**	**CMMNOO**	eddied
CHILLY	**CHMSTU**	incult	script	common	**DDDEET**
chilly	smutch	**CILOPU**	**CIPRSY**	**CMMOOS**	tedded
CHILMO	**CHNOOP**	oilcup	crispy	commos	**DDDEEW**
holmic	poncho	**CILOPY**	**CIRRSU**	**CMMRUY**	wedded
CHILOR	**CHNPUY**	policy	cirrus	crummy	**DDDEFI**
orchil	punchy	**CILORT**	**CIRSTT**	**CMMSUY**	fidded
CHIMNY	**CHNTUU**	lictor	strict	scummy	**DDDEGO**
hymnic	tuchun	**CILOTU**	**CIRSTU**	**CMNNOO**	dodged
CHIMRS	**CHOORT**	coutil	citrus	noncom	**DDDEIK**
chrism	cohort	**CILOYZ**	rustic	**CMOOSS**	kidded
smirch	**CHOOSY**	cozily	**CISSUV**	cosmos	**DDDEIL**
CHIMSS	choosy	**CIMMOS**	viscus	**CMOOSU**	diddle
schism	**CHOPPY**	commis	**CKLNOU**	comous	lidded
CHIMST	choppy	**CIMMOT**	unlock	**CMOSTU**	**DDDEIR**
smitch	**CHOPSY**	commit	**CKLOPU**	custom	didder
CHIMTY	psycho	**CIMMOX**	lockup	**CMOSUU**	ridded
mythic	**CHORRU**	commix	**CKLPUY**	mucous	**DDDELO**
CHINOP	churro	**CIMNOR**	plucky	**CMSTUU**	doddle
chopin	**CHORSU**	micron	**CKNORU**	scutum	**DDDEMU**
phonic	chorus	**CIMNOU**	uncork	**CNOOPU**	mudded
CHINOT	**CHOSTU**	conium	**CKOSTY**	coupon	**DDDENO**
chiton	schout	**CIMOPY**	stocky	**CNOORT**	nodded
CHINRU	scouth	myopic	**CKRSTU**	croton	**DDDEOP**
urchin	**CHOTUY**	**CIMORU**	struck	**CNOOST**	podded
CHINST	touchy	corium	**CKRSUU**	nostoc	**DDDEOR**
snitch	**CHSSSU**	**CIMOST**	ruckus	**CNOOTT**	dodder
CHINTZ	schuss	sitcom	**CLLOOP**	cotton	rodded
chintz	**CIILMU**	**CIMOTY**	collop	**CNOOTY**	**DDDEOS**
CHIORS	cilium	comity	**CLLOOY**	tycoon	sodded
orchis	**CIIMOT**	**CIMPRS**	coolly	**CNOOVY**	**DDDEEH**
CHIPPY	miotic	scrimp	**CLLORS**	convoy	heeded
chippy	**CIIMSV**	**CIMPRY**	scroll	**CNOTUY**	**DDDEEM**
CHIPRY	civism	crimpy	**CLMNOU**	county	deemed

DDEEEN	redden	hodden	noddle	**DDILNR**	**DEEEPP**
needed	**DDEENT**	**DDEHOO**	**DDELOO**	dirndl	peeped
DDEEER	dented	hooded	doodle	**DDILTY**	**DEEEPR**
reeded	tended	**DDEHOR**	**DDELOR**	tiddly	deeper
DDEEES	**DDEENU**	horded	lorded	**DDIOPY**	peered
seeded	denude	**DDEIIO**	**DDELOT**	dipody	**DEEEPS**
DDEEEW	endued	iodide	toddle	**DDIORS**	seeped
weeded	**DDEENV**	**DDEIIT**	**DDELOY**	sordid	**DEEEPV**
DDEEFI	vended	tidied	yodled	**DDIOTY**	peeved
defied	**DDEENW**	**DDEIIV**	**DDELPU**	oddity	**DEEERR**
DDEEFN	wended	divide	puddle	**DDLPUY**	reeder
defend	**DDEEOR**	**DDEIKL**	**DDEMOO**	puddly	**DEEERS**
fended	eroded	kiddle	doomed	**DDMMUU**	seeder
DDEEFU	**DDEERR**	**DDEIKR**	**DDEMPU**	dumdum	**DEEERV**
feuded	redder	dirked	dumped	**DDPSUY**	veered
DDEEGG	**DDEESS**	kidder	**DDEMRU**	spuddy	**DEEERW**
degged	dessed	**DDEILM**	mudder	**DEEEFR**	weeder
DDEEGH	**DDEEUX**	middle	**DDENNO**	feeder	**DEEERY**
hedged	exuded	**DDEILO**	donned	reefed	redeye
DDEEGK	**DDEFFO**	loided	**DDENNU**	**DEEEFZ**	**DEEFGL**
kedged	doffed	**DDEILP**	dunned	feezed	fledge
DDEEGL	**DDEFGU**	piddle	**DDENOP**	**DEEEGR**	**DEEFHT**
gelded	fudged	**DDEILR**	ponded	degree	hefted
DDEEGR	**DDEFIL**	dirled	**DDENOR**	**DEEEHL**	**DEEFIL**
dredge	fiddle	riddle	droned	heeled	defile
DDEEGW	**DDEFLO**	**DDEILS**	**DDENOS**	**DEEEHR**	**DEEFIN**
wedged	folded	sidled	sodden	heeder	define
DDEEHL	**DDEFLU**	**DDEILT**	**DDENOW**	**DEEEJR**	**DEEFIR**
heddle	fuddle	tiddle	downed	jeered	defier
DDEEHR	**DDEFNU**	**DDEIMM**	**DDENSU**	jereed	**DEEFIS**
herded	funded	dimmed	sudden	**DEEEKK**	defies
DDEEIL	**DDEFOR**	**DDEIMN**	**DDEOOR**	keeked	**DEEFKR**
elided	fodder	midden	odored	**DEEEKL**	kerfed
DDEEIN	forded	minded	**DDEOOS**	keeled	**DEEFLL**
denied	**DDEGGO**	**DDEIMS**	dodoes	**DEEEKN**	felled
indeed	dogged	desmid	**DDEOOW**	keened	**DEEFLT**
DDEEIR	**DDEGIL**	**DDEINN**	wooded	**DEEEKP**	felted
deride	gilded	dinned	**DDEORT**	peeked	**DEEFLU**
DDEEIS	glided	**DDEINR**	dorted	**DEEEKR**	fueled
eddies	**DDEGIN**	ridden	**DDEORV**	reeked	**DEEFLW**
DDEEIT	dinged	rinded	droved	**DEEELN**	flewed
dieted	nidged	**DDEINT**	**DDEORW**	needle	**DEEFLX**
edited	**DDEGIR**	dinted	worded	**DEEELP**	flexed
DDEELM	girded	**DDEINU**	**DDEOSU**	peeled	**DEEFNR**
meddle	grided	indued	doused	**DEEELR**	fender
melded	ridged	**DDEINW**	**DDEOSW**	leered	**DEEFRT**
DDEELP	**DDEGIU**	dwined	dowsed	reeled	defter
peddle	guided	winded	**DDEOTT**	**DEEELT**	**DEEFSU**
DDEELU	**DDEGJU**	**DDEIOS**	dotted	delete	defuse
delude	judged	didoes	**DDEPRU**	**DEEELV**	**DEEGGL**
dueled	**DDEGLO**	**DDEIOV**	pudder	leveed	legged
eluded	lodged	devoid	**DDERRU**	**DEEEMR**	**DEEGGP**
DDEELV	**DDEGNU**	voided	rudder	redeem	pegged
delved	dunged	**DDEIPP**	**DDESTU**	**DEEEMS**	**DEEGHR**
DDEELW	nudged	dipped	dusted	seemed	hedger
welded	**DDEGOR**	**DDEIPR**	**DDFIOR**	**DEEEMT**	**DEEGIR**
DDEEMN	dodger	prided	fordid	teemed	edgier
mended	**DDEGRU**	**DDELLU**	**DDHISU**	**DEEENP**	**DEEGIS**
DDEENN	drudge	dulled	dudish	deepen	sieged
denned	**DDEHIN**	**DDELMO**	**DDHOSY**	**DEEENR**	**DEEGLL**
DDEENP	hidden	molded	shoddy	needer	gelled
depend	**DDEHLU**	**DDELMU**	**DDIIMS**	**DEEENV**	**DEEGLN**
pended	huddle	muddle	misdid	evened	legend
DDEENR	**DDEHNO**	**DDELNO**		vendee	**DEEGLP**

pledge	denier	**DEELLY**	nepped	desert	fledgy
DEEGLR	reined	yelled	**DEENPX**	rested	**DEFGOO**
gelder	**DEEINS**	**DEELMT**	expend	**DEERSU**	goofed
ledger	denies	melted	**DEENRR**	reused	**DEFGOR**
DEEGLS	seined	**DEELMY**	render	**DEERSV**	forged
sledge	**DEEINV**	medley	**DEENRS**	served	**DEFHIS**
DEEGLU	devein	**DEELNR**	denser	versed	fished
deluge	endive	lender	sender	**DEERTT**	**DEFHOO**
DEEGMM	envied	**DEELNW**	**DEENRT**	retted	hoofed
gemmed	**DEEIPS**	wedeln	rented	**DEERTX**	**DEFIKN**
DEEGMR	espied	**DEELNY**	tender	dexter	knifed
merged	peised	needly	**DEENRU**	**DEERVV**	**DEFIKR**
DEEGNR	**DEEIRS**	**DEELOP**	endure	revved	firked
gender	desire	eloped	**DEENRV**	**DEESTT**	**DEFILL**
DEEGNU	reside	**DEELPT**	nerved	detest	filled
dengue	**DEEIRT**	pelted	**DEENSS**	tested	**DEFILM**
DEEGNV	retied	**DEELPY**	sensed	**DEESTV**	filmed
venged	**DEEIRV**	deeply	**DEENST**	devest	**DEFILO**
DEEGRV	derive	yelped	nested	**DEESTW**	foiled
verged	**DEEIRW**	**DEELRU**	sedent	stewed	**DEFILR**
DEEGRY	dewier	dueler	tensed	**DEESTZ**	rifled
greedy	**DEEISS**	eluder	**DEENSU**	zested	**DEFILT**
DEEGSU	dieses	**DEELRW**	ensued	**DEETTV**	flited
segued	**DEEISV**	welder	**DEENTT**	vetted	lifted
DEEHLM	devise	**DEELST**	detent	**DEETTW**	**DEFIMR**
helmed	sieved	eldest	netted	wetted	firmed
DEEHLP	**DEEISX**	**DEELTU**	tented	**DEETWY**	**DEFINN**
helped	dexies	eluted	**DEENTU**	tweedy	finned
DEEHLV	**DEEISZ**	teledu	detune	**DEFFHU**	**DEFINR**
helved	seized	**DEELTW**	**DEENTV**	huffed	finder
DEEHMM	**DEEITV**	welted	vented	**DEFFIM**	friend
hemmed	evited	**DEELUX**	**DEENTX**	miffed	redfin
DEEHMS	**DEEITX**	deluxe	extend	**DEFFIR**	**DEFIRT**
meshed	exited	**DEEMNO**	**DEENUV**	differ	rifted
DEEHRR	**DEEIVW**	omened	vendue	**DEFFIT**	**DEFIRV**
herder	viewed	**DEEMNR**	**DEEOPS**	tiffed	fervid
DEEHSW	**DEEJKR**	mender	depose	**DEFFLU**	**DEFIST**
shewed	jerked	**DEEMNT**	**DEEORT**	duffel	fisted
DEEILR	**DEEJLL**	dement	teredo	duffle	sifted
lieder	jelled	**DEEMOT**	**DEEORZ**	luffed	**DEFITT**
relied	**DEEJSS**	demote	zeroed	**DEFFMU**	fitted
DEEILS	jessed	emoted	**DEEOTV**	muffed	**DEFIZZ**
diesel	**DEEJST**	**DEEMRT**	devote	**DEFFNO**	fizzed
sedile	jested	termed	vetoed	offend	**DEFKLU**
seidel	**DEEJTT**	**DEEMRU**	**DEEPPP**	**DEFFOR**	fluked
DEEILV	jetted	demure	pepped	doffer	**DEFKNU**
levied	**DEEKLP**	**DEEMRY**	**DEEPRS**	**DEFFPU**	funked
veiled	kelped	remedy	spreed	puffed	**DEFKOR**
DEEILX	**DEEKNN**	**DEEMSS**	**DEEPRU**	**DEFFRU**	forked
exiled	kenned	messed	perdue	duffer	**DEFLMU**
DEEILY	**DEEKNR**	**DEENNP**	pureed	**DEFGGI**	flumed
eyelid	kerned	penned	**DEEPRY**	figged	**DEFLNO**
DEEIMN	**DEEKNT**	**DEENNT**	preyed	**DEFGGO**	enfold
medine	kented	dennet	**DEEPSW**	fogged	fondle
DEEIMP	**DEEKOV**	**DEENNY**	spewed	**DEFGIR**	**DEFLOO**
impede	evoked	yenned	**DEEPSY**	fridge	fooled
DEEIMS	**DEEKPP**	**DEENOP**	speedy	**DEFGIT**	**DEFLOR**
demies	kepped	depone	**DEEPTT**	fidget	folder
demise	**DEEKPR**	opened	petted	gifted	**DEFLOT**
DEEIMT	perked	**DEENOR**	**DEEPTU**	**DEFGLO**	lofted
itemed	**DEEKRY**	redone	depute	golfed	**DEFLOU**
DEEINN	yerked	**DEENOT**	**DEEQUU**	**DEFGLU**	fouled
indene	**DEEKSW**	denote	queued	gulfed	**DEFLOW**
DEEINR	skewed	**DEENPP**	**DEERST**	**DEFGLY**	flowed

fowled	gorged	girder	**DEHHSU**	hurdle	**DEIINS**
DEFLRU	**DEGGOT**	**DEGIST**	hushed	hurled	inside
furled	togged	digest	**DEHIKT**	**DEHMMU**	**DEIINT**
DEFLTU	**DEGGOU**	**DEGITW**	kithed	hummed	indite
fluted	gouged	widget	**DEHILL**	**DEHMNY**	tineid
DEFLTY	**DEGGPU**	**DEGJRU**	hilled	hymned	**DEIINV**
deftly	pugged	judger	**DEHILS**	**DEHMOT**	divine
DEFLUU	**DEGGRU**	**DEGLLU**	shield	method	**DEIIOZ**
dueful	grudge	gulled	**DEHILT**	**DEHMPU**	iodize
DEFLUX	**DEGGRY**	**DEGLNO**	hilted	humped	**DEIIPT**
fluxed	dreggy	golden	**DEHILW**	**DEHMRY**	pitied
DEFMOR	**DEGGTU**	longed	whiled	rhymed	**DEIIRS**
deform	tugged	**DEGLNU**	**DEHINO**	**DEHMSU**	irides
formed	**DEGHIN**	gulden	hoiden	mushed	**DEIIRT**
DEFNNU	hinged	lunged	honied	**DEHNOP**	tidier
funned	**DEGHIS**	**DEGLOP**	**DEHINR**	phoned	**DEIISS**
DEFNOU	sighed	plodge	hinder	**DEHNOR**	diesis
fondue	**DEGHSU**	**DEGLOR**	**DEHINS**	horned	**DEIIST**
DEFNRU	gushed	lodger	shined	**DEHNOS**	tidies
refund	**DEGIIR**	**DEGLOV**	**DEHINT**	noshed	**DEIJKN**
DEFOOR	dirgie	gloved	hinted	**DEHNOY**	jinked
roofed	**DEGILL**	**DEGLOW**	**DEHINW**	hoyden	**DEIJLT**
DEFOOT	gilled	glowed	whined	**DEHNTU**	jilted
footed	**DEGILM**	**DEGLOZ**	**DEHIOW**	hunted	**DEIJNO**
DEFRRU	midleg	glozed	howdie	**DEHOOP**	joined
furred	**DEGILN**	**DEGLPU**	**DEHIPP**	hooped	**DEIKKN**
DEFSSU	dingle	gulped	hipped	**DEHOOS**	kinked
fussed	elding	**DEGLSU**	**DEHIRT**	shooed	**DEIKLL**
DEFTTU	**DEGILR**	sludge	dither	**DEHOOT**	killed
tufted	gilder	**DEGMMU**	**DEHISS**	hooted	**DEIKLM**
DEGGGI	girdle	gummed	dishes	**DEHOPP**	milked
gigged	glider	**DEGMSU**	hissed	hopped	**DEIKLN**
DEGGHO	**DEGIMP**	smudge	**DEHISW**	**DEHOPY**	kindle
hogged	gimped	**DEGNNU**	wished	hypoed	linked
DEGGHU	**DEGIMR**	gunned	**DEHITT**	**DEHORS**	**DEIKLO**
hugged	grimed	**DEGNOT**	tithed	dehors	keloid
DEGGIJ	**DEGIMT**	tonged	**DEHITW**	horsed	**DEIKLT**
jigged	midget	**DEGNOW**	whited	shored	kilted
DEGGIN	**DEGINN**	gowned	withed	**DEHORW**	**DEIKNP**
edging	ending	**DEGNRU**	**DEHJOS**	whored	pinked
DEGGIP	ginned	gerund	joshed	**DEHOST**	**DEIKNR**
pigged	**DEGINP**	**DEGOOS**	**DEHKLU**	hosted	kinder
DEGGIR	pinged	goosed	hulked	**DEHOSU**	**DEIKNT**
digger	**DEGINR**	**DEGOPR**	**DEHKNO**	housed	tinked
rigged	engird	groped	honked	**DEHOSV**	**DEIKNW**
DEGGIW	ringed	**DEGORU**	**DEHKOO**	shoved	winked
wigged	**DEGINS**	drogue	hooked	**DEHOSW**	**DEIKNY**
DEGGIZ	design	gourde	**DEHKOW**	showed	dinkey
zigged	signed	rouged	howked	**DEHOTT**	kidney
DEGGJO	singed	**DEGOST**	**DEHKSU**	hotted	**DEIKPS**
jogged	**DEGINT**	stodge	husked	**DEHPSU**	spiked
DEGGJU	tinged	**DEGPPY**	**DEHLLU**	pushed	**DEIKRS**
jugged	**DEGINW**	gypped	hulled	**DEHRSU**	risked
DEGGLO	dewing	**DEGPRU**	**DEHLNO**	rushed	**DEIKSS**
dogleg	winged	purged	holden	**DEHRSW**	kissed
logged	**DEGINY**	**DEGRSU**	**DEHLOR**	shrewd	**DEIKSV**
DEGGLU	dingey	surged	holder	**DEHTTU**	skived
lugged	dyeing	**DEGRTU**	**DEHLOT**	hutted	**DEIKTT**
DEGGMU	**DEGIPP**	trudge	tholed	**DEHUZZ**	kitted
mugged	gipped	**DEGSTU**	**DEHLOW**	huzzed	**DEILLM**
DEGGNO	**DEGIPR**	degust	howled	**DEIILL**	milled
gonged	griped	gusted	**DEHLPU**	lilied	**DEILLP**
DEGGOR	**DEGIRR**	**DEGTTU**	upheld	**DEIINO**	pilled
dogger		gutted	**DEHLRU**	iodine	**DEILLR**

rilled	dilute	**DEINPR**	piqued	**DEKLSU**	nurled
DEILLT	**DEILTW**	pinder	**DEIPRS**	sulked	rundle
lilted	wilted	**DEINPS**	spider	**DEKMOS**	**DELNUV**
tilled	**DEILWY**	sniped	spired	smoked	vulned
DEILLW	dewily	spined	**DEIPRZ**	**DEKNOY**	**DELNUY**
willed	widely	**DEINRS**	prized	donkey	nudely
DEILMN	wieldy	rinsed	**DEIPSS**	**DEKNOZ**	**DELOOP**
milden	**DEIMMR**	**DEINRT**	pissed	zonked	looped
DEILMO	dimmer	rident	**DEIPST**	**DEKNRU**	poodle
moiled	rimmed	tinder	spited	dunker	pooled
DEILMP	**DEIMMU**	**DEINRU**	**DEIPSU**	**DEKOOR**	**DELOOS**
dimple	medium	inured	upside	rooked	loosed
limped	**DEIMNO**	ruined	**DEIPSW**	**DEKOPS**	oodles
DEILMR	domine	**DEINRV**	swiped	spoked	**DELOOT**
milder	medino	driven	**DEIPTT**	**DEKORW**	looted
DEILMS	**DEIMNP**	verdin	pitted	worked	tooled
misled	impend	**DEINRW**	**DEIQRU**	**DEKOST**	**DELOPP**
slimed	**DEIMNR**	rewind	quired	stoked	lopped
smiled	remind	winder	**DEIRRS**	**DELLLO**	**DELOPR**
DEILMW	**DEIMNT**	**DEINSU**	derris	lolled	polder
mildew	minted	undies	sirred	**DELLLU**	**DELOPS**
DEILNN	**DEIMOR**	**DEINTT**	**DEIRRV**	lulled	sloped
linden	dormie	tinted	driver	**DELLMU**	**DELOPW**
DEILNT	moider	**DEINTU**	**DEIRRY**	mulled	plowed
dentil	**DEIMPR**	united	yirred	**DELLNU**	**DELOPY**
linted	primed	untied	**DEIRST**	nulled	deploy
DEILNW	**DEIMRS**	**DEINTW**	direst	**DELLOP**	**DELORS**
windle	dermis	twined	driest	polled	solder
DEILOP	**DEIMSS**	**DEIOOX**	stride	**DELLOR**	**DELORT**
dipole	missed	exodoi	**DEIRTV**	rolled	retold
DEILOR	**DEIMST**	**DEIOPR**	divert	**DELLOT**	**DELORU**
roiled	misted	dopier	**DEISST**	tolled	louder
DEILOS	**DEIMSU**	period	desist	**DELLPU**	**DELOST**
soiled	medius	**DEIOPS**	sisted	pulled	oldest
DEILOT	**DEIMTU**	poised	**DEISSU**	**DELLRU**	**DELOSV**
toiled	tedium	**DEIORS**	disuse	duller	solved
DEILPP	**DEINNO**	dories	issued	**DELLWY**	**DELOSW**
lipped	ondine	**DEIORT**	**DEISTU**	lewdly	slowed
DEILPS	**DEINNP**	editor	duties	**DELMNO**	**DELOTT**
dispel	pinned	rioted	suited	dolmen	dottle
lisped	**DEINNR**	triode	**DEISTV**	**DELMOO**	lotted
DEILPX	dinner	**DEIORV**	divest	loomed	**DELOWY**
diplex	**DEINNS**	devoir	**DEISTW**	**DELMOR**	yowled
DEILRS	sinned	voider	widest	molder	**DELPPU**
slider	**DEINNT**	**DEIORW**	**DEISZZ**	**DELMOS**	pulped
DEILRT	dentin	weirdo	sizzed	seldom	**DELPRU**
tirled	indent	**DEIORZ**	**DEITTW**	**DELMOT**	drupel
DEILRV	intend	dozier	witted	molted	purled
drivel	tinned	**DEIOSX**	**DEJKNU**	**DELMOU**	**DELPUX**
DEILRW	**DEINNU**	doxies	junked	**DELMOY**	duplex
wilder	undine	**DEIPPP**	**DEJLOT**	melody	**DELRUY**
DEILRY	**DEINOP**	pipped	jolted	**DELMPU**	rudely
direly	opined	**DEIPPR**	**DEJLOW**	lumped	**DELSTU**
ridley	**DEINOR**	dipper	jowled	plumed	lusted
DEILST	dinero	ripped	**DEJMPU**	**DELNOO**	**DELSTY**
idlest	ironed	**DEIPPS**	jumped	noodle	styled
listed	**DEINOS**	sipped	**DEJOTT**	**DELNOR**	**DEMMSU**
silted	donsie	**DEIPPT**	jotted	rondel	summed
DEILSV	noised	tipped	**DEJTTU**	rondle	**DEMNOO**
slived	onside	**DEIPPY**	jutted	**DELNOU**	mooned
DEILTT	**DEINOT**	yipped	**DEKLOO**	louden	**DEMNOR**
tilted	ditone	**DEIPPZ**	looked	nodule	modern
titled	**DEINPP**	zipped	**DEKLRU**	**DELNRU**	**DEMOOR**
DEILTU	nipped	**DEIPQU**	lurked		moored

roomed	wonted	rossed	**DERTTU**	doming	**DHOOOO**
DEMOOZ	**DENPRU**	sordes	rutted	**DGINOP**	hoodoo
zoomed	pruned	**DEORST**	**DETTTU**	doping	**DHORSU**
DEMOPP	**DENPTU**	sorted	tutted	**DGINOS**	shroud
mopped	punted	stored	**DFGIIR**	dosing	**DIILMP**
DEMOPR	**DENRSU**	strode	frigid	**DGINOT**	limpid
romped	nursed	**DEORSU**	**DFGILU**	doting	**DIILQU**
DEMORR	sunder	roused	fulgid	**DGINOU**	liquid
dormer	**DENRTU**	soured	**DFHLOU**	guidon	**DIIMNU**
DEMORW	turned	**DEORSW**	hodful	**DGINOV**	indium
wormed	**DENRTY**	drowse	**DFIINY**	doving	**DIIMTW**
DEMOST	trendy	**DEORTT**	nidify	**DGINOW**	dimwit
modest	**DENSUU**	rotted	**DFIIRT**	dowing	**DIIMTY**
DEMOSU	unused	**DEORTU**	trifid	**DGINOZ**	dimity
moused	**DENSUW**	detour	**DFILNO**	dozing	**DIINNW**
DEMPPU	sundew	routed	infold	**DGINPU**	inwind
pumped	**DENTTU**	toured	**DFILOR**	duping	**DIKLNY**
DEMPRU	nutted	**DEORTW**	florid	**DGINRU**	kindly
dumper	**DEOOPP**	trowed	**DFILUV**	during	**DIKMNU**
DEMPSU	pooped	**DEORUV**	fulvid	**DGINRY**	dinkum
spumed	**DEOORT**	devour	**DFIMOY**	drying	**DIKNNU**
DEMRRU	rooted	**DEOSST**	modify	**DGINSU**	nudnik
murder	**DEOORV**	tossed	**DFIRTY**	dingus	unkind
DEMSSU	overdo	**DEOSSU**	drifty	**DGIRTU**	**DILLMY**
mussed	**DEOOST**	soused	**DFLNOU**	turgid	mildly
DENNOT	sooted	**DEOSTT**	unfold	**DGLOOY**	**DILLWY**
tendon	**DEOOTT**	sotted	**DFLNOY**	goodly	wildly
DENNOU	tooted	**DEOSTU**	fondly	**DGLSUY**	**DILMOR**
undone	**DEOPPP**	ousted	**DFNSUU**	sludgy	milord
DENNOW	popped	toused	fundus	**DGMSUY**	**DILMOU**
wonned	**DEOPPS**	**DEOSTV**	**DFOORX**	smudgy	dolium
DENNPU	sopped	stoved	oxford	**DGNOOS**	**DILMPY**
punned	**DEOPPT**	**DEOSTW**	**DGHIIN**	godson	dimply
DENNRU	topped	stowed	hiding	**DGNOOW**	**DILNTU**
dunner	**DEOPRS**	**DEOSUX**	**DGHINY**	godown	indult
DENNSU	prosed	exodus	dinghy	**DGNORU**	**DILOST**
sunned	**DEOPRT**	**DEOTTT**	**DGHOUY**	ground	stolid
DENNTU	ported	totted	doughy	**DGNOSU**	**DILOXY**
tunned	redtop	**DEOTTU**	**DGIIKN**	sundog	xyloid
DENOOS	**DEOPRU**	touted	diking	**DGOTUU**	**DIMNOO**
nodose	poured	**DEOTUV**	**DGIILN**	dugout	domino
noosed	**DEOPRV**	devout	idling	**DHIIPS**	**DIMNSU**
DENOOW	proved	**DEOTUX**	**DGIINN**	hispid	nudism
wooden	**DEOPRW**	tuxedo	dining	**DHIISW**	**DIMOPU**
DENOPR	powder	**DEPPPU**	indign	widish	podium
ponder	**DEOPST**	pupped	**DGIINO**	**DHILOS**	**DIMOSU**
DENORS	despot	**DEPPSU**	indigo	oldish	modius
snored	posted	supped	**DGIINP**	**DHIMOS**	**DIMOSW**
DENORT	stoped	**DEPRRU**	pidgin	modish	wisdom
rodent	**DEOPTT**	purred	**DGIINR**	**DHINSY**	**DINNUW**
DENORU	potted	**DEPRSU**	riding	shindy	unwind
enduro	**DEOPTU**	pursed	**DGIINS**	**DHIORR**	**DINOOR**
DENORV	pouted	**DEPRUY**	siding	horrid	indoor
vendor	**DEOQTU**	dupery	**DGIINT**	**DHIOST**	**DINOSW**
DENORW	quoted	**DEPTUY**	tiding	dotish	disown
downer	**DEORRU**	deputy	**DGIINV**	**DHIOSV**	**DINOWW**
wonder	ordure	**DERSSU**	diving	dovish	window
DENORY	**DEORRV**	duress	**DGIKNY**	**DHLOPU**	**DINPTU**
yonder	drover	**DERSSY**	dyking	holdup	pundit
DENOST	**DEORRW**	dressy	**DGILNO**	uphold	**DINPUW**
stoned	reword	**DERSTU**	doling	**DHLOSU**	upwind
DENOSW	**DEORSS**	duster	**DGILOT**	should	windup
snowed	dosser	rudest	diglot		**DINSTU**
DENOTW		rusted	**DGIMNO**		

nudist	dropsy	sememe	fennel	leglet	enmesh
DINTUY	**DORSSY**	**EEEMRT**	**EEFLNS**	**EEGLMN**	**EEHMRT**
nudity	drossy	teemer	flense	legmen	mether
untidy	**DORSTU**	**EEEMST**	**EEFLRT**	**EEGLMU**	**EEHMSS**
DIOOPS	stroud	esteem	reflet	legume	meshes
isopod	**DORSWY**	**EEENRS**	telfer	**EEGLNT**	**EEHMUX**
DIOOSU	drowsy	serene	**EEFLRU**	gentle	exhume
iodous	**DPSTUU**	**EEENRT**	ferule	**EEGLRT**	**EEHNOR**
odious	dustup	entree	refuel	reglet	hereon
DIOOTX	**DRSTUY**	eterne	**EEFLRX**	**EEGMNT**	**EEHNPW**
toxoid	sturdy	teener	reflex	tegmen	nephew
DIOPRT	**EEEEPT**	**EEENRV**	**EEFLRY**	**EEGMOT**	**EEHNRT**
torpid	teepee	veneer	freely	gemote	nether
tripod	**EEEFFT**	**EEENSZ**	**EEFLSX**	**EEGMRR**	**EEHORS**
DIORRT	effete	sneeze	flexes	merger	heroes
torrid	**EEEFLR**	**EEEOPP**	**EEFLTT**	**EEGNOP**	**EEHORT**
DIOSTU	feeler	epopee	fettle	pongee	hereto
studio	**EEEFRR**	**EEEPPR**	**EEFLUY**	**EEGNOX**	**EEHPRS**
DIPPRY	reefer	peeper	eyeful	exogen	herpes
drippy	**EEEFRZ**	**EEEPRW**	**EEFMNN**	**EEGNRT**	sphere
DIPRTU	freeze	weeper	fenmen	regent	**EEHRSU**
putrid	**EEEGLN**	**EEERRV**	**EEFMNO**	**EEGNRY**	rushee
DIPSTU	elenge	revere	foemen	energy	**EEHRSY**
stupid	**EEEGMR**	**EEERSV**	**EEFPRR**	greeny	heresy
DJNNOO	emerge	severe	prefer	**EGGNST**	**EEHRTT**
donjon	**EEEGNR**	**EEERTT**	**EEFPTY**	gentes	tether
DKOOOO	renege	teeter	tepefy	**EEGPRU**	**EEHRTW**
koodoo	**EEEGRZ**	terete	**EEFRRT**	pugree	wether
DLLOOP	geezer	**EEERVW**	ferret	**EEGRRT**	**EEHSST**
dollop	**EEEHLR**	weever	**EEFRST**	regret	theses
DLLORY	heeler	**EEESTT**	fester	**EEGRRV**	**EEHWYZ**
drolly	**EEEHST**	settee	freest	verger	wheezy
lordly	seethe	testee	**EEFRSU**	**EEGRSS**	**EEIJNN**
DLLOUY	**EEEHTT**	**EEESTV**	refuse	egress	jinnee
loudly	teethe	steeve	**EEFRTT**	**EEGRSY**	**EEIKLP**
DLNOTU	**EEEHWZ**	vestee	fetter	geyser	kelpie
untold	wheeze	**EEETWZ**	**EEFRTU**	**EEGRTT**	pelike
DLNUUY	**EEEINW**	tweeze	refute	getter	**EEILMN**
unduly	weenie	**EEFFOT**	**EEFSTW**	**EEHIIN**	meline
DLOOPS	**EEEIRR**	toffee	fewest	heinie	**EEILNR**
podsol	eerier	**EEFFSU**	**EEFSZZ**	**EEHINR**	lierne
DMNOOY	**EEEJRR**	effuse	fezzes	herein	**EEILNS**
monody	jeerer	**EEFGIN**	**EEGGIN**	inhere	senile
DMNOSU	**EEEKLR**	feeing	geeing	**EEHINT**	**EEILOT**
osmund	keeler	**EEFGRU**	**EEGIJN**	theine	etoile
DMOOSY	**EEEKMR**	refuge	jeeing	**EEHIRT**	**EEILPT**
sodomy	meeker	**EEFHIR**	**EEGILT**	either	pelite
DMORSU	**EEEKNR**	heifer	elegit	**EEHITV**	**EEILRV**
dorsum	keener	**EEFHOR**	**EEGIMR**	thieve	relive
DNORTU	**EEEKPR**	hereof	emigre	**EEHKLS**	revile
rotund	keeper	**EEFILN**	regime	shekel	**EEILRY**
DNOSUZ	**EEEKRS**	feline	**EEGINN**	**EEHLLR**	eerily
zounds	seeker	**EEFILR**	engine	heller	**EEILSV**
DNRSUY	**EEELNV**	relief	**EEGINP**	**EEHLMT**	levies
sundry	eleven	**EEFINR**	peeing	helmet	**EEILVW**
DOOOOV	**EEELPR**	ferine	**EEGINS**	**EEHLPR**	weevil
voodoo	peeler	refine	seeing	helper	**EEIMNP**
DOOPRU	**EEELSS**	**EEFIRZ**	**EEGINT**	**EEHLSV**	piemen
uropod	lessee	frieze	teeing	shelve	**EEIMNR**
DOOPRY	**EEELSV**	**EEFLLO**	**EEGIRV**	**EEHMMR**	ermine
droopy	sleeve	felloe	grieve	hemmer	**EEIMPR**
DOOSWY	**EEELTY**	feller	**EEGKLR**	**EEHMNP**	empire
woodsy	eyelet	**EEFLNN**	kegler	hempen	premie
DOPRSY	**EEEMMS**	**EEFLNN**	**EEGLLT**	**EEHMNS**	**EEIMRS**

remise
EEIMRT
metier
EEIMSS
emesis
EEINQU
equine
EEINRS
serein
serine
EEINRT
entire
nerite
EEINRV
envier
EEINRW
wiener
EEINSV
envies
EEIORS
soiree
EEIPPY
yippie
EEIPRS
espier
EEIPRX
expire
EEIPTT
petite
EEIRRS
sirree
EEIRRT
retire
EEIRRW
rewire
EEIRSS
series
EEIRSV
revise
EEIRSX
sexier
EEIRSZ
seizer
EEIRVV
revive
EEIRVW
review
viewer
EEJJNU
jejune
EEJNNT
jennet
EEJRST
jester
EEJRSY
jersey
EEJSSS
jesses
EEKLMY
meekly
EEKLNN
kennel
EEKLNR
kernel

EEKLNY
keenly
EEKLTT
kettle
EEKLWY
weekly
EEKMRS
kermes
EEKNOT
ketone
EEKORV
revoke
EEKPPU
upkeep
EEKPRU
peruke
EEKRSW
skewer
EEKRSY
kersey
EELLPT
pellet
EELLRS
seller
EELLRT
retell
teller
EELLRU
ruelle
EELLRY
yeller
EELMOT
omelet
EELMPT
temple
EELMRY
merely
EELMSY
seemly
EELMTT
mettle
EELNNT
lenten
EELNOV
elevon
EELNPS
spleen
EELNRT
relent
EELNSS
lenses
lessen
EELNST
nestle
EELNTT
nettle
EELNVY
evenly
EELNXY
xylene
EELOPP
people
EELOPR
eloper

EELOPT
pelote
EELORS
resole
EELOVV
evolve
EELPRT
pelter
petrel
EELPRY
yelper
EELPST
pestle
EELPSV
pelves
EELPSY
sleepy
EELQSU
sequel
EELRSS
lesser
EELRTT
letter
EELRTW
welter
EELRUV
velure
EELSSV
selves
vessel
EELSTT
settle
EELSTV
svelte
EELSTY
sleety
steely
EELTVV
velvet
EELTVW
twelve
EEMMNR
mermen
EEMNNP
penmen
EEMNOR
moreen
EEMNOY
yeomen
EEMNSS
menses
EEMNYZ
enzyme
EEMOPT
metope
EEMORT
emoter
meteor
remote
EEMORV
remove
EEMPRS
sempre
EEMPRT

temper
EEMPRY
empery
EEMPTX
exempt
EEMRRT
termer
EEMRST
merest
EEMRSU
resume
EENNPR
penner
EENNRT
rennet
tenner
EENNST
sennet
EENNSU
unseen
EENNUV
uneven
EENOPR
opener
reopen
EENOPT
poteen
EENORW
erenow
EENOVZ
evzone
EENPRT
repent
EENPRY
pyrene
EENRRT
renter
EENRST
nester
resent
tenser
EENRSU
ensure
EENRTT
netter
tenter
EENRTU
neuter
tenure
tureen
EENRTV
venter
EENRTX
extern
EENRUV
veneur
EENRVY
venery
EENSTU
tenues
EENSTV
steven
EENSTW
newest

EENTTX
extent
EENTUX
exeunt
EEOPRS
repose
EEOPSX
expose
EEOPTU
toupee
EEOPTY
peyote
EEORST
stereo
EEORSV
soever
EEORSZ
zeroes
EEOSST
setose
EEOSTV
vetoes
EEPPPR
pepper
EEPPST
steppe
EEPRST
pester
EEPRSU
peruse
EEPRSV
vesper
EEPRTU
repute
EEPRTW
pewter
EEPRTX
expert
EEPRTY
retype
EEPSTT
septet
EEPSWY
sweepy
EEQUXY
exequy
EERRST
terser
EERRSV
revers
server
EERRTT
terret
EERRTU
ureter
EERRTV
revert
EERRVY
revery
EERSTT
setter
street
tester
EERSTW

wester
EERSTY
yester
EERSVW
swerve
EERTTT
tetter
EERTTW
wetter
EERTVV
vervet
EERTVX
vertex
EESSTT
sestet
EESTTU
suttee
EESTTX
sextet
EFFGIR
griffe
EFFGIY
effigy
EFFGOR
goffer
EFFILP
piffle
EFFILR
riffle
EFFINR
niffer
EFFLMU
muffle
EFFLRU
ruffle
EFFLUX
efflux
EFFOPU
pouffe
EFFORT
effort
EFFOST
offset
setoff
EFFPRU
puffer
EFFRSU
suffer
EFGINR
finger
fringe
EFGINT
feting
EFGIOS
fogies
EFGIRU
figure
EFGLNU
engulf
EFGLOR
golfer
EFGOOR

forego	infest	fleury	**EGGIJT**	**EGHITY**	geonim
EFGORR	**EFINSU**	**EFLSUU**	jigget	eighty	**EGIMNT**
forger	infuse	useful	**EGGILN**	**EGHLMP**	meting
EFGORT	**EFIORX**	**EFLSUX**	niggle	phlegm	**EGIMNW**
forget	foxier	fluxes	**EGGILR**	**EGHLNT**	mewing
EFHILS	**EFIOST**	**EFMNOT**	ligger	length	**EGIMOS**
elfish	softie	foment	**EGGILT**	**EGHLUY**	egosim
EFHIRS	**EFIPRX**	**EFMNRU**	giglet	hugely	**EGIMPU**
fisher	prefix	frenum	**EGGILW**	**EGHNOU**	guimpe
sherif	**EFIRST**	**EFMORR**	wiggle	enough	**EGINNS**
EFHISS	sifter	former	**EGGINR**	**EGHNRU**	ensign
fishes	strife	reform	ginger	hunger	**EGINNW**
EFHIST	**EFIRSU**	**EFMTUY**	**EGGIRR**	**EGHOPR**	newing
fetish	furies	tumefy	rigger	gopher	**EGINOP**
EFHLSY	**EFIRTT**	**EFNORZ**	**EGGJLO**	**EGHOTT**	pigeon
fleshy	fitter	frozen	joggle	ghetto	**EGINOR**
EFHOOR	**EFIRTY**	**EFNOST**	**EGGJLM**	**EGHRSU**	eringo
hoofer	ferity	fontes	juggle	gusher	ignore
EFHORT	**EFIRVY**	soften	**EGGJOR**	**EGHSSU**	region
fother	verify	**EFNRYZ**	jogger	gushes	**EGINOS**
EFIINT	**EFISTY**	frenzy	**EGGLOR**	**EGHSTU**	gonies
finite	feisty	**EFNSTU**	logger	hugest	soigne
EFIKNR	**EFLLOS**	funest	**EGGLOT**	**EGIILR**	**EGINOT**
knifer	folles	**EFOORR**	goglet	girlie	toeing
EFILLR	**EFLLOW**	roofer	toggle	**EGIINP**	**EGINPP**
filler	fellow	**EFOORW**	**EGGLRU**	pieing	pigpen
refill	**EFLLRU**	woofer	gurgle	**EGIINT**	**EGINRR**
EFILLT	fuller	**EFORRU**	lugger	ignite	erring
fillet	**EFLMNY**	furore	**EGGMRU**	**EGIJLN**	ringer
EFILNO	flymen	**EFORRV**	mugger	jingle	**EGINRS**
olefin	**EFLMSY**	fervor	**EGGNTU**	**EGIKNY**	resign
EFILNY	myself	**EFORST**	nugget	keying	singer
finely	**EFLNNU**	forest	**EGGORR**	**EGILLN**	**EGINRZ**
EFILOS	funnel	fortes	gorger	lingel	zinger
filose	**EFLNOY**	foster	**EGGORT**	**EGILLR**	**EGINSS**
EFILPP	felony	softer	gorget	grille	gneiss
fipple	**EFLNTU**	**EFORTW**	**EGGORU**	**EGILLU**	**EGINST**
EFILPR	fluent	twofer	gouger	ligule	ingest
pilfer	unfelt	**EFRRSU**	**EGGRRU**	**EGILMN**	signet
EFILRT	**EFLOOR**	surfer	rugger	mingle	**EGINSU**
filter	fooler	**EFRTTY**	**EGHHIR**	**EGILMT**	genius
lifter	**EFLOOY**	fretty	higher	gimlet	**EGINSW**
trifle	flooey	**EFRTUU**	**EGHHIT**	**EGILNO**	sewing
EFILRU	**EFLOOZ**	future	eighth	eloign	swinge
ireful	foozle	**EGGGIL**	height	legion	**EGINSX**
EFILSS	**EFLORT**	giggle	**EGHIIN**	**EGILNR**	sexing
fissle	floret	**EGGGIN**	hieing	linger	**EGINTH**
EFILST	**EFLORU**	egging	**EGHILS**	**EGILNS**	tewing
itself	fouler	**EGGGLO**	sleigh	single	twinge
stifle	furole	goggle	**EGHINO**	**EGILNT**	**EGINVX**
EFILSX	**EFLORW**	**EGGGLU**	hoeing	tingle	vexing
flixes	flower	guggle	**EGHINR**	**EGILOR**	**EGIOPS**
EFILTU	fowler	**EGGGNO**	hinger	logier	pogies
futile	**EFLORX**	eggnog	nigher	**EGILRS**	**EGIORR**
EFILWY	flexor	**EGGHIL**	**EGHINW**	grilse	gorier
wifely	**EFLOUW**	higgle	hewing	**EGILRU**	**EGIORS**
EFILZZ	woeful	**EGGHOR**	**EGHINX**	ligure	orgies
fizzle	**EFLPRU**	hogger	hexing	uglier	**EGIORT**
EFIMRR	purfle	**EGGHRU**	**EGHIOT**	**EGILST**	goiter
firmer	**EFLRUU**	hugger	hogtie	legist	**EGIOST**
EFINRY	rueful	**EGGIJL**	**EGHIRS**	**EGIMMR**	egoist
finery	**EFLRUX**	jiggle	sigher	gimmer	**EGIPPR**
EFINST	reflux	**EGGIJR**	**EGHITW**	megrim	gipper
finest	**EFLRUY**	jigger	weight	**EGIMNO**	grippe

EGIPRR	govern	**EHILOT**	**EHIRTT**	**EHLOSV**	**EHORTT**
griper	**EGNOTT**	eolith	hitter	shovel	hotter
EGIRSU	gotten	**EHILPR**	tither	**EHLRRU**	**EHORTV**
regius	**EGNOTU**	hirple	**EHIRTV**	hurler	throve
EGIRTV	tongue	**EHILRS**	thrive	**EHLRTU**	**EHORTX**
grivet	**EGNOXY**	hirsel	**EHIRTW**	hurtle	exhort
EGITYZ	oxygen	relish	whiter	**EHLRUY**	**EHORTY**
zygite	**EGNRTU**	**EHILRT**	wither	hurley	theory
EGJLNU	urgent	lither	writhe	**EHLSSU**	**EHPRSU**
jungle	**EGNRTY**	**EHILSV**	**EHIRTZ**	lushes	pusher
EGLLTU	gentry	elvish	zither	**EHLSTU**	**EHPRSY**
gullet	**EGOORV**	**EHIMNR**	**EHISST**	hustle	sphery
EGLNNU	groove	menhir	thesis	sleuth	**EHPRYZ**
gunnel	**EGOOST**	**EHIMNS**	**EHISSW**	**EHLSTY**	zephyr
EGLNOR	stooge	inmesh	wishes	shelty	**EHPSSU**
longer	**EGOPRR**	**EHIMNU**	**EHISTT**	**EHLSVY**	pushes
EGLNOU	groper	inhume	theist	shelvy	**EHPSSY**
longue	**EGORRS**	**EHIMOR**	**EHITWY**	**EHMMRU**	physes
lounge	groser	homier	whitey	hummer	**EHRRSU**
EGLNPU	grower	**EHIMRT**	**EHJOPS**	**EHMORT**	rusher
plunge	**EGORRW**	hermit	joseph	mother	**EHRRSY**
EGLNTU	grower	**EHIMRU**	**EHJORS**	**EHMSSU**	sherry
gluten	**EGORRZ**	humeri	josher	mushes	**EHRRTU**
EGLNTY	grozer	**EHIMST**	**EHKLPT**	**EHNOPY**	hurter
gently	**EGORSS**	theism	klepht	phoney	**EHRRWY**
EGLOPR	ogress	**EHINNN**	**EHKNOR**	**EHNORS**	wherry
proleg	**EGORSU**	hennin	honker	senhor	**EHRSSU**
EGLOPS	grouse	**EHINOR**	**EHKNRU**	**EHNORT**	rhesus
gospel	rugose	heroin	hunker	hornet	rushes
EGLORV	**EGOSTY**	hieron	**EHKOOR**	throne	**EHSSTY**
glover	stogey	**EHINPX**	hooker	**EHNOST**	shyest
grovel	**EGOTYZ**	phenix	**EHKOOY**	honest	**EIIKLT**
EGLORW	zygote	**EHINRS**	hookey	**EHNRTU**	kiltie
glower	**EGPRRU**	shiner	**EHKORS**	hunter	**EIIKNP**
EGLOUY	purger	shrine	kosher	**EHOOOP**	pinkie
eulogy	**EGRTTU**	**EHINRT**	**EHKRSU**	hoopoe	**EIIKNR**
EGLTTU	gutter	hinter	husker	**EHOOPR**	inkier
guttle	**EGRUVY**	**EHINRW**	**EHLLOR**	hooper	**EIILLN**
EGLUZZ	guyver	whiner	holler	**EHOOPY**	nielli
guzzle	**EGSSTU**	**EHINSW**	**EHLLRU**	phooey	**EIILLS**
EGMMNU	gusset	newish	huller	**EHOORT**	lillies
gunmen	**EHHIRT**	**EHINTW**	**EHLLSY**	hooter	**EIILMR**
EGMNOO	hither	whiten	shelly	**EHOOST**	limier
mongoe	**EHHNPY**	**EHINTZ**	**EHLMOP**	soothe	**EIILMS**
EGMNOR	hyphen	zenith	phloem	**EHOOSV**	simile
monger	**EHHRST**	**EHIOPR**	**EHLMOY**	hooves	**EIILMU**
morgen	thresh	ephori	homely	**EHOPPR**	milieu
EGMNRU	**EHHSSU**	**EHIOPT**	**EHLMTY**	hopper	**EIILNR**
regnum	hushes	ophite	methyl	**EHOPPS**	inlier
EGMNTU	**EHIIPP**	**EHIORS**	**EHLNOP**	shoppe	linier
nutmeg	hippie	hosier	holpen	**EHOPPT**	**EIILOR**
EGMORU	**EHIKKS**	**EHIORT**	**EHLNOR**	hoppet	oilier
morgue	kishke	heriot	phenol	**EHOPRT**	**EIILOT**
EGMRTU	**EHIKRS**	**EHIPPR**	**EHLNPY**	pother	tolite
tergum	shriek	hipper	phenyl	thorpe	**EIILRV**
EGNNOO	shrike	**EHIPRS**	**EHLOOP**	**EHORRT**	virile
nonego	**EHIKSS**	perish	hoople	rhetor	**EIILRW**
EGNNRU	kishes	**EHIRSS**	**EHLOPP**	**EHORSV**	wilier
gunner	**EHILMU**	hisser	hopple	shover	**EIILRX**
EGNOPS	helium	**EHIRSV**	**EHLORW**	shrove	elixir
sponge	**EHILOR**	shiver	howler	**EHORSW**	**EIIMRR**
EGNORT	holier	shrive	**EHLOST**	shower	mirier
tonger	**EHILOS**	**EHIRSW**	hostel	**EHORSY**	rimier
EGNORV	holies	wisher	**EHLOSU**	horsey	**EIINOZ**
	isohel		housel		

ionize	**EIKLRT**	**EILMNR**	lenity	**EILTTT**	remiss
EIINPR	kilter	limner	**EILNUV**	tittle	**EIMRST**
pinier	kirtle	merlin	unveil	**EILTVY**	mister
EIINPT	**EIKLST**	**EILMNS**	**EILOOR**	levity	smiter
tiepin	likest	simnel	oriole	**EIMMNU**	**EIMRSV**
EIINRT	**EIKLTT**	**EILMOT**	**EILOOT**	immune	verism
tinier	kittel	mottle	oolite	**EIMMOR**	vermis
EIINRV	kittle	**EILMPP**	**EILOPS**	memoir	**EIMRSY**
vinier	**EIKMRS**	pimple	pilose	**EIMMRS**	misery
EIINRW	kermis	**EILMPR**	**EILOPT**	simmer	**EIMSST**
winier	**EIKMST**	limper	polite	**EIMMRU**	tmesis
EIINSZ	kismet	rimple	**EILORT**	immure	**EIMSSU**
seizin	**EIKNOV**	**EILMPS**	loiter	**EIMNNT**	misuse
EIINTV	invoke	simple	toiler	tinmen	**EIMSSX**
invite	**EIKNPU**	**EILMPT**	**EILORV**	**EIMNOR**	sexism
EIIPPR	punkie	limpet	oliver	merino	**EIMSTY**
pipier	**EIKNRS**	**EILMPW**	**EILORW**	**EIMNOS**	stymie
EIIPST	sinker	wimple	lowrie	monies	**EINNNR**
pities	**EIKNRT**	**EILMRS**	**EILOTT**	**EIMNRU**	rennin
EIIRRW	tinker	smiler	toilet	murine	**EINNOT**
wirier	**EIKNSV**	**EILMTU**	**EILOTV**	**EIMNRV**	intone
EIIRSS	knives	telium	olivet	vermin	**EINNRS**
irises	**EIKNTT**	**EILMTY**	violet	**EIMNSU**	sinner
EIIRVZ	kitten	timely	**EILPPR**	senium	**EINNRT**
vizier	**EIKOOR**	**EILMZZ**	lipper	**EIMNTT**	intern
EIJKNR	rookie	mizzle	ripple	mitten	tinner
jerkin	**EIKOPR**	**EILNNT**	**EILPPT**	**EIMNTU**	**EINNST**
EIJKNU	pokier	linnet	tipple	minuet	sennit
junkie	**EIKPPR**	**EILNNY**	**EILPRS**	minute	tennis
EIJLRT	kipper	lineny	lisper	**EIMNTY**	**EINNTT**
jilter	**EIKRSS**	**EILNOP**	**EILPRT**	emnity	intent
EIJNNO	kisser	pinole	triple	**EIMNUX**	**EINNTV**
enjoin	**EIKRST**	**EILNOS**	**EILPRY**	xenium	invent
EIJNOR	strike	insole	ripely	**EIMNZZ**	**EINNTY**
joiner	**EIKRSV**	lesion	**EILPST**	mizzen	ninety
rejoin	skiver	selion	stipel	**EIMOPS**	**EINOPR**
EIJNRU	**EIKSTW**	**EILNOT**	**EILPSU**	impose	opiner
injure	weskit	entoil	pileus	**EIMORS**	orpine
EIJNTY	**EILLMR**	**EILNPP**	**EILPSV**	isomer	**EINOPS**
jitney	'miller	lippen	pelvis	rimose	ponies
EIJRSU	**EILLMT**	nipple	**EILPTU**	**EIMOSS**	**EINOPT**
juries	millet	**EILNPS**	plutei	mioses	pointe
EIJRTT	**EILLMU**	spinel	puteli	**EIMOST**	**EINORR**
jitter	illume	spline	**EILPZZ**	somite	ironer
trijet	**EILLNO**	**EILNPT**	pizzle	**EIMOSX**	**EINORS**
EIKKLN	niello	pintle	**EILRST**	exomis	nosier
kinkle	**EILLNT**	**EILNPU**	lister	**EIMOTV**	senior
EIKKOO	lentil	lupine	**EILRSV**	motive	**EINORT**
kookie	lintel	**EILNRU**	silver	**EIMOTY**	norite
EIKLLR	**EILLRT**	lunier	sliver	moiety	orient
killer	tiller	**EILNST**	**EILRTT**	**EIMPRR**	**ENIORV**
EIKLLY	**EILLST**	enlist	litter	primer	renvoi
likely	illest	listen	**EILRVY**	**EIMPRS**	**EINOSS**
EIKLMR	listel	silent	livery	simper	noesis
milker	**EILLTT**	tinsel	verily	**EIMPRT**	**EINOSW**
EIKLNS	little	**EILNSU**	**EILSTV**	permit	nowise
silken	**EILLTU**	lunies	livest	**EIMPRU**	**EINOVW**
EIKLNT	tuille	**EILNSV**	vilest	impure	inwove
tinkle	**EILLVY**	snivel	**EILSVW**	umpire	**EINPPR**
EIKLNU	evilly	**EILNSY**	**EILSWY**	**EIMPSU**	nipper
unlike	lively	linsey	wisely	sepium	**EINPPS**
EIKLNW	vilely	**EILNTV**	**EILSZZ**	**EIMPTU**	pepsin
welkin	**EILMNO**	ventil	sizzle	impute	**EINPRS**
winkle	moline	**EILNTY**		**EIMRSS**	sniper

EINPRT	otiose	triter	**EKLNOS**	**ELLOWY**	lentor
nipter	**EIOPPT**	**EIRRTW**	kelson	yellow	**ELNOSS**
EINPRU	potpie	writer	**EKLNRU**	**ELLPTU**	lesson
punier	**EIOPRS**	**EIRSST**	runkle	pullet	**ELNOST**
unripe	persio	resist	**EKLOOR**	**ELLPUY**	telson
EINPRY	**EIOPSS**	sister	looker	pulley	**ELNOSV**
pinery	posies	**EIRSSU**	**EKMNOY**	**ELMMOP**	sloven
EINPST	**EIOPST**	issuer	monkey	pommel	**ELNOTT**
instep	sopite	uresis	**EKMORS**	**ELMNOR**	tonlet
spinet	**EIOPTT**	**EIRSTT**	smoker	merlon	**ELNOUZ**
EINPSU	tiptoe	sitter	**EKMSTU**	**ELMNOS**	zonule
puisne	**EIORRS**	**EIRSTV**	musket	solemn	**ELNOZZ**
supine	rosier	stiver	**EKNNSU**	**ELMNOT**	nozzle
EINQSU	**EIORRT**	strive	sunken	loment	**ELNPTU**
sequin	rioter	**EIRSTW**	**EKNOPS**	molten	penult
EINQUU	**EIORST**	wriest	spoken	**ELMNOY**	**ELNPTY**
unique	sortie	**EIRSVV**	**EKNORR**	lemony	plenty
EINRRS	**EIORSX**	vivers	kroner	**ELMNPU**	**ELNRTU**
rinser	orexis	**EIRTTT**	**EKNORW**	lumpen	runlet
EINRST	**EIORSZ**	titter	knower	**ELMOOP**	**ELNRUZ**
estrin	seizor	**EIRTTV**	**EKOORT**	pomelo	luzern
insert	**EIOSTV**	trivet	retook	**ELMOPY**	**ELNSSU**
sinter	soviet	**EIRTUV**	**EKORRW**	employ	unless
triens	**EIOTVV**	virtue	worker	**ELMORS**	**ELNSXY**
EINRSU	votive	**EIRTVY**	**EKORST**	morsel	lynxes
insure	**EIPPRR**	verity	stoker	**ELMOST**	**ELNTTU**
ursine	ripper	**EISSTT**	stroke	molest	nutlet
EINRTT	**EIPPRS**	testis	**EKRRSY**	**ELMOTT**	**ELNTXY**
tinter	sipper	**EISSTU**	skryer	mottle	nextly
EINRTU	**EIPPRT**	tissue	**EKRTUY**	**ELMOTY**	**ELNUZZ**
triune	tipper	**EISSTW**	turkey	motley	nuzzle
EINRTV	**EIPPRZ**	wisest	**ELLLOR**	**ELMOUV**	**ELOOPR**
invert	zipper	**EISSIX**	loller	volume	looper
EINRTW	**EIPPST**	sexist	**ELLMOW**	**ELMPPU**	**ELOORS**
winter	sippet	**EISSZZ**	mellow	peplum	looser
EINRTY	**EIPPTT**	sizzes	**ELLMSY**	**ELMPRU**	**ELOORT**
nitery	tippet	**EISTUX**	smelly	rumple	looter
EINRVW	**EIPQTU**	exitus	**ELLMTU**	**ELMRTY**	**ELOOTT**
wivern	piquet	**EJKNRU**	mullet	myrtle	tottle
EINRVY	**EIPRST**	junker	**ELLMUV**	**ELMSSU**	**ELOPPP**
vinery	esprit	**EJKNTU**	vellum	mussel	popple
EINRWY	priest	junket	**ELLNOP**	**ELMTUU**	**ELOPPR**
winery	ripest	**EJLORT**	pollen	mutuel	lopper
EINSTT	sprite	jolter	**ELLNOR**	mutule	**ELOPPS**
sitten	stripe	**EJLORW**	enroll	**ELMUZZ**	peplos
EINSTU	**EIPRSU**	jowler	**ELLNOV**	muzzle	**ELOPPT**
tenuis	unprise	**EJLOST**	vellon	**ELNNOS**	topple
EINSTV	**EIPRTV**	jostle	**ELLNOY**	nelson	**ELOPRT**
invest	privet	**EJLSTU**	lonely	**ELNNRU**	petrol
EINSTW	**EIPRTY**	justle	**ELLNSU**	runnel	**ELOPRV**
wisent	pyrite	**EJMOST**	sullen	**ELNNTU**	plover
EINSUW	**EIPRXY**	jetsom	**ELLNUU**	tunnel	**ELOPRX**
unwise	expiry	**EJMPRU**	lunule	**ELNOOS**	plexor
EINSUX	**EIPSSS**	jumper	**ELLNUW**	loosen	**ELOPTT**
unisex	sepsis	**EJNOTT**	unwell	**ELNOOW**	pottle
EINSWY	speiss	jetton	**ELLOPX**	woolen	**ELOPTU**
sinewy	**EIQRUS**	**EJOPRT**	pollex	**ELNOOY**	tupelo
EINTTU	risque	projet	**ELLORR**	looney	**ELORRS**
tenuti	squire	**EJORTT**	roller	**ELNOPT**	sorrel
EINTTY	**EIQRUV**	jotter	**ELLOSY**	lepton	**ELORSS**
entity	quiver	**EJRSTU**	solely	**ELNOPY**	lessor
EIOORZ	**EIQTUY**	juster	**ELLOVY**	openly	**ELORST**
oozier	equity	**EKLMMU**	lovely	poleyn	
EIOOST	**EIRRTT**	kummel	volley	**ELNORT**	

ostler	tussle	neuron	nuzzer	**EORRSY**	**ERRTTU**
sterol	**ELSSTY**	**ENNORW**	**ENRVWY**	rosery	turret
torsel	slyest	renown	wyvern	**EORRTT**	**ERSSST**
ELORSV	**ELSTTY**	**ENNOST**	**ENSSTU**	retort	stress
solver	stylet	sonnet	sunset	rotter	**ERSSTU**
ELORSW	**EMMMRU**	tenson	**ENTTWY**	**EORRTU**	estrus
slower	mummer	newton	twenty	router	russet
ELORSY	**EMMNOT**	**ENNOTW**	**EOOPPS**	**EORRTV**	surest
sorely	moment	**ENNRRU**	oppose	trover	**ERSSTY**
ELORTV	**EMMNTU**	runner	**EOOPRR**	**EORSST**	syrtes
revolt	mentum	**ENOORS**	poorer	sorest	**ERSSUU**
ELORTW	**EMMORY**	seroon	**EOORRT**	**EORSSU**	uruses
trowel	memory	sooner	rooter	serous	**ERSSUV**
ELORUV	**EMMRRU**	**ENOOSZ**	torero	**EORSTU**	versus
louver	rummer	snooze	**EOPPPR**	ouster	**ERSTTU**
louvre	**EMMRSU**	**ENOPRR**	popper	**EORSTV**	truest
velour	summer	perron	**EOPPRR**	stover	**ERSTUU**
ELORVY	**EMMSUU**	**ENOPRS**	proper	strove	suture
overly	museum	person	**EOPPRT**	**EORSTW**	uterus
ELORWY	**EMNOPY**	**ENOPRT**	topper	stower	**ERSTUY**
lowery	eponym	pteron	**EOPPRY**	**EORSTY**	surety
ELOSSS	**EMNORS**	**ENOPRV**	popery	oyster	**ERSTVY**
losses	sermon	proven	**EOPRRT**	**EORSTZ**	vestry
ELOSTU	**EMNORT**	**ENOPST**	porter	zoster	**ERSTXY**
solute	mentor	pontes	pretor	**EORSWW**	xyster
tousle	**EMNOST**	**ENORRS**	report	wowser	**ERSUVY**
ELOSTW	montes	snorer	troper	**EORSXY**	survey
lowest	**EMNOTY**	**ENORRY**	**EOPRRY**	oryxes	**ESTTUX**
ELOSVW	etymon	ornery	ropery	**EORTTT**	textus
wolves	**EMNSSU**	**ENORSS**	**EOPRST**	totter	**FFFLUY**
ELOSZZ	sensum	sensor	poster	**EORTTX**	fluffy
sozzle	**EMOORR**	**ENORST**	presto	extort	**FFGIIN**
ELOTTU	romero	tensor	**EOPRSU**	**EORTVX**	fifing
outlet	roomer	**ENORSW**	poseur	vortex	**FFGINO**
ELOTUV	**EMOORS**	worsen	uprose	**EORUVY**	offing
volute	morose	**ENORTT**	**EOPRSY**	voyeur	**FFHIOS**
ELPPRU	**EMOOSS**	rotten	osprey	**EOSTTU**	offish
purple	osmose	**ENOSSU**	**EOPRTT**	outset	**FFHORS**
ELPPSU	**EMOPPT**	onuses	potter	**EPPPTU**	shroff
supple	moppet	**ENOSTT**	**EOPRTU**	puppet	**FFIINT**
ELPQUU	**EMOPRR**	teston	troupe	**EPPRSU**	tiffin
pulque	romper	**ENOSTX**	**EOPRTX**	supper	**FFILLU**
ELPRTY	**EMOQSU**	sexton	export	**EPRRSU**	fulfil
peltry	mosque	**ENOSUV**	**EOPRTY**	purser	**FFILTU**
pertly	**EMORRT**	venous	poetry	**EPRRSY**	fitful
ELPRUY	termor	**ENOTTU**	**EOPSST**	spryer	**FFIMNU**
purely	tremor	tenuto	posset	**EPRSTU**	muffin
ELPSUX	**EMORSU**	**ENPRTU**	**EOPSSU**	purest	**FFINPU**
plexus	mouser	punter	opuses	**EPRSUU**	puffin
ELPUZZ	**EMOSSU**	**ENPRUY**	spouse	pursue	**FFINSY**
puzzle	mousse	penury	**EOQRTU**	**EPRTTU**	sniffy
ELRSTU	**EMPPRU**	**ENRRTU**	quoter	putter	**FFIOPR**
luster	pumper	return	roquet	**EPRTTY**	ripoff
result	**EMPSTU**	**ENRSTU**	torque	pretty	**FFIOST**
rustle	septum	unrest	**EORRRT**	**EPRTUU**	soffit
sutler	**EMRSTU**	**ENRSTW**	terror	puture	**FFIPSY**
ulster	muster	strewn	**EORRRY**	**EPRUVY**	spiffy
ELRSUY	**EMRTTU**	**ENRSTY**	orrery	purvey	**FFISUX**
surely	mutter	sentry	**EORRST**	**ERRSTU**	suffix
ELRTTU	**EMSSTY**	**ENRTUU**	resort	rustre	**FFLUTY**
turtle	system	untrue	roster	**ERRSUU**	fylfot
ELRTTY	**ENNNOP**	**ENRUZZ**	sorter	usurer	**FFNORU**
tetryl	pennon		**EORRSU**	**ERRSUY**	runoff
ELSSTU	**ENNORU**		sourer	surrey	**FFNSUY**

snuffy	vilify	typify	ginkgo	**GHIORS**	**GIIMNR**
FFRRUU	**FIIMNR**	**FIRTUY**	**GGILNO**	ogrish	miring
furfur	infirm	fruity	ogling	**GHIRTW**	riming
FFSTUY	**FIIMNY**	**FIRYZZ**	**GGILNU**	wright	**GIIMNT**
stuffy	minify	frizzy	gluing	**GHIRTY**	miting
FGGORY	**FIIMST**	**FJLOUY**	**GGILOO**	righty	timing
froggy	misfit	joyful	gigolo	**GHLOSU**	**GIIMNX**
FGHILT	**FIITXY**	**FKLNUY**	**GGILWY**	slough	mixing
flight	fixity	flunky	wiggly	**GHNORT**	**GIINNN**
FGHIRT	**FIIVVY**	**FKLOSY**	**GGINNO**	throng	inning
fright	vivify	folksy	noggin	**GHNOSU**	**GIINNP**
FGHOTU	**FIJLOR**	**FLLOOW**	**GGINOR**	shogun	pining
fought	frijol	follow	goring	**GHNOTU**	**GIINNW**
FGIIKN	**FIKRSY**	**FLLOUY**	**GGINRU**	nought	wining
fiking	frisky	foully	gringo	**GHNRUY**	**GIINNX**
FGIILN	**FILLOS**	**FLNRUU**	urging	hungry	nixing
filing	follis	unfurl	**GGINUY**	**GHORTU**	**GIINOR**
FGIINN	**FILLUW**	**FLOOYZ**	guying	trough	origin
fining	wilful	floozy	**GGINVY**	**GHORTW**	**GIINOY**
FGIINR	**FILMOU**	**FLOPPY**	gyving	growth	yogini
firing	folium	floppy	**GGITWY**	**GHOSTU**	**GIINPP**
FGIINX	**FILMRY**	**FLOPTU**	twiggy	sought	piping
fixing	firmly	potful	**GGLOOO**	**GHRRUY**	**GIINPR**
FGILNU	**FILMSY**	**FLORUY**	googol	ghurry	riping
ingulf	flimsy	floury	**GGLOOY**	**GIIJNV**	**GIINPS**
FGILNY	**FILMUY**	**FLOSSY**	googly	jiving	siping
flying	fumily	flossy	**GGNOOR**	**GIIKLN**	**GIINPW**
FGILUY	**FILNOR**	**FLOSTY**	gorgon	liking	wiping
uglify	florin	softly	**GGNRUY**	**GIIKNN**	**GIINRS**
FGIMNU	**FILNOW**	**FLOTUY**	grungy	inking	rising
fuming	inflow	outfly	**GHHILY**	**GIIKNP**	siring
FGINOX	**FILNSU**	**FLRRUY**	highly	piking	**GIINRT**
foxing	sinful	flurry	**GHHOTU**	**GIIKNR**	tiring
FGINRY	**FILNTY**	**FLRSUU**	though	irking	**GIINRV**
frying	flinty	sulfur	**GHIIKN**	**GIIKNS**	riving
FGINSU	**FILNUX**	**FMOSUO**	hiking	skiing	virgin
fusing	influx	fumous	**GHIINR**	**GIIKNT**	**GIINRW**
FGINUZ	**FILOSS**	**FMPRUY**	hiring	kiting	wiring
fuzing	fossil	frumpy	**GHIINV**	**GIILMN**	**GIINST**
FGJLUU	**FILPTU**	**FMRTUU**	hiving	liming	siting
jugful	uplift	furtum	**GHIKNT**	**GIILNN**	**GIINSV**
FGNSUU	**FIMNOR**	**FOORSS**	knight	lignin	vising
fungus	inform	fossor	**GHILNO**	**GIILNO**	**GIINSW**
FGOORT	**FINORT**	**FOOTUX**	holing	oiling	wising
forgot	forint	outfox	**GHILPT**	**GIILNP**	**GIINSZ**
FHIINS	**FINORX**	**FORRUW**	plight	piling	sizing
finish	fornix	furrow	**GHILST**	**GIILNR**	**GIINTW**
FHILTY	**FINOSU**	**FORSTY**	slight	riling	witing
filthy	fusion	frosty	**GHIMNO**	**GIILNT**	**GIINVW**
FHIRST	**FINOTY**	**FORSUU**	homing	tiling	wiving
shrift	notify	rufous	**GHIMTY**	**GIILNV**	**GIJKNO**
FHIRTT	**FINTUX**	**FORWYZ**	mighty	living	joking
thrift	unfixt	frowzy	**GHINNO**	**GIILNW**	**GIJKNU**
FHISTY	**FIOPRT**	**GGGILY**	honing	wiling	juking
shifty	profit	giggly	**GHINOP**	**GIILOS**	**GIJLNY**
FHORTU	**FIORST**	**GGGORY**	hoping	sigloi	jingly
fourth	fortis	groggy	**GHINOS**	**GIIMMN**	**GIJNOW**
FHORTY	**FIOSSY**	**GGIINV**	hosing	miming	jowing
frothy	ossify	giving	**GHINPY**	**GIIMNN**	**GIKLNY**
FIIKNR	**FIOTTU**	**GGIIRR**	hyping	mining	kingly
firkin	outfit	grigri	**GHINSY**	**GIIMNP**	**GIKNOP**
FIILLP	**FIPRUY**	**GGIJLY**	shying	imping	poking
fillip	purify	jiggly	**GHINTY**	**GIIMNP**	**GIKNOY**
FIILVY	**FIPTYY**	**GGIKNO**	nighty	imping	yoking

GIKNPU
puking
GILLOY
logily
GILLUY
uglily
GILMNU
lignum
GILMRY
grimly
GILNOO
looing
GILNOP
loping
poling
GILNOS
losing
GILNOV
loving
GILNOW
lowing
GILNPU
puling
GILNPY
plying
GILNRU
luring
ruling
GILNSU
sluing
GILNSY
lysing
singly
GILNTU
luting
GILNUX
luxing
GILNUY
lungyi
GILOSS
siglos
GILRSY
grisly
GILTUY
guilty
GIMNNO
mignon
GIMNOO
mooing
GIMNOP
moping
GIMNOU
gonium
GIMNOV
moving
GIMNOW
mowing
GIMNPU
impugn
GIMNSU
musing
GIMNTU
muting
GIMNUX

muxing
GINNOP
pignon
GINNOS
nosing
GINNOT
noting
toning
GINNOW
owning
GINNOZ
zoning
GINNTU
tuning
GINOOS
isogon
GINOOW
wooing
GINOOZ
oozing
GINOPR
poring
roping
GINOPS
posing
GINOPT
poting
toping
GINORS
rosing
signor
GINORT
roting
trigon
GINORV
roving
GINORW
rowing
GINOSS
gnosis
GINOSW
sowing
GINOTT
toting
GINOTU
outing
GINOTV
voting
GINOTW
towing
GINOTY
toying
GINOVW
vowing
GINPRS
spring
GINPRU
puring
GINPRY
prying
GINPSU
pignus
GINPSY
spying

GINPTU
pignut
GINPTY
typing
GINRRU
runrig
GINRST
string
GINRTU
truing
GINRTY
trying
GINSTY
stingy
GINSUU
unguis
GINSWY
swingy
GIOPSS
gossip
GIOPST
spigot
GIPSTY
pigsty
GIRTTY
gritty
GJLNUY
jungly
GJNOOU
goujon
GLLMUY
glumly
GLLNOY
longly
GLMOOY
gloomy
GLMSUY
smugly
GLNOOO
oolong
GLNPUU
unplug
GLNSUY
snugly
GLOOOY
oology
GLOPTU
putlog
GLOSSY
glossy
GMNNOO
gnomon
GMNOST
mongst
GMOOPR
pogrom
GMPRUY
grumpy
GMPSUY
gypsum
GNNSUU
unsung
GNOPPU
oppugn

popgun
GNOPSY
spongy
GNORST
strong
GNPRSU
sprung
GNRSTU
strung
GOORTT
grotto
GOORVY
groovy
GOPPRU
gruppo
GORTTU
rotgut
GORTUY
yogurt
GSYYYZ
syzygy
HHIMOS
homish
HHMRTY
rhythm
HHOOSW
whoosh
HHRSTU
thrush
HIIMNS
minish
HIIMOR
hirmoi
HIIMPS
impish
HIIMST
isthmi
HIINTW
within
HIIOPT
pithoi
HIITZZ
zizith
HIKMUZ
muzhik
HIKNRS
shrink
HIKSWY
whisky
HILLOY
holily
HILLPU
uphill
HILLRS
shrill
HILLRT
thrill
HILMOS
holism
HILMOY
homily
HILMSU
mulish
HILNPT

plinth
HILNTY
thinly
HILOOT
tholoi
HILOPS
polish
HILOST
holist
HILOSW
owlish
HILPST
splith
HILSTW
whilst
HIMMSY
shimmy
HIMNOY
hominy
HIMOPS
mopish
HIMORS
hirmos
HIMPRS
shrimp
HIMSTY
smithy
HIMSWY
whimsy
HINNSY
shinny
HINNWY
whinny
HINOPS
siphon
HINPSU
punish
HINPSX
sphinx
HINRSU
inrush
HIOPRT
trophi
HIOPST
pithos
HIPPSU
hippus
uppish
HIPSSY
physis
HIQSSU
squish
HIRSTT
thirst
HIRSTY
thyrsi
HIRTTY
thirty
HISSWY
swishy
HISTTY
stithy
HKNOOU

unhook
HKNRSU
shrunk
HKOOPU
hookup
HLLOOO
holloo
HLLOOW
hollow
HLLOWY
wholly
HLLSUY
lushly
HLMOTY
thymol
HLMPUY
phylum
HLNOPY
phylon
HLNOUY
unholy
HLOOST
tholos
HLOPSS
splosh
HLORUY
hourly
HLOSSY
sloshy
HLSSUY
slushy
HLSTUY
thusly
HMNOPY
nympho
HMOOST
smooth
HMOTUY
mouthy
HMSTUY
thymus
HMTUYZ
zythum
HNOOPT
photon
HNOPSY
syphon
HNOPTY
typhon
HNORSU
onrush
HNORTW
thrown
HNORTY
rhyton
thorny
HOOPSW
whoops
HOORRR
horror
HOOSSW
swoosh
HOOTTY
toothy

HOPRTY	spirit	quinol	monist	turnip	knotty
trophy	**IJNORU**	**ILNOST**	**IMNOSY**	**INQSTU**	**KNPSUY**
HOPSSY	junior	tonsil	simony	squint	spunky
hyssop	**IJNRUY**	**ILNPRU**	**IMNTUY**	**INQSUY**	**KNRRUY**
sposhy	injury	purlin	mutiny	quinsy	knurry
HOPSTU	**IJRSTU**	**ILNPST**	**IMOPRS**	**INRSXY**	**KOOPSY**
upshot	jurist	splint	porism	syrinx	spooky
HORSTY	**IKLNSY**	**ILNSTU**	**IMOPRT**	**INRTWY**	**KOOTWW**
shorty	slinky	insult	import	wintry	kowtow
HORTWY	**IKLNTY**	**ILOORT**	**IMOPST**	**IOPPTT**	**LLLOOP**
worthy	tinkly	loriot	impost	tiptop	lollop
HOSTTY	**IKMNOO**	**ILOOYZ**	**IMORRR**	**IOPRRY**	**LLNORU**
shotty	kimono	oozily	mirror	priory	unroll
HPSTUY	**IKMNOR**	**ILOPRX**	**IMOSSU**	**IOPRST**	**LLOOWY**
typhus	mikron	prolix	simous	tripos	woolly
HRSTTU	**IKMOSU**	**ILOPRY**	**IMPRSU**	**IOPSST**	**LLORST**
thrust	koumis	ropily	purism	ptosis	stroll
IIRST	**IKMPSY**	**ILOPST**	**IMPRSY**	**IORRTY**	**LLOSWY**
iritis	skimpy	pistol	prismy	riotry	slowly
IIJMNY	**IKMSSU**	**ILOPTY**	**IMQRSU**	**IORSTU**	**LMMOUX**
jiminy	kumiss	polity	squirm	suitor	lummox
IIKNPP	**IKNNSY**	**ILOQRU**	**IMRSTU**	**IOTTUW**	**LMOORU**
pipkin	skinny	liquor	truism	outwit	ormolu
IIKNSS	**IKNOOR**	**ILORSY**	**IMSSSU**	**IPPTUY**	**LMOSTY**
siskin	krooni	rosily	missus	uppity	mostly
IILMMU	**IKNOPT**	**ILPPRY**	**INNOOT**	**IPRRTU**	**LMPRUY**
milium	inkpot	ripply	notion	irrupt	rumply
IILNNU	**IKNOST**	**ILPPSY**	**INNOOY**	**IPRSST**	**LMTTUU**
inulin	stinko	slippy	oniony	stirps	tumult
IILNOV	**IKNSTY**	**ILPPTU**	**INNOSU**	**IPRSSY**	**LNOPTU**
violin	stinky	pulpit	unison	prissy	pluton
IILNST	**IKQRUY**	**ILPRTY**	**INNOTW**	**IPRSTU**	**LNRUUY**
instil	quirky	triply	intown	purist	unruly
IILNTY	**ILLMPY**	**ILPTTU**	**INNOWW**	**IPRSTY**	**LOOPRY**
tinily	limply	uptilt	winnow	stripy	poorly
IILPST	**ILLOPW**	**ILRSWY**	**INOOPS**	**IPRTUY**	**LOOSTV**
pistil	pillow	swirly	poison	purity	volost
IILRWY	**ILLOWW**	**ILSTTU**	**INOOPT**	**IPSTTY**	**LOOVVX**
wirily	willow	lutist	option	typist	volvox
IIMMNU	**ILLQSU**	**IMMMOS**	**INOORS**	**IPTTTU**	**LOPPRY**
minium	squill	momism	orison	tittup	propyl
IIMNNO	**ILLSTY**	**IMMNOS**	**INOPRS**	**IQRSTU**	**LOPPSY**
minion	stilly	monism	prison	squirt	sloppy
IIMNOU	**ILMNSU**	**IMMNOU**	**INOPRU**	**IRSSTY**	**LOPRTY**
ionium	muslin	omnium	inpour	syrtis	portly
IIMOSS	**ILMOTU**	**IMMOOS**	**INOPST**	**ISSSTU**	**LORSUY**
miosis	ultimo	simoom	piston	tussis	sourly
IIMSTT	**ILMPPY**	**IMMOSU**	**INOPTY**	**JLSTUY**	**LPPSUY**
timist	pimply	osmium	spinto	justly	supply
IINNOP	**ILMPRY**	**IMMSTU**	**INOPTY**	**JNSTUU**	**LPRSYY**
pinion	primly	summit	pointy	unjust	spryly
IINOSV	**ILMPSY**	**IMNNOW**	**INORSY**	**JOOSUY**	**LRRSUY**
vision	simply	minnow	rosiny	joyous	slurry
IINPPP	**ILMRTY**	**IMNNTU**	**INORTT**	**KKLMUU**	**LRSTUY**
pippin	trimly	muntin	triton	mukluk	sultry
IINSST	**ILMSTU**	**IMNOOR**	**INOSUV**	**KLLNOY**	**LRUUXY**
insist	litmus	morion	vinous	knolly	luxury
IINTTU	**ILNOOT**	**IMNOOS**	**INOSXY**	**KLNRUY**	**LSSTUY**
intuit	lotion	simoon	onyxis	knurly	stylus
IINTTW	**ILNOPP**	**IMNOOT**	**INPPSY**	**KNORRU**	**MMNOSU**
nitwit	poplin	motion	snippy	kronur	summon
IIOSTT	**ILNOPT**	**IMNOST**	**INPRST**	**KNORUY**	**MMOOPP**
otitis	pontil	inmost	sprint	koruny	pompom
IIPRST	**ILNOQU**		**INPRTU**	**KNOTTY**	**MMOOTT**

motmot	prompt	sputum	uptown	porous	**OPSSTU**
MMRRUU	**MOPSSU**	**MPSTUY**	**NORTUU**	**OOPRTU**	tossup
murmur	possum	stumpy	outrun	uproot	**OPSTTY**
MMUUUU	**MOPSTU**	**MSTTUY**	**NOSTTY**	**OOPWWW**	spotty
muumuu	upmost	smutty	snotty	powwow	**OPTTUU**
MNNOUW	**MOQRUU**	**NOOPRT**	**NOSTUY**	**OORRSW**	output
unmown	quorum	pronto	snouty	sorrow	**ORTTUY**
MNOOPP	**MOQTUU**	proton	**NPRSTU**	**OORSTU**	tryout
pompon	quotum	**NOOPSY**	sprunt	torous	**PRRSUY**
MNOOTU	**MORSTY**	snoopy	**NPRTUU**	**OOSTTY**	spurry
mouton	stormy	spoony	upturn	tootsy	**PRSUYY**
MNOTTU	**MOSTTU**	**NOORST**	**OOPPRT**	**OPRSTU**	syrupy
mutton	utmost	tonsor	troppo	sprout	**RSTTUY**
MOORRW	**MPRSUU**	**NOORTU**	**OOPRRT**	stupor	trusty
morrow	rumpus	notour	torpor	**OPRSTY**	**SSTUXY**
MOPPRT	**MPSTUU**	**NOPTUW**	**OOPRSU**	sporty	xystus

7-LETTER WORDS

AAAABNT	cassava	tantara	**AABDELW**	labiate
anabata	**AAADGJN**	tartana	wadable	**AABEISS**
AAABBKL	jangada	**AAARTTT**	**AABDEMS**	abaisse
kabbala	**AAADMNT**	ratatat	sambaed	**AABEKLM**
AAABCCR	adamant	**AAARTXY**	**AABDENU**	makable
baccara	**AAAEGLT**	ataraxy	bandeau	**AABELLN**
AAABDNN	galatea	**AABBCEG**	**AABDGHN**	balneal
bandana	**AAAFFLL**	cabbage	handbag	**AABELLS**
AAABGGL	alfalfa	**AABBINU**	**AABDGNS**	salable
baggala	**AAAFIRT**	babuina	sandbag	**AABELLT**
AAABKLV	ratafia	**AABCCER**	**AABDHNT**	tabella
baklava	**AAAFRWY**	braccae	hatband	**AABELMN**
AAABMST	faraway	**AABCCET**	**AABDHRU**	namable
mastaba	**AAAGHPR**	baccate	bahadur	**AABELMT**
AAACCRS	agrapha	**AABCELN**	**AABDIKR**	tamable
cascara	**AAAGLMM**	balance	bidarka	**AABELNO**
AAACCTT	amalgam	**AABCELP**	**AABDIMR**	abalone
attacca	**AAAGMMT**	capable	barmaid	**AABELNS**
AAACDLU	magmata	**AABCEMR**	**AABDLRW**	sanable
acaudal	**AAAGMNR**	macabre	bradawl	**AABELPR**
AAACDMM	anagram	**AABCERT**	**AABDNNO**	parable
macadam	**AAAGMNS**	cabaret	abandon	**AABELPY**
AAACENP	sagaman	**AABCFKT**	**AABDORV**	payable
panacea	**AAAHHLL**	fatback	bravado	**AABELRT**
AAACHLZ	halalah	**AABCHIR**	**AABDORX**	ratable
chalaza	**AAAHIPS**	brachia	broadax	**AABELSV**
AAACHNT	aphasia	**AABCHOR**	**AABDRST**	savable
acantha	**AAAHMMT**	abroach	bastard	**AABELSY**
AAACILM	mahatma	**AABCIST**	**AABDRSU**	sayable
malacia	**AAAILMR**	abacist	subadar	**AABELTU**
AAACJMR	malaria	**AABCITX**	**AABEELT**	tableau
jacamar	**AAAILRT**	taxicab	eatable	tabulae
AAACLMN	talaria	**AABCKRR**	**AABEERT**	**AABELTX**
almanac	**AAAIPRX**	barrack	trabeae	taxable
AAACLPT	apraxia	**AABCLPY**	**AABEFFL**	**AABEMNS**
catalpa	**AAAIQRU**	capably	affable	baseman
AAACLRZ	aquaria	**AABCNOR**	**AABEFGL**	**AABENTY**
alcazar	**AAAJMPS**	carbona	fleabag	abeyant
AAACMRS	pajamas	**AABCORT**	**AABEGGG**	**AABERST**
marasca	**AAAKKMR**	acrobat	baggage	abreast
mascara	markkaa	**AABCOTT**	**AABEGGR**	**AABERTT**
AAACNPT	**AAALLPT**	catboat	garbage	tabaret
catapan	palatal	**AABDDEL**	**AABEGLR**	**AABETUX**
AAACNRT	**AAAMORT**	addable	algebra	bateaux
nacarat	tamarao	**AABDDER**	**AABEGRR**	**AABFILU**
AAACNRV	**AAAMPRT**	abraded	barrage	fabliau
caravan	patamar	**AABDEGM**	**AABEHLT**	**AABFFLY**
AAACNST	**AAAMRSS**	gambade	hatable	affably
canasta	samsara	**AABDEGN**	**AABEHSS**	**AABGLIM**
AAACNTT	**AAAMRTU**	bandage	abashes	mailbag
cantata	tamarau	**AABDEHS**	**AABEILM**	**AABGINR**
AAACRWY	**AAANNSV**	abashed	amiable	bargain
caraway	savanna	**AABDEIS**	**AABEILT**	**AABGINS**
AAACSSV	**AAANRTT**	diabase	bialate	abasing

AABGINT	**AACCELO**	antacid	**AACEIRV**	guanaco
abating	cloacae	**AACDJKW**	avarice	**AACHHKR**
AABHINT	**AACCELT**	jackdaw	**AACEKNP**	charkha
habitan	laccate	**AACDLNO**	pancake	**AACHHLL**
AABHITT	**AACCEST**	calando	**AACEKNS**	challah
habitat	saccate	**AACDLNS**	askance	**AACHIKN**
AABHLTY	**AACCHIR**	scandal	**AACEKOT**	kachina
bathyal	archaic	**AACDLOR**	oatcake	**AACHILT**
AABIILX	**AACCIIN**	carload	**AACELLT**	calathi
biaxial	acaciin	**AACDLPR**	lacteal	**AACHIPS**
AABILMY	**AACCILM**	placard	**AACELMN**	aphasic
amiably	acclaim	**AACDOOV**	manacle	**AACHIRT**
AABILNT	**AACCITT**	avocado	**AACELMR**	cithara
tablina	atactic	**AACDRSZ**	cameral	**AACHITY**
AABILRS	**AACCLLT**	czardas	caramel	chaitya
basilar	catcall	**AACEEGR**	**AACELMU**	**AACHKMN**
AABIMMR	**AACCLRU**	acreage	maculae	hackman
marimba	accrual	**AACEEHR**	**AACELNU**	**AACHKRT**
AABINST	caracul	earache	lacunae	hatrack
abstain	**AACCLSU**	**AACEEKT**	**AACELNV**	**AACHKRY**
AABKNRT	accusal	teácake	valance	hayrack
tanbark	**AACCNVY**	**AACEENT**	**AACELPT**	**AACHKSW**
AABKOOZ	vacancy	catenae	placate	hacksaw
bazooka	**AACCORU**	**AACEERT**	**AACELRV**	**AACHLPS**
AABLLST	curacao	acerate	caravel	paschal
ballast	**AACCOTT**	**AACEEST**	**AACELTT**	**AACHNRV**
AABLLWY	toccata	caseate	lactate	navarch
wallaby	**AACCRSS**	**AACEETT**	**AACEMMR**	**AACHNRY**
AABLMRU	carcass	acetate	macrame	anarchy
labarum	**AACCRVY**	**AACEFIS**	**AACEMNV**	**AACHRRT**
AABLMSY	vaccary	fasciae	caveman	catarrh
abysmal	**AACDEEM**	**AACEFLT**	**AACEMQU**	**AACHRWY**
balsamy	academe	falcate	macaque	archway
AABLNTT	**AACDEHM**	**AACEFLU**	**AACENNY**	**AACIILN**
blatant	chamade	faculae	cyanean	ancilia
AABLORR	**AACDEHR**	**AACEFRR**	**AACEOPT**	lacinia
arboral	charade	carfare	peacoat	**AACIITV**
AABLRTU	**AACDEHT**	**AACEGKP**	**AACERTT**	viatica
tabular	cathead	package	teacart	**AACIJLP**
AABLSSY	**AACDELN**	**AACEGKS**	**AACERTU**	jalapic
abyssal	decanal	sackage	arcuate	**AACILNR**
AABLTTU	**AACDELR**	**AACEGNR**	**AACERWY**	cranial
abuttal	caldera	carnage	raceway	**AACILOS**
AABMNOT	**AACDEMY**	cranage	**AACESST**	asocial
boatman	academy	**AACEGRT**	cassate	**AACILOX**
AABMNST	**AACDENV**	cartage	**AACETTU**	coaxial
batsman	advance	**AACEHNP**	actuate	**AACILPS**
AABMORU	**AACDENZ**	panache	**AACFINT**	spacial
marabou	cadenza	**AACEHPS**	fanatic	**AACILPT**
AABMRTU	**AACDERV**	apaches	**AACFLLY**	capital
tambura	cadaver	**AACEHPT**	fallacy	**AACILTT**
AABNNOZ	**AACDETU**	patache	**AACFLRT**	cattail
bonanza	caudate	**AACEHPU**	flatcar	**ACCILTV**
AABRRUV	**AACDETV**	chapeau	**AACFLTU**	vatical
bravura	vacated	**AACEHRT**	factual	**AACINNT**
AABSTUX	**AACDFRT**	trachea	**AACGILL**	cantina
saxtuba	adcraft	**AACEHTT**	glacial	**AACINOR**
AACCDEI	**AACDHMR**	attache	**AACGILM**	ocarina
cicadae	drachma	**AACEHTU**	magical	**AACINPT**
AACCDES	**AACDHNR**	chateau	**AACGINT**	captain
cascade	handcar	**AACEINR**	agnatic	**AACINRZ**
saccade	**AACDILR**	carinae	**AACGLOT**	czarina
AACCDIR	radical	**AACEIQU**	catalog	**AACINST**
cardiac	**AACDINT**	acequia	**AACGNOU**	satanic

AACIOPT	**AADDEIL**	**AADELRY**	**AADIILR**	**AADOPRX**
tapioca	alidade	already	diarial	paradox
AACIQTU	**AADDENP**	**AADELTU**	**AADILMR**	**AADOPSS**
aquatic	deadpan	adulate	admiral	passado
AACISTT	**AADDEPR**	**AADEMNT**	**AADILMT**	**AADORWY**
astatic	paraded	mandate	matilda	roadway
AACJKSS	**AADDEPT**	**AADEMRY**	**AADILNP**	**AADQRTU**
jackass	adapted	daymare	paladin	quadrat
AACKLTW	**AADDERW**	**AADEMSS**	**AADILNR**	**AADRSTY**
catwalk	awarded	amassed	laniard	daystar
AACKMNP	**AADDHKR**	**AADENNT**	**AADILPS**	**AADRWWY**
packman	khaddar	andante	apsidal	wayward
AACKNRS	**AADDRST**	**AADENRV**	**AADILWY**	**AAEEFGL**
ransack	dastard	veranda	waylaid	leafage
AACLMNO	**AADEEMT**	**AADEPRT**	**AADIMOR**	**AAEEGKL**
malacon	edemata	adapter	diorama	leakage
AACLMNT	**AADEERT**	**AADEPSS**	**AADIMCZ**	**AAEEGLN**
clamant	aerated	passade	diazoma	lagenae
AACLMRU	**AADEFHT**	**AADEQRU**	**AADINRT**	**AAEEGRV**
macular	fathead	quadrae	radiant	average
AACLMSU	**AADEGMN**	**AADERRY**	**AADKNRT**	**AAEEHRT**
calamus	managed	arrayed	tankard	hetaera
AACLNNO	**AADEGRT**	**AADERSW**	**AADKRWW**	**AAEELOR**
anconal	gradate	seaward	awkward	areolae
AACLNNU	**AADEGRV**	**AADERSY**	**AADLLMR**	**AAEELTX**
cannula	ravaged	daresay	mallard	exalate
AACLNRU	**AADEGRY**	**AADESSY**	**AADLLPU**	**AAEEMNT**
lacunar	drayage	assayed	paludal	emanate
AACLOST	**AADEGRY**	**AADGGHR**	**AADLMNN**	**AAEEMNT**
coastal	yardage	haggard	landman	manatee
AACLOTV	**AADEGSV**	**AADGGLR**	**AADLMNU**	**AAEEPPS**
octaval	savaged	laggard	ladanum	appease
AACLPSU	**AADEHMN**	**AADGIMR**	**AADLNRY**	**AAEFFNR**
scapula	headman	diagram	lanyard	fanfare
AACLRVY	**AADEHMS**	**AADGIMS**	**AADLOPY**	**AAEFFTT**
cavalry	ashamed	magadis	payload	taffeta
AACLTTU	**AADEHMT**	**AADGLLW**	**AADLPPU**	**AAEFRRW**
tactual	hamated	gadwall	applaud	warfare
AACMNOR	**AADEHPS**	**AADGLNR**	**AADMNNO**	**AAEFRWY**
narcoma	saphead	garland	madonna	wayfare
AACMNRT	**AADEHRW**	**AADGLRU**	**AADMNNS**	**AAEGGNO**
cartman	rawhead	gradual	sandman	anagoge
AACMNRU	**AADEHRW**	**AADGMNR**	**AADMNOR**	**AAEGHLU**
arcanum	warhead	dragman	madrona	haulage
AACMORS	**AADEHWY**	**AADGMNR**	**AADMNRS**	**AAEGILR**
sarcoma	headway	grandam	mansard	regalia
AACMRSS	**AADEILV**	**AADGMRA**	**AADMNRY**	**AAEGINV**
sarcasm	availed	grandma	drayman	vaginae
AACNPST	**AADEINS**	**AADGMOT**	**AADMNRY**	**AAEGISS**
capstan	naiades	dogmata	yardman	assegai
AACNSSV	**AADEIRT**	**AADGNPR**	**AADMNSY**	**AAEGITT**
canvass	radiate	grandpa	daysman	agitate
AACRTTT	**AADEITV**	**AADGNRT**	**AADMNSY**	**AAEGKOS**
attract	aviated	gardant	mandyas	soakage
AACRTUY	**AADEITW**	**AADHHRT**	**AADMORT**	**AAEGLLT**
actuary	awaited	hardhat	matador	tallage
AACRTWY	**AADELLY**	**AADHLRY**	**AADMRRY**	**AAEGLNS**
cartway	allayed	halyard	yardarm	lasagne
AACTUWY	**AADELMO**	**AADHNPR**	**AADMRZZ**	**AAEGLOP**
cutaway	alamode	hardpan	mazzard	apogeal
AADDDEN	**AADELMR**	**AADHNSW**	**AADNOPR**	**AAEGLST**
addenda	alarmed	handsaw	pandora	lastage
AADDEGM	**AADELNR**	**AADHRWY**	**AADNPRU**	**AAEGLSV**
damaged	adrenal	hayward	pandura	salvage
	AADELPT	**AADHSWY**	**AADOPRS**	**AAEGMNR**
	palated	washday	parados	

manager	hastate	planeta	farrago	angular
AAEGMNT	**AAEILLX**	plantae	**AAFHLWY**	**AAGLRST**
gateman	axillae	**AAELNRS**	halfway	gastral
magenta	**AAEILMN**	arsenal	**AAFILNT**	**AAGMMRR**
magnate	laminae	**AAELNST**	fantail	grammar
nametag	**AAEILMS**	sealant	**AAFINNT**	**AAGMOPY**
AAEGMPR	malaise	**AAELNYZ**	infanta	apogamy
rampage	**AAEILPT**	analyze	**AAFIPRT**	**AAGNOPR**
AAEGMSS	pileata	**AAELORR**	parfait	paragon
massage	**AAEILRV**	areolar	**AAFIRWY**	**AAGNORZ**
AAEGNNP	velaria	**AAELORU**	fairway	organza
pannage	**AAEILSS**	aureola	**AAFLLTY**	**AAGNRRY**
AAEGNOP	aliases	**AAELPPR**	fatally	granary
apogean	**AAEIMMT**	apparel	**AAFLNOR**	**AAGNRTV**
AAEGNPT	imamate	**AAELPPT**	forlana	vagrant
pageant	**AAEIMNS**	palpate	**AAFMNST**	**AAGOPSS**
AAEGNRR	amnesia	**AAELPRT**	fantasm	sapsago
arrange	**AAEIMNT**	apteral	**AAFNSTT**	**AAGORSU**
AAEGNRT	animate	**AAELPRV**	fantast	saguaro
tanager	**AAEIMTV**	palaver	**AAFFNSTY**	**AAHHNPT**
AAEGNTV	amative	**AAELPTU**	fantasy	naphtha
vantage	**AAEINNO**	plateau	**AAGGILN**	**AAHIIMT**
AAEGPRR	aeonian	**AAELQRU**	ganglia	himatia
parerga	**AAEINNT**	laquear	**AAGGNWY**	**AAHIKRT**
AAEGPSS	anatine	**AAELRTV**	gangway	kithara
passage	**AAEIPRR**	larvate	**AAGHMNN**	**AAHINOP**
AAEGPSY	pareira	**AAELSST**	hangman	aphonia
paysage	**AAEIPRT**	atlases	**AAGHMPR**	**AAHINPR**
AAEGQUY	apteria	**AAELSUX**	phragma	piranha
quayage	**AAEIRST**	asexual	**AAGHRSW**	**AAHJKWY**
AAEGRST	aristae	**AAELTUV**	washrag	jayhawk
teargas	asteria	valuate	**AAGIKNW**	**AAHKLRS**
AAEGRTT	atresia	**AAELTVV**	awaking	lashkar
regatta	**AAEIRTT**	valvate	**AAGILNN**	**AAHKMSY**
AAEGSSU	arietta	**AAEMMMR**	anginal	yashmak
assuage	**AAEISTT**	maremma	**AAGILNV**	**AAHLLWY**
sausage	satiate	**AAEMNNT**	vaginal	hallway
AAEGSTW	**AAEJOPR**	emanant	**AAGIMNO**	**AAHLMRS**
wastage	aparejo	**AAEMNTU**	angioma	marshal
AAEGTTW	**AAEKMRR**	manteau	**AAGIMNS**	**AAHLMRU**
wattage	earmark	**AAEMRTU**	siamang	hamular
AAEGTWY	**AAEKPRT**	amateur	**AAGIMNZ**	**AAHLNPX**
gateway	partake	**AAENNNT**	amazing	phalanx
getaway	**AAELLLM**	antenna	**AAGINRR**	**AAHLNRW**
AAEHHPT	lamella	**AAENPST**	arraign	narwhal
aphthae	**AAELLPT**	anapest	**AAGINRS**	**AAHLPRS**
AAEHILP	patella	peasant	sangria	phrasal
aphelia	**AAELLRT**	**AAENRRT**	**AAGINRU**	**AAHLPST**
phialae	lateral	narrate	guarani	asphalt
AAEHIRT	**AAELLTV**	**AAENRUW**	**AAGINST**	taplash
hetaira	vallate	unaware	against	**AAHMOPR**
AAEHKNT	**AAELMMS**	**AAEORRT**	**AAGINSY**	amphora
khanate	melasma	aerator	gainsay	**AAHMQSU**
AAEHLMT	**AAELMMT**	**AAEPPRT**	**AAGIOTT**	quamash
hematal	lemmata	parapet	agitato	**AAHNNOS**
AAEHLPS	**AAELMNU**	**AAERRRS**	**AAGISTT**	hosanna
phaesal	alumnae	arrears	sagitta	**AAHNRTX**
AAEHLPX	**AAELMOT**	**AAERSSY**	**AAGLLNT**	anthrax
hexapla	oatmeal	assayer	gallant	**AAHPRTW**
AAEHNPR	**AAELMPT**	**AAFFINT**	**AAGLNOR**	warpath
hanaper	palmate	affiant	granola	**AAHPTWY**
AAEHRSY	**AAELMST**	**AAFGLMN**	**AAGLNOY**	pathway
hearsay	maltase	flagman	analogy	**AAHRSTY**
AAEHSTT	**AAELNPT**	**AAFGORR**	**AAGLNRU**	ashtray

AAHRTTW
athwart
AAIILMR
airmail
AAIJMQU
jaquima
AAIKPPR
paprika
AAILLMN
manilla
AAILLMX
maxilla
AAILLNV
vanilla
AAILLPP
papilla
AAILLRX
axillar
AAILLXY
axially
AAILMMN
mailman
AAILMMX
maximal
AAILMNR
laminar
AAILMNT
matinal
AAILMRT
marital
martial
AAILNPT
platina
AAILNTV
valiant
AAILORS
rosalia
AAILPRT
partial
patrial
AAILPST
spatial
AAILRRV
arrival
AAILRTT
rattail
AAILRTV
travail
AAILRWY
railway
AAILSSW
wassail
AAIMMNO
ammonia
AAIMNOS
anosmia
AAIMNRT
tamarin
AAIMNST
stamina
AAIMRSU
samurai
AAIMSTV
atavism

AAINNRV
nirvana
AAINOPS
paisano
AAINRST
artisan
tsarina
AAINRSU
saurian
AAINRTV
variant
AAINRTW
antiwar
AAINTTT
attaint
AAIORTV
aviator
AAIPPTT
pitapat
AAIPRTT
partita
AAIQSSU
quassia
AAJKLWY
jaywalk
AAJMNZZ
jazzman
AAKKLRU
karakul
AAKLOOP
palooka
AAKLOOT
talooka
AAKLWWY
walkway
AAKMRUZ
mazurka
AAKPRWY
parkway
AALLMPU
ampulla
palmula
AALLNSY
nasally
AALMMNS
almsman
AALMNOY
anomaly
AALMORY
mayoral
AALMPRY
palmary
palmyra
AALNNRU
annular
AALNPRT
plantar
AALNRTU
natural
AALNSTT
saltant
AALNSTU
sultana

analyst
AALOPRS
parasol
AALORRU
auroral
AALORSU
arousal
AALOSTT
saltato
AALPSTU
spatula
AALRSTU
austral
AALRSTY
astylar
AALSSTU
assault
AAMMMRY
mammary
AAMNORS
oarsman
AAMNOTY
anatomy
AAMNPRT
rampant
AAMORSV
samovar
AAMORTY
amatory
AAMOSTT
stomata
AAMOTTU
automat
AAMPRRT
rampart
AAMRTWY
tramway
AANPSST
passant
AANQRTU
quartan
AANRRTW
warrant
AANRUWY
runaway
AANSTTT
statant
AAORSVV
vavasor
AAOTWWY
towaway
AAPRRTT
rattrap
AAPRSTY
satrapy
ABBBDEL
babbled
blabbed
ABBBELR
babbler
blabber
ABBBITT
babbitt
ABBCDER

crabbed
ABBCDES
scabbed
ABBCEIS
cabbies
ABBCELR
clabber
ABBCELS
scabble
ABBCGIN
cabbing
ABBCIKT
backbit
ABBCRYY
crybaby
ABBDDEL
dabbled
ABBDDER
drabbed
ABBDEGL
gabbled
ABBDEGR
grabbed
ABBDEIT
tabbied
ABBDELR
drabble
rabbled
ABBDELS
slabbed
ABBDERR
drabber
ABBDEST
stabbed
ABBDESW
swabbed
ABBDGIN
dabbing
ABBDILR
baldrib
ABBDMOR
bombard
ABBDNOX
bandbox
ABBEGIR
gabbier
ABBEGLR
gabbler
grabble
ABBEGNU
bugbane
ABBEGRR
grabber
ABBEGRU
bugbear
ABBEIST
tabbies
ABBELLR
barbell
ABBELMR
bramble
ABBELOR
belabor
ABBELRS

slabber
ABBELRU
barbule
ABBEORR
barbero
ABBERSW
swabber
ABBGGIN
gabbing
ABBGIJN
jabbing
ABBGINN
nabbing
ABBGINR
barbing
ABBGINT
tabbing
ABBGINY
babying
ABBGOOU
bugaboo
ABBHISY
babyish
ABBHRRU
rhubarb
ABBHTTU
bathtub
ABBILOT
bobtail
ABBIMNO
bambino
ABBINOR
rabboni
ABBLMRY
brambly
ABBMOST
bombast
ABBMOTU
bumboat
ABBQSUY
squabby
ABCCILU
cubical
ABCCIMR
cambric
ABCCINU
buccina
ABCCICO
baiocco
ABCCIOR
braccio
ABCCKTU
cutback
ABCCOCR
boccaro
ABCCOOT
tobacco
ABCCSUU
succuba
ABCDEEH
beached
ABCDEEL
debacle
ABCDEHT

batched	wetback	caribou	**ABDEELT**	**ABDEIRW**
ABCDEHU	**ABCELMO**	**ABCIOUV**	belated	bawdier
debauch	cembalo	bivouac	bleated	**ABDEIRZ**
ABCDEIN	**ABCELMR**	**ABCIRTY**	**ABDEELY**	braized
cabined	clamber	barytic	belayed	**ABDEJRU**
ABCDEIP	**ABCELOP**	**ABCISSS**	**ABDEEMY**	abjured
pedicab	placebo	absciss	embayed	**ABDEKLN**
ABCDEIR	**ABCELOV**	**ABCJOSU**	**ABDEEMZ**	blanked
carbide	vocable	jacobus	bemazed	**ABDELMR**
ABCDEKL	**ABCELRU**	**ABCKLLY**	**ABDEERS**	marbled
blacked	curable	blackly	sabered	rambled
ABCDEOR	**ABCELSU**	**ABCKMRU**	**ABDEERT**	**ABDELMW**
brocade	bascule	buckram	berated	wambled
ABCDERU	**ABCENOW**	**ABCKNRU**	rebated	**ABDELOR**
cudbear	cowbane	runback	**ABDEERW**	labored
ABCDILR	**ABCEOOS**	**ABCKOTO**	bewared	**ABDELOT**
baldric	caboose	backout	**ABDEETT**	bloated
ABCDIRS	**ABCEORR**	outback	abetted	**ABDELOW**
scabrid	bracero	**ABCKSTU**	**ABDEFFL**	dowable
ABCDNOS	**ABCESSS**	sackbut	baffled	**ABDELPU**
abscond	abscess	**ABCKSUW**	**ABDEFOR**	dupable
ABCDOOR	**ABCFIKN**	bucksaw	forbade	**ABDELRU**
cordoba	finback	**ABCLLOY**	**ABDEFST**	durable
ABCDORR	**ABCFILO**	callboy	bedfast	**ABDELRW**
brocard	bifocal	**ABCLNOY**	**ABDEGGR**	brawled
ABCEEHS	**ABCGHKO**	balcony	bragged	warbled
beaches	hogback	**ABCLOVY**	**ABDEGIN**	**ABDELST**
ABCEEMR	**ABCGIKN**	vocably	beading	baldest
embrace	backing	**ABCORRW**	**ABDEGIR**	blasted
ABCEENS	**ABCGILN**	crowbar	abridge	stabled
absence	cabling	**ABDDEER**	brigade	**ABDELTT**
ABCEERR	**ABCGINR**	bearded	**ABDEGJU**	battled
cerebra	bracing	breaded	abjudge	blatted
ABCEESU	**ABCGKLO**	**ABDDEES**	**ABDEGLM**	**ABDEMNO**
because	backlog	debased	gambled	abdomen
ABCEGOS	**ABCHHII**	**ABDDEET**	**ABDEGLR**	**ABDENNR**
boscage	hibachi	debated	garbled	branned
ABCEHMR	**ABCHIOT**	**ABDDEIL**	**ABDEGNO**	**ABDENOR**
chamber	cohabit	addible	bondage	bandore
ABCEILR	**ABCHKTU**	**ABDDEIN**	dogbane	broaden
caliber	hackbut	bandied	**ABDEHLR**	**ABDENRT**
ABCEINR	**ABCHNRY**	**ABDDEIR**	halberd	bartend
carbine	branchy	braided	**ABDEHOW**	**ABDENSS**
ABCEINT	**ABCHORU**	**ABDDELR**	bowhead	badness
cabinet	bourach	bladder	**ABDEHRT**	**ABDEOOT**
ABCEIOR	**ABCHOSX**	**ABDDENR**	breadth	tabooed
aerobic	cashbox	branded	**ABDEHSU**	**ABDEORR**
ABCEIOT	**ABCIILL**	**ABDDEOR**	subhead	boarder
iceboat	bacilli	boarded	**ABDEILP**	broader
ABCEIRS	**ABCIILS**	roadbed	bipedal	**ABDEORT**
ascribe	basilic	**ABDDERW**	piebald	aborted
caribes	**ABCIIOR**	bedward	**ABDEILR**	**ABDEORV**
ABCEISS	ciboria	**ABDDINS**	bedrail	bravoed
abscise	**ABCIIOT**	disband	ridable	**ABDEOST**
scabies	abiotic	**ABDDLLO**	**ABDEILS**	boasted
ABCEKLN	**ABCILRS**	oddball	disable	**ABDERST**
blacken	scribal	**ABDEEHV**	**ABDEILU**	dabster
ABCEKLR	**ABCILTU**	behaved	audible	**ABDETTU**
blacker	cubital	**ABDEEIR**	**ABDEINR**	abutted
ABCEKRT	**ABCIMMU**	beadier	brained	**ABDGGIN**
bracket	cambium	**ABDEELL**	**ABDEINS**	badging
ABCEKST	**ABCIMST**	labeled	bandies	**ABDGIN**
setback	cambist	**ABDEELN**	**ABDEIRS**	abiding
ABCEKTW	**ABCIORU**	enabled	braised	**ABDGILN**

balding
ABDGINN
banding
ABDGINO
aboding
ABDGINR
brigand
ABDGINT
dingbat
ABDGINU
daubing
ABDGINW
windbag
ABDGLUY
ladybug
ABDHNSU
husband
ABDIJRY
jaybird
ABDILOT
tabloid
ABDILUY
audibly
ABDIMNR
birdman
ABDINOR
inboard
ABDINRU
unbraid
ABDIPRU
upbraid
ABDKOOY
daybook
ABDLLNY
blandly
ABDLLOR
bollard
ABDLORY
broadly
ABDLRUY
durably
ABDNOOR
onboard
ABDNOSX
sandbox
ABDNOYY
anybody
ABDNRSU
sandbur
ABDRUZZ
buzzard
ABEEELS
seeable
ABEEERV
bereave
ABEEFFL
effable
ABEEGHR
herbage
ABEEGLT
getable
ABEEGRW
brewage
ABEEHNN

henbane
ABEEHNS
banshee
ABEEHNT
beneath
ABEEHRT
breathe
ABEEIMR
beamier
ABEEIST
beastie
ABEEKLR
bleaker
ABEEKNT
betaken
ABEEKPS
bespeak
ABEEKRR
breaker
ABEELLR
labeler
ABEELLY
eyeball
ABEELMZ
emblaze
ABEELNR
enabler
ABEELNT
tenable
ABEELNU
nebulae
ABEELQU
equable
ABEELRR
errable
ABEELSU
useable
ABEEMNS
basemen
ABEEMRS
besmear
ABEENRV
verbena
ABEESWX
beeswax
ABEFFLR
baffler
ABEFFOT
offbeat
ABEFGST
gabfest
ABEFILN
finable
ABEFILR
friable
ABEFILU
fibulae
ABEFILX
fixable
ABEFITY
beatify
ABEFLLU
baleful
ABEFLNU

baneful
ABEFORR
forbear
ABEFORY
forebay
ABEGGIR
baggier
ABEGGRR
bragger
ABEGGRU
burgage
ABEGGRY
beggary
ABEGHNS
shebang
ABEGIMN
beaming
ABEGINN
beaning
ABEGINO
begonia
ABEGINR
bearing
ABEGINT
beating
ABEGIPP
bagpipe
ABEGLMR
gambler
gambrel
ABEGLRR
garbler
ABEGMOR
embargo
ABEGMRU
umbrage
ABEGOPY
pageboy
ABEGORX
gearbox
ABEGOSS
bossage
ABEHIRS
bearish
ABEHISU
beauish
ABEHITU
habitue
ABEHKRU
hauberk
ABEHLMS
shamble
ABEHLRT
blather
ABEHRRS
brasher
ABEHRRY
herbary
ABEHRTY
breathy
ABEIKLL
likable
ABEIKLS
skiable

ABEIKNT
beatnik
ABEIKWY
bikeway
ABEILLP
pliable
ABEILLR
liberal
ABEILLS
sebilla
ABEILLV
livable
ABEILMR
balmier
ABEILMT
limbate
timbale
ABEILMX
mixable
ABEILMY
beamily
ABEILNP
biplane
ABEILNS
lesbian
ABEILRT
librate
ABEILST
bestial
blastie
stabile
ABEILSZ
sizable
ABEILVV
bivalve
ABEIMNS
ambiens
ABEIMNT
ambient
ABEIMRR
barmier
ABEIMRS
ambries
ABEINRT
rabinet
ABEINST
basinet
ABEIORS
isobare
ABEIOTV
obviate
ABEIPST
baptise
ABEIPTZ
baptize
ABEIRRR
barrier
ABEIRRT
arbiter
rarebit
ABEIRRZ
bizarre
brazier
ABEIRSS

brassie
ABEIRTT
battier
biretta
ABEIRTV
vibrate
ABEIRUX
exurbia
ABEISTT
batiste
ABEISUV
abusive
ABEITUX
bauxite
ABEJMNO
jambone
ABEJNOW
jawbone
ABEJRRU
abjurer
ABEKLLY
bleakly
ABEKLNT
blanket
ABEKPRU
breakup
ABELLOV
lovable
ABELLRU
rubella
rulable
ABELLTU
bullate
ABELMMR
membral
ABELMNT
lambent
ABELMNU
albumen
ABELMOV
movable
ABELMRR
rambler
ABELMRT
lambert
ABELMTU
mutable
ABELNOT
notable
ABELNOY
baloney
ABELNRU
nebular
ABELNRY
blarney
ABELNTU
bleaunt
tunable
ABELNTY
tenably
ABELOPT
potable
ABELORR
laborer

ABELORT
bloater
ABELOSV
absolve
ABELOTV
votable
ABELPRU
puberal
ABELQUY
equably
ABELRRW
brawler
warbler
ABELRSS
braless
ABELRTT
battler
ABELRVY
bravely
ABELSTU
balteus
sublate
ABELSTY
beastly
ABELTWY
beltway
ABEMNOT
boatmen
ABEMNST
batsmen
ABEMNSU
sunbeam
ABEMORT
bromate
ABEMSSY
embassy
ABENORT
baronet
ABENOSY
soybean
ABENOTY
bayonet
ABENQTU
banquet
ABENTYZ
bezanty
ABEOOTV
obovate
ABEOPRT
probate
ABEOQRU
baroque
ABEORRS
arbores
ABEORST
boaster
ABEORTT
taboret
ABERRVY
bravery
ABERSSZ
zebrass
ABERSTV
bravest

ABERTTU
abutter
batture
ABERTTY
battery
ABFFIIL
bailiff
ABFFLOU
buffalo
ABFGILN
fabling
ABFHIST
batfish
ABFHLSU
bashful
ABFIILR
bifilar
ABFILRU
fibular
ABFLOTY
flyboat
ABGGGIN
bagging
ABGGIIT
gigabit
ABGGINN
banging
ABGGINR
barging
garbing
ABGHINS
bashing
ABGHINT
bathing
ABGHNOR
hagborn
ABGIILN
bailing
ABGIINS
biasing
ABGIINT
baiting
ABGIKNN
banking
ABGIKNR
barking
braking
ABGIKNS
basking
ABGILLN
balling
ABGILMN
ambling
blaming
ABGILNR
blaring
ABGILNT
tabling
ABGILNZ
blazing
ABGIMMN
bamming
AGBIMST
gambist

ABGINNN
banning
ABGINOT
boating
ABGINRR
barring
ABGINRV
braving
ABGINRY
braying
ABGINRZ
brazing
ABGINST
basting
ABGINSU
abusing
ABGINTT
batting
ABGIOPT
pigboat
ABGLMOU
lumbago
ABGLNOO
bologna
ABGLRRU
burglar
ABGNOTU
gunboat
ABGOTTU
tugboat
ABHHSUY
hushaby
ABHIINT
inhabit
ABHILNO
hobnail
ABHILOS
abolish
ABHILTU
halibut
ABHIORS
boarish
ABHIOST
isobath
ABHKLSY
bashlyk
ABHMNSU
bushman
ABHOTUY
hautboy
ABHRSTU
tarbush
ABHSTUW
washtub
ABIILMU
bulimia
ABIILTY
ability
ABIIOSS
abiosis
ABIKLMN
lambkin
ABIKLOR
kilobar

ABIKMNR
barmkin
ABIKRST
britska
ABILLMY
balmily
ABILLNP
pinball
ABILLPY
pliably
ABILLSW
sawbill
ABILMNU
albumin
ABILMOX
mailbox
ABILOPR
bipolar
ABILORT
orbital
ABILORV
bolivar
ABILOST
oblasti
ABILOTU
bailout
ABILRRY
library
ABILSYZ
sizably
ABIMPST
baptism
ABIMSTU
ambitus
ABINORW
rainbow
ABINOST
bastion
ABINRTV
vibrant
ABIORTV
vibrato
ABIPSTT
baptist
ABISSST
bassist
ABKLLNY
blankly
ABKLRUW
bulwark
ABKMNOO
bookman
ABLLLUY
lullaby
ABLLNOO
balloon
ABLLOTY
tallboy
ABLLRUY
bullary
ABLMPUU
pabulum
ABLNOTY

notably
ABLOPYY
playboy
ABLORST
borstal
ABLRRUY
barruly
ABLRTUU
tubular
ABMOORR
barroom
ABMORTU
tambour
ABNOOSS
bassoon
ABNOTUY
buoyant
ABOOPSX
soapbox
ABOORTW
rowboat
ABOOTTW
towboat
ABRRSUY
bursary
ACCCILY
acyclic
ACCDDEE
acceded
ACCDEEN
cadence
ACCDEHN
chanced
ACCDEHO
coached
ACCDEKL
cackled
clacked
ACCDEKO
cockade
ACCDEKR
cracked
ACCDENY
cadency
ACCDEOT
coacted
ACCDERU
accrued
cardecu
ACCDESU
accused
ACCDFIL
flaccid
ACCDILS
scaldic
ACCDINR
cancrid
ACCEELN
cenacle
ACCEERT
accrete
ACCEFLU
felucca
ACCEHIL

chalice	saccule	**ACCMOOT**	**ACDEEKR**	cordage
ACCEHIN	**ACCENOV**	cocomat	creaked	**ACDEHHT**
chicane	concave	**ACCMOPT**	**ACDEELL**	hatched
ACCEHKL	**ACCENPT**	compact	cadelle	**ACDEHIN**
chackle	peccant	**ACCNOOR**	**ACDEELN**	chained
ACCEHLN	**ACCEOPY**	raccoon	cleaned	**ACDEHIR**
chancel	cacoepy	**ACCNOTT**	**ACDEELR**	chaired
ACCEHLO	**ACCEPRY**	contact	declare	**ACDEHKL**
cochlea	peccary	**ACCNOTU**	**ACDEELT**	chalked
ACCEHNO	**ACCERRS**	account	cleated	**ACDEHKS**
conchae	scarcer	**ACCOPTY**	**ACDEELV**	shacked
ACCEHNR	**ACCERSU**	copycat	cleaved	**ACDEHKW**
chancre	accuser	**ACCORSS**	**ACDEEMN**	whacked
ACCEHOR	**ACCFIIP**	corcass	menaced	**ACDEHLR**
caroche	pacific	**ACDDDEI**	**ACDEEMO**	chalder
coacher	**ACCFILY**	caddied	cameoed	**ACDEHLS**
ACCEHOS	calcify	**ACDDDEU**	**ACDEEMR**	clashed
coaches	**ACCGHIN**	adduced	creamed	**ACDEHLT**
ACCEHPU	caching	**ACDDEEF**	**ACDEEMV**	latched
capuche	**ACCHIOT**	defaced	medevac	**ACDEHMP**
ACCEHRT	chaotic	**ACDDEEY**	**ACDEENS**	champed
catcher	**ACCHKOY**	decayed	encased	**ACDEHMR**
ACCEHTU	haycock	**ACDDEIN**	**ACDEENT**	charmed
catechu	**ACCHPTU**	candied	enacted	marched
ACCEHXY	catchup	**ACDDEIS**	**ACDEEPR**	**ACDEHMS**
cachexy	**ACCHRRU**	caddies	capered	chasmed
ACCEILS	currach	**ACDDELN**	**ACDEEPS**	**ACDEHMT**
calices	**ACCHRST**	candled	escaped	matched
ACCEILT	scratch	**ACDDELR**	**ACDEERS**	**ACDEHNR**
calcite	**ACCIIST**	cradled	creased	ranched
ACCEIMR	sciatic	**ACDDELS**	**ACDEERT**	**ACDEHNT**
ceramic	**ACCIKRS**	scalded	catered	chanted
ACCEINO	carsick	**ACDDEOP**	cerated	**ACDEHOP**
cocaine	**ACCILLU**	decapod	created	poached
oceanic	calculi	**ACDDHIS**	reacted	**ACDEHOT**
ACCEINV	**ACCILMO**	caddish	**ACDEETU**	cathode
vaccine	comical	**ACDDHKO**	educate	**ACDEHPP**
ACCEIPR	**ACCILMU**	haddock	**ACDEETX**	chapped
caprice	calcium	**ACDDIRS**	exacted	**ACDEHPR**
ACCEIQU	**ACCILNO**	discard	**ACDEFFH**	parched
cacique	conical	**ACDDIRY**	chaffed	**ACDEHPT**
ACCEIRT	laconic	dryadic	**ACDEFGO**	patched
creatic	**ACCILNY**	**ACDDKOP**	dogface	**ACDEHRR**
ACCEIST	cynical	paddock	**ACDEFIN**	charred
ascetic	**ACCILOR**	**ACDEEES**	fancied	**ACDEHRS**
ACCEKLR	caloric	decease	**ACDEFRS**	crashed
cackler	**ACCILOV**	**ACDEEFF**	scarfed	**ACDEHRT**
clacker	vocalic	effaced	**ACDEFRT**	charted
crackle	**ACCILRU**	**ACDEEFN**	crafted	**ACDEHST**
ACCEKOP	crucial	enfaced	fracted	scathed
peacock	**ACCILRY**	**ACDEEFT**	**ACDEGGR**	**ACDEHTT**
ACCEKOS	acrylic	faceted	cragged	chatted
seacock	**ACCILSS**	**ACDEEGN**	**ACDEGHN**	**ACDEHTW**
ACCEKPU	classic	engaged	changed	watched
cupcake	**ACCILST**	**ACDEEHL**	**ACDEGHR**	**ACDEHTY**
ACCEKRR	clastic	leached	charged	yachted
cracker	**ACCISTU**	**ACDEEHR**	**ACDEGKO**	**ACDEILL**
ACCELLY	caustic	reached	duckage	cedilla
cecally	**ACCKLRY**	**ACDEEHT**	**ACDEGLN**	**ACDEILM**
ACCELNO	crackly	cheated	clanged	claimed
conceal	**ACCKMMO**	**ACDEEIR**	glanced	decimal
ACCELOR	cammock	deciare	**ACDEGNO**	declaim
coracle	**ACCKOSS**	**ACDEEJT**	decagon	medical
ACCELSU	cassock	dejecta	**ACDEGOR**	**ACDEILR**

decrial	**ACDELOR**	scatted	carotid	**ACEEHPS**
radicle	caroled	**ACDFITT**	**ACDIOTY**	peaches
ACDEILT	coraled	fatidic	dacoity	**ACEEHRS**
citadel	**ACDELOT**	**ACDFIIY**	**ACDIQRU**	reaches
deltaic	located	acidify	quadric	**ACEEHRT**
dialect	**ACDELPP**	**ACDGGIN**	**ACDIRST**	cheater
edictal	clapped	cadging	drastic	hectare
ACDEINR	**ACDELPS**	**ACDGINN**	**ACDITUV**	teacher
cairned	clasped	dancing	viaduct	**ACEEHST**
ACDEINS	scalped	**ACDGINR**	**ACDJNTU**	escheat
candies	**ACDELRW**	carding	adjunct	teaches
incased	crawled	**ACDGORT**	**ACDKLOP**	**ACEEILP**
ACDEINY	**ACDELSS**	dogcart	padlock	calipee
cyanide	classed	**ACDHIIL**	**ACDLLOR**	**ACEEKNP**
ACDEIRR	declass	chiliad	collard	kneecap
carried	**ACDELST**	**ACDHIRY**	**ACDLNOR**	**ACEELLN**
ACDEIRS	castled	diarchy	caldron	nacelle
radices	**ACDEMMR**	**ACDHLOR**	**ACDMMNO**	**ACEELMP**
sidecar	crammed	dorlach	command	emplace
ACDEITT	**ACDEMNU**	**ACDHNOO**	**ACDMORZ**	**ACEELNR**
dictate	decuman	chandoo	czardom	cleaner
ACDEITY	**ACDEMOR**	**ACDHNOW**	**ACDNOOR**	**ACEELNS**
edacity	caromed	cowhand	cardoon	cleanse
ACDEJLO	comrade	**ACDHOPR**	**ACDORST**	scalene
cajoled	**ACDEMPR**	pochard	costard	**ACEELNV**
ACDEKKN	cramped	**ACDHORR**	**ACDORSU**	enclave
knacked	**ACDEMPS**	orchard	crusado	valence
ACDEKLM	scamped	**ACDHRUY**	**ACDORUZ**	**ACEELPR**
mackled	**ACDENNS**	duarchy	cruzado	percale
ACDEKLN	scanned	**ACDHRYY**	**ACDRSTU**	replace
clanked	**ACDENPR**	dyarchy	custard	**ACEELRR**
ACDEKLO	pranced	**ACDIIIN**	**ACEEEUV**	clearer
cloaked	**ACDENPT**	indicia	evacuee	**ACEELRT**
ACDEKLS	pandect	**ACDIIRS**	**ACEEFFR**	treacle
slacked	**ACDENRU**	cidaris	effacer	**ACEELRV**
ACDEKLT	durance	**ACDIITY**	**ACEEFIN**	cleaver
tackled	**ACDENRY**	acidity	faience	**ACEELST**
talcked	ardency	**ACDILMO**	fiancee	celesta
ACDEKLU	**ACDENST**	domical	**ACEEFLU**	**ACEELVX**
caulked	descant	**ACDILNO**	feculae	exclave
ACDEKMS	scanted	nodical	**ACEEFPR**	**ACEEMNR**
smacked	**ACDEORR**	**ACDILOP**	preface	menacer
ACDEKNR	corrade	placoid	**ACEEGIL**	**ACEEMNV**
cranked	**ACDEORT**	**ACDILOR**	elegiac	cavemen
ACDEKNS	cordate	cordial	**ACEEHHT**	**ACEEMRR**
snacked	redcoat	**ACDILOT**	cheetah	creamer
ACDEKOR	**ACDEOST**	cotidal	**ACEEHIV**	**ACEEMRT**
croaked	coasted	**ACDILRY**	achieve	cremate
ACDEKQU	**ACDEOUV**	acridly	**ACEEHKO**	**ACEENNP**
quacked	couvade	**ACDILTW**	hoecake	penance
ACDEKRT	**ACDEPPR**	wildcat	**ACEEHLR**	**ACEENNT**
tracked	crapped	**ACDIMMU**	leacher	canteen
ACDEKST	**ACDEPRS**	cadmium	**ACEEHMR**	**ACEENNY**
stacked	scarped	**ACDIMNO**	machree	cayenne
ACDELMM	scraped	nomadic	**ACEEHMT**	**ACEENOT**
clammed	**ACDERRS**	**ACDIMNY**	machete	acetone
ACDELMP	scarred	dynamic	**ACEEHNN**	**ACEENRT**
clamped	**ACDERSU**	**ACDINST**	enhance	crenate
ACDELNO	crusade	discant	**ACEEHNP**	reenact
celadon	**ACDERTT**	**ACDIOPR**	cheapen	**ACEENTU**
ACDELNS	detract	picador	**ACEEHNS**	cuneate
calends	**ACDERTU**	**ACDIORR**	enchase	**ACEEPRR**
ACDELNU	traduce	corrida	**ACEEHPR**	caperer
unlaced	**ACDESTT**	**ACDIORT**	cheaper	**ACEEPRS**

escaper	apogeic	hackney	**ACEHPRT**	**ACEILRU**
ACEERRT	**ACEGIST**	**ACEHKRY**	chapter	auricle
caterer	cagiest	hackery	**ACEHPRY**	**ACEILRV**
retrace	**ACEGJKL**	**ACEHLLS**	eparchy	caviler
terrace	jackleg	shellac	**ACEHPST**	clavier
ACEERSU	**ACEGKLR**	**ACEHLLT**	patches	**ACEILST**
cesurae	grackle	hellcat	**ACEHRRT**	elastic
ACEERTX	**ACEGKOR**	**ACEHLMY**	charter	laciest
exacter	corkage	alchemy	**ACEHRRX**	latices
excreta	**ACEGLLO**	**ACEHLNN**	xerarch	**ACEILTT**
ACEFFHR	collage	channel	**ACEHRRY**	lattice
chaffer	**ACEGLNO**	**ACEHLNR**	archery	tactile
ACEFHMR	congeal	charnel	**ACEHRSS**	**ACEIMNO**
chamfer	**ACEGNOT**	**ACEHLOP**	crashes	encomia
ACEFILL	cognate	epochal	**ACEHRSY**	**ACEIMNR**
icefall	**ACEGORS**	**ACEHLOR**	hyraces	carmine
ACEFILM	cargoes	cholera	**ACEHRTT**	**ACEIMNS**
malefic	corsage	chorale	chatter	amnesic
ACEFINN	**ACEGORU**	**ACEHLPT**	ratchet	**ACEIMPR**
finance	courage	chaplet	**ACEHRTW**	campier
ACEFINR	**ACEGOTT**	**ACEHLPY**	watcher	**ACEIMST**
fancier	cottage	cheaply	**ACEHSTW**	sematic
ACEFINS	**ACEGSTU**	**ACEHLSS**	watches	**ACEINNP**
fancies	scutage	clashes	**ACEIILT**	pinnace
fascine	**ACEHHRT**	**ACEHLST**	ciliate	**ACEINNR**
ACEFINU	hatcher	latches	**ACEIKRT**	cannier
uniface	**ACEHHRU**	satchel	tackier	**ACEINNT**
ACEFITY	hachure	**ACEHLTT**	**ACEIKRW**	ancient
acetify	**ACEHHST**	chattel	wackier	**ACEINPR**
ACEFLRU	hatches	latchet	**ACEIKSS**	caprine
careful	**ACEHHTT**	**ACEHMNT**	seasick	**ACEINRS**
ACEFNRU	hatchet	manchet	**ACEILLX**	arsenic
furnace	**ACEHILL**	**ACEHMRR**	lexical	**ACEINRT**
ACEFRRT	helical	marcher	**ACEILMR**	certain
refract	**ACEHILT**	**ACEHMRS**	miracle	**ACEINSS**
ACEFRRU	ethical	marches	reclaim	cassine
farceur	**ACEHIMN**	mesarch	**ACEILMT**	**ACEINTT**
ACEFRSU	machine	**ACEHMRT**	climate	nictate
surface	**ACEHIMP**	marchet	**ACEILMX**	**ACEINTX**
ACEFRTU	impeach	rematch	exclaim	inexact
facture	**ACEHIMR**	**ACEHMST**	**ACEILNP**	**ACEINTZ**
furcate	chimera	matches	capelin	zincate
ACEGHNR	**ACEHIMT**	**ACEHNNR**	pelican	**ACEIOPT**
changer	hematic	channer	**ACEILNR**	ectopia
ACEGHOU	**ACEHINN**	**ACEHNNT**	carline	**ACEIORS**
gouache	enchain	enchant	**ACEILNS**	scoriae
ACEGHRR	**ACEHIPT**	**ACEHNRR**	sanicle	**ACEIORT**
charger	aphetic	rancher	**ACEILOR**	erotica
ACEGILN	hepatic	**ACEHNRS**	calorie	**ACEIPPR**
angelic	**ACEHIRR**	ranches	cariole	crappie
ACEGILP	charier	**ACEHNRT**	loricae	epicarp
pelagic	**ACEHIRS**	chanter	**ACEILPR**	**ACEIPST**
ACEGILR	cashier	**ACEHNST**	caliper	aseptic
glacier	**ACEHIRT**	chasten	replica	**ACEIPSU**
gracile	theriac	**ACEHNTY**	**ACEILPS**	auspice
ACEGIMR	**ACEHIRV**	chantey	special	**ACEIPSZ**
grimace	archive	**ACEHOPS**	**ACEILPT**	capsize
ACEGINO	**ACEHKLR**	poaches	plicate	**ACEIPTV**
coinage	hackler	**ACEHORS**	**ACEILRS**	captive
ACEGINP	**ACEHKLS**	roaches	claries	**ACEIQRU**
peacing	shackle	**ACEHPPS**	scalier	acquire
ACEGINS	**ACEHKMN**	schappe	**ACEILRT**	**ACEIRRR**
ceasing	hackmen	**ACEHPRS**	article	carrier
ACEGIOP	**ACEHKNY**	parches	recital	**ACEIRRS**

carries
scarier
ACEIRRT
cirrate
erratic
ACEIRRZ
crazier
ACEIRST
raciest
stearic
ACEIRSU
saucier
ACEIRSV
varices
viscera
ACEIRSZ
crazies
ACEIRTT
cattier
citrate
ACEITUX
auxetic
ACEJLOR
cajoler
ACEJNOT
jaconet
ACEJNOY
joyance
ACEKKNR
knacker
ACEKLNS
slacken
ACEKLPT
placket
ACEKLRS
slacker
ACEKMNP
packmen
ACEKMOR
comaker
ACEKNTU
nutcake
ACEKORR
croaker
ACEKRRT
tracker
ACELLMO
calomel
ACELLNY
cleanly
ACELLOT
collate
ACELLPS
scalpel
ACELLRY
clearly
ACELMMR
clammer
ACELMRY
camelry
ACELMST
calmest
ACELMTU
calumet

ACELNNU
unclean
ACELNNY
lyncean
ACELNOR
corneal
ACELNPS
enclasp
spancel
ACELNPU
cleanup
ACELNRT
central
ACELNRU
lucarne
nuclear
unclear
ACELNRY
larceny
ACELNTY
latency
ACELOPT
polecat
ACELOPU
copulae
ACELOQU
coequal
ACELORR
correal
ACELORT
locater
ACELORY
caloyer
ACELOST
lactose
ACELOTT
calotte
ACELOTY
acolyte
ACELOUV
vacuole
ACELPPR
clapper
ACELPRS
scalper
ACELPRT
plectra
ACELPRY
prelacy
ACELPSU
capsule
specula
ACELQRU
lacquer
ACELRST
scarlet
ACELRSU
secular
ACELRTT
clatter
ACELSSS
classes
ACELSTU
sulcate

ACELSTY
scytale
ACELSXY
calyxes
ACELTUY
acutely
ACELTXY
exactly
ACEMNOR
romance
ACEMNRT
cartmen
ACEMOPR
compare
ACEMORU
morceau
ACEMPRS
scamper
ACENNOS
ancones
ACENNOT
connate
ACENNOZ
canzone
ACENNRY
cannery
ACENNST
nascent
ACENNTY
tenancy
ACENOOR
coronae
ACENORS
coarsen
narcose
ACENORT
enactor
ACENOSS
cassone
ACENOST
costean
ACENOTV
centavo
ACENPTT
pentact
ACENPTY
patency
ACENRRY
errancy
ACENRTU
centaur
uncrate
ACENRTY
nectary
ACEOOPP
apocope
ACEOPRX
exocarp
ACEORRS
coarser
ACEORRT
creator
reactor
ACEORST

coaster
ACEORSU
carouse
ACEOSSU
caseous
ACEOSTT
costate
ACEOSTU
acetous
ACEOTTV
cavetto
ACEOTUU
couteau
ACEPPRR
crapper
ACEPRRS
scarper
scraper
ACEPRST
spectra
ACEPRTU
capture
ACEQRTU
racquet
ACEQSTU
acquest
ACERRSS
crasser
ACERRTT
retract
ACERRTY
tracery
ACERSST
actress
ACERSSV
scarves
ACERSTT
scatter
ACERSTU
crustae
ACERSTY
sectary
ACERTTX
extract
ACESSTY
ecstasy
ACFFIIT
caitiff
ACFFILT
afflict
ACFFIRT
traffic
ACFFOST
castoff
offcast
ACFGHIN
chafing
ACFHIST
catfish
ACFHISU
fuchsia
ACFIILN
finical
ACFILRY

clarify
ACFINNY
infancy
ACFINOT
faction
ACFINRT
frantic
infarct
infract
ACFIRSY
scarify
ACFISST
fascist
ACFLRUU
furcula
ACFLTTU
tactful
ACFLTUY
faculty
ACFORTY
factory
ACGGINR
gracing
ACGGRSY
scraggy
ACGHIKN
hacking
ACGHINR
arching
chagrin
ACGHINS
cashing
chasing
ACGHIPR
graphic
ACGIJKN
jacking
ACGIKLN
lacking
ACGIKNP
packing
ACGIKNR
carking
racking
ACGIKNS
sacking
ACGIKNT
tacking
ACGIKNU
cauking
ACGILLN
calling
ACGILLO
logical
ACGILMN
calming
ACGILNN
lancing
ACGILNO
coaling
ACGILNP
placing
ACGILNS
scaling

ACGILNT	**ACHHIRS**	scholar	musical	**ACINOPT**
catling	rhachis	**ACHLORT**	**ACILNNY**	caption
talcing	**ACHIIPS**	trochal	cannily	paction
ACGILNV	pachisi	**ACHMNOR**	**ACILNOR**	**ACINOQU**
calving	**ACHIJNT**	monarch	carlino	coquina
ACGILNW	jacinth	nomarch	carolin	**ACINORR**
clawing	**ACHIKRY**	**ACHMOPR**	clarion	carrion
ACGILNY	hayrick	camphor	**ACILNPY**	**ACINORT**
claying	**ACHILLP**	**ACHMOST**	pliancy	carotin
ACGIMNO	phallic	stomach	**ACILNTU**	**ACINOSS**
coaming	**ACHILLS**	**ACHMSUW**	lunatic	caisson
ACGIMNP	challis	cumshaw	**ACILNTY**	cassoni
camping	**ACHILMO**	**ACHNNOS**	anticly	**ACINOSU**
ACGINNN	mochila	chanson	**ACILNUV**	acinous
canning	**ACHILOS**	**ACHNOVY**	vincula	**ACINOTT**
ACGINNR	scholia	anchovy	**ACILOPT**	taction
craning	**ACHILRY**	**ACHNPUY**	optical	**ACINOTU**
ACGINNT	charily	paunchy	topical	auction
canting	**ACHILSY**	**ACHNRTY**	**ACILORV**	caution
ACGINOR	clayish	chantry	corival	**ACINPRT**
organic	**ACHIMOS**	**ACHNRUY**	**ACILOST**	cantrip
ACGINOT	chamiso	raunchy	stoical	**ACINQTU**
coating	chamois	**ACHNSTU**	**ACILOTV**	quantic
ACGINOX	**ACHIMRS**	canthus	voltaic	**ACINRTU**
coaxing	charism	staunch	**ACILPST**	curtain
ACGINPP	chrisma	**ACHOPRT**	plastic	**ACIOPRT**
capping	**ACHINNU**	toparch	**ACILPTY**	apricot
ACGINPR	unchain	**ACHPTUZ**	typical	parotic
carping	**ACHINOP**	chutzpa	**ACILRTU**	**ACIOPTY**
craping	aphonic	**ACHRSTY**	curtail	opacity
ACGINPS	**ACHINPS**	starchy	**ACILRTY**	**ACIORRS**
scaping	spinach	**ACHSTUY**	clarity	corsair
spacing	**ACHINTX**	cyathus	**ACILRYZ**	**ACIORSU**
ACGINRS	xanthic	**ACIIKRS**	crazily	carious
sacring	**ACHIOPT**	airsick	**ACILSSS**	curiosa
scaring	aphotic	**ACIILLP**	classis	**ACIORTT**
ACGINRT	**ACHIORT**	capilli	**ACILSUY**	citator
carting	chariot	**ACIILNV**	saucily	ricotta
crating	haricot	vicinal	**ACILTTY**	**ACIPRSY**
tracing	**ACHIQRU**	**ACIILRY**	tacitly	piscary
ACGINRV	charqui	ciliary	**ACILTUV**	**ACIPRTT**
carving	**ACHIRTU**	**ACIIMOT**	victual	tipcart
craving	haircut	comitia	**ACIMNOS**	**ACIPRVY**
ACGINRZ	**ACHIRTY**	**ACIINPS**	masonic	privacy
crazing	charity	piscina	**ACIMNRS**	**ACIPSST**
ACGINSS	**ACHISSS**	**ACIINTT**	narcism	spastic
cassing	chassis	titanic	**ACIMNRU**	**ACIPTUY**
ACGINST	**ACHISTT**	**ACIIRST**	cranium	paucity
casting	cattish	satiric	**ACIMOPT**	**ACIQRTU**
ACGINSU	**ACHKLSY**	**ACIKLWY**	potamic	quartic
causing	shackly	wackily	**ACIMOST**	**ACIRSST**
saucing	**ACHKMMO**	**ACIKMNP**	somatic	sacrist
ACGINTT	hammock	pickman	**ACIMPRT**	**ACIRSSU**
catting	**ACHKOSS**	**ACIKNPY**	crampit	cuirass
ACGIRST	hassock	panicky	ptarmic	**ACIRSTT**
gastric	**ACHLLOO**	**ACIKNST**	**ACIMPRY**	astrict
ACGLNOR	alcohol	catskin	primacy	**ACIRSTY**
clangor	**ACHLLOR**	**ACILLLO**	**ACIMRSZ**	satyric
ACGNNOR	chloral	illocal	czarism	**ACIRSTZ**
crannog	**ACHLMSY**	**ACILLRY**	**ACIMSST**	czarist
ACGNOOT	chlamys	lyrical	miscast	**ACISSTU**
octagon	**ACHLNOY**	**ACILMPS**	**ACINNOT**	casuist
ACGNORU	halcyon	plasmic	actinon	**ACISTUV**
cougnar	**ACHLORS**	**ACILMSU**	contain	vacuist

ACITUVY	crassly	scrappy	gladden	**ADDELTW**
vacuity	**ACLRSTY**	**ADDDEER**	**ADDEGLR**	twaddle
ACJKKSY	crystal	dreaded	gladder	**ADDELZZ**
skyjack	**ACLRSWY**	**ADDDEIS**	**ADDEGRU**	dazzled
ACJKLOW	scrawly	daddies	guarded	**ADDEMMR**
lockjaw	**ACLSSTU**	**ADDDELM**	**ADDEHLN**	drammed
ACJKOPT	cutlass	maddled	handled	**ADDEMOP**
jackpot	**ACMNOPR**	**ADDDELN**	**ADDEHOR**	pomaded
ACJLORU	crampon	dandled	hoarded	**ADDEMST**
jocular	**ACMNOPY**	**ADDDELP**	**ADDEILL**	maddest
ACJMNTU	company	paddled	dallied	**ADDENOR**
muntjac	**ACMNORY**	**ADDDELR**	**ADDEILT**	adorned
ACKLLOP	acronym	raddled	dilated	**ADDENOT**
pollack	**ACMNSTU**	**ADDDELS**	**ADDEIMR**	donated
ACKLLSY	sanctum	saddled	admired	nodated
slackly	**ACMOPSS**	**ADDDELW**	**ADDEIMX**	**ADDENPU**
ACKLOOR	compass	dawdled	admixed	pudenda
oarlock	**ACMQTUU**	waddled	**ADDEINO**	**ADDENTU**
ACKLORW	cumquat	**ADDDELY**	adenoid	daunted
warlock	**ACMRSTU**	addedly	**ADDEINP**	undated
ACKMMMO	castrum	**ADDDENO**	pandied	**ADDEOPT**
mammock	**ACNNNUY**	deodand	**ADDEINR**	adopted
ACKMOTT	uncanny	**ADDDEQU**	dandier	**ADDEPTU**
mattock	**ACNOORT**	quadded	drained	updated
ACLLLOY	cartoon	**ADDEEEY**	**ADDEINS**	**ADDERSS**
locally	**ACNOPSW**	deadeye	dandies	address
ACLLOOR	snowcap	**ADDEEFM**	**ADDEINU**	**ADDERTT**
corolla	**ACNORTU**	defamed	unaided	dratted
ACLLOPS	courant	**ADDEEGR**	**ADDEINV**	**ADDESST**
scallop	**ACNORXY**	degrade	invaded	saddest
ACLLOSU	acronyx	**ADDEEHR**	**ADDEIOT**	**ADDFHIS**
callous	**ACNOSTT**	adhered	toadied	faddish
ACLLOVY	constat	redhead	**ADDEIOV**	**ADDFINY**
vocally	**ACNOSTU**	**ADDEEIR**	avoided	dandify
ACLMNCU	conatus	readied	**ADDEIPS**	**ADDFIST**
columna	**ACNRRTU**	**ADDEEIT**	paddies	faddist
ACLMNUY	currant	ideated	**ADDEISV**	**ADDGGIN**
calumny	**ACNRSWY**	**ADDEEKN**	advised	gadding
ACLMORU	scrawny	kneaded	**ADDEISW**	**ADDGILN**
clamour	**ACNRTUY**	**ADDEELP**	waddies	addling
ACLNOOR	truancy	pedaled	**ADDEISY**	**ADDGIMN**
coronal	**ACOOPRR**	pleaded	dayside	madding
ACLNOOT	corpora	**ADDEELT**	**ADDEITU**	**ADDGINP**
coolant	**ACOOPTT**	delated	audited	padding
ACLNOOV	topcoat	**ADDEELY**	**ADDEJLY**	**ADDGINW**
volcano	**ACOPRRT**	delayed	jadedly	wadding
ACLNPSU	carport	**ADDEEMN**	**ADDEKLR**	**ADDGMNO**
unclasp	**ACORRTT**	amended	darkled	goddamn
ACLNSTY	tractor	**ADDEEMR**	**ADDELLU**	**ADDHITY**
scantly	**ACORRTU**	dreamed	alluded	hydatid
ACLOORT	curator	**ADDEEST**	**ADDELPP**	**ADDIINS**
crotalo	**ACORRTY**	sedated	dappled	disdain
ACLOPRT	carroty	**ADDEFRT**	**ADDELPR**	**ADDIKTY**
caltrop	**ACORSSU**	drafted	paddler	katydid
ACLOPSU	sarcous	**ADDEFRU**	**ADDELRS**	**ADDILMN**
scopula	**ACORSTU**	defraud	saddler	midland
ACLORST	surcoat	**ADDEFRW**	**ADDELRT**	**ADDILNY**
scrotal	**ACORSUU**	dwarfed	dartled	dandily
ACLORSU	raucous	**ADDEGGL**	**ADDELRW**	**ADDIMNO**
carolus	**ACOSTTU**	daggled	drawled	diamond
oscular	outcast	**ADDEGGR**	**ADDELST**	**ADDINOR**
ACLPRUU	**ACOSUUV**	dragged	staddle	android
cupular	vacuous	**ADDEGLN**	**ADDELSW**	**ADDLLRU**
ACLRSSY	**ACPPRSY**	dangled	swaddle	dullard

ADEEELS	**ADEEILM**	**ADEELRW**	essayed	flapped
easeled	limeade	leeward	**ADEESTT**	**ADEFLTU**
ADEEESW	**ADEEILN**	**ADEELRX**	estated	default
seaweed	delaine	relaxed	**ADEESTU**	faulted
ADEEFLR	**ADEEILR**	**ADEELRY**	sauteed	**ADEFOOS**
federal	leadier	relayed	**ADEESTW**	seafood
ADEEFLT	**ADEEIMT**	**ADEELTX**	sweated	**ADEFORV**
deflate	mediate	exalted	**ADEESTY**	favored
ADEEFRT	**ADEEINS**	**ADEELUV**	yeasted	**ADEFORY**
draftee	aniseed	devalue	**ADEEWWX**	forayed
ADEEFST	**ADEEIRS**	**ADEEMNR**	waxweed	**ADEFPPR**
deafest	dearies	amender	**ADEFFIP**	frapped
feasted	readies	meander	piaffed	**ADEFRST**
ADEEGGH	**ADEEIRW**	renamed	**ADEFFIR**	strafed
egghead	wearied	**ADEEMNS**	daffier	**ADEFSTT**
ADEEGGN	**ADEEISS**	seedman	**ADEFFIX**	daftest
engaged	disease	**ADEEMRS**	affixed	**ADEGGGL**
ADEEGLL	seaside	smeared	**ADEFFLO**	gaggled
alleged	**ADEEISV**	**ADEEMST**	leadoff	**ADEGGHL**
ADEEGLM	advisee	steamed	**ADEFFLR**	haggled
gleamed	**ADEEITV**	**ADEEMSU**	raffled	**ADEGGHS**
ADEEGLN	deviate	medusae	**ADEFFLW**	shagged
gleaned	**ADEEKNP**	**ADEENNX**	waffled	**ADEGGLN**
ADEEGLV	kneepad	annexed	**ADEFFQU**	naggled
gaveled	**ADEEKNR**	**ADEENPS**	quaffed	**ADEGGLR**
ADEEGLZ	kneader	sneaped	**ADEFFST**	draggle
deglaze	**ADEEKNS**	**ADEENRV**	staffed	gargled
ADEEGNR	sneaked	ravened	**ADEFGGL**	**ADEGGLS**
angered	**ADEEKRW**	**ADEENRY**	flagged	slagged
derange	wreaked	deanery	**ADEFGGR**	**ADEGGLW**
enraged	**ADEEKTW**	yearned	fragged	waggled
grandee	tweaked	**ADEENTT**	**ADEFGLN**	**ADEGGNS**
grenade	**ADEEKWY**	dentate	fangled	snagged
ADEEGNT	weekday	**ADEEPPR**	flanged	**ADEGGRY**
negated	**ADEELLS**	papered	**ADEFGOR**	raggedy
ADEEGNV	allseed	**ADEEPRS**	foraged	**ADEGGST**
avenged	**ADEELLY**	speared	**ADEFGRT**	stagged
ADEEGRS	alleyed	**ADEEPRT**	grafted	**ADEGHIN**
greased	**ADEELMP**	predate	**ADEFHLS**	heading
ADEEGRT	empaled	tapered	flashed	**ADEGHLU**
gerated	**ADEELMR**	**ADEEPRV**	**ADEFHST**	laughed
ADEEGRW	emerald	deprave	shafted	**ADEGHMO**
ragweed	**ADEELMT**	pervade	**ADEFILL**	homaged
wagered	metaled	repaved	flailed	**ADEGHNS**
ADEEHIR	**ADEELNP**	**ADEEQTU**	**ADEFINT**	gnashed
headier	deplane	equated	defiant	**ADEGHPR**
ADEEHLS	paneled	**ADEERRT**	fainted	graphed
leashed	**ADEELNR**	retread	**ADEFITX**	**ADEGILN**
ADEEHLX	learned	**ADEERRV**	fixated	aligned
exhaled	**ADEELPR**	averred	**ADEFKLN**	dealing
ADEEHMN	pearled	**ADEERST**	flanked	leading
headmen	**ADEELPS**	dearest	**ADEFKNR**	**ADEGILS**
ADEEHRS	elapsed	estrade	franked	silaged
sheared	pleased	**ADEERSV**	**ADEFLLN**	**ADEGILT**
ADEEHRT	**ADEELPT**	adverse	elfland	ligated
hearted	petaled	**ADEERTT**	**ADEFLLW**	**ADEGINR**
ADEEHST	**ADEELQU**	treated	dewfall	grained
headset	equaled	**ADEERTV**	**ADEFLMM**	reading
ADEEHSV	**ADEELRT**	averted	flammed	**ADEGINV**
sheaved	altered	**ADEERTW**	**ADEFLNN**	evading
ADEEHSY	related	watered	flanned	**ADEGINW**
hayseed	treadle	**ADEERVW**	**ADEFLOT**	windage
ADEEIJT	**ADEELRV**	wavered	floated	**ADEGIRU**
jadeite	raveled	**ADEESSY**	**ADEFLPP**	gaudier

ADEGJLN	**ADEHHOT**	**ADEHORR**	aliunde	invader
jangled	hothead	hoarder	**ADEILOP**	**ADEINST**
ADEGLMN	**ADEHILN**	**ADEHOTW**	oedipal	instead
mangled	inhaled	towhead	**ADEILPP**	sainted
ADEGLMO	**ADEHILP**	**ADEHPRS**	applied	satined
gloamed	helipad	phrased	**ADEILPR**	stained
ADEGLMU	**ADEHILY**	sharped	predial	**ADEINTT**
glaumed	headily	**ADEHPSW**	**ADEILPS**	tainted
ADEGLNR	**ADEHINP**	pshawed	lapides	**ADEINTU**
gnarled	headpin	**ADEHQSU**	palsied	audient
ADEGLNT	pinhead	quashed	**ADEILPT**	**ADEINTV**
tangled	**ADEHINR**	**ADEHRST**	plaited	deviant
ADEGLNW	handier	hardest	**ADEILQU**	**ADEIOPT**
wangled	**ADEHIRR**	trashed	quailed	opiated
ADEGLOT	hardier	**ADEHRTW**	**ADEILRR**	**ADEIORV**
gloated	harried	thrawed	lardier	avoider
ADEGLPU	**ADEHIRS**	**ADEHRTY**	**ADEILRT**	**ADEIORX**
plagued	dashier	hydrate	redtail	exordia
ADEGLSS	hardies	thready	trailed	**ADEIOST**
glassed	shadier	**ADEHSST**	**ADEILRV**	toadies
ADEGMNR	**ADEHIRW**	stashed	rivaled	**ADEIPPR**
dragmen	rawhide	**ADEHSSW**	**ADEILRY**	prepaid
ADEGMNU	**ADEHIRY**	swashed	readily	**ADEIPRR**
agendum	hayride	**ADEHSTW**	**ADEILSV**	parried
ADEGMOP	hydriae	swathed	devisal	**ADEIPRS**
megapod	**ADEHKNS**	**ADEIILR**	**ADEILYZ**	aspired
ADEGNNO	shanked	deliria	dialyze	despair
nonaged	**ADEHKNT**	**ADEIILS**	**ADEIMMR**	praised
ADEGNNU	thanked	dailies	mermaid	**ADEIPRT**
dunnage	**ADEHKRS**	sedilia	**ADEIMNS**	partied
ADEGNOR	sharked	**ADEIINR**	sideman	pirated
groaned	**ADEHLLO**	denarii	**ADEIMNT**	**ADEIPSS**
ADEGNOT	halloed	**ADEIINT**	mediant	apsides
tangoed	**ADEHLNR**	inedita	**ADEIMRR**	**ADEIRRT**
ADEGNPU	handler	**ADEIIRS**	admirer	tardier
unpaged	**ADEHLNS**	dairies	married	tarried
ADEGNRR	handsel	diaries	**ADEIMRS**	**ADEIRRV**
gnarred	**ADEHLOS**	**ADEIIRZ**	misread	arrived
grander	shoaled	diarize	sidearm	**ADEIRST**
ADEGNRT	**ADEHLOT**	**ADEIISS**	**ADEIMRT**	astride
dragnet	loathed	daisies	readmit	diaster
granted	**ADEHLPS**	**ADEIKRS**	**ADEIMRY**	**ADEIRSV**
ADEGNTW	plashed	darkies	midyear	adviser
twanged	**ADEHLSS**	**ADEILLR**	**ADEIMTY**	**ADEIRTT**
ADEGORW	hassled	dallier	daytime	attired
dowager	slashed	rallied	**ADEINOV**	**ADEIRTY**
ADEGOVY	**ADEHLTY**	**ADEILLS**	naevoid	dietary
voyaged	deathly	dallies	**ADEINPS**	**ADEISTW**
ADEGPRS	**ADEHMMS**	sallied	pandies	waisted
grasped	shammed	**ADEILLT**	pansied	**ADEISVV**
sparged	**ADEHMNR**	tallied	**ADEINPT**	savvied
ADEGPRU	herdman	**ADEILLY**	depaint	**ADEISWY**
upgrade	**ADEHMSS**	ideally	painted	wayside
ADEGRSS	smashed	**ADEILMM**	**ADEINRR**	**ADEJMOR**
grassed	**ADEHNRU**	dilemma	drainer	majored
ADEGRSU	unheard	**ADEILMP**	**ADEINRS**	**ADEJNRU**
sugared	**ADEHNST**	impaled	randies	jaunder
ADEGRTY	handset	implead	sandier	**ADEJNTU**
gyrated	**ADEHNTU**	**ADEILMS**	sardine	jaunted
tragedy	haunted	misdeal	**ADEINRT**	**ADEJOPR**
ADEGRUU	**ADEHOPT**	mislead	trained	jeopard
augured	pothead	**ADEILNN**	**ADEINRU**	**ADEKLNP**
ADEHHOP	**ADEHOPX**	annelid	unaired	planked
hophead	hexapod	**ADEILNU**	**ADEINRV**	**ADEKLNR**

rankled	roulade	dampest	**ADEORSU**	sandfly
ADEKLNS	**ADELOSS**	stamped	aroused	**ADFLORU**
kalends	lassoed	**ADEMPSW**	**ADEORSV**	foulard
ADEKLNY	**ADELOTT**	swamped	savored	**ADFORRW**
nakedly	totaled	**ADEMRRU**	**ADEORTT**	forward
ADEKLOP	**ADELPPS**	eardrum	rotated	**ADFPRTU**
polkaed	slapped	**ADEMRST**	**ADEORTU**	updraft
ADEKLST	**ADELPST**	smarted	readout	**ADGGGIN**
stalked	stapled	**ADEMRSW**	**ADEOSTT**	dagging
ADEKNPS	**ADELPSY**	swarmed	toasted	**ADGGHNO**
spanked	splayed	**ADEMRTU**	**ADEOTTU**	hangdog
ADEKNST	**ADELPTT**	matured	outdate	**ADGGINO**
dankest	platted	**ADEMSSU**	**ADEPPRT**	goading
ADEKPRS	**ADELPTY**	assumed	trapped	**ADGGINR**
sparked	adeptly	**ADEMTTU**	**ADEPPRW**	grading
ADEKRST	**ADELQRU**	mutated	wrapped	niggard
darkest	quadrel	**ADENNOY**	**ADEPPSW**	**ADGGINU**
ADELLMU	**ADELRRU**	annoyed	swapped	gauding
medulla	ruderal	anodyne	**ADEPPTU**	**ADGHILO**
ADELLOW	**ADELRTT**	**ADENNPS**	pupated	hidalgo
allowed	rattled	spanned	**ADEPRRS**	**ADGHINN**
ADELLOY	**ADELRTW**	**ADENNPT**	sparred	handing
alloyed	trawled	pendant	**ADEPRRY**	**ADGHINS**
ADELLRU	**ADELRTX**	**ADENOPR**	drapery	dashing
allured	dextral	padrone	**ADEPRSY**	shading
ADELLST	**ADELSTT**	**ADENOPS**	sprayed	**ADGHIRS**
stalled	slatted	espadon	**ADEPSTT**	dishrag
ADELMMS	**ADELSTU**	**ADENORU**	spatted	**ADGHNNU**
slammed	saluted	rondeau	**ADEQRSU**	handgun
ADELMNR	**ADELTTT**	**ADENOTT**	squared	**ADGHNOS**
mandrel	tattled	notated	**ADERRST**	sandhog
ADELMNS	**ADELTTW**	**ADENPPS**	starred	**ADGHRTU**
sledman	wattled	snapped	**ADERSSU**	draught
ADELMNT	**ADELTUV**	**ADENPRR**	assured	**ADGIILN**
mantled	vaulted	pardner	**ADERSTT**	dialing
ADELMOR	**ADELTUX**	**ADENPSW**	started	**ADGIILT**
earldom	luxated	spawned	**ADERSTV**	digital
ADELMPS	**ADELTWZ**	**ADENPUV**	starved	**ADGIINR**
sampled	waltzed	unpaved	**ADERSTW**	gradini
ADELNNP	**ADEMNNU**	**ADENRSU**	steward	raiding
planned	mundane	asunder	strawed	**ADGILLN**
ADELNOT	unnamed	danseur	**ADERSTY**	ladling
taloned	**ADEMNOR**	**ADENRTV**	strayed	**ADGILNN**
ADELNPT	madrone	verdant	**ADESTTU**	landing
planted	**ADEMNRU**	**ADENRTY**	statued	**ADGILNO**
ADELNRS	manured	dentary	**ADESTTW**	loading
slander	maunder	**ADENRUY**	swatted	**ADGILNR**
snarled	unarmed	unready	**ADFFGIN**	darling
ADELNRU	**ADEMNRY**	**ADENSSS**	daffing	larding
launder	draymen	sadness	**ADFFHNO**	**ADGILNU**
rundale	yardmen	**ADENSWY**	offhand	languid
ADELNST	**ADEMNSS**	endways	**ADFFIST**	lauding
slanted	madness	**ADENTTU**	distaff	**ADGILOR**
ADELOPR	**ADEMNSU**	attuned	**ADFGINS**	goliard
leopard	medusan	taunted	fadging	**ADGIMMN**
paroled	**ADEMORR**	**ADENTUV**	**ADFGGIN**	damming
ADELOPS	armored	vaunted	fadging	**ADGIMNN**
deposal	**ADEMOSY**	**ADEOPPS**	**ADFHLNU**	damning
ADELOPT	someday	apposed	handful	**ADGINNR**
tadpole	**ADEMOWY**	**ADEOPQU**	**ADFHOOS**	darning
ADELORT	meadowy	opaqued	shadoof	**ADGINNS**
delator	**ADEMPRT**	**ADEORST**	**ADFINRT**	sanding
leotard	tramped	roasted	indraft	**ADGINNW**
ADELORU	**ADEMPST**	torsade	**ADFLNOP**	dawning
			plafond	
			ADFLNSY	

ADGINOR
adoring
gradino
ADGINPP
dapping
ADGINPR
draping
ADGINPS
spading
ADGINRT
darting
trading
ADGINRW
drawing
ADGINRY
draying
yarding
ADGIRZZ
gizzard
ADGLNOO
gondola
ADGLNOY
daylong
ADGLNRY
grandly
ADGMNOO
goodman
ADGMNOR
gormand
ADGNOOR
dragoon
ADGNORU
aground
ADGNORY
organdy
ADHIIKS
dashiki
ADHILMO
halidom
ADHILNY
handily
ADHILOP
haploid
ADHILOY
holiday
hyaloid
hyoidal
ADHILRY
hardily
ADHILSY
ladyish
shadily
ADHINPS
dishpan
ADHINPU
dauphin
ADHLMPY
lymphad
ADHMNOO
manhood
ADHNOTU
handout
ADHNRTY
hydrant

ADHOOPT
hoptoad
ADHOPRT
hardtop
ADHOSWY
shadowy
ADIILMS
mislaid
ADIILNV
invalid
ADIIMPV
impavid
ADIINST
distain
ADIIRST
diarist
ADIIRTY
aridity
ADIITVY
avidity
ADIKLOS
odalisk
ADIKMNN
mankind
ADIKOTY
dakoity
ADILLSY
disally
ADILMNR
mandril
ADILMNU
maudlin
ADILMOP
diploma
ADILMSU
dualism
ADILNOR
ordinal
ADILNRU
diurnal
ADILNSU
sundial
ADILOPR
dipolar
ADILOPS
psaloid
ADILOPT
platoid
ADILORT
dilator
ADILOSU
diaulos
ADILPRY
rapidly
ADILPST
plastid
ADILPSY
display
ADILPTU
plaudit
ADILPVY
vapidly
ADILQSU
squalid

ADILRTY
tardily
ADILSTU
dualist
ADILTUY
duality
ADIMORR
mirador
ADIMOST
mastoid
ADIMOTT
mattoid
ADIMPRY
pyramid
ADIMSTU
stadium
ADINNOR
andiron
ADINNRS
innards
ADINNRW
indrawn
ADINOPP
oppidan
ADINORS
sadiron
ADINOTX
oxidant
ADINPST
sandpit
ADINSTT
distant
ADINTTY
dittany
ADIOPRR
airdrop
ADIOPRT
parotid
ADIORSU
sauroid
ADIORTU
auditor
ADIOSVW
disavow
ADJLMOR
jarldom
ADJNORU
adjourn
ADKORWY
workday
ADKRSWY
skyward
ADLLMOY
modally
ADLLNOW
lowland
ADLLOPR
pollard
ADLLRWY
drywall
ADLMOOR
malodor
ADLMORU
modular

ADLNNOR
norland
ADLNOOR
lardoon
ADLNOPU
poundal
ADLNORU
nodular
ADLNOST
sandlot
ADLNOSY
synodal
ADLNOTU
outland
ADLNRUY
laundry
ADLOPRU
poulard
ADMNOOR
doorman
madrono
ADMNOOW
woodman
ADMNORS
rodsman
ADMNORT
dormant
mordant
ADMNSTU
dustman
ADMOORT
doormat
ADMORST
stardom
ADMRSTU
mustard
ADNNOOY
noonday
ADNNOTU
daunton
ADNOORT
donator
odorant
tornado
ADNOSTU
astound
ADNPSTU
dustpan
ADNRTUU
rutunda
ADNSTYY
dynasty
ADOOPRS
parodos
ADOOPSU
apodous
ADOOPSW
sapwood
ADOORWY
doorway
ADORSUU
arduous
ADORTUW
outward

ADSSTUW
sawdust
AEEEGLT
legatee
AEEEGPR
peerage
AEEEGPS
seepage
AEEEGRT
etagere
AEEELRS
release
AEEELTV
elevate
AEEFHRT
feather
AEEFILR
leafier
AEEFILW
alewife
AEEFIRS
faeries
AEEFLLT
leaflet
AEEFLMN
enflame
AEEFLRW
welfare
AEEFLRZ
alferez
AEEFLSU
easeful
AEEFMNR
freeman
AEEFRST
feaster
AEEFRTU
feature
AEEFRWY
freeway
AEEGGNR
engager
AEEGILL
galilee
AEEGILM
mileage
AEEGILN
lineage
AEEGILP
epigeal
AEEGKLL
kleagle
AEEGLLZ
gazelle
AEEGLMN
gleeman
melange
AEEGLNR
enlarge
general
gleaner
AEEGLNT
angelet
elegant

AEEGLNV	**AEEHLSY**	**AEEIPRT**	**AEELORU**	eastern
evangel	eyelash	peatier	aureole	nearest
AEEGLRU	**AEEHLTT**	**AEEIPSV**	**AEELPRS**	**AEENRTT**
leaguer	athlete	peavies	relapse	entreat
regulae	**AEEHMNT**	**AEEIPTX**	**AEELPRT**	ternate
AEEGLRY	methane	expiate	prelate	**AEENRTV**
eagerly	**AEEHMRT**	**AEEIRRW**	palette	veteran
AEEGLSS	thermae	wearier	**AEELPTT**	**AEENSST**
ageless	**AEEHNPT**	**AEEIRST**	palette	sensate
AEEGLSV	heptane	seriate	**AEELPTU**	**AEENSTT**
selvage	**AEEHNRT**	**AEEIRSW**	epaulet	neatest
AEEGLTV	earthen	wearies	sequela	**AEENTTV**
vegetal	hearten	**AEEIRTT**	**AEELRSS**	navette
AEEGMNR	**AEEHNTW**	ariette	earless	**AEEOPRT**
germane	wheaten	iterate	**AEELRST**	operate
AEEGMNT	**AEEHRSW**	**AEEISST**	stealer	**AEEORST**
gatemen	whereas	easiest	**AEELRSV**	roseate
AEEGMSS	**AEEHRTT**	**AEEISVV**	several	**AEEORTV**
message	theater	evasive	**AEELRSX**	overate
AEEGNOP	theatre	**AEEKLNT**	relaxes	overeat
peonage	**AEEHRTW**	kantele	**AEELRSY**	**AEEPPRR**
AEEGNPP	weather	**AEEKMNS**	sealery	prepare
genappe	wreathe	kamseen	**AEELRTX**	**AEEPRSS**
AEEGNRT	**AEEHSSV**	**AEEKNNN**	exalter	asperse
grantee	sheaves	nankeen	**AEELSSW**	**AEEPRTZ**
greaten	**AEEHSWY**	**AEEKNNP**	aweless	trapeze
reagent	eyewash	kneepan	**AEELSTX**	**AEEPSTT**
AEEGNRV	**AEEIKLR**	**AEEKNRS**	latexes	septate
avenger	leakier	sneaker	**AEELTTY**	**AEERRST**
engrave	**AEEILMR**	**AEEKNRT**	layette	serrate
AEEGNTV	mealier	retaken	**AEEMMRT**	**AEERRSU**
ventage	**AEEILNO**	**AEEKPRS**	ammeter	erasure
AEEGORV	aeoline	speaker	**AEEMNNO**	**AEERRTT**
overage	**AEEILNT**	**AEEKSTW**	anemone	retreat
AEEGPRS	lineate	weakest	**AEEMNST**	**AEERRVW**
presage	**AEEILPT**	**AEELLWY**	meanest	waverer
AEEGRRS	pileate	walleye	**AEEMOSW**	**AEERSST**
greaser	**AEEILRR**	**AEELMNP**	awesome	tessera
AEEGRRT	earlier	empanel	**AEEMPRT**	**AEERSSY**
greater	**AEEILRT**	**AEELMNV**	tempera	essayer
AEEGRSV	atelier	velamen	**AEEMPTU**	**AEERSTT**
greaves	**AEEILRZ**	**AEELMPR**	amputee	estreat
AEEGTTZ	realize	empaler	**AEEMQRU**	restate
gazette	**AEEILTV**	**AEELMPX**	marquee	**AEERSTU**
AEEHHNT	elative	example	**AEEMRST**	austere
heathen	**AEEIMNS**	exempla	steamer	**AEERSTW**
AEEHHRT	meanies	**AEELMSS**	**AEEMRSU**	sweater
heather	**AEEIMNT**	measles	measure	**AEESTTT**
AEEHHST	matinee	**AEELMTU**	**AEENNOV**	testate
sheathe	**AEEIMNX**	emulate	novenae	**AEFFGIR**
AEEHINR	examine	**AEELNRR**	**AEENNRX**	giraffe
herniae	**AEEIMRS**	learner	reannex	**AEFFKOT**
AEEHIRV	seamier	**AEELNRT**	**AEENNTU**	takeoff
heavier	**AEEIMRT**	enteral	uneaten	**AEFFLLY**
AEEHKRT	emirate	eternal	**AEENOSU**	flyleaf
hektare	meatier	teleran	aeneous	**AEFFLNS**
AEEHKWY	**AEEINRT**	**AEELNRW**	**AEENPST**	snaffle
hawkeye	trainee	renewal	penates	**AEFFLRU**
AEEHLPT	**AEEINST**	**AEELNST**	**AEENPSX**	fearful
heeltap	etesian	leanest	expanse	**AEFFLRW**
AEEHLRT	**AEEINTV**	**AEELNSV**	**AEENRRT**	waffler
leather	naivete	enslave	terrane	**AEFFLTU**
AEEHLSS	**AEEINVW**	**AEELOPR**	**AEENRST**	fateful
leashes	inweave	parolee	earnest	**AEFFMRU**

earmuff	**AEFIMRR**	frazzle	**AEGHMOR**	mangier
AEFFRST	firearm	**AEFLSST**	homager	reaming
staffer	**AEFINNS**	falsest	**AEGHNOX**	**AEGIMNS**
AEFGGLR	fannies	**AEFMNOR**	hexagon	seaming
flagger	**AEFINNT**	foramen	**AEGHNSS**	**AEGIMNT**
AEFGGRY	infante	foreman	gnashes	mintage
faggery	**AEFINRR**	**AEFMORR**	**AEGHOPY**	teaming
AEFGILN	refrain	forearm	hypogea	tegmina
finagle	**AEFINRT**	**AEFNOPR**	**AEGHOST**	**AEGIMOS**
leafing	fainter	profane	hostage	imagoes
AEFGILO	**AEFINRX**	**AEFNRSS**	**AEGIIMN**	**AEGIMPR**
foliage	xerafin	farness	imagine	epigram
AEFGILR	**AEFINSW**	**AEFNSST**	**AEGIKLN**	**AEGIMRR**
fragile	fanwise	fatness	leaking	armiger
AEFGINR	**AEFINTX**	**AEFOPRW**	linkage	**AEGIMRT**
fearing	antefix	forepaw	**AEGIKNP**	migrate
AEFGIRT	**AEFIQRU**	**AEFORRV**	peaking	ragtime
frigate	aquifer	favorer	**AEGIKNS**	**AEGIMRY**
AEFGITU	**AEFIRRR**	**AEFORRY**	sinkage	imagery
fatigue	farrier	forayer	**AEGIKRW**	**AEGIMST**
AEFGLMN	**AEFIRST**	**AEFORSW**	gawkier	gamiest
flagmen	fairest	foresaw	**AEGILLL**	**AEGINNR**
AEFGLRU	**AEFKLNR**	**AEFORSY**	illegal	earning
rageful	flanker	foresay	**AEGILLN**	nearing
AEFGNTU	**AEFKLUW**	**AEFSSTT**	gallein	**AEGINNT**
fungate	wakeful	fastest	**AEGILLP**	anteing
AEFGOOT	**AEFKNRR**	**AEFSTTT**	pillage	antigen
footage	franker	fattest	**AEGILLT**	gentian
AEFGORR	**AEFKORS**	**AEGGGLU**	tillage	**AEGINNU**
forager	forsake	luggage	**AEGILLV**	anguine
AEFGORV	**AEFLLNN**	**AEGGHLR**	village	**AEGINNW**
forgave	flannel	haggler	**AEGILLY**	weaning
AEFGRRT	**AEFLLSY**	**AEGGIJR**	agilely	**AEGINNY**
grafter	falsely	jaggier	**AEGILMR**	yeaning
AEFHLRS	**AEFLMOR**	**AEGGINR**	gremial	**AEGINOS**
flasher	femoral	gearing	**AEGILNN**	agonies
AEFHLSS	**AEFLNRU**	**AEGGIOS**	eanling	**AEGINOZ**
flashes	flaneur	isagoge	leaning	agonize
AEFHLTU	funeral	**AEGGLNR**	**AEGILNP**	**AEGINPR**
hateful	**AEFLNTT**	gangrel	leaping	reaping
AEFHRRT	flatten	**AEGGNRR**	pealing	**AEGINPS**
farther	**AEFLOPW**	granger	**AEGILNR**	spaeing
AEFIILT	peafowl	**AEGGRST**	learing	**AEGINRR**
filiate	**AEFLORS**	stagger	realign	angrier
AEFIIRS	safrole	**AEGGRSW**	**AEGILNS**	earring
fairies	**AEFLORT**	swagger	leasing	grainer
AEFIKLR	floater	**AEGGRWY**	sealing	rearing
flakier	**AEFLOSW**	waggery	**AEGILNT**	**AEGINRS**
AEFILMN	seafowl	**AEGHILN**	elating	erasing
inflame	**AEFLPPR**	healing	gelatin	searing
AEFILMR	flapper	**AEGHINP**	genital	seringa
flamier	**AEFLPRS**	heaping	**AEGILNU**	**AEGINRT**
AEFILNT	felspar	**AEGHINR**	linguae	granite
inflate	**AEFLPRY**	hearing	**AEGILNV**	ingrate
AEFILNU	palfrey	**AEGHINT**	leaving	tangier
infulae	**AEFLQSU**	heating	**AEGILOU**	tearing
AEFILOT	flasque	**AEGHINV**	eulogia	**AEGINRV**
foliate	**AEFLRSU**	heaving	**AEGILRZ**	reaving
AEFILRU	refusal	**AEGHLNO**	glazier	vinegar
failure	**AEFLRTT**	halogen	**AEGILTY**	**AEGINRW**
AEFIMNR	flatter	**AEGHRLU**	egality	wearing
fireman	**AEFLRTU**	laugher	**AEGIMNN**	**AEGINST**
AEFIMOR	tearful	**AEGHMNN**	meaning	easting
foamier	**AEFLRZZ**	hangmen	**AEGIMNR**	ingesta

seating	voltage	nosegay	**AEHILRT**	unleash
signate	**AEGLPPR**	**AEGNRRT**	lathier	**AEHLOPT**
teasing	grapple	granter	**AEHILST**	taphole
AEGINTV	**AEGLPRU**	**AEGNRST**	heliast	**AEHLORT**
vintage	earplug	strange	**AEHILTY**	rathole
AEGINVW	**AEGLRRU**	**AEGNSSU**	hyalite	**AEHLPRS**
weaving	regular	sangsue	**AEHILVY**	spheral
AEGIPRS	**AEGLRSS**	**AEGNSSY**	heavily	**AEHLPSS**
prisage	largess	gayness	**AEHIMMR**	hapless
AEGIRRZ	**AEGLRST**	**AEGOPRT**	hammier	**AEHLPSY**
grazier	largest	portage	**AEHIMST**	shapely
AEGIRSS	**AELGRTY**	**AEGOPST**	atheism	**AEHLRST**
gassier	greatly	postage	**AEHINNT**	slather
AEGIRST	**AEGLRVY**	pottage	anthine	**AEHLRTY**
seagirt	gravely	**AEGORRT**	**AEHIORR**	earthly
AEGIRSV	**AEGLSSS**	garrote	hoarier	**AEHLSSS**
gravies	glasses	**AEGORRT**	**AEHIPPR**	slashes
AEGIRTV	**AEGLSTT**	storage	happier	**AEHLSTT**
virgate	gestalt	**AEGORST**	**AEHIPPT**	stealth
AEGJLNR	**AEGLUVY**	**AEGORTT**	epitaph	**AEHLTWY**
jangler	vaguely	garotte	**AEHIPRS**	wealthy
AEGLLLY	**AEGMMRU**	**AEGORTU**	harpies	**AEHMMRS**
legally	rummage	outrage	sharpie	shammer
AEGLLNO	**AEGMNOR**	**AEGORVY**	**AEHIPSS**	**AEHMNOR**
galleon	megaron	voyager	aphesis	menorah
AEGLLOR	**AEGMNOS**	**AEGOSSU**	**AEHIRRR**	**AEHMNPY**
allegro	mangoes	gaseous	harrier	nymphae
AEGLLOT	**AEGMNOT**	**AEGOSTW**	**AEHIRRS**	**AEHMOPT**
tollage	magneto	stowage	harries	apothem
AEGLLRY	megaton	**AEGPRRS**	**AEHIRST**	**AEHMPTY**
allergy	montage	grasper	hastier	empathy
gallery	**AEGMNPY**	**AEGPRRY**	**AEHIRSW**	**AEHMRSS**
largely	pygmean	grapery	washier	marshes
AEGLMOU	**AEGMNRT**	**AEGPSTU**	**AEHIRWY**	smasher
moulage	garment	upstage	haywire	**AEHMRST**
AEGLMPU	**AEGMNTU**	**AEGRRUV**	**AEHISST**	hamster
plumage	augment	gravure	ashiest	**AEHMSSS**
AEGLNOT	**AEGMOOR**	**AEGRSSS**	**AEHISTT**	smashes
angelot	moorage	grasses	atheist	**AEHMUZZ**
tangelo	**AEGMOXY**	**AEGRSTV**	**AEHISTZ**	mezuzah
AEGLNPR	exogamy	gravest	haziest	**AEHNOPT**
grapnel	**AEGMPPU**	**AEGRSTY**	**AEHISVY**	phaeton
AEGLNPS	pumpage	grayest	yeshiva	phonate
spangle	**AEGNNOT**	**AEGSTUV**	**AEHITTW**	**AEHNORS**
AEGLNRT	tonnage	vaguest	thwaite	hoarsen
tangler	**AEGNNRT**	**AEHHLTY**	**AEHKNRT**	senhora
AEGLNRU	regnant	healthy	thanker	**AEHNORT**
granule	**AEGNNTT**	**AEHHNRS**	**AEHKOSS**	another
AEGLNRW	tangent	harshen	shakoes	**AEHNPRS**
wrangle	**AEGNNTU**	**AEHHRRS**	**AEHLLUV**	sharpen
AEGLNTT	tunnage	harsher	helluva	**AEHNPRT**
gantlet	**AEGNOOR**	**AEHIIRR**	**AEHLLYZ**	panther
AEGLNUU	oregano	hairier	hazelly	**AEHNRSS**
ungulae	**AEGNOPT**	**AEHIKNS**	**AEHLMNO**	harness
AEGLNUW	pontage	hankies	manhole	**AEHNRTU**
gunwale	**AEGNORR**	**AEHIKRS**	**AEHLMOR**	haunter
AEGLOPR	groaner	shakier	armhole	unearth
pergola	**AEGNORT**	**AEHILNR**	**AEHLMRT**	**AEHNRTX**
AEGLORT	negator	hernial	thermal	narthex
gloater	**AEGNORW**	**AEHILNY**	**AEHLMRU**	**AEHNSTY**
legator	wagoner	hyaline	humeral	shantey
AEGLOSS	**AEGNOST**	**AEHILPR**	**AEHLNOT**	**AEHORRS**
glossae	onstage	harelip	ethanol	hoarser
AEGLOTV	**AEGNOSY**		**AEHLNSU**	**AEHORST**

earshot	javelin	**AEILMPR**	**AEILRSS**	pastime
AEHORTX	**AEIJMNS**	lempira	airless	**AEIMRRS**
oxheart	jasmine	palmier	**AEILRST**	marries
AEHPPRS	**AEIJRZZ**	**AEILMRR**	realist	**AEIMRST**
perhaps	jazzier	larmier	saltier	maestri
AEHPRRS	**AEIKLLW**	**AEILMRS**	saltire	**AEIMRTT**
sharper	lawlike	realism	**AEILRSV**	martite
AEHPRTY	**AEIKLNO**	**AEILMRT**	revisal	**AEIMRTU**
therapy	kaoline	maltier	**AEILRTT**	muriate
AEHQSSU	**AEIKLNR**	**AEILMSS**	tertial	**AEIMRTW**
quashes	lankier	aimless	**AEILRTY**	wartime
AEHRRST	**AEIKLOT**	**AEILNNY**	irately	**AEIMSST**
trasher	keitloa	inanely	reality	tamises
AEHRRTU	**AEIKLRW**	**AEILNOP**	tearily	**AEIMSSV**
urethra	warlike	opaline	**AEILRVV**	massive
AEHRSST	**AEIKMST**	**AEILNOR**	revival	**AEIMSSW**
rashest	mistake	aileron	**AEILRVY**	swamies
AEHRSTT	**AEIKNRS**	**AEILNOT**	virelay	**AEIMSTZ**
shatter	snakier	elation	**AEILRWY**	maziest
AEHRSTV	**AEIKNRT**	**AEILNPR**	wearily	**AEINNNS**
harvest	keratin	plainer	**AEILSTV**	nannies
AEHRSVW	**AEIKPRW**	praline	estival	**AEINNPR**
wharves	pawkier	**AEILNPS**	**AEILSTZ**	pannier
AEHRSXY	**AEIKQRU**	spaniel	laziest	**AEINNPT**
hyraxes	quakier	**AEILNPT**	**AEILTVY**	pinnate
AEHRTUU	**AEIKRSW**	pantile	vilayet	**AEINOPS**
hauteur	skiwear	**AEILNPX**	**AEIMMMS**	epinaos
AEHSSST	**AEILLOV**	explain	mammies	**AEINORS**
stashes	alveoli	**AEILNRT**	**AEIMNOR**	erasion
AEHSSSW	**AEILLPS**	entrail	moraine	**AEINOSV**
swashes	illapse	latrine	romaine	evasion
AEHSTUX	**AEILLRS**	ratline	**AEIMNRR**	**AEINPPP**
exhaust	rallies	reliant	mariner	panpipe
AEIILNN	**AEILLRT**	**AEILNRY**	**AEIMNRS**	**AEINPRR**
aniline	literal	nailery	seminar	nappier
AEIILNR	**AEILLSS**	**AEILNST**	**AEIMNRT**	**AEINPPS**
airline	sallies	elastin	minaret	nappies
AEIILSS	**AEILLST**	salient	raiment	**AEINPRT**
silesia	tallies	saltine	**AEIMNRV**	painter
AEIILTX	**AEILLUV**	**AEILNVY**	vermian	pertain
exitial	eluvial	naively	**AEIMNSS**	**AEINPSS**
AEIIMNT	**AEILLVX**	**AEILOST**	samisen	pansies
intimae	vexilla	isolate	**AEIMNST**	**AEINPST**
AEIIMPR	**AEILMMN**	**AEILOTV**	inmeats	panties
imperia	mailmen	violate	**AEIMNTY**	sapient
AEIIMRT	**AEILMMS**	**AEILPPS**	amenity	**AEINPTT**
airtime	melisma	applies	anytime	patient
AEIIMTT	**AEILMNN**	**AEILPRT**	**AEIMORR**	**AEINPTU**
imitate	lineman	partile	armoire	petunia
AEIINNS	**AEILMNP**	**AEILPRV**	**AEIMOST**	**AEINQTU**
asinine	impanel	prevail	atomies	antique
AEIINRR	maniple	**AEILPSS**	**AEIMOTX**	quinate
rainier	**AEILMNR**	palsies	toxemia	**AEINRRT**
AEIINRT	manlier	**AEILPST**	**AEIMOTZ**	terrain
inertia	marline	talipes	atomize	trainer
AEIIPRR	mineral	**AEILPSY**	**AEIMPRS**	**AEINRST**
prairie	**AEILMNS**	paisley	impresa	nastier
AEIIRST	malines	**AEILQTU**	**AEIMPRT**	stainer
airiest	seminal	liquate	primate	**AEINRTT**
AEIITTV	**AEILMNT**	tequila	**AEIMPRV**	iterant
vitiate	ailment	**AEILRRT**	vampire	nattier
AEIJKLW	aliment	retrial	**AEIMPSS**	nitrate
jawlike	**AEILMOR**	trailer	impasse	tertian
AEIJLNV	loamier		**AEIMPST**	**AEINRTU**

ruinate	pyrexia	klavern	trammel	trental
taurine	**AEIPSSS**	**AEKLPRS**	**AELMMSY**	**AELNRTU**
urinate	asepsis	sparkle	malmsey	neutral
AEINRTW	**AEIPSST**	**AEKNOOR**	**AELMNOR**	**AELNRTV**
tawnier	pasties	roanoke	nemoral	ventral
tinware	patsies	**AEKNPRS**	**AELMNOT**	**AELNRUV**
AEINSST	**AEIPSSV**	spanker	telamon	unravel
entasis	passive	**AEKNRST**	**AELMNRU**	**AELNSSU**
sestina	**AEIPSTT**	rankest	numeral	sensual
tansies	patties	**AEKNRVY**	**AELMNSS**	**AELNSSX**
AEINSTT	**AEIRRRT**	knavery	manless	laxness
satinet	tarrier	**AEKNSSU**	**AELMNSU**	**AELOORS**
AEINSTU	**AEIRRST**	ankuses	mensual	aerosol
sinuate	tarries	**AEKOPRS**	**AELMOPR**	roseola
AEINSTW	tarsier	presoak	pleroma	**AELOPRT**
waniest	**AEIRRTT**	**AEKOTTU**	**AELMORV**	prolate
AEINSTX	rattier	takeout	removal	**AELOPRV**
sextain	**AIERRTW**	**AEKPRRS**	**AELMOST**	overlap
AEINSTZ	wartier	sparker	maltose	**AELOPST**
zaniest	**AEIRSSS**	**AEKPSSY**	**AELMOSY**	apostle
AEINSVV	sassier	passkey	amylose	**AELOPTT**
navvies	**AEIRSSU**	**AEKQSUY**	**AELMPRS**	paletot
AEINSWY	sauries	squeaky	sampler	**AELORSS**
anywise	**AEIRSTT**	**AEKRSTY**	**AELMPRT**	lassoer
AEINTVY	artiste	streaky	templar	oarless
naivety	striate	**AELLMRS**	trample	**AELORTV**
AEINTXY	tastier	smaller	**AELMPRY**	levator
anxiety	**AEIRSTW**	**AELLMSU**	lamprey	**AELORUU**
AEIOPRS	wariest	malleus	**AELMPST**	rouleau
soapier	**AEIRTTT**	**AELLMSY**	amplest	**AELORVY**
AEIOQSU	titrate	mesally	**AELMRSS**	layover
sequoia	**AEIRTUY**	**AELLMWX**	armless	overlay
AEIORST	aureity	maxwell	**AELMRTT**	**AELOSSS**
otaries	**AEIRTUZ**	**AELLNOV**	martlet	lassoes
AEIORSV	azurite	novella	**AELMSST**	**AELOSSV**
ovaries	**AEIRTVY**	**AELLNVY**	matless	salvoes
AEIOTZZ	variety	venally	**AELNNRT**	**AELOSTV**
azotize	**AEISSUV**	**AELLORS**	lantern	solvate
AEIPPRS	suasive	rosella	**AELNNRU**	**AELOSUZ**
apprise	**AEISSUX**	**AELLORV**	unlearn	zealous
sappier	auxesis	overall	**AELNNTU**	**AELOTUV**
AEIPRRS	**AEISTTU**	**AELLPRU**	annulet	ovulate
aspirer	situate	pleural	**AELNOPT**	**AELPPRY**
parries	**AEISTTY**	**AELLQUY**	polenta	reapply
praiser	satiety	equally	**AELNOTV**	**AELPRST**
raspier	**AEISTVW**	**AELLRST**	volante	plaster
AEIPRSS	waviest	stellar	**AELNPPY**	psalter
paresis	**AEISTWX**	**AELLRTY**	playpen	stapler
AEIPRST	waxiest	alertly	**AELNPRT**	**AELPRSU**
parties	**AEJLNUV**	**AELLSSW**	pantler	perusal
pastier	juvenal	lawless	planter	**AELPRSY**
piaster	**AEJLOSU**	**AELLSTT**	**AELNPRY**	parsley
traipse	jealous	tallest	plenary	sparely
AEIPRSU	**AEJLSSW**	**AELLSTW**	**AELNPSS**	**AELPRTT**
upraise	jawless	setwall	napless	partlet
AEIPRSW	**AEJMNZZ**	**AELLTUU**	**AELNPTY**	platter
waspier	jazzmen	ululate	aplenty	prattle
AEIPRTT	**AEJMSTY**	**AELMMNO**	penalty	**AELPRTY**
partite	majesty	mamelon	**AELNQUU**	peytral
AEIPRTV	**AEJNNOS**	**AELMMOY**	unequal	pteryla
private	joannes	myeloma	**AELNRST**	**AELPRUV**
AEIPRTW	**AEJOOPV**	**AELMMRS**	saltern	parvule
wiretap	apojove	slammer	sternal	**AELPSSS**
AEIPRXY	**AEKLNRV**	**AELMMRT**	**AELNRTT**	sapless

AELPSTU	oarsmen	**AENNPRS**	praetor	**AERSTUY**
pulsate	**AEMNORU**	spanner	**AEOPRST**	estuary
AELQRRU	enamour	**AENNRTT**	seaport	**AESSTUV**
quarrel	**AEMNPTY**	entrant	**AEOPRWY**	suavest
AELQTUZ	payment	**AENNRTY**	ropeway	**AESTTTU**
quetzal	**AEMNRST**	tannery	**AEOQRTU**	statute
AELRRTT	smarten	**AENNSSW**	equator	**AFFGGIN**
rattler	**AEMNRSU**	wanness	**AEOQRUV**	gaffing
AELRRTW	surname	**AENNSTT**	vaquero	**AFFHIRS**
trawler	**AEMNSTY**	tannest	**AEOQSUU**	raffish
AELRSST	amnesty	**AENNSTW**	aqueous	**AFFILSY**
artless	**AEMNTTU**	wannest	**AEORRST**	falsify
AELRSSY	nutmeat	**AENOPPR**	roaster	**AFFIMST**
rayless	**AEMOORT**	propane	**AEORRSV**	mastiff
AELRSTT	tearoom	**AENOPRS**	savorer	**AFFINRU**
slatter	**AEMOOSV**	persona	**AEORSTT**	ruffian
starlet	vamoose	**AENOPRT**	toaster	**AFFINTY**
startle	**AEMOPPR**	operant	**AEORSUU**	tiffany
AELRSTU	pampero	**AENORRV**	aureous	**AFFNORS**
saluter	**AEMOPRT**	overran	**AEORSVW**	saffron
AELRSTV	pteroma	**AENORST**	oversaw	**AFFNORT**
vestral	**AEMORRR**	senator	**AEORTUW**	affront
AELRSTW	armorer	treason	outwear	**AFGGGIN**
wastrel	**AEMORST**	**AENOSVW**	**AEORTVX**	fagging
AELRSVY	maestro	waveson	overtax	**AFGHHIS**
slavery	**AEMOSUZ**	**AENPPRS**	**AEPPRRT**	hagfish
AELRTTT	zamouse	snapper	trapper	**AFGHINS**
tartlet	**AEMOSWY**	**AENPRRT**	**AEPPRRW**	fashing
tattler	someway	partner	wrapper	**AFGHINT**
AELRTUV	**AEMOTTZ**	**AENPRRW**	**AEPQRTU**	hafting
vaulter	mozetta	prewarn	parquet	**AFGHIRS**
AELRTWZ	**AEMPRST**	**AENPRST**	**AEPRRSS**	garfish
waltzer	stamper	pastern	sparser	**AFGHRTU**
AELSSTT	**AEMPRTU**	**AENPRTT**	**AEPRRSY**	fraught
stalest	tempura	pattern	sprayer	**AFGIIKN**
AELSSTU	**AEMPTTT**	**AENPRUV**	**AEPRRTU**	faiking
taluses	attempt	parvenu	rapture	**AFGIILN**
AELSSTX	**AEMQRSU**	**AENPSST**	**AEPRSST**	failing
taxless	masquer	aptness	sparest	**AFGIINR**
AELSTTY	**AEMRRRY**	patness	**AEPRSSY**	fairing
stately	remarry	**AENPSSY**	pessary	**AFGIKLN**
AELSTWZ	**AEMRRST**	synapse	**AEPRSTT**	flaking
waltzes	armrest	**AENPSTW**	spatter	**AFGILMN**
AELSUVY	**AEMRRTU**	stewpan	tapster	flaming
suavely	smarter	**AENRRTY**	**AEPRSTU**	**AFGILNO**
AELTTTW	erratum	ternary	pasture	foaling
twattle	**AEMRRSU**	**AENRSTU**	**AEPRTXY**	loafing
AELTTUX	masseur	saunter	apteryx	**AFGILNR**
textual	**AEMRSTT**	**AENRSTV**	**AEPSSTU**	flaring
AEMMMOS	smatter	servant	petasus	**AFGILNS**
mammose	**AEMRSTU**	versant	**AEQRRSU**	falsing
AEMMNOT	strumae	**AENRTTU**	squarer	**AFGILNT**
momenta	**AEMRSTW**	taunter	**AEQRRTU**	fatling
AEMMRST	warmest	**AENSSTU**	quarter	**AFGILNU**
stammer	**AEMRSTY**	senatus	**AEQRTTU**	gainful
AEMMNOT	mastery	**AENSTTU**	quartet	**AFGILNW**
montane	**AEMRTTX**	tetanus	**AEQRUVY**	flawing
AEMNNOU	martext	**AENSTTX**	quavery	**AFGILNY**
noumena	**AEMRTUU**	sextant	**AERRSTT**	flaying
AEMNNRT	trumeau	**AEOOPPS**	starter	**AFGIMNO**
remnant	**AENNNPT**	papoose	**AERSTTU**	foaming
AEMNNSW	pennant	**AEOPPRV**	stature	**AFGIMNR**
newsman	**AENNOTU**	approve	**AERSTTW**	farming
AEMNORS	tonneau	**AEOPRRT**	swatter	framing

AFGIMNY	amplify	fanwort	arguing	**AGHINPP**
magnify	**AFILNPU**	**AFOSTUU**	**AGGINRV**	happing
AFGINNN	painful	fatuous	graving	**AGHINPR**
fanning	**AFILNTY**	**AGGGGIN**	**AGGINRY**	harping
AFGINNW	faintly	gagging	graying	**AGHINPS**
fawning	**AFILORW**	**AGGGIJN**	**AGGINRZ**	hasping
AFGINRT	airflow	jagging	grazing	phasing
farting	**AFILOTX**	**AGGGILN**	**AGGINSS**	shaping
rafting	foxtail	lagging	gassing	**AGHINPT**
AFGINRY	**AFILQUY**	**AGGGINN**	**AGGINST**	pathing
fraying	qualify	ganging	staging	**AGHINRS**
AFGINRZ	**AFILRTY**	nagging	**AGGISTW**	garnish
frazing	frailty	**AGGGINR**	waggist	sharing
AFGINST	**AFILSSY**	ragging	**AGGMOTY**	**AGHINSS**
fasting	salsify	**AGGGINS**	maggoty	sashing
AFGINTT	**AFILSTU**	sagging	**AGHHINS**	**AGHINST**
fatting	fistula	**AGGGINT**	hashing	hasting
AFGINTW	**AFILSTY**	tagging	**AGHHIWY**	**AGHINSU**
wafting	falsity	**AGGGINU**	highway	anguish
AFGIRTY	**AFINNOT**	gauging	**AGHHMOT**	**AGHINSV**
gratify	fontina	**AGGGINW**	hagmoth	shaving
AFGMNOR	**AFINORS**	wagging	**AGHHOSW**	**AGHINSW**
frogman	insofar	**AGGHHIS**	hogwash	washing
AFGOOTT	**AFINSTU**	haggish	**AGHHTUY**	**AGHINTT**
fagotto	fustian	**AGGHIMN**	haughty	hatting
AFHIIRS	**AFISSTT**	gingham	**AGHIILN**	**AGHINTW**
fairish	sitfast	**AGGHINN**	hailing	thawing
AFHIMNU	**AFISSTY**	hanging	**AGHIKNN**	**AGHIOST**
hafnium	satisfy	**AGGHINS**	hanking	goatish
AFHINOS	**AFITTUY**	gashing	**AGHIKNR**	**AGHKOSW**
fashion	fatuity	**AGGIIMN**	harking	goshawk
AFHINPS	**AFKLNRY**	imaging	**AGHIKNS**	**AGHLMPU**
panfish	frankly	**AGGIINN**	shaking	glaumph
AFHIORS	**AFKLNTU**	gaining	**AGHIKNW**	**AGHLOSU**
oarfish	tankful	**AGGIKNW**	hawking	goulash
AFHISSW	**AFLLOTU**	gawking	**AGHILNO**	**AGHLSTY**
sawfish	fallout	**AGGILLN**	haloing	ghastly
AFHISTT	**AFLLPUY**	galling	**AGHILNR**	**AGHNOTU**
fattish	playful	**AGGILNN**	harling	hangout
AFHISWY	**AFLLUWY**	angling	**AGHILNS**	**AGHNTUY**
fishway	awfully	**AGGILNR**	lashing	naughty
AFHKORY	**AFLMORU**	glaring	shaling	**AGIIJLN**
hayfork	formula	**AGGILNZ**	**AGHILNT**	jailing
AFHLMRU	**AFLMOST**	glazing	halting	**AGIILMN**
harmful	flotsam	**AGGIMMN**	lathing	mailing
AFHLOTY	**AFLMSUU**	gamming	**AGHILNU**	**AGIILNN**
hayloft	famulus	**AGGIMNU**	hauling	alining
AFIILOR	**AFLNORT**	gauming	**AGHILNV**	nailing
airfoil	frontal	**AGGINNR**	halving	**AGIILNR**
AFIILRT	**AFLNTUY**	ranging	**AGHILNW**	railing
airlift	flaunty	**AGGINNT**	whaling	**AGIILNS**
AFIKNRT	**AFLOPTT**	tanging	**AGHILOT**	sailing
ratfink	flattop	**AGGINNU**	goliath	**AGIILNT**
AFILLNY	**AFLPRTY**	unaging	**AGHILRS**	tailing
finally	flytrap	**AGGINNW**	largish	**AGIILNV**
AFILLPT	**AFMNOOT**	gnawing	**AGHIMMN**	vailing
pitfall	footman	**AGGINPP**	hamming	**AGIILNW**
AFILLPU	**AFMNRSU**	gapping	**AGHIMNR**	wailing
pailful	surfman	**AGGINPS**	harming	**AGIILPT**
AFILLUV	**AFMORST**	gasping	**AGHIMNS**	pigtail
fluvial	farmost	**AGGINRT**	mashing	**AGIILTY**
AFILLUW	**AFMOSTU**	grating	shaming	agility
wailful	sfumato	targing	**AGHINOX**	**AGIIMMN**
AFILMPY	**AFNORTW**	**AGGINRU**	hoaxing	maiming

AGIIMMS	skating	valuing	pignora	razzing
imagism	staking	**AGILNVV**	**AGINOPS**	**AGINSSS**
AGIIMOR	tasking	valving	soaping	sassing
origami	**AGILLLN**	**AGILNWY**	**AGINORR**	**AGINSTT**
AGIINNP	lalling	yawning	roaring	stating
paining	**AGILLMN**	**AGILORS**	**AGINORS**	tasting
AGIINNR	malling	girasol	signora	**AGINSTV**
ingrain	**AGILLMU**	**AGIMMNR**	soaring	staving
raining	gallium	ramming	**AGINORT**	**AGINSTW**
AGIINPR	**AGILLNP**	**AGIMNNN**	orating	wasting
pairing	palling	manning	**AGINOST**	**AGINSTY**
AGIINRS	**AGILLNU**	**AGIMNNO**	agonist	staying
raising	lingual	moaning	**AGINOVW**	**AGINSWY**
AGIINSV	lingula	**AGIMNOR**	avowing	swaying
visaing	**AGILLNW**	roaming	**AGINPPP**	**AGINTTT**
AGIINTW	walling	**AGIMNPP**	papping	tatting
waiting	**AGILLNY**	mapping	**AGINPPR**	**AGINTTV**
AGIINTX	allying	**AGIMNPR**	rapping	vatting
taxiing	**AGILLOR**	ramping	**AGINPPS**	**AGINTXY**
AGIINVW	gorilla	**AGIMNPT**	sapping	taxying
waiving	**AGILLOT**	tamping	**AGINPPT**	**AGIRTVY**
AGIJMMN	galliot	**AGIMNPV**	tapping	gravity
jamming	**AGILMMN**	vamping	**AGINPPW**	**AGJLRUU**
AGIJNPU	lamming	**AGIMNRR**	wapping	jugular
jauping	**AGILMNO**	marring	**AGINPPY**	**AGKMNOP**
AGIJNRR	loaming	**AGIMNRT**	yapping	kampong
jarring	**AGILMNP**	migrant	**AGINPPZ**	**AGLLNOO**
AGIJNSW	palming	**AGIMNRW**	zapping	galloon
jigsawn	**AGILMNT**	warming	**AGINPRR**	**AGLLNTU**
AGIJNZZ	malting	**AGIMNSS**	parring	gallnut
jazzing	**AGILMNU**	massing	**AGINPRS**	**AGLLOOT**
AGIKKNY	mauling	**AGIMNSU**	parsing	galloot
yakking	**AGILNNO**	amusing	rasping	**AGLLOSS**
AGIKLNO	loaning	**AGIMNTT**	sparing	glossal
oakling	**AGILNNP**	matting	**AGINPRT**	**AGLLOSW**
AGIKLNR	planing	**AGIMORU**	parting	gallows
larking	**AGILNNS**	gourami	prating	**AGLLOTT**
AGIKLNS	linsang	**AGINNNP**	**AGINPRW**	glottal
slaking	**AGILNPP**	panning	warping	**AGLMORU**
AGIKLNT	lapping	**AGINNNT**	**AGINPRY**	glamour
talking	**AGILNPR**	tanning	praying	**AGLNORU**
AGIKLNW	parling	**AGINNNW**	**AGINPSS**	languor
walking	**AGILNPS**	wanning	passing	**AGLNPSY**
AGIKMNR	lapsing	**AGINNOT**	**AGINPST**	spangly
marking	sapling	atoning	pasting	**AGLNTUY**
AGIKMNS	**AGILNPT**	**AGINNPP**	**AGINPSU**	gauntly
masking	plating	napping	pausing	**AGLOOPY**
AGIKNNR	**AGILNPW**	**AGINNPT**	**AGINPSY**	apology
ranking	lapwing	panting	spaying	**AGLSYYZ**
AGIKNNS	**AGILNPY**	**AGINNPW**	**AGINPTT**	syzygal
snaking	playing	pawning	patting	**AGMNNOS**
AGIKNNT	**AGILNRY**	**AGINNRS**	**AGINQUY**	songman
tanking	angrily	snaring	quaying	**AGMNORU**
AGIKNNY	**AGILNST**	**AGINNRT**	**AGINRRT**	organum
yanking	lasting	ranting	tarring	**AGMNOST**
AGIKNOS	salting	**AGINNRW**	**AGINRRW**	amongst
soaking	slating	warning	warring	**AGMNSTU**
AGIKNOY	staling	**AGINNRY**	**AGINRST**	mustang
kayoing	**AGILNSV**	yarning	staring	**AGMNSTY**
AGIKNPR	salving	**AGINNTW**	**AGINRTT**	gymnast
parking	slaving	wanting	ratting	**AGMOPRR**
AGIKNQU	**AGILNSY**	**AGINNWY**	**AGINRVY**	program
quaking	slaying	yawning	varying	**AGNNNOO**
AGIKNST	**AGILNUV**	**AGINOPR**	**AGINRZZ**	nonagon

AGNNOOR	azimuth	**AHMNORY**	**AIIMNPT**	**AILMNNO**
organon	**AHINNST**	harmony	timpani	nominal
AGNORRT	tannish	**AHMNOSW**	**AIIMNRT**	**AILMNOS**
grantor	**AHINNTX**	showman	martini	malison
AGNRTUY	xanthin	**AHMOOPS**	**AIIMNST**	**AILMNOY**
gauntry	**AHINORT**	shampoo	animist	alimony
AGOPPST	orthian	**AHMORST**	**AIIMNTU**	**AILMNPT**
stopgap	**AHINOTZ**	harmost	minutia	implant
AGORRTW	hoatzin	**AHNOOPR**	**AIIMNTV**	**AILMOPT**
ragwort	**AHINRST**	harpoon	vitamin	optimal
AGOSUYZ	tarnish	**AHNORSX**	**AIIMRST**	**AILMPST**
azygous	**AHINRSV**	saxhorn	simitar	palmist
AHHHISS	varnish	**AHNOTTW**	**AIINNTY**	**AILMPSY**
hashish	**AHIORST**	whatnot	inanity	misplay
AHHIKSW	shortia	**AHNPPUY**	**AIINOTT**	**AILMRST**
hawkish	**AHIPRST**	unhappy	notitia	mistral
AHHISTT	harpist	**AHNPRXY**	**AIINPRS**	**AILNNOT**
shittah	**AHIPRSW**	pharynx	aspirin	antlion
AHHLRSY	warship	**AHOPRTY**	**AIINPST**	**AILNPSX**
harshly	**AHIPSSW**	atrophy	pianist	salpinx
AHHOPRS	waspish	**AHOPTTW**	**AIIPTTU**	**AILNPTU**
shophar	**AHIPSWW**	towpath	pituita	nuptial
AHIIKRS	whipsaw	**AHORTTY**	**AIJMMS**	**AILNPTY**
rikisha	**AHIPSWY**	throaty	jimjams	inaptly
shikari	shipway	**AHOSTUW**	**AIJLYZZ**	ptyalin
AHIINPR	**AHIRSTT**	washout	jazzily	**AILNQTU**
hairpin	athirst	**AHPRRTY**	**AIJNORT**	quintal
AHIIPRS	**AHKMORR**	phratry	janitor	**AILNRUS**
airship	markhor	**AHQSSUY**	**AIKKMNR**	insular
AHIKMNS	**AHLLOPS**	squashy	kirkman	**AILNSTY**
khamsin	shallop	**AHRSTWY**	**AIKLLNY**	nastily
AHIKMRS	**AHLLOST**	swarthy	lankily	saintly
kashmir	shallot	**AHRTUWY**	**AIKLMMN**	**AILNTTY**
AHIKMSW	**AHLLOSW**	thruway	milkman	nattily
mawkish	shallow	**AIIILMT**	**AIKLQUY**	**AILOPST**
AHIKNSV	**AHLLOTY**	militia	quakily	apostil
knavish	loathly	**AIIILNT**	**AIKLRTT**	topsail
AHIKPRS	tallyho	initial	titlark	**AILOPTV**
parkish	**AHLLPSU**	**AIIKMNN**	**AIKLSSY**	pivotal
AHILLST	phallus	manikin	skysail	**AILOQTU**
tallish	**AHLMNPY**	**AIILLLP**	**AIKMNNS**	aliquot
AHILLTT	nymphal	lapilli	kinsman	**AILORUX**
tallith	**AHLMNUY**	**AIILLMN**	**AILLMOT**	uxorial
AHILNPS	humanly	liminal	maillot	**AILORVY**
planish	**AHLMORU**	**AIILLNV**	**AILLMPU**	olivary
AHILPPY	humoral	villain	pallium	**AILPPTY**
happily	**AHLMSUU**	**AIILLQU**	**AILLMSW**	platypi
AHILPSY	hamulus	quillai	sawmill	**AILPQSU**
apishly	**AHLNOPR**	**AIILMMN**	**AILLNNO**	pasquil
AHILSST	alphorn	minimal	lanolin	**AILPSWY**
saltish	**AHLPRSY**	**AIILMRS**	**AILLNPY**	slipway
AHILSSV	sharply	. similar	plainly	**AILQTUY**
slavish	**AHLPRUY**	**AIILNOS**	**AILLNST**	quality
AHILSTU	hypural	liaison	install	**AILRRVY**
halitus	**AHLPSSY**	**AIILNPT**	**AILLORT**	rivalry
AHILSTY	splashy	pintail	litoral	**AILRSTT**
hastily	**AHMMMOT**	**AIILNTU**	**AILLPUV**	starlit
AHIMNNS	mammoth	nautili	pluvial	**AILRTTU**
mannish	**AHMNNTU**	**AIILORV**	**AILLSTY**	titular
AHIMNNU	manhunt	ravioli	saltily	**AILRTUV**
inhuman	**AHMNOPS**	**AIILRTV**	**AILLTVY**	virtual
AHIMNPS	shopman	trivial	vitally	**AILSTTY**
shipman	**AHMNOPT**	**AIIMMNS**	**AILMMOR**	tastily
AHIMTUZ	phantom	animism	immoral	**AILSTUW**

lawsuit	**AINOSSU**	suavity	usually	paronym
AIMMMUX	sanious	**AJKMNNU**	**ALMNNUY**	**AMNOPST**
maximum	suasion	junkman	unmanly	postman
AIMMNTU	**AINOSTT**	**AJLLRUY**	**ALMNOOP**	**AMNORST**
manumit	station	jurally	lampoon	transom
AIMMOST	**AINOSUX**	**AJLNORU**	**ALMNOPW**	**AMNORSY**
atomism	anxious	journal	plowman	masonry
AIMNNOS	**AINPPRS**	**AJMNRUY**	**ALMNOWY**	**AMNOSST**
mansion	parsnip	juryman	womanly	stamnos
onanism	**AINPQSU**	**AKKLRSY**	**ALMNSUU**	**AMNPTYY**
AIMNOOS	pasquin	skylark	alumnus	tympany
animoso	**AINPQTU**	**AKLOTUW**	**ALMOPRT**	**AMNQTUU**
AIMNOPR	piquant	walkout	marplot	quantum
rampion	**AINPRST**	**AKLRSTY**	**ALMOTTU**	**AMNRTTU**
AIMNOPT	spirant	starkly	mulatto	tantrum
maintop	**AINPRTU**	**AKMNORW**	**ALMRSTY**	**AMOOORS**
tampion	puritan	workman	smartly	amoroso
AIMNOTU	**AINQRUY**	**AKMORST**	**ALMSSUY**	**AMOOPRT**
manitou	quinary	ostmark	alyssum	taproom
tinamou	**AINQSTU**	**AKMQTUU**	**ALNNSUU**	**AMOORSU**
AIMNRRU	asquint	kumquat	annulus	amorous
murrain	**AINRRUY**	**AKMRSTU**	**ALNOOPT**	**AMORRWY**
AIMNRTV	urinary	muskrat	platoon	marrowy
varmint	**AINRSTT**	**AKNORTU**	**ALNOORT**	**AMRSTTU**
AIMNRUU	transit	outrank	ortolan	stratum
uranium	**AINRTUY**	**AKOOPRT**	**ALNOPPY**	**AMRTUUY**
AIMNSTU	unitary	partook	panoply	mutuary
tsunami	**AINSSTU**	**AKORRTW**	**ALNPTUY**	**ANNRTYY**
AIMNSYZ	issuant	artwork	unaptly	tyranny
zanyism	sustain	**AKORWWX**	**ALNSUUU**	**ANOOPRS**
AIMOPST	**AINSSXY**	waxwork	unusual	pronaos
impasto	synaxis	**ALLLOYY**	**ALOPPRU**	soprano
AIMORRU	**AINTTVY**	loyally	popular	**ANOOPRT**
orarium	tantivy	**ALLMORY**	**ALOPRSU**	patroon
AIMORST	**AIOPRRT**	morally	parlous	**ANOORTT**
amorist	airport	**ALLNOTY**	**ALOPSSU**	notator
AIMOSTT	**AIOPRTT**	tonally	spousal	**ANORSTU**
atomist	patriot	**ALLNOYZ**	**ALOQRRU**	rousant
AIMPRRY	**AIOPRTY**	zonally	rorqual	**ANPRTYY**
primary	topiary	**ALLNRUU**	**ALOQRSU**	prytany
AIMQRSU	**AIORRRW**	lunular	squalor	**AOOPPRS**
marquis	warrior	**ALLNTUU**	**ALORRST**	apropos
AINNQTU	**AIORRTT**	ululant	rostral	**AOOPRTT**
quintan	traitor	**ALLOOTX**	**ALORTYY**	taproot
AINNRTT	**AIORRTX**	axolotl	royalty	**AOORRTT**
intrant	oratrix	**ALLOPRY**	**ALOSTTU**	rotator
AINNSTT	**AIORSTT**	payroll	outlast	**AOORRTY**
instant	sortita	**ALLORWY**	**AMMNRUY**	oratory
AINNTUY	**AIORSTV**	rollway	nummary	**AOPPRRT**
annuity	travois	**ALLORYY**	**AMMRSUY**	rapport
AINOORR	**AIORSTY**	royally	summary	**AOPRRSW**
orarion	ostiary	**ALLOSWW**	**AMNNOSW**	sparrow
AINOORT	**AIORSUV**	swallow	snowman	**AOPRRTY**
oration	saviour	**ALLOTTY**	**AMNNOTY**	portray
AINOOTV	various	totally	antonym	**AOPRSTW**
ovation	**AIPRSTV**	**ALLOTWY**	**AMNOOPP**	postwar
AINOPPT	pristav	tallowy	pompano	**AOPSTUY**
appoint	**AIPRTVY**	**ALLOTYY**	**AMNOOTT**	autopsy
AINOPSS	pravity	loyalty	ottoman	**AOQRTUU**
passion	**AIRSSTT**	**ALLQSUY**	**AMNOPPR**	quatuor
AINORSW	tsarist	squally	propan	**AORRTWY**
warison	**AIRSTVY**	**ALLRSTU**	**AMNOPRT**	ryotwar
AINORTU	varsity	lustral	portman	**AORSSUY**
rainout	**AISTUVY**	**ALLSUUY**	**AMNOPRY**	ossuary

AORSUVY	**BBDEILN**	boobies	**BBGINTU**	**BCDENOU**
savoury	nibbled	**BBEIRRY**	tubbing	bounced
APPRSUY	**BBDEILO**	bribery	**BBGIOSU**	buncoed
papyrus	lobbied	**BBEIRTU**	gibbous	**BCDESUU**
APRSSSU	**BBDEILR**	tubbier	**BBHIRSU**	subduce
surpass	dribble	**BBEISSU**	rubbish	**BCDIORW**
APRSTTU	**BBDEIOS**	busbies	**BBHRSUY**	cowbird
upstart	dobbies	**BBEJORY**	shrubby	**BCDKORU**
AQRTUYZ	**BBDEKNO**	jobbery	**BBIKTUZ**	burdock
quartzy	knobbed	**BBELLOY**	kibbutz	**BCDSTUU**
AQSTTUY	**BBDELMU**	bellboy	**BBILNOY**	subduct
squatty	bumbled	**BBELMRU**	nobbily	**BCEEEHS**
ARSSTTU	**BBDELNO**	bumbler	**BBLOSUU**	beseech
stratus	nobbled	**BBELNOR**	bulbous	**BCEEFIN**
BBBDELO	**BBDELOS**	nobbler	**BCCEILO**	benefic
blobbed	bobsled	**BBELORS**	ecbolic	**BCEEGIR**
bobbled	**BBDELOW**	slobber	**BCCEILU**	iceberg
BBBDELU	wobbled	**BBELORW**	cubicle	**BCEEHLS**
bubbled	**BBDELRU**	wobbler	**BCCEILY**	belches
BBBELRU	burbled	**BBELSTU**	bicycle	**BCEEHNR**
blubber	**BBDELSU**	stubble	**BCCILOU**	bencher
bubbler	slubbed	**BBENRSU**	bucolic	**BCEEHOU**
BBBGIIN	**BBDENSU**	snubber	**BCCINOO**	bouchee
bibbing	snubbed	**BBEORRY**	obconic	**BCEEIRS**
BBBGINO	**BBDESTU**	robbery	**BCCISUU**	escribe
bobbing	stubbed	**BBERRUY**	succubi	**BCEEIRT**
BBCCIKO	**BBDGINU**	rubbery	**BCCMOOX**	terebic
bibcock	dubbing	**BBFGIIN**	coxcomb	**BCEEKUY**
BBCDEIR	**BBEEIRW**	fibbing	**BCCMSUU**	buckeye
cribbed	webbier	**BBFGINO**	succumb	**BCEENOS**
BBCDELO	**BBEFILR**	fobbing	**BCCNOOR**	obscene
cobbled	fribble	**BBGGIIN**	corncob	**BCEHINR**
BBCDELU	**BBEGILR**	gibbing	**BCDDEOU**	birchen
clubbed	glibber	**BBGGINO**	obduced	**BCEHIOR**
BBCEILR	gribble	gobbing	**BCDEEHL**	brioche
cribble	**BBEGINW**	**BBGIIJN**	belched	**BCEHITW**
BBCEISU	webbing	jibbing	**BCDEEHN**	bewitch
cubbies	**BBEGLOR**	**BBGIINN**	benched	**BCEHLRU**
BBCELOR	gobbler	nibbing	**BCDEEIL**	blucher
cobbler	**BBEHINS**	**BBGIINR**	decibel	**BCEHNSU**
BBCGINU	nebbish	bribing	**BCDEHNU**	bunches
cubbing	**BBEHIOS**	ribbing	bunched	**BCEHORT**
BBCINOU	hobbies	**BBGIJNO**	**BCDEHOT**	botcher
bubonic	**BBEHISU**	jobbing	botched	**BCEHOST**
BBCRSUY	hubbies	**BBGILNO**	**BCDEHOU**	botches
scrubby	**BBEHLOR**	lobbing	debouch	**BCEHRTU**
BBDDEIL	hobbler	**BBGILNU**	**BCDEIKR**	butcher
dibbled	**BBEIIMR**	bulbing	bricked	**BCEIKLR**
BBDDERU	imbiber	**BBGIMNO**	**BCDEIKS**	brickle
drubbed	**BBEILNR**	bombing	sickbed	**BCEILMO**
BBDEELP	nibbler	mobbing	**BCDEILM**	embolic
pebbled	**BBEILOS**	**BBGINNO**	climbed	**BCEILMR**
BBDEFLU	bilboes	nobbing	**BCDEIRS**	climber
flubbed	**BBEILOT**	**BBGINNU**	scribed	**BCEILOR**
BBDEGLO	bibelot	nubbing	**BCDEKLO**	bricole
gobbled	**BBEILQU**	**BBGINOR**	blocked	corbeil
BBDEGRU	quibble	robbing	**BCDEKLU**	**BCEIMNO**
grubbed	**BBEINOR**	**BBGINOS**	buckled	combine
BBDEHLO	biberon	sobbing	**BCDEKOR**	**BCEIMOR**
hobbled	nobbier	**BBGINRU**	bedrock	microbe
BBDEIIM	**BBEINRU**	rubbing	**BCDELOU**	**BCEINOZ**
imbibed	nubbier	**BBGINSU**	becloud	benzoic
BBDEIKL	**BBEIOOS**	gubbins	**BCDEMRU**	**BCEIRRS**
kibbled		subbing	crumbed	scriber

BCEJSTU	boycott	**BDEEHRT**	**BDEHLSU**	plumbed
subject	**BDDEEES**	berthed	blushed	**BDELMRU**
BCEKLOR	seedbed	**BDEEILL**	**BDEHMTU**	rumbled
blocker	**BDDEEIS**	bellied	thumbed	**BDELMTU**
BCEKLRU	bedside	libeled	**BDEHORY**	tumbled
buckler	**BDDEEIT**	**BDEEILV**	herdboy	**BDELNRU**
BCEKORU	betided	bedevil	**BDEHRSU**	blunder
roebuck	debited	**BDEEIMR**	brushed	**BDELNTU**
BCEKOSU	**BDDEELN**	bemired	**BDEIKLN**	blunted
buckoes	blended	**BDEEIMT**	blinked	**BDELOOR**
BCELLOW	**BDDEENO**	bedtime	**BDEILLU**	boodler
cowbell	deboned	**BDEEINR**	bullied	**BDELORU**
BCELMRU	**BDDEGIN**	inbreed	**BDEILMW**	boulder
crumble	bedding	**BDEEINZ**	wimbled	**BDELOST**
BCENORU	**BDDEGIR**	bedizen	**BDEILNR**	boldest
bouncer	bridged	**BDEEIRR**	blinder	**BDELOSU**
BCEORSU	**BDDEIIR**	berried	brindle	bloused
obscure	birdied	**BDEEIRS**	**BDEILOR**	**BDELOTT**
BCGIKNU	**BDDEIIS**	derbies	broiled	blotted
bucking	biddies	**BDEEKRU**	**BDEILPP**	bottled
BCGIMNO	**BDDEILN**	rebuked	blipped	**BDELOTU**
combing	blinded	**BDEELNR**	**BDEILRT**	doublet
BCGINRU	**BDDEILR**	blender	driblet	**BDELRRU**
curbing	bridled	**BDEELNT**	**BDEILRU**	blurred
BCHIKSU	**BDDEINR**	bendlet	builder	**BDELRTU**
buckish	brinded	**BDEELOV**	rebuild	blurted
BCHIMOR	**BDDEISU**	beloved	**BDEIMMR**	**BDELSSU**
rhombic	buddies	**BDEELOW**	brimmed	budless
BCHIOPR	**BDDELNU**	elbowed	**BDEIMNR**	**BDELSTU**
pibroch	bundled	**BDEELRT**	birdmen	bustled
BCHLOTY	**BDDELOO**	trebled	**BDEIMOR**	**BDEMOOR**
blotchy	blooded	**BDEELSS**	bromide	bedroom
BCHORST	**BDDELOU**	bedless	**BDEIMRU**	boredom
borscht	doubled	blessed	imbrued	**BDEMOOS**
BCIIKLN	**BDDENOU**	**BDEEMOW**	**BDEINRY**	bosomed
niblick	bounded	embowed	bindery	**BDEMSTU**
BCIILMU	**BDDEOOR**	**BDEEMRU**	**BDEIORS**	dumbest
bulimic	brooded	embrued	disrobe	**BDENORU**
umbilic	**BDDEOTU**	umbered	**BDEIORT**	bounder
BCIILSY	doubted	**BDEEMSU**	debitor	rebound
sibylic	**BDDESUU**	bemused	orbited	**BDENORW**
BCIINOS	subdued	**BDEENPR**	**BDEIORV**	browned
bionics	**BDDGIIN**	prebend	overbid	**BDENORZ**
BCIISTU	bidding	**BDEEORS**	**BDEIOSY**	bronzed
biscuit	**BDDGINU**	bedsore	disobey	**BDENSUY**
BCILOOR	budding	sobered	**BDEIRSU**	sebundy
bicolor	**BDEEELR**	**BDEFFLU**	bruised	**BDEOORR**
BCINORU	bleeder	bluffed	**BDEIRTU**	brooder
rubicon	**BDEEELT**	**BDEFLMU**	bruited	**BDEOOST**
BCINSUU	beetled	fumbled	**BDEISSU**	boosted
incubus	**BDEEELV**	**BDEGGLO**	subside	**BDEOPST**
BCKLLOU	beveled	boggled	**BDEITUY**	bedpost
bullock	**BDEEELZ**	**BDEGILO**	dubiety	**BDEORRU**
BCKOTTU	bezeled	obliged	**BDEJLMU**	bordure
buttock	**BDEEERR**	**BDEGINN**	jumbled	**BDEORSU**
BCLMOOU	breeder	bending	**BDEKOOR**	rosebud
coulomb	**BDEEERZ**	**BDEGIOT**	brooked	**BDEORSW**
BCLMRUY	breezed	bigoted	**BDELLOR**	browsed
crumbly	**BDEEFIR**	**BDEGLNU**	bedroll	**BDEORTU**
BCMOSTU	briefed	bungled	**BDELMMU**	doubter
combust	debrief	**BDEGLRU**	mumbled	obtrude
BCOOPYY	fibered	burgled	**BDELMOO**	redoubt
copyboy	**BDEEGOY**	**BDEHLMU**	bloomed	**BDGGINU**
BCOOTTY	bogeyed	humbled	**BDELMPU**	budging

BDGIINN
binding
BDGILOO
globoid
BDGINNO
bonding
BDGINOY
bodying
BDGLLOU
bulldog
BDHOOOY
boyhood
BDILLNY
blindly
BDINNOU
inbound
BDINOOR
bridoon
BDINRSU
sunbird
BDINSTU
dustbin
BDIOORU
boudoir
BDIOSUU
dubious
BDIRSTU
disturb
BDISSUY
subsidy
BDLOOOX
oxblood
BDNOORU
bourdon
BDNORUW
rubdown
BDOOOWX
boxwood
BEEEFIR
beefier
freebie
BEEEFLR
feebler
BEEEGIS
besiege
BEEEHIV
beehive
BEEEILN
beeline
BEEEILV
believe
BEEEIRR
beerier
BEEEJLW
bejewel
BEEENNZ
benzene
BEEENTW
between
BEEFGIN
beefing
BEEFILR
febrile
BEEFINT

benefit
BEEGILL
legible
BEEGILU
beguile
BEEGINU
beguine
BEEHIRR
herbier
BEEHOOV
behoove
BEEHRST
sherbet
BEEHRSW
beshrew
BEEHRTY
thereby
BEEHRWY
whereby
BEEHSTY
bheesty
BEEIJLU
jubilee
BEEIKLW
weblike
BEEILLR
libeler
BEEILLS
bellies
BEEILOS
obelise
BEEILOZ
obelize
BEEIMST
betimes
BEEINNS
bennies
BEEINNZ
benzine
BEEINOS
ebonies
BEEINOT
ebonite
BEEINOZ
ebonize
BEEINRZ
zebrine
BEEIQUZ
bezique
BEEIRRS
berries
BEEIRRV
brevier
BEEKNOT
betoken
BEEKOPS
bespoke
BEEKRRS
berserk
BEELMRT
tremble
BEELNNO
ennoble
BEELOSY

obesely
BEEMORW
embower
BEEMRTU
embrute
BEENOST
boneset
BEENSUV
subvene
BEEORRU
bourree
BEEORSV
observe
obverse
verbose
BEEORWY
eyebrow
BEEQSTU
bequest
BEERRWY
brewery
BEERSSU
rebuses
BEERTTU
burette
BEFFIRU
buffier
BEFFLRU
bluffer
BEFGIIL
filibeg
BEFGIRU
firebug
BEFILRT
filbert
BEFILRY
briefly
BEFILSU
fusible
BEFINOR
bonfire
BEFIRST
fibster
BEFIRVY
verbify
BEFOORR
forbore
BEFOOTW
webfoot
BEGGGIN
begging
BEGGIRU
buggier
BEGGIST
biggest
BEGGISU
buggies
BEGGLOR
boggler
BEGHRRU
burgher
BEGIINN
inbeing
BEGILLN

belling
BEGILLY
legibly
BEGILNO
ignoble
BEGILNT
belting
BEGILNU
blueing
BEGILNY
belying
BEGILRT
gilbert
BEGIMSU
gumbies
BEGINOY
biogeny
obeying
BEGINRW
brewing
BEGINSS
bigness
BEGINTT
betting
BEGKMOS
gemsbok
BEGLLOU
globule
BEGLMRU
grumble
BEGLNRU
bungler
BEGLOOT
bootleg
BEGNORU
burgeon
BEGRSSU
burgess
BEHIITX
exhibit
BEHIKLO
hoblike
BEHILMS
blemish
BEHILMT
thimble
BEHINOP
hipbone
BEHIOTW
howbeit
BEHIRRT
rebirth
BEHIRSU
bushier
BEHLLOP
bellhop
BEHLLOX
hellbox
BEHLMRU
humbler
BEHLORT
brothel
BEHLRSU
blusher

BEHLSSU
blushes
BEHMNSU
bushmen
BEHNOST
benthos
BEHOORT
theorbo
BEHOPRT
potherb
BEHORRT
brother
BEHORTT
betroth
BEHRSSU
brushes
BEIILLS
billies
BEIILRS
risible
BEIILSV
visible
BEIINRR
brinier
BEIKLNR
blinker
BEIKLOS
obelisk
BEIKLRU
bulkier
BEIKORS
boskier
BEIKRST
brisket
BEILLSU
bullies
BEILMNR
nimbler
BEILMOR
embroil
BEILMRT
timbrel
BEILMSU
sublime
BEILNOW
bowline
BEILNTZ
blintze
BEILOOS
loobies
BEILOQU
oblique
BEILORR
broiler
BEILORW
blowier
BEILRRU
burlier
BEILRSS
ribless
BEILRST
blister
bristle
BEILRTT

brittle	**BEKLOOT**	**BEMORST**	bushing	**BGINOSS**
BEILRTU	booklet	mobster	**BGHMORU**	bossing
rebuilt	**BEKMNOO**	**BENNORW**	homburg	**BGINOSU**
BEILRTY	bookmen	newborn	**BGHOORU**	bousing
liberty	**BEKNORS**	**BENORRW**	borough	**BGINOUY**
BEILSTU	bonkers	browner	**BGHORTU**	bouying
subtile	**BELLOSU**	**BENOSSU**	brought	**BGINRRU**
BEIMMRR	soluble	bonuses	**BGIIKLN**	burring
brimmer	**BELLOUV**	**BENOSWY**	bilking	**BGINRUY**
BEIMNOR	voluble	newsboy	**BGIILLN**	burying
bromine	**BELMMRU**	**BEOORST**	billing	**BGINSSU**
BEIMNTU	mumbler	booster	**BGIILNO**	bussing
bitumen	**BELMNSU**	**BEOORTY**	boiling	**BGINSUY**
BEIMPRU	numbles	bootery	**BGIILNR**	busying
bumpier	**BELMOOR**	**BEOPRRV**	birling	**BGINTTU**
BEINNOR	bloomer	proverb	**BGIILNS**	butting
bonnier	**BELMOOT**	**BEOQSUY**	sibling	**BGIORTY**
BEINNSU	boomlet	obsequy	**BGIIMNU**	bigotry
bunnies	**BELMOPR**	**BEOQTUU**	imbuing	**BGKLOOO**
BEINOOS	problem	bouquet	**BGIINNN**	logbook
boonies	**BELMORT**	**BEORRSW**	binning	**BGLNOOW**
BEINORW	temblor	browser	**BGIINNR**	longbow
brownie	**BELMOSU**	**BEORUVY**	brining	**BGLNOUW**
BEINOST	embolus	overbuy	**BGIKLNU**	blowgun
boniest	**BELMPRU**	**BEPRRTU**	bulking	**BHIIINT**
BEINOTT	plumber	perturb	**BGIKNNU**	inhibit
bottine	**BELMRSU**	**BEPRTUY**	bunking	**BHIKOOS**
BEINRTT	slumber	puberty	**BGIKNOO**	bookish
bittern	**BELMRTU**	**BEQRSUU**	booking	**BHILLSU**
BEINRTU	tumbler	brusque	**BGIKNRU**	bullish
tribune	tumbrel	**BERSTUV**	burking	**BHILPSU**
turbine	**BELMRTY**	subvert	**BGILLNU**	publish
BEIOOST	trembly	**BERTTUY**	bulling	**BHIMSTU**
booties	**BELMSTU**	buttery	**BGILNOT**	bismuth
BEIORRT	stumble	**BFFGINU**	bolting	**BHINRSU**
orbiter	**BELNOOY**	buffing	**BGILNOW**	burnish
BEIORSS	boloney	**BFFNOOU**	blowing	**BHIOORS**
bossier	**BELNOYZ**	buffoon	bowling	boorish
BEIOSSU	benzoyl	**BFHIRSU**	**BGILNOY**	**BHIRSTU**
soubise	**BELORST**	furbish	ignobly	brutish
BEIOSTX	bolster	**BFILMRU**	**BGILNRU**	**BHLRSUU**
boxiest	lobster	brimful	burling	bulrush
BEIOSTY	**BELORSY**	**BFIORSU**	**BGILOOY**	**BHMORSU**
obesity	soberly	fibrous	biology	rhombus
BEIQRTU	**BELORTT**	**BGGGINO**	**BGIMMNU**	**BHOOPSY**
briquet	blotter	bogging	bumming	shopboy
BEIRRSU	bottler	**BGGGINU**	**BGIMMNU**	**BHPRSUU**
bruiser	**BELORTU**	bugging	numbing	brushup
BEIRTTU	trouble	**BGGHIIS**	**BGIMNOO**	**BIILLNO**
tribute	**BELOSSU**	biggish	booming	billion
BEIRTVY	boluses	**BGGIILN**	**BGIMNPU**	**BIILOSU**
brevity	**BELOSTU**	bilging	bumping	bilious
BEIRUZZ	boletus	**BGGILNO**	**BGINNRU**	**BIILSVY**
buzzier	**BELRSTU**	globing	burning	visibly
BEISSTU	bluster	**BGGILNU**	**BGINNTU**	**BIIMNOU**
busiest	bustler	bugling	bunting	niobium
BEITTWX	**BELRTUY**	bulging	**BGINOOT**	**BIIMNSU**
betwixt	brutely	**BGGINNU**	booting	minibus
BEJKOUX	**BEMMOOS**	bunging	**BGINOOZ**	minisub
jukebox	embosom	**BGHHIOY**	boozing	**BIJNOSU**
BEJLMRU	**BEMNOSU**	highboy	**BGINOPP**	subjoin
jumbler	umbones	**BGHINOR**	bopping	**BIKLNOY**
BEJLOSS	**BEMNSTU**	bighorn	**BGINOPR**	linkboy
jobless	numbest	**BGHINSU**	probing	**BIKLRSY**

briskly	buttony	**CCEEHRS**	centric	**CCHNRSU**
BIKMNPU	**BOOPSTX**	screech	**CCEIOPP**	scrunch
bumpkin	postbox	**CCEEINS**	coppice	**CCHNRUY**
BILLNOU	**BOOPSTY**	science	**CCEIOPT**	crunchy
bullion	postboy	**CCEEIRV**	ectopic	**CCIILRU**
BILLOPX	**CCCNOOT**	crevice	**CCEIPST**	circuli
pillbox	concoct	**CCEEKOY**	sceptic	**CCIIRTU**
BILLOWY	**CCDEEHK**	cockeye	**CCEKNOY**	circuit
billowy	checked	**CCEELRY**	cockney	**CCIKLOW**
BILMNOR	**CCDEENO**	recycle	**CCEKOPT**	cowlick
nombril	concede	**CCEEORR**	petcock	**CCIKLOY**
BILOSSU	**CCDEENY**	coercer	**CCEKRT**	colicky
subsoil	decency	**CCEERSY**	crocket	**CCIKOPT**
BILRSTY	**CCDEEOR**	secrecy	**CCELLOT**	cockpit
bristly	coerced	**CCEFNOT**	collect	**CCILNOU**
BILRTUY	**CCDEESU**	confect	**CCELNOY**	council
tilbury	succeed	**CCEHIKN**	cyclone	**CCILOOP**
BIMNOSU	**CCDEHIN**	chicken	**CCENNOR**	piccolo
omnibus	cinched	**CCEHINS**	concern	**CCILSTY**
BIMOSSS	**CCDEHKO**	cinches	**CCENNOT**	cyclist
bossism	chocked	**CCEHINT**	concent	**CCINOOT**
BIOOSUV	**CCDEHKU**	technic	**CCENNOT**	coction
obvious	chucked	**CCEHIOR**	connect	**CCINOTV**
BIOPRTY	**CCDEHOU**	choicer	**CCENOPT**	convict
probity	couched	choreic	concept	**CCIOORS**
BISSSTU	**CCDEIIL**	**CCEHKLU**	**CCENORT**	sirocco
subsist	icicled	chuckle	concert	**CCIOPTU**
BKNOOTW	**CCDEIIT**	**CCEHKPU**	**CCENOTV**	occiput
bowknot	deictic	checkup	convect	**CCIPRTY**
BLLNTUY	**CCDEIKL**	**CCEHLRU**	**CCEOOTT**	cryptic
bluntly	clicked	cleruch	cocotte	**CCKOOPW**
BLLOSUU	**CCDEIKR**	**CCEHNOS**	**CCEORRT**	cowpock
bullous	cricked	conches	correct	**CCNOOTU**
BLLOSUY	**CCDEILR**	**CCEHORT**	**CCESSSU**	coconut
solubly	circled	crochet	success	**CCSSSUU**
BLLOUVY	**CCDEIOS**	**CCEHOSU**	**CCFIRUY**	succuss
volubly	codices	couches	crucify	**CDDDEEI**
BLMOOSS	**CCDEKLO**	**CCEIIRT**	**CCFLOSU**	decided
blossom	clocked	icteric	floccus	**CDDDEEO**
BLMOUXY	**CCDEKLU**	**CCEIKLR**	**CCGIKNO**	decoded
buxomly	clucked	clicker	cocking	**CDDDEEU**
BLMSTUY	**CCDEKOR**	**CCEIKLT**	**CCGILNY**	deduced
stumbly	crocked	clicket	cycling	**CDDDELO**
BLOOOTX	**CCDELOU**	**CCEIKOR**	**CCHHINY**	coddled
toolbox	occlude	cockier	chinchy	**CDDDELU**
BLOOQUY	**CCDENOS**	**CCEIKRT**	**CCHIIST**	cuddled
obloquy	sconced	cricket	stichic	**CDDDERU**
BLOORWW	**CCDENOU**	**CCEILNO**	**CCHILOR**	crudded
lowbrow	conduce	conicle	chloric	**CDDDESU**
BLOOTUW	**CCDIILO**	**CCEILOT**	**CCHIMOR**	scudded
blowout	codicil	coctile	chromic	**CDDEEER**
BLOPSTU	**CCDIIOR**	**CCEILRT**	**CCHINOR**	decreed
subplot	cricoid	circlet	chronic	receded
BMORSUU	**CCDILOY**	**CCEILSY**	**CCHIORY**	**CDDEEES**
brumous	cycloid	cylices	chicory	seceded
BNNRSUU	**CCDKLOU**	**CCEILTU**	**CCHIPSY**	**CDDEEII**
sunburn	cuckold	cuticle	psychic	deicide
BNOOTTY	**CCDNOOR**	**CCEINOR**	**CCHIRST**	**CDDEEIR**
bottony	concord	cornice	scritch	decried
BNORSUU	**CCDNOTU**	**CCEINOS**	**CCHKLOS**	**CDDEEIX**
burnous	conduct	concise	schlock	excided
BNORTUU	**CCEEHKR**	**CCEINOT**	**CCHKMSU**	**CDDEENO**
burnout	checker	conceit	schmuck	encoded
BNOTTUY		**CCEINRT**	**CCHKPUU**	**CDDEENS**
			upchuck	

descend	**CDEEHIP**	**CDEENST**	decking	chromed
scended	cepheid	descent	**CDEGILN**	**CDEHMOU**
CDDEEOY	**CDEEHIV**	scented	clinged	mouched
decoyed	chevied	**CDEEOPR**	**CDEGINO**	**CDEHNOT**
CDDEERU	**CDEEHKL**	proceed	coigned	notched
reduced	heckled	**CDEEORV**	**CDEGINR**	**CDEHNPU**
CDDEESU	**CDEEHLT**	covered	cringed	punched
seduced	letched	**CDEEORW**	**CDEGINU**	**CDEHNRU**
CDDEHIN	**CDEEHMS**	cowered	educing	churned
chidden	schemed	**CDEEOTV**	**CDEGIOR**	**CDEHOPP**
CDDEHIT	**CDEEHNW**	coveted	ergodic	chopped
ditched	wenched	**CDEERRU**	**CDEHHIT**	**CDEHOPU**
CDDEHOU	**CDEEHOR**	reducer	hitched	pouched
douched	cohered	**CDEERST**	**CDEHHNU**	**CDEHORT**
CDDEINU	**CDEEHPR**	crested	hunched	torched
induced	perched	**CDEERSU**	**CDEHIKN**	**CDEHORW**
CDDEISU	**CDEEHTT**	recused	chinked	chowder
cuddies	tetched	rescued	**CDEHILL**	cowherd
CDDELOS	**CDEEIIT**	secured	chilled	**CDEHOSU**
scolded	eidetic	seducer	**CDEHIMR**	choused
CDDELOU	**CDEEILN**	**CDEERSW**	chirmed	hocused
clouded	decline	screwed	**CDEHINN**	**CDEHOTU**
CDDELRU	**CDEEIMN**	**CDEESUX**	chinned	touched
curdled	endemic	excused	**CDEHINP**	**CDEHOUV**
CDDEORW	**CDEEINO**	**CDEETUW**	pinched	vouched
crowded	codeine	cutweed	**CDEHINS**	**CDEHPSY**
CDDGINO	**CDEEINT**	**CDEFFHU**	chinsed	psyched
codding	enticed	chuffed	**CDEHINW**	**CDEHRSU**
CDDIIOS	**CDEEINV**	**CDEFFOS**	winched	crushed
discoid	evinced	scoffed	**CDEHIOR**	**CDEHSSU**
CDDIORS	**CDEEIOS**	**CDEFFSU**	choired	duchess
discord	diocese	scuffed	**CDEHIOW**	**CDEHSTY**
CDDKORU	**CDEEIPR**	**CDEFHIL**	cowhide	scythed
ruddock	pierced	filched	**CDEHIPP**	**CDEIIKS**
CDEEEFL	**CDEEIRT**	**CDEFHIT**	chipped	dickies
fleeced	recited	fitched	**CDEHIPR**	**CDEIINS**
CDEEEHL	tierced	**CDEFIIT**	chirped	incised
leeched	**CDEEISX**	deficit	**CDEHIPT**	indices
CDEEEHP	excised	**CDEFIKL**	pitched	**CDEIINT**
cheeped	**CDEEITV**	flicked	**CDEHIST**	incited
CDEEEHR	evicted	**CDEFINO**	ditches	**CDEIIST**
cheered	**CDEEITX**	confide	**CDEHISU**	deistic
CDEEEIV	excited	**CDEFKLO**	duchies	diciest
deceive	**CDEEKKL**	flocked	**CDEHITT**	**CDEIISU**
CDEEEJT	keckled	**CDEFKOR**	chitted	suicide
ejected	**CDEEKLR**	defrock	**CDEHKOS**	**CDEIKLN**
CDEEELT	clerked	frocked	shocked	clinked
elected	**CDEEKNR**	**CDEFNOR**	**CDEHKSU**	**CDEIKLP**
CDEEEPR	redneck	cornfed	shucked	pickled
precede	**CDEEKRW**	**CDEFNTU**	**CDEHLMU**	**CDEIKLT**
CDEEERS	wrecked	defunct	mulched	tickled
seceder	**CDEELMM**	**CDEFORT**	**CDEHLNU**	**CDEIKNS**
CDEEERT	clemmed	crofted	lunched	dickens
erected	**CDEELPU**	**CDEFOSU**	**CDEHLNY**	snicked
CDEEFHT	cupeled	focused	lynched	**CDEIKNZ**
fetched	**CDEELSU**	**CDEGGHU**	**CDEHLOT**	zincked
CDEEFII	seclude	chugged	clothed	**CDEIKPR**
edifice	**CDEELUX**	**CDEGGLO**	**CDEHLRU**	pricked
CDEEFKL	exclude	clogged	lurched	**CDEIKQU**
flecked	**CDEENOR**	**CDEGHOU**	**CDEHMMU**	quicked
CDEEFLT	encoder	coughed	chummed	**CDEIKRR**
deflect	encored	**CDEGIIN**	**CDEHMNU**	derrick
CDEEFOR	**CDEENOZ**	deicing	munched	**CDEIKRT**
deforce	cozened	**CDEGIKN**	**CDEHMOR**	tricked

CDEIKRU
duckier
CDEIKST
sticked
CDEILLO
collide
collied
CDEILMO
melodic
CDEILNU
include
nuclide
CDEILOP
policed
CDEILPP
clipped
CDEILPS
spliced
CDEILTU
ductile
CDEIMNO
demonic
CDEIMOR
dormice
CDEIMOT
demotic
CDEIMPR
crimped
CDEIMPU
pumiced
CDEIMSU
miscued
CDEINOS
secondi
CDEINOT
ctenoid
noticed
CDEINPR
princed
CDEINRS
discern
rescind
CDEINRY
cindery
CDEINSU
incudes
CDEINSX
exscind
CDEIORT
cordite
CDEIORV
divorce
CDEIORW
crowdie
CDEIPRS
crisped
CDEIPRT
predict
CDEIRRU
curried
CDEIRSU
cruised
CDEIRTV
verdict

CDEISST
dissect
CDEJNOU
jounced
CDEKKNO
knocked
CDEKLNU
clunked
CDEKLOW
wedlock
CDEKLPU
plucked
CDEKLSU
suckled
CDEKMOS
smocked
CDEKOOR
crooked
CDEKOST
stocked
CDEKRTU
trucked
CDELLOU
collude
CDELMPU
clumped
CDELMSU
muscled
CDELMTU
mulcted
CDELNOO
condole
CDELNOW
clowned
CDELNOY
condyle
CDELOOR
colored
decolor
CDELOPP
coppled
CDELOPU
coupled
CDELORS
scolder
CDELORW
clowder
crowled
CDELOST
coldest
CDELOSW
scowled
CDELOTT
clotted
CDELOTU
clouted
CDELRUY
crudely
CDEMMNO
commend
CDEMMOO
commode
CDEMMSU
scummed

CDEMNNO
condemn
CDEMORU
decorum
CDEMPRU
crumped
CDENNOO
condone
CDENNOT
contend
CDENOOR
crooned
CDENOOS
secondo
CDENOPU
pounced
CDENORS
scorned
CDENORW
crowned
CDENOTU
counted
CDENRUU
uncured
CDEOOPS
scooped
CDEOOPT
coopted
CDEOORR
corrode
CDEOOST
scooted
CDEOPPR
cropped
CDEOPRU
produce
CDEORSS
crossed
CDEORSU
coursed
scoured
CDEORTU
courted
CDEORUU
douceur
CDEOSTU
scouted
CDEPRSU
spruced
CDERSTU
crudest
crusted
CDFHIOS
codfish
CDFILUY
dulcify
CDGHIIN
chiding
CDGIKNO
docking
CDGIKNU
ducking
CDGILNO
codling

CDGINNO
condign
CDGINOR
cording
CDGINRU
curding
CDHIIST
distich
CDHILLY
childly
CDHIPTY
diptych
CDIIIOT
idiotic
CDIIJRU
juridic
CDIILLY
idyllic
CDIINOR
crinoid
CDIINOT
diction
CDIIORS
cirsoid
CDIIOSS
cissoid
CDIKNOR
dornick
CDIKNPU
duckpin
CDILLOO
colloid
CDILLUY
lucidly
CDIMMOU
mocicum
CDINOTU
conduit
noctuid
CDIOSTY
cystoid
CDIOTUV
oviduct
CDIRTUY
crudity
CDISSSU
discuss
CDOOOPT
octopod
CDOOTUW
woodcut
CDOPRTU
product
CDOSTUY
custody

essence
CEEEPRR
creeper
CEEERST
secrete
CEEERTX
excrete
CEEETUX
execute
CEEFFNO
offence
CEEFHRT
fetcher
CEEFHST
fetches
CEEFIRR
fiercer
CEEFKLR
freckle
CEEFLRT
reflect
CEEFNOR
enforce
CEEFPRT
perfect
prefect
CEEGINR
generic
CEEGINT
genetic
CEEGINU
eugenic
CEEGLLO
college
CEEGLNT
neglect
CEEGLOU
eclogue
CEEGNRY
regency
CEEGORT
cortege
CEEHILS
helices
CEEHILV
vehicle
CEEHIMR
chimere
CEEHIMS
chemise
CEEHIOR
cheerio
CEEHIRT
heretic
CEEHIRW
chewier
CEEHISV
chevies
CEEHKLR
heckler
CEEHKNP
henpeck
CEEHLNO
echelon

CEEHLRY
lechery
CEEHMRS
schemer
CEEHNPU
penuche
CEEHNRW
wencher
CEEHNST
tenches
CEEHNSW
wenches
CEEHORT
trochee
CEEHPRS
perches
CEEHRST
retches
CEEIJOR
rejoice
CEEIKNT
necktie
CEEILLM
micelle
CEEILNO
cineole
CEEILNR
recline
CEEILNS
license
silence
CEEILPS
eclipse
CEEILRT
reticle
tiercel
CEEILSS
iceless
CEEILST
sectile
CEEILSV
vesicle
CEEILTU
leucite
CEEIMNT
centime
CEEIMRS
mercies
CEEINNS
incense
CEEINRS
sincere
CEEINRT
enteric
CEEINRV
cervine
CEEIOPT
picotee
CEEIORT
coterie
CEEIPPR
precipe
CEEIPRR
piercer

CEEIPRS
precise
CEEIPRT
receipt
CEEIPRU
epicure
CEEIPSS
species
CEEIQSU
quiesce
CEEIRSV
service
CEEIRTX
exciter
CEEITTZ
zetetic
CEEJORT
ejector
CEEKLNT
necklet
CEEKLPS
speckle
CEEKRRW
wrecker
CEELLLU
cellule
CEELLNO
colleen
CEELMNT
clement
CEELMOW
welcome
CEELNOS
enclose
CEELNRT
lectern
CEELORT
elector
electro
CEELPRT
prelect
CEELRRU
crueler
CEELRSU
recluse
CEELRTU
lecture
CEELRTY
erectly
CEELTTU
lettuce
CEEMNRU
cerumen
CEEMOPR
compeer
CEEMOPT
compete
CEENNOV
convene
CEENNRT
centner
CEENOOT
ecotone
CEENOPT

potence
CEENORS
necrose
CEENPRS
spencer
CEENPRT
percent
CEENRSU
censure
CEENRSY
scenery
CEENTTU
cunette
CEEOPTY
ecotype
CEEORRT
erector
CEEORRV
recover
CEEPPRT
percept
precept
CEEPRST
respect
scepter
sceptre
specter
CEEPRTX
excerpt
CEERRSU
securer
CEERSST
cresset
CEERTTU
curette
CEETTUV
cuvette
CEFFIOR
officer
CEFFISU
suffice
CEFFLSU
scuffle
CEFFORS
scoffer
CEFGINN
fencing
CEFHILS
filches
CEFHILY
chiefly
CEFHINS
finches
CEFHITW
fitchew
CEFHORU
fourche
CEFIILT
fictile
CEFIIOR
orifice
CEFIITV
fictive
CEFIKLR

flicker
CEFILNT
inflect
CEFILNU
funicle
CEFIMOR
comfier
CEFINNO
confine
CEFINOR
conifer
CEFIPSY
specify
CEFIRTY
certify
rectify
CEFKLLO
elflock
CEFKLOT
fetlock
CEFKLRY
freckly
CEFLNOU
flounce
CEFLNUY
fluency
CEFMORY
comfrey
CEFNORU
frounce
CEFNOSS
confess
CEFNOSU
confuse
CEFNOTU
confute
CEFOPRS
forceps
CEFORRT
crofter
CEFOSSU
focuses
CEGGHIR
chigger
CEGGIOR
georgic
CEGHILN
leching
CEGHINO
echoing
CEGHINT
etching
CEGHINW
chewing
CEGHLSU
gulches
CEGIILN
ceiling
CEGIINP
piecing
CEGIINZ
ecizing
CEGIKKN
kecking

CEGIKNN
necking
CEGIKNP
pecking
CEGIKNR
recking
CEGILNR
cringle
CEGILNW
clewing
CEGINNS
censing
CEGINOZ
cognize
CEGINRW
crewing
CEGLNOO
cologne
CEGLOOY
ecology
CEGLOSU
glucose
GEGNORY
cryogen
CEGNOST
congest
CEGNRUY
urgency
CEGORRY
grocery
CEGORSU
scourge
CEHHIOO
hoochie
CEHHIRS
cherish
CEHHIST
hitches
CEHHNSU
hunches
CEHIINR
hircine
CEHIINT
ichnite
CEHIIRT
itchier
CEHIKNT
kitchen
thicken
CEHIKNW
chewink
CEHIKRT
thicker
CEHIKTT
thicket
CEHILLR
chiller
CEHILNO
choline
helicon
CEHILRV
chervil
CEHIMNY
chimney

CEHIMOS
echoism
CEHIMRT
thermic
CEHIMST
chemist
CEHINOP
chopine
CEHINPR
phrenic
CEHINPS
pinches
CEHINRT
cithern
CEHINST
sthenic
CEHINSW
winches
CEHIOPS
hospice
CEHIOPT
potiche
CEHIPPR
chipper
CEHIPRS
spheric
CEHIPRT
pitcher
CEHIPST
pitches
CEHIRST
richest
CEHIRSU
cushier
CEHIRSZ
scherzi
CEHIRTT
chitter
CEHISSS
schesis
CEHISTW
witches
CEHKKRU
chukker
CEHKLMO
hemlock
CEHKOOR
kerchoo
CEHKORS
shocker
CEHKPTU
ketchup
CEHKRSU
shucker
CEHKSTY
sketchy
CEHLNRY
lyncher
CEHLORT
chortle
CEHLPPS
schlepp
CEHLQSU
squelch

CEHLRSU
lurches
CEHMNSU
munches
CEHMOOR
moocher
CEHMOOS
mooches
CEHMOSS
schmoes
CEHMOSU
mouches
CEHNNSU
nunches
CEHNOOR
coehorn
CEHNORV
chevron
CEHNOST
notches
CEHNPST
pschent
CEHNPSU
punches
CEHNTUY
chutney
CEHOORT
cheroot
CEHOPPR
chopper
CEHOPRS
porches
CEHOPSU
pouches
CEHORST
torches
CEHORSU
choreus
CEHORSZ
scherzo
CEHORTU
retouch
CEHORUV
voucher
CEHOSUV
vouches
CEHRRSU
crusher
CEHRSSU
crushes
CEHRSTT
stretch
CEIIJRU
juicier
CEIIKNT
kinetic
CEIIKPR
pickier
CEIIKQU
quickie
CEIIKST
ickiest
CEIILNN
incline

CEIIMNS
menisci
CEIIMOT
meiotic
CEIIMPR
empiric
CEIIMSS
seismic
CEIIMTT
titmice
CEIINOR
oneiric
CEIINOV
invoice
CEIINRS
sericin
CEIINRT
citrine
crinite
inciter
neritic
CEIINSS
iciness
CEIINSU
cuisine
CEIINTZ
citizen
zincite
CEIIOPZ
epizoic
CEIIPRS
spicier
CEIIRST
eristic
CEIIRSU
ericius
CEIISVV
civvies
CEIJSTU
justice
CEIKLNR
clinker
crinkle
CEIKLPR
prickle
CEIKLRS
slicker
CEIKLRT
tickler
trickle
CEIKLRU
luckier
CEIKLST
stickle
CEIKMRU
muckier
CEIKNQU
quicken
CEIKNRS
snicker
CEIKORR
corkier
rockier
CEIKPRT

pricket
CEIKPST
skeptic
CEIKQRU
quicker
CEIKRST
rickets
sticker
CEIKRTY
rickety
CEIKSST
sickest
CEILLNO
lioncel
CEILLOR
collier
CEILLST
cellist
CEILLSU
cullies
CEILMOP
compile
polemic
CEILMPR
crimple
CEILNOS
inclose
CEILNOT
lection
CEILNOX
lexicon
CEILNST
stencil
CEILORT
cortile
CEILOSS
ossicle
CEILPPR
clipper
cripple
CEILPRS
splicer
CEILRSY
clerisy
CEILRZZ
crizzle
CEIMNOR
incomer
CEIMNOT
centimo
CEIMOPT
metopic
CEIMOQU
comique
CEIMOST
comites
CEIMOTT
totemic
CEIMOTV
vicomte
CEIMRTU
tumeric
CEINNOV
connive

CEINOPR
porcine
CEINOPT
nepotic
CEINORR
cornier
CEINORS
cronies
CEINORV
corvine
CEINOSS
cession
CEINOST
section
CEINOTT
entotic
CEINOVV
convive
CEINPRS
pincers
CEINPST
inspect
CEINRST
cistern
CEINRTT
cittern
CEINSTY
cystine
CEINTTX
extinct
CEIOPPS
coppies
CEIOPSU
piceous
CEIORRS
cirrose
crosier
CEIORRU
courier
CEIORRZ
crozier
CEIORTT
cottier
CEIORVY
viceroy
CEIOSST
cosiest
CEIOSTV
costive
CEIOSTX
coexist
CEIOSTY
society
CEIOSTZ
coziest
CEIPRRS
crisper
CEIPRSY
spicery
CEIPRTU
picture
CEIPRTY
pyretic
CEIRRRU

currier	counsel	crumpet	procure	**CFLNOUX**
CEIRRSU	**CELNSUU**	**CEMRRUY**	**CEOPRSS**	conflux
cruiser	nucleus	mercury	process	**CFMNOOR**
curries	**CELOOST**	**CENNOOT**	**CEOPRTT**	conform
CEIRRTT	coolest	connote	protect	**CFMOORT**
critter	**CELOPRU**	**CENNOST**	**CEOQRTU**	comfort
CEIRRTU	coupler	consent	croquet	**CFOSSUU**
recruit	**CELOPTU**	**CENNOTT**	**CEORRSS**	fuscous
CEIRRUV	couplet	content	crosser	**CGGGINO**
curvier	octuple	**CENNOTV**	**CEORRSU**	cogging
CEIRSTU	**CELORST**	convent	courser	**CGHIIMN**
icterus	corslet	**CENNRSU**	scourer	chiming
CEIRSUV	costrel	scunner	**CEORRSY**	**CGHIINN**
cursive	**CELORSU**	**CENOORR**	sorcery	inching
CEIRTTX	closure	coroner	**CEORRTY**	niching
tectrix	**CELORTU**	**CENOORT**	rectory	**CGHIINT**
CEISSTU	cloture	coronet	**CEORSSS**	itching
ictuses	coulter	**CENOPSY**	crosses	**CGHIKNO**
CEJNORU	**CELORVY**	syncope	**CEORSSU**	choking
conjure	clovery	**CENOPTY**	sucrose	hocking
CEJOPRT	**CELOSST**	potency	**CEORSTU**	**CGHILPY**
project	closest	**CENOQRU**	scouter	glyphic
CEKKLNU	**CELPRSU**	conquer	**CEORTUU**	**CGHINNO**
knuckle	scruple	**CENORRS**	couture	chignon
CEKKNOR	**CELPSUY**	scorner	**CEPPRRU**	**CGHINOS**
knocker	clypeus	**CENORTU**	crupper	coshing
CEKLLRY	**CELRSTU**	counter	**CEPPRSU**	**CGHINTU**
clerkly	cluster	recount	scupper	chuting
CEKLRTU	**CELRTTU**	**CENORTV**	**CEPRRSU**	**CGHORUY**
truckle	clutter	convert	sprucer	grouchy
CEKMORY	**CELRTUU**	**CENORTW**	**CEPRSSU**	**CGIIJNU**
mockery	culture	crownet	percuss	juicing
CEKNOOV	**CELRTUV**	**CENORUV**	**CEPRSSY**	**CGIIKKN**
convoke	culvert	uncover	cypress	kicking
CEKOOPW	**CELRTUY**	**CENOSSY**	**CEPRSUW**	**CGIIKLN**
cowpoke	cruelty	coyness	screwup	licking
CEKOORY	cutlery	**CENOSTT**	**CEPSSTU**	**CGIIKMM**
cookery	**CELSTTU**	contest	suspect	gimmick
CEKORST	scuttle	**CENOSTU**	**CERSTUY**	**CGIIKNN**
restock	**CEMMNOT**	contuse	curtsey	nicking
CEKPRUY	comment	**CENOTTX**	**CFFGINU**	**CGIIKNP**
puckery	**CEMMNOU**	context	cuffing	picking
CEKRRTU	commune	**CENRRTU**	**CFFHINO**	**CGIIKNS**
trucker	**CEMMOTU**	current	chiffon	sicking
CELLNOO	commute	**CENRSTU**	**CFFIKKO**	**CGIIKNT**
colonel	**CEMNNOT**	encrust	kickoff	ticking
CELLOSY	contemn	**CENRSUW**	**CFFRSUY**	**CGIILLO**
closely	**CEMNOOY**	unscrew	scruffy	illogic
CELLRRU	economy	**CENRTUY**	**CFGINOR**	**CGIILNO**
cruller	**CEMNOSU**	century	forcing	coiling
CELLRUY	consume	**CEOOPRY**	**CFIIKNY**	**CGIILNS**
cruelly	**CEMNRTU**	coopery	finicky	slicing
CELMNOO	centrum	**CEOORST**	**CFIILNT**	**CGIIMNN**
monocle	**CEMOOPS**	scooter	inflict	mincing
CELMOPX	compose	**CEOPRRR**	**CFIINOT**	**CGIINNO**
complex	**CEMOOPT**	cropper	fiction	coining
CELMPRU	compote	**CEOPPRY**	**CFIMNOR**	**CGIINNW**
crumple	**CEMOOTU**	coppery	confirm	wincing
CELNNOU	outcome	**CEOPRRS**	**CFINORY**	**CGIINOV**
nucleon	**CEMOPTU**	scorper	cornify	voicing
CELNOOS	compute	**CEOPRRT**	**CFKOTTU**	**CGIINPR**
colones	**CEMOSTU**	porrect	futtock	pricing
console	costume	**CEOPRRU**	**CFLMRUU**	**CDIINPS**
CELNOSU	**CEMPRTU**		fulcrum	spicing

CGIINRT	crowing	schnook	**CIKLQUY**	**CINOSTU**
tricing	**CGINORZ**	**CHLOPST**	quickly	suction
CGIKLNO	crozing	splotch	**CIKNOSW**	**CINRSTU**
locking	**CGINOST**	**CHLOSUY**	cowskin	incrust
CGIKMNO	costing	slouchy	**CIKNPTU**	**CIOOPRT**
mocking	gnostic	**CHNNOOR**	nutpick	portico
CGIKMNU	**CGINOSU**	chronon	**CIKNSTU**	**CIOOPSU**
mucking	congius	**CHNNOSU**	unstick	copious
CGIKNNO	**CGINOSW**	nonsuch	**CIKPSTU**	**CIOOQTU**
nocking	scowing	**CHNOTUU**	stickup	coquito
CGIKNOO	**CGINPPU**	uncouth	**CILLOOR**	**CIOPSTY**
cocking	cupping	**CHPSSUY**	criollo	copyist
CGIKNOR	**CGINRSU**	scyphus	**CILMNOP**	**CIOQRSU**
corking	cursing	**CIIILLT**	complin	croquis
rocking	**CGINRUV**	illicit	**CILMSTU**	**CIORSSS**
CGIKNOS	curving	**CIIILNV**	cultism	scissor
socking	**CGINSSU**	incivil	**CILNOOS**	**CIORSTU**
CGIKNPU	cussing	**CIIINPT**	cloison	citrous
kingcup	**CGINTTU**	incipit	**CILNOTU**	**CIORSUU**
CGIKNRU	cutting	**CIIJLUY**	linocut	curious
rucking	**CGIOOOS**	juicily	**CILOOPT**	**CIORTVY**
CGIKNSU	giocoso	**CIIKKLL**	copilot	victory
sucking	**CHHISTY**	killick	**CILOORU**	**CIOSSUV**
CGIKNTU	ichthys	**CIIKNPT**	couloir	viscous
tucking	**CHIIKSS**	nitpick	**CILOOSS**	**CIPSTTY**
CGILLNO	sickish	**CIILLTY**	colossi	styptic
colling	**CHIIMSU**	licitly	**CILOOST**	**CIRTUVY**
CGILLNU	ischium	**CIILLVY**	sciolto	curvity
culling	**CHIKLLO**	civilly	**CILOPRY**	**CJNORUY**
CGILNNO	hillock	**CIILNOS**	pyloric	conjury
cloning	**CHIKLTY**	silicon	**CILOPSW**	**CKKLNUY**
CGILNOO	thickly	**CIILNUV**	cowslip	knuckly
cooling	**CHIKORY**	uncivil	**CILOSTU**	**CKLLOOP**
CGILNOS	hickory	**CIILOPT**	oculist	pollock
closing	**CHILNSY**	politic	**CILPRSY**	**CKLNOTU**
CGILNOW	lychnis	**CIILOST**	crisply	locknut
cowling	**CHILOST**	colitis	**CILPRTU**	**CKLNUUY**
CGILNOY	coltish	solicit	culprit	unlucky
cloying	**CHIMMOR**	**CIIMMRY**	**CILRRSU**	**CKLOORW**
CGILNRU	microhm	mimicry	scurril	rowlock
curling	**CHIMOPR**	**CIIMNOT**	**CILSTTU**	**CKLOOTU**
CGILORW	morphic	miction	cultist	lockout
cowgirl	**CHIMORS**	**CIINORS**	**CIMMOSS**	**CKLOPTU**
CGILPTY	chrisom	incisor	cosmism	potluck
glyptic	**CHINOSU**	**CIINQTU**	**CIMNOOR**	**CKNSTUU**
CGIMNOP	cushion	quintic	omicron	unstuck
comping	**CHIOPRT**	**CIIOSTX**	**CIMNORS**	**CKOOOTU**
CGINNNU	trophic	coxitis	crimson	cookout
cunning	**CHIOPST**	**CIIOSUV**	**CIMOOST**	**CKORTUW**
CGINNOR	photics	vicious	osmotic	cutwork
corning	**CHIORST**	**CIIPRTY**	**CIMOTYZ**	**CKOSSTU**
CGINNOS	chorist	pyritic	zymotic	tussock
consign	ostrich	**CIJNNOO**	**CIMPRSY**	**CLLOOPS**
CGINOOP	**CHIOSST**	conjoin	scrimpy	scollop
cooping	stichos	**CIKKLLO**	**CINNORU**	**CLMOOPT**
CGINOPP	**CHIPRRU**	killock	unicorn	complot
copping	chirrup	**CIKLLOR**	**CINNOTU**	**CLMSUUU**
CGINOPS	**CHIPRRY**	rollick	unction	cumulus
copsing	pyrrhic	**CIKLLUY**	**CINORRT**	**CLNOORT**
CGINOPY	**CHKMMOO**	luckily	tricorn	control
copying	hommock	**CIKLNRY**	**CINORTU**	**CLNOOSS**
CGINORS	**CHKMMOU**	crinkly	ruction	consols
scoring	hummock	**CIKLPRY**	**CINOSST**	**CLNOOSU**
CGINORW	**CHKNOOS**	prickly	consist	colonus

CLNOSTU
consult
CLORSSY
crossly
CLORTUY
courtly
CMNOOPY
compony
CMOOPRT
comport
CMOOPST
compost
CMOOSTY
scotomy
CMORSTU
scrotum
CMORTUW
cutworm
CNNORTU
nocturn
CNOOPPR
popcorn
CNOOPSU
soupcon
CNOORST
consort
CNOORTT
contort
CNOORTU
contour
crouton
CNOOSUU
nocuous
CNOOTTY
cottony
CNORTUY
country
CNPSTUU
punctus
COOPRRT
proctor
COOPRTU
outcrop
COOPSTU
octupus
COPRRTU
corrupt
COPRSUU
cuprous
CORRSUY
cursory
DDDDEIL
diddled
DDDDELO
doddled
DDDEEGR
dredged
DDDEEIR
derided
DDDEELM
meddled
DDDEELP
peddled
DDDEELS

sledded
DDDEELU
deluded
DDDEEMO
demoded
DDDEENU
denuded
DDDEFIL
fiddled
DDDEFLU
fuddled
DDDEGRU
drudged
DDDEHLU
huddled
DDDEHTU
thudded
DDDEIIV
divided
DDDEIKS
skidded
DDDEILM
middled
DDDEILP
piddled
DDDEILR
riddled
DDDEILT
tiddled
DDDEIMU
muddied
DDDEIRU
ruddied
DDDELMU
muddled
DDDELNO
noddled
DDDELOO
doodled
DDDELOP
plodded
DDDELOT
toddled
DDDELPU
puddled
DDDEOPR
prodded
DDDEPSU
spudded
DDDESTU
studded
DDEEELN
needled
DDEEELT
deleted
DDEEELV
develed
DDEEEMN
emended
DDEEEPS
speeded
DDEEFGL
fledged
DDEEFII

deified
edified
DDEEFIL
defiled
fielded
DDEEFIN
defined
DDEEFLU
deedful
DDEEFSU
defused
DDEEGIN
deeding
deigned
DDEEGLP
pledged
DDEEGLS
sledged
DDEEGLU
deluged
DDEEHRS
shedder
DDEEILR
dreidel
DDEEILV
deviled
DDEEILW
wielded
DDEEILY
yielded
DDEEIMP
impeded
DDEEIMS
demised
misdeed
DDEEINW
widened
DDEEINX
indexed
DDEEINZ
dizened
DDEEIRS
desired
resided
DDEEIRV
derived
DDEEIST
teddies
DDEEISV
devised
DDEELLW
dwelled
DDEELMO
modeled
DDEELMR
meddler
DDEELOW
doweled
DDEELOY
yodeled
DDEELPR
peddler
DDEELRS
sledder

DDEEMOT
demoted
DDEENOP
deponed
DDEENOT
denoted
DDEENOW
endowed
DDEENPU
upended
DDEENRU
endured
DDEENTU
detuned
DDEEOPS
deposed
DDEEORR
ordered
DDEEORW
dowered
DDEEOTV
devoted
DDEEPTU
deputed
DDEERSS
dressed
DDEERST
reddest
DDEERTU
detrude
DDEFILR
fiddler
DDEFLNO
fondled
DDEFLOO
flooded
DDEFLRU
fuddler
DDEFNOU
founded
DDEGGRU
drugged
grudged
DDEGIIR
giddier
DDEGILR
girdled
griddle
DDEGIMO
demigod
DDEGINT
tedding
DDEGINW
wedding
DDEGINY
eddying
DDEGLOP
plodged
DDEGMSU
smudged
DDEGNOS
godsend
DDEGNOU
dudgeon

DDEGORY
dodgery
DDEGRTU
trudged
DDEHIRS
reddish
DDEHIRY
hydride
DDEHLRU
huddler
hurdled
DDEHNOS
shodden
DDEHNOU
hounded
DDEHNRU
hundred
DDEHRSU
shudder
DDEHRSY
shreddy
DDEIIKS
kiddies
DDEIIMS
middies
DDEIINT
indited
DDEIINV
divined
DDEIIOX
dioxide
DDEIIOZ
idiozed
DDEIIRT
dirtied
DDEIIRV
divider
DDEIIVV
divvied
DDEIIZZ
dizzied
DDEIKLN
kindled
DDEIKNR
kindred
DDEIKOS
kiddoes
DDEILLR
drilled
DDEILMP
dimpled
DDEILNW
dwindle
DDEILOT
deltoid
DDEILTU
diluted
DDEILTW
twiddle
DDEIMOS
desmoid
DDEIMRU
muddier
DDEINOS

noddies
DDEINOT
dentoid
DDEINPU
nudiped
DDEINST
distend
DDEIORW
dowdier
DDEIOSW
dowdies
DDEIOTT
dittoed
DDEIOWW
widowed
DDEIPPR
dripped
DDEIRRU
ruddier
DDEISSU
disused
DDEISTU
studied
DDELLOR
drolled
DDELMRU
muddler
DDELNOO
noodled
DDELNOU
noduled
DDELOOR
drooled
DDELORT
toddler
DDELPRU
puddler
DDELPSU
spuddle
DDEMMRU
drummed
DDEMMSU
smeddum
DDEMNOT
oddment
DDEMNOU
mounded
DDENOPS
despond
DDENOPU
pounded
DDENORT
trodden
DDENORU
redound
rounded
underdo
DDENORW
drowned
DDENOSS
oddness
DDENOSU
sounded
DDENOUW

wounded
DDEOOPR
drooped
DDEOORW
redwood
DDEOPPR
dropped
DDEOPRW
dewdrop
DDEORSW
drowsed
DDFGIIN
fidding
DDGGINO
dodging
DDGIIKN
kidding
DDGIILY
giddily
DDGIINR
ridding•
DDGIMNU
mudding
DDGINNO
nodding
DDGINOP
podding
DDGINOS
sodding
DDGINPU
pudding
DDGOOOW
dogwood
DDHIORY
hydroid
DDIILOP
diploid
DDIKOOS
skiddoo
DDILOWY
dowdily
DDILRUY
ruddily
DDMNOOR
dromond
DEEEFNS
defense
DEEEFRV
fevered
DEEEGMR
emerged
DEEEGNR
greened
reneged
DEEEGRT
deterge
greeted
DEEEGST
egested
DEEEHLW
wheedle
DEEEHNS
sheened
DEEEHRS

heredes
sheered
DEEEHST
seethed
sheeted
DEEEHTT
teethed
DEEEHWZ
wheezed
DEEEINR
needier
DEEEIRS
seedier
DEEEIRW
weedier
DEEEJLW
jeweled
DEEEJRR
jerreed
DEEEKLN
kneeled
DEEEKNW
weekend
DEEELLV
leveled
DEEELNR
needler
DEEELPT
deplete
DEEELRV
levered
reveled
DEEELST
sleeted
steeled
DEEELSV
sleeved
DEEELTW
tweedle
DEEEMNS
demesne
seedmen
DEEEMRS
emersed
DEEEMRT
metered
DEEENPR
preened
DEEENQU
queened
DEEENRS
sneered
DEEENRT
entered
DEEENRW
renewed
DEEENSZ
sneezed
DEEENTT
detente
DEEEOTV
devotee
DEEEPRS
speeder

DEEEPRT
petered
DEEEPST
deepest
steeped
DEEERRV
revered
DEEERST
steered
DEEERSV
deserve
severed
DEEERSW
sewered
DEEERTV
everted
DEEERTX
exerted
DEEETTV
vedette
DEEETTW
tweeted
DEEETWZ
tweezed
DEEFFIN
effendi
DEEFFOR
offered
DEEFFSU
effused
DEEFGIN
feeding
feigned
DEEFGRU
refuged
DEEFHLS
fleshed
DEEFHLU
heedful
DEEFIIR
edifier
reified
DEEFIIS
deifies
edifies
DEEFILR
fielder
DEEFINR
refined
DEEFINT
feinted
DEEFIRR
ferried
refired
DEEFIRZ
friezed
DEEFLNS
flensed
DEEFLNU
needful
DEEFLOT
feedlot
DEEFLRU
feruled

DEEFLSU
seedful
DEEFLTT
fettled
DEEFMOR
freedom
DEEFRSU
refused
DEEFRTT
fretted
DEEFRTU
refuted
DEEFSTT
deftest
DEEGHIN
heeding
neighed
DEEGHIW
weighed
DEEGHOW
hogweed
DEEGILN
deleing
DEEGILR
ledgier
DEEGIMN
deeming
DEEGINN
needing
DEEGINR
dreeing
reeding
reigned
DEEGINS
seeding
DEEGINW
weeding
DEEGIPW
pigweed
DEEGIRV
diverge
grieved
DEEGIRW
wedgier
DEEGIST
edgiest
DEEGLNT
gentled
DEEGLPR
pledger
DEEGLPT
pledget
DEEGOSY
geodesy
DEEGSSU
guessed
DEEHIKV
khedive
DEEHINR
inhered
DEEHIST
heisted
DEEHITV
thieved

DEEHLLO	**DEEIMRS**	diverse	delouse	**DEEORRS**
helloed	remised	revised	**DEELOTV**	reredos
DEEHLLS	**DEEIMRT**	**DEEIRTU**	dovelet	**DEEORST**
shelled	demerit	erudite	**DEELOTW**	oersted
DEEHLOV	dimeter	**DEEIRTV**	toweled	**DEEORTT**
hoveled	merited	riveted	**DDELOVV**	tetrode
DEEHLPW	mitered	**DEEIRVV**	evolved	**DEEORTW**
whelped	**DEEIMRX**	revived	**DEELPRU**	towered
DEEHLSV	remixed	**DEEISTW**	prelude	**DEEORUV**
shelved	**DEEIMTT**	dewiest	**DEEPLST**	overdue
DEEHLSW	emitted	**DEEISTX**	pestled	**DEEORXX**
welshed	**DEEINNZ**	existed	**DEELRUV**	xeroxed
DEEHMNR	denizen	**DEEJNOY**	velured	**DEEPPPR**
herdmen	**DEEINPR**	enjoyed	**DEELSSW**	prepped
DEEHMUX	ripened	**DEEKKRT**	dewless	**DEEPPST**
exhumed	**DEEINRW**	trekked	**DEELSTT**	stepped
DEEHNOY	widener	**DEEKLLN**	settled	**DEEPRRU**
honeyed	**DEEINRX**	knelled	**DEELTUX**	perdure
DEEHORV	indexer	**DEEKLPS**	exulted	**DEEPRSS**
hovered	**DEEINST**	skelped	**DEEMMST**	depress
DEEHPRS	destine	**DEEKORV**	stemmed	pressed
sphered	**DEEINSW**	revoked	**DEEMNOU**	**DEEPRSU**
DEEHRSW	sinewed	**DEELLMS**	eudemon	perused
shrewed	**DEEINSX**	smelled	**DEEMNOY**	**DEEPRTU**
DEEHTTW	indexes	**DEELLPS**	moneyed	erupted
whetted	**DEEINTT**	spelled	**DEEMORV**	reputed
DEEIIST	detinet	**DEELLQU**	removed	**DEEPRTY**
deities	dinette	quelled	**DEEMOSY**	retyped
DEEIJLL	**DEEINTU**	**DEELLRW**	moseyed	**DEEQSTU**
jellied	detinue	dweller	**DEEMPTT**	quested
DEEIJMM	**DEEINTV**	**DEELLRY**	tempted	**DEERRSS**
jemmied	evident	elderly	**DEEMRRU**	dresser
DEEIJTT	**DEEINWZ**	**DEELLSW**	demurer	redress
jettied	wizened	swelled	**DEEMRSU**	**DEERRUV**
DEEIKLL	**DEEIOPS**	**DEELMOR**	resumed	verdure
kellied	episode	remodel	**DEENNPT**	**DEERSSS**
DEEIKLN	**DEEIOPT**	**DEELMST**	pendent	dresses
likened	epidote	smelted	**DEENORS**	**DEERSST**
DEEIKMW	**DEEIORS**	**DEELNRS**	endorse	dessert
midweek	osiered	slender	**DEENORT**	**DEERSTW**
DEEILNS	**DEEIPPT**	**DEELNRT**	erodent	strewed
linseed	peptide	trendle	**DEENPPR**	wrested
DEEILNV	**DEEIPRS**	**DEELNSS**	perpend	**DEERSVW**
livened	preside	endless	**DEENPRT**	swerved
DEEILPR	**DEEIPRV**	**DEELNST**	pretend	**DEERTTU**
periled	deprive	nestled	**DEENRSU**	uttered
replied	**DEEIPRX**	**DEELNSY**	ensured	**DEERTUX**
DEEILRV	expired	densely	**DEENRTU**	extrude
deliver	**DEEIPSS**	**DEELNTT**	denture	**DEFFFLU**
relived	despise	nettled	**DEENSST**	fluffed
reviled	**DEEIPST**	**DEELOPP**	densest	**DEFFHIW**
DEEILRW	despite	peopled	**DEENUVX**	whiffed
wielder	**DEEIQRU**	**DEELOPR**	unvexed	**DEFFILR**
DEEILRY	queried	deplore	**DEEOPPY**	riffled
yielder	**DEEIQTU**	**DEELOPV**	popeyed	**DEFFINS**
DEEILSS	quieted	develop	**DEEOPRS**	sniffed
idlesse	**DEEIRRS**	**DEELOPX**	reposed	**DEFFIOS**
DEEIMNS	derries	explode	**DEEOPST**	offside
sidemen	**DEEIRRT**	**DEELORS**	estoped	**DEFFISU**
DEEIMPR	retired	resoled	**DEEOPSX**	diffuse
demirep	retried	**DEELORW**	exposed	**DEFFLMU**
impeder	**DEEIRSU**	lowered	**DEEORRR**	muffled
DEEIMPT	residue	roweled	orderer	**DEFFLRU**
emptied	**DEEIRSV**	**DEELOSU**	reorder	ruffled

DEFFLSU	**DEFIMOR**	thigged	ghosted	vending
sluffed	deiform	**DEGGHOS**	**DEGIILN**	**DEGINNW**
DEFFNSU	**DEFINSU**	shogged	eliding	wending
snuffed	infused	**DEGGIJL**	**DEGIINN**	**DEGINNY**
DEFFSTU	**DEFINUX**	jiggled	indigen	denying
stuffed	unfixed	**DEGGIKN**	**DEGIINT**	**DEGINOR**
DEFGGIR	**DEFIOST**	kedging	dieting	eroding
frigged	foisted	**DEGGILN**	editing	groined
DEFGGLO	**DEFIPRY**	gelding	ignited	ignored
flogged	perfidy	niggled	**DEGIIRR**	redoing
DEFGGOR	**DEFIRRT**	**DEGGILW**	ridgier	**DEGINOS**
frogged	drifter	wiggled	**DEGIIRZ**	dingoes
DEFGINN	**DEFIRTU**	**DEGGINW**	dizgier	**DEGINRR**
fending	fruited	wedging	**DEGIJLN**	grinder
DEFGINR	**DEFIRZZ**	**DEGGIOR**	jingled	**DEGINRW**
fringed	frizzed	doggier	**DEGIKLO**	wringed
DEFGINU	**DEFISTU**	**DEGGIOS**	godlike	**DEGINSS**
feuding	feudist	doggies	**DEGILLR**	dessing
DEFGINY	**DEFKLNU**	**DEGGIPR**	grilled	**DEGINSW**
defying	flunked	prigged	**DEGILMN**	swinged
DEFGIRU	**DEFLLOU**	**DEGGISW**	melding	**DEGINTW**
figured	doleful	swigged	mingled	twinged
DEFGITY	**DEFLNOT**	**DEGGJLO**	**DEGILNN**	**DEGINUX**
fidgety	tenfold	joggled	lending	exuding
DEFHIST	**DEFLOOR**	**DEGGJLU**	**DEGILNS**	**DEGIOOS**
shifted	floored	juggled	singled	goodies
DEFHLSU	**DEFLOOZ**	**DEGGLOS**	**DEGILNT**	**DEGIPPR**
flushed	foozled	slogged	glinted	gripped
DEFHORT	**DEFLOPP**	**DEGGLPU**	tingled	**DEGIPRU**
frothed	flopped	plugged	**DEGILNU**	pudgier
DEFIILN	**DEFLORU**	**DEGGLRU**	dueling	**DEGIRSS**
infidel	floured	gurgled	eluding	digress
infield	**DEFLOTU**	**DEGGLSU**	indulge	**DEGIRSU**
DEFIIMW	flouted	slugged	**DEGILNV**	gurdies
midwife	**DEFLPRU**	**DEGGMSU**	delving	**DEGIRTT**
DEFIINU	purfled	smugged	**DEGILNW**	gritted
unified	**DEFMORS**	**DEGGNOO**	welding	**DEGLMOO**
DEFIINX	serfdom	doggone	**DEGILOR**	gloomed
infixed	**DEFNOOR**	**DEGGNOU**	gloried	**DEGLNOO**
DEFIKRS	fordone	gudgeon	**DEGILRU**	endlong
frisked	**DEFNORT**	**DEGGNSU**	guilder	**DEGLNOU**
DEFILLR	fronted	snugged	**DEGILRW**	lounged
frilled	**DEFNORU**	**DEGGOPR**	wergild	**DEGLNPU**
DEFILOW	founder	progged	**DEGILUV**	plunged
oldwife	**DEFNORW**	**DEGGORY**	divulge	**DEGLORW**
DEFILPP	frowned	doggery	**DEGIMNN**	growled
flipped	**DEFOOPS**	**DEGGRTU**	mending	**DEGLOSS**
DEFILRT	spoofed	drugget	**DEGIMNS**	glossed
flirted	**DEFORST**	**DEGHILT**	smidgen	godless
trifled	defrost	delight	**DEGINNN**	**DEGLTTU**
DEFILRU	frosted	lighted	denning	glutted
direful	**DEGGGIL**	**DEGHINR**	**DEGINNP**	guttled
DEFILSS	giggled	herding	pending	**DEGLUZZ**
fissled	**DEGGGIN**	**DEGHINT**	**DEGINNR**	guzzled
DEFILST	degging	nighted	grinned	**DEGMNOO**
stifled	**DEGGGLO**	**DEGHIOT**	rending	goodmen
DEFILSU	goggled	hogtied	**DEGINNS**	**DEGMOOR**
sulfide	**DEGGGLU**	**DEGHIRT**	sending	groomed
DEFILTT	guggled	righted	**DEGINNT**	**DEGNNOU**
flitted	**DEGGHIL**	**DEGHIST**	denting	dungeon
DEFILXY	higgled	sighted	tending	**DEGNOPR**
fixedly	**DEGGHIN**	**DEGHORU**	**DEGINNU**	pronged
DEFILZZ	hedging	roughed	enduing	**DEGNOPS**
fizzled	**DEGGHIT**	**DEGHOST**	**DEGINNV**	sponged

DEGNORU	**DEHIRTV**	dislike	**DEIJNRU**	**DEILLRT**
guerdon	thrived	**DEIIKNR**	injured	trilled
undergo	**DEHIRTW**	dinkier	**DEIJOST**	**DEILLSS**
DEGNORW	writhed	**DEIIKNS**	joisted	lidless
wronged	**DEHISSW**	dinkies	**DEIKKLN**	**DEILLST**
DEGNOTU	swished	**DEIILLS**	kinkled	stilled
tongued	**DEHIWZZ**	dillies	**DEIKKNS**	**DEILLSU**
DEGNRTU	whizzed	**DEIILMP**	skinked	sullied
grunted	**DEHLOOT**	implied	**DEIKLLS**	**DEILLSW**
DEGOORV	toehold	**DEIILMT**	skilled	swilled
grooved	**DEHLOPP**	delimit	**DEIKLNP**	**DEILLTW**
DEGOPRU	hoppled	limited	plinked	twilled
grouped	**DEHLORW**	**DEIILNS**	**DEIKLNT**	**DEILMMS**
DEGORTU	whorled	lindies	tinkled	slimmed
grouted	**DEHLOSS**	**DEIILOS**	**DEIKLNW**	**DEILMOP**
DEHHISW	sloshed	doilies	winkled	implode
whished	**DEHLRRU**	**DEIILOZ**	**DEIKLRS**	**DEILMOR**
DEHIKRS	hurdler	idolize	skirled	moldier
shirked	**DEHLRTU**	**DEIIMMX**	**DEIKLRT**	**DEILMPP**
DEHIKSW	hurtled	immixed	kirtled	pimpled
whisked	**DEHLSTU**	**DEIIMNO**	**DEIKLTT**	**DEILMPR**
DEHILPR	hustled	dominie	kittled	rimpled
hirpled	**DEHMORU**	**DEIINOT**	**DEIKMMS**	**DEILMPW**
DEHILRT	humored	edition	skimmed	wimpled
thirled	**DEHMOTU**	**DEIINOZ**	**DEIKMPS**	**DEILMST**
DEHILRW	mouthed	ionized	skimped	mildest
whirled	**DEHMPTU**	**DEIINRS**	**DEIKMRS**	**DEILMZZ**
DEHIMMS	thumped	insider	smirked	mizzled
shimmed	**DEHNNSU**	**DEIINRT**	**DEIKNNS**	**DEILNNU**
DEHIMNU	shunned	inditer	skinned	unlined
inhumed	**DEHNOOR**	nitride	**DEIKNOS**	**DEILNOO**
DEHIMOR	honored	**DEIINRW**	doeskin	eidolon
heirdom	**DEHNOOW**	windier	**DEIKNOV**	**DEILNPP**
DEHINNS	hoedown	**DEIINTV**	invoked	nippled
shinned	**DEHNORT**	invited	**DEIKNRS**	**DEILNPS**
DEHINNT	thorned	**DEIIORT**	redskin	spindle
thinned	throned	diorite	**DEIKNST**	splined
DEHINOY	**DEHNORU**	**DEIIORV**	kindest	**DEILNRT**
hyenoid	hounder	ivoried	**DEIKNTT**	tendril
DEHINRS	**DEHNRTU**	**DEIIORZ**	knitted	**DEILNSW**
shrined	thunder	iodizer	**DEIKOSY**	swindle
DEHIORT	**DEHNSTU**	**DEIIOXZ**	disyoke	**DEILNTU**
theroid	shunted	oxidize	**DEIKPPS**	diluent
DEHIOST	**DEHOOPW**	**DEIIPPR**	skipped	**DEILNTW**
hoisted	whooped	dippier	**DEIKRRS**	indwelt
DEHIOSU	**DEHOOST**	**DEIIRRT**	skirred	**DEILOOS**
hideous	soothed	dirtier	**DEIKRST**	doolies
DEHIOTU	**DEHOOTT**	**DEIIRST**	skirted	**DEILOPS**
hideout	toothed	dirties	**DEIKRSU**	despoil
DEHIPPS	**DEHOPPS**	**DEIIRZZ**	duskier	spoiled
shipped	shopped	dizzier	**DEIKSTT**	**DEILOPT**
DEHIPPW	**DEHOPPW**	**DEIISTT**	skitted	piloted
whipped	whopped	ditties	**DEIKSVY**	**DEILORS**
DEHIRRS	**DEHORST**	tidiest	skydive	soldier
shirred	shorted	**DEIISTV**	**DEILLMU**	**DEILPPR**
DEHIRRU	**DEHOSTT**	visited	illumed	rippled
hurried	shotted	**DEIISZZ**	**DEILLNW**	**DEILPPS**
DEHIRRW	**DEHOSTU**	dizzies	indwell	slipped
whirred	shouted	**DEIJLLO**	**DEILLOS**	**DEILPPT**
DEHIRST	**DEIIIRZ**	jollied	dollies	tippled
shirted	iridize	**DEIJNOR**	**DEILLPS**	**DEILPRT**
DEHIRSV	**DEIIJMM**	joinder	spilled	tripled
dervish	jimmied	**DEIJNOT**	**DEILLQU**	**DEILPTY**
shrived	**DEIIKLS**	jointed	quilled	tepidly

DEILQTU	**DEINNRU**	**DEIORSV**	knurled	**DELOPRT**
quilted	inurned	devisor	**DEKNNOS**	droplet
DEILRSW	**DEINNTW**	**DEIORSW**	nonsked	**DELOPTT**
swirled	twinned	dowries	**DEKNNRU**	plotted
DEILRTW	**DEINOPT**	**DEIORSW**	drunken	**DELORRY**
twirled	pointed	rowdies	**DEKNOTT**	orderly
DEILRVY	**DEINORS**	**DEIORTT**	knotted	**DELORST**
devilry	indorse	dottier	**DEKNOTU**	oldster
DEILRWY	ordines	**DEIORTU**	knouted	**DELOSTT**
wierdly	rosined	outride	**DEKOOPS**	slotted
DEILRZZ	**DEINORW**	**DEIORWW**	spooked	**DELOSTU**
drizzle	downier	widower	**DEKOOTW**	loudest
DEILSTT	**DEINPPS**	**DEIOSTU**	kotowed	tousled
slitted	snipped	outside	**DEKORST**	**DELOSZZ**
stilted	**DEINPRT**	tedious	stroked	sozzled
DEILSTU	printed	**DEIOSTZ**	**DELLORT**	**DELOTUV**
duelist	**DEINPST**	doziest	trolled	voluted
DEILSTW	stipend	**DEIOSUV**	**DELLSTU**	**DELPPRU**
wildest	**DEINRSU**	devious	dullest	purpled
DEILSZZ	insured	**DEIPPQU**	**DELMMSU**	**DELPPSU**
sizzled	**DEINRTT**	quipped	slummed	suppled
DEIMMPR	trident	**DEIPPRT**	**DELMORS**	**DELPRSU**
primmed	**DEINRTU**	tripped	smolder	slurped
DEIMMRT	intrude	**DEIPRST**	**DELMOTT**	**DELPUZZ**
midterm	untried	striped	mottled	puzzled
trimmed	**DEINRTY**	**DEIPRSY**	**DELMPPU**	**DELRRSU**
DEIMMRU	tindery	spidery	plumped	slurred
immured	**DEINSST**	**DEIPSTU**	**DELMPRU**	**DELRSTU**
DEIMMST	dissent	dispute	rumpled	rustled
dimmest	**DEINSTT**	**DEIPSXY**	**DELMPSU**	strudel
DEIMMSU	dentist	pyxides	slumped	**DELSSTU**
dummies	distent	**DEIPTTU**	**DELMUZZ**	tussled
DEIMNNU	stinted	puttied	muzzled	**DEMMRRU**
minuend	**DEINSTY**	**DEIQRSU**	**DELNORU**	drummer
DEIMNOS	density	squired	roundel	**DEMMSTU**
misdone	destiny	**DEIQTTU**	**DELNOSS**	stummed
DEIMNUX	**DEIOORW**	quitted	oldness	**DEMNOOR**
unmixed	woodier	**DEIQUZZ**	**DELNOTW**	doormen
DEIMOOR	**DEIOOST**	quizzed	letdown	**DEMNOOW**
moidore	osteoid	**DEIRRST**	**DELNOTY**	woodmen
moodier	**DEIOPRT**	stirred	notedly	**DEMNORS**
DEIMOPS	diopter	**DEIRSTU**	**DELNOUV**	rodsmen
imposed	**DEIOPRV**	dustier	unloved	**DEMNORT**
DEIMORS	provide	**DEISSTU**	**DELNPRU**	mordent
misdoer	**DEIOPSS**	studies	plunder	**DEMNORU**
DEIMOST	dispose	tissued	**DELNRTU**	mourned
modiste	**DEIOPST**	**DEISTTW**	trundle	**DEMNOST**
DEIMOTT	deposit	twisted	**DELNRUY**	endmost
omitted	dopiest	**DEITTTW**	underly	**DEMNOTU**
DEIMOTV	posited	twitted	**DELNUZZ**	mounted
vomited	topside	**DEJLOST**	nuzzled	**DEMNSTU**
DEIMPPR	**DEIOPTT**	jostled	**DELOOPS**	dustmen
primped	tiptoed	**DEJLSTU**	spooled	**DEMOOPP**
DEIMPRU	**DEIOPTV**	justled	**DELOOST**	popedom
dumpier	pivoted	**DEJOSTU**	stooled	**DEMOOPR**
umpired	**DEIORRW**	jousted	**DELOOTT**	predoom
DEIMPTU	rowdier	**DEKKLSU**	tootled	**DEMOORT**
imputed	wordier	skulked	**DELOPPP**	motored
DEIMSSU	worried	**DEKKNSU**	plopped	**DEMOOSS**
misused	**DEIORSS**	skunked	**DELOPPS**	osmosed
DEIMSTY	dossier	**DEKLLNO**	poppled	**DEMOPST**
stymied	**DEIORST**	knolled	**DELOPPS**	stomped
DEINNOT	steroid	**DEKLNPU**	slopped	**DEMORRU**
intoned	storied	plunked	**DELOPPT**	rumored
		DEKLNRU	toppled	

DEMORST	**DEOOPST**	finding	hording	**DGINNNU**
stormed	stooped	**DFGIINY**	**DGHINTU**	dunning
DEMOSTY	**DEOOPSW**	dignify	hindgut	**DGINNOP**
modesty	swooped	**DFGILNO**	**DGHIOOS**	ponding
DEMPRTU	**DEOORST**	folding	goodish	**DGINNOR**
trumped	roosted	**DFGINNU**	**DGHIOPS**	droning
DEMPSTU	**DEOORTU**	funding	godship	**DGINNOU**
stumped	outrode	**DFGINOR**	**DGHORTU**	undoing
DEMSTTU	**DEOPPPR**	fording	drought	**DGINNOW**
smutted	propped	**DFGINOU**	**DGHOTUY**	downing
DENNOOW	**DEOPPRR**	fungoid	doughty	**DGINNUY**
unowned	dropper	**DFHILSU**	**DGIIKNR**	undying
DENNSTU	**DEOPPST**	dishful	dirking	**DGINORT**
stunned	stopped	**DFILLUY**	**DGIILNO**	dorting
DENOOPS	**DEOPRST**	fluidly	loiding	**DGINORV**
snooped	sported	**DFILMNU**	**DGIILNR**	droving
spooned	**DEOPRWY**	mindful	dirling	**DGINORW**
DENOOSW	powdery	**DFILNOP**	**DGIILNS**	wording
swooned	**DEOPSTT**	pinfold	sidling	**DGINOSU**
DENOOSZ	spotted	**DFILOSX**	sliding	dousing
snoozed	**DEOPSTU**	sixfold	**DGIILRY**	**DGINOSW**
DENOOTU	spouted	**DFILTUU**	rigidly	dowsing
duotone	**DEORRST**	dutiful	**DGIIMMN**	**DGINOTT**
DENOPPR	rodster	**DFIMNUY**	dimming	dotting
propend	**DEORSTW**	mundify	**DGIIMNN**	**DGINSTU**
DENOPRS	worsted	**DFLOOTW**	minding	dusting
respond	**DEORSTY**	twofold	**DGIINNN**	**DGIOPRY**
DENOPRT	destroy	**DFNORUY**	dinning	prodigy
portend	**DEORTTT**	foundry	**DGIINNR**	**DGLNOUY**
protend	trotted	**DGGGIIN**	rinding	ungodly
DENOPRU	**DEORTTU**	digging	**DGIINNT**	**DGLOOOW**
pounder	tutored	**DGGGINO**	dinting	logwood
DENOPUX	**DEOSTTU**	dogging	**DGIINNU**	**DGMOPRU**
expound	testudo	**DGGHIOS**	induing	gumdrop
DENORRU	**DEOSTUU**	doggish	**DGIINNW**	**DGOORTT**
rounder	duteous	**DGGIILN**	dwining	dogtrot
DENORST	**DEPRRSU**	gilding	winding	**DHIILOT**
snorted	spurred	gliding	**DGIINOV**	lithoid
DENORSU	**DEPRRUY**	**DGGIINN**	voiding	**DHIIMNO**
resound	prudery	dinging	**DGIINPP**	hominid
sounder	**DEPRSTU**	nidging	dipping	**DHIIOPX**
DENOSTU	spurted	**DGGIINR**	**DGIINPR**	xiphoid
snouted	**DEPRSUU**	girding	priding	**DHIIORZ**
DENPRSU	pursued	griding	**DGIINPU**	rhizoid
spurned	usurped	ridging	pinguid	**DHIKSSU**
DENPRTU	**DERSSTU**	**DGGIINU**	**DGIINTY**	duskish
prudent	trussed	guiding	dignity	**DHILLSU**
uptrend	**DERSTTU**	**DGGIJNU**	tidying	dullish
DENPSSU	trusted	judging	**DGIKMNO**	**DHILMUY**
suspend	**DERSTTY**	**DGGILNO**	kingdom	humidly
DENRSSU	trysted	godling	**DGILLNU**	**DHILNOP**
undress	**DERSTUU**	lodging	dulling	dolphin
DENRSSY	sutured	**DGGINNU**	**DGILMNO**	**DHILPSY**
dryness	**DFFGINO**	dunging	molding	sylphid
DENSTTU	doffing	nudging	**DGILNOR**	**DHILRTY**
student	**DFFIIMR**	**DGHIILN**	lording	thirdly
stunted	midriff	hilding	**DGILNOY**	**DHIMOPR**
DEOOPPS	**DFFIMOR**	**DGHIINS**	yodling	dimorph
opposed	difform	shindig	**DGIMNOO**	**DHIMORU**
DEOOPRS	**DFGGINU**	**DGHILNO**	dooming	humidor
spoored	fudging	holding	**DGIMNPU**	rhodium
DEOOPRT	**DFGHIOS**	**DGHINOO**	dumping	**DHIMPSU**
torpedo	dogfish	hooding	**DGINNNO**	dumpish
trooped	**DFGIINN**	**DGHINOR**	donning	**DHINNOS**

donnish	dipylon	prosody	**EEEIRST**	sweeper
DHIOPTY	**DILNPSY**	**DOOPRTU**	eeriest	**EEEQRRU**
typhoid	spindly	dropout	**EEEIRSV**	queerer
DHIORTY	**DILORWY**	**EEEEFRR**	veeries	**EEEQSUZ**
thyroid	wordily	referee	**EEEIRSW**	squeeze
DHIPRSU	**DILOSTY**	**EEEFGRU**	eweries	**EEERRSV**
prudish	styloid	refugee	**EEEISTW**	reserve
DHJOPRU	**DILRYZZ**	**EEEFMNR**	sweetie	reverse
jodhpur	drizzly	freemen	**EEEJLRW**	severer
DHKORSY	**DIMMOST**	**EEEFORS**	jeweler	**EEERSSS**
droshky	midmost	foresee	**EEEJPRS**	seeress
DHLMOOU	**DIMNOPU**	**EEEFRRZ**	jeepers	**EEERSTW**
hoodlum	impound	freezer	**EEEKLNR**	sweeter
DHLOOTU	**DIMNOTW**	**EEEGILS**	kneeler	**EEERTTW**
holdout	midtown	elegies	**EEEKLRS**	tweeter
DHMMRUU	**DIMRTUU**	elegise	sleeker	**EEFFGLU**
humdrum	triduum	**EEEGILZ**	**EEEKMST**	effulge
DHMNOYY	**DIMRUUV**	elegize	meekest	**EEFFINT**
hymnody	duumvir	**EEEGIPR**	**EEEKNST**	fifteen
DHORSUY	**DINNOUW**	perigee	keenest	**EEFFNOS**
hydrous	inwound	**EEEGKLR**	**EEELLRV**	offense
DIIIMRU	**DINOOST**	kegeler	leveler	**EEFFORR**
iridium	isodont	**EEEGLMN**	**EEELMNT**	offerer
DIIINPS	**DINORWW**	gleemen	element	**EEFGILN**
insipid	windrow	**EEEGLNT**	**EEELPRS**	feeling
DIIJNOS	**DIOORTT**	genteel	sleeper	fleeing
disjoin	ridotto	**EEEGNPR**	**EEELPRT**	**EFFGINR**
DIIKKNS	**DIORSTT**	epergne	replete	feering
kidskin	distort	**EEEGNRR**	**EEELPST**	feigner
DIILLST	**DIPRSTU**	greener	steeple	freeing
distill	disrupt	**EEEGNRV**	**EEELRTV**	reefing
DIILLVY	**DLLORWY**	revenge	leveret	**EEFGINZ**
lividly	worldly	**EEEGNSS**	**EEELSSY**	feezing
DIILMTY	**DLNOPSY**	geneses	eyeless	**EEFGLLU**
timidly	spondyl	**EEEGRRT**	**EEEMNSS**	gleeful
DIILVVY	**DLNORUY**	greeter	nemeses	**EEFGLOR**
vividly	roundly	**EEEGRUX**	**EEEMRTX**	foreleg
DIILYZZ	**DLNOSUY**	exergue	extreme	**EEFGORY**
dizzily	soundly	**EEEHILW**	**EEENNTT**	frogeye
DIIMNOR	**DLOOPPY**	wheelie	entente	**EEFHINW**
miridon	polypod	**EEEHLOY**	**EEENPRT**	henwife
DIIMSSS	**DLOOPWY**	eyehole	preteen	**EEFHIRT**
dismiss	plywood	**EEEHSTT**	**EEENPST**	heftier
DIIMSUV	**DLOOSTU**	esthete	steepen	**EEFHLRS**
vidimus	outsold	**EEEILRR**	**EEENPSX**	herself
DIINOQU	**DLOPRUY**	leerier	expense	**EEFHLSS**
quinoid	proudly	**EEEILRV**	**EEENRRT**	fleshes
DIIORSV	**DNNOSUU**	relieve	reenter	**EEFHNRS**
divisor	unsound	**EEEIMNS**	terrene	freshen
DIJOSTU	**DNNOSUW**	enemies	**EEENRRV**	**EEFHORT**
judoist	sundown	**EEEIMRT**	venerer	thereof
DIKLSUY	**DNNOUUW**	eremite	**EEENRUV**	**EEFHORW**
duskily	unwound	**EEEINRT**	revenue	whereof
DIKNNOS	**DNOORTU**	teenier	**EEENSTW**	**EEFHRRS**
nonskid	orotund	**EEEINST**	sweeten	fresher
DILLOSY	**DNOOTUW**	teenies	**EEEORSV**	refresh
solidly	nutwood	**EEEIPRS**	oversee	**EEFHRST**
DILLRUY	**DNOPRUU**	seepier	**EEEORSY**	freshet
luridly	roundup	**EEEIPRW**	eyesore	**EEFIIMN**
DILMNRU	**DOOORSU**	weepier	**EEEPRSS**	feminie
drumlin	odorous	**EEEIPST**	peeress	**EEFIIRR**
DILMOOY	**DOOORTU**	epeeist	**EEEPRST**	fierier
moodily	outdoor	**EEEIRRV**	estrepe	**EEFILLS**
DILNOPY	**DOOPRSY**	reverie	**EEEPRSW**	fellies

EEFILLX	hegumen	**EEGIOTZ**	**EEHISTV**	jetties
flexile	**EEGIJNR**	egotize	thieves	**EEIKNPY**
EEFILRT	jeering	**EEGIRRV**	**EEHKLOY**	pinkeye
fertile	**EEGIKKN**	griever	keyhole	**EEIKPRR**
EEFILST	keeking	**EEGISTV**	**EEHLLRS**	perkier
felsite	**EEGIKLL**	vestige	sheller	**EEIKPRS**
lefties	leglike	**EEGLLSS**	**EEHLPRT**	peskier
EEFIMNR	**EEGIKLN**	legless	telpher	**EEIKRRS**
firemen	keeling	**EEGLMMU**	**EEHLRST**	kerries
EFFINSS	**EEGIKNN**	gemmule	shelter	**EEIKRST**
finesse	keening	**EEGLMOR**	**EEHLRSW**	keister
EEFIRRS	kneeing	gomerel	welsher	**EEIKTTT**
ferries	**EEGIKNP**	**EEGLNOR**	**EEHLRSY**	tektite
EDFIRRT	keeping	erelong	sheerly	**EEILLPS**
ferrite	peeking	**EEGLNOZ**	**EEHLSSU**	ellipse
EEFISTV	**EEGIKNR**	lozenge	hueless	**EEILLRY**
festive	reeking	**EEGLNRT**	**EEHLSSW**	leerily
EEFLLTY	**EEGIKNS**	gentler	welshes	**EEILLST**
fleetly	seeking	**EEGLNRY**	**EEHMORT**	tellies
EEFLNOS	**EEGILNP**	greenly	theorem	**EEILMNN**
oneself	epingle	**EEGMNST**	**EEHNNRY**	linemen
EEFLNRS	peeling	segment	hennery	**EEILMRV**
fresnel	**EEGILNR**	**EEGNPUX**	**EEHNOOR**	vermeil
EEFLRRU	leering	expunge	honoree	**EEILNNO**
ferrule	reeling	**EEGNSSU**	**EEHNORT**	leonine
EEFLRTU	**EEGILNT**	genuses	thereon	**EEILNNT**
fleuret	gentile	neguses	**EEHNORW**	lenient
EEFLRUX	**EEGILST**	**EEGOPRT**	nowhere	**EEILNNV**
flexure	elegist	protege	**EEHNPRS**	enliven
EEFMNOR	**EEGIMNR**	**EEGRRSS**	phrenes	**EEILNPS**
foremen	regimen	regress	**EEHNSTV**	pensile
EEFMNRT	**EEGIMNS**	**EEGRSTU**	seventh	**EEILNRV**
ferment	seeming	gesture	**EEHORRV**	livener
EEFMOTT	**EEGIMNT**	**EEHHRTW**	hoverer	**EEILNST**
mofette	meeting	whether	**EEHORTT**	tensile
EEFMPRU	teeming	**EEHIKLN**	thereto	**EEILNTT**
perfume	**EEGIMRS**	henlike	**EEHORTW**	entitle
EEFMTTU	remiges	**EEHIKLO**	whereto	**EEILOPT**
fumette	**EEGINNU**	hoelike ·	**EEHORVW**	petiole
EEFNRRY	genuine	**EEHILMN**	however	**EEILORV**
fernery	ingenue	hemline	whoever	overlie
EEFNRTV	**EEGINNV**	**EEHILPS**	**EEHOSTY**	**EEILOST**
fervent	evening	ephelis ·	eyeshot	estoile
EEFNSSW	**EEGINOP**	**EEHILSX**	**EEHRSTZ**	**EEILPRS**
fewness	epigone	helixes	hertzes	replies
EEFORRV	**EEGINPP**	**EEHINOR**	**EEIIMTZ**	spieler
forever	peeping	heroine	itemize	**EEILPRT**
EEFPRSU	**EEGINPR**	**EEHINRS**	**EEIINRV**	perlite
perfuse	peering	henries	veinier	reptile
EEFSSTU	**EEGINPS**	**EEHINRT**	**EEIIPST**	**EEILPRU**
fetuses	seeping	neither	pieties	puerile
EEGGHTU	**EEGINPV**	therein	**EEIIRRV**	**EEILPSS**
thuggee	peeving	**EEHINRW**	riviere	pelisse
EEGGILR	**EEGINPW**	wherein	**EEIJKRR**	**EEILPST**
leggier	weeping	**EEHIPSV**	jerkier	epistle
EEGGNOR	**EEGINRT**	peevish	**EEIJLLS**	**EEILRSS**
engorge	integer	**EEHIPTT**	jellies	ireless
EEGHILN	treeing	epithet	**EEIJMMS**	**EEILRST**
heeling	**EEGINRV**	**EEHIRSS**	jemmies	leister
EEGHINY	veering	heiress	**EEIJNNS**	sterile
hygiene	**EEGINSS**	**EEHIRST**	jennies	**EEILRSU**
EEGHIRW	genesis	heister	**EEIJRRS**	leisure
weigher	**EEGINTX**	**EEHISST**	jerries	**EEILRSV**
EEGHMNU	exigent	hessite	**EEIJSTT**	servile

EEILSSS
sessile
EEILSST
telesis
EEILSTV
velties
EEILSTX
sextile
EEILSUV
elusive
EEILTTX
textile
EEIMMNS
immense
EEIMMRS
immerse
EEIMNNO
nominee
EEIMNNT
eminent
EEIMNSS
nemesis
siemens
EEIMOPT
epitome
EEIMOTV
emotive
EEIMPRR
premier
EEIMPRS
emprise
imprese
premise
EEIMPRT
emptier
EEIMPST
septime
EEIMQRU
requiem
EEIMRRR
merrier
EEIMRRT
trireme
EEIMRSS
messier
EEIMRTT
termite
EEINNPS
pennies
EEINNRT
interne
EEINNRV
nervine
EEINNST
intense
EEINNTW
entwine
EEINOPR
pioneer
EEINOPS
peonies
EEINPSS
penises
EEINPSV

pensive
EEINQTU
quieten
EEINRRT
terrine
EEINRRV
nervier
vernier
EEINRST
entries
EEINRSV
inverse
EEINRSW
newsier
EEINRTU
retinue
reunite
uterine
EEINSST
sestine
EEINSTX
sixteen
EEIOPSS
poesies
EEIOPSX
epoxies
EEIOPTZ
poetize
EEIORSV
erosive
EEIPPPR
peppier
EEIPPTT
pipette
EEIPQRU
perique
EEIPRRR
perrier
EEIPRRS
perries
reprise
respire
EEIPRSV
previse
EEIPRSX
prexies
EEIPRTT
pettier
EEIPRTY
yperite
EEIPRVW
preview
EEIQRRU
require
EEIQRSU
esquire
queries
EEIQRTU
quieter
EEIQSTU
equites
EEIRRRT

terrier
EEIRRSV
reversi
EEIRRTV
riveter
EEIRRTW
rewrite
EEIRSSU
reissue
EEIRSTT
testier
EEIRSTV
restive
veriest
EEIRSTX
exister
EEIRSUZ
seizure
EEISSTX
sexiest
EEJLLMU
jumelle
EEJLRWY
jewelry
EEJPRRU
perjure
EEKKRRT
trekker
EEKLLUU
ukulele
EEKLNOS
keelson
EEKLRST
kestrel
EEKLSSY
keyless
EEKMRSS
kermess
EEKNOTY
keynote
EEKNSTU
netsuke
EELLLVY
levelly
EELLNOV
novelle
EELLOPT
pellote
EELLPRS
speller
EELMORW
eelworm
EELMPTT
templet
EELMRST
smelter
EELMRSU
lemures
EELNOPV
envelop
EELNPSY
spleeny
EELNQUY
queenly

EELNRST
nestler
EELNSTY
tensely
EELNTTU
lunette
EELOPRS
leprose
EELOPRX
explore
EELOPTU
eelpout
EELORSV
resolve
EELORTT
lorette
EELORVV
evolver
revolve
EELOSST
toeless
EELOTUV
veloute
EELPPRX
perplex
EELPRSU
repulse
EELPRTZ
pretzel
EELPRUX
plexure
EELPSTY
steeply
EELQRUY
queerly
EELRRVY
revelry
EELRSTT
settler
trestle
EELRSTW
swelter
wrestle
EELRSTY
tersely
EELRSTZ
seltzer
EELSSSU
useless
EELSSSX
sexless
EELSTUY
eustyle
EELSTWY
sweetly
EELTVVY
velvety
EEMMNOT
memento
EEMMRST
stemmer
EEMNNOV
envenom
EEMNNSW

newsmen
EEMNOOS
someone
EEMNOOY
mooneye
EEMNOST
temenos
EEMNPTU
umpteen
EEMOOSW
woesome
EEMOPRR
emperor
EEMOPRW
empower
EEMORRS
remorse
EEMORRT
remoter
EEMPPRT
preempt
EEMPRSS
empress
EEMPRSU
presume
supreme
EEMPRTT
tempter
EEMPRTU
permute
EEMPSTT
tempest
EEMSTTU
musette
EENNOSS
oneness
EENNRUV
unnerve
EENNSSW
newness
EENOPPT
peptone
EENORSS
senores
EENORSV
nervose
EENOTTT
tonette
EENPRST
present
serpent
EENPRTV
prevent
EENQSTU
sequent
EENRRST
sterner
EENRRTY
reentry
EENRRUV
nervure
EENRSTT
stenter
EENRSTW

western	tresses	freight	further	inferno
EENRSTY	**EERSSTT**	**EFGIKNR**	**EFIILLS**	**ERINNRU**
styrene	tersest	kerfing	fillies	funnier
EENRTUV	**EERSTTU**	**EFGILLN**	**EFIILMR**	**EFINNSU**
venture	trustee	felling	filmier	funnies
EENSSST	**EERSTUV**	**EFGILNT**	**EFIILMS**	**EFINRST**
setness	vesture	felting	misfile	snifter
EENSSTT	**EERTTUX**	**EFGILNU**	**EFIILRY**	**EFINRSU**
tensest	texture	fueling	fierily	infuser
EENSSTW	**EESTTTW**	**EFGILNX**	**EFIIMRS**	**EFINRUY**
wetness	wettest	flexing	misfire	reunify
EENSSUX	**EFFFINO**	**EFGIMNT**	**EFIINRT**	**EFINSST**
nexuses	infeoff	figment	niftier	fitness
EENSTVY	**EFFHILW**	**EFGINNP**	**EFIINSU**	**EFIOOST**
seventy	whiffle	pfennig	unifies	footsie
EEOOPRS	**EFFHIRS**	**EFGINOR**	**EFIIRZZ**	**EFIORRT**
operose	sheriff	foreign	fizzier	rotifer
EEOPPRS	**EFFHIRU**	**EFGINRU**	**EFIJLOR**	**EFIORST**
prepose	huffier	gunfire	frijole	foister
EEOPRRV	**EFFHLSU**	**EFGIOOR**	**EFIKNRU**	**EFIORST**
reprove	shuffle	goofier	funkier	forties
EEOPRTT	**EFFIIJS**	**EFGIORV**	**EFIKRRS**	**EFIOSRU**
treetop	jiffies	forgive	frisker	fisoure
EEOPSST	**EFFIKLS**	**EFGIRRT**	**EFILLOS**	**EFIOSTX**
poetess	skiffle	grifter	follies	foxiest
EEOPSSU	**EFFILNS**	**EFGLNTU**	**EFILLOW**	**EFIPRTY**
espouse	sniffle	fulgent	lowlife	petrify
EEORRST	**EFFILRY**	**EFGLOSS**	**EFILNOX**	**EFIRRRU**
restore	firefly	fogless	flexion	furrier
EEORRTU	**EFFINST**	**EFGNOOR**	**EFILNSS**	**EFIRRSU**
reroute	stiffen	forgone	finless	friseur
EEORRTW	**EFFIOPR**	**EFGNOSU**	**EFILOOS**	**EFIRRTT**
rewrote	piffero	fungoes	foliose	fritter
EEORSTT	**EFFIORT**	**EFGOORR**	**EFILOPR**	**EFIRRTY**
rosette	forfeit	forgoer	profile	terrify
EEORSTY	**EFFIPRU**	**EFGORRY**	**EFILORT**	**EFIRSSU**
esotery	puffier	forgery	loftier	fissure
EEPPPRY	**EFFIRST**	**EFHIIRS**	trefoil	fussier
peppery	stiffer	fishier	**EFILOSX**	**EFIRSTU**
EEPPRST	**EFFLMRU**	**EFHILMS**	sexfoil	surfeit
stepper	muffler	himself	**EFILPPR**	**EFIRSTW**
EEPRRSS	**EFFLNSU**	**EFHILSS**	flipper	swifter
presser	snuffle	selfish	**EFILPPU**	**EFIRSVY**
repress	**EFFLOSU**	**EFHINST**	pipeful	versify
EEPRRSU	souffle	fishnet	**EFILQUY**	**EFIRTUV**
peruser	**EFFLRRU**	**EFHIRST**	liquefy	furtive
EEPRRTV	ruffler	shifter	**EFILRRT**	**EFIRTUX**
pervert	**EFFLRTU**	**EFHIRSY**	trifler	fixture
EEPRSSS	fretful	fishery	**EFILRRY**	**EFIRUZZ**
presses	truffle	**EFHLLPU**	riflery	fuzzier
EEPRSSX	**EFFNRSU**	helpful	**EFILRTT**	**EFISTTT**
express	snuffer	**EFHLOPU**	flitter	fittest
EEPRSTT	**EFFOPRR**	hopeful	**EFILRVV**	**EFISTTY**
pretest	proffer	**EFHLRSU**	flivver	testify
EEPRTTX	**EFFPRUY**	flusher	**EFILRZZ**	**EFJLSTU**
pretext	puffery	**EFHLRSY**	fizzler	jestful
EEQRRUY	**EFFSSUU**	freshly	frizzle	**EFKLMNO**
equerry	suffuse	**EFHLSSU**	**EFILSTT**	menfolk
EEQRSTU	**EFGGLOR**	flushes	leftist	**EFLLSTU**
quester	flogger	**EFHLSTY**	**EFIMRST**	fullest
request	**EFGHINT**	thyself	firmest	**EFLMOSU**
EERRTTU	hefting	**EFHLTTW**	**EFIMRTY**	fulsome
utterer	**EFGHIRT**	twelfth	metrify	**EFLNORY**
EERSSST	fighter	**EFHRRTU**	**EFINNOR**	felonry

EFLNTUU	pegging	inveigh	lignite	kepping
tuneful	**EGGHILR**	**EGHIKLO**	**EGIILNV**	**EGIKNPR**
EFLOORT	higgler	hoglike	veiling	perking
rooflet	**EGGHORY**	**EGHIKNR**	**EGIILNX**	**EGIKNRY**
EFLOORY	hoggery	gherkin	exiling	yerking
foolery	**EGGIINS**	**EGHILMN**	**EGIIMNP**	**EGIKNSW**
EFLORSU	sieging	helming	impinge	skewing
ourself	**EGGIIPS**	**EGHILNP**	**EGIIMNT**	**EGILLNS**
EFLORTU	piggies	helping	iteming	selling
flouter	**EGGILLN**	**EGHILNS**	**EGIIMRR**	**EGILLNT**
EFLORUY	gelling	shingle	grimier	telling
fleuroy	**EGGILNR**	**EGHILNT**	**EGIINNR**	**EGILLNY**
EFLORWW	niggler	lighten	reining	yelling
werwolf	**EGGILRW**	**EGHILNV**	**EGIINNS**	**EGILLSU**
EFLORWY	wriggle	helving	insigne	gullies
flowery	**EGGIMMN**	**EGHILRT**	seining	**EGILMMN**
EFLRSTU	gemming	lighter	**EGIINPS**	lemming
fluster	**EGGIMNR**	**EGHILST**	peising	**EGILMMR**
restful	merging	sleight	**EGIINRT**	glimmer
EFLRTTU	**EGGINNS**	**EGHIMMN**	igniter	**EGILMNR**
flutter	ginseng	hemming	tigrine	gremlin
EFLSTUZ	**EGGINNV**	**EGHIMNS**	**EGIINSV**	mingler
zestful	venging	meshing	sieving	**EGILMNT**
EFMNOOT	**EGGINRS**	**EGHINNT**	**EGIINSZ**	melting
footmen	snigger	henting	seizing	**EGILMPS**
EFMOPRR	**EGGINRV**	**EGHINOS**	**EGIINTV**	glimpse
perform	verging	shoeing	eviting	**EGILNOP**
preform	**EGGINRY**	**EGHINRR**	**EGIINTX**	eloping
EFMPRUY	gingery	herring	exiting	**EGILNOS**
perfumy	**EGGINTT**	**EGHINRT**	**EGIINVW**	lingoes
EFNOOST	getting	righten	viewing	**EGILNOT**
eftsoon	**EGGIORS**	**EGHINST**	**EGIIPRW**	lentigo
festoon	soggier	nighest	periwig	**EGILNPT**
EFNORRW	**EGGIRRT**	**EGHINSW**	**EGIJKNR**	pelting
frowner	trigger	shewing	jerking	**EGILNPY**
EFNORTU	**EGGJLRU**	**EGHINTT**	**EGIJLLN**	yelping
fortune	juggler	tighten	jelling	**EGILNRT**
EFNORTW	**EGGLMSU**	**EGHIORS**	**EGIJLNR**	ringlet
forwent	smuggle	ogreish	jingler	tingler
EFOOPRR	**EGGLNSU**	**EGHIOTU**	**EGIJLNT**	tringle
reproof	snuggle	toughie	jinglet	**EGILNRY**
EFOOPRT	**EGGLOOY**	**EGHIRRT**	**EGIJNOS**	relying
foretop	geology	righter	jingoes	**EGILNST**
EFOPPRY	**EGGLORS**	**EGHIRTT**	**EGIJNSS**	glisten
foppery	slogger	tighter	jessing	singlet
EFOPRSS	**EGGLRSU**	**EGHITWY**	**EGIJNST**	**EGILNSW**
profess	slugger	weighty	jesting	swingle
EFOPRSU	**EGGLRTU**	**EGHLMPY**	**EGIJNTT**	**EGILNTT**
profuse	gurglet	phlegmy	jetting	letting
EFORRSU	**EGGNRSU**	**EGHLNOR**	**EGIKLNP**	**EGILNTU**
ferrous	snugger	leghorn	kelping	eluting
EFORRTY	**EGGNTUY**	**EGHLNTY**	**EGIKLNR**	**EGILNTW**
torrefy	nuggety	lengthy	erlking	welting
EFOSSTT	**EGGORTY**	**EGHMOSU**	**EGIKLNT**	**EGILNVY**
softest	toggery	gumshoe	kinglet	levying
EFPRTUY	**EGGSSTU**	**EGHNORU**	**EGIKNNN**	**EGILORS**
putrefy	suggest	roughen	kenning	glories
EFPSTUY	**EGHHHIT**	**EGHNOTU**	**EGIKNNR**	**EGILOST**
stupefy	heighth	toughen	kerning	elogist
EGGGILN	**EGHHIST**	**EGHORRU**	**EGIKNNT**	logiest
legging	highest	roughen	kenting	**EGILRST**
EGGGILR	**EGHIINT**	**EGHRTTUY**	**EGIKNOV**	gristle
giggler	nightie	theurgy	evoking	**EGILRTT**
EGGGINP	**EGHIINV**	**EGIILNT**	**EGIKNPP**	glitter

EGILRZZ	springe	tigress	upsurge	**EHILRSU**
grizzle	**EGINPRU**	**EGKLORW**	**EGRRSUY**	hurlies
EGILSSW	pureing	legwork	surgery	**EHILRSV**
wigless	**EGINPRY**	**EGLLOSY**	**EHHILLS**	shrivel
EGILSTU	preying	sylloge	hellish	**EHILSST**
ugliest	**EGINPSU**	**EGLMMRU**	**EHHIRTT**	hitless
EGIMMRR	pungies	glummer	thither	**EHILSTT**
grimmer	**EGINPSW**	**EGLMNOR**	**EHHIRTW**	lithest
EGIMNNO	spewing	mongrel	whither	thistle
omening	**EGINPSY**	**EGLMOOR**	**EHIKLP**	**EHILSTW**
EGIMNOT	espying	legroom	hiplike	whistle
emoting	**EGINPTT**	**EGLNOOY**	**EHIILLR**	**EHILTTW**
EGIMNPT	petting	neology	hillier	whittle
pigment	**EGINQUU**	**EGLNORU**	**EHIINNS**	**EHILTWY**
EGIMNRT	queuing	lounger	hinnies	whitely
terming	**EGINRRW**	**EGLNOST**	**EHIINRS**	**EHIMMRS**
EGIMNSS	wringer	longest	shinier	shimmer
messing	**EGINRSS**	**EGLORRW**	**EHIINRT**	**EHIMNRU**
EGIMOST	ingress	growler	inherit	rhenium
egotism	**EGINRST**	**EGLOSSS**	**EHIIPRT**	**EHIMORS**
EGINNNP	resting	glosses	pithier	heroism
penning	stinger	**EGLPRSU**	**EHIISTW**	**EHIMORZ**
EGINNNY	**EGINRSU**	splurge	withies	rhizome
yenning	reusing	**EGLRUZZ**	**EHIKLRU**	**EHIMOST**
EGINNOP	**EGINRSV**	guzzler	hulkier	homiest
opening	serving	**EGLSTUU**	**EHIKNOS**	**EHIMPRU**
EGINNPP	versing	gluteus	honkies	humpier
nepping	**EGINRSW**	**EGMMORT**	**EHIKNRT**	**EHIMPRW**
EGINNPU	swinger	grommet	thinker	whimper
penguin	**EGINRSY**	**EGMNORU**	**EHIKNSU**	**EHIMRSU**
EGINNRT	syringe	murgeon	hunkies	mushier
renting	**EGINRTT**	**EGMORTU**	**EHIKRRS**	**EHINNRT**
EGINNRV	gittern	gourmet	shirker	thinner
nerving	retting	**EGNNPTU**	**EHIKRSU**	**EHINOPR**
EGINNSS	**EGINRTY**	pungent	huskier	phonier
sensing	retying	**EGNNRUY**	**EHIKRSY**	**EHINOPS**
EGINNST	**EGINRVV**	gunnery	shrieky	phonies
nesting	revving	**EGNNTUU**	**EHIKSSU**	**EHINOPX**
tensing	**EGINSTT**	unguent	huskies	phoenix
EGINNSU	setting	**EGNOPRS**	**EHIKSWY**	**EHINORR**
ensuing	testing	sponger	whiskey	hornier
gunnies	**EGINSTW**	**EGNOPRY**	**EHILLNO**	**EHINORS**
EGINNTT	stewing	progeny	hellion	inshore
netting	westing	**EGNORRU**	**EHILLOS**	**EHINOSU**
tenting	**EGINSTZ**	rongeur	hollies	heinous
EGINNTV	zesting	**EGNORSS**	**EHILLTY**	**EHINRTV**
venting	**EGINTTV**	engross	lithely	thriven
EGINNVY	vetting	**EGNORSU**	**EHILNOP**	**EHIORRS**
envying	**EGINTTW**	surgeon	pinhole	horsier
EGINORR	wetting	**EGNORTZ**	**EHILNOT**	**EHIORRT**
ignorer	**EGIOPRU**	grotzen	neolith	heritor
EGINORS	groupie	**EGNORUY**	**EHILNPS**	**EHIORST**
signore	pirogue	younger	plenish	hoister
EGINORZ	**EGIORST**	**EGNRSTU**	**EHILOPT**	shortie
zeroing	goriest	surgent	hoplite	**EHIORSW**
EGINOSU	**EGIORTV**	**EGOPRRU**	**EHILOST**	showier
igneous	vertigo	grouper	holiest	**EHIORSY**
EGINOSY	**EGIOSTT**	**EGORRUY**	hostile	hosiery
isogeny	egotist	roguery	**EHILPRT**	**EHIPPRS**
EGINOTV	**EGIPRUU**	**EGORSSS**	philter	shipper
vetoing	guipure	grosses	**EHILPSS**	**EHIPPST**
EGINPPP	**EGIPSSY**	**EGPRRUY**	hipless	hippest
pepping	gypsies	purgery	**EHILRST**	**EHIPPTW**
EGINPRS	**EGIRSST**	**EGPRSUU**	slither	whippet

EHIPRST
hipster
EHIPRSU
pushier
EHIPRSW
whisper
EHIPSTT
pettish
EHIRRSU
hurries
rushier
EHIRSTU
hirsute
EHIRSTW
swither
EHIRSVY
shivery
EHISSSU
hussies
EHISSSW
swishes
EHISTTW
wettish
whitest
EHLMNOT
menthol
EHLNTTY
tenthly
EHLOOPT
pothole
EHLORST
holster
hostler
EHLORTY
helotry
EHLOSSS
sloshes
EHLPRSU
plusher
EHLRSTU
hustler
EHLSTTU
shuttle
EHMNOOR
hormone
EHMNOPS
shopmen
EHMNOSW
showmen
EHMNPTY
nymphet
EHMNTTU
hutment
EHMOOSW
somehow
EHMORST
smother
EHMPRTU
thumper
EHMRSUU
humerus
EHNNRSU
shunner
EHNOORR

honorer
EHNOORS
onshore
EHNOPRY
hyperon
EHNOPUY
euphony
EHNORRT
horrent
norther
EHNORST
shorten
EHNOSST
hotness
EHNOSTT
shotten
EHNOSTY
honesty
EHNSSSY
shyness
EHOORST
shooter
EHOPPRS
shopper
EHOPPRT
prophet
EHOPPRW
whopper
EHOPRRY
orphrey
EHOPRST
strophe
EHORSTU
shouter
souther
EHORSWY
showery
EHOSSST
hostess
EHOSTTT
hottest
EHRSSTY
shyster
EHRSTTU
shutter
EIIILST
ileitis
EIIJMMS
jimmies
EIIKKNR
kinkier
EIIKLMR
milkier
EIIKLNT
tinlike
EIIKLRS
silkier
EIIKNPS
pinkies
EIIKNST
inkiest
EIIKRRS
riskier
EIIKSTT

kitties
EIILLMM
millime
EIILLMN
milline
EIILLMR
millier
EIILLNV
villein
EIILLRS
sillier
EIILLSS
sillies
EIILMPR
imperil
EIILMPS
implies
EIILMRS
milreis
slimier
EIILMRT
limiter
EIILMSS
missile
EIILMST
elitism
limiest
limites
EIILMUX
milieux
EIILNOS
elision
EIILNOZ
lionize
EIILNRT
lintier
EIILNST
liniest
EIILNTU
inutile
EIILOST
oiliest
EIILQSU
silique
EIILRST
siltier
EIILSTT
elitist
EIILSTW
wiliest
EIILTUZ
utilize
EIIMMSS
mimesis
EIIMNRT
interim
mintier
termini
EIIMNRV
miniver
EIIMNTY
nimiety
EIIMOSS
meiosis

EIIMPTY
impiety
EIIMRST
miriest
mistier
rimiest
EIIMSSV
missive
EIINNNS
ninnies
EIINNQU
quinine
EIINNRT
tinnier
EIINORS
ironies
EIINORZ
ironize
EIINPPR
nippier
EIINPRS
inspire
spinier
EIINPST
piniest
EIINQRU
inquire
EIINRTT
nitrite
EIINRTV
inviter
vitrine
EIINSTT
tiniest
EIINSTU
unities
EIINSTV
viniest
EIINSTW
winiest
EIINTUZ
unitize
EIIORSV
ivories
EIIPPRZ
zippier
EIIPPST
pipiest
EIIPRST
tipsier
EIIPRSW
wispier
EIIRRTZ
ritzier
EIIRSTV
revisit
EIIRSTW
wiriest
EIIRTTW
wittier
EIISSSS
sissies
EIISSTX

sixties
EIISTZZ
tizzies
EIJKLRY
jerkily
EIJLLOR
jollier
EIJLLOS
jollies
EIJLORT
joltier
EIJLORW
jowlier
EIJMPRU
jumpier
EIJNORT
jointer
EIJNORY
joinery
EIJNPRU
juniper
EIJNRRU
injurer
EIJRTTY
jittery
EIJSSUV
jussive
EIKKMNR
kirkmen
EIKKOOR
kookier
EIKLLNW
inkwell
EIKLLST
skillet
EIKLMMN
milkmen
EIKLNRW
wrinkle
EIKLNSY
skyline
EIKLNTT
knittle
EIKLNTW
twinkle
EIKLPRY
perkily
EIKLRSU
sulkier
EIKLRTT
kittler
EIKLSSU
sulkies
EIKLSTT
skittle
EIKMMRR
krimmer
EIKMMRS
skimmer
EIKMNNS
kinsmen
EIKMNOR
moniker
EIKMNRY

minkery	**EILMPRY**	rissole	**EIMMMSU**	misstep
EIKMORS	primely	**EILORSU**	mummies	**EIMPSTU**
irksome	**EILMPST**	lousier	**EIMMPRR**	impetus
smokier	limpest	**EILORSW**	primmer	**EIMRSSU**
EIKMRSS	**EILMPSU**	lowries	**EIMMPRU**	surmise
kirmess	impulse	**EILORTT**	premium	**EIMRSTT**
skinner	**EILMPSX**	tortile	**EIMMRRT**	metrist
EIKNORV	simplex	**EILORTU**	trimmer	**EIMRTUX**
invoker	**EILMPTY**	outlier	**EIMMRSU**	mixture
EIKNOSS	emptily	**EILOSTT**	rummies	**EIMSSTY**
kenosis	**EILMRRY**	litotes	**EIMMRSW**	stymies
EIKNRST	merrily	**EILOTUV**	swimmer	**EINNOPS**
stinker	**EILMRSS**	outlive	**EIMMRUY**	pension
EIKNRTT	rimless	**EILPPRS**	yummier	**EINNORT**
knitter	**EILMRSU**	slipper	**EIMMSTU**	intoner
trinket	misrule	**EILPPRT**	tummies	ternion
EIKNOPR	**EILMRSY**	tippler	**EIMNNOT**	**EINNORU**
porkpie	miserly	**EILPPRU**	mention	reunion
EIKOPRR	**EILMUUV**	pulpier	**EIMNOOR**	**EINNORV**
porkier	eluvium	**EILPPST**	ionomer	environ
EIKOPST	**EILNOOR**	stipple	**EIMNOOS**	**EINNOST**
pokiest	loonier	**EILPPSW**	noisome	tension
EIKPPRS	**EILNOPS**	swipple	**EIMNOOT**	**EINNOSV**
skipper	epsilon	**EILPRSU**	emotion	venison
EIKPPST	**EILNOSS**	pluries	**EIMNOPT**	**EINNOTT**
skippet	lioness	**EILPRTT**	pimento	tontine
EIKPSSS	**EILNOSU**	triplet	**EIMNOST**	**EINNOVW**
skepsis	elusion	**EILPRTX**	moisten	inwoven
EIKRRST	**EILNOTU**	triplex	**EIMNOSW**	**EINNPRS**
striker	outline	**EILPRUU**	winsome	spinner
EIKRSTT	**EILNOTV**	purlieu	**EIMNOTY**	**EINNPST**
skitter	violent	**EILPSST**	omneity	tenpins
EILLLOS	**EILNOVV**	tipless	**EIMNPTU**	**EINNPSY**
lollies	involve	**EILPSTT**	pinetum	spinney
EILLMOS	**EILNPTY**	spittle	**EIMNRST**	**EINNRRU**
mollies	ineptly	**EILPSTU**	minster	runnier
EILLMOT	**EILNPUV**	stipule	**EIMNSTT**	**EINNRSU**
melilot	vulpine	**EILPSUV**	smitten	sunnier
EILLNSS	**EILNRSV**	pulsive	**EIMNUZZ**	**EINNRTV**
illness	silvern	**EILQRTU**	muezzin	vintner
EILLORW	**EILNRTY**	quilter	**EIMOORR**	**EINOORS**
lowlier	inertly	**EILQRUU**	roomier	erosion
EILLOSV	**EILNRVY**	liqueur	**EIMOPRS**	**EINOOST**
vollies	nervily	**EILQTUY**	imposer	isotone
EILLRST	**EILNSSS**	quietly	promise	**EINOPPR**
stiller	sinless	**EILRRTW**	semipro	propine
trellis	**EILNSTU**	twirler	**EIMOPRV**	**EINOPRT**
EILLRTT	luniest	**EILRSTU**	improve	pointer
littler	utensil	lustier	**EIMORRW**	protein
EILLSSU	**EILOOST**	**EILRSVY**	wormier	**EINOPRV**
sullies	ostiole	silvery	**EIMORSS**	provine
EILMMRS	**EILOPPR**	**EILRTUV**	mossier	**EINOQUX**
slimmer	loppier	rivulet	**EIMORST**	equinox
EILMOPR	**EILOPRS**	**EILSSTW**	moister	**EINORST**
implore	spoiler	witless	mortise	oestrin
EILMORR	**EILOPST**	**EILSTTY**	**EIMORSU**	stonier
lorimer	pistole	stylite	mousier	**EINORSV**
EILMOSS	**EILOPSU**	testily	**EIMOSTZ**	version
lissome	pileous	**EILSTYZ**	mestizo	**EINORSW**
EILMPRS	**EILOPTX**	stylize	**EIMPRSS**	snowier
simpler	exploit	**EILSWZZ**	impress	**EINORTU**
EILMPRU	**EILORRS**	swizzle	**EIMPRST**	routine
lumpier	lorries	**EIMMMOS**	imprest	**EINOSSS**
	EILORSS	mommies	**EIMPSST**	session

EINOSST	potties	tritest	novelly	**ELPPRSU**
nosiest	**EIOPSTU**	**EIRSTTW**	**ELLOOSY**	suppler
EINOSUV	piteous	twister	loosely	**ELPRUZZ**
envious	**EIOPTUW**	**EIRSUVV**	pollute	puzzler
niveous	wipeout	survive	**ELLOPTU**	**ELPSTUU**
EINPPRS	**EIORRRS**	**EIRTTTW**	pollute	pluteus
snipper	sorrier	twitter	**ELLORTY**	pustule
EINPPST	**EIORRRW**	**EJJMNNUU**	trolley	**ELRRSTU**
snippet	worrier	jejunum	**ELLOSTU**	rustler
EINPRRT	**EIORRSW**	**EJKMNNU**	outsell	**ELRTTUY**
printer	worries	junkmen	sellout	utterly
reprint	**EIORSST**	**EJLORST**	**ELLOWYY**	**ELRTUUV**
EINPRSU	rosiest	jostler	yellowy	vulture
uprisen	sorites	**EJLOSSY**	**ELMMPTU**	**ELSSTYY**
EINPSTU	stories	joyless	plummet	systyle
puniest	**EIORSSU**	**EJMNRUY**	**ELMOORT**	**EMMNOTY**
punties	serious	jurymen	tremolo	metonym
EINPSTW	**EIOSTUZ**	**EJNORUY**	**ELMOPRY**	**EMMRSUY**
inswept	outsize	journey	polymer	summery
EINPTTY	**EIPPPSU**	**EJOORVY**	**ELMOSUU**	**EMNOORT**
tintype	puppies	overjoy	emulous	montero
EINQSTU	**EIPPRRT**	**EJOPPRT**	**ELMPRUY**	**EMNOPST**
inquest	tripper	propjet	plumery	postmen
EINQTTU	**EIPRRST**	**EJOPRTT**	**ELMSSSU**	**EMNOPSU**
quintet	striper	jetport	sumless	spumone
EINRRSU	**EIPRRSU**	**EJORSTU**	**ELNOPTU**	**EMNORRU**
insurer	pursier	jouster	opulent	mourner
EINRRTU	**EIPRSST**	**EJPRRUY**	**ELNORTY**	**EMNORST**
runtier	persist	perjury	elytron	monster
EINRSSU	stirpes	**EKLLNOR**	**ELNOSTV**	**EMNORTT**
sunrise	**EIPRSSU**	knoller	solvent	torment
EINRSTV	pussier	**EKLLRRU**	**ELNOTVY**	**EMNORTU**
striven	suspire	kruller	novelty	monture
EINRSWY	**EIPRSTT**	**EKLNORS**	**ELNRSTY**	remount
swinery	spitter	snorkel	sternly	**EMNRSTU**
EINRTTU	tipster	**EKMNORW**	**ELNSSSU**	sternum
nuttier	**EIPRSUU**	workmen	sunless	**EMOOPRT**
EINRTTW	euripus	**EKMNPTU**	**ELNSSSY**	promote
written	**EIPRUVW**	unkempt	slyness	**EMOOSTT**
EINSSSU	purview	**EKNOORS**	**ELOORTT**	mottoes
sinuses	**EIPSSSU**	snooker	rootlet	**EMOOSTW**
EINSSTW	pussies	**EKNORTW**	**ELOOSST**	twosome
witness	**EIPSTTU**	network	loosest	**EMORRSU**
EIOOPST	putties	**EKNORUY**	**ELOPPST**	morsure
isotope	**EIQRSTU**	younker	stopple	**EMORSUY**
EIOORRT	querist	**EKNRTUY**	**ELOPRRW**	mousery
rootier	**EIQRTTU**	turnkey	prowler	**EMOSTVZ**
EIOORST	quitter	**EKOOPRV**	**ELOPRSU**	zemstvo
sootier	**EIQRUVY**	provoke	leprous	**EMPRSTU**
EIOORWZ	quivery	**EKOORRY**	**ELOPRSY**	stumper
woozier	**EIQRUZZ**	rookery	leprosy	sumpter
EIOOSTZ	quizzer	**EKOORTW**	**ELOPRTY**	**EMPRTTU**
ooziest	**EIQSTUU**	kotower	protyle	trumpet
EIOPPPS	quietus	**EKPPSUU**	**ELOPSST**	**EMRSTYY**
poppies	**EIQSUZZ**	seppuku	topless	mystery
EIOPRRS	quizzes	**EKPRSTY**	**ELORSUY**	**ENNNRUY**
prosier	**EIRRSTU**	psykter	elusory	nunnery
EIOPRST	rustier	**ELLMOOR**	**ELORTTY**	**ENNORSU**
riposte	**EIRSSUU**	morello	lottery	nonuser
EIOPRSU	usuries	**ELLMPUU**	**ELOSSTU**	**ENNORTU**
soupier	**EIRSSUV**	plumule	lotuses	neutron
EIOPRSX	viruses	**ELLNOSW**	**ELOSSTW**	**ENNRSTU**
proxies	**EIRSTTT**	swollen	slowest	stunner
EIOPSTT	stretti	**ELLNOVY**	**ELOSSTY**	**ENOOPPR**
			systole	

propone
ENOORSU
onerous.
ENOPRST
postern
ENOPRTT
portent
ENOPRTY
entropy
ENOPSST
stepson
ENOQTUU
unquote
ENORRTT
torrent
ENORRUV
overrun
runover
ENORSSY
sensory
ENORSTT
stentor
ENORSTU
tonsure
ENORSUV
nervous
ENORTUY
tourney
ENOSTUU
tenuous
ENPRSTU
punster
ENRRSUY
nursery
ENRRTUU
nurture
ENRSSWY
wryness
ENRSTTU
entrust
EOOPPRS
opposer
propose
EOOPPRV
popover
EOOPRRT
trooper
EOOPRST
poorest
EOOPRTW
towrope
EOORRST
rooster
EOORRTY
rootery
EOORTUW
outwore
EOOSSSU
osseous
EOPPRRS
prosper
EOPPRSS
oppress
EOPPRST

stopper
EOPPRSU
purpose
EOPPSSU
suppose
EOPRRST
presort
EOPRRTU
trouper
EOPRSSW
prowess
EOPRSTT
protest
spotter
EOPRSTU
petrous
posture
EOPRTTY
pottery
EOPRTVY
poverty
EOPSSSS
possess
EOQRSTU
questor
EORRSTT
stertor
EORRTTT
trotter
EORRTTU
torture
EORSSTU
oestrus
sourest
EORSTTT
stretto
EPPSTUW
upswept
EPRRSUU
usurper
EPRRTUU
rupture
EPRSSTY
spryest
EPRSTTU
sputter
ERSSTUY
russety
ERSTTTU
stutter
FFGHINU
huffing
FFGIIMN
miffing
FFGIINR
griffin
FFGIINT
tiffing
FFGILNU
luffing
FFGIMNU
muffing
FFGINPU
puffing

FFGLRUY
gruffly
FFHHISU
huffish
FFHOSTU
shutoff
FFILOST
sifflot
FFILPUY
puffily
FFILSTU
fistful
FFILSTY
stiffly
FFINOPT
pontiff
FFIORTY
fortify
FFNORTU
turnoff
FGGGIIN
figging
FGGGINO
fogging
FGGILNO
golfing
FGGILNU
gulfing
FGGILOY
foggily
FGGINOO
goofing
FGGINOR
forging
FGHHIOS
hogfish
FGHIINS
fishing
FGHILTY
flighty
FGHINOO
hoofing
FGHNOOR
foghorn
FGIIKNN
knifing
FGIIKNR
firking
FGIILLN
filling
FGIILMN
filming
FGIILNO
foiling
FGIILNR
rifling
FGIILNT
fliting
lifting
FGIILNY
lignify
FGIIMNR
firming
FGIINRT

rifting
FGIINST
sifting
FGIINSY
signify
FGIINTT
fitting
FGIINZZ
fizzing
FGIKNNU
funking
FGIKNOR
forking
FGILMNU
fluming
FGILNOO
fooling
FGILNOT
lofting
FGILNOU
fouling
FGILNOW
flowing
fowling
FGILNRU
furling
FGILNTU
fluting
FGILNUX
fluxing
FGILORY
glorify
FGIMNOR
forming
FGINNNU
funning
FGINOOR
roofing
FGINOOT
footing
FGINRRU
furring
FGINRSU
surfing
FGINSSU
fussing
FGINTTU
tufting
FGLLOWY
glowfly
FGLNORU
furlong
FGNOSUU
fungous
FHIINPS
pinfish
FHILOOS
foolish
FHILOSW
wolfish
FHILSUW
wishful
FHINRSU
furnish

FHINSSU
sunfish
FHIOPPS
foppish
FHIORRY
horrify
FHIRTTY
thrifty
FHIRTUY
thurify
FHLOOSY
shoofly
FHLRTUU
hurtful
ruthful
FHOOOTT
hotfoot
FIILLMO
milfoil
FIILPTU
pitiful
FIINOSS
fission
FIINRTY
nitrify
FIIRTVY
vitrify
FIJLLOY
jollify
FIJSTUY
justify
FIKKLNO
kinfolk
FIKLLSU
skilful
FIKLNSU
skinful
FIKLRSU
riskful
FILLMOY
mollify
FILLNUY
nullify
FILLOTY
loftily
FILLSTU
listful
FILNNUY
funnily
FILNOUX
fluxion
FILORST
florist
FILPPUY
pulpify
FILRSTY
firstly
FILSSUY
fussily
FILSTTU
flutist
FILSTUW
wistful
FILSTWY

swiftly	logging	glowing	insight	hunting
FILUYZZ	**GGGILNU**	**GGILNOZ**	**GHIINSW**	**GHINOOP**
fuzzily	lugging	glozing	wishing	hooping
FIMMMUY	**GGGIMNU**	**GGILNPU**	**GHIINTT**	**GHINOOS**
mummify	mugging	gulping	hitting	shooing
FIMNORU	**GGGINNO**	**GGILRWY**	tithing	**GHINOOT**
uniform	nogging	wriggly	**GHIINTW**	hooting
FIMORTY	**GGGINOR**	**GGIMMNU**	whiting	**GHINOPP**
mortify	gorging	gumming	withing	hopping
FIMSTYY	**GGGINOT**	**GGINNNU**	**GHIJNOS**	**GHINOPY**
mystify	togging	gunning	joshing	hypoing
FINRTUY	**GGGINOU**	**GGINNOO**	**GHIKLNU**	**GHINORS**
nutrify	gouging	ongoing	hulking	horsing
FIOORSU	**GGGINPU**	**GGINNOT**	**GHIKNNO**	shoring
furioso	pugging	tonging	honking	**GHINORW**
FIOPRTY	**GGGINTU**	**GGINNOW**	**GHIKNOO**	whoring
torpify	tugging	gowning	hooking	**GHINOST**
FIOPSTX	**GGHHIOS**	**GGINOOS**	**GHIKNOS**	hosting
postfix	hoggish	goosing	hogskin	**GHINOSU**
FIORSUU	**GGHIINN**	**GGINOPR**	**GHIKNOW**	housing
furious	hinging	groping	howking	**GHINOSV**
FKOOORS	**GGHIINS**	**GGINORU**	**GHIKNSU**	shoving
forsook	sighing	rouging	husking	**GHINOSW**
FLLOSUU	**GGHIIRS**	**GGINORW**	**GHILLNU**	showing
soulful	riggish	growing	hulling	**GHINOTT**
FLLSTUU	**GGHINSU**	**GGINPPY**	**GHILLTY**	hotting
lustful	gushing	gypping	lightly	tonight
FLMMOUX	**GGIILLN**	**GGINPRU**	**GHILNOS**	**GHINPSU**
flummox	gilling	purging	longish	pushing
FLMOORU	**GGIIMNP**	**GGINRSU**	**GHILNOT**	**GHINRSU**
roomful	gimping	surging	tholing	rushing
FLNOORR	**GGIIMNR**	**GGINSTU**	**GHILNOW**	**GHINRTU**
forlorn	griming	gusting	howling	hurting
FLOOTUW	**GGIINNN**	**GGINTTU**	**GHILNRU**	**GHINTTU**
outflow	ginning	gutting	hurling	hutting
FLOSUUV	**GGIINNO**	**GGIPRSY**	**GHILNSY**	**GHINUZZ**
fulvous	ingoing	spriggy	shingly	huzzing
FMRSTUU	**GGIINNP**	**GHHINSU**	**GHILNTY**	**GHIORSU**
frustum	pinging	hushing	nightly	rougish
FNOORSU	**GGIINNR**	**GHHORTU**	**GHILRTY**	**GHIPRTU**
sunroof	ringing	through	rightly	upright
FOOOPRT	**GGIINNS**	**GHHOTTU**	**GHILSTY**	**GHIPTTU**
rooftop	signing	thought	sightly	uptight
GGGGIIN	**GGIINNT**	**GHIIKNT**	**GHILTTY**	**GHLORUY**
gigging	tinging	kithing	tightly	roughly
GGGHINO	**GGIINNW**	**GHIILLN**	**GHIMMNU**	**GHLOSTY**
hogging	winging	hilling	humming	ghostly
GGGHINU	**GGIINPP**	**GHIILNT**	**GHIMNNY**	**GHMORSU**
hugging	gipping	hilting	hymning	sorghum
GGGIIJN	**GGIINPR**	**GHIILNW**	**GHIMNPU**	**GHNOSTU**
jigging	griping	whiling	humping	gunshot
GGGIINP	**GGILLNU**	**GHIILRS**	**GHIMNRY**	shotgun
pigging	gulling	girlish	rhyming	**GHORTUW**
GGGIINR	**GGILNNO**	**GHIINNS**	**GHIMNSU**	wrought
rigging	longing	shining	mushing	**GHORTUY**
GGGIINW	**GGILNNU**	**GHIINNT**	**GHINNOP**	yoghurt
wigging	lunging	hinting	phoning	**GIIJKNN**
GGGIINZ	**GGILNOS**	**GHIINNW**	**GHINNOR**	jinking
zigging	gosling	whining	horning	**GIIJLNT**
GGGIJNO	**GGILNOV**	**GHIINPP**	**GHINNOS**	jilting
jogging	gloving	hipping	noshing	**GIIJNNO**
GGGIJNU	**GGILNOW**	**GHIINSS**	**GHINNOT**	joining
jugging		hissing	nothing	**GIIKKNN**
GGGILNO		**GHIINST**	**GHINNTU**	kinking

GIIKLLN
killing
GIIKLMN
milking
GIIKLNN
inkling
linking
GIIKLNT
kilting
kitling
GIIKNNP
kingpin
pinking
GIIKNNS
sinking
GIIKNNT
tinking
GIIKNNW
winking
GIIKNPS
pigskin
spiking
GIIKNRS
risking
GIIKNSS
kissing
GIIKNSV
skiving
GIIKNTT
kitting
GIILLMN
milling
GIILLNP
pilling
GIILLNR
rilling
GIILLNT
lilting
tilling
GIILLNW
willing
GIILMNO
moiling
GIILMNP
limping
GIILMNS
sliming
smiling
GIILMPR
pilgrim
GIILNNT
linting
GIILNOR
ligroin
roiling
GIILNOS
soiling
GIILNOT
toiling
GIILNPP
lipping
GIILNPS
lisping
GIILNRT

tirling
GIILNST
listing
silting
GIILNSV
sliving
GIILNTT
tilting
titling
GIILNTW
wilting
GIIMMNR
rimming
GIIMMNT
minting
GIIMNPP
pimping
GIIMNPR
priming
GIIMNSS
missing
GIIMNST
misting
smiting
GIINNNP
pinning
GIINNNS
sinning
GIINNNT
tinning
GIINNNW
winning
GIINNOP
opining
GIINNOR
ironing
GIINNOS
noising
GIINNPP
nipping
GIINNPS
sniping
GIINNRS
rinsing
GIINNRU
inuring
ruining
GIINNTT
tinting
GIINNTU
uniting
GIINNTW
twining
GIINOPS
poising
GIINORS
signior
signori
GIINORT
rioting
GIINPPP
pipping
GIINPPR
ripping

GIINPPS
sipping
GINNPPT
tipping
GIINPPY
yipping
GIINPPZ
zipping
GIINPQU
piquing
GIINPRS
spiring
GIINPRZ
prizing
GIINPSS
pissing
GIINPST
spiting
GIINPSW
swiping
GIINPTT
pitting
GIINPTY
pitying
GIINQRU
quiring
GIINRRS
sirring
GIINRRY
yirring
GIINRTW
writing
GIINSST
sisting
GIINSSU
issuing
GIINSTT
sitting
GIINSTU
suiting
GIINSZZ
sizzing
GIINTTW
witting
GIJKNNU
junking
GIJLNOT
jolting
GIJMNPU
jumping
GIJNOTT
jotting
GIJNTTU
jutting
GIKLNOO
looking
GIKLNRU
lurking
GIKLNSU
sulking
GIKMNOS
smoking
GIKNNOW
knowing

GIKNOOR
rooking
GIKNOPS
spoking
GIKNORW
working
GIKNOST
stoking
GILLLNO
lolling
GILLLNU
lulling
GILLMNU
mulling
GILLNNU
nulling
GILLNOP
polling
GILLNOR
rolling
GILLNOT
tolling
GILLNPU
pulling
GILMNOO
looming
GILMNOT
molting
GILMNPU
lumping
pluming
GILNNRU
nurling
GILNOOP
looping
pooling
GILNOOS
loosing
GILNOOT
looting
tooling
GILNOPP
lopping
GILNOPS
sloping
GILNOPW
plowing
GILNOSV
solving
GILNOSW
slowing
GILNOTT
lotting
GILNOWY
yowling
GILNPPU
pulping
GILNPRU
purling
GILNSTU
lusting
GILNSTY
styling
GILORTY

trilogy
GILOSTT
glottis
GILRSTY
gristly
GILRTUY
liturgy
GILRYZZ
grizzly
GIMMNSU
summing
GIMNNOO
mooning
GIMNNOR
morning
GIMNOOR
mooring
rooming
GIMNOOZ
zooming
GIMNOPP
mopping
GIMNOPR
romping
GIMNORW
worming
GIMNOSU
mousing
GIMNPPU
pumping
GIMNPSU
spuming
GIMNSSU
mussing
GINNNOO
nooning
GINNNOW
wonning
GINNNPU
punning
GINNNRU
running
GINNNSU
sunning
GINNNTU
tunning
GINNOOS
noosing
GINNORS
snoring
GINNORW
ingrown
GINNOST
stoning
GINNOSW
snowing
GINNOTW
wonting
GINNPRU
pruning
GINNPTU
punting
GINNRSU
nursing

GINNRTU turning	stoving **GINOSTW** stowing	grownup **GOORTUW** outgrow	**HIMOTTY** timothy	**IILLMNO** million
GINNTTU nutting	**GINOTTT** totting	**HHIISTW** whitish	**HIMPRTU** triumph	**IILLMSY** slimily
GINNTUY untying	**GINOTTU** touting	**HHIOPST** hipshot	**HIMSSTU** isthmus	**IILLNOP** pillion
GINOOPP pogonip pooping	**GINPPPU** pupping	**HHIORSW** whorish	**HINNNSU** nunnish	**IILLNOZ** zillion
GINOORT rooting	**GINPPSU** supping	**HHOOSTT** hotshot	**HINNORT** tinhorn	**IILLNST** instill
GINOOST sooting	**GINPRRU** purring	**HIIJKNS** hijinks	**HINOORT** hornito	**IILMNOS** lionism
GINOOTT tooting	**GINPRSU** pursing	**HIIKNPS** kinship pinkish	**HINOORZ** horizon	**IILMSTU** stimuli
GINOPPP popping	**GINPRSY** springy	**HIILMTU** lithium	**HINORSU** nourish	**IILNNSU** insulin
GINOPPS sopping	**GINPSUW** upswing	**HIILPST** shilpit	**HIOPRSW** worship	**IILNORS** sirloin
GINOPPT topping	**GINPTTU** putting	**HIILPTY** pithily	**HIOPSST** sophist	**IILNOSY** noisily
GINOPRS prosing	**GINRSTU** rusting	**HIIMNSX** minxish	**HIORSTY** history	**IILORTV** vitriol
GINOPRT porting	**GINRSTY** stringy	**HIIMSTT** shittim	**HIOSSTT** sottish	**IILOSTV** violist
GINOPRU ingroup pouring	**GINRTTU** rutting	**HIINORS** ironish	**HIOTTUW** without	**IILPRVY** privily
GINOPRV proving	**GINTTTU** tutting	**HIINSSW** swinish	**HIQSSUY** squishy	**IILPSWY** wispily
GINOPST posting stoping	**GIOPRRU** prurigo	**HIKLSUY** huskily	**HIRSTTU** ruttish	**IILSTTT** titlist
GINOPTT potting	**GIOPSSY** gossipy	**HIKMNOS** monkish	**HIRSTTY** thirsty	**IILTTUY** utility
GINOPTU pouting	**GIOSSYZ** zygosis	**HIKNNOR** inkhorn	**HKKLOOZ** kolkhoz	**IILTTWY** wittily
GINOQTU quoting	**GLLLOOR** logroll	**HILLOPT** hilltop	**HKOOOPT** pothook	**IIMMMNU** minimum
GINORSS rossing	**GLNNOOR** lorgnon	**HILLRSY** shrilly	**HLMNOTY** monthly	**IIMNOSS** mission
GINORST sorting storing	**GLNOOPR** prolong	**HILMMOU** holmium	**HLORSTY** shortly	**IIMNOTX** mixtion
GINORSU rousing souring	**GLNOOPY** polygon	**HILMPSU** lumpish	**HLPRSUU** sulphur	**IIMNPRT** imprint
GINORTT rotting	**GLNORWY** wrongly	**HILMSUY** mushily	**HMMNOOY** homonym	**IIMOPSU** impious
GINORTU routing touring	**GLNOTTU** glutton	**HILMTUU** thulium	**HMOPRSU** rumshop	**IIMOSST** mitosis
GINORTW trowing	**GLNOUYY** youngly	**HILNNTY** ninthly	**HNOOPTY** typhoon	**IINNOOP** opinion
GINOSST tossing	**GLOOORY** orology	**HILNORY** hornily	**HOPRSTU** hotspur	**IINOPSS** sinopis
GINOSSU sousing	**GLOOOYZ** zoology	**HILOSTU** loutish	**HOSTTUU** shutout	**IINORST** ironist
GINOSTT sotting	**GLOORUY** urology	**HILSSTY** stylish	**HPRTTUU** thruput	**IINOTTU** tuition
GINOSTU ousting tousing	**GLORSSY** grossly	**HIMNSTY** hymnist	**HRSSTUY** thyrsus	**IINQRUY** inquiry
GINOSTV	**GMMPUUW** mugwump	**HIMOORS** moorish	**IIJLLNO** jillion	**IINRTTY** trinity
	GMRUYYZ zymurgy	**HIMOPSS** sophism	**IIKLMNP** limpkin	**IIORSTV** visitor
	GNOOOSS gossoon	**HIMORTU** thorium	**IIKLNOS** oilskin	**IJJSTUU** jujitsu
	GNOPRUW		**IIKMNOR** kirimon	

IJKLLOY	**ILMORTU**	proximo	**IORSTTU**	monsoon
killjoy	turmoil	**IMOOSSS**	tourist	**MNNOSYY**
IJLLLOY	**ILMOSTY**	osmosis	**IPRRSTU**	synonym
jollily	moistly	**IMOPRST**	stirrup	**MNORSTU**
IJLLOTY	**ILNOPRU**	tropism	**IPRSTUU**	nostrum
jollity	purloin	**IMORSTU**	pursuit	**MOOOTYZ**
IJLMPUY	**ILNOPSU**	tourism	**JNOORSU**	zootomy
jumpily	pulsion	**IMOSSYZ**	sojourn	**MOOPPSU**
IJLNOQU	upsilon	zymosis	**KLLMOSU**	pompous
jonquil	**ILNORST**	**IMOSTUV**	mollusk	**MOOPSSU**
IJLNOTY	nostril	vomitus	**KLOOOTU**	opossum
jointly	**ILNOSTY**	**IMRSSTU**	lookout	**MOOPSTT**
IKKMNOU	stonily	sistrum	outlook	topmost
kikumon	**ILNTTUY**	**IMRTTUY**	**KNNNOUW**	**MOOSTTU**
IKLMOPS	nuttily	yttrium	unknown	outmost
milksop	**ILOOORS**	**INNOOPS**	**KNOOPTT**	**MOPSSUU**
IKLNOOS	rosolio	opsonin	topknot	spumous
skolion	**ILLOPST**	**INNOSTU**	**KNOPRTY**	**MORRSTU**
IKLNOOT	topsoil	nonsuit	krypton	rostrum
kiloton	**ILOORTY**	**INOOPRT**	**KOOPRTW**	**NNOOOPT**
IKLNRWY	olitory	portion	potwork	pontoon
wrinkly	**ILOOSST**	**INOORST**	**KOORTUW**	**NNOOPRU**
IKMNPPU	soloist	torsion	workout	pronoun
pumpkin	**ILOPRRY**	**INOORTT**	**LLMPPUY**	**NNOOPSS**
IKMOOST	priorly	tortoni	plumply	sponson
mistook	**ILOPSTU**	**INOOSUX**	**LLOOPRT**	**NNOOPST**
IKNORTW	slipout	noxious	trollop	nonstop
tinwork	**ILORRSY**	**INOPSSU**	**LMRSTUU**	**NOOPRSS**
IKNPSTU	sorrily	spinous	lustrum	sponsor
sputnik	**ILRSTUY**	**INOPSTU**	**LMSTUUU**	**NOORTUW**
ILLMNOU	rustily	spinout	tumulus	outworn
mullion	**ILSSTTY**	**INORSTU**	**LNNOPSU**	**NOPSSTU**
ILLNOQU	stylist	nitrous	nonplus	sunspot
quillon	**IMMOPTU**	**INORSUU**	**LOPPSUU**	**NORTTUU**
ILLNORU	optimum	ruinous	pulpous	turnout
rullion	**IMMSSTU**	urinous	**LOPPSUY**	**OOPRSTV**
ILLNTUY	summist	**INOSSUU**	polypus	provost
nullity	**IMNNOOR**	sinuous	**LOPRSUY**	**OOPSTTU**
ILLOPRY	norimon	**INQSTUY**	pylorus	outpost
pillory	**IMNOORT**	squinty	**LOPRTUY**	**OPPRRTU**
ILLOPWY	monitor	**IOOPRSV**	poultry	purport
pillowy	**IMNOOSU**	proviso	**LOSTTUY**	**OPPRSTU**
ILLOSUY	ominous	**IOORSTU**	stoutly	support
lousily	**IMNOOSY**	riotous	**LPRSSUU**	**ORSTTUU**
ILLOWWY	isonomy	**IOOSSST**	surplus	surtout
willowy	**IMNOPRW**	ostosis	**MMOPSTY**	
ILLSTUY	pinworm	**IOQRTTU**	symptom	
lustily	**IMOOPRX**	quittor	**MNNOOOS**	

8-LETTER WORDS

AAAAGLMT
agalmata
AAAAIMPR
arapaima
AAAAIRTX
ataraxia
AAABBELT
abatable
AAABCCRT
baccarat
AAABCHLS
calabash
AAABCNRR
barranca
AAABDNNN
bandanna
AAABDNRS
saraband
AAABEHNR
habanera
AAABGRTU
rutabaga
AAABINSS
anabasis
AAABLOPR
parabola
AAACCELN
calcanea
AAACCEPR
carapace
AAACCILR
calcaria
AAACCRTT
cataract
AAACDHLN
chandala
AAACDNNO
anaconda
AAACELNT
analecta
AAACGLSW
scalawag
AAACHIPS
aphasiac
AAACILMN
maniacal
AAACINTV
cavatina
AAACIRRS
sacraria
AAACSTWY
castaway
AAADELMS
salaamed

AAADHMRS
madrasah
AAADKRRV
aardvark
AAAEGLMX
malaxage
AAAEGNPP
appanage
AAAEHMNT
anathema
AAAELMTX
malaxate
AAAELNPT
panatela
AAAFINST
fantasia
AAAGGLOP
galapago
AAAGHNTY
yataghan
AAAGINRR
agrarian
AAAGLRST
astragal
AAAGMPRR
paragram
AAAHIMRT
hamartia
AAAHMNRT
amaranth
AAAHNNSV
savannah
AAAHNOPR
anaphora
AAAIINPR
apiarian
AAAILLMR
malarial
AAAILLPT
palatial
AAAILPRV
paravail
AAAIMNRR
marinara
AAAINOPR
paranoia
AAALLPRX
parallax
AAAMNOPR
panorama
AAAMOTTU
automata
AAAMRTTU
traumata

AAANORSY
sayonara
AAANQTUU
aquanaut
AAAPQRTU
paraquat
AAAPRSST
parastas
AABBCDEG
cabbaged
AABBCDRS
scabbard
AABBCEKR
bareback
AABBCINR
barbican
AABBCIRR
barbaric
AABBEELR
bearable
AABBELLM
blamable
AABBELLS
baseball
AABBELRY
bearably
AABBLLMY
blamably
AABCCEHK
backache
AABCCKKP
backpack
AABCCKLL
callback
AABCCKLP
blackcap
AABCCKLW
clawback
AABCCMOT
catacomb
AABCDEIN
abidance
AABCDEIT
abdicate
AABCDELL
caballed
AABCDELN
balanced
AABCDHKN
backhand
AABCDHKR
hardback
AABCDILU
bicaudal

AABCDKRW
backward
AABCEENY
abeyance
AABCEERT
acerbate
AABCEGOT
cabotage
AABCEHLS
chasable
AABCEILM
amicable
AABCEIRT
bacteria
AABCEKLM
clambake
AABCELLP
placable
AABCELLR
caballer
AABCELLS
scalable
AABCELNR
balancer
AABCELOR
albacore
AABCELWY
cableway
AABCEMRV
vambrace
AABCESST
cabasset
AABCESSU
abacuses
AABCFHKL
halfback
AABCFKLL
backfall
AABCFKST
fastback
AABCHILR
brachial
AABCHINR
branchia
AABCHKLS
backlash
AABCHKRS
shabrack
AABCHKSW
backwash
AABCHMRY
chambray

AABCIILS
basilica
AABCIKLT
tailback
AABCILMS
cabalism
AABCILMY
amicably
AABCILNN
cannibal
AABCILST
basaltic
cabalist
AABCINNR
cinnabar
AABCINNS
cannabis
AABCKLPY
playback
AABCKSTY
backstay
AABCRSTT
abstract
AABDDEET
deadbeat
AABDDEGN
bandaged
AABDDEHN
headband
AABDDLNS
badlands
AABDEELR
readable
AABDEGIN
badinage
AABDEKRY
daybreak
AABDELLU
laudable
AABDELOR
adorable
AABDELPT
baldpate
AABDELRY
readably
AABDENTU
unabated
AABDENUX
bandeaux
AABDEORS
seaboard
AABDEQRU
quebrada
AABDERTV

vartabed
AABDGINR
abrading
AABDGNOV
vagabond
AABDGOTU
gadabout
AABDHLLN
handball
AABDHLLR
hardball
AABDINNR
rainband
AABDKNNS
sandbank
AABDKLLRY
balladry
AABDLLUY
laudably
AABDLMNY
damnably
AABDLMRU
adumbral
AABDLOOT
boatload
AABDLOPR
lapboard
AABDLORR
larboard
AABDLORY
adorably
AABDMNNS
bandsman
AABDNNTU
abundant
AABDNRRY
barnyard
AABDORTY
boatyard
AABEEGKR
breakage
AABEEGLT
ablegate
AABEEGNT
abnegate
AABEEHLT
hateable
AABEEKMT
makebate
AABEELLS
saleable
sealable
AABEELMN
amenable
nameable
AABEELRS
erasable
AABEELRW
wearable
AABEELSV
saveable
AABEENOR
anaerobe
AABEERRT

aberrate
AABEFHKL
halfbeak
AABEFLLL
flabella
AABEFLMR
farmable
AABEFLMU
flambeau
AABEGHLN
hangable
AABEGMNR
bargeman
AABEGNOR
baronage
AABEGORT
abrogate
AABEGOST
sabotage
AABEGRSS
brassage
AABEHLPS
shapable
AABEHLPT
alphabet
AABEHLSV
shavable
AABEHLSW
washable
AABEILLM
mailable
AABEILRV
variable
AABEILST
satiable
AABEILTV
ablative
AABEIRSV
abrasive
AABEKMNR
brakeman
AABELLMT
meatball
AABELLPP
palpable
AABELLPY
playable
AABELLSV
salvable
AABELLSY
saleably
AABELLUV
valuable
AABELMNY
amenably
AABELMST
blastema
lambaste
AABELMSU
amusable
AABELMTU
ambulate
AABELNOT
atonable

AABELNPW
pawnable
AABELNRY
balneary
AABELORR
arboreal
AABELOSV
lavaboes
AABELOVW
avowable
AABELPRS
sparable
AABELPSS
passable
AABELRTY
betrayal
AABELTTU
tabulate
AABELTUX
tableaux
AABENRRT
aberrant
AABENRST
ratsbane
AABFILUX
fabliaux
AABFLOTT
flatboat
AABGGRRT
braggart
AABGHKRS
shagbark
AABGIMNS
sambaing
AABHHORU
brouhaha
AABHILTU
habitual
AABHINTT
habitant
AABIIJLT
jailbait
AABILLLY
labially
AABILLST
ballista
AABILNNU
biannual
AABILNOR
baronial
AABILNOT
ablation
AABILNTY
banality
AABILOST
sailboat
AABILRRT
arbitral
AABILRST
arbalist
AABILRVY
variably
AABIMORS
ambrosia

AABINNPR
brainpan
AABINORS
abrasion
AABINRTZ
bartizan
AABIORTT
abattoir
AABISTUZ
zaibatsu
AABLLPPY
palpably
AABLLSTU
blastula
AABLLSVY
salvably
AABLMNOR
abnormal
AABLPSSY
passably
AABMORTU
tamboura
AABORRRT
barrator
AABRRRTY
barratry
AABRRSST
brassart
AACCCRUY
accuracy
AACCDDES
cascaded
AACCDEIM
academic
AACCDELO
accolade
AACCDENU
caducean
AACCDOVY
advocacy
AACCEENT
cetacean
AACCEGRU
carucage
AACCELOR
caracole
AACCELPT
placcate
AACCENRT
carcanet
AACCERTU
accurate
AACCFILR
farcical
AACCGILT
galactic
AACCHLOR
charcoal
AACCHLOT
cachalot
AACCHMNO
coachman
AACCIIST

sciatica
AACCILTT
tactical
AACCIPTY
capacity
AACCJORU
carcajou
AACCOSTT
staccato
AACDDEHI
acidhead
AACDDENT
decanted
AACDDENV
advanced
AACDDETU
caudated
AACDDINR
radicand
AACDEEHH
headache
AACDEEHR
headrace
AACDEELS
escalade
AACDEEPS
escapade
AACDEEST
caseated
AACDEFLT
falcated
AACDEGKP
packaged
AACDEGMR
decagram
AACDEHHY
headachy
AACDEHIN
hacienda
AACDEHLP
cephalad
AACDEHRT
cathedra
AACDEHTT
attached
AACDEINR
radiance
AACDEIRT
radicate
AACDEJNT
adjacent
AACDEKNP
pancaked
AACDEKTT
attacked
AACDELLN
canalled
AACDELMN
manacled
AACDELNR
calendar
AACDELOS
caseload
AACDELPT

placated
AACDELTT lactated
AACDENSV canvased
AACDEOTV advocate
AACDEQUY adequacy
AACDERST cadaster
AACDETTU actuated
AACDFHRU fauchard
AACDGGHI haggadic
AACDGINR cardigan
AACDHINP handicap
AACDHINR arachnid
AACDHKRT hardtack
AACDHNRT handcart
AACDILMO malacoid
AACDILMT dalmatic
AACDILNO diaconal
AACDILNR cardinal
AACDILOZ zodiacal
AACDIMRT dramatic
AACDIRTY caryatid
AACDITUY audacity
AACDJQRU jacquard
AACDLORT cartload
AACDMMOR cardamom
AACDMNOR marcando
AACEEFLP paleface
AACEEGLR clearage
AACEEGLV cleavage
AACEEHRT tracheae
AACEEIMT emaciate
AACEEINN encaenia
AACEELRT lacerate

AACEELST escalate
AACEEMRT macerate
AACEEMST casemate
AACEENTT catenate
AACEEPSS seascape
AACEETUV evacuate
AACEETVX excavate
AACEFFIN affiance
AACEFIST fasciate
AACEGILT glaciate
AACEGIRR carriage
AACEGIRV vicarage
AACEHHRU huarache
AACEHILL heliacal
AACEHIRZ archaize
AACEHLSS calashes
AACEHMRS marchesa
AACEHMST schemata
AACEHPUX chapeaux
AACEHTUX chateaux
AACEIILN laciniae
AACEILLN alliance
AACEILMN calamine
AACEILNZ canalize
AACEILOP alopecia
AACEILRV cavalier
AACEINRS canaries
AACEINRT carinate
AACEINRV variance
AACEIPPS papacies
AACEITTV activate

AACEKKLW cakewalk
AACELLOT allocate
AACELMTU maculate
AACELNPR parlance
AACELNPT placenta
AACELNST analects
AACELORV cavalero
AACELPSU scapulae
AACEMNPS spaceman
AACEMRSS massacre
AACENOTU oceanaut
AACENPRS pancreas
AACENPSU saucepan
AACENRST canaster
AACENRVZ czarevna
AACENSTT castanet
AACEOSST seacoast
AACERRTU arcature
AACERSTT castrate
AACERTTT tractate
AACESUWY causeway
AACFHMST camshaft
AACFILLY facially
AACFIRRT aircraft
AACFIRTT artifact
AACFJKLP flapjack
AACGGINO anagogic
AACGIIMN magician
AACGILNV galvanic
AACGILOX coxalgia
AACGIMMT magmatic
AACGIMNP campaign

AACGINTV vacating
AACGISTY sagacity
AACGLMOU glaucoma
AACGNRVY vagrancy
AACHHTWY hatchway
AACHIIMR mariachi
AACHILMS chamisal
AACHILNP chaplain
AACHILPS calipash
AACHILRV archival
AACHIMNN chainman
AACHIMNR chairman
AACHIMRR armchair
AACHIMRS archaism / charisma
AACHIMST cathisma
AACHIRTX taxiarch
AACHKSTY haystack
AACHLMNO monachal
AACHLSTU calathus
AACHMNNR ranchman
AACHMNTW watchman
AACHMNUY naumachy
AACHMPRY pharmacy
AACHOPPR approach
AACHPPRY paparchy
AACHRTUY autarchy
AACIJLMO majolica
AACIKMNW mackinaw
AACILLPY apically
AACILMNT claimant
AACILMTY calamity
AACILNRV carnival

AACILNTU nautical
AACILNTY analytic
AACILOTT coattail
AACILPRU piacular
AACILPTY atypical
AACILRTY alacrity
AACIMNOR macaroni
AACIMORT aromatic
AACINORT raincoat
AACINOTV vacation
AACINQTU acquaint
AACIPRTY rapacity
AACIRRTT tartaric
AACIRSTT castrati
AACIRTZZ czaritza
AACJKLPS slapjack
AACJKSTY jackstay
AACKKNPS knapsack
AACKMNST tacksman
AACKORWY rockaway
AACLLNRY carnally
AACLLRRY carryall
AACLLSUY casually / causally
AACLLTUY actually
AACLMNNS clansman
AACLORRU oracular
AACLORSU carousal
AACLPPRT claptrap
AACLPRSU capsular / scapular
AACLPRTY calyptra
AACLPTTU

catapult	awakened	**AADEHRSS**	**AADFGNNO**	**AADILMNN**	
AACLRSUV	**AADEELNN**	harassed	fandango	mainland	
vascular	annealed	**AADEHSSY**	**AADFINRU**	**AADILNPR**	
AACLSTTY	**AADEELPP**	sashayed	unafraid	prandial	
catalyst	appealed	**AADEILMS**	**AADFLLLN**	**AADILORR**	
AACLSTUY	**AADEEMNT**	maladies	landfall	railroad	
casualty	emanated	**AADEILPS**	**AADFLNST**	**AADILPRY**	
AACMNOOR	**AADEENTT**	palisade	fastland	lapidary	
macaroon	antedate	**AADEILRS**	**AADFLORW**	**AADIMNNR**	
AACMNORS	**AADEEPPR**	salaried	aardwolf	mandarin	
mascaron	appeared	**AADEILSS**	**AADFLOWY**	**AADIMNRT**	
AACNRSTT	**AADEEPPS**	assailed	foldaway	tamarind	
transact	appeased	**AADEILTV**	**AADFMRRY**	**AADIMNRY**	
AACORSTT	**AADEEQTU**	validate	farmyard	dairyman	
castrato	adequate	**AADEIMNR**	**AADGGIMN**	**AADIMNUV**	
AACORTTU	**AADEFHLT**	marinade	damaging	vanadium	
autocrat	flathead	**AADEIMNT**	**AADGGLNN**	**AADIMSTZ**	
AADDDEEH	**AADEFIRZ**	animated	gangland	samizdat	
deadhead	faradize	**AADEIMRV**	**AADGHIPR**	**AADINOPS**	
AADDDGNR	**AADEFLLR**	maravedi	diagraph	diapason	
granddad	falderal	**AADEIMST**	**AADGIINS**	**AADINOPT**	
AADDEFLL	**AADEFLRY**	diastema	gainsaid	adaption	
deadfall	defrayal	**AADEINTT**	**AADGILLR**	**AADIORRT**	
AADDEGRT	**AADEFRWY**	attained	galliard	radiator	
gradated	wayfared	**AADEIPRS**	**AADGILMR**	**AADIRRSY**	
AADDEHHR	**AADEGHRY**	paradise	madrigal	disarray	
hardhead	grayhead	**AADEIPTV**	**AADGILNO**	**AADJNTTU**	
AADDEHLN	**AADEGINR**	adaptive	diagonal	adjutant	
headland	drainage	**AADEIRST**	**AADGIMPR**	**AADKLMNR**	
AADDEHMN	gardenia	dataries	paradigm	landmark	
handmade	**AADEGITT**	**AADEISST**	**AADGINPR**	**AADKLNPR**	
AADDEHRZ	agitated	diastase	parading	parkland	
hazarded	**AADEGLSV**	**AADEISTT**	**AADGINPT**	**AADKORWY**	
AADDEIRT	salvaged	satiated	adapting	workaday	
radiated	**AADEGMPR**	**AADEJNNP**	**AADGINRU**	**AADLMNNS**	
AADDELNS	rampaged	japanned	guardian	landsman	
sandaled	**AADEGMSS**	**AADEKMNR**	**AADGINRW**	**AADLMNOR**	
AADDELTU	massaged	mandrake	awarding	mandorla	
adulated	**AADEGNRR**	**AADELLPP**	**AADGIQRU**	**AADLMNUU**	
AADDEMNT	arranged	appalled	quadriga	laudanum	
mandated	**AADEGPSS**	**AADELMNR**	**AADGMNOR**	**AADMMNOW**	
AADDEMRU	passaged	alderman	dragoman	madwoman	
marauded	**AADEGRTU**	**AADELMPT**	**AADGMNOS**	**AADMMNSU**	
AADDEMRY	graduate	palmated	goadsman	mandamus	
daydream	**AADEGRTW**	**AADELMYZ**	**AADGNRUV**	**AADMNORS**	
AADDHIMN	gateward	amazedly	vanguard	roadsman	
handmaid	**AADEGSSU**	**AADELNYZ**	**AADHHIPS**	**AADMNORT**	
AADDLLNY	assuaged	analyzed	padishah	mandator	
landlady	**AADEHILN**	**AADELPPT**	**AADHILLR**	**AADMNRSW**	
AADDLNRW	nailhead	palpated	halliard	wardsman	
landward	**AADEHILS**	**AADELTUV**	**AADHILNR**	**AADNOSWY**	
AADDNRST	headsail	valuated	handrail	nowadays	
standard	**AADEHIRR**	**AADEMRRU**	**AADHINRR**	**AADNQRSU**	
AADEEGHR	diarrhea	marauder	harridan	quadrans	
headgear	**AADEHIWY**	**AADENRRT**	**AADHLPSS**	**AADNQRTU**	
AADEEGLT	hideaway	narrated	slapdash	quadrant	
galeated	**AADEHLLO**	**AADENRTT**	**AADHMNNY**	**AADNQRUY**	
AADEEGRV	halloaed	rattaned	handyman	quandary	
averaged	**AADEHMNS**	**AADEQRTU**	**AADHMNOU**	**AADNRSTU**	
AADEEHMT	headsman	quadrate	omadhaun	tarandus	
meathead	**AADEHMST**	**AADERRRW**	**AADIKLLO**	**AADOPSUY**	
AADEEIRT	masthead	rearward	alkaloid	paduasoy	
eradiate	**AADEHRRW**	**AADERSTW**	**AADILLLO**	**AAEEEHRT**	
AADEEKNW	hardware	eastward	allodial	hetaerae	

AAEEFRRS
seafarer
AAEEGMPR
amperage
AAEEGRTW
waterage
AAEEHSTT
attaches
AAEEILNT
alienate
AAEEKMNS
namesake
AAEEKPRT
parakeet
AAEEKQSU
seaquake
AAEELLLM
lamellae
AAEELLMT
malleate
AAEELLPT
patellae
AAEELNPS
seaplane
AAEELORT
areolate
AAEELRTU
laureate
AAEELTUV
evaluate
AAEEMMTT
teammate
AAEENNNT
antennae
AAEENORS
araneose
AAEENRST
serenata
AAEENSTU
nauseate
AAEEPPRR
rapparee
reappear
AAEEPRST
separate
AAEFGLLL
flagella
AAEFIKLT
kalifate
AAEFIMRR
airframe
AAEFKMST
makefast
AAEFLRTW
flatware
AAEFRRWY
wayfarer
AAEGGLNU
language
AAEGHMRX
hexagram
AAEGHNRU
harangue
AAEGILSX

galaxies
AAEGILTT
tailgate
AAEGIMNO
egomania
AAEGIMNS
magnesia
AAEGIMNT
enigmata
AAEGIMNZ
magazine
AAEGIMRR
marriage
AAEGIMST
sagamite
AAEGINPT
paginate
AAEGINRT
aerating
AAEGINTV
navigate
AAEGIPRU
periagua
AAEGIRSV
vagaries
AAEGIVWY
giveaway
AAEGLLPR
pellagra
AAEGLLST
stallage
AAEGLNOU
analogue
AAEGLNTU
angulate
AAEGLSVY
savagely
AAEGMNRV
gravamen
AAEGMORS
sagamore
AAEGMRRV
margrave
AAEGMTTW
megawatt
AAEGNRTU
runagate
AAEGNSTT
stagnate
AAEGORRT
arrogate
AAEGRSVY
savagery
AAEHIMNT
anthemia
AAEHINST
asthenia
AAEHKMRY
haymaker
AAEHLPUV
upheaval
AAEHMNRT
earthman
AAEHMOPR

amphorae
AAEHMORT
atheroma
AAEHNPST
pheasant
AAEHRRSS
harasser
AAEIIPRS
apiaries
AAEIIRSV
aviaries
AAEIKLLN
alkaline
AAEIKLLS
alkalies
AAEIKLLZ
alkalize
AAEILLPP
papillae
AAEILLPT
palliate
AAEILLRY
aerially
AAEILMNT
laminate
AAEILMNV
velamina
AAEILMRT
material
AAEILNPR
airplane
AAEILNPT
palatine
AAEILNSZ
nasalize
AAEILPPZ
papalize
AAEILPRT
parietal
AAEILPRX
preaxial
AAEILRRT
arterial
AAEILRSS
salaries
AAEILRST
asterial
AAEILRTV
varietal
AAEILSTV
salivate
AAEILSTX
saxatile
AAEILTVX
laxative
AAEIMNRT
marinate
AAEIMNRZ
mazarine
AAEINORT
aeration
AAEINORX
anorexia
AAEINRRW

rainwear
AAEINRST
seatrain
AAEINSTT
astatine
AAEINSTV
sanative
AAEIPPRS
appraise
AAEIPRST
parasite
AAEIRRRT
terraria
AAEIRSTT
aristate
AAEIRSVW
airwaves
AAEJNNPR
japanner
AAEKLMRW
lawmaker
AAEKLMRY
malarkey
AAEKNPRT
partaken
AAEKPRRT
partaker
AAELLLPR
parallel
AAELLMPU
ampullae
AAELLWYY
alleyway
AAELMMNO
melanoma
AAELMMTU
malamute
AAELMNRT
maternal
AAELMNSS
salesman
AAELMNST
talesman
AAELMPRT
malapert
AAELMPTY
playmate
AAELMRSY
lamasery
AAELMRTT
maltreat
AAELNNTU
annulate
AAELNOSS
seasonal
AAELNPRT
parental
AAELNPRT
paternal
AAELNPRW
warplane
AAELNPST
pleasant
AAELNRST

asternal
AAELNSSY
analyses
AAELNSTT
atlantes
AAELPPSU
applause
AAELPRST
palestra
AAELPRYZ
paralyze
AAELPTUX
plateaux
AAELRUZZ
zarzuela
AAELRWYY
waylayer
AAEMMNRT
armament
AAEMNORT
emanator
AAEMNPRT
parament
AAEMNRST
sarmenta
AAEMNTUX
manteaux
AAEMOTTU
automate
AAEMPTTU
amputate
AAEMRRTU
armature
AAEMRTTU
maturate
AAENNOTT
annotate
AAENNSTU
nauseant
AAENORTU
aeronaut
AAENPPRT
apparent
AAEOPSTT
apostate
AAEPRTXY
taxpayer
AAERSTTU
saturate
AAERTWWY
waterway
AAFFILRT
taffrail
AAFFINPR
paraffin
AAFFLPST
palstaff
AAFGLNRT
flagrant
AAFGNRRT
fragrant
AAFHRSUU
hausfrau
AAFIILLM

familial	**AAGKNOOR**	mammilla	aspirant	**AAOPSSTY**
AAFIILMR	kangaroo	**AAILLMNT**	partisan	apostasy
familiar	**AAGLNRRU**	mantilla	**AAINQRTU**	**AAOSTWWY**
AAFILLNR	granular	**AAILLRXY**	quatrain	stowaway
rainfall	**AAGMOTUY**	axillary	**AAINQTTU**	**ABBBEILR**
AAFILMST	autogamy	**AAILMMRS**	aquatint	bribable
fatalism	**AAGMOTYZ**	alarmism	**AAINRRSZ**	**ABBBGILN**
AAFILSTT	zygomata	**AAILMMNOR**	sarrazin	babbling
fatalist	**AAGNNOST**	manorial	**AAINRSTY**	blabbing
AAFILTTY	anagnost	**AAILMNST**	sanitary	**ABBCDELS**
fatality	**AAGNNSTT**	talisman	**AAINSSSS**	scabbled
AAFLLPRT	stagnant	**AAILMOPT**	assassin	**ABBCEERU**
pratfall	**AAGNORRT**	lipomata	**AAINSSTT**	barbecue
AAGGIMNN	arrogant	**AAILMORR**	satanist	**ABBCEGIR**
managing	**AAGNRTUY**	armorial	**AAIRSTWY**	cribbage
AAGGINRV	guaranty	**AAILMRST**	stairway	**ABBCEHOU**
ravaging	**AAGORSSS**	alarmist	**AAJMMORR**	babouche
AAGGINSV	sargasso	**AAILMTTU**	marjoram	**ABBCEHOY**
savaging	**AAHIILRT**	ultimata	**AAKMMNRS**	beachboy
AAGGITTW	hairtail	**AAILNNOT**	marksman	**ABBCEIKT**
gigawatt	**AAHILNNT**	national	**AAKMORUZ**	backbite
AAGHHINS	inhalant	**AAILNNPT**	mazourka	**ABBCEIRR**
shanghai	**AAHILNOT**	plantain	**AALLMNTY**	crabbier
AAGHILNN	halation	**AAILNNST**	tallyman	**ABBCEIRS**
hangnail	**AAHIPSXY**	annalist	**AALLMNUY**	scabbier
AAGHKMNY	asphyxia	**AAILNORT**	manually	**ABBCEKNO**
gymkhana	**AAHKLLMR**	notarial	**AALLNNUY**	backbone
AAGHLNPY	hallmark	rational	annually	**ABBCELRS**
anaglyph	**AAHKMOTW**	**AAILNOTV**	**AALLORWY**	scrabble
AAGHMNOY	tomahawk	lavation	rollaway	**ABBCERRY**
mahogany	**AAHLMSTU**	**AAILNQTU**	**AALMNORU**	crabbery
AAGIILNV	thalamus	aliquant	monaural	**ABBCGINR**
availing	**AAHMNORT**	**AAILNSSY**	**AALMNTTU**	crabbing
AAGIINTV	marathon	analysis	tantalum	**ABBCGINS**
aviating	**AAHMNPST**	**AAILNSTY**	**AALMNTUU**	scabbing
AAGIINTW	phantasm	nasality	autumnal	**ABBCIILL**
awaiting	**AAHOPRTU**	**AAILPPST**	**AALMOPPR**	biblical
AAGILLNY	autoharp	papalist	malaprop	**ABBCIINR**
allaying	**AAIILMNS**	**AAILRSVY**	**AALNNTTY**	rabbinic
AAGILMNO	mainsail	salivary	natantly	**ABBCIKRT**
magnolia	**AAIIMMNT**	**AAIMMMNST**	**AALOPPRV**	brickbat
AAGILMNR	maintain	mainmast	approval	**ABBCILSY**
alarming	**AAIINOTV**	**AAIMNORT**	**AALOPRST**	scabbily
marginal	aviation	animator	pastoral	**ABBDDELR**
AAGILNPT	**AAIINPRR**	**AAIMNPRZ**	**AALORTVY**	drabbled
palating	riparian	marzipan	lavatory	**ABBDEEJR**
AAGILPRY	**AAIINRST**	**AAIMNSST**	**AALRSSVY**	jabbered
plagiary	intarsia	mantissa	vassalry	**ABBDEELN**
AAGIMNPS	**AAIIPRST**	satanism	**AALRSTTW**	bendable
paganism	apiarist	**AAIMNSTY**	stalwart	**ABBDEERR**
AAGIMNSS	**AAIIPRVV**	mainstay	**AALRSTUY**	barbered
amassing	vivipara	**AAIMPRST**	salutary	**ABBDEGLR**
AAGIMSSV	**AAIIRTVX**	pastrami	**AAMMRSSU**	grabbled
savagism	aviatrix	**AAIMQRUU**	marasmus	**ABBDELMR**
AAGIMSTT	**AAIKMNST**	aquarium	**AAMOPRRU**	brambled
stigmata	antimask	**AAINNOTT**	paramour	**ABBDELRR**
AAGINRRY	**AAIKMRST**	natation	**AANNOSST**	drabbler
arraying	tamarisk	**AAINNSST**	assonant	**ABBDEORS**
AAGINSST	**AAIKSSTW**	naissant	**AANNRSTY**	absorbed
assignat	swastika	**AAINORRS**	stannary	**ABBDEQSU**
AAGINSSY	**AAILLLUV**	rosarian	**AANORRRT**	squabbed
assaying	alluvial	**AAINOTTX**	narrator	**ABBDERST**
AAGIORTT	**AAILLMMM**	taxation	**AANRRTWY**	drabbest
agitator		**AAINPRST**	warranty	**ABBDGILN**

dabbling	comeback	**ABCDHKLO**	brisance	**ABCIISTY**
ABBDGINR	**ABCCHISU**	holdback	**ABCEINRV**	basicity
drabbing	bacchius	**ABCDIILO**	vibrance	**ABCILLSU**
ABBDHOOY	**ABCCHNOO**	diabolic	**ABCEINTU**	bacillus
babyhood	cabochon	**ABCDKOPR**	incubate	**ABCILLSY**
ABBEEJRR	**ABCCHOSU**	backdrop	**ABCEIRRT**	syllabic
jabberer	chubasco	**ABCDOPRU**	cribrate	**ABCILNPU**
ABBEERTT	**ABCCIKKK**	cupboard	**ABCEIRTT**	publican
barbette	kickback	**ABCDORTU**	brattice	**ABCILRRU**
ABBEFILR	**ABCCILOR**	abductor	**ABCEIRTY**	bicrural
flabbier	carbolic	**ABCEEHLM**	acerbity	**ABCIMORR**
ABBEGIST	**ABCCINOR**	bechamel	**ABCEJLTY**	microbar
gabbiest	carbonic	**ABCEEHLR**	abjectly	**ABCIOSSU**
ABBEHIRS	**ABCCKOOT**	bleacher	**ABCEKLST**	scabious
shabbier	cockboat	**ABCEEHLS**	blackest	**ABCJKOOT**
ABBEHORT	**ABCDDEOR**	bleaches	**ABCEKOOS**	bootjack
bathrobe	brocaded	**ABCEEHRS**	bookcase	jackboot
ABBELNRU	**ABCDDETU**	breaches	casebook	**ABCKKOOR**
burnable	abducted	**ABCEEILT**	**ABCEKRST**	bookrack
ABBELOPR	**ABCDEEFK**	celibate	backrest	**ABCKLLOR**
probable	feedback	**ABCEEIMN**	**ABCELLPU**	rollback
ABBELQSU	bleached	ambience	culpable	**ABCKLOPT**
squabble	**ABCDEEHL**	**ABCEELRR**	**ABCELMRS**	blacktop
ABBELRSY	**ABCDEEHR**	cerebral	scramble	**ABCKLOTU**
slabbery	breached	**ABCEELRT**	**ABCELMRY**	blackout
ABBEORRS	**ABCDEELL**	bracelet	cymbaler	**ABCKMOSS**
reabsorb	becalled	**ABCEEMRR**	**ABCELNOT**	mossback
ABBEORTW	**ABCDEELM**	embracer	balconet	**ABCKMOST**
browbeat	becalmed	**ABCEFIIT**	**ABCELORT**	backmost
ABBERRYY	**ABCDEELU**	beatific	brocatel	**ABCKOORU**
bayberry	educable	**ABCEFIKR**	**ABCELOST**	buckaroo
ABBGGILN	**ABCDEEMR**	backfire	obstacle	**ABCKOPST**
gabbling	cambered	fireback	**ABCELOTU**	backstop
ABBGGINR	embraced	**ABCEGHIN**	bluecoat	**ABCLLNOR**
grabbing	**ABCDEFLO**	beaching	**ABCFIKLL**	cornball
ABBGILNR	boldface	**ABCEGKLO**	backfill	**ABCLLPUY**
rabbling	**ABCDEHLN**	blockage	**ABCFKLLU**	culpably
ABBGILNS	blanched	**ABCEGKOR**	fullback	**ABCLNORY**
slabbing	**ABCDEHNR**	brockage	**ABCGHINT**	carbonyl
ABBGINST	branched	**ABCEHLNR**	batching	**ABCLORXY**
stabbing	**ABCDEHOR**	blancher	**ABCGIINN**	carboxyl
ABBGINSW	broached	**ABCEHLNS**	cabining	**ABCLSSSU**
swabbing	**ABCDEHOS**	blanches	**ABCGIKLN**	subclass
ABBGINTY	caboshed	**ABCEHLOR**	blacking	**ABCNOUYY**
tabbying	**ABCDEIIT**	bachelor	**ABCHIKLS**	buoyancy
ABBHILSY	diabetic	**ABCEHLSU**	blackish	**ABCORRSS**
shabbily	**ABCDEIKS**	chasuble	**ABCHIKRS**	crossbar
ABBIRRTY	backside	**ABCEHMOT**	brackish	**ABCORRSU**
rabbitry	**ABCDEIRS**	hecatomb	**ABCHIMRU**	scabrous
ABBIRSUU	ascribed	**ABCEHNRR**	brachium	**ABCRSTTU**
suburbia	**ABCDEISS**	brancher	**ABCHINOR**	subtract
ABBLOPRY	abscised	**ABCEHORS**	bronchia	**ABDDEEEH**
probably	**ABCDEKLO**	broaches	**ABCHKMPU**	beheaded
ABBNRSUU	blockade	**ABCEHORU**	humpback	**ABDDEEGR**
suburban	**ABCDEKNN**	barouche	**ABCHKOOP**	badgered
ABCCDHIK	neckband	**ABCEIKWZ**	chapbook	**ABDDEEHT**
dabchick	**ABCDEKNU**	zwieback	**ABCHLLUU**	deathbed
ABCCEELP	unbacked	**ABCEILNN**	clubhaul	**ABDDEEKR**
peccable	**ABCDELOO**	binnacle	**ABCHMOTX**	debarked
ABCCEEOR	caboodle	**ABCEILOR**	matchbox	**ABDDEERR**
caboceer	**ABCDEMOT**	cabriole	**ABCIILOT**	debarred
ABCCEILY	combated	**ABCEILOS**	biotical	**ABDDEEST**
celibacy	**ABCDENTU**	sociable	**ABCIIORS**	bedstead
ABCCEKMO	abducent	**ABCEINRS**	isobaric	**ABDDEGIR**

abridged
brigaded
ABDDEHMO
hebdomad
ABDDEILS
disabled
ABDDEINR
brandied
ABDDENST
bedstand
ABDDIRRY
yardbird
ABDEEEMN
bemeaned
bereaved
ABDEEFMR
bedframe
ABDEEHRT
breathed
ABDEEILN
deniable
ABDEEILR
rideable
ABDEEILW
bewailed
ABDEEIST
beadiest
diabetes
ABDEEKMN
embanked
ABDEEKMR
embarked
ABDEEKST
basketed
ABDEELLL
labelled
ABDEELLW
weldable
ABDEELMM
embalmed
ABDEELMN
mendable
ABDEELMZ
emblazed
ABDEELNS
sendable
ABDEELOR
leeboard
ABDEELRR
barreled
ABDEELRT
baltered
ABDEEMNO
bemoaned
ABDEENNR
bannered
ABDEENRT
bantered
ABDEENTT
battened
ABDEERRT
bartered
ABDEERST

breasted
ABDEERTT
battered
ABDEERTW
waterbed
ABDEERTY
betrayed
ABDEFFST
bedstaff
ABDEFIIS
basified
ABDEFLOR
fordable
ABDEGINR
breading
ABDEGINS
debasing
ABDEGINT
debating
ABDEGLMO
gamboled
ABDEGOPR
pegboard
ABDEHINS
banished
ABDEHITU
habitude
ABDEHKLU
bulkhead
ABDEHLLU
bullhead
ABDEHLMS
shambled
ABDEHMSU
ambushed
ABDEHORR
abhorred
ABDEIIRT
diatribe
ABDEIKNU
baudekin
ABDEILMN
mandible
ABDEILNR
bilander
ABDEILOV
voidable
ABDEILRT
librated
ABDEILVV
bivalved
ABDEINNR
endbrain
ABDEINOR
debonair
ABDEINOT
obtained
ABDEINSU
unbiased
ABDEIOTV
obviated
ABDEIPST
baptised

ABDEIPTZ
baptized
ABDEIRTV
vibrated
ABDEISSU
disabuse
ABDEISTW
bawdiest
ABDEJNOW
jawboned
ABDEKORW
beadwork
ABDEKORY
keyboard
ABDELLMO
moldable
ABDELLOT
balloted
ABDELLTU
bullated
ABDELNOZ
blazoned
ABDELNSS
baldness
ABDELOSV
absolved
ABDELSTU
sublated
ABDEMNNS
bandsmen
ABDEMRTU
drumbeat
umbrated
ABDENNOS
noseband
ABDENOTW
downbeat
ABDENTTU
debutant
ABDEOORW
bearwood
ABDEOPRT
probated
ABDEORRW
wardrobe
ABDEORST
broadest
ABDEORTU
obdurate
ABDGHINR
hangbird
ABDGIINR
braiding
ABDGINNR
branding
ABDGINNY
bandying
ABDGINOR
boarding
ABDHILLN
handbill
ABDHILNS
blandish
ABDHINRS

brandish
ABDHIRTY
birthday
ABDHKNOO
handbook
ABDHMOTU
badmouth
ABDIIJLR
jailbird
ABDIIMNR
midbrain
ABDIINOS
obsidian
ABDIINTT
banditti
ABDILMNN
blindman
ABDILRRY
ribaldry
ABDILRZZ
blizzard
ABDINOTT
banditto
ABDINOTY
antibody
ABDJMOOR
doorjamb
ABDLRSUY
absurdly
ABDMNNOS
bondsman
ABDNORUY
boundary
ABDOORTU
outboard
ABDOOSSW
basswood
ABEEEGRV
beverage
ABEEELLR
reelable
ABEEENST
absentee
ABEEENTZ
bezantee
ABEEFILS
feasible
ABEEFILT
fleabite
ABEEFLLL
fellable
ABEEFLLN
befallen
ABEEFORR
forebear
ABEEFRRY
feaberry
ABEEGHRT
berthage
ABEEGIRV
verbiage
ABEEGMNR
bargemen
ABEEGTTU

baguette
ABEEHLLR
harebell
ABEEHQTU
bequeath
ABEEHRRT
breather
ABEEIKRS
bakeries
ABEEILLR
reliable
ABEEILLV
liveable
ABEEILNP
plebeian
ABEEILNV
enviable
ABEEILPX
expiable
ABEEILRT
iterable
liberate
ABEEILSZ
sizeable
ABEEIMST
beamiest
ABEEIPRS
bepraise
ABEEISTU
beauties
ABEEJMOR
jamboree
ABEEKLOT
keelboat
ABEEKLST
bleakest
ABEEKMNR
brakemen
ABEEKMRR
reembark
ABEEKOOP
peekaboo
ABEELLLS
sellable
ABEELLMT
meltable
ABEELLSS
baleless
ABEELMMR
embalmer
ABEELMOV
moveable
ABEELMPR
preamble
ABEELMRZ
emblazer
ABEELMSS
assemble
ABEELMTT
embattle
ABEELNOP
beanpole
ABEELNTT
nettable

ABEELOPR
operable
ABEELORX
exorable
ABEELRSU
reusable
ABEELRSV
servable
ABEELSSS
baseless
ABEELSSU
sublease
ABEELTTW
wettable
ABEEMMNR
membrane
ABEEMNST
basement
ABEENNRT
banneret
ABEENNTU
unbeaten
ABEENORS
seaborne
ABEENRRT
banterer
ABEENRSS
bareness
ABEENSSS
baseness
ABEEORRV
overbear
ABEERRRT
barterer
ABEERRTT
barrette
berretta
ABEERRTV
vertebra
ABEERRTY
betrayer
ABEFILLL
fallible
ABEFILLR
fireball
ABEFILLT
liftable
ABEFILOT
lifeboat
ABEFILRS
barflies
ABEFILSY
feasibly
ABEFITUY
beautify
ABEFLLTU
tableful
ABEFOORT
barefoot
ABEGGIST
baggiest
ABEGGLRY
beggarly
ABEGHINV

behaving
ABEGHRRY
hagberry
ABEGIJTU
bijugate
ABEGIKNR
breaking
ABEGIKNT
betaking
ABEGILLN
labeling
ABEGILNN
enabling
ABEGILNT
bleating
tangible
ABEGILNY
belaying
ABEGILOT
obligate
ABEGIMNY
embaying
ABEGINRS
sabering
ABEGINRT
berating
rebating
ABEGINRW
bewaring
ABEGINTT
abetting
ABEGIPPR
bagpiper
ABEGMNOS
gambeson
ABEGMNOY
bogeyman
ABEGMORT
bergamot
ABEHIKLS
bleakish
ABEHILNR
hibernal
ABEHILTT
tithable
ABEHINRS
banisher
ABEHINSS
banishes
ABEHINST
absinthe
ABEHIORV
behavior
ABEHMNOR
hornbeam
ABEHMSSU
ambushes
ABEHNSTU
sunbathe
ABEHORRR
harborer
ABEHRSST
brashest
ABEIILMT

imitable
ABEIILNN
biennial
ABEIILPT
pitiable
ABEIILST
sibilate
ABEIINRS
binaries
ABEIJLNO
joinable
ABEIJLTU
jubilate
ABEIJMNN
benjamin
ABEIKLLM
lamblike
ABEIKLLN
balkline
ABEIKLSS
kissable
ABEIKNRS
bearskin
ABEILLLT
tillable
ABEILLOV
violable
ABEILLST
bastille
ABEILMST
balmiest
ABEILNOP
opinable
ABEILNTV
bivalent
ABEILNVY
enviably
ABEILPRT
partible
ABEILPRZ
prizable
ABEILPSS
passible
ABEILSTU
suitable
ABEILSUX
bisexual
ABEIMRST
barmiest
ABEIMRTV
verbatim
ABEIMSSU
iambuses
ABEINNRR
brannier
ABEINORR
airborne
ABEINORS
baronies
ABEINORT
baritone
ABEINQSU
basquine
ABEINRRW

brawnier
ABEINRST
banister
ABEINRUZ
urbanize
ABEINSSS
biasness
ABEINSST
bassinet
ABEIORST
sabotier
ABEIORTV
abortive
ABEIPRRS
sparerib
ABEIPRTZ
baptizer
ABEIRRSS
brassier
ABEIRRTT
brattier
ABEIRRVY
breviary
ABEIRSTY
bestiary
ABEISTTT
battiest
ABEKLNOW
knowable
ABEKLORW
workable
ABEKNSSY
sneaksby
ABEKOORY
yearbook
ABEKORTU
breakout
outbreak
ABEKRSTY
basketry
ABELLLOR
rollable
ABELLLSY
syllable
ABELLMRU
umbrella
ABELLNOT
ballonet
ABELLORT
balloter
ABELLOSV
solvable
ABELLOTY
oblately
ABELLRVY
verbally
ABELMNNO
nobleman
ABELMNOZ
emblazon
ABELMNST
semblant
ABELMSSY
assembly

ABELNRRY
barrenly
ABELNRUY
urbanely
ABELNRYZ
brazenly
ABELNSTU
unstable
ABELNSTY
absently
ABELOPRT
portable
ABELOPRV
provable
ABELOPRY
operably
ABELOQTU
quotable
ABELORST
sortable
storable
ABELOSTU
absolute
ABELOSTW
bestowal
ABELRSTU
baluster
ABELRTTU
burletta
rebuttal
ABELSTUY
baetylus
ABEMMNOO
moonbeam
ABEMNPRU
penumbra
ABEMNTTU
abutment
ABENOPSU
subpoena
ABENORSS
baroness
ABENORTT
betatron
ABENORTW
banewort
ABENORTY
barytone
ABENOSSW
sawbones
ABEORSTU
saboteur
ABEORTTU
obturate
tabouret
ABEOSSST
asbestos
ABEOSTWX
sweatbox
ABEQRSUU
arquebus
ABERSSTU
abstruse
ABFFGILN

baffling
ABFFLLPU
puffball
ABFFNOTU
bouffant
ABFIILLR
fibrilla
ABFILLLY
fallibly
ABFILSTU
fabulist
ABFLLOOT
football
ABFLLOST
softball
ABFLLUZZ
fuzzball
ABFLOSTU
boastful
ABFLOSUU
fabulous
ABGGGINR
bragging
ABGGILMN
gambling
ABGGILNR
garbling
ABGGNOOT
toboggan
ABGHHILL
highball
ABGHMORU
brougham
ABGIIMST
bigamist
ABGIINNR
braining
ABGIINRS
braising
ABGIINRZ
braizing
ABGIJNRU
abjuring
ABGIKLNN
blanking
ABGILMNR
marbling
rambling
ABGILMNW
wambling
ABGILNNT
bantling
ABGILNOR
laboring
ABGILNOT
bloating
ABGILNRW
brawling
warbling
ABGILNST
blasting
stabling
ABGILNTT
battling

blatting
ABGILNTY
tangibly
ABGILOOT
obligato
ABGIMOSU
bigamous
ABGINNNR
branning
ABGINORV
bravoing
ABGINOST
boasting
bostangi
ABGINTTU
abutting
ABGLNOOT
longboat
ABGLNOUW
bungalow
ABGLORSU
glabrous
ABGLRRUY
burglary
ABGNORSU
osnaburg
ABHIKLLW
hawkbill
ABHIKLOR
kohlrabi
ABHIRRSU
airbrush
ABHLLMOT
mothball
ABHLLOOY
ballyhoo
ABHLOSWW
washbowl
ABHMNSUU
subhuman
ABHMOORT
bathroom
ABHOORST
tarboosh
ABHOOSTW
showboat
ABIIKLSS
basilisk
ABIILLMR
millibar
ABIILMNO
binomial
ABIILMNS
albinism
ABIILNOT
libation
ABIILNST
sibilant
ABIIMNOT
ambition
ABIJLNTU
jubilant
ABIJNOST
banjoist

ABIKNORR
ironbark
ABILLLPY
playbill
ABILLPST
spitball
ABILMNTU
tablinum
ABILNOOT
oblation
ABILNOTU
ablution
ABILNRTU
tribunal
ABILSTUY
suitably
ABIMNRSU
urbanism
ABINOORT
abortion
ABINOSTT
botanist
ABINRSTU
urbanist
ABINRTUY
urbanity
ABIORRTV
vibrator
ABIORTUY
obituary
ABIRRSTU
airburst
ABKKMOOR
bookmark
ABKLLNOR
bankroll
ABKNNOSW
snowbank
ABKNPRTU
bankrupt
ABKOOPSS
passbook
ABLLMOOR
ballroom
ABLLNOSW
snowball
ABLLORSU
sourball
ABLLRTUY
brutally
ABLLSSUY
syllabus
ABLNORYZ
blazonry
ABLOORST
barstool
ABLOPRVY
provably
ABLOQTUY
quotably
ABLOSTTU
subtotal
ABLPRTUY
abruptly

ABNOORRT
roborant
ABNORTUU
runabout
ACCDDEEN
cadenced
ACCDDEOR
accorded
ACCDDIIT
didactic
ACCDDIIT
didactic
ACCDEELN
canceled
ACCDEENT
accented
ACCDEEPT
accepted
ACCDEERT
accreted
ACCDEGIN
acceding
ACCDEHIL
chaliced
ACCDEHIN
chicaned
ACCDEILY
delicacy
ACCDEINT
accident
ACCDEIRT
accredit
ACCDEISU
caudices
ACCDEKLR
crackled
ACCDENOV
concaved
ACCDEOST
accosted
ACCDESUU
caduceus
ACCDILTY
dactylic
ACCDIOOR
coracoid
ACCDOOXY
cacodoxy
ACCEEHLO
cochleae
ACCEEILS
ecclesia
ACCEEKLN
necklace
ACCEELNR
canceler
clarence
ACCEELOS
coalesce
ACCEERSU
reaccuse
ACCEFFIY
efficacy
ACCEFILS
fascicle

ACCEGKMO
gamecock
ACCEHHKT
hatcheck
ACCEHIKP
chickpea
ACCEHILM
chemical
ACCEHILP
cephalic
ACCEHIMN
mechanic
ACCEHIRT
catchier
ACCEHKPY
paycheck
ACCEHLST
clatches
ACCEHMNO
coachmen
ACCEHNNO
chaconne
ACCEHNOR
encroach
ACCEHNRY
chancery
ACCEHOPT
cachepot
ACCEIKRR
crackier
ACCEILLN
cancelli
ACCEILLR
clerical
ACCEILLV
clavicle
ACCEILNT
canticle
ACCEILRV
cervical
ACCEINPU
capucine
ACCEINRT
acentric
ACCEIOTV
coactive
ACCEIPRT
practice
ACCEIRSU
curacies
ACCEIRTU
cruciate
ACCEISTT
ecstatic
ACCEKLNR
cracknel
ACCELNOV
conclave
ACCELNRU
caruncle
ACCELRSY
scarcely
ACCENNSY
nascency

ACCENOST
cosecant
ACCERSST
scarcest
ACCESSTU
cactuses
ACCESSUU
caucuses
ACCFIILT
lactific
ACCFLNOO
confocal
ACCGHINN
chancing
ACCGHINO
coaching
ACCGHINT
catching
ACCGIKLN
cackling
clacking
ACCGIKMR
gimcrack
ACCGIKNR
cracking
ACCGILOX
coxalgic
ACCGINOT
coacting
ACCGINRU
accruing
ACCGINSU
accusing
ACCGLOOY
cacology
ACCHHITT
chitchat
ACCHILOT
catholic
ACCHINPU
capuchin
ACCHIORT
thoracic
ACCHKLOR
charlock
ACCHNOTU
coughant
ACCHORTY
octarchy
ACCHRSTY
scratchy
ACCIILLN
clinical
ACCIILMT
climatic
ACCIILNO
concilia
iconical
ACCIILRT
critical
ACCIIRTX
cicatrix
ACCIKKNN
nicknack

ACCIKKRR
rickrack
ACCIKLOT
cocktail
ACCILNOV
volcanic
ACCILORT
cortical
ACCILRRU
circular
ACCILTUU
cuticula
ACCIMNOS
moccasin
ACCINOOS
occasion
ACCINOOT
coaction
ACCINORT
narcotic
ACCINRSU
carcinus
ACCIORST
acrostic
ACCIOSTU
acoustic
ACCIRSTY
scarcity
ACCKKRSU
rucksack
ACCKOOOT
cockatoo
ACCKOPRT
crackpot
ACCLLOSU
occlusal
ACCLLSUU
calculus
ACCMOSTU
accustom
ACCNOOTU
cocoanut
ACCNOPTU
occupant
ACCNORTT
contract
ACCDDEIT
addicted
ACDDEEES
deceased
ACDDEEHT
detached
ACDDEEIT
dedicate
ACDDEELR
declared
ACDDEEMP
decamped
ACDDEENS
ascended
ACDDEENT
decadent
ACDDEETU
educated

ACDDEIIM
medicaid
ACDDEINR
riddance
ACDDEITT
dictated
ACDDEKLO
deadlock
ACDDEORR
corraded
ACDDERSU
crusaded
ACDDERTU
traduced
ACDDGILN
cladding
ACDDGINU
adducing
ACDDGINY
caddying
ACDDHKOS
shaddock
ACDDIIOR
cardioid
ACDDILNY
candidly
ACDDKORY
dockyard
ACDDORTU
adductor
ACDEEEFT
defecate
ACDEEEKS
seedcake
ACDEEENR
careened
ACDEEERS
decrease
ACDEEESS
seedcase
ACDEEFFT
affected
ACDEEFIN
defiance
ACDEEFIS
casefied
ACDEEFPR
prefaced
ACDEEFRY
federacy
ACDEEHIV
achieved
ACDEEHLP
chapeled
pleached
ACDEEHNN
enhanced
ACDEEHNR
enarched
ACDEEHNS
enchased
ACDEEHPR
preached
ACDEEHRS

searched
ACDEEHST
detaches
ACDEEILT
delicate
ACDEEIMR
medicare
ACDEEIMT
decimate
medicate
ACDEEINU
audience
ACDEEJKT
jacketed
ACDEEKNR
cankered
ACDEEKPT
packeted
ACDEEKRS
screaked
ACDEEKRT
racketed
ACDEELLR
cellared
recalled
ACDEELMP
emplaced
ACDEELNR
calender
ACDEELNS
cleansed
ACDEELPR
parceled
replaced
ACDEEMRS
screamed
ACDEEMRT
cremated
ACDEENNP
penanced
ACDEENOT
anecdote
ACDEENRT
cantered
decanter
nectared
recanted
ACDEENRV
caverned
ACDEENRZ
credenza
ACDEEORT
decorate
ACDEEPPR
recapped
ACDEEPRS
escarped
ACDEEPRT
carpeted
ACDEERRT
retraced
terraced
ACDEERSS
caressed

ACDEFFLS
sclaffed
ACDEFGIN
defacing
ACDEFHLN
flanched
ACDEFHLO
headlocf
ACDEFIIP
pacified
ACDEFILN
canfield
ACDEFINN
financed
ACDEFNRU
furnaced
ACDEFORT
factored
ACDEFRSU
surfaced
ACDEFRTU
furcated
ACDEGIMR
decigram
grimaced
ACDEGINU
guidance
ACDEGINY
decaying
ACDEGIRS
disgrace
ACDEHHNU
haunched
ACDEHHTT
thatched
ACDEHIJK
hijacked
ACDEHILR
heraldic
ACDEHIMN
machined
ACDEHKLO
headlock
ACDEHKLS
shackled
ACDEHKOV
havocked
ACDEHKRU
archduke
ACDEHKTW
thwacked
ACDEHLNR
chandler
ACDEHLNU
launched
ACDEHNOR
anchored
rondache
ACDEHNST
snatched
ACDEHNSU
uncashed
ACDEHPST
despatch

ACDEHRST starched	callused	dialogic	**ACDLNORU** cauldron	**ACEEHMRS** cashmere
ACDEIINT indicate	**ACDELMOR** clamored	**ACDGILNN** candling	**ACDLOORT** doctoral	marchese
ACDEIITV cavitied	**ACDELMSU** muscadel	**ACDGILNR** cradling	**ACDLORWY** cowardly	**ACEEHNRS** enchaser
vaticide	**ACDELNOR** colander	**ACDGILNS** scalding	**ACDMMNOO** commando	**ACEEHPRR** preacher
ACDEIJNU jaundice	**ACDELOPT** clodpate	**ACDGIMOT** dogmatic	**ACDMNORY** dormancy	**ACEEHPRS** preaches
ACDEIKNP panicked	**ACDELRSW** scrawled	**ACDGINNY** candying	**ACDNOORV** cordovan	**ACEEHPST** cheapest
ACDEIKPX pickaxed	**ACDELRSY** sacredly	**ACDHINSW** sandwich	**ACDNOSTW** downcast	**ACEEHRRS** research
ACDEILMT maledict	**ACDEMNOR** romanced	**ACDHIOPS** scaphoid	**ACEEEFRR** carefree	searcher
ACDEILMX climaxed	**ACDEMOPR** compared	**ACDHIPST** dispatch	**ACEEEGLN** elegance	**ACEEHRSS** searches
ACDEILPS displace	**ACDEMORT** democrat	**ACDHLNOR** chaldron	**ACEEELMR** cameleer	**ACEEHRTT** catheter
ACDEILRT articled	**ACDEMUUV** vacuumed	**ACDIIJLU** judicial	**ACEEENSV** evanesce	**ACEEHSTX** cathexes
ACDEILTT latticed	**ACDENNOR** ordnance	**ACDIILMS** disclaim	**ACEEERRT** recreate	**ACEEIKNP** peacenik
ACDEIMNO comedian	**ACDENNOT** cantoned	**ACDIILSU** suicidal	**ACEEERTT** etcetera	**ACEEIKRR** creakier
demoniac	**ACDENORY** deaconry	**ACDIILTY** dialytic	**ACEEFFIN** caffeine	**ACEEILMN** cameline
ACDEIMNP pandemic	**ACDENOPR** crayoned	**ACDIINOT** diatonic	**ACEEFLPU** peaceful	**ACEEILNR** reliance
ACDEIMPT impacted	**ACDENPPU** uncapped	**ACDIIRST** carditis	**ACEEFLSS** faceless	**ACEEILNS** salience
ACDEIMRT timecard	**ACDENRTU** uncrated	**ACDIIRTY** acridity	**ACEEFPRR** prefacer	**ACEEILPS** especial
ACDEINNR crannied	**ACDENRVY** verdancy	**ACDIISST** sadistic	**ACEEFPRT** perfecta	**ACEEIMRR** creamier
ACDEINOS diocesan	**ACDEOPRS** scorepad	**ACDIKLTU** ducktail	**ACEEFPTY** typeface	**ACEEINPS** sapience
ACDEINOV voidance	**ACDEORSU** caroused	**ACDILNOO** conoidal	**ACEEGHNX** exchange	**ACEEINPT** patience
ACDEINPT pedantic	**ACDEORTU** educator	**ACDILNOR** ironclad	**ACEEGILS** legacies	**ACEEINRS** increase
ACDEINST distance	**ACDEORTV** cavorted	**ACDILPSU** cuspidal	**ACEEGINS** agencies	**ACEEINRT** iterance
ACDEINTT nictated	**ACDEPPRS** scrapped	**ACDIMNSU** muscadin	**ACEEGKRW** wreckage	**ACEEINTV** enactive
ACDEIORT ceratoid	**ACDEPRTU** captured	**ACDINORS** sardonic	**ACEEGNOZ** cozenage	**ACEEIRSW** wiseacre
ACDEIOSU edacious	**ACDEPSTU** cuspated	**ACDINORW** cordwain	**ACEEGNSV** scavenge	**ACEEIRTV** creative
ACDEIPSZ capsized	**ACDEQTUU** aqueduct	**ACDINSTY** dynastic	**ACEEGORV** coverage	reactive
ACDEIQRU acquired	**ACDERRSU** crusader	**ACDIOPRS** sporadic	**ACEEHINT** echinate	**ACEEKLMR** mackerel
ACDEKNPU unpacked	**ACDERRTU** traducer	**ACDIORTT** dictator	**ACEEHIRV** achiever	**ACEEKNRW** neckwear
ACDEKOST stockade	**ACDFFHNU** handcuff	**ACDIOSTU** custodia	**ACEEHIPR** peachier	**ACEEKRRT** racketer
ACDELLNU uncalled	**ACDFFIRT** diffract	**ACDIRSTT** distract	**ACEEHLOS** shoelace	**ACEELLNT** lancelet
ACDELLOR carolled	**ACDFFLOS** scaffold	**ACDIRTWY** cityward	**ACEEHLTV** chevalet	**ACEELLRR** cellarer
collared	**ACDGHOTW** watchdog	**ACDJOSTU** coadjust	**ACEEHMNR** menarche	**ACEELLRT** cellaret
ACDELLOT collated	**ACDGIILO**		**ACEEHMNR** menarche	**ACEELMNT** cemental
ACDELLSU				**ACEELNPT**

pentacle	chaffier	clearing	hatchery	**ACEHLNSU**
ACEELNRS	**ACEFGINN**	**ACEGILNT**	**ACEHHSTT**	launches
cleanser	enfacing	cleating	thatches	**ACEHLORT**
ACEELNRU	**ACEFGINT**	**ACEGILNV**	**ACEHIIRT**	chlorate
cerulean	faceting	cleaving	hieratic	**ACEHLOST**
ACEELNST	**ACEFGLRU**	**ACEGILRS**	**ACEHIJKR**	eschalot
cleanest	graceful	graciles	hijacker	**ACEHLPRY**
ACEELNTT	**ACEFIIPR**	**ACEGILRV**	**ACEHIKLR**	chapelry
tentacle	pacifier	claviger	chalkier	**ACEHMNRT**
ACEELNTU	**ACEFIIPS**	**ACEGIMNN**	**ACEHIKRW**	merchant
nucleate	pacifies	menacing	whackier	**ACEHMNSS**
ACEELOPS	**ACEFIIRT**	**ACEGIMNO**	**ACEHILLT**	chessman
opalesce	artifice	cameoing	hellicat	**ACEHMNTW**
ACEELORS	**ACEFIMPR**	**ACEGIMNR**	**ACEHILNT**	watchmen
escarole	campfire	creaming	chainlet	**ACEHMORT**
ACEELORT	**ACEFINRX**	germanic	ethnical	chromate
relocate	carnifex	**ACEGIMNT**	**ACEHILTT**	**ACEHMSTU**
ACEELPTU	**ACEFINST**	magnetic	athletic	mustache
peculate	fanciest	**ACEGINNO**	**ACEHIMNR**	**ACEHNNPT**
ACEELRSS	**ACEFIOSS**	canoeing	chairmen	penchant
careless	fiascoes	**ACEGINNS**	**ACEHIMPT**	**ACEHNOPR**
ACEELRST	**ACEFIRRT**	encasing	empathic	chaperon
clearest	craftier	**ACEGINNT**	emphatic	**ACEHNOPT**
ACEELRTU	**ACEFIRTT**	enacting	**ACEHIMRS**	cenotaph
ulcerate	trifecta	**ACEGINOS**	marchesi	**ACEHNORR**
ACEELSTT	**ACEFLMNO**	cosinage	**ACEHIMTT**	ranchero
telecast	flamenco	**ACEGINPR**	thematic	**ACEHNRSS**
ACEEMNST	**ACEFLNOR**	capering	**ACEHINOT**	archness
casement	falconer	**ACEGINPS**	inchoate	**ACEHOPRR**
ACEEMOPR	**ACEFLNOT**	escaping	**ACEHINST**	reproach
camporee	conflate	**ACEGINRS**	asthenic	**ACEHORTT**
ACEEMORV	falconet	creasing	**ACEHIOPR**	theocrat
overcame	**ACEFLRUU**	**ACEGINRT**	ecphoria	**ACEHORTU**
ACEEMRRS	furculae	argentic	**ACEHIPRS**	outreach
screamer	**ACEFNORV**	catering	seraphic	**ACEHOSSW**
ACEEMRRY	conferva	creating	**ACEHIPRT**	showcase
creamery	**ACEFORST**	reacting	patchier	**ACEHOSTU**
ACEENNRT	forecast	**ACEGINSS**	phreatic	cathouse
entrance	**ACEFRRTU**	caginess	**ACEHIPST**	**ACEHPRSU**
ACEENORT	fracture	**ACEGINTX**	pastiche	purchase
carotene	**ACEGGINN**	exacting	**ACEHIPTT**	**ACEHRRTT**
ACEENPRR	encaging	**ACEGIOTT**	pathetic	tetrarch
parcener	**ACEGGIRR**	cogitate	**ACEHIPTW**	**ACEHRSST**
ACEENRRT	craggier	**ACEGKLOV**	whitecap	starches
recreant	**ACEGHILN**	gavelock	**ACEHIRST**	**ACEHRSSU**
ACEENRST	leaching	**ACEGLNOT**	chariest	chasseur
sarcenet	**ACEGHINR**	octangle	**ACEHIRTT**	**ACEHSSSU**
ACEEOPST	reaching	**ACEGMNOY**	chattier	chausses
escopeta	**ACEGHINT**	geomancy	**ACEHISST**	**ACEHSSTW**
ACEEORST	cheating	**ACEGNNTY**	chastise	swatches
ceratose	teaching	tangency	**ACEHISTX**	**ACEIILST**
ACEEPRTU	**ACEGHLRS**	**ACEGORTT**	cathexis	silicate
peracute	schlager	cottager	**ACEHKLOV**	**ACEIIMTU**
ACEERRTU	**ACEGIINV**	**ACEGORTY**	havelock	maieutic
creature	vicinage	category	**ACEHKLTY**	**ACEIINTV**
ACEERSSV	**ACEGIKNR**	**ACEHHIRR**	latchkey	inactive
crevasse	creaking	hierarch	**ACEHKOPS**	**ACEIIPRS**
ACEERTTU	**ACEGILLR**	**ACEHMMNN**	shoepack	piracies
eructate	allergic	henchman	**ACEHLLSU**	**ACEIISTV**
ACEESSTT	**ACEGILMU**	**ACEHHNSU**	halluces	cavities
cassette	mucilage	haunches	**ACEHLNPT**	**ACEIJMST**
ACEFFGIN	**ACEGILNN**	**ACEHHRTT**	planchet	majestic
effacing	cleaning	thatcher	**ACEHLNRU**	**ACEIKMNN**
ACEFFHIR	**ACEGILNR**	**ACEHHRTY**	launcher	nickname

ACEIKMRV	**ACEILRSS**	canister	escallop	**ACEMPSSU**
maverick	classier	scantier	**ACELLORT**	campuses
ACEIKNRR	**ACEILRSV**	**ACEINRTT**	collaret	**ACENNNOU**
crankier	visceral	interact	**ACELLOSW**	announce
ACEIKPSX	**ACEILRTT**	**ACEINRTV**	coleslaw	**ACENNOSS**
pickaxes	tractile	navicert	**ACELLSSU**	canoness
ACEIKSTT	**ACEILRTV**	**ACEINSSU**	calluses	**ACENNOTT**
tackiest	vertical	issuance	**ACELMMOU**	cotenant
ACEIKSTW	**ACEILRTY**	**ACEINTTX**	mameluco	**ACENNOTV**
wackiest	literacy	excitant	**ACELMNNS**	covenant
ACEILLMR	**ACEILSST**	**ACEINTTY**	clansmen	**ACENOORT**
millrace	scaliest	tenacity	**ACELMNSS**	coronate
ACEILLMT	**ACEILTVY**	**ACEIOPRT**	calmness	**ACENOPST**
metallic	actively	aporetic	**ACELMORY**	capstone
ACEILLNT	**ACEIMMRU**	operatic	claymore	**ACENOQTU**
cliental	americum	**ACEIORSV**	**ACELMOSU**	cotquean
ACEILLOP	**ACEIMNRU**	varicose	maculose	**ACENORRW**
calliope	manicure	**ACEIOTVV**	**ACELMSTU**	careworn
ACEILLOR	**ACEIMNTU**	vocative	muscatel	**ACENORST**
rocaille	neumatic	**ACEIPPRR**	**ACELMTUU**	ancestor
ACEILLOZ	**ACEIMPRR**	crappier	cumulate	**ACENORSU**
localize	crampier	**ACEIPRST**	**ACELNNRS**	nacreous
ACEILLPS	**ACEIMPSS**	practise	scrannel	**ACENORTT**
allspice	escapism	**ACEIPSSU**	**ACELNORV**	contrate
ACEILMMO	**ACEIMPST**	auspices	novercal	**ACENORTU**
camomile	campiest	**ACEIRRTX**	**ACELNOTV**	courante
ACEILMMR	**ACEIMRST**	creatrix	covalent	**ACENORTY**
clammier	matrices	**ACEIRSST**	**ACELOPPU**	enactory
ACEILMNP	**ACEIMRTU**	scariest	populace	**ACENOSTT**
manciple	muricate	**ACEIRSTZ**	**ACELOPRT**	constate
ACEILMOS	**ACEINNOZ**	craziest	pectoral	**ACENPTTU**
camisole	canonize	**ACEIRTUV**	**ACELOPTU**	punctate
ACEILMPS	**ACEINNRS**	curative	copulate	**ACENRSTY**
misplace	crannies	**ACEIRTVY**	**ACELORSS**	ancestry
ACEILMRT	**ACEINNST**	veracity	lacrosse	**ACENRTTU**
metrical	canniest	**ACEISSSU**	**ACELORSY**	truncate
ACEILMSX	instance	saucisse	coarsely	**ACENSSTW**
climaxes	**ACEINNSU**	**ACEISSTU**	**ACELOSTU**	newscast
ACEILNNP	nuisance	sauciest	lacteous	**ACEOORTV**
pinnacle	**ACEINNTU**	suitcase	osculate	overcoat
ACEILNRT	uncinate	**ACEISTTT**	**ACELPPRS**	**ACEORRSU**
clarinet	**ACEINOPS**	cattiest	scrapple	carouser
ACEILOPR	canopies	**ACEJLORY**	**ACELPRST**	**ACEORRTT**
capriole	**ACEINOPZ**	cajolery	spectral	retroact
ACEILOPT	caponize	**ACEJNRRY**	**ACELPRSU**	**ACEORSST**
poetical	**ACEINORS**	jerrycan	specular	coarsest
ACEILORR	scenario	**ACEKLSSS**	**ACELQRUU**	**ACEORSTV**
carriole	**ACEINORT**	sackless	claqueur	overcast
ACEILORS	creation	**ACEKMNST**	**ACELRRSW**	**ACEOSTTU**
calories	reaction	tacksmen	scrawler	outcaste
ACEILORT	**ACEINORV**	**ACEKNORW**	**ACELRSSS**	**ACEOTUUX**
loricate	veronica	canework	scarless	couteaux
ACEILOTV	**ACEINOST**	**ACEKOORW**	**ACELRTTU**	**ACEPSTTY**
locative	canoeist	cookware	cultrate	typecast
ACEILOVZ	**ACEINOTX**	**ACEKORSW**	**ACELSSTT**	**ACERSSST**
vocalize	exaction	casework	tactless	crassest
ACEILPRS	**ACEINPTT**	**ACEKQRUY**	**ACEMNORR**	**ACERSTTY**
spiracle	pittance	quackery	romancer	cytaster
ACEILPRT	**ACEINPUY**	**ACELLLRU**	**ACEMOOST**	**ACERTTUW**
particle	picayune	cellular	comatose	cutwater
ACEILPRU	**ACEINRRY**	**ACELLMSU**	**ACEMORSY**	**ACFFGHIN**
peculiar	cinerary	sacellum	sycamore	chaffing
ACEILPSS	**ACEINRST**	**ACELLOPS**	**ACEMORUX**	**ACFFIILO**
slipcase		collapse	morceaux	official

ACFFILNU
fanciful
ACFFKORT
offtrack
ACFFLOSW
scofflaw
ACFGIIMN
magnific
ACFGIIPR
caprifig
ACFGINNY
fancying
ACFGINRS
scarfing
ACFGINRT
crafting
ACFHILNO
falchion
ACFHILOS
coalfish
ACFHIRSW
crawfish
ACFHIRSY
crayfish
ACFHLTUW
watchful
ACFHMNOR
chamfron
ACFHNNOR
chanfron
ACFIILTY
facility
ACFIIMPS
pacifism
ACFIIPST
pacifist
ACFIKLNS
calfskin
ACFILRTY
craftily
ACFILSSY
classify
ACFINORT
fraction
ACFINSTY
sanctify
ACFIOSTU
factious
ACFLNORY
falconry
ACFLOOPS
foolscap
ACFMOTTU
factotum
ACGGHINN
changing
ACGGHINR
charging
ACGGHLUU
chugalug
ACGGIINT
gigantic
ACGGIIOS
isagogic

ACGGILNN
clanging
ACGGILNN
glancing
ACGGLRSY
scraggly
ACGHHINT
hatching
ACGHIINN
chaining
ACGHIINR
chairing
ACGHIKLN
chalking
ACGHIKLN
hackling
ACGHIKNS
shacking
ACGHIKNW
whacking
ACGHILNS
clashing
ACGHILNT
latching
ACGHILNY
achingly
ACGHILOR
oligarch
ACGHIMNP
champing
ACGHIMNR
charming
ACGHIMNR
marching
ACGHIMNT
matching
ACGHINNR
ranching
ACGHINNT
chanting
ACGHINOP
poaching
ACGHINPP
chapping
ACGHINPR
parching
ACGHINPT
nightcap
ACGHINPT
patching
ACGHINRR
charring
ACGHINRS
crashing
ACGHINRT
charting
ACGHINST
scathing
ACGHINTT
chatting
ACGHINTW
watching
ACGHINTY
yachting
ACGHNRYY
gynarchy
ACGIILMN
claiming

ACGIILNO
logician
ACGIILNV
caviling
ACGIILRS
gracilis
ACGIINNS
incasing
ACGIINRT
granitic
ACGIJLNO
cajoling
ACGIKKNN
knacking
ACGIKLMN
mackling
ACGIKLNN
clanking
ACGIKLNO
cloaking
ACGIKLNS
slacking
ACGIKLNT
tackling
ACGIKLNT
talcking
ACGIKLNU
caulking
ACGIKLRY
garlicky
ACGIKMNS
smacking
ACGIKNNR
cranking
ACGIKNNS
snacking
ACGIKNOR
croaking
ACGIKNQU
quacking
ACGIKNRT
tracking
ACGIKNST
stacking
ACGIKPRS
gripsack
ACGILMMN
clamming
ACGILMNP
clamping
ACGILNNU
unlacing
ACGILNOR
caroling
ACGILNOR
coraling
ACGILNOT
locating
ACGILNPP
clapping
ACGILNPS
clasping
ACGILNPS
scalping
ACGILNRW
crawling
ACGILNSS

classing
ACGILNST
castling
ACGILRSU
surgical
ACGIMMNR
cramming
ACGIMNOR
caroming
ACGIMNPR
cramping
ACGIMNPS
scamping
ACGIMORS
orgasmic
ACGINNNS
scanning
ACGINNPR
prancing
ACGINNRU
uncaring
ACGINNST
scanting
ACGINORY
congiary
ACGINOST
agnostic
coasting
ACGINPPR
crapping
ACGINPRS
scarping
scraping
ACGINRRS
scarring
ACGINRRY
carrying
ACGINSTT
scatting
ACGIOORS
gracioso
ACGIORST
orgastic
ACGIORSU
gracious
ACGJLNOU
conjugal
ACGLOSUU
glaucous
ACHHINTY
hyacinth
ACHHIPPR
hipparch
ACHHLPRY
phylarch
ACHHNTTU
nuthatch
ACHIIRST
rachitis
ACHIKKSW
kickshaw
ACHIKQSU
quackish
ACHIKRSW

rickshaw
ACHILMRS
chrismal
ACHILMTY
mythical
ACHILNNS
clannish
ACHILNPS
clanship
ACHILPSY
physical
ACHILRVY
chivalry
ACHIMMOS
machismo
ACHIMMST
mismatch
ACHIMNOP
champion
ACHIMNOR
harmonic
ACHIMPSS
scampish
ACHIMRRY
myriarch
ACHINORT
anorthic
ACHIOPRT
atrophic
ACHIRSTT
chartist
ACHISTTY
chastity
ACHKMORS
shamrock
ACHLLORY
chorally
ACHLMSTZ
schmaltz
ACHLOPTT
potlatch
ACHMNORY
monarchy
nomarchy
ACHNPPSS
schnapps
ACHOORTU
coauthor
ACHOPRTY
toparchy
ACHOTTUW
watchout
ACHPRSTU
pushcart
ACIIILMN
inimical
ACIIILNV
civilian
ACIIKNNN
cannikin
ACIILLTV
villatic
ACIILMNR
criminal

ACIILMOT
comitial
ACIILNOR
ironical
ACIIMNSU
musician
ACIIMNTY
intimacy
ACIIMRST
scimitar
ACIIMSTV
activism
ACIIMTUV
viaticum
ACIINNOT
inaction
ACIINNQU
cinquain
ACIINOPT
optician
ACIINOSV
avionics
ACIINOTT
citation
ACIINRSS
narcissi
ACIIRSTT
artistic
ACIISTTV
activist
ACIITTVY
activity
ACIITVVY
vivacity
ACIJKKPS
skipjack
ACILLMOS
localism
ACILLNOO
colonial
ACILLNOR
carillon
ACILLNOS
scallion
ACILLOSY
socially
ACILLOTY
locality
ACILMNOP
complain
ACILMOPR
proclaim
ACILMOSV
vocalism
ACILMSTY
mystical
ACILNOOT
colation
ACILNORT
contrail
ACILNOSU
unsocial
ACILNRUY
culinary

ACILNSTY
scantily
ACILOPRT
tropical
ACILORRV
corrival
ACILOSTV
vocalist
ACILPRTU
pictural
ACIMNNNO
cinnamon
ACIMNNRU
manurinc
ACIMNORT
romantic
ACIMNORY
acrimony
ACIMNOST
monastic
ACIMRRSY
miscarry
ACINNOOT
conation
ACINNORS
nasicorn
ACINNOSS
scansion
ACINNOST
canonist
sanction
ACINOOPR
picaroon
ACINOOTV
vocation
ACINOPPT
panoptic
ACINORSS
narcosis
ACINORST
cantoris
ACINORTT
traction
ACINOSSY
cyanosis
ACINOSTW
wainscot
coxswain
ACINOTTX
toxicant
ACINPQUY
piquancy
ACINRTTU
taciturn
ACINSTTY
sanctity
ACIOPRST
piscator
ACIOPSSU
spacious
ACIOPSTU
captious
ACIORSSU

scarious
ACIORTTY
atrocity
citatory
ACIORTVY
voracity
ACIOSTUU
cautious
ACIRSSTY
sacristy
ACKKMOPR
pockmark
ACKKORRW
rackwork
ACKLLPSU
skullcap
ACKMNOST
stockman
ACLLMNOU
columnal
ACLLOORT
collator
ACLLOOSS
colossal
ACLLRTUU
cultural
ACLMMNOU
communal
ACLMNORU
columnar
ACLMNORY
normalcy
ACLMNTUU
cumulant
ACLMORTU
crotalum
ACLMRSUU
muscular
ACLNOORT
colorant
ACLNORSU
consular
ACLNORTU
calutron
ACLNPTUU
punctual
ACLOOPRR
corporal
ACMNOORT
monocrat
ACMNOPRS
corpsman
ACMOOSTU
comatous
ACMORSTY
costmary
ACNNNORY
cannonry
ACNNOSTT
constant
ACNOOORY
coronary
ACNORRTY
contrary

ACNORSTT
contrast
ACNORTTU
turncoat
ACOPRRTT
protract
ACPSSTUY
pussycat
ADDDEEGR
degraded
ADDDEEIM
diademed
ADDDEEMN
demanded
maddened
ADDDEENS
saddened
ADDDELSW
swaddled
ADDDELTW
twaddled
ADDDEMNU
addendum
ADDEEEFN
deafened
ADDEEEFT
defeated
ADDEEEMN
demeaned
ADDEEENR
endeared
ADDEEFKL
defalked
ADDEEFLT
deflated
ADDEEFRY
defrayed
ADDEEGGR
daggered
ADDEEGLZ
deglazed
ADDEEGNR
deranged
gandered
gardened
ADDEEGRR
regarded
ADDEEGSS
degassed
ADDEEHLR
heralded
ADDEEHNR
hardened
ADDEEHRT
threaded
ADDEEILN
deadline
ADEEILR
deadlier
derailed
ADDEEILT
detailed
ADDEEIMT
mediated

ADDEEINT
detained
ADDEEIPR
diapered
ADDEEISS
diseased
ADDEEIST
steadied
ADDEEITV
deviated
ADDEEKNR
darkened
ADDEELNU
unleaded
ADDEELOR
reloaded
ADDEELRT
treadled
ADDEELUV
devalued
ADDEEMNR
remanded
ADDEENPP
appended
ADDEENPR
pandered
ADDEENPX
expanded
ADDEENRW
wandered
ADDEENSS
deadness
ADDEENTT
attended
ADDEEPRT
departed
predated
ADDEEPRV
depraved
pervaded
ADDEERRT
retarded
ADDEERRW
rewarded
ADDEFLRU
dreadful
ADDEGGLR
draggled
ADDEGINR
dreading
ADDEGLST
gladdest
ADDEGPRU
upgraded
ADDEHILR
dihedral
ADDEHINW
headwind
ADDEHLLU
dullhead
ADDEHMRU
drumhead
ADDEHOSW
shadowed

ADDEIIRZ	**ADDGINQU**	repeated	presaged	**ADEEIJMR**
diarized	quadding	**ADDEFFOR**	**ADEEGPRT**	jeremiad
ADDEIITV	**ADDGMRUU**	afforded	pargeted	**ADEEILMR**
additive	mudguard	**ADEEFHOR**	**ADEEGRRT**	remedial
ADDEIJNO	**ADDHHLNO**	forehead	garreted	**ADEEILMV**
adjoined	handhold	**ADEEFHRT**	gartered	medieval
ADDEILNS	**ADDHOORW**	fathered	**ADEEGRSS**	**ADEEILNT**
landside	hardwood	**ADEEFIRR**	dressage	entailed
ADDEILNT	**ADDIILUV**	rarefied	**ADEEGRTT**	**ADEEILPT**
tideland	dividual	**ADEEFLMN**	targeted	depilate
ADDEILYZ	**ADDIINOT**	enflamed	**ADEEGSWY**	**ADEEILRS**
dialyzed	addition	**ADEEFLOR**	edgeways	sidereal
ADDEIMRS	**ADDINRWW**	freeload	**ADEEGTTZ**	**ADEEILRT**
disarmed	windward	**ADEEFLRR**	gazetted	retailed
ADDEIMSY	**ADDKNRRU**	deferral	**ADEEHHRS**	**ADEEILRZ**
dismayed	drunkard	**ADEEFLRT**	rehashed	realized
ADDEIMTT	**ADDLLNOR**	faltered	**ADEEHHST**	**ADEEILST**
admitted	landlord	**ADEEFLSX**	sheathed	leadiest
ADDEINOR	**ADDLNOOW**	flaxseed	**ADEEHILN**	**ADEEIMNR**
ordained	woodland	**ADEEFMNR**	headline	remained
ADDEINST	**ADDLORTY**	freedman	**ADEEHIST**	**ADEEIMNT**
dandiest	dotardly	**ADEEFNSS**	headiest	dementia
ADDEIOPR	**ADDMOOSY**	deafness	**ADEEHISV**	**ADEEIMNX**
parodied	doomsday	**ADEEFNST**	adhesive	examined
ADDEIORS	**ADDNOPWY**	fastened	**ADEEHKNR**	**ADEEIMRR**
roadside	pandowdy	**ADEEFNTT**	hankered	dreamier
ADDEISSU	**ADDNORWW**	fattened	**ADEEHKNR**	**ADEEIMRT**
dissuade	downward	**ADEEFORT**	harkened	diameter
ADDEJSTU	**ADEEEFNY**	foredate	**ADEEHKWW**	**ADEEIMTT**
adjusted	fedayeen	**ADEEFRTU**	hawkweed	meditate
ADDELNOU	**ADEEEFRT**	featured	**ADEEHLLW**	**ADEEINRS**
duodenal	federate	**ADEEGGWW**	wellhead	denaries
unloaded	**ADEEEGLT**	gewgawed	**ADEEHLRT**	**ADEEINRT**
ADDELNSU	delegate	**ADEEGHRT**	lathered	retained
unsaddle	**ADEEEGNR**	gathered	**ADEEHLSS**	**ADEEINVW**
ADDELRST	renegade	**ADEEGINR**	headless	inweaved
straddle	**ADEEEGRS**	regained	**ADEEHMMO**	**ADEEIPRR**
ADDELRSY	degrease	**ADEEGIRS**	homemade	repaired
saddlery	**ADEEEHHW**	disagree	**ADEEHMMR**	**ADEEIPTX**
ADDELRTW	heehawed	**ADEEGKST**	hammered	expiated
twaddler	**ADEEEHRT**	gasketed	**ADEEHMNS**	**ADEEIRRR**
ADDENOPR	reheated	**ADEEGLLT**	headsmen	drearier
pardoned	**ADEEEHSY**	galleted	**ADEEHMPR**	**ADEEIRRS**
ADDENRST	eyeshade	**ADEEGLNR**	hampered	drearies
stranded	**ADEEEKNW**	enlarged	**ADEEHNPP**	**ADEEIRST**
ADDEOTTU	weakened	**ADEEGLRV**	happened	seriated
outdated	**ADEEELMN**	glavered	**ADEEHNRR**	**ADEEIRTT**
ADDFFILO	enameled	graveled	hardener	iterated
daffodil	**ADEEELNV**	**ADEEGMNR**	**ADEEHNRT**	**ADEEISST**
ADDFFNRU	leavened	gendarme	neatherd	steadies
dandruff	**ADEEELPR**	**ADEEGMSS**	**ADEEHNST**	**ADEEISTV**
ADDGILMN	repealed	messaged	hastened	sedative
maddling	**ADEEELRS**	**ADEEGNNR**	**ADEEHORS**	**ADEEKMRR**
ADDGILNN	released	endanger	sorehead	remarked
dandling	**ADEEELRV**	**ADEEGNRR**	**ADEEHORV**	**ADEEKMRT**
ADDGILNP	revealed	gardener	overhead	marketed
paddling	**ADEEELTV**	garnered	**ADEEHRRT**	**ADEEKQSU**
ADDGILNR	elevated	**ADEEGNRU**	threader	squeaked
raddling	**ADEEENRS**	dungaree	**ADEEHRST**	**ADEEKRST**
ADDGILNS	serenade	**ADEEGNRV**	headrest	streaked
saddling	**ADEEENTT**	engraved	**ADEEHRTW**	**ADEELLRU**
ADDGILNW	edentate	**ADEEGORT**	wreathed	laureled
dawdling	**ADEEEPRT**	derogate	**ADEEIILZ**	**ADEELLTY**
waddling	departee	**ADEEGPRS**	idealize	

elatedly
ADEELLWY
walleyed
ADEELMNO
lemonade
ADEELMNR
aldermen
ADEELMNT
lamented
ADEELMRV
marveled
ADEELMTU
emulated
ADEELNOR
oleander
ADEELNRT
antlered
ADEELNRV
lavender
ADEELNSU
unleased
ADEELNSV
enslaved
ADEELNTT
talented
ADEELOST
desolate
ADEELPRS
relapsed
ADEELPRT
paltered
ADEELPRY
parleyed
ADEELPST
pedestal
ADEELQSU
squealed
ADEELRTV
traveled
ADEELSST
dateless
tasseled
ADEELSTY
sedately
ADEEMMRY
yammered
ADEEMMSS
mesdames
ADEEMNNR
mannered
ADEEMNOR
demeanor
ADEEMNOT
nematode
ADEEMORT
moderate
ADEEMPPR
pampered
ADEEMPRT
tampered
ADEEMPRV
revamped
ADEEMPST
stampede

ADEEMRST
mastered
streamed
ADEEMRSU
measured
ADEEMRTT
mattered
ADEENNRU
unearned
ADEENORS
reasoned
ADEENORV
endeavor
ADEENOSS
seasoned
ADEENOTT
detonate
ADEENPPS
sandpeep
ADEENPTT
patented
ADEENRRW
wanderer
ADEENRSS
dearness
ADEENRSU
undersea
ADEENRSW
answered
ADEENRTT
nattered
ADEENRTU
denature
ADEENSST
assented
ADEENSSU
danseuse
ADEENSTU
unseated
ADEENTTV
vendetta
ADEEOPRT
operated
ADEEPPRR
prepared
ADEEPPRS
spreader
ADEEPRSS
aspersed
ADEEPRST
pederast
ADEEPRSU
persuade
ADEEPRTT
pattered
ADEEPRTU
depurate
ADEEPSWY
speedway
ADEEQRUV
quavered
ADEERRST
arrested
serrated

ADEERSST
asserted
ADEERSTT
restated
ADEERTTT
tattered
ADEERVYY
everyday
ADEESTTT
attested
ADEFFIMR
affirmed
ADEFFIST
daffiest
ADEFFLNS
snaffled
ADEFGIIS
gasified
ADEFGILS
gadflies
ADEFGIMN
defaming
ADEFGITU
fatigued
ADEFGLOT
gatefold
ADEFGNTU
fungated
ADEFHIMS
famished
ADEFHLTU
deathful
ADEFHMOT
fathomed
ADEFHNOR
forehand
ADEFHORR
forehand
ADEFIILM
familied
ADEFIILR
airfield
ADEFIILS
salified
ADEFIILT
filiated
ADEFIIMR
ramified
ADEFIIRT
ratified
ADEFILMN
inflamed
ADEFILNT
inflated
ADEFILOT
foliated
ADEFINRR
infrared
ADEFIORS
foresaid
ADEFIRRT
draftier
ADEFLLUY
feudally

ADEFLNOR
foreland
ADEFLNTU
flaunted
ADEFLORV
flavored
ADEFLPRS
feldspar
ADEFLRSW
selfward
ADEFLRTW
leftward
ADEFLRZZ
frazzled
ADEFNOPR
profaned
ADEFNSST
daftness
ADEGGJLY
jaggedly
ADEGGLRY
raggedly
ADEGGMOY
demagogy
ADEGGOPY
pedagogy
ADEGHHOS
hogshead
ADEGHILT
alighted
ADEGHINR
adhering
ADEGHLNO
headlong
ADEGHORT
goatherd
ADEGHRTU
daughter
ADEGIILP
diplegia
ADEGIIMN
imagined
ADEGIINT
ideating
ADEGIITT
digitate
ADEGIJSW
jigsawed
ADEGIKNN
kneading
ADEGILLP
pillaged
ADEGILMN
maligned
ADEGILNP
pedaling
pleading
ADEGILNR
dragline
ADEGILNS
signaled
ADEGILNT
delating
ADEGILNY

delaying
ADEGILOU
dialogue
ADEGILSS
glissade
ADEGIMNN
amending
ADEGIMNR
dreaming
ADEGIMRT
migrated
ADEGINOS
diagnose
ADEGINOZ
agonized
ADEGINRT
gradient
treading
ADEGINRY
readying
ADEGINSS
assigned
ADEGINST
sedating
ADEGISTU
gaudiest
ADEGLLOP
galloped
ADEGLNPS
spangled
ADEGLNRW
wrangled
ADEGLNSS
gladness
ADEGLPPR
grappled
ADEGMMRU
rummaged
ADEGMNOR
dragomen
ADEGMNOT
megadont
ADEGNNRU
grandeur
ADEGNRST
grandest
ADEGOPRT
portaged
ADEGORRT
garroted
ADEGORTT
garotted
ADEGORTU
outraged
ADEGRSSU
graduses
ADEHHRST
thrashed
ADEHIKLN
handlike
ADEHILLO
hilloaed
ADEHILLP
pillhead

ADEHIMMS	sunshade	**ADEILORT**	**ADEINORT**	**ADEISSWY**
shammied	**ADEHNNSU**	idolater	ordinate	sideways
ADEHINOP	unwashed	tailored	rationed	**ADEISTTU**
diaphone	**ADEHOPXY**	**ADEILORV**	**ADEINOST**	situated
ADEHINOS	hexapody	overlaid	sedation	**ADEITTTU**
adhesion	**ADEHORRW**	**ADEILOST**	**ADEINOTT**	attitude
ADEHINOY	harrowed	diastole	antidote	**ADEJOPRY**
hyoidean	**ADEHQSSU**	isolated	**ADEINPPX**	jeopardy
ADEHINST	squashed	**ADEILOTV**	appendix	**ADEJRSTU**
handiest	**ADEHRTTW**	dovetail	**ADEINPRS**	adjuster
ADEHINSV	thwarted	violated	sprained	readjust
vanished	**ADEIILMS**	**ADEILPRS**	**ADEINQTU**	**ADEKLMRY**
ADEHIRSS	idealism	spiraled	antiqued	markedly
radishes	**ADEIILST**	**ADEILPRT**	**ADEINRSS**	**ADEKLPRS**
ADEHIRST	idealist	dipteral	aridness	sparkled
hardiest	**ADEIIMNR**	**ADEILQTU**	**ADEINRST**	**ADEKMNRU**
ADEHIRSV	meridian	liquated	strained	unmarked
ravished	**ADEIIMPR**	**ADEILRRY**	**ADEINRSU**	**ADEKMNSU**
ADEHISST	impaired	drearily	denarius	unmasked
dashiest	**ADEIIMRS**	**ADEILRST**	**ADEINRTT**	**ADEKNNSS**
shadiest	semiarid	lardiest	nitrated	dankness
ADEHLLOW	**ADEEIMTT**	**ADEILRSU**	**ADEINRTU**	**ADEKNRSS**
hallowed	imitated	residual	indurate	darkness
ADEHLMNO	**ADEIINOT**	**ADEILRTT**	ruinated	**ADEKOOTW**
homeland	ideation	detrital	urinated	teakwood
ADEHLNSS	**ADEIINRS**	**ADEILSTY**	**ADEINRVY**	**ADEKQSUW**
handless	draisine	steadily	vineyard	squawked
ADEHLOPS	**ADEIINRT**	**ADEILSWY**	**ADEINSST**	**ADELLNNU**
asphodel	daintier	slideway	sandiest	annulled
ADEHLPSS	**ADEIINST**	**ADEILSXY**	**ADEINSTU**	**ADELLNSS**
splashed	dainties	dyslexia	sinuated	landless
ADEHLRRY	**ADEIIPRR**	**ADEILTTU**	**ADEIOPRS**	**ADELLOTT**
heraldry	prairied	altitude	parodies	allotted
ADEHMNNY	**ADEIITTV**	latitude	**ADEIOPTV**	**ADELLOTW**
handymen	vitiated	**ADEIMNOT**	adoptive	tallowed
ADEHMNOS	**ADEIKLLY**	dominate	**ADEIORST**	**ADELLOWW**
handsome	ladylike	nematoid	asteroid	wallowed
ADEHMNOT	**ADEIKLOT**	**ADEIMNRY**	**ADEIORTT**	**ADELLQSU**
methadon	toadlike	dairymen	teratoid	squalled
ADEHMNRS	**ADEIKLSW**	**ADEIMNRZ**	**ADEIOTZZ**	**ADELLTUU**
herdsman	sidewalk	zemindar	azotized	ululated
ADEHMNRU	**ADEILLNU**	**ADEIMNSS**	**ADEIPPRS**	**ADELMNNS**
unharmed	unallied	sidesman	apprised	landsmen
ADEHMOOR	**ADEILLPR**	**ADEIMNTY**	**ADEIPRST**	**ADELMOTU**
headroom	pillared	dynamite	traipsed	modulate
ADEHMORW	**ADEILLPS**	**ADEIMORT**	**ADEIPRSU**	**ADELMPRT**
homeward	spadille	mediator	upraised	trampled
ADEHMOST	**ADEILLSW**	**ADEIMOTZ**	**ADEIPTTU**	**ADELNORS**
headmost	sidewall	atomized	aptitude	solander
ADEHMOSU	**ADEILMNO**	**ADEIMPRT**	**ADEIQRRU**	**ADELNPRS**
madhouse	melanoid	imparted	quarried	spandrel
ADEHNNSW	**ADEILMNY**	**ADEIMRTU**	**ADEIRSSU**	**ADELNPRU**
handsewn	maidenly	muriated	radiuses	pendular
ADEHNOPR	**ADEILMRY**	**ADEINNOT**	**ADEIRSSU**	**ADELNRTY**
orphaned	dreamily	anointed	disaster	ardently
ADEHNOPT	**ADEILMST**	antinode	**ADEIRSTT**	**ADELNRUY**
phonated	medalist	**ADEINNSX**	striated	underlay
ADEHNORV	misdealt	disannex	tardiest	**ADELNSTU**
overhand	**ADEILNNR**	**ADEINNTU**	**ADEIRVWY**	unsalted
ADEHNRSS	inlander	inundate	driveway	**ADELNTUU**
hardness	**ADEILNRS**	**ADEINOPT**	**ADEISSST**	undulate
ADEHNRTU	islander	antipode	assisted	**ADELOORV**
unthread	**ADEILOPS**	**ADEINORR**	**ADEISSTT**	overload
ADEHNSSU	episodal	ordainer	distaste	**ADELORST**

lodestar
ADELOTUV
ovulated
ADELOVWY
avowedly
ADELPQUX
quadplex
ADELPRSW
sprawled
ADELPRTT
prattled
ADELPSTU
pulsated
ADELRRTU
ultrared
ADELRSTT
startled
ADELRTUY
adultery
ADELTTTW
twattled
ADEMMNNOW
madwomen
ADEMNNNU
unmanned
ADEMNOOR
marooned
ADEMNOPR
pomander
ADEMNORS
ransomed
ADEMNOST
madstone
ADEMNOTU
amounted
ADEMNPSS
dampness
ADEMNRRU
underarm
ADEMNRUW
unwarmed
ADEMNSUU
unamused
ADEMOORT
moderato
ADEMOOSV
vamoosed
ADEMORRT
mortared
ADEMRRTY
martyred
ADENNNTU
untanned
ADENNOTU
unatoned
ADENNTUW
unwanted
ADENOORT
ratooned
ADENOPRR
pardoner
ADENOPSS
spadones
ADENORRW

narrowed
ADENORTT
attorned
ADENORUX
rondeaux
ADENOUVW
unavowed
ADENPRTU
unparted
ADENPRTY
pedantry
ADENPRUY
underpay
ADENQRSU
squander
ADENSTUY
unsteady
ADENSUWY
unswayed
ADEOORRT
toreador
ADEOOTTT
tattooed
ADEOPPRV
approved
ADEOPRRT
parroted
ADEOPRRT
teardrop
ADEOPSTT
postdate
ADEORRST
roadster
ADEORRVW
overdraw
ADEORSST
assorted
ADEORSTX
extrados
ADEORSUV
savoured
ADEPPRST
strapped
ADEPRRTU
raptured
ADEPRSTU
pastured
ADEQSTTU
squatted
ADERSTUX
surtaxed
ADERSTWW
westward
ADFGINRT
drafting
ADFGINRW
dwarfing
ADFHINSS
sandfish
ADFHIRSW
dwarfish
ADFHLOST
holdfast
ADFILLNW
windfall

ADFILMNO
manifold
ADFIORSV
disfavor
ADFLLNOW
downfall
ADGGGILN
daggling
ADGGGINR
dragging
ADGGILNN
dangling
ADGGINRU
guarding
ADGGLRSU
sluggard
ADGHHILN
highland
ADGHHIOR
highroad
ADGHILNN
handling
ADGHILTY
daylight
ADGHINOR
hoarding
ADGHINPR
handgrip
ADGHITTW
tightwad
ADGIILLO
gladioli
ADGIILNT
dilating
ADGIIMNR
admiring
ADGIIMNX
admixing
ADGIINNR
draining
ADGIINNV
invading
ADGIINOV
avoiding
ADGIINRY
dairying
ADGIINSV
advising
ADGIINTU
auditing
ADGIKLNR
darkling
ADGILLNU
alluding
ADGILLNY
dallying
ADGILMOR
marigold
ADGILNPP
dappling
ADGILNRT
dartling
ADGILNRW
drawling

ADGILNZZ
dazzling
ADGILOPR
prodigal
ADGIMMNR
dramming
ADGIMNOP
pomading
ADGINNOR
adorning
ADGINNOT
donating
ADGINNST
standing
ADGINNTU
daunting
ADGINOOR
rigadoon
ADGINOPT
adopting
ADGINOTY
toadying
ADGINPTU
updating
ADGINRTT
dratting
ADGNNORS
grandson
ADHHIPRS
hardship
ADHIINOP
ophidian
ADHILOPS
shipload
ADHILPSY
ladyship
ADHIMNOS
admonish
ADHIMOPP
amphipod
ADHINOPY
diaphony
ADHINRTW
handwrit
ADHINSST
standish
ADHIPRSY
shipyard
ADHIRTWW
withdraw
ADHKNORW
handwork
ADHLMNOO
handloom
ADHLNOUW
downhaul
ADHNOSTU
thousand
ADHOPRSY
rhapsody
ADIIIQRU
daiquiri
ADIIKLMM
milkmaid

ADIILLMR
milliard
ADIILLUV
diluvial
ADIILNOT
dilation
ADIILNTW
tailwind
ADIILNTY
daintily
ADIILSSY
dialysis
ADIILTVY
validity
ADIINOTU
audition
ADIIPRTY
rapidity
ADIIPSTY
sapidity
ADIJRTUX
adjutrix
ADIKNNST
inkstand
ADIKNRST
stinkard
ADILLLPY
pallidly
ADILLMNR
mandrill
ADILLMSY
dismally
ADILLNPS
landslip
ADILLOSW
disallow
ADILLOSY
disloyal
ADILLSTY
distally
ADILMNNO
mandolin
ADILMOPT
diplomat
ADILMOPY
olympiad
ADILMOTY
modality
ADILMPRY
lampyrid
ADILNRWY
inwardly
ADILNSSW
windlass
ADILOPSS
disposal
ADILORSY
solidary
ADILORTY
idolatry
ADILOSTY
sodality

ADIMMNOS nomadism	**ADLPRUWY** upwardly	**AEEELNRV** veneral	**AEEGGINR** agreeing	**AEEGNRST** estrange
ADIMMNSY dynamism	**ADMNNORY** monandry	**AEEELQSU** sequelae	**AEEGGIRV** aggrieve	**AEEGNRST** segreant sergeant
ADIMMNOT dominant	**ADMNOOST** mastodon	**AEEELRTX** axletree	**AEEGGNNR** gangrene	**AEEGNSSS** sageness
ADIMNOST saintdom	**ADMNOOSW** woodsman	**AEEELSSS** easeless	**AEEGHIRT** heritage	**AEEGRSTT** greatest
ADIMOPRY myriapod	**ADMNORSW** sandworm	**AEEEMNST** easement	**AEEGHNRS** shagreen	**AEEHHRSS** rehashes
ADINNNTU inundant	**ADMOORRW** wardroom	**AEEEMPRT** permeate	**AEEGHRRT** gatherer	**AEEHHRTY** heathery
ADINNOOT donation	**ADNNORTY** dynatron	**AEEENRTV** enervate venerate	**AEEGIIST** gaieties	**AEEHIRRT** earthier heartier
ADINNORY nondairy	**ADNOOQRU** quadroon	**AEEEPPRT** repartee repeater	**AEEGILLZ** legalize	**AEEHIRSV** shivaree
ADINOOPT adoption	**ADNOOSVW** advowson		**AEEGILTV** levigate	**AEEHISST** esthesia
ADINOOTT dotation	**ADNOQRSU** squadron	**AEEFFLNR** fernleaf	**AEEGIMNT** geminate	**AEEHISTT** hesitate
ADINOPRR raindrop	**ADNORSTW** sandwort	**AEEFGLNR** ferngale	**AEEGIMRT** emigrate	**AEEHISTV** heaviest
ADINORRY ordinary	**ADNORSXY** sardonyx	**AEEFGLSU** fuselage	**AEEGINSS** agenesis	**AEEHKLLU** keelhaul
ADINORST intrados	**ADNORTUW** untoward	**AEEFHRTY** feathery	**AEEGINSV** envisage	**AEEHKNRR** harkener
ADINORSU dinosaur	**ADNOSTTU** standout	**AEEFILST** fealties leafiest	**AEEGINTV** negative	**AEEHLLSS** seashell
ADINORTU duration	**ADOPRSSW** password	**AEEFIRRS** rarefies	**AEEGIPQU** equipage	**AEEHLMNY** hymeneal
ADIOPRST parodist	**ADOPSSSU** soapsuds	**AEEFISST** safeties	**AEEGIRRS** greasier	**AEEHLMPT** helpmate
ADIORSVY advisory	**AEEEGLRT** relegate	**AEEFKOPR** forepeak	**AEEGLMRT** telegram	**AEEHLNPT** elephant
ADIORTUY auditory	**AEEEGLRV** leverage	**AEEFLLRW** farewell	**AEEGLMRY** meagerly	**AEEHLNRT** leathern
ADIRRWYZ wizardry	**AEEEGNRT** generate renegate teenager	**AEEFLLSS** leafless	**AEEGLNNT** entangle	**AEEHLNVY** heavenly
ADJKNRUY junkyard		**AEEFLMSS** fameless selfsame	**AEEGLNOT** elongate	**AEEHLRST** halteres
ADJORSTU adjustor	**AEEEGRST** steerage	**AEEFLNRU** funereal	**AEEGLNRR** enlarger	**AEEHLRTY** leathery
ADKLOORW workload	**AEEEGRSW** sewerage	**AEEFLORV** overleaf	**AEEGLPRT** grapelet	**AEEHLSST** hateless
ADKMOORR darkroom	**AEEEGTTV** vegetate	**AEEFLRRT** falterer	**AEEGLRSS** eelgrass	**AEEHLSST** heatless
ADKOORRW roadwork	**AEEEHKLL** keelhale	**AEEFLRSS** fearless	**AEEGLRSS** largesse	**AEEHMMRR** hammerer
ADLLNOPW plowland	**AEEEHLRT** ethereal	**AEEFLRRT** falterer	**AEEGLRTU** regulate	**AEEHMNPS** sheepman
ADLLORSY dorsally	**AEEEHMPR** ephemera	**AEEFMNOR** forename	**AEEGLSST** gateless	**AEEHMNRT** earthmen
ADLMNOOR moorland	**AEEEHRRS** rehearse	**AEEFMORS** fearsome	**AEEGLSSZ** gazeless	**AEEHMPRR** hamperer
ADLMNORY randomly	**AEEEHSTT** aesthete	**AEEFNRST** fastener	**AEEGLTTU** tutelage	**AEEHMPSS** emphases
ADLMOPSY psalmody	**AEEEIMNX** examinee	**AEEFNRTT** fattener	**AEEGMNSS** gameness	**AEEHNOPR** earphone
ADLNNTUU undulant	**AEEEIRST** eateries	**AEEFNSSS** safeness	**AEEGMRST** gamester	**AEEHNPST** stephane
ADLNOPRU pauldron	**AEEEKKPS** keepsake	**AEEFNSST** featness	**AEEGMSSU** messuage	**AEEHNRST** hastener
ADLNOPWY downplay	**AEEELMNR** enameler	**AEEGGHIW** weighage	**AEEGNRRV** engraver	**AEEHNRTT** threaten

AEEHNRTU urethane
AEEHNRWY anywhere
AEEHNSTS snatches
AEEHORRV overhear
AEEHORSS seashore
AEEHORTV overheat
AEEHOSTU teahouse
AEEHRTVW whatever
AEEHSTTW sawteeth
AEEIKLMU leukemia
AEEIKLMZ mazelike
AEEIKLRW weaklier
AEEIKLST leakiest
AEEIKLVW wavelike
AEEIKNRS sneakier
AEEILMMT mealtime
AEEILMRT materiel
AEEILMST mealiest
AEEILMTZ metalize
AEEILNPZ penalize
AEEILNSV vaseline
AEEILPRR pearlier
AEEILPRS espalier
AEEILPSW palewise
AEEILQTU eliquate
AEEILQUX exequial
AEEILQUZ equalize
AEEILRRT retailer
AEEILRST earliest / realties
AEEILRSZ sleazier
AEEILRTT literate
AEEILRTV levirate / relative
AEEILTTV levitate
AEEIMMNT meantime
AEEIMNNO neomenia
AEEIMNRX examiner
AEEIMNST seminate
AEEIMRRS smearier
AEEIMRST steamier
AEEIMSST seamiest
AEEIMSTT estimate / meatiest
AEEINNRS anserine
AEEINPRT aperient
AEEINRRT retainer
AEIINRSS airiness
AEEINSSS easiness
AEEINSTT anisette
AEEIPPSU eupepsia
AEEIPPTT appetite
AEEIPRST parietes / petaries
AEEIPSTT peatiest
AEEIQRSU queasier
AEEIRRST arteries
AEEIRSTT treaties / treatise
AEEIRSTW sweatier / weariest
AEEISTTV estivate
AEEKLLST skeletal
AEEKLMRT telemark
AEEKMRRT marketer
AEEKNSSW weakness
AEEKORTV overtake / takeover
AEEKQRSU squeaker
AEELLLTT telltale
AEELLMSS mealless
AEELLPTT platelet
AEELLSTT stellate
AEELMMTU malemute
AEELMNRT lamenter
AEELMNSS lameness / nameless / salesman
AEELMOTT matelote
AEELMPRY empyreal
AEELMPTT template
AEELMSST meatless
AEELNNRT lanneret
AEELNNSS leanness
AEELNOPT antelope
AEELORTV elevator
AEELNPSS paleness
AEELNRTV relevant
AEELNRTX external
AEELNSST lateness
AEELNTUV eventual
AEELOPSX poleaxes
AEELORTT tolerate
AEELPRSU pleasure
AEELPRSV vesperal
AEELQRSU squealer
AEELRRSV reversal
AEELRRTV traveler
AEELRSST tearless
AEELRSTY easterly
AEELSSVW waveless
AEEMNNSS meanness
AEEMNPRY empyrean
AEEMNPTV pavement
AEEMNRUV maneuver
AEEMNSSS sameness
AEEMNSST tameness
AEEMNSTU mansuete
AEEMPPRR pamperer
AEEMPRRT tamperer
AEEMRRST streamer
AEEMRRSU measurer
AEEMRSST masseter
AEEMRSTT teamster
AEEMRSTW stemware
AEEMSSSU masseuse
AEENNRSS nearness
AEENNSSS saneness
AEENNSST neatness
AEENOPRS personae
AEENORSS seasoner
AEENORST resonate
AEENORTV renovate
AEENORVW ovenware
AEENPTTY antetype
AEENRRSS rareness
AEENRSTU sauterne
AEENRTTV antevert
AEENRTTY entreaty
AEEOPRTT operetta
AEEORRTV overrate
AEEORSSV overseas
AEEPRRRT parterre
AEEPRRTU aperture
AEEQRRUV quaverer
AEEQRTTU raquette
AEERRRST arrester
AEERRSST reassert
AEERRSSU reassure
AEERRSTU treasure
AEERRSTV traverse
AEERSSSS reassess
AEERSSUU uraeuses
AEERSTTT attester
AEFFGIIL effigial
AEFFGOST offstage
AEFFGRSU suffrage
AEFFHILL halflife
AEFFIMRR reaffirm
AEFFLNTU affluent
AEFFLSTU feastful
AEFFLSUX affluxes
AEFGHINR hangfire
AEFGIISS gasifies
AEFGIMTU fumigate
AEFGINST feasting
AEFGLLOP flagpole
AEFGLMNU fugleman
AEFGLOPR leapfrog
AEFGLRTU grateful
AEFGMNRT fragment
AEFGNORT frontage
AEFGOORT footgear
AEFHIKRS freakish

AEFHIKSW	festival	funerary	**AEGHINSV**	villager
weakfish	**AEFILTUU**	**AEFNSSST**	sheaving	**AEGILLST**
AEFHILRS	fauteuil	fastness	**AEGHIPPR**	legalist
flashier	**AEFIMNST**	**AEFORRSW**	epigraph	stillage
AEFHIMSS	manifest	forswear	**AEGHIPRT**	**AEGILLTY**
famishes	**AEFIMOST**	**AEFORSTW**	graphite	legality
AEFHLMSU	foamiest	software	**AEGHIRRS**	**AEGILMMR**
shameful	**AEFINOPR**	**AEFORSTY**	gharries	aglimmer
AEFHLNOT	pinafore	forestay	**AEGHLOPY**	**AEGILMNP**
halftone	**AEFINOTT**	**AEGGGINN**	hypogeal	empaling
AEFHLNSS	fetation	engaging	**AEGHLOSS**	**AEGILMNR**
halfness	**AEFINRSS**	**AEGGHIRS**	galoshes	germinal
AEFHLRTY	fairness	shaggier	**AEGHLRTU**	maligner
fatherly	**AEFINSTT**	**AEGGHORU**	laughter	malinger
AEFHMNRS	faintest	roughage	**AEGHLRTY**	**AEGILMNT**
freshman	**AEFIORTV**	**AEGGIILR**	lethargy	ligament
AEFHRSTT	favorite	gigelira	**AEGHMNOY**	metaling
farthest	**AEFIPRRT**	**AEGGIJST**	hogmenay	**AEGILNNP**
AEFIILMS	firetrap	jaggiest	**AEGHMOPT**	paneling
families	**AEFKNORS**	**AEGGIKNR**	apothegm	**AEGILNNR**
AEFIILNZ	forsaken	knaggier	**AEGHNOPT**	learning
finalize	**AEFKOPRS**	**AEGGILLN**	heptagon	**AEGILNNT**
AEFIILRT	forspeak	alleging	**AEGHNORV**	gantline
firetail	**AEFLIISS**	**AEGGILLR**	hangover	**AEGILNNY**
AEFIIMNS	salifies	grillage	overhang	yeanling
infamies	**AEFLLPTU**	**AEGGILMN**	**AEGHORST**	**AEGILNOR**
AEFIIMRS	plateful	gleaming	shortage	regional
ramifies	**AEFLLSSW**	**AEGGILNN**	**AEGIILTT**	**AEGILNOS**
AEFIINRV	flawless	gleaning	litigate	gasoline
vinifera	**AEFLLSTY**	**AEGGINNR**	**AEGIIMNR**	**AEGILNOT**
AEFIIPRT	festally	angering	imaginer	legation
aperitif	**AEFLMORU**	enraging	migraine	**AEGILNPR**
AEFIIRRS	formulae	**AEGGINNT**	**AEGIIMTT**	pearling
friaries	**AEFLNOPT**	negating	mitigate	**AEGILNPS**
AEFIIRST	pantofle	**AEGGINNV**	**AEGIINRR**	elapsing
ratifies	**AEFLNRTU**	avenging	grainier	pleasing
AEFIITVX	flaunter	**AEGGINOS**	**AEGIIRRT**	**AEGILNQU**
fixative	**AEFLNSST**	seagoing	irrigate	equaling
AEFIKLST	flatness	**AEGGINRS**	**AEGIKLNW**	**AEGILNRS**
flakiest	**AEFLOPRY**	greasing	weakling	signaler
AEFILMNR	foreplay	**AEGGINRW**	**AEGIKMNR**	**AEGILNRT**
inflamer	**AEFLOSTT**	wagering	remaking	alerting
rifleman	falsetto	**AEGGIOPR**	**AEGIKNNS**	altering
AEFILMNT	**AEFLPPRY**	arpeggio	sneaking	integral
filament	flypaper	**AEGGIQRU**	**AEGIKNPS**	relating
AEFILMST	**AEFLRTTY**	quaggier	speaking	triangle
flamiest	flattery	**AEGGLNPT**	**AEGIKNRT**	**AEGILNRV**
AEFILMSY	**AEFLSTTT**	eggplant	retaking	raveling
mayflies	flattest	**AEGGLORY**	**AEGIKNRW**	**AEGILNRX**
AEFILNNR	**AEFLSTTU**	gargoyle	wreaking	relaxing
infernal	tasteful	**AEGGLRST**	**AEGIKNTW**	**AEGILNRY**
AEFILNRT	**AEFLSTUW**	straggle	tweaking	relaying
inflater	wasteful	**AEGGMORT**	**AEGIKSTW**	yearling
AEFILORS	**AEFMNRRY**	mortgage	gawkiest	**AEGILNST**
foresail	ferryman	**AEGGNRST**	**AEGILLMS**	eastling
AEFILRTT	**AEFMORST**	gangster	legalism	stealing
filtrate	foremast	**AEGHILMT**	**AEGILLNU**	**AEGILNTX**
AEFILRTU	**AEFNNSTU**	megalith	lingulae	exalting
faultier	unfasten	**AEGHILNS**	**AEGILLNY**	**AEGILOPS**
AEFILSSW	**AEFNORRW**	leashing	genially	spoilage
sawflies	forewarn	**AEGHILNX**	**AEGILLPS**	**AEGILORS**
AEFILSTU	**AEFNRRST**	exhaling	spillage	seraglio
fistulae	transfer	**AEGHINRS**	**AEGILLRV**	**AEGILPPS**
AEFILSTV	**AEFNRRUY**	shearing		slippage

AEGILPPU	**AEGINRTT**	playgoer	**AEHILORS**	**AEHIRRST**
pupilage	treating	**AEGLORTW**	shoalier	trashier
AEGILRTT	**AEGINRTV**	waterlog	**AEHILPRS**	**AEHIRRSV**
aglitter	averting	**AEGMNNOT**	earlship	ravisher
AEGILRTU	**AEGINRTW**	magneton	**AEHILRSS**	**AEHIRSSV**
ligature	watering	**AEGMNORV**	hairless	ravishes
AEGILRVW	**AEGINRVW**	mangrove	**AEHILRSV**	**AEHIRSTU**
lawgiver	wavering	**AEGMNRTU**	lavisher	thesauri
AEGIMNNR	**AEGINRWY**	argument	shrieval	**AEHIRSTW**
renaming	wearying	**AEGMORSS**	**AEHILRTY**	waterish
AEGIMNRS	**AEGINSST**	gossamer	heartily	**AEHIRSTY**
smearing	giantess	**AEGMPSTU**	**AEHILSTT**	hysteria
AEGIMNRT	**AEGINSSY**	stumpage	lathiest	**AEHISSTT**
emigrant	essaying	**AEGNNOPT**	**AEHIMMSS**	hastiest
AEGIMNRU	**AEGINSTT**	pentagon	shammies	**AEHISSTU**
geranium	estating	**AEGNNPRT**	**AEHIMMST**	hiatuses
AEGIMNST	tangiest	pregnant	hammiest	**AEHISSTW**
mangiest	**AEGINSTW**	**AEGNOPRR**	**AEHIMMSW**	washiest
steaming	sweating	parergon	whammies	**AEHJNNOS**
AEGIMPRU	yeasting	**AEGNORST**	**AEHIMNNU**	johannes
umpirage	**AEGIORSS**	ragstone	inhumane	**AEHKNNSU**
AEGIMQRU	argosies	**AEGNORTT**	**AEHIMNUZ**	unshaken
quagmire	**AEGIORSV**	tetragon	humanize	**AEHKNOSW**
AEGIMRST	viragoes	**AEGNORTY**	**AEHIMPRS**	hawknose
magister	**AEGIRRSS**	negatory	samphire	**AEHLLMNS**
AEGIMNNX	grassier	**AEGNOTUY**	seraphim	shellman
annexing	**AEGIRSUU**	autogeny	**AEHIMPRT**	**AEHLLNRT**
AEGINNOT	auguries	**AEGNRRST**	teraphim	enthrall
negation	**AEGISSST**	stranger	**AEHIMPSS**	**AEHLLSST**
AEGINNPS	gassiest	**AEGNRSSY**	emphasis	haltless
sneaping	**AEGLLOPR**	grayness	misshape	**AEHLMMNS**
AEGINNRS	galloper	**AEGOPPST**	**AEHIMPST**	helmsman
grannies	**AEGLLORY**	stoppage	shipmate	**AEHLMNUY**
AEGINNRV	allegory	**AEGOPSTT**	**AEHIMRRS**	humanely
ravening	**AEGLLOTT**	gatepost	marshier	**AEHLMPPT**
AEGINNRY	tollgate	**AEGORUVY**	**AEHINORT**	pamphlet
yearning	**AEGLLSSU**	voyageur	antihero	**AEHLMRSS**
AEGINNSU	galluses	**AEGRSTTY**	**AEHINPPY**	harmless
sanguine	**AEGLMNNO**	strategy	epiphany	**AEHLNPRS**
AEGINORZ	mangonel	**AEHHRSST**	**AEHINPST**	shrapnel
organize	**AEGLMOTV**	harshest	thespian	**AEHLNTUZ**
AEGINPPR	megavolt	thrashes	**AEHINRSV**	hazelnut
papering	**AEGLNNTU**	**AEHIIKLR**	vanisher	**AEHLOPRT**
AEGINPRS	untangle	hairlike	**AEHINSST**	plethora
spearing	**AEGLNORY**	**AEHIILNR**	anthesis	**AEHLORSY**
AEGINPRT	yearlong	hairline	shanties	hoarsely
tapering	**AEGLNOSU**	**AEHIIMNT**	**AEHINSSV**	**AEHLORUV**
AEGINPRV	angulose	thiamine	vanishes	overhaul
repaving	**AEGLNPSS**	**AEHIIMOP**	**AEHINSSZ**	**AEHLPSSS**
AEGINPRY	pangless	hemiopia	haziness	splashes
repaying	**AEGLNRRW**	**AEHIIRRW**	**AEHINSTT**	**AEHLPSST**
AEGINQTU	wrangler	wirehair	hesitant	pathless
equating	**AEGLNRST**	**AEHIIRST**	**AEHIOPPR**	**AEHLPSTU**
AEGINRRV	strangle	hairiest	epiphora	sulphate
averring	**AEGLNRSY**	**AEHIKKLW**	**AEHIOPRU**	**AEHLSTTY**
AEGINRVY	laryngas	hawklike	euphoria	stealthy
vinegary	**AEGLNTTU**	**AEHIKLLO**	**AEHIOPRZ**	**AEHMNNPY**
AEGINRSS	gauntlet	halolike	aphorize	nymphean
assigner	**AEGLNTUU**	**AEHIKSST**	**AEHIORST**	**AEHMNORS**
AEGINRST	ungulate	shakiest	hoariest	horseman
angriest	**AEGLOOPU**	**AEHILNOP**	**AEHIPPRS**	**AEHMNPRU**
gantries	apologue	aphelion	sapphire	prehuman
AEGINRSW	**AEGLOPRY**	**AEHILNTZ**	**AEHIPPST**	**AEHMOPRT**
swearing		zenithal	happiest	metaphor

AEHMOSTT
hemostat
AEHMOSTW
somewhat
AEHMSSSU
shamuses
AEHMSTTY
amethyst
AEHNNOPT
pantheon
AEHNOPST
stanhope
AEHNRSSS
rashness
AEHNSTUW
unswathe
AEHOPRRY
pyorrhea
AEHOPRSS
pharoses
AEHORRRW
harrower
AEHORSST
hoarsest
AEHORSSW
sawhorse
AEHORSTT
rheostat
AEHPRSST
sharpest
AEHPRSUX
haruspex
AEHQSSSU
squashes
AEHRSTTY
shattery
AEIIINTT
initiate
AEIIKLLT
taillike
AEIILLTV
illative
AEIILMPR
imperial
AEIILMTT
militate
AEIILNQU
aquiline
AEIILNRR
airliner
AEIILNRT
inertial
AEIILNST
litanies
AEIILPPT
tailpipe
AEIILRTT
literati
AEIILTVZ
vitalize
AEIIMMRT
maritime
AEIIMMXZ
maximize

AEIIMNTT
intimate
AEIIMNTU
minutiae
AEIIMRST
seriatim
AEIINRST
rainiest
AEIINSTV
vanities
AEIINSTZ
sanitize
AEIINSVV
invasive
AEIIPRZZ
pizzeria
AEIIPSST
epitasis
AEIIRRST
rarities
AEIIRRTT
irritate
AEIIRSTW
wisteria
AEIIRSTZ
saterize
AEIJLOPS
jalopies
AEIJLOSU
jalousie
AEIJNRTU
jauntier
AEIJSTZZ
jazziest
AEIKLLMS
selamlik
AEIKLNPS
skiplane
AEIKLNSS
sealskin
AEIKLNST
lankiest
AEIKLRST
starlike
AEIKMNST
mistaken
AEIKNRTW
knitwear
AEIKNSST
snakiest
AEIKPSTW
pawkiest
AEIKQSTU
quakiest
AEIKRSST
asterisk
AEILLLMO
malleoli
AEILLLNY
lineally
AEILLNQU
quinella
AEILLNRY
linearly

AEILLOTV
volatile
AEILLPRT
pillaret
AEILLPST
pastille
AEILLRRU
railleur
AEILLRRY
raillery
AEILLRSY
serially
AEILLSST
tailless
AEILLSUV
allusive
AEILMMOR
memorial
AEILMMOT
immolate
AEILMNNS
linesman
AEILMNOS
semolina
AEILMNRT
terminal
AEILMNST
manliest
AEILMORZ
moralize
AEILMOST
loamiest
AEILMPRV
primeval
AEILMPST
palmiest
AEILMPTY
playtime
AEILMRTT
remittal
AEILMRUV
velarium
AEILMSTT
maltiest
AEILMSTU
simulate
AEILMTTU
mutilate
ultimate
AEILNNRT
internal
AEILNNSY
insanely
AEILNNTY
innately
AEILNOPT
antipole
AEILNOPU
poulaine
AEILNORT
oriental
relation
AEILNPPT

pieplant
AEILNPSS
painless
AEILNPST
panelist
plainest
AEILNPTT
tinplate
AEILNRSS
rainless
AEILNRTV
interval
AEILNSSZ
laziness
AEILNSTU
insulate
AEILNSUY
uneasily
AEILNTVY
natively
venality
AEILOPPT
oppilate
AEILOPRZ
polarize
AEILOPST
spoliate
AEILORSZ
solarize
AEILORTV
violater
AEILPPQU
applique
AEILPRRS
reprisal
AEILPRRT
paltrier
AEILPRST
pilaster
AEILPSUV
plausive
AEILQRTU
quartile
requital
AEILQSUY
queasily
AEILQTUY
equality
AEILRRTY
literary
AEILRRUZ
ruralize
AEILRSST
slaister
AEILSSTT
saltiest
AEIMMNNT
immanent
AEIMMRTU
immature
AEIMNNOT
nominate
AEIMNNRT
trainmen

AEIMNOST
masonite
AEIMNRSU
aneurism
AEIMNRSY
seminary
AEIMNRTT
martinet
AEIMNRTU
ruminate
AEIMNSST
mantises
AEIMOPST
epistoma
AEIMORRS
armories
AEIMORTT
amoretti
AEIMORTZ
amortize
atomizer
AEIMOTTV
motivate
AEIMPRRT
imparter
AEIMPRST
mispreat
AEIMPRTU
apterium
AEIMQRSU
marquise
AEIMRSST
asterism
AEIMRSSY
emissary
AEIMRSTX
matrixes
AEIMRSWW
swimwear
AEIMSSTT
misstate
AEINNORT
anointer
AEINNOTT
intonate
AEINNOTV
innovate
AEINNSSV
vainness
AEINNSSZ
zaniness
AEINOPPT
antipope
AEINOPRT
atropine
AEINOQTU
equation
AEINORRT
anterior
AEINORRW
ironware
AEINORST
notaries
senorita

AEINORSV	pastries	**AELLNPRU**	platyope	tapeworm
aversion	raspiest	prunella	**AELOPPXY**	**AEMORRST**
AEINORTZ	**AEIPRSSV**	**AELLNRUY**	apoplexy	rearmost
notarize	parvises	neurally	**AELOPQUY**	**AEMORRSY**
AEINOTVX	**AEIPRSSX**	**AELLNSST**	opaquely	rosemary
vexation	praxises	tallness	**AELOPRVY**	**AEMORSSY**
AEINPPRS	**AEIPRSTY**	**AELLNTTY**	overplay	mayoress
snappier	asperity	latently	**AELOPSSU**	**AEMPRSTU**
AEINPPST	**AEIPRSVY**	**AELLOSUV**	espousal	upstream
nappiest	vespiary	alveolus	**AELOPSTU**	**AEMQRSSU**
AEINPRRT	**AEIPRTVY**	**AELLSSST**	petalous	marquess
terrapin	varitype	saltless	**AELORTYZ**	**AEMRSSTT**
AEINPRST	**AEIPSSTT**	**AELLSUXY**	zealotry	mattress
pantries	pastiest	sexually	**AELPRRTT**	smartest
AEINPTTY	**AEIPSSTW**	**AELMNNOT**	prattler	**AEMRSTTU**
antitype	waspiest	nonmetal	**AELPRSSY**	testamur
AEINQRTU	**AEIPTTUV**	**AELMNNRY**	sparsely	**AEMRTUUX**
quainter	putative	mannerly	**AELPRSTT**	trumeaux
AEINQTTU	**AEIQRRRU**	**AELMNOPS**	splatter	**AENNORST**
equitant	quarrier	neoplasm	**AELQRSUY**	resonant
AEINQTUZ	**AEIQRRSU**	**AELMNOSU**	squarely	**AENNORSU**
quantize	quarries	melanous	**AELRSSST**	unreason
AEINRRST	**AEIRRTTY**	**AELMOOPT**	starless	**AENOOPST**
restrain	tertiary	omoplate	**AELRSSUW**	teaspoon
strainer	**AEIRSSTW**	**AELMOPRR**	walruses	**AENOPRWY**
AEINRSSW	waitress	premolar	**AELRSTTU**	weaponry
wariness	**AEIRSTTT**	**AELMOPRT**	lustrate	**AENORRRW**
AEINRSTT	rattiest	temporal	**AELSTTUY**	narrower
straiten	**AEIRSTTW**	**AELMOPSY**	astutely	**AENORSST**
AEINRSUZ	wartiest	playsome	**AEMMOORT**	assentor
suzerain	**AEIRSTVY**	**AELMORTU**	roommate	**AENORSUV**
AEINSSTT	vestiary	emulator	**AEMMORST**	ravenous
nastiest	**AEIRTTTW**	**AELMOSSS**	marmoset	**AENORTTY**
AEINSSVW	atwitter	molasses	**AEMNNORT**	attorney
waviness	**AEISSSST**	**AELMRRST**	ornament	**AENOSSUU**
AEINSSWX	sassiest	maltster	**AEMNNOST**	nauseous
waxiness	**AEISSSTY**	**AELMRSTY**	stoneman	**AENPRSTT**
AEINSTTT	essayist	masterly	**AEMNNRTY**	transept
nattiest	**AEISSTTT**	**AELMRTUY**	entryman	**AENQRRTU**
AEINSTTW	tastiest	maturely	**AEMNOORT**	quartern
tawniest	**AEJLOSUY**	**AELMSSSS**	anteroom	**AENRSSTT**
AEIOPPST	jealousy	massless	**AEMNOPRW**	tartness
apposite	**AEKLMRUW**	**AELMSSST**	manpower	**AENRSTWY**
AEIOPRRT	lukewarm	mastless	**AEMNORST**	sternway
priorate	**AEKLMRUY**	**AELNNOOP**	storeman	**AENRTWYY**
AEIOPRVZ	yarmulke	napoleon	**AEMNORTY**	entryway
vaporize	**AEKLNNSS**	**AELNOPRS**	monetary	**AENSSSTV**
AEIOPSST	lankness	personal	**AEMNORYY**	vastness
soapiest	**AEKLPRRS**	**AELNORTT**	yeomanry	**AENSSTTU**
AEIOPTTV	sparkler	tolerant	**AEMNOSTU**	tautness
optative	**AEKMMNRS**	**AELNORTY**	seamount	**AEOOPPPS**
AEIORRSS	marksmen	ornately	**AEMNPRSS**	pappoose
rosaries	**AEKMORTW**	**AELNPRSU**	pressman	**AEOOPRRT**
AEIORRST	teamwork	purslane	**AEMNPRSU**	operator
rotaries	**AEKNNRSS**	supernal	superman	**AEOOPSTT**
AEIORRSV	rankness	**AELNPTTU**	**AEMOORRW**	potatoes
savorier	**AEKOSTTU**	petulant	wareroom	**AEOORTTT**
AEIORTTV	stakeout	**AELNRSTT**	**AEMOORTT**	tattooer
rotative	**AELLMNTY**	slattern	amoretto	**AEOPRSSV**
AEIPPSST	mentally	**AELNSSST**	**AEMOOSST**	overpass
sappiest	**AELLMOTT**	saltness	maestoso	**AEOPRSTT**
AEIPQRTU	maletolt	**AELOPPTU**	**AEMOOSTT**	prostate
pratique	**AELLMSST**	populate	tomatoes	**AEOPRSTU**
AEIPRSST	smallest	**AELOPPTY**	**AEMOPRTW**	apterous

AEOPSSTT
potestas
AEOPTTUY
autotype
AEOQRSTU
quaestor
AEOQRTUZ
quatorze
AEORRSTT
rostrate
AEORRTZZ
terrazzo
AEORSSSS
assessor
AEORSTTT
attestor
testator
AEORSTVY
overstay
AEPPRRST
strapper
AEPRSSST
sparsest
trespass
AEPRSTTY
tapestry
AEPSSSSU
passuses
AEQRSSTU
squarest
AEQRSTTU
squatter
AERRSTUY
treasury
AERSSTUX
surtaxes
AERSTTVY
travesty
AFFFFIRR
riffraff
AFFGHIRT
affright
AFFGIINP
piaffing
AFFGIINX
affixing
AFFGIIRT
graffiti
AFFGILNR
raffling
AFFGILNW
waffling
AFFGINQU
quaffing
AFFGINST
staffing
AFFGIORT
graffito
AFFHILLS
fallfish
AFFHILST
flatfish
AFFHILTU
faithful

AFFIINTY
affinity
AFFILLMM
flimflam
AFFINOSU
affusion
AFFIPSTT
tipstaff
AFFLLOOT
footfall
AFFLOOTT
flatfoot
AFGGGILN
flagging
AFGGGINR
fragging
AFGGILNN
flanging
AFGGINOR
foraging
AFGGINOT
fagoting
AFGGINRT
grafting
AFGHILLN
halfling
AFGHILNS
flashing
AFGHILPS
flagship
AFGHINRT
farthing
AFGHINST
shafting
AFGIILLN
flailing
AFGIINNT
fainting
AFGIINTX
fixating
AFGIKLNN
flanking
AFGIKNNR
franking
AFGILMMN
flamming
AFGILMNO
flamingo
AFGILNNN
flanning
AFGILNOT
floating
AFGILNPP
flapping
AFGILNTU
faulting
AFGINORV
favoring
AFGINPPR
frapping
AFGINRST
strafing

AFGLLRUY
frugally
AFGLLSSU
glassful
AFGLNNOO
gonfalon
AFHIILSS
sailfish
AFHIILST
fishtail
AFHILLSY
flashily
AFHILOSY
oafishly
AFHIRSST
starfish
AFHKLNTU
thankful
AFHLLOTU
loathful
AFHLRTUW
wrathful
AFHOOPTT
footpath
AFIILNST
finalist
AFIILNTY
finality
AFIINNOS
sinfonia
AFIINOTX
fixation
AFIJMNOR
janiform
AFIKLNNR
franklin
AFILLLOT
flotilla
AFILLTUY
faultily
AFILMNOR
informal
AFILNORT
inflator
AFILNOTU
flautino
AFILNPPT
flippant
AFILNRUY
unfairly
AFILRSTU
fistular
AFILSTTU
flautist
AFIMNOPR
napiform
AFIMNOSU
infamous
AFINNOTU
fountain
AFINNRTY
infantry
AFINQTUY
quantify

AFINRSTX
transfix
AFIRSTTY
stratify
AFKLNOTU
outflank
AFKMOORT
footmark
AFLLLUWY
lawfully
AFLLMNUY
manfully
AFLLMORY
formally
AFLLNOSW
snowfall
AFLLNUUW
unlawful
AFLLRTUY
artfully
AFLMOPRT
platform
AFLMORTW
flatworm
AFLMOSUY
famously
AFLNTUUV
vauntful
AFLOSTUU
flatuous
AGGGGILN
gaggling
AGGGHILN
haggling
AGGGHINS
shagging
AGGGILNN
gangling
naggling
AGGGILNR
gargling
AGGGILNS
slagging
AGGGILNW
waggling
AGGGINNS
snagging
AGGGINST
stagging
AGGHILNU
laughing
AGGHILST
gaslight
AGGHIMNO
homaging
AGGHINNS
gnashing
AGGHINPR
graphing
AGGIILNN
aligning
AGGIILNS
silaging
AGGIILNT

AGGIILNT
ligating
AGGIILNV
gingival
AGGIINNR
graining
AGGIJLNN
jangling
AGGILMNN
mangling
AGGILMNO
gloaming
AGGILMNU
glauming
AGGILNNO
ganglion
AGGILNNR
gnarling
AGGILNNT
gnailing
tangling
AGGILNNW
wangling
AGGILNOT
gloating
AGGILNPU
plaguing
AGGILNPY
gapingly
AGGILNSS
glassing
AGGINNOR
groaning
AGGINNOT
tangoing
AGGINNRR
gnarring
AGGINNRT
granting
AGGINNTW
twanging
AGGINOVY
voyaging
AGGINPRS
grasping
sparging
AGGINRSS
grassing
AGGINRSU
sugaring
AGGINRTY
gyrating
AGGINRUU
auguring
AGGIRTUZ
ziggurat
AGGLLLOY
lollygag
AGGLMOOR
logogram
AGGLRSTY
straggly
AGHHIILT
hightail
AGHHLOTU

although	garookuh	jaunting	**AGILNOTT**	**AGIMORRT**
AHGIILNN	**AGHLMOOR**	**AGIKLMOR**	totaling	migrator
inhaling	hologram	kilogram	**AGILNOTY**	**AGIMQRUY**
AGHIIRTT	**AGHMMOOY**	**AGIKLNNP**	antilogy	quagmiry
airtight	homogamy	planking	**AGILNPPS**	**AGINNNOY**
AGHIKNNS	**AGHNPRSY**	**AGIKLNNR**	slapping	annoying
shanking	syngraph	rankling	**AGILNPPY**	**AGINNNPS**
AGHIKNNT	**AGIIINNS**	**AGIKLNOP**	applying	spanning
thanking	insignia	polkaing	**AGILNPST**	**AGINNOPT**
AGHIKNRS	**AGIILMNP**	**AGIKLNST**	stapling	poignant
sharking	impaling	stalking	**AGILNPSY**	**AGINNORT**
AGHILLNO	**AGIILNNU**	**AGIKNNPS**	palsying	ignorant
halloing	inguinal	spanking	splaying	**AGINNOTT**
AGHILMTY	**AGIILNNY**	**AGIKNOST**	**AGILNPTT**	notating
almighty	inlaying	goatskin	platting	**AGINNPPS**
AGHILNOO	**AGIILNOR**	**AGIKNPRS**	**AGILNRST**	snapping
hooligan	original	sparking	starling	**AGINNPSW**
AGHILNOR	**AGIILNOT**	**AGILLMNU**	**AGILNRSU**	spawning
longhair	intaglio	mulligan	singular	wingspan
AGHILNOS	ligation	**AGILLMNY**	**AGILNRTT**	**AGINNTTU**
shoaling	**AGIILNPT**	malignly	rattling	attuning
AGHILNOT	plaiting	**AGILLNOW**	**AGILNRTW**	taunting
loathing	**AGIILNQU**	allowing	trawling	**AGINNTUV**
AGHILNPS	quailing	**AGILLNOY**	**AGILNSTT**	vaunting
plashing	**AGIILNRT**	alloying	slatting	**AGINOORT**
AGHILNSS	ringtail	**AGILLNRU**	**AGILNSTU**	rogation
hassling	trailing	alluring	saluting	**AGINOPPS**
slashing	**AGIILNRV**	**AGILLNRY**	**AGILNTTT**	apposing
AGHILNSU	rivaling	rallying	tattling	**AGINOPQU**
languish	virginal	**AGILLNST**	**AGILNTTW**	opaquing
AGHILRSY	**AGIILNTT**	stalling	wattling	**AGINORRS**
garishly	litigant	**AGILLNSY**	**AGILNTUV**	garrison
AGHIMMNS	**AGIILNTV**	sallying	vaulting	**AGINORSS**
shamming	vigilant	signally	**AGILNTUX**	assignor
AGHIMNSS	**AGIIMNTT**	**AGILLNTY**	luxating	**AGINORST**
smashing	mitigant	tallying	**AGILNTWZ**	roasting
AGHINNTU	**AGIINNPT**	**AGILLOPT**	waltzing	**AGINORSU**
haunting	painting	gallipot	**AGILOOPY**	arousing
AGHINNTY	**AGIINNRT**	**AGILLSSY**	apiology	**AGINORSV**
anything	training	glassily	**AGIMMOSY**	savoring
AGHINPRS	**AGIINNST**	**AGILMMNS**	misogamy	**AGINORTT**
phrasing	sainting	slamming	**AGIMNNRU**	rotating
sharping	satining	**AGILMNNT**	manuring	**AGINORTY**
AGHINPSW	staining	mantling	unarming	gyration
pshawing	**AGIINNTT**	**AGILMNPS**	**AGIMNORS**	**AGINOSTT**
AGHINQSU	tainting	sampling	organism	toasting
quashing	**AGIINOPT**	**AGILMORS**	**AGIMNPRT**	**AGINPPRT**
AGHINRRY	opiating	algorism	tramping	trapping
harrying	**AGIINORT**	**AGILNNNP**	**AGIMNPST**	**AGINPPRW**
AGHINRST	rigatoni	planning	stamping	wrapping
trashing	**AGIINPRS**	**AGILNNPT**	**AGIMNPSW**	**AGINPPSW**
AGHINRTW	aspiring	planting	swamping	swapping
thrawing	praising	**AGILNNRS**	**AGIMNRRY**	**AGINPPTU**
AGHINSST	**AGIINPRT**	snarling	marrying	pupating
stashing	pirating	**AGILNNST**	**AGIMNRST**	**AGINPRRS**
AGHINSSW	**AGIINRRV**	slanting	smarting	sparring
swashing	arriving	**AGILNNUY**	**AGIMNRSW**	**AGINPRRY**
AGHINSTW	**AGIINRTT**	ungainly	swarming	parrying
swathing	attiring	**AGILNOPR**	**AGIMNRTU**	**AGINPRSY**
AGHIOPRS	**AGIJLNPY**	paroling	maturing	spraying
isograph	japingly	**AGILNORT**	**AGIMNSSU**	**AGINPRTY**
AGHIRSTT	**AGIJMNOR**	trigonal	assuming	partying
straight	majoring	**AGILNOSS**	**AGIMNTTU**	**AGINPSTT**
AGHKOORU	**AGIJNNTU**	lassoing	mutating	

spatting	**AHHMPRRU**	**AHLORRTY**	**AIIMORTT**	**AILMMORS**
AGINQRSU	harrumph	harlotry	imitator	moralism
squaring	**AHHNORTW**	**AHMNNSTU**	**AIIMRUVV**	**AILMMORT**
AGINRRST	hawthorn	huntsman	vivarium	immortal
starring	**AHIIILMN**	**AHMOORSW**	**AIIMSSTT**	**AILMNNSU**
AGINRRTY	malihini	washroom	mastitis	annulism
tarrying	**AHIILRTY**	**AHMOPTYY**	**AIINNOSV**	**AILMNOOP**
AGINRSSU	hilarity	myopathy	invasion	palomino
assuring	**AHIIMNOT**	**AHMPSTYY**	**AIINNQTU**	**AILMNOOR**
AGINRSTT	himation	sympathy	quintain	monorail
starting	**AHIIMNST**	**AHNOORRY**	**AIINNSTY**	**AILMNPTU**
AGINRSTV	isthmian	honorary	insanity	platinum
starving	**AHIINSST**	**AHNOPPSW**	**AIINRRTT**	**AILMNRUY**
AGINRSTW	saintish	pawnshop	irritant	luminary
strawing	**AHIKPRSS**	**AHNOPSST**	**AIINSTTV**	**AILMORST**
AGINRSTY	sparkish	snapshot	nativist	moralist
stingray	**AHILLMSS**	**AHNOSTUX**	**AIINSTTV**	**AILMORSU**
straying	smallish	xanthous	visitant	solarium
AGINSTTW	**AHILLSVY**	**AHOOSSTY**	**AIINTTVY**	**AILMORTY**
swatting	lavishly	soothsay	nativity	morality
AGINSVVY	**AHILMQSU**	**AHOOSTTW**	**AIIPRRST**	**AILMOSTU**
savvying	qualmish	sawtooth	airstrip	solatium
AGIOORSZ	**AHILNOPS**	**AHOPSTUW**	**AIIRSSTT**	**AILMPSST**
grazioso	siphonal	southpaw	satirist	psalmist
AGIORRTT	**AHILNORT**	**AIIIRSSS**	**AIJKKNOU**	**AILMPSTY**
grattoir	horntail	siriasis	kinkajou	ptyalism
AGIRTTUY	**AHILOPST**	**AIIJNRTX**	**AIJLLOVY**	**AILMRRSU**
gratuity	hospital	janitrix	jovially	ruralism
AGLMOPRY	**AHIMMNSU**	**AIIKKSUY**	**AIJLNTUY**	**AILMRSTU**
polygram	humanism	sukiyaki	jauntily	altruism
AGLMOPYY	**AHIMNOSW**	**AIIKNNNP**	**AIJMORTY**	ultraism
polygamy	womanish	pannikin	majority	**AILNNOOT**
AGLMORUY	**AHIMNSTU**	**AIIKORTY**	**AIKLOTTW**	notional
glamoury	humanist	yakitori	kilowatt	**AILNOOPT**
AGLNOOSY	**AHIMNTUY**	**AIILLLUV**	**AIKMRSTZ**	optional
nasology	humanity	illuvial	sitzmark	**AILNOPTY**
AGLNOSUU	**AHIMOPRS**	**AIILLMRY**	**AIKNNOOS**	ponytail
angulous	aphorism	milliary	nainsook	**AILNOTTY**
AGLNOSWY	**AHIMORRW**	**AIILLNNV**	**AIKNNSSW**	tonality
longways	hairworm	vanillin	swanskin	**AILNOTUX**
AGLORSSY	**AHIMPPSS**	**AIILLNOT**	**AIKNOSTT**	luxation
glossary	sapphism	illation	stotinka	**AILNQRTU**
AGLPSSSY	**AHINNOPT**	**AIILLNVY**	**AILLLPSU**	tranquil
spyglass	antiphon	villainy	lapillus	**AILNQTUY**
AGLRTTUU	**AHINOSST**	**AIILMNTT**	**AILLMUUV**	quaintly
guttural	astonish	militant	alluvium	**AILNSTUU**
AGLSTUUY	**AHINPPSS**	**AIILMRST**	**AILLNOPP**	nautilus
augustly	snappish	mistrial	papillon	**AILOORTT**
AGMMNOOR	**AHINPSWW**	**AIILMRTY**	**AILLNOST**	totorial
monogram	whipsawn	military	stallion	**AILOORTV**
AGMMNOOY	**AHINQSUV**	**AIILMSTV**	**AILLNOSU**	violator
monogamy	vanquish	vitalism	allusion	**AILOPRTY**
AGMNNOSW	**AHIOPRST**	**AIILNOPV**	**AILLNPTU**	polarity
gownsman	aphorist	pavilion	puntilla	**AILORSTY**
AGMNORST	**AHKLOPST**	**AIILNPST**	**AILLORTT**	royalist
angstrom	shoptalk	tailspin	littoral	**AILORSTY**
AGNORTUY	**AHLLNOOS**	**AIILLTTVY**	**AILLOSTY**	solitary
nugatory	shalloon	vitality	loyalist	**AILOTTTY**
AGOORTUY	**AHLMNOOR**	**AIIMNNOS**	**AILLPSWY**	totality
autogyro	hormonal	insomnia	spillway	**AILPSTUY**
AHHILPSW	**AHLMOOPS**	**AIIMNSTV**	**AILLSUVY**	playsuit
whiplash	omphalos	nativism	visually	**AILRRSTU**
AHHIMMSS	**AHLNNORT**	**AIIMNTTU**	**AILMMNUU**	ruralist
mishmash	lanthorn	titanium	aluminum	**AILRSTTU**
				altruist

ultraist	upstairs	paroxysm	**BBDEILQU**	**BBGIIIMN**
AILRSTTY	**AIPRSSTY**	**AMORRTUY**	quibbled	imbibing
straitly	sparsity	mortuary	**BBDEILRU**	**BBGIIKLN**
AILRSUVV	**AIRRSTTY**	**AMORSTTU**	bluebird	kibbling
survival	artistry	outsmart	**BBDEINOR**	**BBGIILNN**
AILRTTUY	**AKLMNOOW**	**ANORSUVY**	ribboned	nibbling
titulary	moonwalk	unsavory	**BBDEIQSU**	**BBGIKNNO**
AIMMNORT	**AKLNNOPT**	**ANPRSTUU**	squibbed	knobbing
mortmain	plankton	pursuant	**BBDELLMU**	**BBGILMNU**
AIMNNOTU	**AKLPRRSU**	**AOOPRSSU**	dumbbell	bumbling
mountain	larkspur	saporous	**BBDGIILN**	**BBGILNNO**
AIMNNOTY	**AKMOPRST**	**AOOPRSUV**	dibbling	nobbling
antimony	postmark	vaporous	**BBDGINRU**	**BBGILNOW**
antinomy	**ALLLPRUY**	**AOORRTTY**	drubbing	wobbling
AIMNNRTU	plurally	rotatory	**BBDOSUYY**	**BBGILNOY**
ruminant	**ALLMNORY**	**AOPPRSST**	busybody	lobbying
AIMNORTY	normally	passport	**BBEEIIRR**	**BBGILNRU**
minatory	**ALLMOPSX**	**AOPRSTTY**	beriberi	burbling
AIMNOSST	smallpox	pyrostat	**BBEEISTW**	**BBGILNSU**
stasimon	**ALLMORTY**	**BBBCEOWY**	webbiest	slubbing
AIMNOTTU	mortally	cobwebby	**BBEELLLU**	**BBGINNSU**
mutation	**ALLMTUUY**	**BBBEILRU**	bluebell	snubbing
AIMNRSTT	mutually	bubblier	**BBEGILNP**	**BBGINSTU**
transmit	**ALMNORTY**	**BBBELRUY**	pebbling	stubbing
AIMNRSTU	matronly	blubbery	**BBEGILST**	**BBHINOSS**
naturism	**ALMOOPRY**	**BBBGILNO**	glibbest	snobbish
AIMOPRST	playroom	blobbing	**BBEGIRRU**	**BBHIOSTY**
atropism	**ALMOPPRS**	bobbling	grubbier	hobbyist
AIMORRSU	proplasm	**BBBGILNU**	**BBEHIOTW**	**BBIKLNOO**
rosarium	**ALMOPPST**	bubbling	bobwhite	bobolink
AIMPRSTY	lamppost	**BBCDEILR**	**BBEILNRU**	**BBILOSTY**
partyism	**ALNNOTWY**	cribbled	nubblier	lobbyist
AIMRTTUY	wantonly	**BBCDERSU**	**BBEILORW**	**BBILOSUU**
maturity	**ALNOPRST**	scrubbed	wobblier	bibulous
AINNOOTT	plastron	**BBCEHIRU**	**BBEILQRU**	**BBIMNOSS**
notation	**ALNORRWY**	chubbier	quibbler	snobbism
AINNOOTV	narrowly	**BBCEILRS**	**BBEILRRY**	**BBNORSTU**
novation	**ALNPPSTU**	scribble	bilberry	stubborn
AINOOPTT	supplant	**BBCERRSU**	**BBEILRST**	**BCCDEILY**
potation	**ALOOPPRS**	scrubber	stibbler	bicycled
AINOORTT	proposal	**BBCGIINR**	**BBEINORS**	**BCCEEIRR**
rotation	**ALOORSUV**	cribbing	snobbier	cerebric
AINOOSTT	valorous	**BBCGILNO**	**BBEINOST**	**BCCEHIRU**
ostinato	**ALOPPSSU**	cobbling	nobbiest	cherubic
AINOPPTU	supposal	**BBCGILNU**	**BBEINSTU**	**BCCEHORU**
pupation	**ALOPRSTT**	clubbing	nubbiest	bucchero
AINORTVY	portlast	**BBCHILSU**	**BBEIRSTU**	**BCCEILRU**
vanitory	**ALOPRSTU**	clubbish	stubbier	crucible
AINPSSTU	pulsator	**BBDDEEMO**	**BBEISTTU**	**BCCEMRUU**
puissant	**ALORSTTW**	demobbed	tubbiest	cucumber
AINPSTTU	saltwort	**BBDDEILR**	**BBELORSY**	**BCCIIMOR**
pantsuit	**ALPPSTUY**	dribbled	slobbery	microbic
AINQTTUY	platypus	**BBDEEGIR**	**BBENORSY**	**BCCILOOR**
quantity	**AMMNOORT**	gibbered	snobbery	broccoli
AINRSTTU	motorman	**BBDEEGIT**	**BBEORRXY**	**BCCINORR**
naturist	**AMMNPTUY**	gibbeted	boxberry	corncrib
AIOOORRT	tympanum	**BBDEEMNU**	**BBFGILNU**	**BCCIRTUU**
oratorio	**AMNNOSTW**	benumbed	flubbing	cucurbit
AIOPRRTT	townsman	**BBDEFILR**	**BBGGILNO**	**BCCSSUUU**
portrait	**AMNOOTUY**	fribbled	gobbling	succubus
AIOPRSST	autonomy	**BBDEHORT**	**BBGGINRU**	**BCDDEEEK**
prosaist	**AMNOOTXY**	throbbed	grubbing	bedecked
protasis	taxonomy	**BBDEHRSU**	**BBGHILNO**	**BCDDEHIL**
AIPRSSTU	**AMOPRSXY**	shrubbed	hobbling	childbed

BCDDESUU	**BCEGHILN**	**BCGIINRS**	birdseed	beholden
subduced	belching	scribing	**BDDEENRU**	**BDEEHLOR**
BCDEEEHR	**BCEGIMNO**	**BCGIKLNO**	burdened	beholder
breeched	becoming	blocking	**BDDEEORR**	**BDEEHLSU**
BCDEEIKR	**BCEHIMRS**	**BCGIKLNU**	bordered	busheled
bickered	besmirch	buckling	**BDDEILNR**	**BDEEHOOV**
BCDEEILR	**BCEHIMRU**	**BCGIMNRU**	brindled	behooved
credible	cherubim	crumbing	**BDDEILOO**	**BDEEHORT**
BCDEEILU	**BCEHINRU**	**BCGINNOU**	bloodied	bothered
educible	bunchier	bouncing	**BDDEINNU**	**BDEEIILN**
BCDEEINT	**BCEHIORT**	buncoing	unbidden	inedible
benedict	botchier	**BCHIISSU**	**BDDEINRU**	**BDEEILLL**
BCDEEIRS	**BCEHIRST**	hibiscus	underbid	libelled
describe	britches	**BCHIKLOS**	**BDDEIORS**	**BDEEILLT**
BCDEEJOT	**BCEHLOST**	blockish	disrobed	billeted
objected	blotches	**BCHIOORY**	**BDDEISSU**	**BDEEILMR**
BCDEEKNO	**BCEHOORS**	choirboy	subsided	limbered
beckoned	brooches	**BCHKOSTU**	**BDDEORTU**	**BDEEILNV**
BCDEEKTU	**BCEHORRU**	buckshot	obtruded	vendible
bucketed	brochure	**BCHNORSU**	**BDEEEEMS**	**BDEEILOS**
BCDEELOR	**BCEHRTUY**	bronchus	beseemed	besoiled
corbeled	butchery	**BCIIMORU**	**BDEEEGIS**	obelised
BCDEEMRU	**BCEIILMS**	ciborium	besieged	**BDEEILOZ**
cumbered	miscible	**BCIKKNSU**	**BDEEEGNO**	obelized
BCDEEOTT	**BCEIILNV**	buckskin	edgebone	**BDEEILRW**
obtected	vincible	**BCIKLOOT**	**BDEEEHTU**	bewilder
BCDEHLOT	**BCEIIMRS**	bootlick	hebetude	**BDEEIMOR**
blotched	imbrices	**BCILLPUY**	**BDEEEILV**	embodier
BCDEIMNO	**BCEIINRS**	publicly	believed	**BDEEIMOS**
combined	inscribe	**BCILMOOU**	**BDEEELLR**	embodies
BCDELMRU	**BCEIKLOR**	colobium	rebelled	**BDEEIMRT**
crumbled	blockier	**BCILMOSY**	**BDEEELMM**	timbered
BCDEORSU	**BCEILPRU**	symbolic	emblemed	**BDEEINOT**
obscured	republic	**BCINOSSU**	**BDEEFFRU**	obedient
BCDGINOU	**BCEIMNOR**	subsonic	buffered	**BDEEINOZ**
obducing	combiner	**BCIOPSTU**	rebuffed	ebonized
BCDIIPSU	**BCEINORU**	subtopic	**BDEEFFTU**	**BDEEIRRV**
bicuspid	bouncier	**BCKKOOOO**	buffeted	riverbed
BCDIKLLU	**BCEIORST**	cookbook	**BDEEFGGO**	**BDEEIRST**
duckbill	bisector	**BCKOOOPY**	befogged	bistered
BCDINRUU	**BCEJOORT**	copybook	**BDEEFINR**	**BDEEIRSU**
rubicund	objector	**BCMORSUU**	befriend	debruise
BCEEEEFIN	**BCEKLNUU**	cumbrous	**BDEEFITT**	**BDEEIRTT**
benefice	unbuckle	**BCOORSSW**	befitted	bittered
BCEEEHRS	**BCELRSTU**	crossbow	**BDEEFLOU**	**BDEELLOW**
breeches	clubster	**BCORSTTU**	befouled	bellowed
BCEEFLTU	**BCEORRSU**	obstruct	**BDEEFOOR**	**BDEELMNO**
clubfeet	obscurer	**BDDDEEEM**	forebode	embolden
BCEEHNTU	**BCFIIMOR**	embedded	**BDEEFSUU**	**BDEELMRT**
beechnut	morbific	**BDDDEEIM**	subfeued	trembled
BCEEIILM	**BCFILORY**	imbedded	**BDEEGGIW**	**BDEELMRU**
imbecile	forcibly	**BBDEEFLU**	bewigged	lumbered
BCEEIKRR	**BCFIMORU**	befuddle	**BDEEGGRU**	**BDEELNNO**
bickerer	cubiform	**BDDEEGGU**	begrudge	ennobled
BCEEINOT	**BCFLOOTU**	debugged	debugger	**BDEELORU**
cenobite	clubfoot	**BDDEEGTU**	**BDEEGILN**	redouble
BCEEMNRU	**BCGHINNU**	budgeted	bleeding	**BDEEMNOT**
encumber	bunching	**BDDEEIMM**	**BDEEGILU**	entombed
BCEEMRRU	**BCGHINOT**	bedimmed	beguiled	**BDEEMNRU**
cerebrum	botching	**BDDEEIMO**	**BDEEGINR**	numbered
BCEFFIIR	**BCGIIKNR**	embodied	breeding	**BDEEMOSS**
febrific	bricking	**BDDEEINT**	**BDEEGLNO**	embossed
BCEFILOR	**BCGIILMN**	indebted	belonged	**BDEEMRTU**
forcible	climbing	**BDDEEIRS**	**BDEEHLNO**	embruted

BDEENNOT bonneted
BDEENSUV subvened
BDEEOORRS resorbed
BDEEORSV observed
BDEEOSSS obsessed
BDEEOSTT besotted
BDEEOSTW bestowed
BDEEPRRU purebred
BDEERRWY dewberry
BDEERTTU buttered / rebutted
BDEFIIIR ribified
BDEFIIRR firebird
BDEFOORY forebody
BDEGHHIR highbred
BDEGHILT blighted
BDEGIINT betiding / debiting
BDEGILNN blending
BDEGINNO deboning
BDEGLMRU grumbled
BDEGLNOU bludgeon
BDEGORRY dogberry
BDEHMOOY homebody
BDEHOOOO boohooed
BDEIIKTZ kibitzed
BDEIILTY debility
BDEIKNSU buskined
BDEILLOW billowed
BDEILMNN blindmen
BDEILMSU sublimed
BDEILNRU unbridle
BDEILOOR bloodier

BDEILOOS bloodies
BDEILORV lovebird
BDEILOSS bodiless
BDEILRST bristled
BDEIMNSU nimbused
BDEINOOS nobodies
BDEINOOW woodbine
BDEIOORR broodier
BDEIRSSU disburse
BDEIRTUY rubedity
BDELLOOR bordello / doorbell
BDELLOUZ bulldoze
BDELMSTU stumbled
BDELNOOS doblones
BDELNOSS boldness / bondless
BDELNOTU unbolted
BDELORTU troubled
BDELORUU doublure
BDEMNNOS bondsmen
BDEMNSSU dumbness
BDEMOOSY somebody
BDEMOOTT bottomed
BDENNRUU unburden
BDENOOTW bentwood
BDENORSU suborned
BDENOTTU buttoned
BDENRUUY underbuy
BDEOORRW borrowed
BDEORRTU obtruder
BDEORRUW burrowed
BDFGNOOU fogbound

BDFILLLO billfold
BDFLOTUU doubtful
BDGGIINR bridging
BDGHOOUY doughboy
BDGIILNN blinding
BDGIILNR bridling
BDGIILNU building
BDGILNNU bundling
BDGILNOU doubling
BDGINNOU bounding
BDGINOOR brooding
BDGINORS songbird
BDGINOTU doubting
BDGINSUU subduing
BDHIMOOR rhomboid
BDIIMRUU rubidium
BDILLOOY bloodily
BDILMORY morbidly
BDILNPRU purblind
BDILRTUY turbidly
BDIMNORU moribund
BDINNRUW windburn
BDINORSW snowbird
BDIOSTUY bodysuit
BDKNOOOR doorknob
BDKOOORW wordbook
BDLNOOOU doubloon
BDNOOTUU outbound

BEEEILRV believer
BEEEIRRZ breezier
BEEEIRST beeriest
BEEELMNS ensemble
BEEELMRS resemble
BEEELMZZ embezzle
BEEEMMRR remember
BEEFILLX flexible
BEEFILRS belfries
BEEFNORR freeborn
BEEGIILL eligible
BEEGILNT beetling
BEEGILNV beveling
BEEGILNZ bezeling
BEEGILRU beguiler
BEEGINNR beginner
BEEGINRZ breezing
BEEGINSW beeswing
BEEGMRSU submerge
BEEGNOTT begotten
BEEHHMOT behemoth
BEEHIRST herbiest
BEEHLLNT hellbent
BEEHLRSS herbless
BEEHNRRT brethren
BEEIILNZ zibeline
BEEIINRT benitier
BEEIKLWY biweekly
BEEILLTT belittle
BEEILMOS embolies
BEEILNSS sensible
BEEILNUZ nebulize

BEEILRRT terrible
BEEILRYZ breezily
BEEIMRTT embitter
BEEINRSS nebrises
BEEIORSW boweries
BEEIORTV overbite
BEELMNNO noblemen
BEELMRRT trembler
BEELNOSS boneless / noblesse
BEELNOSU bluenose / nebulose
BEELNSSU blueness
BEELOOST obsolete
BEELOQRU breloque
BEELPUZZ bepuzzle
BEEMNRRU numberer
BEEMORSS embosser
BEEMRSSU submerse
BEENRTTU brunette
BEEOORRV overbore
BEEOORRSV observer
BEEORSTW bestower
BEEORTTU brouette
BEERSSUV subserve
BEFFISTU buffiest
BEFGIINR briefing
BEFGILNU fungible
BEFHILSU bluefish
BEFILLUX fluxible
BEFILOST botflies

BEFNOORR
forborne
BEGGINOY
bogeying
BEGGISTU
buggiest
BEGHINOR
neighbor
BEGHINRT
berthing
brighten
BEGHIRRT
brighter
BEGHNOTU
boughten
BEGHOSTU
besought
BEGIILLN
libeling
BEGIILLY
eligibly
BEGIIMNR
bemiring
BEGIKNRU
rebuking
BEGILLLU
bluegill
gullible
BEGILLNY
bellying
benignly
BEGILNOW
elbowing
BEGILNRT
trebling
BEGILNSS
blessing
glibness
BEGILNTT
bletting
BEGIMNOW
embowing
BEGIMNRU
embruing
umbering
BEGIMNSU
bemusing
BEGINORS
sobering
BEGINRRY
berrying
BEGLMRRU
grumbler
BEGNORTU
burgonet
BEGNSSUU
subgenus
BEHILLTY
blithely
BEHILMRW
whimbrel
BEHILORR
rible

BEHILRTU
thurible
BEHIMNOO
bonhomie
BEHINNOS
shinbone
BEHINOSW
wishbone
BEHISSTU
bushiest
BEHLMSTU
humblest
BEHORSSU
rosebush
BEIIIKMN
minibike
BEIIKRTZ
kibitzer
BEIILMMO
immobile
BEIILMOZ
mobilize
BEIILRTT
libretti
BEIINORS
brionies
BEIINRST
briniest
BEIIOPSS
biopsies
BEIKLMOT
tomblake
BEIKLSTU
bulkiest
BEIKOSST
boskiest
BEILLNTU
bulletin
BEILLOSU
libelous
BEILMMOS
embolism
BEILMNOU
nobelium
BEILMNST
nimblest
BEILMOOR
bloomier
BEILNNTU
buntline
BEILNOPS
bonspiel
BEILNSSY
sensibly
BEILOPPW
blowpipe
BEILORST
strobile
BEILORSU
blousier
BEILORSW
blowsier
BEILORTT
blottier

libretto
BEILORWZ
blowzier
BEILOSTW
blowiest
BEILRRTY
terribly
BEILRSTU
burliest
BEILRTTY
bitterly
BEILSTTU
subtitle
BEIMNSSU
nimbuses
BEIMORTY
biometry
BEIMPSTU
bumpiest
BEINNOSS
boniness
BEINNOST
bonniest
BEINOSTU
bounties
BEINSSSU
business
BEIORSTY
sobriety
BEIOSSST
bossiest
BEISTUZZ
buzziest
BEJORTTU
turbojet
BEKNNORU
unbroken
BEKNOOOT
notebook
BEKOOTTX
textbook
BELLNORW
wellborn
BELLOPTY
potbelly
BELLORTW
bellwort
BELLOSST
boltless
BELMORSY
somberly
BELMRRUY
mulberry
BELNOSUU
nebulous
BELOOSST
bootless
BELOSTUY
obtusely
BELRSTUY
blustery
BELSTTUY
subtlety
BEMNNSSU

numbness
BEMNOORT
trombone
BEMNORTU
bronteum
BEMOORRS
sombrero
BENOORSU
burncose
BENORSTU
burstone
rubstone
BENORSTW
brownest
BENSSSUY
busyness
BEOORRRW
borrower
BEORRRUW
burrower
BERSSTTU
buttress
BESSSSUY
byssuses
BFFGILNU
bluffing
BFFNOSUX
snuffbox
BFGILMNU
fumbling
BFGLLORU
bullfrog
BFHILOSW
blowfish
BFHIMNSU
numbfish
BFIIORSS
fibrosis
BFILLSSU
blissful
BFLLNOWY
flyblown
BGGGILNO
boggling
BGGIILNO
obliging
BGGIINNR
bringing
BGGILNNU
bungling
BGGILNRU
burgling
BGHHINOR
highborn
BGHHIORW
highbrow
BGHILMNU
humbling
BGHILNSU
blushing
BGHILRTY
brightly
BGHIMNTU
thumbing

BGHIMOTU
bigmouth
BGHINRSU
brushing
BGIIKLNN
blinking
BGIILMNW
wimbling
BGIILNOR
broiling
BGIILNPP
blipping
BGIILNRS
brisling
BGIILNTY
bitingly
BGIIMMNR
brimming
BGIIMNRU
imbruing
BGIINORT
orbiting
BGIINRSU
bruising
BGIINRTU
bruiting
BGIJLMNU
jumbling
BGIJOSUU
bijugous
BGIKNOOR
brooking
BGILLNRU
bullring
BGILLNUY
bullying
BGILMMNU
mumbling
BGILMNOO
blooming
BGILMNPU
plumbing
BGILMNRU
rumbling
BGILMNTU
tumbling
BGILNNTU
blunting
BGILNOSU
blousing
BGILNOTT
blotting
BGILNOTT
bottling
BGILNOWY
bowingly
BGILNRRU
blurring
BGILNRTU
blurting
BGILNSTU
bustling
BGINNORW
browning
BGINNORZ

bronzing	sunburst	occupied	**CCEGINOR**	**CCEILNUY**
BGINOOST	**BOOPRSSU**	**CCDEKOOU**	coercing	unicycle
boosting	bosporus	cuckooed	**CCEHHRSU**	**CCEILRRU**
BGINORSW	**BORSTTUU**	**CCDELNOU**	churches	curricle
browsing	outburst	conclude	**CCEHIIMR**	**CCEILRTY**
BGINRSTU	**CCCEEILT**	**CCDEORRU**	chimeric	tricycle
bursting	eclectic	occurred	**CCEHILNR**	**CCEILRUU**
BGLOORYY	**CCCEEGOSY**	**CCDEORSU**	clincher	curlicue
bryology	coccyges	succored	**CCEHILNS**	**CCEIMNOO**
BHIILMPS	**CCCILNOY**	**CCDHINOO**	clinches	economic
blimpish	cyclonic	conchoid	**CCEHILOR**	**CCEIMOST**
BHIIOPRT	**CCCILOPY**	**CCDIINOO**	choleric	cosmetic
prohibit	cyclopic	conicoid	**CCEHILOY**	**CCEIMRRU**
BHILLNOR	**CCCINSTU**	**CCDKOOOW**	choicely	mercuric
hornbill	succinct	woodcock	**CCEHILTY**	**CCEINNOV**
BHILLPUW	**CCDDEENO**	**CCEEHLNS**	hecticly	convince
bullwhip	conceded	clenches	**CCEHINOR**	**CCEINOOR**
BHILORRY	**CCDDEEOT**	**CCEEHRSY**	enchoric	coercion
horribly	decocted	screechy	**CCEHINOZ**	**CCEINORT**
BHILOSYY	**CCDDELOU**	**CCEEIILS**	zecchino	necrotic
boyishly	occluded	cicelies	**CCEHIORT**	**CCEINOTT**
BHKNOOOR	**CCDDENOU**	**CCEEILNR**	ricochet	concetti
hornbook	conduced	encircle	**CCEHIOST**	**CCEINOTT**
BHLLRSUU	**CCDEEENR**	**CCEEILNT**	choicest	tectonic
bullrush	credence	elenctic	**CCEHKOTU**	**CCEINPRT**
BIILMOTY	**CCDEEHLN**	**CCEEILPY**	checkout	precinct
mobility	clenched	epicycle	**CCEHLMOR**	**CCEINRTU**
BIILNOOV	**CCDEEIOP**	**CCEEILRT**	cromlech	cincture
oblivion	codpiece	electric	**CCEHLNNU**	**CCEIOPSU**
BIILNOTY	**CCDEEIRV**	**CCEEINOR**	unclench	occupies
nobility	creviced	cicerone	**CCEHLSTU**	**CCEIOPTY**
BIIQTUUY	**CCDEEKOR**	**CCEEINOV**	clutches	ecotypic
ubiquity	cockered	conceive	**CCEHNRSU**	**CCEIORST**
BIIRSSTU	**CCDEEKOY**	**CCEEIORV**	crunches	cortices
bursitis	cockeyed	coercive	**CCEHORRS**	**CCEIRSSU**
BIJNOSTU	**CCDEELRY**	**CCEEIRSV**	scorcher	circuses
subjoint	recycled	cervices	**CCEHORSS**	**CCEKORRY**
BIKOOUUZ	**CCDEHILN**	**CCEEIRSV**	scorches	crockery
bouzouki	clinched	crescive	**CCEHORST**	**CCEKORSU**
BILLNOOU	**CCDEHIPU**	**CCEEITTU**	crotches	cocksure
bouillon	hiccuped	eutectic	**CCEHORSU**	**CCENOORT**
BILLOSWY	**CCDEHKLU**	**CCEEKLOR**	crouches	concerto
blowsily	chuckled	cockerel	**CCEHORTT**	**CCENOOTT**
BILMOSTU	**CCDEHLTU**	**CCEELMNY**	crotchet	concetto
botulism	clutched	clemency	**CCEHOSST**	**CCENRRUY**
BILOPSSY	**CCDEHNRU**	**CCEEMMNO**	scotches	currency
possibly	crunched	commence	**CCEHRSTU**	**CCEORSSU**
BIOPRSTW	**CCDEHORS**	**CCEEMMOR**	crutches	crocuses
bowsprit	scorched	commerce	**CCEHRTUY**	**CCFIIRUX**
BIORSTUY	**CCDEHORT**	**CCEENNOS**	cutchery	crucifix
bistoury	crotched	ensconce	**CCEIILNR**	**CCFILNOT**
BKMOOORW	**CCDEHORU**	**CCEENORT**	circline	conflict
bookworm	crouched	concrete	**CCEIILNT**	**CCFKLOOT**
BLMOOOTY	**CCDEHOST**	**CCEENRST**	enclitic	cockloft
lobotomy	scotched	crescent	**CCEIILOP**	**CCFLOOOO**
BLMOOSSY	**CCDEHRTU**	**CCEFFHKO**	epicolic	locofoco
blossomy	crutched	checkoff	**CCEIILOR**	**CCGHHIOU**
BNNOTTUU	**CCDEIINO**	**CCEFIIPS**	licorice	hiccough
unbutton	coincide	specific	**CCEIILPT**	**CCGHIINN**
BNRRSTUU	**CCDEINOR**	**CCEFIRRU**	ecliptic	cinching
sunburnt	corniced	crucifer	**CCEIILST**	**CCGHIKNO**
BNOORTUW	**CCDEINOT**	**CCEFLOOS**	scilicet	chocking
brownout	occident	floccose	**CCEIKCST**	**CCGHIKNU**
BNRSSTUU	**CCDEIOPU**	**CCEGHIKN**	**CCEIKCST**	chucking
		checking	cockiest	**CCGHINOU**

couching	CDDEEENT	corroded	defector	pendicle
CCGIIKLN	decedent	**CDDEEOORT**	**CDEEGIIR**	**CDEEILNR**
clicking	**CDDEEEPR**	doctored	regicide	reclined
CCGIIKNR	preceded	**CDDEOPRU**	**CDEEGINO**	**CDEEILNS**
cricking	**CDDEEEET**	produced	genocide	licensed
CCGIILNR	detected	**CDDGHILO**	**CDEEGINR**	silenced
circling	**CDDEEFOR**	godchild	receding	**CDEEILNT**
CCGIKLNO	deforced	**CDDGILNO**	**CDEEGINS**	denticle
clocking	**CDDEEEGLU**	coddling	seceding	**CDEEILOR**
cockling	cudgeled	**CDDGILNU**	**CDEEGIOS**	recoiled
CCGIKLNU	**CDDEEHNR**	cuddling	geodesic	**CDEEILPS**
clucking	drenched	**CDDGINRU**	**CDEEGIOT**	eclipsed
CCGIKNOR	**CDDEEIKR**	crudding	geodetic	**CDEEILRT**
crocking	dickered	**CDDGINSU**	**CDEEHILS**	derelict
CCGINNOS	**CDDEEILN**	scudding	chiseled	**CDEEIMNR**
sconcing	declined	**CDDHILOS**	**CDEEHINR**	endermic
CCHHIITY	**CDDEEINR**	cloddish	enriched	**CDEEIMOR**
ichthyic	cindered	**CDDOOORW**	**CDEEHIPR**	mediocre
CCHHLRUY	**CDDEEIPT**	cordwood	ciphered	**CDEEIMOS**
churchly	depicted	**CDEEEFFT**	decipher	comedies
CCHIINUZ	**CDDEEIRS**	effected	**CDEEHKST**	**CDEEIMRV**
zucchini	descried	**CDEEEHLR**	sketched	decemvir
CCHKLOSY	**CDDEEIRT**	lechered	**CDEEHLSU**	**CDEEINNS**
schlocky	credited	**CDEEEHSW**	schedule	incensed
CCIIKKPW	directed	eschewed	**CDEEHNQU**	**CDEEINNT**
pickwick	**CDDEEKOT**	**CDEEINV**	quenched	indecent
CCIIMNSY	docketed	evidence	**CDEEHNRS**	**CDEEINTU**
cynicism	**CDDEELSU**	**CDEEEIRV**	drenches	inductee
CCIINOOS	secluded	received	**CDEEHNRT**	**CDEEINTV**
occision	**CDDEELUX**	**CDEEEJRT**	trenched	invected
CCIINOTY	excluded	rejected	**CDEEHNRW**	**CDEEIPRT**
conicity	**CDDEENOS**	**CDEEEKNW**	wrenched	decrepit
CCIIRTUY	seconded	neckweed	**CDEEHORT**	**CDEEIPRU**
circuity	**CDDEEORR**	**CDEEELLX**	hectored	pedicure
CCIKKLOP	recorded	excelled	**CDEEHPRU**	**CDEEIQSU**
picklock	**CDDEERUV**	**CDEEELST**	cheruped	quiesced
CCIKKOTT	decurved	selected	**CDEEHRTW**	**CDEEIRRT**
ticktock	**CDDEFIIO**	**CDEEEMNT**	wretched	redirect
CCILRSUU	codified	cemented	**CDEEIILT**	**CDEEIRSS**
circulus	**CDDEFINO**	**CDEEENRS**	elicited	descries
CCINOPRT	confided	screened	**CDEEIIMN**	**CDEEIRST**
procinct	**CDDEGIIN**	secerned	medicine	discreet
CCINORSY	deciding	**CDEEENRT**	**CDEEIIMP**	discrete
cryonics	**CDDEGINO**	centered	epidemic	**CDEEIRSU**
CCJNNOTU	decoding	**CDEEEPTX**	**CDEEIIRT**	decuries
conjunct	**CDDEGINU**	excepted	dieretic	**CDEEIRSV**
CCLNOOOR	deducing	expected	**CDEEIISV**	serviced
concolor	**CDDEIINT**	**CDEEERSS**	decisive	**CDEEITUV**
CCOOSSUU	indicted	recessed	**CDEEIITT**	eductive
couscous	**CDDEILLO**	**CDEEERST**	dietetic	**CDEEJKOY**
CCORSSTU	collided	secreted	**CDEEIJNT**	jockeyed
crosscut	**CDDEILNU**	**CDEEERTX**	injected	**CDEEKLPS**
CDDDEETU	included	excreted	**CDEEIJOR**	speckled
deducted	**CDDEINTU**	**CDEEETUX**	rejoiced	**CDEEKNOR**
CDDDEORS	inducted	executed	**CDEEIKLN**	reckoned
scrodded	**CDDEIORV**	**CDEEFIIT**	nickeled	**CDEEKOPT**
CDDEEEEX	divorced	feticide	**CDEEIKNS**	pocketed
exceeded	**CDDELLOU**	**CDEEFINT**	sickened	**CDEEKORT**
CDDEEEFT	colluded	infected	**CDEEIKPT**	rocketed
defected	**CDDELNOO**	**CDEEFKLR**	picketed	**CDEEKORW**
CDDEEEIV	condoled	freckled	**CDEEIKTT**	rockweed
deceived	**CDDENNOO**	**CDEEFNOR**	ticketed	**CDEEKPRU**
CDDEEEJT	condoned	enforced	**CDEEILNP**	puckered
dejected	**CDDEOORR**	**CDEEFORT**	penciled	**CDEELLOR**

cordelle	CDEEOSST	CDEHINST	CDEIKLWY	CDEKLRTU
CDEELMOW	cosseted	snitched	wickedly	truckled
welcomed	**CDEERRRU**	**CDEHIOTY**	**CDEIKSTU**	**CDEKNOOU**
CDEELNOS	recurred	theodicy	duckiest	uncooked
enclosed	**CDEESSUX**	**CDEHISTT**	**CDEILLPU**	**CDEKNOOV**
CDEELNPU	excussed	stitched	pellucid	convoked
peduncle	**CDEFFISU**	**CDEHISTW**	**CDEILMOP**	**CDEKNORU**
CDEELNTY	sufficed	switched	compiled	uncorked
decently	**CDEFFLSU**	**CDEHITTW**	complied	**CDELLNUU**
CDEELOOW	scuffled	twitched	**CDEILMRU**	unculled
locoweed	**CDEFHILN**	**CDEHLOOS**	dulcimer	**CDELLORS**
CDEELOST	flinched	schooled	**CDEILNRY**	scrolled
closeted	**CDEFHIMO**	**CDEHLORT**	cylinder	**CDELLOTU**
CDEELPRU	chiefdom	chortled	**CDEILORU**	cloudlet
preclude	**CDEFIIIT**	**CDEHLOSU**	cloudier	**CDELMNOU**
lectured	citified	slouched	**CDEILOSS**	columned
CDEELRUX	**CDEFIIOR**	**CDEHMOOS**	disclose	**CDELMPRU**
excluder	codifier	smooched	**CDEILPPR**	crumpled
CDEEMOPT	**CDEFIIOS**	**CDEHMOSU**	crippled	**CDELNOOS**
competed	codifies	smouched	**CDEILRTY**	consoled
ectoderm	**CDEFINNO**	**CDEHMSTU**	directly	**CDELNOSS**
CDEEMORT	confined	smutched	**CDEIMOST**	coldness
CDEENNOS	**CDEFINOR**	**CDEHSSSU**	domestic	**CDELNOSY**
condense	confider	schussed	**CDEIMPRS**	secondly
CDEENNOU	**CDEFLNOU**	**CDEIIIOS**	scrimped	**CDELNRUU**
denounce	flounced	idiocies	**CDEINNOV**	uncurled
CDEENNOV	**CDEFNORU**	**CDEIIKKS**	connived	**CDELOPTU**
convened	frounced	sidekick	**CDEINORS**	octupled
CDEENNPY	**CDEFNOSU**	**CDEIIKMM**	consider	**CDELORSS**
pendency	confused	mimicked	**CDEINORT**	cordless
CDEENNTY	**CDEFNOTU**	**CDEIILMO**	doctrine	**CDELORSU**
tendency	confuted	domicile	**CDEINORU**	closured
CDEENORR	**CDEGIINX**	**CDEIILNN**	decurion	**CDELPRSU**
cornered	exciding	inclined	**CDEINOTU**	scrupled
CDEENORS	**CDEGINNO**	**CDEIILNO**	eduction	**CDELPSTU**
necrosed	encoding	indocile	**CDEINPRS**	sculpted
CDEENOVX	**CDEGINNS**	**CDEIILPS**	prescind	**CDELRSUY**
convexed	scending	disciple	**CDEINRRU**	cursedly
CDEENOVY	**CDEGINOY**	**CDEIILRU**	incurred	**CDELRTUU**
conveyed	decoying	ridicule	**CDEIOPST**	cultured
CDEENPRU	**CDEGINOZ**	**CDEIINNT**	despotic	**CDELSSTU**
prudence	cognized	incident	**CDEIORRT**	ductless
CDEENRSU	**CDEGINRU**	**CDEIINOR**	creditor	**CDELSTTU**
censured	reducing	dicerion	director	scuttled
CDEENRUV	**CDEGINRY**	**CDEIINOS**	**CDEIORSV**	**CDEMMNOU**
verecund	decrying	decision	discover	communed
CDEENSTY	**CDEGINSU**	**CDEIINRT**	**CDEIORTU**	**CDEMMOTU**
encysted	seducing	indirect	outcried	commuted
CDEEOOPR	**CDEGORSU**	**CDEIIOPR**	**CDEIPRST**	**CDEMNOOW**
coopered	scourged	periodic	scripted	comedown
CDEEOOTV	**CDEHIILO**	**CDEIIOPS**	**CDEIPRTU**	downcome
dovecote	helicoid	episodic	pictured	**CDEMNOSU**
CDEEOPPR	**CDEHIIMO**	**CDEIIOSU**	**CDEIRRSU**	consumed
coppered	homicide	diecious	scurried	**CDEMNOTU**
CDEEOPRU	**CDEHILNR**	**CDEIIRTU**	**CDEIRSTU**	document
recouped	children	diuretic	curtsied	**CDEMOOPS**
CDEEOPRW	**CDEHILOR**	**CDEIKLNR**	**CDEISSSU**	composed
cropweed	chloride	crinkled	discuses	**CDEMOPTU**
CDEEORRR	**CDEHILRT**	**CDEIKLPR**	**CDEJNORU**	computed
recorder	eldritch	prickled	conjured	**CDEMOSTU**
CDEEORST	**CDEHIMRS**	**CDEIKLRT**	**CDEKKLNU**	costumed
corseted	smirched	trickled	knuckled	**CDENNOOT**
escorted	**CDEHINOS**	**CDEIKLST**	**CDEKLNOU**	connoted
	hedonics	stickled	unlocked	**CDENOOTT**

cottoned
CDENOOVY
convoyed
CDENORTU
trounced
CDENOSTU
contused
CDENRTUU
undercut
CDEOOPRS
scrooped
CDEOORSU
decorous
CDEOPRRU
procured
producer
CDERSTTU
destruct
CDFNNOOU
confound
CDGHIINT
ditching
CDGHINOU
douching
CDGIINNU
inducing
CDGIKLNU
duckling
CDGILNOS
scolding
CDGILNOU
clouding
CDGILNRU
curdling
CDGINORW
crowding
CDHHIILS
childish
CDHIIOSZ
schizoid
CDHLOOPY
copyhold
CDIIIMNU
indicium
CDIILOTY
docility
CDIILTUY
lucidity
CDIINSTT
distinct
CDIIOPRT
dioptric
CDIIPTUY
cupidity
pudicity
CDIIRSTT
district
CDIJNSTU
disjunct
CDILLOUY
cloudily
CDILOORS
discolor
CDIMOORT

microdot
CDINNQUU
quidnunc
CDINORTU
inductor
CDINOSTU
discount
CDIOORRR
corridor
CDIOPRSU
cuspidor
CDJLNOUY
jocundly
CDLLLOOP
clodpoll
COMNOOPU
compound
CDMNORUU
corundum
CDOORRUY
corduroy
CEEEEIPY
eyepiece
CEEEELST
selectee
CEEEFFRT
effecter
CEEEFNOR
conferee
CEEEGIMN
emceeing
CEEEGLNY
elegency
CEEEHIKR
cheekier
CEEEHIRR
cheerier
CEEEHPSS
speeches
CEEEIJTV
ejective
CEEEILNS
licensee
CEEEILRT
erectile
CEEEILTV
elective
CEEEIMNN
eminence
CEEEINNT
enceinte
CEEEIPRR
creepier
CEEEIPRV
perceive
CEEEIRRV
receiver
CEEEIRSX
exercise
CEEELLNR
crenelle
CEEELRRV
cleverer
CEEEMNRT

cerement
CEEEMRTY
cemetery
CEEENNST
sentence
CEEENPRS
presence
CEEENQSU
sequence
CEEENRRS
screener
CEEERSSS
recesses
CEEERSST
sesterce
CEEERSSU
cereuses
CEEERTUX
executer
CEEFFORT
effector
CEEFGILN
fleecing
CEEFHIKR
kerchief
CEEFHLRT
fletcher
CEEFHLRU
cheerful
CEEFILRY
fiercely
CEEFINRT
frenetic
infecter
CEEFIRST
fiercest
CEEFKLSS
feckless
CEEFLNTU
feculent
CEEFNORR
confrere
enforcer
CEEFNRVY
fervency
CEEFOPRR
perforce
CEEFORSS
frescoes
CEEFORTW
crowfeet
CEEGHILN
leeching
CEEGHINP
cheeping
CEEGHINR
cheering
CEEGIINP
epigenic
CEEGIJNT
ejecting
CEEGILNT
electing
CEEGILRS

clergies
CEEGINPR
creeping
CEEGINRT
erecting
CEEGINXY
exigency
CEEGNNPU
pungence
CEEGNORV
converge
CEEHHMNN
henchmen
CEEHILLN
chenille
CEEHILRS
chiseler
CEEHILRY
cheerily
CEEHIMRT
hermetic
CEEHINPR
encipher
CEEHINRS
enriches
CEEHIOSU
icehouse
CEEHIOSV
cohesive
CEEHIRRS
cherries
CEEHISTT
esthetic
CEEHISTW
chewiest
CEEHKRST
sketcher
CEEHKSST
sketches
CEEHLMSZ
schmelze
CEEHLNPU
penuchle
CEEHLNSU
elenchus
CEEHLOSS
echoless
CEEHNQRU
quencher
CEEHNQSU
quenches
CEEHNRRT
retrench
trencher
CEEHNRST
trenches
CEEHNRSW
wrenches
CEEHOPRY
coryphee
CEEHORRT
torchere
CEEHRSTW
wretches

CEEIINRT
icterine
CEEIINST
niceties
CEEIJNOT
ejection
CEEIJRUV
verjuice
CEEIKLNN
neckline
CEEIKLPR
pickerel
CEEILLLP
pellicle
CEEILMOR
comelier
CEEILMPS
semplice
CEEILNNY
leniency
CEEILNOT
election
CEEILNOV
violence
CEEILNRS
silencer
CEEILNRV
vernicle
CEEILOSZ
solecize
CEEILRTU
reticule
CEEILRTY
celerity
CEEILSTT
testicle
CEEIMNNY
eminency
CEEIMNPS
specimen
CEEIMORT
meteoric
CEEINNSS
niceness
CEEINNST
nescient
CEEINORT
neoteric
CEEINPRT
prentice
CEEINPSX
sixpence
CEEINRRS
sincerer
CEEINRSU
insecure
sinecure
CEEINRTT
reticent
CEEIOPPR
pericope
CEEIORST
esoteric

CEEIORSX
exorcise
CEEIORTX
exoteric
CEEIPPTU
eupeptic
CEEIRRSW
screwier
CEEIRSTV
vertices
CEEIRSVX
cervixes
CEEKLNSS
neckless
CEEKLRSS
reckless
CEELLMOU
molecule
CEELLRVY
cleverly
CEELLSTY
selectly
CEELMOPT
complete
CEELMRTU
electrum
CEELNOPU
opulence
CEELNOQU
loquence
CEELNORS
encloser
CEELNORT
electron
CEELNRTY
recently
CEELORSS
coreless
CEELORST
corselet
selector
CEELORTT
cotterel
CEELORTV
coverlet
CEELOSSU
coleuses
CEELRRTU
lecturer
CEELRSTU
cruelest
CEELRSTY
secretly
CEELRSUY
securely
CEEMMNORW
newcomer
CEEMNORY
ceremony
CEEMOORV
overcome
CEENNORT
cretonne
CEENNORU

renounce
CEENNCSX
connexes
CEENOPTW
twopence
CEENORSV
conserve
converse
CEENORVY
conveyer
CEENSSTU
cuteness
CEEOORST
creosote
CEEOQTTU
coquette
CEEORRRS
sorcerer
CEEORRSU
recourse
resource
CEEORRVY
recovery
CEEORTTV
corvette
CEEORTUX
executor
CEERSSTW
setscrew
CEESSSTU
cestuses
CEFFIORU
coiffure
CEFFLORU
forceful
CEFGHINT
fetching
CEFGIKLN
flecking
CEFGLNUY
fulgency
CEFHIIMS
mischief
CEFHILNS
flinches
CEFIIST
citifies
CEFIILTY
felicity
CEFIIRRT
terrific
CEFILLLO
follicle
CEFILMRU
merciful
CEFILNOT
flection
CEFIMOST
comfiest
CEFINORS
forensic
CEFINORT
infector
CEFINOTT

confetti
CEFIORTY
ferocity
CEFKLOOR
forelock
CEFKLPSY
flyspeck
CEFNOOTT
confetto
CEFORSTU
fructose
CEGGILOO
geologic
CEGGILOR
cloggier
CEGGILRS
scriggle
CEGHIINY
hygienic
CEGHIKLN
heckling
CEGHILNT
letching
CEGHIMNS
scheming
CEGHINNW
wenching
CEGHINOR
cohering
CEGHINPR
perching
CEGHINVY
chevying
CEGHNORS
groschen
CEGIILNR
clingier
CEGIINNT
enticing
CEGIINNV
envincing
CEGIINPR
piercing
CEGIINRT
reciting
CEGIINSX
excising
CEGIINTV
evicting
CEGIINTX
exciting
CEGIIOST
egoistic
CEGIKKLN
keckling
CEGIKLNR
clerking
CEGIKNNR
ringneck
CEGIKNRW
wrecking
CEGILMMN
clemming
CEGILMNO

comingle
CEGILNOO
neologic
CEGILNPU
cupeling
CEGILNRY
glycerin
CEGINNOR
encoring
CEGINNOZ
cozening
CEGINNST
scenting
CEGINOOP
geoponic
CEGINORV
covering
CEGINORW
cowering
CEGINOTV
coveting
CEGINRST
cresting
CEGINRSU
recusing
rescuing
securing
CEGINRSW
screwing
CEGINSUX
excusing
CEGLLORY
glycerol
CEGLOOTY
cetology
CEGNNPUY
pungency
CEGNORSS
congress
CEGNORSU
scrounge
CEHIIKNR
chinkier
CEHIILLR
chillier
CEHIILNT
lecithin
CEHIILOT
eulithic
CEHIIMPT
mephitic
CEHIIPPS
chippies
CEHIIPRR
chirpier
CEHIISTT
itchiest
theistic
CEHIKLRS
clerkish
CEHIKMOS
homesick
CEHIKNRU
chunkier

CEHIKSTT
thickest
CEHILLRS
schiller
CEHILLSY
chiselly
CEHILNOP
pinochle
CEHILNOR
chlorine
CEHILORT
clothier
CEHILPTY
phyletic
CEHILSTW
switchel
CEHIMMRU
chummier
CEHIMRSS
smirches
CEHINNRT
intrench
CEHINOOS
cohesion
CEHINOPT
phonetic
CEHINOPU
euphonic
CEHINPRS
pinchers
CEHINRSS
richness
GEHINRST
christen
CEHIOORS
choosier
CEHIOPPR
choppier
CEHIOPRU
euphoric
CEHIORRT
rhetoric
CEHIORTU
touchier
CEHIRSTY
hysteric
CEHIRTWY
witchery
CEHISSTT
stitches
CEHISSTU
cushiest
CEHISSTW
switches
CEHISTTW
twitches
CEHKLORS
sherlock
CEHKNPUY
keypunch
CEHKRSTU
huckster
CEHLNNOU
luncheon

CEHLORSU
sloucher
CEHLOSSU
slouches
CEHLSTUY
lecythus
CEHMOOSS
smooches
CEHMOSSU
smouches
CEHNNOPU
puncheon
CEHNNOSU
nonesuch
CEHNOORS
schooner
CEHNSTTU
chestnut
CEHOPPRY
prophecy
CEHRSTTY
stretchy
CEIIILVZ
civilize
CEIIINSV
incisive
CEIIJSTU
juiciest
CEIIKLMR
limerick
CEIIKLRS
sicklier
CEIIKPST
pickiest
CEIIKRRT
trickier
CEIIKRST
stickier
CEIILLPT
elliptic
CEIILNNR
incliner
CEIILNOS
isocline
silicone
CEIILOPS
policies
CEIILORT
elicitor
CEIILPTX
explicit
CEIILSSS
scissile
CEIIMOST
comities
semiotic
CEIINNOT
nicotine
CEIINORS
recision
CEIINOSX
excision
CEEINOTV
eviction

CEIINRSU
sciurine
CEIIPRRS
crispier
CEIIPSST
spiciest
CEIIQRTU
critique
CEIISTVV
vivisect
CEIJNORT
injector
CEIKKNRS
knickers
CEIKLMSU
scumlike
CEIKLOSV
lovesick
CEIKLPRU
pluckier
CEIKLRST
stickler
strickle
CEIKLSST
slickest
CEIKLSTU
luckiest
CEIKMSTU
muckiest
CEIKNRST
stricken
CEIKNSSS
sickness
CEIKORST
corkiest
rockiest
stockier
CEIKQSTU
quickest
quickset
CEIKRRTY
trickery
CEILLMOY
comelily
CEILLNOT
colletin
CEILLNOU
nucleoli
CEILLOPS
pollices
CEILLOQU
coquille
CEILLORY
colliery
CEILMOPR
compiler
CEILMOPS
complies
CEILMOSS
solecism
CEILMOSU
coliseum
CEILMRSU
clumsier

CEILNOOS
colonies
CEILNOOZ
colonize
CEILNPRY
princely
CEILNRUV
culverin
CEILOPRV
proclive
CEILOPTU
poultice
CEILORST
cloister
coistrel
costlier
CEILOSST
solecist
CEILOSSU
coulisse
CEILOTVY
velocity
CEILPRSU
surplice
CEIMMNNO
mnemonic
CEIMMNOU
encomium
meconium
CEIMMRRU
crummier
CEIMMRSU
scummier
CEIMNNOY
neomycin
CEIMNOPY
eponymic
CEIMNORS
sermonic
CEIMNORT
intercom
CEIMNNSU
meniscus
CEIMOPRS
comprise
CEIMORSX
exorcism
CEIMSSTY
systemic
CEINNNOT
innocent
CEINNORV
conniver
CEINNOTU
continue
CEINOOTZ
entozoic
CEINOPRS
conspire
CEINOPRT
inceptor
CEINOPRV
province

CEINOPTT
entoptic
CEINORSS
necrosis
CEINORST
corniest
CEINORSU
coinsure
CEINORTT
contrite
CEINORTU
neurotic
CEINORTV
contrive
CEINOSTU
counties
CEINPPRS
princeps
CEINPRSS
princess
CEINRSTT
centrist
CEINRTTU
tincture
CEIOORSV
rovescio
CEIOPPRS
croppies
CEIOPRRU
croupier
CEIOPRST
persicot
CEIOPRSU
precious
CEIOPSSU
specious
CEIORRTU
courtier
outcrier
CEIORRUZ
cruzeiro
CEIORSTU
outcries
CEIORSTV
vortices
CEIORSTX
exorcist
CEIPRRST
scripter
CEIPRSTU
crepitus
CEIRRSSU
scurries
CEIRRSTT
restrict
CEIRRSTU
crustier
CEIRSSSU
scissure
CEIRSSTU
citruses
curtsies
CEIRSTUV
curviest

CEIRSTUY
security
CEJLOOSY
jocosely
CEJNORRU
conjurer
CEJNRTUU
juncture
CEKKLNRU
knuckler
CEKLLSSU
luckless
CEKLORSS
rockless
CEKOPRST
sprocket
CEKORRTY
rocketry
CELLNSUU
nucellus
CELLNTUU
luculent
CELLOSSY
cloyless
CELLRSUY
scullery
CELMPRTU
plectrum
CELMPSUU
speculum
CELNOOSS
coolness
CELNOOVV
convolve
CELNOPUU
uncouple
CELNOPUY
opulency
CELNORWY
clownery
CELNOSUV
convulse
CELNOSVY
solvency
CELNOVXY
convexly
CELOOPSS
cesspool
CELOOSTU
closeout
CELOPTTU
octuplet
CELORSST
crosslet
CELORSUU
ulcerous
urceolus
CELORTVY
covertly
CELOSTTU
culottes
CELRSTUY
clustery
CELSSTUU

cultuses	**CFFGINSU**	**CGGIINNO**	**CGHINOPP**	cruising
CEMMNOOR	scuffing	coigning	chopping	**CGIJNNOU**
commoner	**CFFIRTUY**	**CGGIINNR**	**CGHINOPU**	jouncing
CEMMNOOS	fructify	cringing	pouching	**CGIKKNNO**
consomme	**CFGHIILN**	**CGHHIINT**	**CGHINORT**	knocking
CEMMORTU	filching	hitching	torching	**CGIKLNNU**
commuter	**CFGIIKLN**	**CGHHINNU**	**CGHINOSU**	clunking
CEMNOPRS	flicking	hunching	chousing	**CGIKLNPU**
corpsmen	**CFGIKLNO**	**CGHIIKNN**	hocusing	plucking
CEMNOPTT	flocking	chinking	**CGHINOTU**	**CGIKLNSU**
contempt	**CFGIKNOR**	**CGHIILLN**	touching	suckling
CEMNORSU	frocking	chilling	**CGHINOUV**	**CGIKMNOS**
consumer	**CFGINORT**	**CGHIIMNR**	vouching	smocking
CEMOOPRS	crofting	chirming	**CGHINPSY**	**CGIKNOOR**
composer	**CFGINOSU**	**CGHIINNN**	psyching	crooking
CEMOPRSS	focusing	chinning	**CGHINRSU**	**CGIKNOST**
compress	**CFHIINOO**	**CGHIINNP**	crushing	stocking
CEMOPRTU	finochio	pinching	**CGHINSTY**	**CGIKNRTU**
computer	**CFHIIORR**	**CGHIINNS**	scything	trucking
CEMORSTU	horrific	chinsing	**CGIIINNS**	**CGILLNOY**
customer	**CFHIKORS**	**CGHIINNW**	incising	collying
CEMPRSTU	rockfish	winching	**CGIIINNT**	**CGILMNPU**
spectrum	**CFIILNOQ**	**CGHIINOR**	inciting	clumping
CENNORTU	cinqfoil	choiring	**CGIIKLNN**	**CGILMNSU**
nocturne	**CFIILNUU**	**CGHIINPP**	clinking	muscling
CENOORSU	funiculi	chipping	**CGIIKLNP**	**CGILMNTU**
corneous	**CFIILOPR**	**CGHIINPR**	pickling	mulcting
CENOORVY	prolific	chirping	**CGIIKLNT**	**CGILNNOW**
conveyor	**CFIINOPT**	**CGHIINTT**	tickling	clowning
CENOPRSY	pontific	chitting	**CGIIKNNS**	**CGILNOOR**
necropsy	**CFIINORT**	**CGHIINTW**	snicking	coloring
CENOQSTU	friction	witching	**CGIIKNNZ**	**CGILNOPU**
conquest	**CFIKLSTU**	**CGHIKNOS**	zincking	coupling
CENORSTU	stickful	shocking	**CGIIKNPR**	**CGILNORW**
construe	**CFILRSUU**	**CGHIKNSU**	pricking	crowling
CENOSSTU	sulfuric	shucking	**CGIIKNRT**	**CGILNOSW**
countess	**CFIMNOOR**	**CGHILMNU**	tricking	scowling
CENPRTUU	coniform	mulching	**CGIIKNST**	**CGILNOTT**
puncture	**CFIMNORU**	**CGHILNNU**	sticking	clotting
CEOOSTUV	unciform	lunching	**CGIILNOP**	**CGILNOTU**
covetous	**CFINNOTU**	**CGHILNNY**	policing	clouting
CEOPPRST	function	lynching	**CGIILNPP**	**CGIMMNSU**
prospect	**CFLLOORU**	**CGHILNOT**	clipping	scumming
CEOPRRRU	colorful	clothing	**CGIILNPS**	**CGIMNNOO**
procurer	**CFLMRUUU**	**CGHILNRU**	splicing	oncoming
CEOPRSUU	furculum	lurching	**CGILOST**	**CGIMNOPU**
cupreous	**CFLNORSU**	**CGHLOOPSU**	logistic	upcoming
CEOQRTUY	scornful	scoopful	**CGIIMNNO**	**CGIMNPRU**
coquetry	**CFLOOPSU**	**CFNNOORT**	incoming	crumping
CEORSSST	scoopful	confront	**CGIIMNPR**	**CGINNOOR**
crossest	**CFNNOORT**	**CFOOOORTW**	crimping	crooning
CEORSTUY	confront	crowfoot	**CGIIMNPU**	**CGINNOPU**
cosurety	**CFOOOORTW**	**CFRSTUUU**	pumicing	pouncing
courtesy	crowfoot	usufruct	**CGIIMNSU**	**CGINNORS**
CEPPRTUU	**CFRSTUUU**	**CGGGHINU**	miscuing	scorning
uppercut	usufruct	chugging	**CGIINNOT**	**CGINNORW**
CEPRSSTU	**CGGGHINU**	**CGGGILNO**	noticing	crowning
sprucest	chugging	clogging	**CGIINNPR**	**CGINNOTU**
CEPRSTUU	**CGGGILNO**	**CGGHINOU**	princing	counting
cutpurse	clogging	coughing	**CGIINOOS**	**CGINOOPS**
CFFGHINU	**CGGHINOU**	**CGHINNRU**	isogonic	scooping
chuffing	coughing	churning	**CGIINPRS**	**CGINOOPT**
CFFGINOS	**CGGIILNN**	**CGHINOOS**	crisping	coopting
scoffing	clinging	choosing	**CGIINRSU**	**CGINOOST**

scooting
CGINOPPR
cropping
CGINORSS
crossing
CGINORSU
coursing
scouring
CGINORTU
courting
CGINOSTU
scouting
CGINPRSU
sprucing
CGINRRUY
currying
CGINRSTU
crusting
CGLNOOOY
oncology
CGLOOTYY
cytology
CHHIIPST
phthisic
CHHILRSU
churlish
CHHIMRTY
rhythmic
CHHOOPTT
hotchpot
CHIIKLST
ticklish
CHIILNNP
linchpin
CHIILOST
holistic
CHIILQSU
cliquish
CHIINOPS
siphonic
CHIINORT
ornithic
CHIIORST
historic
CHIKMNPU
chipmunk
CHILLOOT
oilcloth
CHILMOSU
scholium
CHILNOSW
clownish
CHILOOOZ
holozoic
CHIMMOOR
micromho
CHIMMORU
chromium
CHIMNORW
inchworm
CHIMNOSU
insomuch
CHIMPSSY
psychism

CHINOPTY
hypnotic
pythonic
CHINOSUY
cushiony
CHIOORSU
ichorous
CHIOPTTU
pitchout
CHIPRTTY
triptych
CHKMMOUY
hummocky
CHLNOOOP
colophon
CHLOORSU
chlorous
CHLOPSTY
splotchy
CHOOOPRS
prochoos
CHORSTTU
shortcut
CIIILMPT
implicit
CIIILTVY
civility
CIIINNOS
incision
CIIINTVY
vicinity
CIIKLPST
lipstick
CIIKNPPR
pinprick
CIIKNPST
stickpin
CIILMOPY
impolicy
CIILMOSS
sciolism
CIILMQSU
cliquism
CIILMRSY
lyricism
CIILORST
clitoris
CIILOSST
sciolist
CIILRSTY
lyricist
CIIMNOST
monistic
CIINNSTT
instinct
CIINOSSS
scission
CIINPSTU
sinciput
CIIOPSTT
opticist
CIIOQTUX
quixotic
CIIOTTXY

toxicity
CIISSTTY
cystitis
CIJKOSTY
joystick
CIJNNOOT
conjoint
CIJNNOTU
junction
CIJOOSTY
jocosity
CIKLOSTY
stockily
CIKMOORS
sickroom
CIKMOPST
mopstick
CIKNNOOS
coonskin
CILLMSUY
clumsily
CILLNOSU
scullion
CILMNUUV
vinculum
CILNOOST
colonist
CILNOOTU
locution
CILOORRT
tricolor
CILOORST
colorist
CILOOSSU
sciolous
CILOSSTY
systolic
CILOSSUU
luscious
CILRSTTY
strictly
CILRSTUY
rusticly
CIMNOSTU
miscount
CINNOOTU
continuo
CINNOOTX
nontoxic
CINNQUUX
quincunx
CINOOPRS
scorpion
CINOOPRT
protonic
CINOPSTY
synoptic
CINORSUY
cousinry
CINOSTUV
viscount
CINRSTTU
instruct
CINRSTUY

scrutiny
CJNOORRU
conjuror
CKKNOOTU
knockout
CKKOORRW
rockwork
CLLOOQUY
colloquy
CLMMNOOY
commonly
CLMOSUUU
cumulous
CLOOOPRT
protocol
CLOOORTW
coolwort
CLOOSSSU
colossus
CLOPRSTU
sculptor
CMMNNOOU
uncommon
CMNOPSTU
consumpt
CNOOOORT
octoroon
CNOSTUUU
unctuous
DDDDEEIR
diddered
DDDDEEOR
doddered
DDDEEEFN
defended
DDDEEENP
depended
DDDEEFOR
foddered
DDDEEHRS
shredded
DDDEENOS
soddened
DDDEERTU
detruded
DDDEIINV
dividend
DDDEILNW
dwindled
DDDEILTW
twiddled
DDDEINOR
dendroid
DDDEINRU
underdid
DDDGIILN
diddling
DDDGILNO
doddling
DDEEEEMR
redeemed
DDEEEFLX
deflexed
DDEEEFNR

defender
DDEEEFRR
deferred
DDEEEGNR
gendered
DDEEEGRT
deterged
DDEEEHLW
wheedled
DDEEEHNU
unheeded
DDEEEIMR
remedied
DDEEELPT
depleted
DDEEELSS
deedless
DDEEELTW
tweedled
DDEEEMNT
demented
DDEEENNU
unneeded
DDEEENPX
expended
DDEEENRR
rendered
DDEEENRT
tendered
DDEEENTX
extended
DDEEERRT
deterred
DDEEERST
deserted
DDEEERSV
deserved
DDEEESTT
detested
DDEEESTV
devested
DDEEFFIR
differed
DDEEFFNO
offended
DDEEFGGO
defogged
DDEEFGIT
fidgeted
DDEEFMOR
deformed
DDEEFNRU
refunded
underfed
DDEEGINR
engirded
DDEEGINS
designed
DDEEGIRV
diverged
DDEEGIST
digested
DDEEGSTU
degusted

DDEEHILS	demurred	unguided	dropsied	spudding
shielded	murdered	**DDEGNORU**	**DDEIOPRV**	**DDGINSTU**
DDEEHINR	**DDEENOPR**	grounded	provided	studding
hindered	pondered	underdog	**DDEIOPSS**	**DDHILOSY**
DDEEHRRS	**DDEENOPW**	**DDEGRRUY**	disposed	shoddily
shredder	pondweed	drudgery	**DDEIORRS**	**DDIIQTUY**
DDEEIINT	**DDEENORS**	**DDEHILOO**	disorder	quiddity
inedited	endorsed	idlehood	**DDEIOSTW**	**DDINNOWW**
DDEEILLW	**DDEENORW**	**DDEHINOR**	dowdiest	downwind
dillweed	wondered	dihedron	**DDEIPSTU**	**DDINOOWW**
DDEEILMW	**DDEENRSU**	**DDEHIORS**	disputed	woodwind
mildewed	sundered	shoddier	**DDEIRSSU**	**DDLMORSU**
DDEEILRV	**DDEEOPRT**	**DDEHIOSS**	druidess	doldrums
driveled	deported	shoddies	**DDEIRSTU**	**DEEEEMRR**
DDEEILRW	**DDEEOPRW**	**DDEHOOSW**	ruddiest	redeemer
wildered	powdered	woodshed	**DDELNRTU**	**DEEEEMST**
DDEEIMNP	**DDEEORRW**	**DDEHORSU**	trundled	esteemed
impended	reworded	shrouded	**DDELNSUY**	**DEEEERTT**
DDEEIMNR	**DDEEORTU**	**DDEHRSUY**	suddenly	teetered
reminded	detoured	shuddery	**DDEMNOUU**	**DEEEFLRU**
DDEEIMOR	**DDEEORUV**	**DDEIIIRZ**	duodenum	refueled
moidered	devoured	iridized	**DDEMNPUU**	**DEEEFLRX**
DDEEIMTT	**DDEEPRRU**	**DDEIIKLS**	pudendum	reflexed
demitted	perdured	disliked	**DDEMOOTU**	**DEEEFMNR**
DDEEINNT	**DDEERTUX**	**DDEIILOZ**	outmoded	freedmen
indented	extruded	idolized	**DDFGIILN**	**DEEEFNRT**
intended	**DDEFFISU**	**DDEIIMTT**	fiddling	deferent
DDEEINRT	diffused	dimitted	**DDFGILNU**	**DEEEFRRR**
dendrite	**DDEFIIIN**	**DDEIIMVW**	fuddling	referred
DDEEINST	nidified	midwived	**DDGGINRU**	**DEEEFRRT**
destined	**DDEFIIMO**	**DDEIINTU**	drudging	ferreted
DDEEIPRS	modified	untidied	**DDGHILNU**	**DEEEFRST**
presided	**DDEFIIMW**	**DDEIIOPS**	huddling	festered
DDEEIPRV	midwifed	dipodies	**DDGHINTU**	**DEEEFRTT**
deprived	**DDEFLNOU**	**DDEIIOST**	thudding	fettered
DDEEIPSS	unfolded	oddities	**DDGIIINV**	**DEEEGILS**
despised	**DDEGGINR**	**DDEIIOXZ**	dividing	elegised
DDEEIPST	dredging	oxidized	**DDGIIKNS**	**DEEEGILZ**
despited	**DDEGGLOY**	**DDEIKOSY**	skidding	elegized
DDEEIRTT	doggedly	disyoked	**DDGIILMN**	**DEEEGINS**
detrited	**DDEGGNOO**	**DDEIKSVY**	middling	designee
DDEEIRTV	doggoned	skydived	**DDGIILNP**	**DEEEGIPR**
diverted	**DDEGHINS**	**DDEILMOP**	piddling	pedigree
DDEEISST	shedding	imploded	**DDGIILNR**	**DEEEGIRR**
desisted	**DDEGIINR**	**DDEILNPS**	riddling	greedier
DDEEISTV	deriding	spindled	**DDGIILNT**	**DEEEGISW**
divested	**DDEGIIST**	splendid	tiddling	edgewise
DDEELLOY	giddiest	**DDEILNSW**	**DDGILMNU**	**DEEEGLSS**
yodelled	**DDEGILMN**	swindled	muddling	edgeless
DDEELOPR	meddling	**DDEILOPS**	**DDGILNNO**	**DEEEGNNR**
deplored	**DDEGILNP**	lopsided	noddling	engender
DDEELOPX	peddling	**DDEILRZZ**	**DDGILNOO**	**DEEEGNRV**
exploded	**DDEGILNS**	drizzled	doodling	revenged
DDEELOPY	sledding	**DDEIMSTU**	**DDGILNOP**	**DEEEHLMT**
deployed	**DDEGILNU**	muddiest	plodding	helmeted
DDEELORS	deluding	**DDEINORS**	**DDGILNOT**	**DEEEHLSS**
soldered	indulged	indorsed	toddling	heedless
DDEELOSU	**DDEGILOS**	**DDEINOSW**	**DDGILNPU**	**DEEEHRTT**
deloused	dislodge	disowned	puddling	tethered
DDEELPRU	**DDEGILUV**	**DDEINRST**	**DDGIMNUY**	**DEEEIKLS**
preluded	divulged	stridden	muddying	seedlike
DDEEMORR	**DDEGINNU**	**DDEINRTU**	**DDGINOPR**	**DEEEILRV**
dormered	denuding	intruded	prodding	relieved
DDEEMRRU	**DDEGINUU**	**DDEIOPRS**	**DDGINPSU**	**DEEEIMRS**

remedies	**DEEENRST**	**DEEFLNOR**	demiurge	**DEEHIRSV**
DEEEIMST	resented	enfolder	**DEEGINOP**	shivered
seedtime	**DEEEPPPR**	**DEEFLORW**	pigeoned	**DEEHIRTW**
DEEEINRR	peppered	deflower	**DEEGINPS**	withered
reindeer	**DEEEPRRT**	flowered	speeding	**DEEHIRTY**
DEEEINST	depreter	**DEEFLPSU**	**DEEGINRS**	heredity
neediest	**DEEEPRST**	speedful	designer	**DEEHKNOS**
DEEEINTV	estreped	**DEEFLRRU**	redesign	keeshond
eventide	pestered	ferruled	resigned	**DEEHKNRU**
DEEEIPRS	**DEEEQSUZ**	**DEEFMNOT**	**DEEGINST**	hunkered
speedier	squeezed	fomented	ingested	**DEEHLLOR**
DEEEIPTX	**DEEERRRV**	**DEEFMORR**	**DEEGIORT**	hollered
expedite	verderer	reformed	goitered	**DEEHLOSV**
DEEEIRRR	**DEEERRSV**	**DEEFMPRU**	**DEEGIOTZ**	shoveled
derriere	reserved	perfumed	egotized	**DEEHLSTU**
DEEEIRSS	reversed	**DEEFNOST**	**DEEGISTW**	sleuthed
diereses	**DEEERRTV**	softened	wedgiest	**DEEHMNRS**
DEEEIRVW	reverted	**DEEFNSST**	**DEEGLLTU**	herdsmen
reviewed	**DEEFFGLU**	deftness	gulleted	**DEEHMORT**
DEEEISST	effulged	**DEEFORST**	**DEEGLMNT**	mothered
seediest	**DEEFFGOR**	forested	ledgment	**DEEHNORT**
DEEEISTW	goffered	fostered	**DEEGLOPR**	dethrone
weediest	**DEEFFINR**	**DEEFPRSU**	pledgeor	**DEEHNOWY**
DEEEKLNN	niffered	perfused	**DEEGLOPS**	honeydew
kenneled	**DEEFFNOR**	**DEEGGHHO**	gospeled	**DEEHORSW**
DEEEKLNR	offender	hedgehog	**DEEGLORV**	showered
kerneled	**DEEFFRSU**	**DEEGGIJR**	groveled	**DEEHORTX**
DEEEKOPW	suffered	jiggered	**DEEGMNOR**	exhorted
pokeweed	**DEEFGGOR**	**DEEGGIJT**	mongered	**DEEHRRSW**
DEEELLLV	defogger	jiggeted	**DEEGNORV**	shrewder
levelled	**DEEFGINR**	**DEEGGIRR**	governed	**DEEIILNS**
DEEELLPR	fingered	dreggier	**DEEGNPUX**	sideline
repelled	**DEEFGLNU**	**DEEGGLOR**	expunged	**DEEIILRV**
DEEELLPT	engulfed	doggerel	**DEEGOSSS**	liveried
pelleted	**DEEFHLOR**	**DEEGGNOR**	godesses	**DEEIILRW**
DEEELLPX	freehold	engorged	**DEEGRSTU**	wieldier
expelled	**DEEFHORT**	**DEEGHILS**	gestured	**DEEIILVZ**
DEEELNRT	fothered	sleighed	**DEEGRTTU**	devilize
relented	**DEEFIINT**	**DEEGHITW**	guttered	**DEEIIMTZ**
DEEELNSS	definite	weighted	**DEEGSSTU**	itemized
lessened	**DEEFIIRS**	**DEEGHNRU**	gusseted	**DEEIIRSS**
needless	fireside	hungered	**DEEHHPRS**	dieresis
DEEELRSS	**DEEFIIRV**	**DEEGHOPR**	shepherd	**DEEIIRST**
reedless	verified	gophered	**DEEHHRST**	siderite
DEEELRTT	**DEEFILLR**	**DEEGHOPS**	threshed	**DEEIIRSV**
lettered	refilled	sheepdog	, **DEEHIKRS**	derisive
DEEELSSS	**DEEFILLT**	**DEEGHORW**	shrieked	**DEEIISSW**
seedless	filleted	hedgerow	**DEEHILRS**	sidewise
DEEELSSV	**DEEFILRT**	**DEEGILNN**	hirseled	**DEEIJNOR**
vesseled	filtered	needling	relished	rejoined
DEEEMPRT	**DEEFIMTU**	**DEEGILNR**	**DEEHILSS**	**DEEIJRTT**
tempered	tumefied	engirdle	hideless	jittered
DEEEMPTX	**DEEFINRR**	lingered	**DEEHILSV**	**DEEIKLLR**
exempted	inferred	**DEEGILNS**	dishevel	killdeer
DEEEMRST	**DEEFINRZ**	seedling	**DEEHIMNS**	**DEEIKLMW**
deemster	frenzied	**DEEGILNT**	inmeshed	milkweed
DEEENOPR	**DEEFINSS**	deleting	**DEEHINRR**	**DEEIKLNR**
reopened	finessed	**DEEGILNV**	hinderer	rekindle
DEEENORS	**DEEFINST**	develing	**DEEHINTW**	**DEEIKLSW**
endorsee	infested	**DEEGILRY**	whitened	silkweed
DEEENPRT	**DEEFIPRX**	greedily	**DEEHIPRS**	**DEEIKNRS**
repented	prefixed	**DEEGIMNN**	perished	deerskin
DEEENRRV	**DEEFLNNU**	emending	**DEEHIRRW**	**DEEIKNRT**
reverend	funneled	**DEEGIMRU**	wherried	tinkered

DEEIKPPR	simpered	quivered	revolved	**DEEOPRST**
kippered	**DEEIMRTT**	**DEEIQTUU**	**DEELPRSU**	dopester
DEEILLMP	remitted	quietude	repulsed	**DEEOPRTX**
impelled	**DEEINNRT**	**DEEIRRSS**	**DEELRSTU**	exported
milleped	interned	dressier	resulted	**DEEOPSSU**
DEEILLNO	**DEEINNTV**	**DEEIRRST**	**DEELRSTW**	espoused
nielloed	invented	destrier	wrestled	**DEEORRST**
DEEILMNU	**DEEINNTW**	**DEEIRSST**	**DEEMMORS**	resorted
demilune	entwined	resisted	mesoderm	restored
DEEILMOS	**DEEINORT**	**DEEIRSSU**	**DEEMMRSU**	**DEEORRTT**
melodies	oriented	reissued	summered	retorted
DEEILMOZ	**DEEINOTV**	**DEEIRTTT**	**DEEMNOQU**	**DEEORRTU**
melodize	denotive	tittered	queendom	rerouted
DEEILNOT	**DEEINPSS**	**DEEJKNTU**	**DEEMOORT**	**DEEORRVW**
deletion	dispense	junketed	odometer	overdrew
DEEILNRU	**DEEINQSU**	**DEEJPRRU**	**DEEMPRSU**	**DEEORSTX**
underlie	sequined	perjured	presumed	dextrose
DEEILNSS	**DEEINRRT**	**DEEKMNOY**	**DEEMPRTU**	**DEEORSTY**
idleness	interred	monkeyed	permuted	oystered
DEEILNST	trendier	**DEEKNOTY**	**DEEMRRRU**	**DEEORTTT**
enlisted	**DEEINRSS**	keynoted	murderer	tottered
listened	direness	**DEELLMOW**	**DEEMRSTU**	**DEEORTTX**
DEEILNSV	**DEEINRST**	mellowed	demurest	extorted
sniveled	inserted	**DEELLNOR**	mustered	**DEEPPRSU**
DEEILNTT	resident	enrolled	**DEEMRTTU**	suppered
entitled	sintered	rondelle	muttered	**DEEPRTTU**
DEEILNUV	**DEEINRTU**	**DEELLOTX**	**DEENNOPU**	puttered
unveiled	reunited	extolled	unopened	**DEEPRUVY**
DEEILORT	**DEEINRTV**	**DEELLOVY**	**DEENNORW**	purveyed
dolerite	inverted	volleyed	renowned	**DEERRTTU**
loitered	**DEEINRTW**	**DEELLOWY**	**DEENNRUV**	turreted
DEEILORV	wintered	yellowed	unnerved	**DEERSSST**
evildoer	**DEEINSSW**	**DEELMMOP**	**DEENNSSU**	stressed
DEEILPSY	dewiness	pommeled	nudeness	**DEERSUVY**
speedily	wideness	**DEELMNOO**	**DEENOORV**	surveyed
DEEILRSV	**DEEINSTV**	melodeon	overdone	**DEERTTUX**
silvered	invested	**DEELMOOS**	**DEENORRW**	textured
slivered	**DEEIOPRX**	dolesome	wonderer	**DEFFHILW**
DEEILRTT	peroxide	**DEELMOPY**	**DEENORSW**	whiffled
littered	**DEEIOPTZ**	employed	worsened	**DEFFHLSU**
DEEILRVY	poetized	**DEELMOST**	**DEENORTU**	shuffled
delivery	**DEEIORRV**	molested	deuteron	**DEFFILNS**
DEEILSUV	override	**DEELMRUY**	**DEENRRTU**	sniffled
delusive	**DEEIPPQU**	demurely	returned	**DEFFILOV**
DEEILSVW	equipped	**DEELNNTU**	**DEENRSSU**	fivefold
swiveled	**DEEIPRRS**	tunneled	rudeness	**DEFFISUX**
DEEILTUY	respired	**DEELNOOS**	**DEENRSUV**	suffixed
yuletide	**DEEIPRSS**	loosened	unversed	**DEFFLNSU**
DEEIMMOS	disperse	**DEELNORT**	**DEENRTUV**	snuffled
semidome	**DEEIPRST**	redolent	ventured	**DEFFSSUU**
DEEIMMRS	respited	rondelet	**DEENSTTU**	suffused
immersed	**DEEIPRSU**	**DEELNRTY**	untested	**DEFFSTUY**
simmered	duperies	tenderly	**DEEOORRV**	dyestuff
DEEIMNOR	**DEEIPRSV**	**DEELNWWY**	overrode	**DEFGIILN**
domineer	prevised	newlywed	**DEEOORSV**	fledging
DEEIMNOZ	**DEEIPRTT**	**DEELOPRX**	overdose	**DEFGIILN**
demonize	prettied	explored	**DEEOPPRS**	defiling
DEEIMNPT	**DEEIPSTU**	**DEELORSV**	preposed	fielding
pediment	deputies	resolved	**DEEOPPST**	**DEFGIILU**
DEEIMNRR	**DEEIPTUZ**	**DEELORTV**	estopped	uglified
reminder	deputize	revolted	**DEEOPRRT**	**DEFGIINN**
DEEIMNST	**DEEIQRRU**	**DEELORTW**	reported	defining
sediment	required	troweled	**DEEOPRRV**	**DEFGIINY**
DEEIMPRS	**DEEIQRUV**	**DEELORVV**	reproved	deifying

edifying	**DEFILOTU**	**DEGGIOST**	ridgiest	**DEGIOPSS**
DEFGILNU	outfield	doggiest	**DEGIISSU**	gossiped
ingulfed	**DEFILPRU**	**DEGGLMSU**	disguise	**DEGIPSTU**
DEFGINSU	prideful	smuggled	**DEGIJMSU**	pudgiest
defusing	**DEFILPTU**	**DEGGLNSU**	misjudge	**DEGJMNTU**
DEFGIOOW	uplifted	snuggled	**DEGILLNW**	judgment
goodwife	**DEFILRRU**	**DEGGLRUY**	dwelling	**DEGLNOOT**
DEFGJORU	flurried	ruggedly	**DEGILMNO**	gondolet
forjudge	**DEFILRVY**	**DEGHHIIT**	modeling	**DEGLPRSU**
DEFHIINS	fervidly	hightide	**DEGILMPS**	splurged
fiendish	**DEFILRZZ**	**DEGHIINS**	glimpsed	**DEGNOOSS**
finished	frizzled	dinghies	**DEGILNOS**	goodness
DEFHIOOW	**DEFIMNOR**	**DEGHIKNT**	sidelong	**DEGNOPPU**
wifehood	informed	knighted	**DEGILNOW**	oppugned
DEFHLOOS	**DEFIMRRU**	**DEGHILNS**	doweling	**DEGNORRU**
selfhood	drumfire	shingled	**DEGILNOY**	grounder
DEFHOORS	**DEFIOORW**	**DEGHILPT**	yodeling	**DEGPRSUU**
serfhood	firewood	plighted	**DEGILNRU**	upsurged
DEFIIILV	**DEFIOPRT**	**DEGHILST**	indulger	**DEHHILTW**
vilified	profited	slighted	**DEGILNSW**	withheld
DEFIIIMN	**DEFIOTXY**	**DEGHIORU**	swingled	**DEHIILLS**
minified	detoxify	doughier	**DEGILOOY**	hillside
DEFIIIVV	**DEFIRSSU**	**DEGHNORT**	ideology	**DEHIILSV**
vivified	fissured	thronged	**DEGILRZZ**	devilish
DEFIILLP	**DEFLLOOR**	**DEGHNORY**	grizzled	**DEHIIMMS**
filliped	folderol	hydrogen	**DEGIMNOT**	shimmied
DEFIILLW	**DEFLLOOW**	**DEGHOOSU**	demoting	**DEHIIMNS**
wildlife	followed	doghouse	**DEGIMNPU**	minished
DEFIILMS	**DEFLLOSS**	**DEGIILNS**	impugned	**DEHIIMST**
misfiled	foldless	sideling	**DEGINNNU**	ditheism
DEFIILRW	**DEFLNORU**	**DEGIILNT**	unending	**DEHIINNS**
wildfire	flounder	diligent	**DEGINNOP**	shinnied
DEFIILTY	**DEFLNRUU**	**DEGIILNV**	deponing	**DEHIINNW**
fidelity	unfurled	deviling	**DEGINNOT**	whinnied
DEFIIMOR	**DEFLNSSU**	**DEGIILNW**	denoting	**DEHIINSS**
modifier	fundless	wielding	**DEGINNOW**	shindies
DEFIIMOS	**DEFLOORT**	**DEGIILNY**	endowing	**DEHIIPSS**
modifies	foretold	yielding	**DEGINNPS**	shipside
DEFIIMRS	**DEFLOOSS**	**DEGIIMNP**	spending	**DEHIIRST**
misfired	foodless	impeding	**DEGINNPU**	disherit
DEFIINOT	**DEFMNORU**	impinged	upending	**DEHIISTT**
notified	unformed	**DEGIIMNS**	**DEGINNRU**	ditheist
DEFIINTY	**DEFNNOSS**	demising	enduring	**DEHIJMNO**
identify	fondness	**DEGIINNT**	**DEGINNTU**	demijohn
DEFIIOSS	**DEFNORRU**	indigent	detuning	**DEHIKMOS**
ossified	frondeur	**DEGIINNW**	untinged	shiekdom
DEFIIPRU	**DEFNORTU**	widening	**DEGINOPS**	**DEHILLRS**
purified	fortuned	**DEGIINNX**	deposing	shrilled
DEFIIPSS	**DEFOORRW**	indexing	**DEGINORR**	**DEHILLRT**
fissiped	foreword	**DEGIINNZ**	ordering	thrilled
DEFIIPTY	**DEFORRUW**	dizening	**DEGINORW**	**DEHILMOS**
typified	furrowed	**DEGIINOS**	dowering	demolish
DEFIIRRT	**DEGGHRSU**	indigoes	**DEGINOTV**	**DEHILOPS**
driftier	shrugged	**DEGIINRS**	devoting	polished
DEFILLNU	**DEGGIINN**	desiring	**DEGINPRS**	**DEHILOTY**
unfilled	deigning	residing	springed	holytide
DEFILNNO	**DEGGILNP**	ringside	**DEGINPTU**	**DEHILSTW**
ninefold	pledging	**DEGIINRV**	deputing	whistled
DEFILNRY	**DEGGILNS**	deriving	**DEGINRSS**	**DEHILTTW**
friendly	sledging	**DEGIINST**	dressing	whittled
DEFILOPR	**DEGGILNU**	dingiest	**DEGINSSU**	**DEHIMNOS**
profiled	deluging	**DEGIINSV**	disguses	hedonism
DEFILORU	**DEGGILRW**	devising	**DEGIOPRR**	**DEHIMPRS**
fluoride	wriggled	**DEGIIRST**	porridge	shrimped

DEHINOPR	**DEIILNVY**	dirtiest	solitude	poisoned
nephroid	divinely	**DEIISTZZ**	**DEILOSVW**	**DEINOOTV**
DEHINOPS	**DEIILNXY**	dizziest	oldwives	devotion
sphenoid	xylidine	**DEIKLLOR**	**DEILPPST**	**DEINOPPR**
DEHINOST	**DEIILORZ**	lordlike	stippled	propined
hedonist	idolizer	**DEIKLNRW**	**DEILPPSU**	**DEINOPRS**
DEHINPSU	**DEIILPSS**	wrinkled	supplied	prisoned
punished	sideslip	**DEIKLNTW**	**DEILRSSY**	**DEINOPRU**
DEHIOPRS	**DEIILTUZ**	twinkled	dressily	inpoured
spheroid	utilized	**DEIKLSTT**	**DEILRTVY**	**DEINOPSU**
DEHIRRST	**DEIIMMTT**	skittled	deviltry	unpoised
redshirt	immitted	**DEIKNNSS**	**DEILSTUY**	**DEINOSTW**
DEHIRSTT	**DEIIMNRT**	kindness	sedulity	downiest
thirsted	diriment	**DEIKSSTU**	**DEILSTYZ**	**DEINPPUZ**
DEHIRTWW	**DEIIMNST**	duskiest	stylized	unzipped
withdrew	identism	**DEILLNTU**	**DEIMMNOS**	**DEINPRST**
DEHKNOOU	**DEIIMNTU**	untilled	demonism	sprinted
unhooked	mutinied	**DEILLOPW**	**DEIMMOST**	**DEINQSTU**
DEHLLOOW	**DEIINORS**	pillowed	immodest	squinted
hollowed	derision	**DEILMNOO**	**DEIMNOOS**	**DEINRRTU**
DEHLOORV	ironside	melodion	dominoes	intruder
holdover	**DEIINORZ**	**DEILMNSS**	**DEIMNOOT**	**DEINRSSU**
DEHLOOST	ironized	mildness	motioned	sundries
toolshed	**DEIINOST**	mindless	**DEIMNOOX**	**DEINRSTT**
DEHLORSU	sedition	**DEILMOOT**	monoxide	strident
shoulder	**DEIINPPW**	dolomite	**DEIMNPTU**	**DEINSTUU**
DEHLRSWY	windpipe	**DEILMOPR**	impudent	unsuited
shrewdly	**DEIINPRS**	implored	**DEIMNRTU**	**DEINTTUW**
DEHLSTTU	inspired	**DEILMOST**	rudiment	unwitted
shuttled	**DEIINPRT**	melodist	**DEIMOOST**	**DEIOOPRR**
DEHMOPRY	intrepid	moldiest	moodiest	droopier
hypoderm	**DEIINQRU**	**DEILMRSU**	**DEIMOPRS**	**DEIOORSW**
DEHNORSU	inquired	misruled	promised	woodsier
enshroud	**DEIINRST**	**DEILNNOT**	**DEIMOPRT**	**DEIOOSTW**
DEHNORTY	disinter	indolent	imported	woodiest
threnody	**DEIINRTU**	**DEILNOOS**	**DEIMOPRV**	**DEIOPRSV**
DEHNRTUY	untidier	solenoid	improved	disprove
thundery	**DEIINSST**	**DEILNOSU**	**DEIMORRR**	**DEIOPRSW**
DEHOOOPP	insisted	delusion	mirrored	dropwise
popehood	**DEIINSTU**	**DEILNOVV**	**DEIMORST**	**DEIORRSS**
DEHOOPRT	tidiness	involved	mortised	drossier
theropod	**DEIINSTU**	**DEILNPST**	**DEIMORUX**	**DEIORRSW**
DEHOOSSW	disunite	splinted	exordium	drowsier
swooshed	nudities	**DEILNRSW**	**DEIMPSTU**	**DEIORRSY**
DEHRRSTU	**DEIINSTW**	swindler	dumpiest	derisory
druthers	windiest	**DEILNSSW**	**DEIMQRSU**	**DEIORRTU**
DEIIIMST	**DEIINTTU**	wildness	squirmed	outrider
dimities	intuited	**DEILNSTU**	**DEIMRSSU**	**DEIORSSU**
DEIIINVZ	**DEIINTTY**	windless	surmised	desirous
divinize	identity	**DEILNSTU**	**DEINNNOU**	**DEIORSTU**
DEIIISVV	**DEIINTUZ**	insulted	innuendo	outsider
divisive	unitized	**DEILNTTU**	**DEINNNPU**	**DEIORSTW**
DEIIKLNR	**DEIIOPRS**	untitled	unpinned	rowdiest
kindlier	presidio	**DEILNUWY**	**DEINNOOT**	**DEIOSTTT**
DEIIKLNV	**DEIIORXZ**	unwieldy	noontide	dottiest
devilkin	oxidizer	**DEILOOPW**	**DEINNORU**	**DEIPPRST**
DEIIKNST	**DEIIPPRR**	woodpile	unironed	stripped
dinkiest	drippier	**DEILOPST**	**DEINNOWW**	**DEIPRRTU**
DEIILMRU	**DEIIPPST**	pistoled	winnowed	irrupted
delirium	dippiest	**DEILORSY**	**DEINNPRU**	**DEIPRSSU**
DEIILNOZ	**DEIIPRST**	soldiery	underpin	suspired
lionized	spirited	**DEILOSSV**	**DEINNRTU**	**DEIQRSTU**
DEIILNPV	**DEIIQSTU**	dissolve	inturned	squirted
vilipend	disquiet	**DEILOSTU**	**DEINOOPS**	
	DEIIRSTT			

DEIRRSTU	**DEMNORSY**	**DFGINOOR**	diluting	midships
sturdier	syndrome	fordoing	**DGIIMNOS**	**DHIIMTUY**
DEIRSSST	**DEMOOPRT**	**DFHIIMUY**	misdoing	humidity
distress	promoted	humidify	**DGIINORR**	**DHIKNOOW**
DEIRSUVV	**DEMOORSU**	**DFHLOOOT**	gridiron	hoodwink
survived	dormouse	foothold	**DGIINOTT**	**DHILLNOW**
DEISSTTU	**DEMOPPRT**	**DFHNOOUX**	dittoing	downhill
dustiest	prompted	foxhound	**DGIINOWW**	**DHILMOSY**
DEKOOPRV	**DENOOPPR**	**DFIILOSY**	widowing	modishly
provoked	proponed	solidify	**DGIINPPR**	**DHILOPRS**
DEKOOTWW	**DENORSTU**	**DFIILTUY**	dripping	lordship
kowtowed	roundest	fluidity	**DGIINRST**	**DHILOPSS**
DELLNSSU	tonsured	**DFILLORY**	striding	slipshod
dullness	**DENORTUW**	floridly	**DGIINRTY**	**DHILORRY**
DELLOPTU	undertow	**DFILLOWW**	dirtying	horridly
polluted	**DENRRTUU**	wildfowl	**DGIINSSU**	**DHIMNOST**
DELLORRY	nurtured	**DFIOOPRS**	disusing	hindmost
drollery	**DEOOORSW**	disproof	**DGIINVVY**	**DHINOORS**
DELLORSS	rosewood	**DFNOOPRU**	divvying	dishonor
lordless	**DEOOPPRS**	profound	**DGIINYZZ**	**DHINORSU**
DELLORST	proposed	**DGGGINRU**	dizzying	roundish
strolled	**DEOOPPRT**	drugging	**DGILLNOR**	**DHINOTUW**
DELMNPUU	pteropod	grudging	drolling	whodunit
pendulum	**DEOOPRRV**	**DGGIILNR**	**DGILMNPU**	**DHLORXYY**
DELMOSTY	provedor	girdling	dumpling	hydroxyl
modestly	**DEOOPRST**	**DGGIINNR**	**DGILNNOO**	**DHLOSSTU**
DELNOOWY	doorstep	grinding	noodling	shouldst
woodenly	**DEOOPRTU**	**DGGILNOP**	**DGILNOOR**	**DHNOOSWW**
DELNOPRS	uprooted	plodging	drooling	showdown
splendor	**DEOPPRST**	**DGGIMNSU**	**DGILNOTY**	**DHNOSTUW**
DELNORTU	stropped	smudging	dotingly	shutdown
roundlet	**DEOPPRSU**	**DGGINRTU**	**DGILRTUY**	**DHOOORTX**
DELNOSSU	purposed	trudging	turgidly	orthodox
loudness	**DEOPPSSU**	**DGGIRSTU**	**DGIMMNRU**	**DHOPRSYY**
DELNOSUV	supposed	druggist	drumming	hydropsy
unsolved	**DEOPRRTU**	**DGHIIMNT**	**DGIMNNOU**	**DIIILTVY**
DELOORRV	protrude	midnight	mounding	lividity
overload	**DEOPRSTU**	**DGHILNRU**	**DGINNOPU**	**DIIIMTTY**
DELOORSS	postured	hurdling	pounding	timidity
odorless	sprouted	**DGHILOOR**	**DGINNORU**	**DIIINOSV**
DELOPSTU	**DEORRTTU**	girlhood	rounding	division
postlude	tortured	**DGHINNOU**	**DGINNORW**	**DIIINTVY**
DELORSSW	**DEORSTUX**	hounding	drowning	divinity
wordless	dextrous	**DGHNOTUU**	**DGINNOSU**	**DIIIRTVY**
DELORSUY	**DEPRRTUU**	doughnut	sounding	viridity
delusory	ruptured	**DGHORTUY**	**DGINNOUW**	**DIIJNOST**
DELOSSUU	**DERSTTTU**	droughty	wounding	disjoint
sedulous	strutted	**DGIIIINNT**	**DGINOOPR**	**DIILLMNW**
DELOTUVY	**DFFLOORU**	inditing	drooping	windmill
devoutly	fourfold	**DGIIINNV**	**DGINOPPR**	**DIILLMPY**
DELSSSTU	**DFFOORUW**	divining	dropping	limpidly
dustless	woodruff	**DGIIINOZ**	**DGINORSW**	**DIILLQUY**
DEMMNNOSU	**DFGGHIOT**	iodizing	drowsing	liquidly
summoned	dogfight	**DGIIIRTY**	**DGINSTUY**	**DIILLSTY**
DEMMRRUU	**DFGHILOS**	rigidity	studying	idyllist
murmured	goldfish	**DGIIKLNN**	**DGLOOOXY**	**DIILMUUV**
DEMMRSTU	**DFGIILRY**	kindling	doxology	diluvium
strummed	frigidly	**DGIILLNR**	**DHHILOTW**	**DIILNOTU**
DEMNOOOP	**DFGILNNO**	drilling	withhold	dilution
monopode	fondling	**DGIILMNP**	**DHIIIMNS**	**DIILOSTY**
DEMNOOST	**DFGILNOO**	dimpling	diminish	solidity
mesodont	flooding	**DGIILNNP**	**DHIIMOST**	**DIIMNNOO**
DEMNOOSW	**DFGINNOU**	pindling	isthmoid	dominion
woodsmen	founding	**DGIILNTU**	**DHIIMPSS**	**DIIMNOPT**

midpoint	downpour	enmeshes	**EEELMRTU**	fleeting
DIIMOPRS	**DNOORSUW**	**EEEHMNTV**	muleteer	**EEFGINRR**
prismoid	wondrous	vehement	**EEELNOPV**	fingerer
DIINSTUY	**DNORRSUU**	**EEEHNNPT**	envelope	**EEFGINRZ**
disunity	surround	nepenthe	**EEELNRSW**	freezing
DIKLNNUY	**DOOOPRST**	**EEEHNRVW**	newsreel	**EEFGLMNU**
unkindly	doorstop	whenever	**EEELNRSY**	fuglemen
DILLMNOP	**DOOPSWWY**	**EEEHORST**	serenely	**EEFGLNUV**
millpond	powsowdy	shoetree	**EEELPRSS**	vengeful
DILLOORS	**EEEEGQSU**	**EEEHRRVW**	peerless	**EEFGNOOR**
doorsill	squeegee ·	wherever	**EEELRSVY**	foregone
DILLOSTY	**EEEFFNRT**	**EEEILLRV**	severely	**EEFGOORR**
stolidly	efferent	reveille	**EEEMNNTT**	foregoer
DILOORSS	**EEEFLRSX**	**EEEILMRS**	tenement	**EEFHILLR**
lordosis	reflexes	seemlier	**EEEMORRV**	hellfire
DILOOSUY	**EEEFNRSS**	**EEEILNRY**	evermore	**EEFHIRSV**
odiously	freeness	eyeliner	**EEEMRRTX**	feverish
DILOPRTY	**EEEFORRS**	**EEEILNST**	extremer	**EEFHISST**
torpidly	foreseer	selenite	**EEEMRSST**	fetishes
DILORSWY	**EEEFRRRT**	**EEEILPRS**	semester	**EEFHISTT**
drowsily	ferreter	sleepier	**EEENNOPR**	heftiest
DILPSTUY	**EEEGGILN**	**EEEILRST**	neoprene	**EEFHLLWY**
stupidly	negligee	leeriest	**EEENNSSV**	flywheel
DILRSTUY	**EEEGHINT**	**EEEILRST**	evenness	**EEFHMNRS**
sturdily	eighteen	steelier	**EEENORSV**	freshmen
DIMNOOOS	**EEEGILNV**	**EEEILSTV**	overseen	**EEFHRSST**
isodomon	leveeing	televise	**EEENORVY**	freshest
DIMNOSTU	**EEEGINNR**	**EEEIMPRR**	everyone	**EEFIIKLL**
dismount	engineer	premiere	**EEENPRST**	lifelike
DINOOORW	**EEEGINRS**	**EEEIMPRS**	pretense	**EEFIIKLW**
ironwood	energies	emperies	**EEENRRTV**	wifelike
DINOOSTY	**EEEGINRS**	**EEEIMRRS**	reverent	**EEFIILMT**
nodosity	energise	miserere	**EEENRRUV**	lifetime
DINRSTUY	**EEEGINRZ**	**EEEINNNT**	revenuer	**EEFIILRW**
industry	energize	nineteen	**EEENRSTY**	wifelier
DIOSSTUU	**EEEGISSX**	**EEEINNRT**	yestreen	**EEFIIMNN**
studious	exegesis	internee	**EEEOORSV**	feminine
DIRSSTTU	**EEEGISTV**	**EEEINPTT**	overseer	**EEFIIMNZ**
distrust	egestive	epinette	**EEEPRRST**	feminize
DKOOORWW	**EEEGMNRT**	**EEEINRSS**	pesterer	**EEFIINRS**
woodwork	emergent	eeriness	**EEEPRRSV**	fineries
DLLMORSU	**EEEGNRRY**	**EEEINSTT**	perverse	**EEFIIRRV**
slumlord	greenery	teeniest	**EEEPRRSV**	verifier
DLNOOSWW	**EEEGNRST**	**EEEIPRRV**	preserve	**EEFIIRST**
slowdown	greenest	reprieve	**EEEQRSTU**	fieriest
DLOOOORS	**EEEHILRW**	**EEEIPSST**	queerest	**EEFIIRSV**
doloroso	erewhile	seepiest	**EEERSSTV**	verifies
DLOOORSU	**EEEHIRSS**	**EEEIPSTW**	severest	**EEFIKLRS**
dolorous	heresies	weepiest	**EEERSTVX**	serflike
DMNOOORT	**EEEHIRWZ**	**EEEIRRTV**	vertexes	**EEFIKNNP**
rodomont	wheezier	retrieve	**EEERSTWZ**	penknife
DMOOORWW	**EEEHKLLR**	**EEEIRTVX**	tweezers	**EEFILLSS**
wormwood	rekehell	exertive	**EEESSTTW**	lifeless
DNNOOPRU	**EEEHLMPT**	**EEEKLSST**	sweetest	**EEFILMNR**
pundonor	helpmeet	sleekest	**EEFFGIIS**	riflemen
DNNOOTWW	**EEEHLNTV**	**EEEKMNSS**	effigies	**EEFILNOS**
downtown	eleventh	meekness	**EEFFISUV**	felonies
DNNORTUW	**EEEHLNTY**	**EEEKNNSS**	effusive	**EEFILPRR**
turndown	ethylene	keenness	**EEFFLNTU**	pilferer
DNOOPPRU	**EEEHLOPP**	**EEEKNORS**	effluent	**EEFILRSS**
propound	peephole	kerosene	**EEFFRRSU**	fireless
DNOOPRSW	**EEEHMNPS**	**EEELLNQU**	sufferer	**EEFINNSS**
snowdrop	sheepmen	quenelle	**EEFGIILR**	fineness
DNOOPRUW	**EEEHMNSS**	**EEELMOPY**	filigree	**EEFINRRR**
		employee	**EEFGILNT**	

inferrer
EEFINRRY
refinery
EEFINRST
infester
EEFINRSZ
frenzies
EEFIPRSX
prefixes
EEFIRSTT
frisette
EEFIRTTZ
frizette
EEFLLNSS
fellness
EEFLLORT
foretell
EEFLLSSS
selfless
EEFLNSSS
selfness
EEFLNTUV
eventful
EEFLORRW
flowerer
EEFLORTV
leftover
EEFLORTW
floweret
EEFLORWW
werewolf
EEFMNORT
fomenter
EEFMNRRY
ferrymen
EEFMORRR
reformer
EEFNORST
softener
EEFNORTU
fourteen
EEFNORTW
forewent
EEFNQRTU
frequent
EEFORRST
forester
reforest
EEGGHLLS
eggshell
EEGGILST
leggiest
EEGGIMNR
emerging
EEGGINNR
greening
reneging
EEGGINRT
greeting
EEGGINST
egesting
EEGGINSU
segueing
EEGHHINT

heighten
EEGHIIST
eighties
EEGHINNS
sheening
EEGHINRS
greenish
sheering
EEGHINST
seething
sheeting
EEGHINTT
teething
EEGHINWZ
wheezing
EEGHISTY
eyesight
EEGHLNNT
lengthen
EEGHMNOY
hegemony
EEGHNOPS
phosgene
EEGHNOPY
hypogene
EEGHNSSU
hugeness
EEGHORTT
together
EEGHOSTT
ghettoes
EEGIILMT
legitime
EEGIILNR
lingerie
EEGIILNV
inveigle
EEGIINTV
genitive
EEGIJLNW
jeweling
EEGIKLNN
kneeling
EEGILLNV
leveling
EEGILNPS
sleeping
EEGILNRV
levering
reveling
EEGILNST
sleeting
steeling
EEGILNSV
sleeving
EEGILOPU
epilogue
EEGILOSU
eulogies
EEGILOUZ
eulogize
EEGIMNRT
metering
regiment

EEGIMNRU
meringue
EEGINNPR
preening
EEGINNQU
queening
EEGINNRS
sneering
EEGINNRT
entering
EEGINNRW
renewing
EEGINNSZ
sneezing
EEGINOST
egestion
EEGINPRS
spreeing
EEGINPRT
petering
EEGINPST
steeping
EEGINPSW
sweeping
EEGINRRV
revering
EEGINRST
steering
EEGINRSU
seigneur
EEGINRSV
severing
EEGINRSW
sewering
EEGINRTV
everting
EEGINRTX
exerting
EEGINSSU
geniuses
EEGINTTV
vignette
EEGINTTW
tweeting
EEGINTWZ
tweezing
EEGIOPSU
epigeous
EEGIPRST
prestige
EEGIRRST
register
EEGIRSTT
grisette
EEGLNSTT
gentlest
EEGLOPRS
gospeler
EEGMNOST
gemstone
EEGMORSU
gruesome
EEGMORTY
geometry

EEGNNOSS
goneness
EEGNNOSV
evensong
EEGNORST
estrogen
EEGNORSU
generous
EEGNRSUY
guernsey
EEGOPRSU
superego
EEGORRVW
overgrew
EEGRRSTU
gesturer
EEHHIPSS
sheepish
EEHHIRTW
herewith
EEHHLLLO
hellhole
EEHHNOSU
henhouse
EEHHRRST
thresher
EEHHRSST
threshes
EEHIKLMO
homelike
EEHIKRRS
shrieker
EEHILLRS
shellier
EEHILMOR
homelier
EEHILORT
hotelier
EEHILRSS
heirless
relishes
EEHILSST
shelties
EEHIMNRT
theremin
EEHIMRTT
thermite
EEHINNRS
enshrine
EEHINNRT
inherent
EEHINORT
hereinto
EEHINPRT
nephrite
EEHINRTT
thirteen
EEHINRTW
whitener
EEHIORST
theories
EEHIORTZ
theorize
EEHIPRSS

perishes
EEHIPUUZ
euphuize
EEHIRRSS
sherries
EEHIRRSV
shiverer
EEHIRRSW
wherries
EEHIRTVY
thievery
EEHLLMSS
helmless
EEHLLOSS
holeless
EEHLLPSS
helpless
EEHLMMNS
helmsmen
EEHLMOSS
homeless
EEHLNOTT
telethon
EEHLOPSS
hopeless
EEHLORST
hosteler
EEHLORSV
shoveler
EEHLOSSS
shoeless
EEHMMORT
ohmmeter
EEHMNORS
horsemen
EEHMORVW
whomever
EEHNNORT
enthrone
EEHNOPRU
hereupon
EEHNOPTY
neophyte
EEHNORSS
senhores
EEHOORSV
overshoe
EEIIKLLR
likelier
EEIIKLLV
veillike
EEIIKLSW
likewise
EEIILLMM
millieme
EEIILLRV
livelier
EEIILNTV
lenitive
EEIILRSV
liveries
EEIIMNST
enmities
EEIIMOST

moieties	timeless	**EEIMSSST**	**EEIPQTTU**	eloquent
EEIIMRSS	**EEILMSUV**	messiest	piquette	**EELNORST**
miseries	emulsive	**EEINNPTT**	**EEIPRRTT**	entresol
EEIIMRTZ	**EEILNNST**	penitent	preterit	**EELNOSSS**
itemizer	sentinel	**EEINNSTT**	prettier	noseless
EEIIMSSV	**EEILNOPR**	sentient	**EEIPRSTX**	**EELNOSST**
emissive	leporine	**EEINOPPR**	preexist	noteless
EEIINNST	**EEILNOVZ**	peperoni	**EEIPRTUV**	**EELNSTTU**
nineties	novelize	**EEINORST**	eruptive	unsettle
EEIINPPR	**EEILNPST**	serotine	**EEIPSTTT**	**EELOPPSS**
piperine	plenties	**EEINORSV**	pettiest	peploses
EEIINPRS	**EEILNRST**	eversion	**EEIQRRUV**	**EELOPPST**
pineries	listener	**EEINORTX**	quiverer	estoppel
EEIINRRV	**EEILNRTY**	exertion	**EEIRRSST**	**EELOPRRX**
riverine	entirely	**EEINPRSS**	resister	explorer
EEIINRST	**EEILNSSV**	ripeness	**EEIRSSTU**	**EELOPTTY**
niteries	evilness	**EEINPRTX**	sureties	telotype
EEIINRSV	**EEILORRT**	inexpert	**EEIRSSTV**	**EELORRVV**
vineries	loiterer	**EEINQRSU**	vestries	revolver
EEIINRSW	**EEILPPSY**	squireen	**EEIRSTVY**	**EELORSTU**
wineries	epilepsy	**EEINRRTX**	severity	resolute
EEIINSTT	**EEILPRST**	interrex	**EEISSTTT**	**EELORTTU**
entities	peltries	**EEINRSST**	testiest	roulette
EEIINSTV	**EEILPSSV**	sentries	**EEJPRSTU**	**EELOSSTV**
veiniest	pelvises	**EEINRSSU**	superjet	voteless
EEIIPRSX	**EEILPSTY**	enuresis	**EEKKORWW**	**EELPPSTU**
expiries	epistyle	**EEINRSTT**	workweek	septuple
EEIIPRTT	**EEILRSSS**	interest	**EEKLNOST**	**EELPRTXY**
epitrite	sireless	**EEINRSTV**	skeleton	expertly
EEIIQSTU	**EEILRSST**	nerviest	**EEKNORTY**	**EELPSTUX**
equities	tireless	reinvest	keynoter	sextuple
EEIIRSTV	**EEILRSSW**	servient	**EEKNOSTY**	**EELRRSTW**
verities	wireless	sirvente	keystone	wrestler
EEIJKRST	**EEILSSVW**	**EEINRSTX**	**EEKRRTUZ**	**EELRSSST**
jerkiest	viewless	intersex	kreutzer	restless
EEIJLNNU	**EEIMMORS**	**EEINRSTY**	**EELLORST**	**EELRSTWY**
julienne	memories	serenity	solleret	westerly
EEIJLNUV	**EEIMMORZ**	**EEINRSUV**	**EELLORWY**	**EEMMNOTV**
juvenile	memorize	universe	yellower	movement
EEIKLNOS	**EEIMMOST**	**EEINRTTY**	**EELLOSSV**	**EEMNNRTY**
noselike	sometime	entirety	loveless	entrymen
EEIKLNSS	**EEIMNORS**	eternity	**EELMMPUX**	**EEMNPRSS**
likeness	emersion	**EEINSSTW**	exemplum	pressmen
EEIKLNST	**EEIMNOST**	newsiest	**EELMNOOS**	**EEMNRSTU**
nestlike	semitone	**EEINSTTW**	lonesome	muenster
EEIKLNTT	**EEIMNRTU**	twenties	**EELMNSUY**	**EEMNSTTV**
tentlike	mutineer	**EEINSTTX**	unseemly	vestment
EEIKPRST	**EEIMORST**	existent	**EELMOPRY**	**EEMOORRV**
perkiest	tiresome	**EEIOPRRT**	employer	moreover
EEIKPSST	**EEIMORTV**	portiere	**EELMORST**	**EEMORSTT**
peskiest	overtime	**EEIOPRST**	molester	remotest
EEILLMPR	**EEIMPSTT**	poetries	**EELMORTY**	**EENNNOSS**
impeller	emptiest	**EEIORRRS**	remotely	nonsense
EEILLMRS	**EEIMQSTU**	orreries	**EELMRSST**	**EENNNOTV**
smellier	mesquite	**EEIORRSS**	termless	nonevent
EEILLNOR	**EEIMRRST**	roseries	**EELMRSTY**	**EENNNPTY**
lonelier	merriest	**EEIORRTX**	smeltery	tenpenny
EEILLORV	**EEIMRRTX**	exterior	**EELNNOSS**	**EENNOPSS**
lovelier	meretrix	**EEIORVVW**	loneness	openness
EEILLPSY	**EEIMRSTU**	overview	**EELNNUVY**	**EENNOPTX**
sleepily	emeritus	**EEIPPPST**	unevenly	exponent
EEILMNSU	**EEIMRTTY**	peppiest	**EELNOPRT**	**EENOORTV**
selenium	temerity	**EEIPPRRS**	petronel	overtone
EEILMSST		perspire	**EELNOQTU**	**EENOPPRS**

propense	forehoof	**EFGIOPTT**	**EFIINNOS**	**EFIORRST**
EENOPRSS	**EFFHOORS**	pettifog	sinfonie	frostier
response	offshore	**EFGIORRV**	**EFIINORR**	**EFIPPRRY**
EENOPRTT	**EFFIIPRS**	forgiver	inferior	frippery
entrepot	spiffier	**EFGLOOVX**	**EFIINORT**	**EFIPRTTY**
EENORRTT	**EFFILMOR**	foxglove	notifier	prettify
rottener	feliform	**EFGLSSTU**	**EFIINOST**	**EFIRRRUY**
EENORSSS	**EFFINOSU**	slugfest	notifies	furriery
soreness	effusion	**EFGNOSST**	**EFIINSTT**	**EFIRRSTU**
EENORSSU	**EFFIPSTU**	songfest	niftiest	furriest
neuroses	puffiest	**EFHIILLT**	**EFIINSUV**	**EFIRRSTU**
EENORSTX	**EFFIRSTU**	helilift	infusive	surfiest
extensor	stuffier	**EFHIILNS**	**EFIIOSSS**	**EFISSSTU**
EENPRSST	**EFFISSTT**	fishline	ossifies	fussiest
pertness	stiffest	**EFHIILRT**	**EFIIPRRU**	**EFISSTTW**
EENPRSSU	**EFFISSUX**	filthier	purifier	swiftest
pureness	suffixes	**EFHIINRS**	**EFIIPRST**	**EFISTUZZ**
EENPSSSU	**EFFOOORT**	finisher	spitfire	fuzziest
suspense	forefoot	refinish	**EFIIPRSU**	**EFKLLOOR**
EENRRTUV	**EFFRRSUU**	**EFHIINSS**	purifies	folklore
venturer	furfures	finishes	**EFIIPSTY**	**EFKORRTW**
EENRSSSU	**EFGGIINN**	**EFHIIRST**	typifies	fretwork
sureness	feigning	shiftier	**EFIIRRTU**	**EFLLLOOW**
EENRSSTT	**EFGGINRU**	**EFHIISST**	fruitier	woolfell
sternest	refuging	fishiest	**EFIISTZZ**	**EFLLLOWY**
EENRSSTU	**EFGHINRT**	**EFHILLSY**	fizziest	fellowly
trueness	frighten	elfishly	**EFIKLORW**	**EFLLNSSU**
EEOPRRRT	**EFGIINNR**	**EFHIOPRS**	lifework	fullness
reporter	infringe	foreship	**EFIKNORS**	**EFLLNTUY**
EEOPRRTX	refining	**EFHIORTT**	foreskin	fluently
exporter	**EFGIINNT**	fortieth	**EFIKNSTU**	**EFLLOORW**
EEOPRSSS	feinting	**EFHIRRTU**	funkiest	follower
espresso	**EFGIINRU**	thurifer	**EFILMSUY**	**EFLLOUWY**
EEOPRSSU	figurine	**EFHKOOOR**	emulsify	woefully
espouser	**EFGIINRY**	forehook	**EFILNNTU**	**EFLLSUUY**
EEOPRSTV	reifying	**EFHLOOSS**	influent	usefully
overstep	**EFGIINRZ**	hoofless	**EFILNORU**	**EFLMMRUY**
EEOPRSUX	friezing	**EFHLOPST**	fluorine	flummery
exposure	**EFGIITUV**	fleshpot	**EFILOOSZ**	**EFLMORRY**
EEORRTUV	fugitive	**EFHLORSY**	floozies	formerly
overture	**EFGILLNO**	horsefly	**EFILOPPR**	**EFLMORSS**
EEORSTVX	lifelong	**EFHLOSUU**	floppier	formless
vortexes	**EFGILLUU**	houseful	**EFILOPST**	**EFLNORTT**
EEPRRSSU	guileful	**EFHLOSUY**	septfoil	frontlet
pressure	**EFGILNNS**	housefly	**EFILOSTT**	**EFLNOSSU**
EFFFILRU	flensing	**EFHRSTTU**	loftiest	foulness
fluffier	**EFGILNRU**	furthest	**EFILPSTU**	**EFLOORSS**
EFFGINOR	feruling	**EFIIILSV**	spiteful	roofless
offering	**EFGILNTT**	vilifies	**EFILRRSU**	**EFLOORVW**
EFFGINSU	fettling	**EFIIINNT**	flurries	overflow
effusing	**EFGILPRU**	infinite	**EFIMNORR**	**EFLOOSST**
EFFHIILS	fireplug	**EFIILMRS**	informer	footless
filefish	**EFGINORV**	flimsier	**EFIMNRSS**	**EFLOPRUW**
EFFHIISW	forgiven	**EFIILMSS**	firmness	powerful
fishwife	**EFGINRRY**	flimsies	**EFIMOQRU**	**EFLORSUY**
EFFHIITT	ferrying	**EFIILMST**	equiform	yourself
fiftieth	**EFGINRSU**	filmiest	**EFINNSTU**	**EFLRSTUU**
EFFHILRW	refusing	**EFIILNTY**	funniest	frustule
whiffler	**EFGINRTT**	felinity	**EFINOPTX**	**EFLRTTUY**
EFFHISTU	fretting	**EFIILNTY**	pontifex	fluttery
huffiest	**EFGINRTU**	finitely	**EFINORRT**	**EFMOORST**
EFFHLRSU	refuting	**EFIILRSU**	frontier	foremost
shuffler	**EFGIOOST**	fusilier	**EFINOSSX**	**EFMOORSU**
EFFHOOOR	goofiest	**EFIIMMNS**	foxiness	foursome
		feminism		

EFNNOOOR
forenoon
EFNOOOTT
footnote
EFNOSSST
softness
EFOOORST
footsore
EFOOPSTT
footstep
EFOORRSW
forswore
EFOORSTT
footrest
EFORRRUW
furrower
EFORRSST
fortress
EFORRSTY
forestry
EGGGIILR
gigglier
EGGHIINN
neighing
EGGHIINW
weighing
EGGIILRW
wigglier
EGGIINNR
reigning
EGGIINNS
singeing
EGGIINNT
tingeing
EGGIINRV
grieving
EGGILNNT
gentling
EGGILNRU
grueling
EGGILNRY
gingerly
EGGILQSU
squiggle
EGGINRRU
grungier
EGGINSSU
guessing
EGGIOSST
soggiest
EGGIPRRY
priggery
EGGLMRSU
smuggler
EGGLRSTU
struggle
EGGNOOSY
geognosy
EGGNSSTU
snuggest
EGGOORSU
gorgeous
EGHHINSS
highness

EGHIILNR
hireling
EGHIIMRT
mightier
EGHIINNR
inhering
EGHIINST
heisting
EGHIINTV
thieving
EGHIIRST
righties
tigerish
EGHILLNO
helloing
EGHILLNS
shelling
EGHILNOV
hoveling
EGHILNPT
penlight
EGHILNPW
whelping
EGHILNRS
shingler
EGHILNSV
shelving
EGHILNSW
welshing
EGHILRST
slighter
EGHILSSS
sighless
EGHILSTT
lightest
EGHIMNUX
exhuming
EGHINNOY
honeying
EGHINNST
sennight
EGHINORV
hovering
EGHINPRS
sphering
EGHINRRU
hungrier
EGHINRSW
shrewing
EGHINTTW
whetting
EGHIOTUW
outweigh
EGHIRRSU
ghurries
EGHIRRUY
hierurgy
EGHIRSTT
rightest
EGHISTTT
tightest
EGHLMNOP
phlegmon
EGHLOOOR

horologe
EGHLOOTY
theology
EGHMNOOY
homogeny
EGHMOPUY
hypogeum
EGHNNOVY
honeyvng
EGHNOOTY
theogony
EGHNORUV
overhung
EGHNRSTT
strength
EGHOOOSW
hoosegow
EGHORSTU
roughest
EGIIKLNN
likening
EGIILNNV
livening
EGIILNOR
religion
EGIILNPR
periling
EGIILNRV
reliving
reviling
EGIILRRS
grislier
EGIILRTU
guiltier
EGIIMNRS
remising
EGIIMNRT
meriting
mitering
EGIIMNRX
remixing
EGIIMNTT
emitting
EGIIMOPT
impetigo
EGIIMRST
grimiest
EGIINNPR
ripening
EGIINNSW
sinewing
EGIINNWZ
wizening
EGIINOPR
peignoir
EGIINORS
seignior
EGIINPRX
expiring
EGIINQTU
quieting
EGIINRRT
retiring
EGIINRST

stingier
EGIINRSV
revising
EGIINRTU
intrigue
EGIINRTV
riveting
EGIINRVV
reviving
EGIINSTX
existing
EGIIPSST
pigsties
EGIJLLNY
jellying
EGIJMMNY
jemmying
EGIJNNOY
enjoying
EGIJNTTY
jettying
EGIKKNRT
trekking
EGIKLLNN
knelling
EGIKLLNY
kellying
EGIKLNOS
songlike
EGIKLNPS
skelping
EGIKLNSS
kingless
EGIKNORV
revoking
EGILLMNS
smelling
EGILLNOV
livelong
EGILLNPS
spelling
EGILLNQU
quelling
EGILLNSW
swelling
EGILMNST
smelting
EGILNNST
nestling
EGILNNTT
nettling
EGILNOPP
peopling
popeling
EGILNORS
resoling
EGILNORW
lowering
roweling
EGILNOSU
ligneous
EGILNOTW
toweling
EGILNOVV

evolving
EGILNPRS
springle
EGILNPRY
replying
EGILNPST
pestling
EGILNRRY
erringly
EGILNRST
sterling
EGILNRUV
veluring
EGILNSSU
ugliness
EGILNSSW
wingless
EGILNSTT
settling
EGILNTUX
exulting
EGILNVXY
vexingly
EGILOSTU
eulogist
EGIMMNST
stemming
EGIMMRST
grimmest
EGIMNORV
removing
EGIMNOSY
moseying
EGIMNPTT
tempting
EGIMNPTY
emptying
EGIMNRSU
resuming
EGINNORT
nitrogen
EGINNRRU
unerring
EGINNRSU
ensuring
EGINOPRS
reposing
EGINOPST
estoping
EGINOPSX
exposing
EGINORTW
towering
EGINORXX
xeroxing
EGINPPPR
prepping
EGINPPST
stepping
EGINPRRS
springer
EGINPRSS
pressing

EGINPRSU perusing	**EGNORSST** songster	**EHIKLNOS** sinkhole	**EHIMSSTU** mushiest	**EHLMORTY** motherly
EGINPRTU erupting reputing	**EGNORSTU** sturgeon	**EHIKLSTU** hulkiest	**EHINNOTW** nonwhite	**EHLMPSSU** humpless
EGINPRTY retyping	**EGNOSTUY** youngest	**EHIKMNST** methinks	**EHINNSST** thinness	**EHLNORSS** hornless
EGINQRUY querying	**EGOORRVW** overgrow	**EHIKNRRS** shrinker	**EHINNSSU** sunshine	**EHLNOSTY** honestly
EGINQSTU questing	**EGOORSTT** grottoes	**EHIKSSTU** huskiest	**EHINNSTT** thinnest	**EHLNSSSU** lushness
EGINRRST stringer	**EGOPRRSS** progress	**EHILLLMO** molehill	**EHINOPPR** hornpipe	**EHLOOPRT** porthole
EGINRRTY retrying	**EHHIIPRS** heirship	**EHILLMOP** philomel	**EHINOPST** phoniest	**EHLOOPTY** holotype
EGINRSTW strewing wresting	**EHHIISTV** thievish	**EHILLRRT** thriller	**EHINORRT** thornier	**EHLORSTY** hostelry
EGINRSVW swerving	**EHHILMNT** helminth	**EHILLSVY** elvishly	**EHINORST** horniest	**EHLORTTT** throttle
EGINRTTU uttering	**EHHIORTT** hitherto	**EHILMOOR** heirloom	**EHINPRSU** punisher	**EHLPSSTU** plushest
EGIOPRSS gossiper	**EHHIRSSW** shrewish	**EHILNORU** unholier	**EHINPSSU** punishes	**EHLRSSTU** ruthless
EGIORSUV grievous	**EHHNOORS** shoehorn	**EHILNOSS** holiness	**EHINPSSX** sphinxes	**EHMMOOOR** homeroom
EGIOSUUX exiguous	**EHHOOSTU** hothouse	**EHILNOTX** xenolith	**EHIOPPPS** popeship	**EHMNOOTW** hometown
EGIRRSTY registry	**EHHRSSTU** thrushes	**EHILOPRT** heliport	**EHIOPPSU** eohippus	**EHMNOPSU** homespun
EGJLNORU jongleur	**EHIIKSSW** whiskies	**EHILOPSS** polishes	**EHIOPRST** trophies	**EHMOORST** smoother
EGLMMSTU glummest	**EHIILLST** hilliest	**EHILORSS** sloshier	**EHIORRTW** worthier	**EHMORSTY** smothery
EGLMNOOY menology	**EHIILMOS** homilies	**EHILPSTU** sulphite	**EHIORSST** horsiest	**EHMORTUV** vermouth
EGLMOPRU promulge	**EHIIMMSS** shimmies	**EHILRSSU** slushier	**EHIORSTT** theorist	**EHMRTUYY** eurythmy
EGLNOOOY oenology	**EHIIMPST** mephitis	**EHILRSTW** whistler	**EHIORSTW** worthies	**EHMSSTUY** thymuses
EGLNOOPY penology	**EHIIMSST** smithies	**EHILSSSW** wishless	**EHIORTWZ** howitzer	**EHNNORRT** northern
EGLNOSSS songless	**EHIIMSSW** whimsies	**EHIMMRSY** shimmery	**EHIOSSTW** showiest	**EHNOOSSW** snowshoe
EGLNRTUY urgently	**EHIINNOS** inhesion	**EHIMNOPR** morphine	**EHIPQSUY** physique	**EHNORSTU** southern
EGLOOPRU prologue	**EHIINNSS** shinnies	**EHIMNORT** thermion	**EHIPSSTU** pushiest	**EHNRSSTU** huntress
EGLOORSY serology	**EHIINSST** shiniest	**EHIMNOTT** monteith	**EHIPSTUU** euphuist	**EHOOPRRT** horopter
EGMNNOSW gownsmen	**EHIINNSW** whinnies	**EHIMNPST** shipment	**EHIQSSSU** squishes	**EHOOPRST** hoopster
EGMNOOOS mongoose	**EHIINSVX** vixenish	**EHIMOOST** smoothie	**EHIRSSTU** rushiest	**EHOOPRTY** orthoepy
EGMNSSSU smugness	**EHIIPRSV** viperish	**EHIMORST** isotherm	**EHKLNOOT** knothole	**EHOOPSTU** housetop
EGNNOOTY ontogeny	**EHIIPSTT** pithiest	**EHIMORTU** mouthier	**EHKMOORW** homework	**EHOORSTV** overshot
EGNNSTTU tungsten	**EHIIRSTT** thirties	**EHIMPPSS** psephism	**EHKMORSW** meshwork	**EHOOSTUU** outhouse
EGNOORRV governor	**EHIISTTX** sixtieth	**EHIMPRRS** shrimper	**EHKNNRSU** shrunken	**EHOPPRSY** prophesy
EGNORRST stronger	**EHIKLMNY** hymnlike	**EHIMPSTU** humpiest	**EHLLNSTU** nutshell	**EHOPRSUV** pushover
	EHIKLNOR hornlike	**EHIMPSUU** euphuism	**EHLLOOOP** loophole	**EIIILPPR** liripipe

EIIIMMNZ	EIILRTUZ	EIINRSTU	EIKNRRRU	looniest
minimize	utilizer	neuritis	knurrier	oilstone
EIIJNRSU	EIILSSTT	EIIOPRRS	EIKOOPRS	EILNOPTY
injuries	siltiest	priories	spookier	linotype
EIIKKLLS	EIIMMNNT	EIIOPSTV	EIKOPRST	EILNORTT
silklike	imminent	positive	porkiest	trotline
EIIKKNST	EIIMMNUZ	EIIORRST	EIKORRWW	EILNOSTV
kinkiest	immunize	riotries	wirework	novelist
EIIKLMST	EIIMMPRU	EIIOSSTT	EIILLMNOU	EILNOTUV
milkiest	imperium	osteitis	linoleum	involute
EIIKLNOR	EIIMNOSS	EIIPPSTZ	EIILLMPSS	EILNPRST
ironlike	emission	zippiest	misspell	splinter
EIIKLSST	EIIMNRST	EIIPRRSS	EIILLMPTU	EILNQUUY
silkiest	minister	prissier	multiple	uniquely
EIIKMPRS	EIIMNRTX	EIIPRSTU	EIILLMUVX	EILNRSTU
skimpier	intermix	purities	vexillum	insulter
EIIKNNRS	EIIMNSTT	EIIPSSTT	EIILLNSTY	EILNRTUV
skinnier	mintiest	tipsiest	silently	virulent
EIIKNNSW	EIIMNSTU	EIIPSSTW	EIILLOORW	EILNSUWY
wineskin	mutinies	wispiest	woollier	unwisely
EIIKRSST	EIIMOPST	EIIQSTTU	EIILLOOSW	EILOPPRS
riskiest	optimise	quietest	woollies	sloppier
EIILLMMR	EIIMOPTZ	EIIRSTTZ	EIILLOPTY	EILOPPST
millirem	optimize	ritziest	politely	loppiest
EIILLMNR	EIIMQSTU	EIISTTTW	EIILLOSTW	EILOPRRT
milliner	quietism	wittiest	lowliest	portlier
EIILLMNU	EIIMSSTT	EIJLLOST	EIILLSSST	EILOPRSU
illumine	mistiest	jolliest	listless	perilous
EIILLPSS	EIINNNPS	EIJLOSTT	EIILLSTT	EILOPRSV
ellipsis	ninepins	joltiest	stillest	slipover
EIILLSST	EIINNOSV	EIJLOSTW	EIILLSTTT	EILORRTU
silliest	envision	jowliest	littlest	ulterior
EIILLSUV	EIINNOUZ	EIJMPSTU	EIILMMSST	EILORTTY
illusive	unionize	jumpiest	slimmest	toiletry
EIILMMOT	EIINNSTT	EIJNORTU	EIILMNOSU	EILOSSTU
immotile	tinniest	jointure	emulsion	lousiest
EIILMNNT	EIINOPRT	EIJNOSTT	EIILMNPSS	EILOSTTT
liniment	pointier	jettison	limpness	stiletto
EIILMOPT	EIINOPTT	EIKKOOST	EIILMNRST	EILPPRSU
impolite	petition	kookiest	minstrel	supplier
EIILMPPR	EIINORRT	EIKLLNUY	EIILMNTUY	EILPPRSY
pimplier	interior	unlikely	minutely	slippery
EIILMSST	EIINORSV	EIKLLORY	EIILMNTUY	EILPPSSU
slimiest	revision	overkill	untimely	supplies
EIILMSTY	EIINOSST	EIKLNPRS	EILMOOST	EILPPSTU
myelitis	noisiest	sprinkle	toilsome	pulpiest
EIILNOSS	EIINPPST	EIKLNRRU	EILMOPRR	EILPRSTY
oiliness	nippiest	knurlier	implorer	priestly
EIILNQTU	EIINPRST	EIKLNSSS	EILMOPST	EILPRSUY
quintile	pristine	skinless	milepost	pleurisy
EIILNSSW	EIINPSST	EIKLSSTU	EILMPPSST	EILPRTTY
wiliness	spiniest	sulkiest	simplest	prettily
EIILNSTT	EIINPTUV	EIKLSTTT	EILMPSTU	EILQRRSU
lintiest	punitive	kittlest	lumpiest	squirrel
EIILNSTY	EIINQRRU	EIKMNOST	EILMRSSY	EILRRSSU
senility	inquirer	tokenism	remissly	slurries
EIILOPST	EIINQTUY	EIKMOSST	EILNNOSS	EILRSSTY
polities	inequity	smokiest	onliness	sisterly
EIILOTVV	EIINRRTW	EIKNORTT	EILNNOST	EILRSTTW
volitive	wintrier	knottiest	insolent	wristlet
EIILPPUZ	EIINRSST	EIKNPRSU	EILNNTTY	EILRSUUX
pupilize	sinister	spunkier	intently	luxuries
EIILPSST	EIINRSSW	EIKNPRTU	EILNOOPP	EILSSTTU
pitiless	wiriness	turnpike	epiploon	lustiest
			EILNOOST	

EIMMMNOOR	**EIMQSTUY**	porpoise	**EKLOOORV**	momentum
monorime	mystique	**EIOOPPST**	overlook	**EMMMNNOTU**
EIMMMNORS	**EIMRSSST**	opposite	**EKLOOPSW**	monument
misnomer	mistress	**EIOORSTT**	slowpoke	**EMMNOTYY**
EIMMOPRU	**EINNOPPT**	rootiest	**ELKORSSW**	metonymy
emporium	penpoint	tortoise	workless	**EMMRSTYY**
EIMMOSTT	**EINNORTU**	**EIOOSSTT**	**EKMRSTUY**	symmetry
totemism	neutrino	sootiest	musketry	**EMNNNOOU**
EIMMPRST	**EINNORTV**	tootsies	**EKNNOPSU**	noumenon
primmest	inventor	**EIOOSTWZ**	unspoken	**EMNNOOOT**
EIMMRSTT	**EINNORWW**	wooziest	**EKOOORTV**	monotone
trimmest	winnower	**EIOPRRSS**	overtook	**EMNOORSU**
EIMMSTUY	**EINNPRSY**	prioress	**EKOORRVW**	enormous
yummiest	spinnery	**EIOPRRST**	overwork	**EMNOORSW**
EIMNNOOT	**EINNPSSU**	sportier	**EKOORTWW**	newsroom
noontime	puniness	**EIOPRRSU**	kowtower	**EMNOOSUV**
EIMNNOTT	**EINNRSTU**	superior	**ELLLMOWY**	venomous
ointment	runniest	**EIOPRSST**	mellowly	**EMNORSUU**
EIMNOPST	**EINNRTTU**	prosiest	**ELLLNSUY**	numerous
nepotism	nutrient	**EIOPRSTT**	sullenly	**EMOPPRRT**
EIMNOPTT	**EINNSSTU**	spottier	**ELLMNOSY**	prompter
impotent	sunniest	**EIOPRSTV**	solemnly	**EMOSSTTW**
EIMNORSU	**EINOPRRS**	sportive	**ELLNOORV**	westmost
monsieur	prisoner	**EIOPRSUV**	lovelorn	**EMPRRTUY**
EIMNORTW	**EINOPRSS**	pervious	**ELLNOSVY**	trumpery
timeworn	pression	previous	slovenly	**EMPRSTTU**
EIMNORTY	**EINOPRTU**	viperous	**ELLOPRST**	strumpet
enormity	eruption	**EIOPSSTU**	pollster	**ENNOOOTZ**
EIMNPRSS	**EINOPSTT**	soupiest	**ELLOPRUV**	entozoon
primness	nepotist	**EIORRRST**	pullover	**ENNOOPPT**
EIMNRSST	**EINOQSTU**	errorist	**ELLORRST**	opponent
trimness	question	**EIORRRTU**	stroller	**ENNOORTV**
EIMNRSTU	**EINOQTTU**	roturier	**ELLOSSSU**	nonvoter
terminus	quotient	**EIORRSST**	soulless	**ENNOPRUV**
EIMOORST	**EINORRTV**	resistor	**ELMNOOSS**	unproven
roomiest	invertor	sorriest	moonless	**ENOOPPST**
EIMOORTZ	**EINORSSS**	**EIORRSTV**	**ELMOORSY**	postpone
motorize	rosiness	servitor	morosely	**ENOOPRSS**
EIMOPPRR	**EINORSSU**	**EIORSTUV**	**ELMPRSSU**	poorness
improper	neurosis	vitreous	rumpless	**ENOPRSUX**
EIMOPRRS	**EINORSSU**	**EIPPRRST**	**ELNNOPTU**	proxenus
primrose	resinous	stripper	nonuplet	**ENOPSSSY**
EIMOPRRT	**EINORSTV**	**EIPQRSTU**	**ELOORSST**	synopses
importer	investor	quipster	rootless	**ENORRTUV**
EIMOPRRV	**EINORSUV**	**EIPRRRSU**	**ELOORSUV**	overturn
improver	souvenir	spurrier	oversoul	turnover
EIMOPRST	**EINOSSTT**	**EIPRRSSU**	**ELOPPRRY**	**ENORSSSU**
imposter	stoniest	surprise	properly	sourness
EIMOQSTU	**EINOSSTW**	**EIPRSSTU**	**ELOPPTYY**	**ENOSSSUU**
misquote	snowiest	pursiest	polytype	sensuous
EIMORRST	**EINPRRTU**	**EIPSSSTU**	**ELOPRSTY**	**EOOORRST**
stormier	prurient	pussiest	prostyle	roseroot
EIMORSTU	**EINPRRTY**	**EIRSSTTU**	**ELOPSSST**	**EOOPRSTV**
moisture	printery	rustiest	spotless	stopover
EIMORSTW	**EINPRSST**	**EJJLNUUY**	**ELOPSSST**	**EOPPRRTY**
wormiest	spinster	jujunely	stopless	property
EIMOSSST	**EINQRTTU**	**EJNSSSTU**	**ELPPSSTU**	**EOPRRUVY**
mossiest	quitrent	justness	supplest	purveyor
EIMOSSTT	**EINRSTTU**	**EKKLNPRU**	**ELPRSSSU**	**EORRRTTU**
moistest	runtiest	kerplunk	spurless	torturer
EIMOSSTU	**EINSSTXY**	**EKKNRSUY**	**ELPRSTTU**	**EORRSSTU**
mousiest	syntexis	skunkery	splutter	trousers
EIMOSTTU	**EINSTTTU**	**EKLNOOOR**	**ELSSSTUY**	**EORRSUVY**
titmouse	nuttiest	onlooker	styluses	surveyor
	EIOOPPRS		**EMMMNOTU**	

EPPPRTUY
puppetry
EPPRSSSU
suppress
FFFGILNU
fluffing
FFGHIINW
whiffing
FFGIILNR
riffling
FFGIINNS
sniffing
FFGILMNU
muffling
FFGILNRU
ruffling
FFGILNSU
sluffing
FFGINNSU
snuffing
FFGINSTU
stuffing
FFHILOSY
offishly
FFHOOOST
offshoot
FFILKORT
forklift
FFILLTUY
fitfully
FFILRTUU
fruitful
FFINOPRT
offprint
FFOORRUU
froufrou
FGGGIINR
frigging
FGGGILNO
flogging
FGGGINOR
frogging
FGGHIINT
fighting
FGGHINTU
gunfight
FGGIILNN
flinging
FGGIINNR
fringing
FGGIINRU
figuring
FGGINOOR
forgoing
FGHIIKNS
kingfish
FGHIINST
shifting
FGHILNSU
flushing
lungfish
FGHILRTU
rightful
FGHINORT

frothing
FGHLORUU
furlough
FGIIIKNN
finiking
FGIIINNX
infixing
FGIIKNRS
frisking
FGIILLNR
frilling
FGIILNPP
flipping
FGIILNRT
flirting
trifling
FGIILNSS
fissling
FGIILNST
stifling
FGIILNTT
flitting
FGIILNZZ
fizzling
FGIINNSU
infusing
FGIINNUX
unfixing
FGIINNUY
unifying
FGIINOST
foisting
FGIINRZZ
frizzing
FGIKLNNU
flunking
FGILNOOR
flooring
FGILNOOZ
foozling
FGILNOPP
flopping
FGILNORU
flouring
FGILNOTU
flouting
FGILNPRU
purfling
FGINNORT
fronting
FGINNORW
frowning
FGINOOPS
spoofing
FGINORST
frosting
FGLNORUW
wrongful
FHHIKOOS
fishhook
FHIILSTY
shiftily
FHILLOOT
foothill

FHILMRTU
mirthful
FHILORSU
flourish
FHIMORSW
fishworm
FHIMPRSU
frumpish
FHLMOTUU
mouthful
FHLORTUY
fourthly
FHLOTUUY
youthful
FHLRTTUU
truthful
FHOOORST
forsooth
FIIINNOX
infixion
FIIINNTY
infinity
FIIKLRSY
friskily
FIILMPSY
simplify
FIILTTUY
futility
FIINNOSU
infusion
FIINORTU
fruition
FIKLLLSU
skillful
FILLLUWY
wilfully
FILLOOPY
polyfoil
FILSTTUY
stultify
FIMOORRT
rotiform
FIMOPPRU
pupiform
FIMORRSU
orsiform
FIORTTUY
fortuity
FIRSTTUU
futurist
FIRTTUUY
futurity
FJLLOUYY
joyfully
FKOOORTW
footwork
FLMNORUU
mournful
FLMORSTU
stormful
FLNOOPSU
spoonful
FLOPRSTU
sportful

FLRSTTUU
trustful
FNOORRSW
forsworn
GGGGIILN
giggling
GGGGILNO
goggling
GGGGILNU
guggling
GGGHIILN
higgling
GGGHIINT
thigging
GGGHINOS
shogging
GGGIIJLN
jiggling
GGGIILNN
niggling
GGGIILNW
wiggling
GGGIINPR
prigging
GGGIINSW
swigging
GGGIJLNO
joggling
GGGIJLNU
juggling
GGGILNOS
slogging
GGGILNPU
plugging
GGGILNRU
gurgling
GGGILNSU
slugging
GGGIMNSU
smugging
GGGINNSU
snugging
GGGINOPR
progging
GGHIILNT
lighting
GGHIINRT
righting
GGHIINST
sighting
GGHIIPRS
priggish
GGHILSSU
sluggish
GGHINORU
roughing
GGHINOST
ghosting
GGHINOTY
hogtying
GGHOOPRS
grogshop
GGIIINNT
igniting

GGIIJLNN
jingling
GGIIILLNR
grilling
GGIILMNN
mingling
GGIILNNS
singling
slinging
GGIILNNT
glinting
tingling
GGIINNNR
grinning
GGIINNOR
groining
ignoring
GGIINNRW
wringing
GGIINNST
stinging
GGIINNSW
swinging
GGIINNTW
twinging
GGIINPPR
gripping
GGIINRTT
gritting
GGILMNOO
glooming
GGILNNOU
lounging
GGILNOPU
plunging
GGILNORW
growling
GGILNORY
glorying
GGILNOSS
glossing
GGILNTTU
glutting
guttling
GGILNUZZ
guzzling
GGIMNOOR
grooming
GGINNOPR
pronging
GGINNOPS
sponging
GGINNORW
wronging
GGINNOSS
singsong
GGINNOTU
tonguing
GGINNRTU
grunting
GGINOORV
grooving
GGINOOTU
outgoing

GGINOPRU	**GHIINWZZ**	shutting	**GIIKNNTT**	**GIILNSTU**
grouping	whizzing	**GHIORTTU**	knitting	linguist
GGINORTU	**GHIIORSV**	outright	**GIIKNPPS**	**GIILNSZZ**
grouting	vigorish	**GHLMOOOY**	skipping	sizzling
GHHIINSW	**GHIIRSTT**	homology	**GIIKNRRS**	**GIILPSTU**
whishing	rightist	**GHLNNOOR**	skirring	pugilist
GHHILOSU	**GHIKLNTY**	longhorn	**GIIKNRST**	**GIIMMNPR**
ghoulish	knightly	**GHLOOORY**	skirting	primming
GHHOORTU	**GHIKLSTY**	horology	striking	**GIIMMNRT**
thorough	skylight	**GHNOSTUU**	**GIIKNSTT**	trimming
GHIIKNNT	**GHILLSTY**	unsought	skitting	**GIIMMNRU**
thinking	slightly	**GIIILMNT**	**GIILLMNU**	immuring
GHIIKNPS	**GHILNOPP**	limiting	illuming	**GIIMMNSW**
kingship	hoppling	**GIIILNNU**	**GIILLNPS**	swimming
GHIIKNRS	**GHILNOSS**	linguini	spilling	**GIIMMNOY**
shirking	sloshing	**GIIIMMNX**	**GIILLNQU**	ignominy
GHIIKNSW	**GHILNRTU**	immixing	quilling	**GIIMNOPS**
whisking	hurtling	**GIIINNOT**	**GIILLNRT**	imposing
GHIILLNS	**GHILNRUY**	ignition	trilling	**GIIMNOTT**
shilling	hungrily	**GIIINNOZ**	**GIILLNST**	omitting
GHIILMTY	**GHILNSTU**	ionizing	stilling	**GIIMNOTV**
mightily	hustling	**GIIINNTV**	**GIILLNSW**	vomiting
GHIILNPR	sunlight	inviting	swilling	**GIIMNPPR**
hirpling	**GHILOPRS**	**GIIINSTV**	**GIILLNTW**	primping
GHIILNRT	shopgirl	visiting	twilling	**GIIMNPRU**
thirling	**GHILPRTY**	**GIIJMMNY**	**GIILMMNS**	umpiring
GHIILNRW	triglyph	jimmying	slimming	**GIIMNPTU**
whirling	**GHIMNORU**	**GIIJMNOS**	**GIILMNPP**	imputing
GHIILTTW	humoring	jingoism	pimpling	**GIIMNSSU**
twilight	**GHIMNOTU**	**GIIJNNOT**	**GIILMNPR**	misusing
GHIIMMNS	mouthing	jointing	rimpling	**GIIMORRS**
shimming	**GHIMNPTU**	**GIIJNNRU**	**GIILMNPW**	rigorism
GHIIMNNU	thumping	injuring	wimpling	**GIINNNOT**
inhuming	**GHIMNSTU**	**GIIJNOST**	**GIILMNPY**	intoning
GHIINNNS	gunsmith	jingoist	implying	**GIINNNPS**
shinning	**GHINNNSU**	joisting	**GIILMNZZ**	spinning
GHIINNNT	shunning	**GIIKKNNS**	mizzling	**GIINNNRU**
thinning	**GHINNOOR**	skinking	**GIILMPSU**	inurning
GHIINNRS	honoring	**GIIKLLNS**	pugilism	**GIINNNTW**
shrining	**GHINNORT**	skilling	**GIILNNPP**	twinning
GHIINOST	northing	**GIIKLNNP**	nippling	**GIINNOPT**
hoisting	throning	plinking	**GIILNOPS**	pointing
GHIINPPS	**GHINNSTU**	**GIIKLNNS**	spoiling	**GIINNPPS**
shipping	shunting	slinking	**GIILNOPT**	snipping
GHIINPPW	**GHINOOPW**	**GIIKLNNT**	piloting	**GIINNPRT**
whipping	whooping	tinkling	**GIILNPPR**	printing
GHIINRRS	**GHINOOST**	**GIIKLNNW**	rippling	**GIINNRSU**
shirring	shooting	winkling	**GIILNPPS**	insuring
GHIINRRW	**GHINOOST**	**GIIKLNRS**	slipping	**GIINNRTU**
whirring	soothing	skirling	**GIILNPPT**	untiring
GHIINRST	**GHINOPPS**	**GIIKLNTT**	tippling	**GIINNSTT**
shirting	shopping	kittling	**GIILNPRT**	stinting
GHIINRSV	**GHINOPPW**	**GIIKMMNS**	tripling	**GIINOPST**
shriving	whopping	skimming	**GIILNQSU**	positing
GHIINRTV	**GHINORST**	**GIIKMNPS**	quisling	**GIINOPTT**
thriving	shorting	skimping	**GIILNQTU**	tiptoing
GHIINRTW	**GHINORTW**	**GIIKMNRS**	quilting	**GIINOPTV**
writhing	throwing	smirking	**GIILNRSW**	pivoting
GHIINSSW	**GHINOSTU**	**GIIKNNNS**	swirling	**GIINPPQU**
swishing	shouting	skinning	**GIILNRTW**	quipping
GHIINSTT	**GHINRRUY**	**GIIKNNOV**	twirling	**GIINPPRT**
shitting	hurrying	invoking	**GIILNSTT**	tripping
GHIINTTW	**GHINSSTU**	**GIIKNNST**	slitting	**GIINPRST**
twinight	hustings	stinking	stilting	striping
	GHINSTTU			

GIINPRSU uprising	**GILMNOTT** mottling	stumming	**GINOPPST** stopping	**GLOOOPSY** posology
GIINPSTT spitting	**GILMNOVY** movingly	**GIMNNORU** mourning	**GINOPRST** sporting	**GLOOOPTY** topology
GIINQRSU squiring	**GILMNPPU** plumping	**GIMNNOTU** mounting	**GINOPSST** signpost	**HHIIPSST** phthisis
GIINQTTU quitting	**GILMNPRU** rumpling	**GIMNNOUV** unmoving	**GINOPSTT** spotting	**HHIORSST** shortish
GIINQUZZ quizzing	**GILMNPSU** slumping	**GIMNOORT** motoring	**GINOPSTU** spouting	**HIIILMNS** nihilism
GIINRRST stirring	**GILMNUZZ** muzzling	**GIMNOOSS** osmosing	**GINORRWY** worrying	**HIIILNST** nihilist
GIINRSTV striving	**GILMOOSY** misology	**GIMNOPST** stomping	**GINORSTY** storying	**HIIILNTY** nihility
GIINSSTU tissuing	**GILNNRSU** nursling	**GIMNOPTU** gumption	**GINORTTT** trotting	**HIIKMRSS** skirmish
GIINSTTW twisting	**GILNNUZZ** nuzzling	**GIMNORRU** rumoring	**GINORTTU** tutoring	**HIIKOPRS** piroshki
GIINTTTW twitting	**GILNOOPS** spooling	**GIMNORRW** ringworm	**GINPRRSU** spurring	**HIIKSSTT** skittish
GIJKLNOY jokingly	**GILNOOST** stooling	**GIMNORST** storming	**GINPRSTU** spurting	**HIILLMMO** millimho
GIJLLNOY jollying	**GILNOOSY** sinology	**GIMNOSYY** misogyny	**GINPRSUU** usurping	**HIILLMOO** milliohm
GIJLNOST jostling	**GILNOOTT** tootling	**GIMNPRTU** trumping	**GINPTTUY** puttying	**HIILMOST** homilist
GIJLNSTU justling	**GILNOOWY** wooingly	**GIMNPSTUS** stumping	**GINRSSTU** trussing	**HIILMPSU** silphium
GIJNOSTU jousting	**GILNOPPP** plopping	**GIMNSTTU** smutting	**GINRSTTU** trusting	**HIILMPSY** impishly
GIKKLNSU skulking	**GILNOPPL** poppling	**GIMNSTYY** stymying	**GINRSTTY** trysting	**HIILMTUY** humility
GIKKNNSU skunking	**GILNOPPS** slopping	**GINNNSTU** stunning	**GINRSTUU** suturing	**HIILPSSY** syphilis
GIKLLNNO knolling	**GILNOPPT** toppling	**GINNOOPS** snooping	**GIOOORSV** vigoroso	**HIIMNSTT** tinsmith
GIKLNNPU plunking	**GILNOPTT** plotting	**GINNOOSW** swooning	**GIOORRSU** rigorous	**HIKNOTTU** outthink
GIKLNNRU knurling	**GILNOSTT** slotting	**GINNOOSZ** snoozing	**GIOORSUV** vigorous	**HIKOOPSS** spookish
GIKLNNUY unkingly	**GILNOSTU** tousling	**GINNOPTU** gunpoint	**GLLOOPTY** polyglot	**HILMNOOT** monolith
GIKNNOTT knotting	**GILNOSZZ** sozzling	**GINNORST** snorting	**GLLOOPWY** pollywog	**HILMPRTU** philtrum
GIKNNOTU knouting	**GILNOTUY** outlying	**GINNOSTU** snouting	**GLMNOOOT** monoglot	**HILNOPSU** unpolish
GIKNOOPS spooking	**GILNPPRU** purpling	**GINNPRSU** spurning	**GLMNOOOY** monology	**HILOOPYZ** zoophily
GIKNOOTW kotowing	**GILNPPSU** suppling	**GINNSTTU** stunting	**GLMNOOOY** nomology	**HILPPRSU** purplish
GIKNORST stroking	**GILNPRSU** slurping	**GINOOPPS** opposing	**GLMOOOPY** pomology	**HILSSTTU** sluttish
GILLNORT trolling	**GILNPRYY** pryingly	**GINOOPRS** spooring	**GLMOORWW** glowworm	**HIMNOPRX** phorminx
GILLNOVY lovingly	**GILNPUZZ** puzzling	**GINOOPRT** trooping	**GLNOOOSY** nosology	**HIMORSTU** humorist
GILLNPUY pulingly	**GILNRRSU** slurring	**GINOOPST** stooping	**GLNOOOTY** ontology	**HINNOORT** ornithon
GILLNSUY sullying	**GILNRSTU** rustling	**GINOOPSW** swooping	**GLNOORUY** runology	**HINNSSUY** sunshiny
GILLOOPW polliwog	**GILNSSTU** tussling	**GINOORST** roosting	**GLNORSTY** strongly	**HINOPSSY** hypnosis
GILMMNSU slumming	**GILOORSU** glorious	**GINOPPPR** propping	**GLNOTTUY** gluttony	**HINOPSTW** township
	GIMMNSTU			**HKOOPRSW**

workshop
HLLLOOWY
hollowly
HLMOOSTY
smoothly
HMMOORSU
mushroom
HMNOOOST
moonshot
HMNOPSYY
symphony
HMOOORSW
showroom
HMOORSUU
humorous
HNOOPRSW
shopworn
HNOORRTW
hornwort
HNORTUWY
unworthy
IIILMRSV
virilism
IIILRTVY
virility
IIIMMPRS
imprimis
IIINQTUY
iniquity
IIJJSTUU
jiujitsu
IIKNOSTT
stotinki
IILLNORT
trillion
IILLNOSU
illusion
IILMOTTY
motility
IILNOOTV
volition
IILOPSST
ptilosis
IILOPSTY
pilosity

IIMMNTUY
immunity
IIMMOPST
optimism
IIMMSTTU
mittimus
IIMNNOOT
monition
IIMNNOSU
unionism
IIMNNOTU
munition
IIMNOOSS
omission
IIMNOPRS
imprison
IIMNORTY
minority
IIMNPRST
misprint
IIMNPTUY
impunity
IIMNRSTY
ministry
IIMOPSTT
optimist
IIMPRTUY
impurity
IIMRRTUV
triumvir
IIMSSTUW
swimsuit
IINNOPPT
pinpoint
IINNOSTU
unionist
IINNSTTU
tinnitus
IINOOPST
position
IIOOSTTY
otiosity
IIOPRRTY
priority
IIORRRSY

irrisory
IIPRSSTU
spiritus
IJJSTUUU
jiujutsu
IKLLOOTV
kilovolt
IKLMORSW
silkworm
IKLNOPST
slipknot
IKNOORRW
ironwork
IKNOPSTT
stinkpot
IKORSTTU
outskirt
ILLLOOPP
lollipop
ILLMPTUY
multiply
ILLOPPSS
slipslop
ILLORSUY
illusory
ILMNOSUU
luminous
ILMSSTUU
stimulus
ILNOOSTU
solution
ILNOOTUV
volution
ILPPRTUY
pulpitry
IMNNOSUU
numinous
IMNOPSTU
sumption
IMNOSTUU
mutinous
IMOOORST
timoroso
IMOOPRST
impostor

IMOOQSTU
mosquito
IMOORSTT
motorist
IMOORSTU
timorous
IMPPPSUY
puppyism
IMRSSTTU
mistrust
INNNNOOU
nonunion
INNNORTU
trunnion
INNORTTU
notturni
INOOPRST
positron
INOOPSTT
spittoon
INOPRTTU
printout
INUPRTUY
punitory
INOPSSSY
synopsis
INOSSTUW
snowsuit
INPRRSTU
surprint
IOORRSTY
sorority
IOORRTTT
trottoir
IOORSSUV
voussoir
IOORSTUV
virtuoso
IOORSUUX
uxorious
IOPRSSUU
spurious
IOPRSTTU
outstrip
IORRSUVV

survivor
IORSSUUU
usurious
IORSTUUV
virtuous
JLNSTUUY
unjustly
JLOOSUYY
joyously
JNNOORRU
nonjuror
KLLMNSUU
numskull
LMNOOOPY
monopoly
LMOOOOPR
poolroom
LMOOOORT
toolroom
LMOOPTYY
polytomy
LNOOOPRT
poltroon
LNOOPSWW
snowplow
LOOPPSUU
populous
LORSSTUU
lustrous
MNNOOOTY
monotony
MNNOSYYY
synonymy
MNORSTUU
surmount
MOOOORRTW
tomorrow
NNOORTTU
notturno
NOOORSSU
sonorous
OORSTTUU
tortuous
OPRSSSUU
sourpuss

9-LETTER WORDS

AAAACMNRT
catamaran
AAAAGLMRS
salagrama
AAAAHHJMR
maharajah
AAAAHINST
athanasia
AAAABBINRR
barbarian
AAABCCHLN
bacchanal
AAABCDRRU
barracuda
AAABCLMRU
ambulacra
AAABDELPT
adaptable
AAABEILLV
available
AAABELLPT
palatable
AAABELMSS
amassable
AAABELRST
alabaster
AAABLLPTY
palatably
AAACCDELV
cavalcade
AAACDLRST
cadastral
AAACEHLNV
avalanche
AAACEMMNR
cameraman
AAACFILNT
fanatical
AAACHLNRT
charlatan
AAACHLPRR
chaparral
AAACILLMR
camarilla
AAACILNST
satanical
AAACILRTU
actuarial
AAACMORST
sarcomata
AAADEGNTV
advantage
AAADELMMR
marmalade

AAADELMTX
malaxated
AAADHHPRZ
haphazard
AAADMNRTY
mandatary
AAAEEHMNR
maharanee
AAAEGGRTV
aggravate
AAAEGLSSV
vassalage
AAAELPRST
palaestra
AAAFRSSSS
sassafras
AAAGHPPRR
paragraph
AAAGILMNS
salaaming
AAAGIMNRV
gravamina
AAAGPRSSU
asparagus
AAAHINPTU
naupathia
AAAIINRST
sanitaria
AAAIJMNRU
marijuana
AAAILMMMN
mammalian
AAAILMORT
amatorial
AAAILNSST
assailant
AAAILPPRS
appraisal
AAAIMNORT
inamorata
AAAINORTT
natatoria
AAALMORTX
malaxator
AAALNRTTU
tarantula
AAAPPRSTU
apparatus
AABBCDKOR
backboard
AABBCGGIN
cabbaging
AABBCKLLL
blackball

AABBDEELT
debatable
AABBDELOR
boardable
AABBDEORS
baseboard
AABBEEKLR
breakable
AABBEHILT
habitable
AABBHILTY
habitably
AABBIMRRS
barbarism
AABBIRRTY
barbarity
AABBORRSU
barbarous
AABCCEHLT
catchable
AABCCEHNT
bacchante
AABCCEKLM
camelback
AABCCHHKT
hatchback
AABCCHKKU
huckaback
AABCCIKKP
pickaback
AABCCIORT
acrobatic
AABCCISSU
abaciscus
AABCCKKRT
backtrack
AABCDDEIT
abdicated
AABCDDORR
cardboard
AABCDEEFR
barefaced
AABCDEEHH
beachhead
AABCDEERT
acerbated
AABCDEIRR
barricade
AABCDEKLP
backpedal
AABCDELNR
barnacled
AABCDEMSU
ambuscade

AABCDENNU
abundance
AABCDHNTW
watchband
AABCDLOPR
clapboard
AABCDNNUY
abundancy
AABCDORST
broadcast
AABCEEELP
peaceable
AABCEEHLT
teachable
AABCEELLV
cleavable
AABCEELNT
enactable
AABCEELPS
escapable
AABCEELPY
peaceably
AABCEENRR
aberrance
AABCEFIRT
fabricate
AABCEFOSU
fabaceous
AABCEGILR
algebraic
AABCEGKST
backstage
AABCEGLMR
cablegram
AABCEHINR
branchiae
AABCEHLMT
matchable
AABCEHLPT
patchable
AABCEILLM
claimable
AABCEILMR
bicameral
AABCEILNP
incapable
AABCEILNT
cantabile
AABCEILRT
bacterial
calibrate
AABCEINOR
anaerobic
AABCEIORT

aerobatic
AABCEKPPR
paperback
AABCELLOR
caballero
AABCELLSS
classable
AABCELMNU
ambulance
AABCELNNU
unbalance
AABCELOOS
calaboose
AABCELRTT
tractable
AABCENORT
carbonate
AABCFHKLS
flashback
AABCGILLN
caballing
AABCGILNN
balancing
AABCHILNR
branchial
AABCIKLLM
blackmail
AABCILNOT
botanical
AABCILOPR
parabolic
AABCKORRZ
razorback
AABCMNOTT
combatant
AABDDEGLS
saddlebag
AABDDEHOR
headboard
AABDDENNO
abandoned
AABDDHORR
hardboard
AABDDHORS
dashboard
AABDDNNST
bandstand
AABDDORRT
dartboard
AABDEELLP
pleadable
AABDEELMN
amendable
AABDEENNO
abandonee
AABDEERRT
aberrated
AABDEFLOR
broadleaf
AABDEGINR
bargained
gabardine
AABDEGORT
abrogated

AABDEGRRY
graybeard
AABDEHLNR
handlebar
AABDEHNSU
unabashed
AABDEILLT
dilatable
AABDEILMR
admirable
AABDEILOV
avoidable
AABDEILRV
adverbial
AABDEILSV
advisable
AABDEINST
abstained
AABDELMST
lambasted
AABDELMTU
ambulated
AABDELOPT
adoptable
AABDELTTU
tabulated
AABDEMORT
dreamboat
AABDENSTW
sweatband
AABDEORSV
bravadoes
AABDEORSX
broadaxes
AABDGGINN
bandaging
AABDGIILR
garibaldi
AABDGNNOW
bandwagon
AABDHORSW
washboard
AABDILLST
balladist
AABDILMNO
abdominal
AABDILSVY
advisably
AABDINSTW
waistband
AABDKLORW
boardwalk
AABDLLORW
wallboard
AABDLNSST
sandblast
AABDLRSTY
bastardly
AABDORRST
starboard
AABEEEGLR
agreeable
AABEEGLLT
bagatelle

AABEEGLRY
agreeably
AABEEHRTT
heartbeat
AABEELLLM
malleable
AABEELLNR
learnable
AABEELORT
elaborate
AABEELPRS
separable
AABEELQTU
equatable
AABEELRTW
tableware
AABEEMNST
abasement
AABEEMNTT
abatement
AABEEQRSU
arabesque
AABEFKRST
breakfast
AABEFLLMM
flammable
AABEFLLPP
flappable
AABEFLMUX
flambeaux
AABEFLORV
favorable
AABEGHLLU
laughable
AABEGHORR
harborage
AABEGILNV
navigable
AABEGINRR
bargainer
AABEHINRR
harebrain
AABEHITTU
habituate
AABEHLOTW
whaleboat
AABEIJKLR
jailbreak
AABEILLNR
ballerina
AABEILLRT
bilateral
AABEILLSW
wallabies
AABEILMNR
lamebrain
AABEILNPT
paintable
AABEILNRT
trainable
AABEIMNOT
abominate
AABEINRST
abstainer

AABEIRRTT
arbitrate
AABEKLNST
beanstalk
AABELLLOW
allowable
AABELLSTU
blastulae
AABELMNNU
unnamable
AABELMNRU
manurable
AABELORST
astrolabe
AABELORTT
rotatable
AABEMOSTT
steamboat
AABEMRRSS
embarrass
AABFLORVY
favorably
AABGHLLUY
laughably
AABGILNVY
navigably
AABGINNTU
unabating
AABGLNOOT
oblongata
AABHIIMNP
amphibian
AABHINRSW
brainwash
AABHIPRRV
vibraharp
AABHMRRTU
barathrum
AABIILLXY
biaxially
AABIILNRR
librarian
AABILMNOS
anabolism
AABILMORS
ambrosial
AABILMPST
baptismal
AABILNOTT
battalion
AABINOSTW
boatswain
AABIRRRTY
arbitrary
AABLLMSYY
abysmally
AABLLNTTY
blatantly
AABLLRTUY
tabularly
AABLORSST
albatross
AABLORTTU
tabulator

AACCDDELO	antarctic	**AACDEINOV**	**AACEEGLSV**
accoladed	**AACCIOPRT**	avoidance	esclavage
AACCDDINY	capacitor	**AACDEINPT**	**AACEEHHRT**
candidacy	**AACCIOPSU**	captained	heartache
AACCDEILM	capacious	**AACDEITTV**	**AACEEJLTU**
acclaimed	**AACCIRSST**	activated	ejaculate
AACCDEJNY	sarcastic	**AACDEKNRS**	**AACEEKMPR**
adjacency	**AACCLMORY**	ransacked	pacemaker
AACCDELLT	cyclorama	**AACDELLOT**	**AACEEKRRT**
catcalled	**AACCLMSTY**	allocated	caretaker
AACCDNORT	cataclysm	**AACDELMTU**	**AACEELNPS**
accordant	**AACCMNOPY**	maculated	pleasance
AACCDGINS	accompany	**AACDELNOT**	**AACEELPRT**
cascading	**AACCOPRRS**	anecdotal	paraclete
AACCDHLRU	sarcocarp	**AACDELNPS**	**AACEELRTT**
archducal	**AACCORTUY**	landscape	altercate
AACCEELNR	autocracy	**AACDELNRT**	**AACEEMMNR**
clearance	**AACDDEELS**	declarant	cameramen
AACCEENRT	escaladed	**AACDEMNTU**	**AACEEOPRS**
reactance	**AACDDEINT**	manducate	aerospace
AACCEHRRT	candidate	**AACDEMRSS**	**AACEFGNRR**
character	**AACDDEIRT**	massacred	fragrance
AACCEILMT	radicated	**AACDENNNO**	**AACEFILLS**
acclimate	**AACDDELNS**	cannonade	fallacies
AACCEILST	scandaled	**AACDENNST**	**AACEFINST**
ascetical	**AACDDEOTV**	ascendant	fascinate
AACCEINSV	advocated	**AACDENORR**	**AACEGHLNR**
vacancies	**AACDEEIMS**	carronade	archangel
AACCEINTV	academies	**AACDENPPT**	**AACEGHNOR**
vaccinate	**AACDEEIMT**	catnapped	anchorage
AACCEIRRT	emaciated	**AACDENSSV**	**AACEGILLN**
ricercata	**AACDEEIRT**	canvassed	angelical
AACCEIRSV	eradicate	**AACDERSTT**	**AACEGILNS**
vaccaries	**AACDEELRT**	castrated	analgesic
AACCEKNRS	lacerated	**AACDERTTT**	**AACEGILRT**
crankcase	**AACDEELST**	attracted	cartilage
AACCELLTU	escalated	**AACDGINNV**	**AACEGINST**
calculate	**AACDEEMRT**	advancing	caseating
AACCELMNU	demarcate	**AACDHINOT**	**AACEGISTT**
calcaneum	macerated	acanthoid	castigate
AACCHINRS	**AACDEETUV**	**AACDHLMNR**	**AACEGLOTU**
saccharin	evacuated	marchland	catalogue
AACCHIRTT	**AACDEETVX**	**AACDHLNPS**	coagulate
cathartic	excavated	handclasp	**AACEGNORR**
AACCIINTT	**AACDEFFIN**	**AACDILLRY**	arrogance
tactician	affianced	radically	**AACEGOPST**
AACCILLSS	**AACDEFIST**	**AACDILMNY**	scapegoat
classical	fasciated	dynamical	**AACEGORTT**
AACCILLUV	**AACDEGILT**	**AACDILORR**	greatcoat
clavicula	glaciated	corradial	**AACEHILMR**
AACCILNNO	**AACDEGLOT**	**AACDIOSUU**	camelhair
canonical	cataloged	audacious	**AACEHILMT**
AACCILNRU	**AACDEGNOS**	**AACDIQRTU**	malachite
canicular	gasconade	quadratic	**AACEHILPT**
AACCILPRT	**AACDEHILN**	**AACDOORTV**	caliphate
practical	enchilada	advocator	**AACEHIMNT**
AACCILTTY	**AACDEHLRT**	**AACDORSTW**	machinate
catalytic	cathedral	coastward	**AACEHIPTT**
AACCIMNOR	**AACDEILLN**	**AACEEFIRT**	apathetic
carcinoma	dalliance	cafeteria	**AACEHKMOR**
macaronic	**AACDEILNZ**	**AACEEFLPT**	hackamore
AACCINPTY	canalized	faceplate	**AACEHKRSV**
captaincy	**AACDEIMPR**	**AACEEGLLR**	haversack
AACCINRTT	paramedic	cellarage	**AACEHNNPS**

snaphance
AACEHNRST
anthraces
AACEHPRTU
parachute
AACEIILNT
laciniate
AACEILLPT
capitella
AACEILLTV
vacillate
AACEILMNP
campanile
AACEILMTV
calmative
AACEILNNT
lancinate
AACEILNPP
appliance
AACEILRSV
cavalries
AACEILTUZ
actualize
AACEIMSTT
masticate
AACEINNRT
incarnate
AACEINNSS
naissance
AACEINRST
ascertain
sectarian
AACEIOSST
associate
AACEIPSTU
auspicate
AACEIPTTV
captivate
AACEIRSST
staircase
AACEIRSTU
actuaries
AACEISTUV
causative
AACELLNOW
allowance
AACELLRST
castellar
AACELMNTT
cattleman
AACELMSST
classmate
AACELNRST
ancestral
AACELORST
escalator
AACELOTUV
autoclave
AACELPRRS
presacral
AACELRTUW
caterwaul
AACEMNNRU
manurance

AACEMNRST
sacrament
AACENNNOY
annoyance
AACENNOSS
assonance
AACENORST
ostracean
AACENRSSU
assurance
AACENRSSV
canvasser
AACEORTVX
excavator
AACFFKPST
packstaff
AACFGLNRY
flagrancy
AACFHJKST
jackshaft
AACFIILNN
financial
AACFILNOT
factional
AACFILORT
factorial
AACFINSTT
fantastic
AACFMNRST
craftsman
AACGGIKNP
packaging
AACGHINTT
attaching
AACGIKNNP
pancaking
AACGIKNTT
attacking
AACGILLLY
glacially
AACGILLMY
magically
AACGILLNN
canalling
AACGILLOS
scagliola
AACGILMNN
manacling
AACGILNPT
placating
AACGILNTT
lactating
AACGIMPRT
pragmatic
AACGINNSV
canvasing
AACGINTTU
actuating
AACGIOSSU
sagacious
AACGLNOOT
octagonal
AACGLNOTU
coagulant

AACHIIPRS
pharisaic
AACHIIRRV
charivari
AACHILOPR
parochial
AACHIMNOR
harmonica
AACHIMNRS
anarchism
AACHIMRRT
matriarch
AACHIMSTT
asthmatic
AACHINRRT
anarthric
AACHINRST
anarchist
AACHIPRRT
patriarch
AACHIRSST
catharsis
AACHLMNOR
monarchal
AACHMNNOR
anchorman
AACHMNOPR
pharmacon
AACHMNSTY
yachtsman
AACHNOSTU
acanthous
AACHOPPRY
apocrypha
AACIILRST
satirical
AACIIMOTX
axiomatic
AACIINPRT
patrician
AACIIPRST
parasitic
AACIISTTV
atavistic
AACILLNRY
ancillary
AACILLOXY
coaxially
AACILLPRY
capillary
AACILLPTY
capitally
AACILNOTT
lactation
AACILNNPPT
applicant
AACILNRST
carnalist
AACILNRUV
navicular
AACILORTU
auctorial
AACILOSSU
salacious

AACILPRTU
capitular
AACILPRTY
paralytic
AACILQTTU
acquittal
AACILSTUY
causality
AACILTTUY
actuality
AACIMNNOPR
panoramic
AACIMNOTT
mactation
AACIMOTTU
automatic
AACIMRRSU
sacrarium
AACIMRTTU
traumatic
AACINNORT
carnation
AACINOOTV
avocation
AACINOPRS
caparison
AACINOSTU
causation
AACINRSST
sacristan
AACIOPRSU
rapacious
AACIOSTTW
waistcoat
AACJKRSTW
jackstraw
AACLLRSTU
claustral
AACLLTTUY
tactually
AACLNRUUV
avuncular
AACLOPRTU
portulaca
AACLPRSUY
scapulary
AACMMOORS
cosmorama
AACMNOTTU
catamount
AACNRSTUY
sanctuary
AADDEEIRT
eradiated
AADDEEMRY
readymade
AADDEENTT
antedated
AADDEGIMR
diagramed
AADDEGLNR
garlanded
AADDEGRTU
graduated

AADDEHNST
headstand
AADDEHRTW
deathward
AADDEILPS
palisaded
AADDEILTV
validated
AADDEIMNR
marinaded
AADDELMNR
dreamland
AADDELRST
astraddle
AADDEQRTU
quadrated
AADDHNNST
handstand
AADDIIMRY
dairymaid
AADDINPRT
dandiprat
AADDLRSTY
dastardly
AADEEGNOR
orangeade
AADEEGNPP
appendage
AADEEHKNS
snakehead
AADEEHPRS
spearhead
AADEEIILNT
alienated
AADEELLMN
allemande
AADEELLMT
malleated
AADEELNPS
esplanade
AADEELPPR
appareled
AADEELPRV
palavered
AADEELTUV
devaluate
evaluated
AADEENSTU
nauseated
AADEEPRST
separated
AADEESTTV
devastate
AADEFGRSU
safeguard
AADEFINST
fantasied
AADEFIORS
aforesaid
AADEFMRST
farmstead
AADEFRRTW
afterward
AADEFSSTT

steadfast
AADEGHNRU
harangued
AADEGHNST
stagehand
AADEGILTT
tailgated
AADEGINPT
paginated
AADEGINRR
arraigned
AADEGINRT
tragedian
AADEGINTV
navigated
AADEGIPRS
disparage
AADEGIQRU
quadrigae
AADEGLLOP
gallopade
AADEGNSTT
stagnated
AADEGORRT
arrogated
AADEGRRVY
graveyard
AADEHHKNS
handshake
AADEHIPRT
apartheid
AADEHLMNN
manhandle
AADEHLMPS
lampshade
AADEHLMRS
marshaled
AADEHLMSY
ashamedly
AADEHLNNP
panhandle
AADEHLNRT
heartland
AADEHLNTW
wheatland
AADEHMNSU
unashamed
AADEHNRTY
anhydrate
AADEHORRW
arrowhead
AADEHPRTT
deathtrap
AADEHRRTW
earthward
AADEIINRT
dietarian
AADEIIRRT
irradiate
AADEIKLLZ
alkalized
AADEILLPT
palliated
AADEILMNT

laminated
AADEILNSZ
nasalized
AADEILNVZ
vandalize
AADEILPPZ
papalized
AADEILRTV
travailed
AADEILSTV
salivated
AADEIMNRT
marinated
AADEIMRTZ
dramatize
AADEINRTT
attainder
AADEINTTT
attainted
AADEIPPRS
appraised
disappear
AADEIPRST
disparate
AADEJKLWY
jaywalked
AADEKMRRT
trademark
AADELLSSY
saleslady
AADELMMOR
melodrama
AADELNNTU
annulated
AADELNSTW
wasteland
AADELPRYZ
paralyzed
AADELSSTU
assaulted
AADEMMNOR
memoranda
AADEMNPRS
ampersand
AADEMNRST
tradesman
AADEMOTTU
automated
AADEMPRRT
ramparted
AADEMPTTU
amputated
AADEMRTTU
maturated
AADENNOTT
annotated
AADENNTTT
attendant
AADENPPRS
sandpaper
AADENRRTW
warranted
AADEOPRSX
paradoxes

AADEOPSSS
passadoes
AADERRSVY
adversary
AADERSTTU
saturated
AADFFIITV
affidavit
AADFILNRY
fairyland
AADFLNOTU
flautando
AADFMNRST
draftsman
AADGGHLRY
haggardly
AADGGINRT
gradating
AADGHIMPR
diaphragm
AADGHINRZ
hazarding
AADGIINRT
radiating
AADGILNNS
sandaling
AADGILNTU
adulating
AADGILORT
gladiator
AADGILRRU
guardrail
AADGIMNNT
mandating
AADGIMNRU
marauding
AADGINORT
gradation
AADGLLNRU
glandular
AADGLLRUY
gradually
AADGLNOOW
wagonload
AADGLNRSS
grassland
AADGMNRSU
guardsman
AADGNNRTU
grandaunt
AADHLMNRS
marshland
AADHNSSTW
washstand
AADHORSUZ
hazardous
AADIINORT
radiation
AADIIORTU
auditoria
AADIIQRUV
quadrivia
AADILLMOR
armadillo

AADILLMPU
palladium
AADILMNSV
vandalism
AADILMOPT
diplomata
AADILMORT
maladroit
AADILMPRY
pyramidal
AADILMRTY
admiralty
AADILNOPT
antipodal
AADILNOTT
antidotal
AADILNOTU
adulation
AADIMNNOT
damnation
AADIMORSS
madarosis
AADIMRSTT
dramatist
AADINNNOT
andantino
AADINOORT
adoration
AADKLRWWY
awkwardly
AADLORTUY
laudatory
AADLRWWYY
waywardly
AADMNORTY
mandatory
AAEEGGGRT
aggregate
AAEEGILNR
generalia
AAEEGIRTV
variegate
AAEEGMNNS
manganese
AAEEGNPRT
parentage
AAEEGNRRR
rearrange
AAEEGNRTU
guarantee
AAEEHLMRX
hexameral
AAEEHLRRS
rehearsal
AAEEHMPST
metaphase
AAEEILLRV
lavaliere
AAEEILLTV
alleviate
AAEEILRTT
retaliate
AAEEKPRRT
parrakeet

AAEELLNPT
panetella
AAEEELLPPT
appellate
AAEELMRTW
metalware
AAEELMSTT
stalemate
AAEELNRTT
alternate
AAEELPRST
palestrae
AAEEMMNTZ
amazement
AAEEMPRRT
parameter
AAEENRRTW
warrantee
AAEENRSSW
awareness
AAEENTTTU
attenuate
AAEEOPRTV
evaporate
AAEEPRTTX
praetexta
AAEFFIILT
affiliate
AAEFGINRS
seafaring
AAEFGIRSX
saxifrage
AAEFGORRS
farragoes
AAEFHMRTT
aftermath
AAEFINSST
fantasies
AAEFINSTZ
fantasize
AAEFINTTU
infatuate
AAEFLLRTW
waterfall
AAEFLNRRT
fraternal
AAEFLNSST
fatalness
AAEGGINNT
gigantean
AAEGGINRV
averaging
AAEGHLNOX
hexagonal
AAEGHNOPR
orphanage
AAEGHNRRU
haranguer
AAEGIKNNW
awakening
AAEGILNNN
annealing
AAEGILNNT
galantine

AAEGILNOS
analogies
AAEGILNOZ
analogize
AAEGILNPP
appealing
AAEGILNRU
neuralgia
AAEGILNVZ
galvanize
AAEGIMMNS
mismanage
AAEGIMNNT
emanating
AAEGIMNNT
manganite
AAEGIMNRR
margarine
AAEGINPPR
appearing
AAEGINPPS
appeasing
AAEGINRRS
granaries
AAEGINRSY
gainsayer
AAEGIRTTV
gravitate
AAEGLNNTT
tangental
AAEGLNRTU
granulate
AAEGLRSSW
glassware
AAEGLRTTU
gratulate
AAEGMNPRT
pentagram
AAEGMRSTT
strategem
AAEGNOPRS
parsonage
AAEGNOPRT
patronage
AAEGNPRTY
pageantry
AAEGOPPRT
propagate
AAEGPRSTU
pasturage
AAEGRRSTZ
stargazer
AAEHILNTV
leviathan
AAEHIMRTU
hematuria
AAEHLNPSX
phalanxes
AAEHMNRSS
sharesman
AAEIILMNZ
animalize
AAEIILRST
aerialist
AAEIIMNNT

inanimate
AAEIKLTTV
talkative
AAEILLMNT
alimental
AAEILLNPS
sailplane
AAEILLPSS
paillasse
AAEILMMNO
melomania
AAEILMNOS
anomalies
AAEILNORT
rationale
AAEILNTTZ
tantalize
AAEILPPTT
palpitate
AAEILRRST
saltierra
AAEIMNNOT
emanation
AAEIMNOST
anatomies
AAEIMNOTZ
anatomize
AAEIMNPRR
repairman
AAEINPPRT
appertain
AAEINQTTU
antiquate
AAEINRRTV
narrative
AAEIPPRRS
appraiser
AAEIPRSST
satrapies
AAEISSSUV
assuasive
AAEJKLRWY
jaywalker
AAEKLPRST
lapstrake
AAEKMRRTW
watermark
AAELLLRTY
laterally
AAELLNPPT
appellant
AAELLPPRW
wallpaper
AAELLSUXY
asexually
AAELMMORR
marmoreal
AAELMMPST
metaplasm
AAELNNOPT
pantaleon
AAELNNRTT
alternant
AAELNPRTY

planetary	japanning	talkathon	antiquary
AAELNPSTT	**AAGIKNPRT**	**AAHKLNOTW**	**AAINSSSTT**
pantalets	partaking	walkathon	assistant
AAELNRSTT	**AAGILLNPP**	**AAHLPPPSY**	**AAIORRTTT**
translate	appalling	slaphappy	trattoria
AAELOPRST	**AAGILLNTV**	**AAHORTWWY**	**AALLNNRUY**
pastorale	gallivant	throwaway	annularly
AAELPRSSY	**AAGILLORT**	**AAIILMMNS**	**AALLNRTUY**
paralyses	alligator	animalism	naturally
AAELRSTTW	**AAGILMNNS**	**AAIILMNST**	**AALLPRSTU**
saltwater	signalman	animalist	plaustral
AAEMNPRTT	**AAGILMNNT**	**AAIILMPRT**	**AALMNOOSU**
apartment	malignant	impartial	anomalous
AAEMNSSTT	**AAGILMNSV**	**AAIILRUXY**	**AALMNOPRT**
statesman	galvanism	auxiliary	patrolman
AAEMPRSTY	**AAGILMNYZ** ₀	**AAIIMNNOT**	**AALMORTYY**
paymaster	amazingly	animation	mayoralty
AAENNNRST	**AAGILMRST**	**AAIIMPPRR**	**AALNNOOPT**
transenna	magistral	primipara	pantaloon
AAENPRSST	**AAGILNNYZ**	**AAIINORTV**	**AALNNRTUU**
apartness	analyzing	variation	unnatural
AAENPRSTY	**AAGILNOST**	**AAILLMMXY**	**AALNOPSST**
peasantry	nostalgia	maximally	postnasal
AAEOPRRST	**AAGILNPPT**	**AAILLMRRY**	**AALOPRRTY**
separator	palpating	armillary	portrayal
AAEOPRSTT	**AAGILNRUU**	**AAILLMRXY**	**AALORSTTY**
pastorate	inaugural	maxillary	saltatory
AAFFFGLST	**AAGILNTUV**	**AAILLNOTV**	**AAMNOOTTU**
flagstaff	valuating	vallation	automaton
AAFGINRWY	**AAGILNWYY**	**AAILLPRTY**	**AAMNOPRTU**
wayfaring	waylaying	partially	paramount
AAGGIINTT	**AAGINNRRT**	**AAILMNPRU**	**AAMNQRRUY**
agitating	narrating	manipular	quarryman
AAGGILNSV	**AAGINNRTT**	**AAILMPRSU**	**AANNOORTT**
salvaging	rattaning	marsupial	annotator
AAGGIMNSS	**AAGINORTV**	**AAILNNPQU**	**AANORSTTU**
massaging	navigator	palanquin	astronaut
AAGGINNRR	**AAGIRSTTY**	**AAILNOSTT**	**AAOOPPRRT**
arranging	sagittary	saltation	paratroop
AAGGINPSS	**AAGLLLNTY**	**AAILNOSTV**	**ABBCDEERU**
passaging	gallantly	salvation	barbecued
AAGGINSSU	**AAGLLNRTY**	**AAILNOTUV**	**ABBCDEFNO**
assuaging	gallantry	valuation	confabbed
AAGHILLNO	**AAGLLNRUY**	**AAILNPRTU**	**ABBCDELRS**
halloaing	angularly	tarpaulin	scrabbled
AAGHINRSS	**AAGLMMMOY**	**AAILORRST**	**ABBCDIKLR**
harassing	mammalogy	sartorial	blackbird
AAGHINSSY	**AAGLNOOSU**	**AAILPRSSY**	**ABBCDKORU**
sashaying	analogous	paralysis	buckboard
AAGHOPRTU	**AAGMOOPSU**	**AAIMMNNOO**	**ABBCEIKRT**
autograph	apogamous	monomania	backbiter
AAGIILNSS	**AAGNNORTU**	**AAIMNOORT**	**ABBCEIRST**
assailing	orangutan	inamorato	crabbiest
AAGIIMNNT	**AAGNORRTU**	**AAIMNOPRY**	**ABBCEIRSY**
animating	guarantor	pyromania	crybabies
AAGIIMNRY	**AAHIMMNSS**	**AAIMNRSTT**	**ABBCEISST**
imaginary	shamanism	tarantism	scabbiest
AAGIINNTT	**AAHINOORR**	**AAINNORRT**	**ABBCGILNS**
attaining	honoraria	narration	scabbling
AAGIINOTT	**AAHINPTTY**	**AAINNORTT**	**ABBCIMOST**
agitation	antipathy	tarnation	bombastic
AAGIINSTT	**AAHIPRRSY**	**AAINOPSTT**	**ABBDDEMOR**
satiating	hairspray	antipasto	bombarded
AAGIJNNNP	**AAHKLNOTT**	**AAINQRTUY**	**ABBDEELOR**

belabored
ABBDEELRS
slabbered
ABBDEILLU
buildable
ABBDEILOT
bobtailed
ABBDEILTU
dubitable
ABBDELOTU
doubtable
ABBDELQSU
squabbled
ABBDGILNR
drabbling
ABBDILLOR
billboard
ABBDIMORR
broadbrim
ABBEFILST
flabbiest
ABBEGIJNR
jabbering
ABBEGINRR
barbering
ABBEHISST
shabbiest
ABBEIMNOZ
bombazine
ABBELMOOZ
bamboozle
ABBELOSTY
stableboy
ABBELQRSU
squabbler
ABBENORST
absorbent
ABBGGILNR
grabbling
ABBGILMNR
brambling
ABBGILOOT
obbligato
ABBGINORS
absorbing
ABBGINQSU
squabbing
ABBHINOOS
baboonish
ABCCEENRU
buccaneer
ABCCELNRU
carbuncle
ABCCEOOST
tobaccoes
ABCCHHKNU
hunchback
ABCCHKOTU
touchback
ABCCIKRST
crabstick
ABCCIRSTU
subarctic
ABCCKORTU

backcourt
ABCCMOORY
mobocracy
ABCDDEEHU
debauched
ABCDDEKLO
blockaded
ABCDDENUS
absconded
ABCDEEHMR
chambered
ABCDEEHSU
debauches
ABCDEEKLN
blackened
ABCDEEKRT
bracketed
ABCDEELMR
clambered
ABCDEFIKL
backfield
ABCDEHIOT
cohabited
ABCDEHKLO
blockhead
ABCDEIKLS
backslide
ABCDEILNO
balconied
ABCDEINTU
incubated
ABCDEIRRV
cabdriver
ABCDEKLOR
blockader
ABCDELMRS
scrambled
ABCDGINOR
brocading
ABCDGINTU
abducting
ABCDHIOPR
chipboard
ABCDIKRRY
brickyard
ABCDILOPR
clipboard
ABCDINOTU
abduction
ABCDKLOOR
roadblock
ABCDKOORR
corkboard
ABCDKOOSW
backwoods
ABCDLNRSU
scrubland
ABCEEELLR
cerebella
ABCEEEILLT
electable
ABCEEEELRT
celebrate
ABCEEEELLRX
erectable

ABCEEELRX
execrable
ABCEEERRT
cerebrate
ABCEEFIRS
briefcase
ABCEEFLOR
forceable
ABCEEGKNR
greenback
ABCEEHLLY
bellyache
ABCEEILPR
priceable
ABCEEILSX
excisable
ABCEEILTX
excitable
ABCEEIMRV
embracive
ABCEEINOS
obeisance
ABCEEKKNR
breakneck
ABCEELMNS
semblance
ABCEELNRT
celebrant
ABCEELNST
albescent
ABCEELOPS
placeboes
ABCEELORV
revocable
ABCEELRSW
screwable
ABCEELRXY
execrably
ABCEELSUX
excusable
ABCEEOSSU
sebaceous
ABCEFHLSU
flashcube
ABCEFIRTU
bifurcate
ABCEFOSTU
obfuscate
ABCEGHILN
bleaching
ABCEGHINR
breaching
ABCEGILLN
becalling
ABCEGILMN
becalming
ABCEGIMNR
cambering
embracing
ABCEHKLLS
shellback
ABCEHKLOS
shoeblack
ABCEHKORS

horseback
ABCEHKRRY
hackberry
ABCEHKTUW
buckwheat
ABCEHLOOS
choosable
ABCEHLOTU
touchable
ABCEHRSSU
subchaser
ABCEIILRS
irascible
ABCEIIMRT
imbricate
ABCEIJNOT
abjection
ABCEILMOT
metabolic
ABCEILNOS
balconies
ABCEILNRU
incurable
ABCEILORT
cabriolet
ABCEILRTU
lubricate
ABCEIMOTV
combative
ABCEIMRTU
bacterium
ABCEINORZ
carbonize
ABCEIRRTU
rubricate
ABCEJNSTU
subjacent
ABCEKLNSS
blackness
ABCELLOOR
colorable
ABCELLRSW
screwball
ABCELMNOY
belomancy
ABCELMOOS
cosmolabe
ABCELMRRS
scrambler
ABCELNOST
constable
ABCELRSTU
scrutable
ABCELRTUU
lucubrate
ABCELSUXY
excusably
ABCEMORSS
crossbeam
ABCENRRRY
cranberry
ABCENRTUU
bucentaur
ABCENSSTU

substance
ABCFHIKLS
blackfish
ABCGGIKPY
piggyback
ABCGHILNN
blanching
ABCGHINNR
branching
ABCGHINOR
broaching
ABCGHLOOS
schoolbag
ABCGIINRS
ascribing
ABCGIINSS
abscising
ABCGIMNOT
combating
ABCHILNOR
bronchial
ABCHILORR
charbroil
ABCHKMOOT
matchbook
ABCHKMTTU
thumbtack
ABCHKORTW
throwback
ABCIIIKLW
bailiwick
ABCIILLMU
umbilical
ABCIILLST
ballistic
ABCIILMOR
microbial
ABCIKLLQU
quillback
ABCIKLLST
blacklist
stickball
ABCILMSTY
cymbalist
ABCILNNOU
connubial
ABCILNORU
binocular
ABCILNRTU
lubricant
ABCILORRU
orbicular
ABCINORTU
incubator
ABCINOSTY
obstinacy
ABCKOOPRS
scrapbook
ABDDDEINS
disbanded
ABDDEEPRS
bedspread
ABDDENHSU
husbanded

ABDDEIORS
broadside
sideboard
ABDDEIPRU
upbraided
ABDDEIRRS
disbarred
ABDDEISSU
disabused
ABDDELOSW
saddlebow
ABDDEORTU
obdurated
ABDDGORUY
bodyguard
ABDDHNORU
hardbound
ABDEEEELMN
emendable
ABDEEEMRS
besmeared
ABDEEFIIT
beatified
ABDEEFILN
definable
ABDEEGGLR
bedraggle
ABDEEGHIN
beheading
ABDEEGINR
gaberdine
ABDEEGMOR
embargoed
ABDEEHLRT
blathered
ABDEEILRS
desirable
ABDEEILRT
liberated
ABDEEILSV
devisable
ABDEEITTU
beatitude
ABDEEKLNT
blanketed
ABDEELMPR
preambled
ABDEELMSS
assembled
ABDEELMTT
embattled
ABDEELNOR
banderole
bandoleer
ABDEELNOT
denotable
ABDEELNRU
endurable
ABDEELRSS
beardless
breadless
ABDEELSSU
subleased
ABDEEMRRW

bedwarmer
ABDEENOTY
bayoneted
ABDEENQTU
banqueted
ABDEENRRT
bartender
ABDEENTTU
debutante
ABDEEOPST
speedboat
ABDEERRST
redbreast
ABDEFINRR
firebrand
ABDEGGINR
badgering
ABDEGIIRR
brigadier
ABDEGIKNR
debarking
ABDEGILOT
obligated
ABDEGINRR
debarring
ABDEHIINT
inhabited
ABDEHILOS
abolished
ABDEHNSTU
sunbathed
ABDEHORSW
showbread
ABDEIILNU
inaudible
ABDEIILST
sibilated
ABDEIJLTU
jubilated
ABDEIKLNR
drinkable
ABDEIKMRS
disembark
ABDEIKNRW
windbreak
ABDEILOPR
parboiled
ABDEILRSY
desirably
ABDEINOST
bastioned
ABDEINRUZ
urbanized
ABDEINSSW
bawdiness
ABDEKNORW
breakdown
ABDELLLSY
syllabled
ABDELLNOO
ballooned
ABDELNNSS
blandness
ABDELNOST

endoblast
ABDELNRUY
endurably
ABDELORUV
boulevard
ABDEMORTU
tamboured
ABDENORSS
broadness
ABDENORST
adsorbent
ABDENOSTU
eastbound
ABDENRSTY
bystander
ABDEOORRV
overboard
ABDEORTTU
obturated
ABDFORRSU
surfboard
ABDGGIINR
abridging
brigading
ABDGIILNS
disabling
ABDGIILNY
abidingly
ABDGINNOU
abounding
ABDGINNRY
brandying
ABDGINORS
signboard
ABDHIMRTY
dithyramb
ABDHINRRT
brandrith
ABDHIOPRS
shipboard
ABDHNRSUY
husbandry
ABDHOOSWX
shadowbox
ABDIILLRS
billiards
ABDIILMOS
diabolism
ABDIMNNOT
badminton
ABDINRSTW
wristband
ABDIRSTUY
absurdity
ABDLMOOOR
broadloom
ABDMMNOSU
ombudsman
ABEEEFKST
beefsteak
ABEEEGGRT
eggbeater
ABEEEGLRU
beleaguer

ABEEEGLTV
vegetable
ABEEELMPR
permeable
ABEEELNRV
venerable
ABEEELRSV
severable
ABEEFFILN
ineffable
ABEEFIIST
beatifies
ABEEFIKRR
firebreak
ABEEGHNOR
habergeon
ABEEGIMNN
bemeaning
ABEEGINRV
bereaving
ABEEGKORR
brokerage
ABEEGLNPR
pregnable
ABEEGMORS
embargoes
ABEEHILRT
heritable
ABEEHIMSV
misbehave
ABEEHINRT
hibernate
ABEEHKOSU
bakehouse
ABEEHLMPS
blaspheme
ABEEHLNOW
whalebone
ABEEHORRS
seborrhea
ABEEHORTU
hereabout
ABEEIINRT
inebriate
ABEEIKLRZ
zebralike
ABEEIKNST
snakebite
ABEEILMRS
miserable
ABEEILMRZ
marbleize
ABEEILMST
estimable
ABEEILMTT
timetable
ABEEILQTU
equitable
ABEEILRST
beastlier
ABEEILRTV
veritable
ABEEILRVZ
verbalize

ABEEIMSSS
embassies
ABEEIRRSS
brasserie
brassiere
ABEEIRRSV
braveries
ABEEIRSTT
batteries
ABEEJLLNY
jellybean
ABEEJLNOY
enjoyable
ABEEKLNNO
anklebone
ABEEKLNSS
bleakness
ABEELLMSS
blameless
ABEELLMTU
umbellate
ABEELLORT
tolerable
ABEELMMOR
memorable
ABEELMNRU
numerable
ABEELMORV
removable
ABEELNNTU
untenable
ABEELNRVY
venerably
ABEELPRSU
superable
ABEELPRTU
reputable
ABEELRRTV
vertebral
ABEEMORRT
barometer
ABEENQRTU
banqueter
ABEENQTTU
banquette
ABEENRSSV
braveness
ABEENRSSZ
brazeness
ABEENRTUX
exuberant
ABEEOSTUU
beauteous
ABEEPRSTT
bespatter
ABEFFILNY
ineffably
ABEFFLOSU
buffaloes
ABEFGILLN
befalling
ABEFGILNR
frangible
ABEFHILST

shiftable
ABEFHIRSZ
zebrafish
ABEFIILLR
fibrillae
ABEFIILNU
unifiable
ABEFIIMRT
fimbriate
ABEFILTUU
beautiful
ABEFINORR
forebrain
ABEFKLSTU
basketful
ABEFLLLMU
flabellum
ABEFLLLUY
balefully
ABEFLLNUY
banefully
ABEFORRTY
ferryboat
ABEFRTTTU
butterfat
ABEGGINSS
bagginess
ABEGHILLT
eightball
ABEGHINRR
harbinger
ABEGHINRT
breathing
ABEGHRSSU
sagebrush
ABEGIILNW
bewailing
ABEGIINOR
aborigine
ABEGIKMNN
embanking
ABEGIKMNR
embarking
ABEGILLLN
labelling
ABEGILMMN
embalming
ABEGILMNY
beamingly
ABEGILMNZ
emblazing
ABEGILNRR
barreling
ABEGILNRT
baltering
ABEGILRTT
litterbag
ABEGIMNNO
bemoaning
ABEGIMRRS
ambergris
ABEGINNRT
bantering
ABEGINNTT

battening
ABEGINRRT
bartering
ABEGINRST
breasting
ABEGINRTT
battering
ABEGINRTY
betraying
ABEGJSTUU
subjugate
ABEGKRSTU
grubstake
ABEGLRSSU
bluegrass
ABEGMNOOR
boomerang
ABEGORSTU
subrogate
ABEHHOSTU
bathhouse
ABEHILRST
herbalist
ABEHILSST
establish
ABEHIMRRU
herbarium
ABEHLMPSY
blasphemy
ABEHLNOOR
honorable
ABEHLOOST
shootable
ABEHLOPRY
hyperbola
ABEHLORTT
betrothal
ABEHNORRT
abhorrent
earthborn
ABEHNRRTU
heartburn
ABEHOOSTU
boathouse
houseboat
ABEIIILST
abilities
ABEIILLLR
illiberal
ABEIILRRS
libraries
ABEIILRRT
irritable
ABEIILSTZ
stabilize
ABEIKNRRV
riverbank
ABEILLLRY
liberally
ABEILLLSU
lullabies
ABEILLNOT
tabellion
ABEILLPSU

plausible
ABEILLSTY
bestially
ABEILLSYZ
syllabize
ABEILMMOV
immovable
ABEILMMTU
immutable
ABEILMRSY
miserably
ABEILMSTU
sublimate
ABEILNPRT
printable
ABEILNRSS
brainless
ABEILNRSU
insurable
ABEILORRT
liberator
ABEILQRTU
quatrible
ABEILQTUY
equitably
ABEILRTUZ
brutalize
ABEILRTVY
veritably
ABEILSTUV
sublative
ABEILSUVY
abusively
ABEIMMNRT
timberman
ABEIMNRST
tribesman
ABEIMNRSU
submarine
ABEINNOST
sanbenito
ABEINNRST
branniest
ABEINNSTT
abstinent
ABEINOSTT
obstinate
ABEINPRST
breastpin
ABEINRSTW
brawniest
ABEIOPRTV
probative
ABEIRRRST
barrister
ABEIRRSSU
bursaries
ABEIRSSST
brassiest
ABEIRSTTT
brattiest
ABEIRTTTU
attribute
ABEKKMOOR

bookmaker
ABEKLNNSS
blankness
ABEKLOOPT
bookplate
ABEKLORTW
worktable
ABELLORTY
tolerably
ABELMMNRU
lumberman
ABELMNOUV
unmovable
ABELNNORV
nonverbal
ABELNOSST
slabstone
ABELNRSTU
subaltern
ABELNRTTU
turntable
ABELOOPPS
opposable
ABELPRSUY
superably
ABEMORRTU
arboretum
ABENORSTV
observant
ABEOPRRSY
soapberry
ABEPRRRSY
raspberry
ABFGIINSY
basifying
ABFHLLSUY
bashfully
ABGGILMNO
gamboling
ABGHIINNS
banishing
ABGHILMNS
shambling
ABGHIMNSU
ambushing
ABGHINORR
abhorring
harboring
ABGHIOPRY
biography
ABGIILLNU
bilingual
ABGIILNRT
librating
ABGIIMTUY
ambiguity
ABGIINNOT
obtaining
ABGIINOTV
obviating
ABGIINPST
baptising
ABGIINPTZ
baptizing

ABGIINRTV
vibrating
ABGIJNNOW
jawboning
ABGILLNOT
balloting
ABGILLNYZ
blazingly
ABGILNNOZ
blazoning
ABGILNOSV
absolving
ABGILNSTU
sublating
ABGIMOSUU
ambiguous
ABGINOPRT
probating
ABHHIRRSU
hairbrush
ABHIKMRRT
birthmark
ABHILMNTU
thumbnail
ABHILNRSU
nailbrush
ABHILNRTY
labyrinth
ABHIOOOPZ
zoophobia
ABHLNOORY
honorably
ABIIILLTY
liability
ABIIILNTY
inability
ABIIILTVY
viability
ABIILLNRT
brilliant
ABIILMRST
tribalism
ABIILNOOT
abolition
ABIILNORT
libration
ABIILNORY
nobiliary
ABIILRRTY
irritably
ABIILSTTY
stability
ABIIMOSTU
ambitious
ABIINORTV
vibration
ABILLMSSY
syllabism
ABILLORRZ
razorbill
ABILLPSUY
plausibly
ABILMMOVY
immovably

ABILMMTUY
immutably
ABILNOSTU
sublation
ABILNRTVY
vibrantly
ABILOORSU
laborious
ABILRTTUY
brutality
ABINOOPRT
probation
ABIRRTTUY
tributary
ABKLMOOPS
psalmbook
ABLNOTUYY
buoyantly
ABMNNORRST
barnstorm
ABMOOOORTT
motorboat
ABNORTTUU
turnabout
ABOOPRSTT
bootstrap
ACCCHKOOR
cockroach
ACCCIILMT
climactic
ACCCNOPUY
occupancy
ACCDDEEEN
decadence
ACCDDEILS
discalced
ACCDEEHIK
chickadee
ACCDEEIST
desiccate
ACCDEEKLN
necklaced
ACCDEEKOP
peacocked
ACCDEELLN
cancelled
ACCDEELNO
concealed
ACCDEELOS
coalesced
ACCDEFIIL
calcified
ACCDEFILY
decalcify
ACCDEGINN
cadencing
ACCDEHRST
scratched
ACCDEIILT
dialectic
ACCDEIORW
cowardice
ACCDEIPRT
practiced

ACCDEMOPT
compacted
ACCDEMORY
democracy
ACCDENOTT
contacted
ACCDENOTU
accounted
ACCDEORRS
scorecard
ACCDFILLY
flaccidly
ACCDGINOR
according
ACCDHHRUY
archduchy
ACCDHORTW
catchword
ACCDIIIRT
diacritic
ACCDINOOR
accordion
ACCDNOORT
concordat
ACCEEEILS
ecclesiae
ACCEEGLMY
megacycle
ACCEEHITZ
catechize
ACCEEHKMT
checkmate
ACCEEHNPR
perchance
ACCEEINNT
accenting
ACCEEIPRS
peccaries
ACCEEIQSU
acquiesce
ACCEEKLOT
cockateel
ACCEELLNR
canceller
ACCEELPST
spectacle
ACCEEOSTU
cetaceous
ACCEFIIRS
sacrifice
ACCEGILNN
canceling
ACCEGINPT
accepting
ACCEGINRT
accreting
ACCEHILNO
cochineal
ACCEHILNT
technical
ACCEHIMST
catechism
schematic
ACCEHIRTT

architect
ACCEHISTT
catchiest
ACCEHLOOT
chocolate
ACCEHORTU
cartouche
ACCEHORTY
theocracy
ACCEHRSST
scratches
ACCEIILMN
calcimine
ACCEIIMNT
cinematic
ACCEIINRT
circinate
ACCEIKLRR
cracklier
ACCEIKRST
crackiest
ACCEIKRSW
wisecrack
ACCEILNTU
inculcate
ACCEILRTU
circulate
ACCEILTUU
cuticulae
ACCEINORT
accretion
ACCEINOSS
accession
ACCEINSTU
encaustic
ACCEIPSTY
cityscape
ACCEJKRSW
jackscrew
ACCELLOOT
collocate
ACCEMOPRT
compacter
ACCENNOTY
cotenancy
ACCENORSU
cancerous
ACCEORRSW
scarecrow
ACCEORRSY
accessory
ACCEORSTU
curuscate
ACCFIILOR
calorific
ACCGHIINN
chicaning
ACCGIKLNR
crackling
ACCGINNOV
concaving
ACCGINOST
accosting
ACCGINSUU

caucusing
ACCHIILRV
chivalric
ACCHILLOO
alcoholic
ACCHIMNOR
monarchic
ACCHIMOST
stomachic
ACCHKLMOT
matchlock
ACCHKLOST
sackcloth
ACCHNOOPY
cacophony
ACCHOSSTU
succotash
ACCIIILNN
clinician
ACCIILNOR
conciliar
ACCIILOPT
occipital
ACCIILTVY
acclivity
ACCIINRST
narcistic
ACCIINRTY
intricacy
ACCIIOPST
pasticcio
ACCIIRSTZ
czaristic
ACCIKNOSW
cockswain
ACCILLMOY
comically
ACCILLNYY
cynically
ACCILRRUU
curricula
ACCINOTVY
concavity
ACCIOPRTY
procacity
ACCLOORST
colorcast
ACCMMOORS
macrocosm
ACCMNOORY
monocracy
nomocracy
ACCMNOTUY
contumacy
ACCMOOPRT
compactor
ACCNNOSTY
constancy
ACCOPRRUY
procuracy
ACDDDEEIT
dedicated
ACDDDEIRS
discarded

ACDDDEKOP
paddocked
ACDDEEEFT
defecated
ACDDEEEERS
decreased
ACDDEEILM
declaimed
ACDDEEIMT
decimated
medicated
ACDDEELSS
declassed
ACDDEEORT
decorated
ACDDEERTT
detracted
ACDDEFIII
acidified
ACDDEGIRS
disgraced
ACDDEIINT
indicated
ACDDEIITV
addictive
ACDDEIJNU
jaundiced
ACDDEILPS
displaced
ACDDEINST
distanced
ACDDEKLOP
padlocked
ACDDEKOST
stockaded
ACDDEMMNO
commanded
ACDDGIINT
addicting
ACDDHHNSU
dachshund
ACDDIINOT
addiction
ACDEEEHNP
cheapened
ACDEEEHNR
adherence
ACDEEEHST
escheated
ACDEEELTT
delectate
ACDEEEMRT
decameter
ACDEEENRT
reenacted
ACDEEENSV
evanesced
ACDEEEPRT
deprecate
ACDEEERRT
recreated
ACDEEERST
decastere
desecrate

ACDEEFFHR
chaffered
ACDEEFHMR
chamfered
ACDEEFIIT
acetified
ACDEEFRRT
refracted
ACDEEGHNX
exchanged
ACDEEGINS
deceasing
ACDEEGLNO
congealed
ACDEEGLOU
decalogue
ACDEEGNSV
scavenged
ACDEEGOPU
decoupage
ACDEEHHTT
hatcheted
ACDEEHIMP
impeached
ACDEEHIRS
cashiered
ACDEEHKNY
hackneyed
ACDEEHLNN
channeled
ACDEEHLPT
chapleted
ACDEEHNNR
channered
ACDEEHNNT
enchanted
ACDEEHNST
chastened
ACDEEHPRT
chaptered
ACDEEHRRT
chartered
ACDEEHRTT
chattered
ACDEEIJTV
adjective
ACDEEILMR
reclaimed
ACDEEILMX
exclaimed
ACDEEILNT
declinate
ACDEEILRT
decaliter
ACDEEILTU
elucidate
ACDEEIMNP
impedance
ACDEEINRS
increased
ACDEEIPRT
predicate
ACDEEISST
ecstasied

ACDEEITUV
educative
ACDEEKLNS
slackened
ACDEELLMR
marcelled
ACDEELLOT
decollate
ocellated
ACDEELNPS
enclasped
ACDEELNTU
nucleated
ACDEELOPS
opalesced
ACDEELORT
relocated
ACDEELPTU
peculated
ACDEELQRU
lacquered
ACDEELRTT
clattered
ACDEELRTU
ulcerated
ACDEEMPRS
scampered
ACDEENNRT
entranced
ACDEENNRU
endurance
ACDEENNRY
decennary
ACDEENORS
coarsened
ACDEENOSS
deaconess
ACDEENRTU
uncreated
ACDEERRTT
retracted
ACDEERSSV
crevassed
ACDEERSTT
scattered
ACDEERTTU
eructated
ACDEERTTX
extracted
ACDEESSTU
decussate
ACDEFFILT
afflicted
ACDEFFMOR
cofferdam
ACDEFGHOU
doughface
ACDEFIIIS
acidifies
ACDEFIILR
clarified
ACDEFIIRS
scarified
ACDEFINRT

infarcted
infracted
ACDEFLNOT
conflated
ACDEFRRTU
fractured
ACDEGGIOP
pedagogic
ACDEGHINR
chagrined
ACDEGHINT
detaching
ACDEGHIRS
discharge
ACDEGHNNU
unchanged
ACDEGILNR
declaring
ACDEGINNS
ascending
ACDEGINNT
decanting
ACDEGINTU
educating
ACDEGIOTT
cogitated
ACDEGIRRT
cartridge
ACDEHHIKT
thickhead
ACDEHHORX
hexachord
ACDEHIIRS
diarchies
ACDEHINNR
hindrance
ACDEHINNU
unchained
ACDEHINSV
cavendish
ACDEHIRSU
duarchies
ACDEHISST
chastised
ACDEHLMSY
chlamydes
ACDEHLNOT
decathlon
ACDEHMOST
stomached
ACDEHMPRY
pachyderm
ACDEHNSTU
unscathed
ACDEHORRV
hardcover
ACDEHPRSU
purchased
ACDEIILMN
medicinal
ACDEIILNT
identical
ACDEIILRV
veridical

ACDEIIMMY
immediacy
ACDEIIMRT
matricide
ACDEIINTV
vindicate
ACDEIIOPR
aperiodic
ACDEIIPRR
parricide
ACDEIIPRT
pediatric
ACDEIKMNN
nicknamed
ACDEIKRST
sidetrack
ACDEILLMY
medically
ACDEILLOZ
localized
ACDEILMNU
unclaimed
ACDEILMPS
misplaced
ACDEILNNP
pinnacled
ACDEILOPR
caprioled
ACDEILORT
loricated
ACDEILOST
dislocate
ACDEILOVZ
vocalized
ACDEILPTU
duplicate
ACDEILRTU
curtailed
ACDEILTUV
victualed
ACDEIMNNT
mendicant
ACDEIMNOP
companied
compendia
ACDEIMNRU
manicured
ACDEIMNTY
mendacity
ACDEINNOR
ordinance
ACDEINNOT
contained
ACDEINNOZ
canonized
ACDEINOPT
captioned
ACDEINORR
coriander
ACDEINOTU
auctioned
cautioned
education
ACDEINPRT

predicant
ACDEINRTU
curtained
ACDEINSTY
syndicate
ACDEIPRST
practised
ACDEIPSTU
cuspidate
ACDEIQTTU
acquitted
ACDEIRSTT
astricted
ACDEJKKSY
skyjacked
ACDEKMMMO
mammocked
ACDELLOPS
collapsed
scalloped
ACDELLORR
corralled
ACDELLOSU
calloused
ACDELMTUU
cumulated
ACDELNNOO
colonnade
ACDELOPTU
copulated
ACDELOSTU
osculated
ACDEMMNOR
commander
ACDEMOORT
motorcade
ACDEMOPSS
compassed
ACDEMORRY
comradery
ACDENNNOU
announced
ACDENNRST
transcend
ACDENOORT
cartooned
coronated
ACDENOOTT
cottonade
ACDENORSY
secondary
ACDENORTU
undercoat
ABDENRTTU
truncated
ACDEOORRT
decorator
ACDEOORTT
doctorate
ACDEORRTT
detractor
ACDFIIRUY
fiduciary
ACDFINNOT

confidant
ACDFOORTW
woodcraft
ACDGIINTT
dictating
ACDGINORR
corrading
ACDGINRSU
crusading
ACDGINRTU
traducing
ACDHIILMO
homicidal
ACDHILRUY
hydraulic
ACDHINORY
diachrony
ACDHORTWW
watchword
ACDIIIMOT
idiomatic
ACDIIJLRU
juridical
ACDIIJRUY
judiciary
ACDIILMNO
dominical
ACDIILSTU
dualistic
ACDIIMPRY
pyramidic
ACDIINORT
indicator
ACDIINOTT
dictation
ACDIIRTTX
dictatrix
ACDIKKNST
kickstand
ACDIKNQSU
quicksand
ACDIKRSTY
yardstick
ACDILLLOO
colloidal
ACDILLORY
cordially
ACDILMOPY
diplomacy
ACDILNORT
doctrinal
ACDILNORU
uncordial
ACDILNOTY
dactylion
ACDILOORT
doctorial
ACDIMORTY
mordacity
ACDINOSTU
custodian
ACDJOORTU
coadjutor
ACDKLORTU

truckload
ACDKORSTY
stockyard
ACDLMNOPW
clampdown
ACDLNOOPT
placodont
ACDMNOORT
macrodont
ACDMOOPRR
comprador
ACDOOORSS
crossroad
ACDORRTUY
courtyard
ACEEEGNNV
vengeance
ACEEEILMP
piecemeal
ACEEEIMPT
peacetime
ACEEEKRRT
racketeer
ACEEELNTY
acetylene
ACEEELSSS
ceaseless
ACEEENRSV
severance
ACEEEPRRT
precreate
ACEEFFLNU
affluence
ACEEFFLTU
effectual
ACEEFHLNP
halfpence
ACEEFILPR
fireplace
ACEEFINNR
refinance
ACEEFINRT
interface
ACEEFIRSS
fricassee
ACEEFLORS
alfrescoe
ACEEGHIRU
gaucherie
ACEEGHLLN
challenge
ACEEGILNV
evangelic
ACEEGILRS
sacrilege
ACEEGINNR
careening
ACEEGINRV
grievance
ACEEGIRTT
cigarette
ACEEGLLOU
colleague
ACEEGLNRT

rectangle
ACEEGLRSS
graceless
ACEEGNORU
encourage
ACEEGNRSV
scavenger
ACEEGOOPR
cooperage
ACEEHIIPR
hairpiece
ACEEHIKRS
hackeries
ACEEHILRT
heretical
ACEEHILRV
chevalier
ACEEHIMNZ
mechanize
ACEEHIMPS
impeaches
ACEEHINST
hesitance
ACEEHIORT
chariotee
ACEEHIPRS
eparchies
parcheesi
ACEEHIPST
peachiest
ACEEHISTT
aesthetic
ACEEHLMNO
chameleon
ACEEHLNRU
herculean
ACEEHLNSS
seneschal
ACEEHLPSS
chapeless
ACEEHLRTW
cartwheel
ACEEHMNRY
archenemy
ACEEHNNRT
enchanter
ACEEHNOPR
canephore
chaperone
ACEEHNRTT
entrechat
ACEEHNSTU
chanteuse
ACEEHPRTY
achetype
ACEEHRRTT
chatterer
ACEEHRRTY
treachery
ACEEIIRSS
scarifies
ACEEIKLNO
oceanlike
ACEEIKRST

creakiest
ACEEILLST
celestial
ACEEILMNS
mescaline
ACEEILNRT
interlace
ACEEILPRS
prelacies
ACEEILPRT
replicate
ACEEILPTX
explicate
ACEEIMMNT
mincemeat
ACEEIMPRT
imprecate
ACEEIMRRS
careerism
ACEEIMRST
creamiest
ACEEINNRS
canneries
ACEEINNRT
nectarine
ACEEINNST
tenancies
ACEEINNTU
enunciate
ACEEINRRS
errancies
ACEEINRST
nectaries
ACEEIORST
esoterica
ACEEIORTX
excoriate
ACEEIRSST
sectaries
ACEEIRTTX
extricate
ACEEIRTUZ
cauterize
ACEEISSST
ecstasies
ACEEISSTZ
ecstasize
ACEELLORT
electoral
ACEELLSSS
scaleless
ACEELMNPT
placement
ACEELMNST
selectman
ACEELMNTT
cattlemen
ACEELMOPS
someplace
ACEELNNSS
cleanness
ACEELNORT
tolerance
ACEELNPTU

petulance
ACEELNRSS
clearness
ACEELNRTU
crenulate
ACEELOPRT
percolate
ACEELORRT
correlate
ACEELORSS
casserole
ACEELPSSS
spaceless
ACEELPSTU
speculate
ACEELRTUY
electuary
ACEELSSSU
causeless
ACEEMNNTT
enactment
ACEEMNRRY
mercenary
ACEENNNOR
cannoneer
ACEENNORS
resonance
ACEENNRTY
centenary
ACEENPRRT
carpenter
ACEENPTTX
expectant
ACEENRSSY
necessary
ACEENRTTU
utterance
ACEENSSTU
acuteness
ACEENSSTX
exactness
ACEEOOPRT
cooperate
ACEERRSST
creatress
ACEERRSTT
streetcar
ACEERRSTY
secretary
ACEERSSST
actresses
ACEFFGINT
affecting
ACEFFHIST
chaffiest
ACEFFHLSS
chaffless
ACEFFHRUU
chauffeur
ACEFFIIOT
officiate
ACEFFINOT
affection
ACEFFOSTU

suffocate
ACEFGHLNU
changeful
ACEFGINPR
prefacing
ACEFHIINT
chieftain
ACEFHINRS
franchise
ACEFHLSTU
scatheful
ACEFHOSUV
vouchsafe
ACEFIILMS
facsimile
ACEFIILRR
clarifier
ACEFIILRS
clarifies
ACEFIINNR
financier
ACEFIINNS
infancies
ACEFIIRRS
scarifier
ACEFIIRRT
artificer
ACEFIJKKN
jackknife
ACEFIKRTU
fruitcake
ACEFILSTU
faculties
ACEFINORT
fornicate
ACEFIORST
factories
ACEFIOSTU
facetious
ACEFIRSTT
craftiest
ACEFLLRUY
carefully
ACEFLNORR
conferral
ACEFLTTUU
fluctuate
ACEGGIRRS
scraggier
ACEGGIRST
craggiest
ACEGHIINV
achieving
ACEGHILNP
chapeling
pleaching
ACEGHILRT
lethargic
ACEGHINNN
enhancing
ACEGHINNS
enchasing
ACEGHINPR
preaching

ACEGHINRS
searching
ACEGHMORT
hectogram
ACEGHOPRR
cerograph
ACEGHRRSU
surcharge
ACEGIILNV
vigilance
ACEGIIMNT
enigmatic
ACEGIIRRT
geriatric
ACEGIJKNT
jacketing
ACEGIKNNR
cankering
ACEGIKNPT
packeting
ACEGIKNRS
screaking
ACEGIKNRT
racketing
ACEGIKPRR
ragpicker
ACEGILLNO
collegian
ACEGILLNR
cellaring
recalling
ACEGILLOT
colligate
ACEGILMNP
emplacing
ACEGILMOP
magalopic
ACEGILNNO
congenial
ACEGILNNS
cleansing
ACEGILNPR
replacing
ACEGILNRU
neuralgic
ACEGIMMRS
scrimmage
ACEGIMNRS
screaming
ACEGIMNRT
centigram
cremating
ACEGINNNP
penancing
ACEGINNOR
ignorance
ACEGINNRT
cantering
recanting
ACEGINNSU
unceasing
ACEGINPPR
recapping
ACEGINPRS

escarping
ACEGINPRT
carpeting
ACEGINPRY
panegyric
ACEGINRRT
retracing
terracing
ACEGINRSS
caressing
ACEGINRST
recasting
ACEGIOPRR
paregoric
ACEGIRSTT
strategic
ACEGJNOTU
conjugate
ACEGLMNRY
clergyman
ACEGNNOTT
cotangent
ACEGNNPRY
pregnancy
ACEGORRTU
corrugate
ACEHHIRRY
hierarchy
ACEHHMNTT
hatchment
ACEHHMOTY
theomachy
ACEHHOOTT
toothache
ACEHIILST
heliastic
ACEHIIRST
charities
ACEHIISTT
atheistic
ACEHIKLST
chalkiest
ACEHIKORT
artichoke
ACEHIKRST
heartsick
ACEHIKSTW
whackiest
ACEHILMST
alchemist
ACEHILNOR
enchorial
ACEHILNTU
unethical
ACEHILPRS
spherical
ACEHILRUV
vehicular
ACEHIMMNS
mechanism
ACEHIMNRY
machinery
ACEHIMRTU
rheumatic

ACEHINORT
anchorite
ACEHINOSV
anchovies
schiavone
ACEHINPRU
paunchier
ACEHINRRU
hurricane
ACEHINRSS
chariness
ACEHINRST
chantries
ACEHINSTY
hesitancy
ACEHINTTU
authentic
ACEHIPPSS
spaceship
ACEHIPSTT
patchiest
ACEHIRSTU
eucharist
ACEHISTTT
chattiest
ACEHKOPRS
packhorse
ACEHKORST
shortcake
ACEHLLLMS
clamshell
ACEHLMSST
matchless
ACEHLOPSU
cephalous
ACEHLOPSW
showplace
ACEHLORTT
charlotte
ACEHMNPRT
parchment
ACEHMNSTY
yachtsmen
ACEHMNTTU
humectant
ACEHMOSTU
moustache
ACEHMPRTY
champerty
ACEHNNRTT
trenchant
ACEHNPRTY
pentarchy
ACEHNRSUZ
schnauzer
ACEHOOSTU
housecoat
ACEHORRST
orchestra
ACEHPRRSU
purchaser
ACEIIILTZ
italicize
ACEIIKMNT

kinematic
ACEIILMPR
empirical
ACEIILMPT
implicate
ACEIILNST
inelastic
scientia
ACEIILOST
socialite
ACEIILOSZ
socialize
ACEIILRST
realistic
ACEIIMPRS
primacies
ACEIIMRST
ameristic
armistice
ACEIINPRS
precision
ACEIINRTT
intricate
ACEIIOPST
opacities
ACEIIPRSS
piscaries
ACEIIPRST
peirastic
ACEIIPRSV
privacies
ACEIISTUV
vacuities
ACEIJKNPS
jacksnipe
ACEIKLPST
skeptical
ACEIKNRST
crankiest
ACEIKNSST
tackiness
ACEIKNSSW
wackiness
ACEILLLNY
cleanlily
ACEILLNOR
collinear
ACEILLOST
oscillate
ACEILLOTV
collative
ACEILLPSY
specially
ACEILLRXY
xerically
ACEILMMST
clammiest
ACEILMNOP
policeman
ACEILMNRU
numerical
ACEILMNSU
calumnies
masculine

ACEILMNTU
culminate
ACEILMOSS
coseismal
ACEILMRRU
mercurial
ACEILNNOT
octennial
ACEILNNTY
anciently
ACEILNOPR
porcelain
ACEILNOST
coastline
sectional
ACEILNOTU
inoculate
ACEILNRTU
centurial
ACEILNRTY
certainly
ACEILNSSS
scaliness
ACEILNUVZ
vulcanize
ACEILOPPS
episcopal
ACEILOQUV
equivocal
ACEILPSTY
specialty
ACEILRTUV
lucrative
ACEILSSST
classiest
ACEILSUWY
sluiceway
ACEILTTUV
cultivate
ACEIMNOPS
companies
ACEIMNORT
cremation
manticore
ACEIMNPTU
pneumatic
ACEIMNRST
miscreant
ACEIMORVW
microwave
ACEIMPRST
crampiest
ACEIMRTTU
micturate
ACEINNNSS
canniness
ACEINNORT
container
ACEINNOSS
ascension
ACEINNRSU
insurance
ACEINNRTU
uncertain

ACEINNSST
incessant
ACEINOOTV
evocation
ACEINOPRS
proscenia
ACEINORRV
carnivore
ACEINORTU
cautioner
ACEINOSST
cessation
ACEINOSTU
tenacious
ACEINPRUY
pecuniary
ACEINPSSU
puissance
ACEINQTTU
quittance
ACEINRRSW
scrawnier
ACEINRSST
scenarist
ACEINRSSZ
craziness
ACEINRTTY
certainty
ACEINSSSU
sauciness
ACEINSSTT
scantiest
ACEIOPTTT
petticoat
ACEIORSTZ
ostracize
ACEIORSUV
veracious
ACEIOSSTW
coastwise
ACEIPPRRS
scrappier
ACEIPPRST
crappiest
ACEIPSSTU
spacesuit
ACEIQSTUY
sequacity
ACEJKKRSY
skyjacker
ACEKKMRRU
muckraker
ACEKLNSSS
slackness
ACEKLRSST
trackless
ACEKNORSU
cankerous
ACEKPRSSU
sapsucker
ACELLMORU
molecular
ACELLNNUY
uncleanly

ACELLNRTY
centrally
ACELLORSS
sclerosal
ACELLORSV
coveralls
ACELLPSSS
scalpless
ACELLSSSS
classless
ACELMMNSU
muscleman
ACELMOPST
ectoplasm
ACELNOOSV
volcanoes
ACELNORSU
larcenous
ACELNOSTU
consulate
ACELNRTTU
reluctant
ACELOOPRR
corporeal
ACELORRSU
carrousel
ACEMMOORT
macrotome
ACEMNOOPS
moonscape
ACEMNOPSS
encompass
ACEMORRTY
crematory
ACEMOSTVY
vasectomy
ACEMPRSUY
supremacy
ACENNNORU
announcer
ACENNSSST
scantness
ACENOOPRT
cooperant
ACENOPRRT
copartner
ACENOPRTY
procreant
ACENOPSTY
syncopate
ACENORRTU
raconteur
ACENORSTU
courtesan
ACENORSUV
cavernous
ACENORTUZ
courtezan
ACENPRRTY
carpentry
ACENPRSUU
pursuance
ACENPTTUU
punctuate
ACENRSSSS

crassness
ACEOOPRRT
corporate
ACEOPRSTT
spectator
ACEORRTTX
extractor
ACERRTUUV
curvature
ACFFGILNS
sclaffing
ACFFIIORY
officiary
ACFGIIMNO
magnifico
ACFGIINNN
financing
ACFGIINPY
pacifying
ACFGINNRU
furnacing
ACFGINORT
factoring
ACFGINRSU
surfacing
ACFGINRTU
furcating
ACFGIOSUU
fugacious
ACFIILLNY
finically
ACFIILNOT
fictional
ACFIIOPRS
saporific
ACFILNOOT
olfaction
ACFILNPPY
flippancy
ACFIMORRY
formicary
ACFINORTU
furcation
ACFIORSTU
fractious
ACFLLTTUY
tactfully
ACFLNTTUU
fluctuant
ACFLOORST
colorfast
ACFLOORTY
olfactory
ACGGIIMNR
grimacing
ACGHHHIIR
highchair
ACGHHINTT
thatching
ACGHIIJKN
hijacking
ACGHIIMNN
machining
ACGHIJKLT

jacklight
ACGHIKLNS
shackling
ACGHIKNOV
havocking
ACGHIKNTW
thwacking
ACGHILNNU
launching
ACGHILORY
oligarchy
ACGHINNOR
anchoring
ACGHINNST
snatching
ACGHINRST
starching
ACGIIKNNP
panicking
ACGIIKNPX
pickaxing
ACGIILLLO
illogical
ACGIILLOR
cigarillo
ACGIILMNX
climaxing
ACGIILNRT
articling
ACGIILNTT
latticing
ACGIIMNPT
impacting
ACGIIMSTT
stigmatic
ACGIINNOR
inorganic
ACGIINNTT
nictating
ACGIINOST
agonistic
ACGIINPSZ
capsizing
ACGIINQRU
acquiring
ACGIINQTU
acquiting
ACGIJLNOU
conjugial
ACGIKNNPU
unpacking
ACGILLLOY
logically
ACGILLNOR
carolling
ACGILLNOR
collaring
ACGILLNOT
collating
ACGILMNOR
clamoring
ACGILNOST
nostalgic
ACGILNOXY
coaxingly

ACGILNRSW
scrawling
ACGIMMORR
microgram
ACGIMNNOR
romancing
ACGIMNOPR
comparing
ACGIMNSTY
gymnastic
ACGIMNUUV
vacuuming
ACGINNNRY
crannying
ACGINNOOT
cognation
contagion
ACGINNORY
crayoning
ACGINNOTZ
cognizant
ACGINNRTU
uncrating
ACGINORSU
carousing
ACGINORTV
cavorting
ACGINPPRS
scrapping
ACGINPRTU
capturing
ACGINPSTU
upcasting
ACGINPTUY
pugnacity
ACGKNNSUY
gunnysack
ACGLMOORY
macrology
ACGLOOSTY
scatology
ACHHILORT
haircloth
ACHHLOSTW
washcloth
ACHIILMSW
whimsical
ACHIIMNST
machinist
ACHIINPSY
physician
ACHIIOPST
pistachio
ACHIIRRTT
arthritic
ACHIIRSTV
archivist
ACHIKLMST
mahlstick
ACHILLOST
sailcloth
ACHILORST
choralist
ACHILRSSY

chrysalis
ACHIMMNOS
monachism
ACHIMMOSS
masochism
ACHIMNORT
chromatin
ACHIMNOST
macintosh
ACHIMOSST
masochist
ACHIMOSTU
mustachio
ACHIMRSSW
scrimshaw
ACHINNOST
stanchion
ACHINOPRT
anthropic
ACHIOPPRS
hippocras
ACHKOPRTW
patchwork
ACHLLORSY
scholarly
ACHLMSTYZ
schmaltzy
ACHLOOSTU
holocaust
ACHLOPRYY
polyarchy
ACHMMNOOY
monomachy
ACHNOPSTY
sycophant
ACHOPSTTW
stopwatch
ACHORTTTU
cutthroat
ACIIILNOS
siciliano
ACIIINPPR
principia
ACIILLNOS
isoclinal
ACIILLNST
scintilla
ACIILLOPT
political
ACIILMNPU
municipal
ACIILMNTY
militancy
ACIILMOSS
socialism
ACIILMOSU
malicious
ACIILMQTU
quitclaim
ACIILNOOT
coalition
ACIILNOPT

plication
ACIILNOVV
convivial
ACIILNPPR
principal
ACIILOPRT
pictorial
ACIILOSST
socialist
ACIILQUZZ
quizzical
ACIIMNNOT
antinomic
ACIIMNOSU
minacious
ACIIMNOTT
manicotti
ACIIMOPRS
micropsia
ACIIMOPST
simpatico
ACIIMPRST
prismatic
ACIINNOTT
nictation
ACIINNOTU
incaution
ACIINPRTU
puritanic
ACIIOPRTT
patriotic
ACIIOPTZZ
pizzicato
ACIIORSUV
vicarious
ACIIOSUVV
vivacious
ACIIPTTVY
captivity
ACIISSTTT
statistic
ACIKLPSST
slapstick
ACILLMSSU
scamillus
ACILLMSUY
musically
ACILLOOQU
colloquia
ACILLORST
cloistral
ACILLPTYY
typically
ACILMMOTT
committal
ACILMNOPT
complaint
compliant
ACILMNOSV
volcanism
ACILMNSUU
unmusical
ACILMSSTU
simulcast

ACILNNOTU
continual
ACILOOPRS
acropolis
ACILOOPST
apostolic
ACILOPPTY
platyopic
ACILOQTUY
loquacity
ACILSSTTY
systaltic
ACIMMORSS
commissar
ACIMNNOOP
companion
ACIMNOOTU
autonomic
ACIMNORST
narcotism
romancist
ACIMORSST
ostracism
ACIMORTTW
microwatt
ACINNORST
constrain
ACINNRTUU
uncurtain
ACINORSST
croissant
ACINORTTU
ructation
ACINRSSSU
narcissus
ACIOORSTU
atrocious
ACIOORSUV
voracious
ACIOPRSTY
piscatory
ACIOPTTUY
autotypic
ACIRSSTUY
casuistry
ACJKOPRST
jockstrap
ACJLLORUY
jocularly
ACKLMOOOR
cloakroom
ACKLNORST
cornstalk
ACKLORSSW
classwork
ACKLORSSW
crosswalk
ACLLLOSUY
callously
ACLLMNOSU
molluscan
ACLLOORRY
corollary
ACLMNOORU
monocular

ACLMOORSS
classroom
ACLMOPSTY
cytoplasm
ACLNNORTU
nocturnal
ACLNOORTT
contralto
ACLOPRTTU
plutocrat
ACMNOORRT
cormorant
ACMNOOSTU
cosmonaut
ACMOORSTU
macrotous
ACMORRSUU
macrurous
ACMORSTUY
customary
ACNNNOOST
consonant
ACNOOPRST
corposant
ADDDEEFRU
defrauded
ADDDEEGLN
gladdened
ADDDEEKLS
skedaddle
ADDDEERSS
addressed
ADDDEFIIN
dandified
ADDDEIINS
disdained
ADDDEISSU
dissuaded
ADDDELNSU
unsaddled
ADDDELRST
straddled
ADDEEEFRT
federated
ADDEEEGHL
headledge
ADDEEEGLT
delegated
ADDEEEGRS
degreased
ADDEEEMNR
meandered
ADDEEENRS
serenaded
ADDEEERSS
addressee
ADDEEFLTU
defaulted
ADDEEFNNT
defendant
ADDEEFORT
foredated
ADDEEGHIP
pigheaded

ADDEEGIRS
disagreed
ADDEEGORT
derogated
ADDEEHILN
headlined
ADDEEHRSS
headdress
ADDEEHRTY
dehydrate
ADDEEIILZ
idealized
ADDEEILMP
impleaded
ADDEEILPT
depilated
ADDEEILRV
daredevil
ADDEEILST
deadliest
ADDEEIMTT
meditated
ADDEEINPT
depainted
ADDEEIPRS
despaired
ADDEEJNRU
jaundered
ADDEEJNSS
jadedness
ADDEELNRS
slandered
ADDEELNRU
laundered
ADDEELOST
desolated
ADDEEMNRU
maundered
ADDEEMORT
moderated
ADDEEMPST
stampeded
ADDEENOTT
detonated
ADDEENRTU
denatured
ADDEEOPRS
desperado
ADDEEPRSU
persuaded
ADDEEPRTU
depurated
ADDEERRSS
readdress
ADDEERSSS
addresses
ADDEERSTW
stewarded
ADDEFIINS
dandifies
ADDEFORRW
forwarded
ADDEGGINR

degrading
ADDEGHINR
hagridden
ADDEGIIMN
diademing
ADDEGIMNN
demanding
maddening
ADDEGINNS
saddening
ADDEGINOS
diagnosed
ADDEGIRRS
disregard
ADDEGLRUY
guardedly
ADDEGNOOR
dragooned
ADDEGNORW
downgrade
ADDEGNRRU
undergrad
ADDEGNRUU
unguarded
ADDEHNNRU
underhand
ADDEIILLS
disallied
ADDEIINST
distained
ADDEIKNPP
kidnapped
ADDEILMMN
middleman
ADDEILMOP
diplomaed
ADDEILNNO
dandelion
ADDEILNRU
underlaid
ADDEILPSY
displayed
ADDEILSVY
advisedly
ADDEIMNOT
dominated
ADDEIMNTY
dynamited
ADDEINNTU
inundated
ADDEINORT
ordinated
ADDEINPRU
underpaid
ADDEINRTU
indurated
ADDEINSUV
unadvised
ADDEIOSVW
disavowed
ADDEISSTT
distasted
ADDELMOTU
modulated

ADDELNTUU
undulated
ADDEMORRY
dromedary
ADDENNORU
unadorned
ADDENNOTU
dauntoned
ADDENNRTU
redundant
ADDENNTUU
undaunted
ADDENOORT
deodorant
ADDENOSTU
astounded
ADDEOPSTT
postdated
ADDEPQRUU
quadruped
ADDFIIQRU
quadrifid
ADDGILNSW
swaddling
ADDGILNTW
twaddling
ADDHHIOOR
hardihood
ADEEEFHRT
feathered
ADEEEGLRT
relegated
ADEEEGLRV
everglade
ADEEEGNRT
generated
ADEEEGTTV
vegetated
ADEEEHLRT
leathered
ADEEEHNRT
heartened
ADEEEHRRS
rehearsed
ADEEEHRTW
weathered
ADEEEILNT
delineate
ADEEEINRS
deaneries
ADEEELMNP
empaneled
ADEEEMPRT
permeated
ADEEENNRX
reannexed
ADEEENRTT
entreated
ADEEENRTV
enervated
veneratad
ADEEEPRST
desperate
ADEEERRTT

retreated
ADEEERSTT
estreated
ADEEFGINN
deafening
ADEEFGINT
defeating
ADEEFIKRR
firedrake
ADEEFILOT
defoliate
ADEEFINRR
refrained
ADEEFLLNN
flanneled
ADEEFLLRY
federally
ADEEFLNTT
flattened
ADEEFLRTT
flattered
ADEEFMNOR
forenamed
ADEEFMORR
forearmed
ADEEGGINS
disengage
ADEEGGIRV
aggrieved
ADEEGGIRW
earwigged
ADEEGGMOU
demagogue
ADEEGGNNR
gangrened
ADEEGGOPU
pedagogue
ADEEGGRST
staggered
ADEEGGRSW
swaggered
ADEEGILLR
galleried
ADEEGILLZ
legalized
ADEEGILNR
realigned
ADEEGILTV
levigated
ADEEGIMNN
demeaning
ADEEGIMRT
emigrated
ADEEGINNR
endearing
grenadine
ADEEGINRR
grenadier
ADEEGINRT
denigrate
ADEEGINST
designate
ADEEGINSV
envisaged

ADEEGINTV
negatived
ADEEGLNNT
entangled
ADEEGLNOT
elongated
ADEEGLNRY
legendary
ADEEGLRTU
regulated
ADEEGMNRT
garmented
ADEEGMNTU
augmented
ADEEGNNUV
unavenged
ADEEGNRST
estranged
ADEEHHNOP
headphone
ADEEHHNRS
harshened
ADEEHILNR
headliner
ADEEHINRT
herniated
ADEEHINSS
headiness
ADEEHIRRV
riverhead
ADEEHISST
diatheses
ADEEHISTT
hesitated
ADEEHKLRS
sheldrake
ADEEHLNSU
unleashed
ADEEHLRST
slathered
ADEEHLSSS
shadeless
ADEEHLSST
deathless
ADEEHMNOT
methadone
ADEEHMOST
homestead
ADEEHNOST
headstone
ADEEHNPPR
apprehend
ADEEHNPRS
sharpened
ADEEHNRSS
harnessed
ADEEHNRTU
unearthed
ADEEHRSTT
shattered
ADEEHRSTV
harvested
ADEEHRSTW
watershed

ADEEHSTUX
exhausted
ADEEIIMMT
immediate
ADEEIIMTV
mediative
ADEEIIRST
dietaries
ADEEILMNP
impaneled
ADEEILMNR
madrilene
ADEEILMPR
epidermal
ADEEILMTZ
metalized
ADEEILNPX
explained
ADEEILNPZ
penalized
ADEEILPPR
reapplied
ADEEILPRV
prevailed
ADEEILPSS
displease
ADEEILQTU
eliquated
ADEEILQUZ
equalized
ADEEILTTV
levitated
ADEEIMNRR
remainder
ADEEIMNST
seminated
ADEEIMRRR
remarried
ADEEIMRST
dreamiest
ADEEIMSST
demitasse
ADEEIMSTT
estimated
ADEEINPRT
pertained
ADEEINRSS
readiness
ADEEIOPTV
videotape
ADEEIPPSS
passepied
ADEEIPRRS
draperies
ADEEIPRTU
repudiate
ADEEIRRST
dreariest
ADEEIRSTV
advertise
ADEEIRSTW
waterside
ADEEIRTTW
tidewater

ADEEIRTTX
extradite
ADEEISSTT
stateside
steadiest
ADEEISTTW
statewide
ADEEKNNSS
nakedness
ADEEKNRTU
undertake
ADEELLMRV
marvelled
ADEELLNRY
learnedly
ADEELNNRU
unlearned
ADEELNRRS
slanderer
ADEELNRRU
launderer
ADEELNRTU
unaltered
ADEELNRUV
unraveled
ADEELORTT
tolerated
ADEELPRST
plastered
ADEELPRSU
pleasured
ADEELQRRU
quarreled
ADEELRRTU
adulterer
ADEELRSTY
steelyard
ADEELRSVY
adversely
ADEEMMNNT
amendment
ADEEMMRST
stammered
ADEEMNOPR
promenade
ADEEMNORT
emendator
ADEEMNRRU
maunderer
ADEEMNRST
smartened
ADEEMNRTY
dynameter
ADEEMPTTT
attempted
ADEEMRSTT
smattered
ADEENNNUX
unannexed
ADEENNORR
nonreader
ADEENORST
resonated
ADEENORTV

renovated
ADEENPPRT
entrapped
ADEENPRRW
prewarned
ADEENPRTT
patterned
ADEENPSST
adeptness
ADEENRRTU
underrate
ADEENRRUW
underwear
ADEENRSTU
sauntered
ADEENRSTY
sedentary
ADEENRTUV
adventure
ADEEOPRSV
eavesdrop
ADEEORRTV
overrated
ADEEORTVX
overtaxed
ADEEPQRTU
parqueted
ADEEPRRTU
departure
ADEEPRSTT
spattered
ADEEPRSTU
depasture
ADEEPRSTY
pederasty
ADEEQRRTU
quartered
ADEERRSSU
reassured
ADEERRSTU
treasured
ADEERRSTV
traversed
ADEERSTYY
yesterday
ADEFFIILS
falsified
ADEFFNORT
affronted
ADEFGHORT
godfather
ADEFGIIMN
magnified
ADEFGIIRT
gratified
ADEFGIKLN
defalking
ADEFGILNT
deflating
ADEFGILRU
lifeguard
ADEFGIMTU
fumigated
ADEFGINRY

defraying
ADEFGLOOT
floodgate
ADEFHINOS
fashioned
ADEFHIRST
headfirst
ADEFHLOOS
falsehood
ADEFIILMP
amplified
ADEFIILNZ
finalized
ADEFIILQU
qualified
ADEFIILRT
airlifted
ADEFIISST
satisfied
ADEFILLSU
fusillade
ADEFILNNZ
zinfandel
ADEFILNOT
deflation
ADEFILNSS
sandflies
ADEFILNTY
defiantly
ADEFILRTT
filtrated
ADEFILSTU
feudalist
ADEFIRSTT
draftiest
ADEFLMMOR
malformed
ADEFMNRST
draftsmen
ADEFOOPRR
proofread
ADEFORRRW
forwarder
ADEFORRTV
overdraft
ADEFORRTW
afterword
ADEGGGINR
daggering
ADEGGGIZZ
zigzagged
ADEGGILNZ
deglazing
ADEGGINNR
deranging
gandering
ADEGGINRR
regarding
ADEGGINSS
degassing
ADEGGLRST
straggled
ADEGGMORT

mortgaged
ADEGGNORU
groundage
ADEGHHILT
headlight
ADEGHILNR
heralding
ADEGHINNR
hardening
ADEGHINRS
garnished
ADEGHINRT
threading
ADEGHINSU
anguished
ADEGHNOUZ
gazehound
ADEGIILNR
derailing
ADEGIILNT
detailing
ADEGIILTT
litigated
ADEGIIMNT
mediating
ADEGIIMTT
mitigated
ADEGIINNR
ingrained
ADEGIINNT
detaining
ADEGIINPR
diapering
ADEGIINSS
diseasing
ADEGIINTV
deviating
ADEGIIRRT
irrigated
ADEGIKLNV
gavelkind
ADEGIKNNR
darkening
ADEGILLNY
leadingly
ADEGILNNU
unaligned
ADEGILNOR
girandole
reloading
ADEGILNOS
alongside
ADEGILNRT
treadling
ADEGILNUV
devaluing
ADEGIMNNR
remanding
ADEGIMNTU
magnitude
ADEGIMOTZ
dogmatize
ADEGINNPP
appending

ADEGINNPR
pandering
ADEGINNPX
expanding
ADEGINNRW
wandering
ADEGINNTT
attending
ADEGINORS
grandiose
ADEGINORZ
organized
ADEGINPRS
spreading
ADEGINPRT
departing
predating
ADEGINPRV
depraving
pervading
ADEGINRRT
retarding
ADEGINRRW
rewarding
ADEGINSTY
steadying
ADEGIPRRT
partridge
ADEGIRTTU
gratitude
ADEGLNNTU
untangled
ADEGLNRST
strangled
ADEGMNRSU
guardsmen
ADEGMOPRR
programed
ADEGNNOPR
pendragon
ADEGNNORW
downrange
ADEGNNORY
androgyne
ADEGNNRSS
grandness
ADEGNORSU
dangerous
ADEHIILNP
delphinia
ADEHIISST
diathesis
ADEHILMNS
mishandle
ADEHILNPR
philander
ADEHIMNRS
sanhedrim
ADEHIMOSU
housemaid
ADEHIMPSS
misshaped
ADEHIMRTY
diathermy

ADEHINNSS
handiness
ADEHINRSS
hardiness
ADEHINRST
tarnished
ADEHINRSV
varnished
ADEHINRTW
handwrite
ADEHINSSS
shadiness
ADEHIOPRT
atrophied
ADEHIOPRZ
aphorized
ADEHIORSW
shadowier
ADEHIPSWW
whipsawed
ADEHIRSTW
dishwater
ADEHKNOSW
shakedown
ADEHLLOSW
shallowed
ADEHMNORS
handsomer
ADEHMOOPS
shampooed
ADEHMOPRY
hypoderma
ADEHNNOVW
handwoven
ADEHNOOPR
harpooned
ADEHNSTUW
unswathed
ADEHOOSTT
statehood
ADEHORRSW
shoreward
ADEIIILNT
initialed
ADEIIINTT
dietitian
initiated
ADEIIIRST
aridities
ADEIIKOST
dakoities
ADEIILLSS
disallies
ADEIILMTT
militated
ADEIILNST
disentail
ADEIILORT
editorial
ADEIILPRS
presidial
ADEIILQTU
liquidate
ADEIILTVZ

vitalized
ADEIIMMXZ
maximized
ADEIIMNOT
mediation
ADEIIMNTT
intimated
ADEIINOTV
deviation
ADEIINPPR
drainpipe
ADEIINSTT
daintiest
dittanies
ADEIINSTZ
sanitized
ADEIIPRRS
disrepair
ADEIIPSST
dissipate
ADEIIRRTT
irritated
ADEIIRSTZ
satirized
ADEIKNPPR
kidnapper
ADEILLMNO
medallion
ADEILLMOT
metalloid
ADEILLMRT
treadmill
ADEILLNST
installed
ADEILLQRU
quadrille
ADEILMMOT
immolated
ADEILMNPT
implanted
ADEILMNST
dismantle
ADEILMOPT
diplomate
ADEILMORZ
moralized
ADEILMPTU
amplitude
ADEILMSTU
simulated
ADEILMTTU
mutilated
ADEILNNRU
underlain
ADEILNOPT
planetoid
ADEILNRSU
laundries
ADEILNSSV
validness
ADEILNSTU
insulated
ADEILOPPT
oppilated

ADEILOPRZ
polarized
ADEILOPST
spoliated
ADEILORSZ
solarized
ADEILPTTU
platitude
ADEILRRUZ
ruralized
ADEILSSTU
lassitude
ADEIMMRST
midstream
ADEIMNNOT
nominated
ADEIMNPRR
reprimand
ADEIMNRRU
unmarried
ADEIMNRSU
nursemaid
ADEIMNRTU
ruminated
ADEIMNRTY
dynamiter
ADEIMORTZ
amortized
ADEIMOTTV
motivated
ADEIMRTUX
admixture
ADEIMRTXY
taxidermy
ADEIMSSTT
misstated
ADEINNOTT
dentation
intonated
ADEINNOTV
innovated
ADEINNRTU
untrained
ADEINNSSS
sandiness
ADEINOPPT
appointed
ADEINOPRR
preordain
ADEINORTZ
notarized
ADEINOSTT
stationed
ADEINPPRS
sandpiper
ADEINPRSS
rapidness
ADEINPSSV
vapidness
ADEINQTUZ
quantized
ADEINRSST
tardiness
ADEINRSTT

transited
ADEINSSTU
sustained
ADEINSSTY
dynasties
ADEIOPRTZ
trapezoid
ADEIOPRVZ
vaporized
ADEIORSTT
storiated
ADEIPPSSY
dyspepsia
ADEIPRTVY
depravity
ADEIRSTVY
adversity
ADEISTTUV
vastitude
ADEJLNORU
journaled
ADDEJNORU
adjourned
ADELLNOPR
landloper
ADELLOPRT
patrolled
ADELLOSWW
swallowed
ADELLRTXY
dextrally
ADELMNNUY
mundanely
ADELMNOOP
lampooned
ADELMSSUY
assumedly
ADELNNORW
landowner
ADELNOOST
loadstone
ADELNORUY
roundelay
ADELNPRUY
underplay
ADELNRSSU
laundress
ADELNSSTU
dauntless
ADELOPPTU
populated
ADELPQRUU
quadruple
ADELRSSUY
assuredly
ADELRSTTU
lustrated
ADEMNNORT
adornment
ADEMOORRT
moderator
ADEMOORST
astrodome
ADENNOSST

sandstone
ADENNOSTY
asyndeton
ADENNSSTW
newsstand
ADENOORST
tornadoes
ADENOORTT
detonator
ADENOPRTV
davenport
ADENORRVW
overdrawn
ADENPRSSU
underpass
ADEOPRRTY
portrayed
predatory
ADEPRSSSU
surpassed
ADFFGINOR
affording
ADFGILNRW
dwarfling
ADFGLNORY
dragonfly
ADFHINRST
firsthand
ADFHLOORY
foolhardy
ADFLLOOST
faldstool
ADFLORRWY
forwardly
ADGGGILNR
draggling
ADGGILNRY
niggardly
ADGGINPRU
upgrading
ADGHIIOPR
idiograph
ADGHILLLU
guildhall
ADGHIINOSW
shadowing
ADGHINRTW
nightward
ADGHNORUY
grayhound
ADGHNOSTU
staghound
ADGIIILST
digitalis
ADGIIINRZ
diarizing
ADGIIJNNO
adjoining
ADGIILMOS
dialogism
ADGIILNYZ
dialyzing
ADGIILOST
dialogist

ADGIIMNRS
disarming
ADGIIMNSY
dismaying
ADGIIMNTT
admitting
ADGIINNNT
indignant
ADGIINNOR
ordaining
ADGIINOSS
diagnosis
ADGIINRTY
dignitary
ADGIJNSTU
adjusting
ADGILLNUY
languidly
ADGILLOSU
gladiolus
ADGILNNOU
unloading
ADGILNORY
adoringly
ADGILNOSS
glissando
ADGILOORY
radiology
ADGIMMOST
dogmatism
ADGIMOSTT
dogmatist
ADGINNOPR
pardoning
ADGINNRST
stranding
ADGINOORS
grandioso
ADGINUPRY
parodying
ADGINOTTU
outdating
ADGINPRSY
dayspring
ADGOOPRST
gastropod
ADHHNOORU
hoarhound
ADHHNORST
shorthand
ADHIIMPSS
amidships
ADHIIOPTY
idiopathy
ADHIKMNNU
humankind
ADHIKNORW
handiwork
ADHINOOST
sainthood
ADHINORTY
hydration
ADHINRTWW
withdrawn

ADHIINSTTW
withstand
ADHLNNORT
northland
ADHMNOOOW
womanhood
ADHMOORSY
hydrosoma
ADHNOORYZ
hydrozoan
ADHNORRTW
northward
ADHOOPRRT
arthropod
ADHORSTTY
hydrostat
ADHORSTUW
southward
ADIILLNVY
invalidly
ADIILMSSS
dismissal
ADIIMNOSS
admission
ADIINOOTX
oxidation
ADIINOQTU
quotidian
ADIINORTT
tradition
ADIIPRSTY
disparity
ADIISSTUY
assiduity
ADIKMNNOW
womankind
ADILLQSUY
squalidly
ADILNSTTY
distantly
ADILORSTW
swordtail
ADINNOORT
antidoron
ADINNOSST
dissonant
ADINOUSTW
satinwood
ADIOQRTUZ
quartzoid
ADIOSSSUU
assiduous
ADJMMOOOR
majordomo
ADLMNORTY
mordantly
ADLNOPRYY
polyandry
ADLOOOSTT
toadstool
ADLOPRSWY
swordplay
ADLORSUUY
arduously

ADLORTUWY
outwardly
ADLPQRUUY
quadruply
ADMMORRTY
martyrdom
ADMNNORSU
roundsman
ADMNORSST
sandstorm
ADMNORSSW
swordsman
ADMOOPPRU
pompadour
AEEEEHMPR
ephemerae
AEEEFHRRT
hereafter
AEEEGGRST
segregate
AEEEGIMNR
menagerie
AEEEGMNRT
agreement
AEEEGNRSS
eagerness
AEEEGRTTZ
gazetteer
AEEEHLMPR
ephemeral
AEEEHLSSY
eyelashes
AEEEHMRTX
hexameter
AEEEIMNRX
reexamine
AEEEIRRTT
reiterate
AEEEKLTTT
teakettle
AEEELLMNT
elemental
AEEELMNTT
elatement
AEEEMNRTU
enumerate
AEEEMORRT
aerometer
AEEEMPRTT
temperate
AEEEMSTTW
sweetmeat
AEEENORTV
overeaten
AEEENORTX
exonerate
AEEENPRTT
penetrate
AEEENRRST
easterner
AEEENTTUX
extenuate
AEEFFILRT
afterlife**

AEEFGLLOT
flageolet
AEEFHLRTT
heartfelt
AEEFILNSS
leafiness
AEEFILOTX
exfoliate
AEEFILRSV
lifesaver
AEEFINSTX
antefixes
AEEFIRRTW
firewater
AEEFLLMSS
flameless
AEEFLLSUY
easefully
AEEFLMRSS
frameless
AEEFLNRST
fenestral
AEEFLNRTT
flattener
AEEFLNSSS
falseness
AEEFLRRTT
flatterer
AEEFMNORS
freemason
AEEFOPRRT
perforate
AEEFORSTT
foretaste
AEEGGLNOY
genealogy
AEEGGMORT
mortgagee
AEEGHHINW
heehawing
AEEGHIMRT
hermitage
AEEGHINRS
garnishee
AEEGHINRT
reheating
AEEGHLPRT
telegraph
AEEGHMNOP
megaphone
AEEGHMRTZ
megahertz
AEEGHOSTU
gatehouse
AEEGIILST
egalities
AEEGIIMRS
imageries
AEEGIKNNW
weakening
AEEGILLRS
allergies
galleries
AEEGILLST

legislate
AEEGILMNN
enameling
AEEGILNNT
eglantine
inelegant
AEEGILNNV
leavening
AEEGILNPR
repealing
AEEGILNRS
releasing
AEEGILNRV
revealing
AEEGILNSS
agileness
AEEGILNTV
elevating
AEEGIMNRT
germinate
AEEGIMNTZ
magnetize
AEEGINNRT
tangerine
AEEGINOPS
espionage
AEEGINOTT
negotiate
AEEGINPRT
repeating
AEEGINPRV
grapevine
AEEGINRTT
integrate
AEEGINSTU
sauteeing
AEEGIPRRS
graperies
AEEGIRSST
greasiest
AEEGLLNRY
generally
AEEGLLNTY
elegantly
AEEGLMNNT
gentleman
AEEGLMNST
segmental
AEEGLMORT
glomerate
AEEGLNRSS
largeness
AEEGLRSSV
graveless
AEEGNOPRS
personage
AEEGNORRT
generator
AEEGNORTU
entourage
AEEGNOTXY
oxygenate
AEEGNPRSS
passenger

AEEGNRSST
greatness
AEEGNSSUV
vagueness
AEEGOPRRT
porterage
AEEHHILRT
healthier
AEEHHNPTY
hyphenate
AEEHHNRTY
heathenry
AEEHILMNW
meanwhile
AEEHILPRS
shapelier
AEEHILRRT
earthlier
AEEHILRTW
wealthier
AEEHIMNPS
misehapen
AEEHIMPRR
epirrhema
AEEHIMPSZ
emphasize
AEEHIMPTZ
empathize
AEEHIMRST
hetaerism
AEEHINPRS
seraphine
AEEHINSSV
heaviness
AEEHIPRST
therapies
AEEHIRSTT
earthiest
heartiest
hesitater
AEEHKLPSW
sheepwalk
AEEHKMMOR
homemaker
AEEHKMORS
shoemaker
AEEHLLOSW
wholesale
AEEHLMSSS
shameless
AEEHLNSST
natheless
AEEHLNSSU
unleashes
AEEHLPSSS
phaseless
shapeless
AEEHLPTTY
telepathy
AEEHLRSST
heartless
AEEHLRTWY
weatherly
AEEHLSTXY

hexastyle
AEEHMMPSY
emphysema
AEEHMNNOP
phenomena
AEEHMOPRS
semaphore
AEEHMPRST
peterhsam
AEEHNPRRS
sharpener
AEEHNRRSS
harnesser
AEEHNRRTY
erythrean
AEEHORRST
heartsore
AEEHORSUW
warehouse
AEEHPRSTU
superheat
AEEHRRSTT
shatterer
AEEHRRSTV
harvester
AEEIILMNT
eliminate
AEEIILRST
realities
AEEIILRSZ
serialize
AEEIIMNST
amenities
AEEIINPTX
inexpiate
AEEIINSTV
naiveties
AEEIINSTX
anxieties
AEEIIRSTV
varieties
AEEIJMSST
majesties
AEEIKKLNS
snakelike
AEEIKLSTW
weakliest
AEEIKNRSV
knaveries
AEEIKNSST
sneakiest
AEEIKQRSU
squeakier
AEEIKRRST
streakier
AEEILLMTZ
metallize
AEEILLPTT
paillette
AEEILLSTT
satellite
AEEILMNNT
lineament
AEEILMNRT

marteline
AEEILMNSS
mealiness
messaline
AEEILMORT
meliorate
AEEILMRTT
altimeter
AEEILMTUV
emulative
AEEILNNPR
perennial
AEEILNNSX
sexennial
AEEILNNTV
valentine
AEEILNOTV
elevation
AEEILNPPP
pineapple
AEEILNPST
penalties
AEEILNRSS
earliness
AEEILNSST
essential
AEEILNTTV
ventilate
AEEILPPRS
reapplies
AEEILPRST
pearliest
AEEILQRUZ
equalizer
AEEILRSTT
statelier
AEEILRSTV
versatile
AEEILSSTZ
sleaziest
AEEILSUXZ
sexualize
AEEILSVVY
evasively
AEEIMNNZZ
mezzanine
AEEIMNPRR
repairmen
AEEIMNRTT
terminate
AEEIMNSSS
seaminess
AEEIMNSST
amnesties
meatiness
AEEIMORSW
wearisome
AEEIMRRRS
remarries
AEEIMRSST
smeariest
AEEIMRSTV
timesaver
AEEIMSSTT

steamiest
AEEINNRST
tanneries
AEEINNRTT
entertain
AEEINOPPT
appointee
AEEINORTT
orientate
AEEINPRSS
parenesis
AEEINRSSW
weariness
AEEINRSTT
reinstate
AEEINRSTY
eyestrain
AEEINSSTV
assentive
AEEINSTTT
intestate
AEEINTTTV
attentive
AEEIOPRTV
operative
AEEIPPRTZ
appetizer
AEEIPRRTV
privateer
AEEIPRSSS
pessaries
AEEIPRSVV
pervasive
AEEIPRTTX
extirpate
AEEIQSSTU
queasiest
AEEIRSSTU
estuaries
AEEIRSSTV
assertive
AEEISSTTW
sweatiest
AEEJKRRTW
jerkwater
AEEJMORTT
majorette
AEEKLLSSS
slakeless
AEEKMNRSW
newsmaker
AEEKMNRTW
newmarket
AEEKNORTV
overtaken
AEELLNRTY
eternally
AEELLRSVY
severally
AEELLSSUV
valueless
AEELMNPSS
ampleness

AEELMNRTT
letterman
AEELMORST
elastomer
AEELMPRXY
exemplary
AEELMRSST
semestral
AEELNNNTU
antennule
AEELNNOSS
aloneness
AEELNPRTV
prevalent
AEELNQSSU
equalness
AEELNRSST
alertness
AEELNRSTY
earnestly
AEELORTVY
elevatory
AEELPPRRU
puerperal
AEELPPRTU
perpetual
AEELPQTTU
plaquette
AEELPRSTT
saltpeter
AEELQRRRU
quarreler
AEELRSSTW
waterless
AEELRSTVY
severalty
AEELSSSTT
tasteless
AEELSSSTW
wasteless
AEEMMNSTU
amusement
AEEMNNOTT
atonement
AEEMNNPRT
permanent
AEEMNOPSU
menopause
AEEMNPSST
passement
AEEMNRTTT
treatment
AEEMNSSTT
statesmen
AEEMNSTTT
statement
testament
AEEMPRRTU
premature
AEENNPRTT
penetrant
AEENOPPRT
notepaper
AEENOPTTT

potentate
AEENORSTW
stoneware
AEENPPRSW
newspaper
AEENPRRTU
enrapture
AEENPRSTY
septenary
AEENSSSUV
suaveness
AEEOPRSTT
poetaster
AEEORSTTV
overstate
AEEPSSSTU
petasuses
AEEQRRRTU
quarterer
AEERRRSTU
treasurer
AEESTTTTU
statuette
AEFFHORST
foreshaft
AEFFIILRS
falsifier
AEFFIILSS
falsifies
AEFFLLRUY
fearfully
AEFFLLTUY
fatefully
AEFFLORSW
safflower
AEFGHINRT
fathering
AEFGHORRT
forgather
AEFGIIMNR
magnifier
AEFGIIMNS
magnifies
AEFGIIRRT
gratifier
AEFGIIRST
gratifies
AEFGILMNN
enflaming
AEFGILNRT
faltering
AEFGINNST
fastening
AEFGINNTT
fattening
AEFGINRRY
rarefying
AEFGINRTU
featuring
AEFGISTTU
fustigate
AEFGLLLMU
flagellum
AEFGLNOST

flagstone
AEFGLRTUU
fulgurate
AEFHHLLTU
healthful
AEFHIKMST
makeshift
AEFHILSST
faithless
flashiest
AEFHIMNRS
fisherman
AEFHINORS
fashioner
AEFHINPSS
panfishes
AEFHLLTUY
hatefully
AEFHLNNPY
halfpenny
AEFHMORSU
farmhouse
AEFIILMNS
semifinal
AEFIILMPR
amplifier
AEFIILMPS
amplifies
AEFIILNNT
infantile
AEFIILQRU
qualifier
AEFIILQSU
qualifies
AEFIILSSS
salsifies
AEFIINRTU
infuriate
AEFIISSST
satisfies
AEFIISTTU
fatuities
AEFIKLNSS
flakiness
AEFILLOOT
foliolate
AEFILMNTU
fulminate
AEFILMORZ
formalize
AEFILMRSW
welfarism
AEFILNNUZ
influenza
AEFILNRSS
frailness
AEFILPRSU
praiseful
AEFILSTTU
faultiest
fistulate
AEFIMMNRT
firmament
AEFIMNOST

manifesto
AEFIMORTV
formative
AEFINNSST
faintness
AEFINORSU
nefarious
AEFINSSTT
fattiness
AEFKLLUWY
wakefully
AEFKLNORT
lakefront
AEFKLNOSW
snowflake
AEFKMORRW
framework
AEFKNNRSS
frankness
AEFLLNTTU
flatulent
AEFLLORST
forestall
AEFLLRTUY
tearfully
AEFLLSSTU
faultless
AEFLMORTU
formulate
AEFLMRSTU
masterful
AEFLNOOSS
aloofness
AEFLORSSV
favorless
AEFLORTWW
waterfowl
AEFLRSTTU
flustrate
AEFMNOORW
forewoman
AEFMORSTT
aftermost
AEFNNOORT
afternoon
AEFNORTTU
fortunate
AEFNRSSTU
transfuse
AEFOPRRTY
prefatory
AEFRRSTTU
frustrate
AEGGHINRT
gathering
AEGGHISST
shaggiest
AEGGHOPRY
geography
AEGGIINNR
regaining
AEGGIKNST
knaggiest
AEGGILLNT

galleting
AEGGILNNR
enlarging
AEGGILNRV
glavering
graveling
AEGGIMNSS
messaging
AEGGINNRR
garnering
AEGGINNRV
engraving
AEGGINOSY
easygoing
AEGGINPRS
presaging
AEGGINPRT
pargeting
AEGGINRRT
gartering
AEGGINRTT
targeting
AEGGINTTZ
gazetting
AEGGIQSTU
quaggiest
AEGGLRRST
straggler
AEGGMORRT
mortgager
AEGGNOSUY
synagogue
AEGGORRSS
aggressor
AEGHHINRS
rehashing
AEGHHINST
sheathing
AEGHHIRTU
haughtier
AEGHIKNNR
hankering
AEGHIKNRS
shrinkage
AEGHILNRS
shearling
AEGHILNRT
earthling
lathering
AEGHIMMNR
hammering
AEGHIMNPR
hampering
AEGHIMNRT
nightmare
AEGHIMORR
hierogram
AEGHINNPP
happening
AEGHINNST
hastening
AEGHINOPS
siphonage

AEGHINRRS
garnisher
AEGHINRSS
garnishes
AEGHINRTU
naughtier
AEGHINRTW
wreathing
AEGHINSSU
anguishes
AEGHIPPRY
epigraphy
AEGHIPSTT
spaghetti
AEGHLMOPR
melograph
AEGHLRSTU
slaughter
AEGHNOORR
gonorrhea
AEGHNPRSY
pharynges
AEGHOPRST
grapeshot
AEGHOPSSU
esophagus
AEGIILNNT
entailing
AEGIILNRT
retailing
AEGIILNRZ
realizing
AEGIILNSZ
signalize
AEGIILNTV
vigilante
AEGIILNTY
geniality
AEGIILSTV
vestigial
AEGIIMMRT
immigrate
AEGIIMNNR
remaining
AEGIIMNNX
examining
AEGIINNRT
retaining
AEGIINNVW
inweaving
AEGIINORT
originate
AEGIINPRR
repairing
AEGIINPTX
expiating
AEGIINRST
grainiest
seriating
AEGIINRTT
iterating
AEGIINRTW
waitering
AEGIINSTT

instigate	**AEGIMMNOT**	**AEGINRSST**	halophyte
AEGIIRSTV	gemmation	asserting	**AEHHNOPTY**
gravities	**AEGIMMNRU**	**AEGINRSTT**	theophany
AEGIKKMNR	germanium	restating	**AEHHNRSSS**
kingmaker	**AEGIMMNRY**	**AEGINRSTU**	harshness
AEGIKMNRR	yammering	gauntries	**AEHHOPPST**
remarking	**AEGIMMNST**	signature	phosphate
AEGIKMNRT	magnetism	**AEGINRTTT**	**AEHIILMTU**
marketing	**AEGIMMNSU**	tattering	humiliate
AEGIKNQSU	magnesium	**AEGINRWZZ**	**AEHIIMNST**
squeaking	**AEGIMNNSS**	zwanziger	histamine
AEGIKNRST	manginess	**AEGINSSST**	**AEHIINRSS**
streaking	**AEGIMNPPR**	staginess	hairiness
AEGIKNSSW	pampering	**AEGINSSUZ**	**AEHIIPSTT**
gawkiness	**AEGIMNPRT**	guaziness	hepatitis
AEGILLLLY	tampering	**AEGINSTTT**	**AEHIJLOSU**
illegally	**AEGIMNPRV**	attesting	jailhouse
AEGILLNPT	revamping	**AEGINSTTU**	**AEHILLOPT**
palleting	**AEGIMNRST**	statueing	paleolith
AEGILLNRU	mastering	**AEGIPRTUV**	**AEHILLPTY**
laureling	streaming	purgative	philately
AEGILLRRU	**AEGIMNRSU**	**AEGIRRRST**	**AEHILMNPS**
guerrilla	measuring	registrar	nephalism
AEGILLRSS	**AEGIMNRTT**	**AEGIRSSST**	**AEHILNOST**
salesgirl	mattering	grassiest	hailstone
AEGILMNNS	**AEGIMNSTT**	**AEGLLNOPW**	**AEHILNPST**
signalmen	magnetist	alpenglow	nephalist
AEGILMNNT	**AEGINNORS**	**AEGLLNOST**	**AEHILNQRU**
alignment	reasoning	gallstone	harlequin
lamenting	**AEGINNOSS**	**AEGLLOOPY**	**AEHILORST**
AEGILMNRV	seasoning	paleology	horsetail
marveling	**AEGINNPTT**	**AEGLMNORW**	**AEHILOSST**
AEGILMNTU	patenting	angleworm	shoaliest
emulating	**AEGINNRSS**	**AEGLNRRST**	**AEHILOSTT**
AEGILMORR	angriness	strangler	heliostat
rigmarole	**AEGINNRSW**	**AEGLNRSTY**	**AEHIMNNOT**
AEGILNNOO	answering	strangely	anthemion
neologian	**AEGINNRTT**	**AEGLORRTU**	**AEHIMNORS**
AEGILNNSV	nattering	regulator	harmonies
enslaving	**AEGINNSST**	**AEGLRSSSU**	**AEHIMNORZ**
AEGILNORY	assenting	sugarless	harmonize
legionary	**AEGINNSTU**	**AEGMNNORT**	**AEHIMNPST**
AEGILNPRS	unseating	magnetron	pantheism
relapsing	**AEGINOPRT**	**AEGMNORRW**	**AEHIMOSST**
AEGILNPRT	operating	warmonger	hematosis
paltering	**AEGINORRZ**	**AEGMOOSUX**	**AEHIMPSST**
AEGILNPRY	organizer	exogamous	steamship
parleying	**AEGINOSTT**	**AEGNNPRTU**	**AEHIMQSSU**
AEGILNQSU	gestation	repugnant	squeamish
squealing	**AEGINPPRR**	**AEGNRSSTT**	**AEHIMRSST**
AEGILNRTV	preparing	strangest	marshiest
traveling	**AEGINPPRY**	**AEGORRSTU**	**AEHINORSS**
AEGILNSST	prepaying	surrogate	hoariness
tasseling	**AEGINPRSS**	**AEHHILLTY**	**AEHINORST**
AEGILNSSW	aspersing	healthily	senhorita
wineglass	**AEGINPRTT**	**AEHHIORRS**	**AEHINPPRU**
AEGILOOPS	pattering	horsehair	unhappier
apologies	**AEGINQRUV**	**AEHHIPPSS**	**AEHINPPSS**
AEGILOOPZ	quavering	shipshape	happiness
apologize	**AEGINRRST**	**AEHHISTWW**	**AEHINPSSS**
AEGILRRRU	arresting	whitewash	apishness
irregular	serrating	**AEHHLNTUY**	**AEHINPSTT**
AEGILRUVZ	**AEGINRRTU**	unhealthy	pantheist
vulgarize	garniture	**AEHHLOPTY**	**AEHINRSST**

tarnishes
AEHINRSSV
varnishes
AEHINSSST
hastiness
AEHIOPRST
atrophies
AEHIORSTT
hesitator
AEHIORTUZ
authorize
AEHIPRRST
phratries
AEHIPRSTT
therapist
AEHIRRSTW
swarthier
AEHIRSSTT
trashiest
AEHKLNSST
thankless
AEHKORRTW
earthwork
AEHLLORSW
shallower
AEHLLPSSY
haplessly
AEHLMOOST
loathsome
AEHLMOSSU
almshouse
AEHLNOSSS
shoalness
AEHLNRTUY
unearthly
AEHLOPRSW
plowshare
AEHLOPRSY
horseplay
AEHLOPSUY
playhouse
AEHMNNSSU
humanness
AEHMORRTW
earthworm
AEHNNRSSU
unharness
AEHNOOPRR
harpooner
AEHNOOPSX
saxophone
AEHNORSTT
northeast
AEHNPRSSS
sharpness
AEHOOPSTT
osteopath
AEHOPSSTT
posthaste
AEHOPSSTW
sweatshop
AEHORSSTU
authoress
AEHORSTVW

shortwave
AEHORSTWY
seaworthy
AEHOSSTTU
southeast
AEHRSSTUU
thesaurus
AEIIIMTTV
imitative
AEIIINNST
inanities
AEIIKLLNS
snaillike
AEIIKLNST
satinlike
AEIILLTTT
titillate
AEIILNOPT
epilation
AEIILNPTV
plaintive
AEIILNPTZ
platinize
AEIILNRST
saintlier
AEIILNSTW
waistline
AEIILORST
solitaire
AEIILQSTU
qualities
AEIILRRSV
rivalries
AEIILRSTY
seriality
AEIILSUVZ
visualize
AEIIMNPTT
impatient
AEIIMNRTU
miniature
AEIIMPRRS
impresari
primaries
AEIIMPSSV
impassive
AEIINNOST
antinoise
AEIINNRSS
raininess
AEIINNRTT
itinerant
AEIINNSTU
annuities
insinuate
AEIINOPTX
expiation
AEIINORTT
iteration
AEIINRRSU
urinaries
AEIINRRTY
itinerary
AEIINSTTV

tantivies
AEIIORSST
ostiaries
AEIIPRSTV
pravities
AEIIPRTTV
partitive
AEIIPSSTX
epistaxis
AEIIRSSTV
varsities
AEIJNSSZZ
jazziness
AEIJNSTTU
jauntiest
AEIKKNNSS
snakeskin
AEIKLQSUY
squeakily
AEIKNNPRS
spinnaker
AEIKNQSSU
quakiness
AEILLLRTY
literally
AEILLMNRY
millenary
AEILLMSSY
aimlessly
AEILLNRTU
tellurian
AEILLOSTY
loyalties
AEILLRRTY
artillery
AEILLRSTW
stairwell
AEILMNNSS
manliness
AEILMNOOT
emotional
AEILMNORZ
normalize
AEILMNOSS
loaminess
AEILMNOTU
emulation
AEILMNPTU
emulation
AEILMNPTU
penultima
AEILMNRSU
semilunar
AEILMNRVY
liveryman
AEILMNSTT
mentalist
AEILMNTTY
mentality
AEILMOPST
epistomal
AEILMORTZ
mortalize
AEILMOSTU

mousetail
AEILMRRSU
semirural
AEILMSSVY
massively
AEILMSTTU
stimulate
AEILNNOPR
nonpareil
AEILNNPSS
plainness
AEILNNPSU
peninsula
AEILNOOPS
polonaise
AEILNOPPS
panoplies
AEILNOPRT
rantipole
AEILNOPTT
potential
AEILNORSS
sensorial
AEILNOSSS
sessional
AEILNPRTY
interplay
AEILNPSTY
sapiently
AEILNPTTY
patiently
AEILNPTUV
pulvinate
AEILNRSUV
universal
AEILNRTUY
unreality
AEILNSSST
saltiness
AEILNSSTS
stainless
AEILNSSTW
slantwise
AEILOPTXY
pleiotaxy
AEILORSTY
royalties
AEILPRSTT
paltriest
AEILPRTVY
privately
AEILPSSVY
passively
AEILPSTTU
stipulate
AEILRTUUX
luxuriate
AEILSSUVY
suasively
AEILSTUXY
sexuality
AEIMMNNRS
mannerism
AEIMMNOPT
pantomime

AEIMMRSSU
summaries
AEIMMRSUZ
summarize
AEIMNNNQU
mannequin
AEIMNNOPU
pneumonia
AEIMNNRST
mannerist
AEIMNORRS
rosmarine
AEIMNORTV
normative
AEIMNORWZ
womanizer
AEIMNPRST
spearmint
AEIMNPSTY
tympanies
AEIMNRTTY
maternity
AEIMNSSSS
massiness
AEIMOPRRT
imperator
AEIMOPRTX
proximate
AEIMORSTT
estimator
AEIMRRRTU
terrarium
AEINNOPSX
expansion
AEINNORTV
nervation
AEINNOSST
sensation
AEINNOTTT
attention
AEINNPPSS
nappiness
AEINNPSST
inaptness
AEINNRSTT
transient
AEINNRSTU
saturnine
AEINNRSTY
tyrannies
AEINNRTYZ
tyrannize
AEINNSSST
nastiness
AEINNSSTT
nattiness
AEINNSSTW
tawniness
AEINOOPRT
operation
AEINOPRRT
pretorian
AEINOPRSS
aspersion

AEINOPRTU
epuration
AEINOPRTZ
patronize
AEINORRST
sepration
AEINORSST
assertion
AEINORSTT
stationer
AEINOSTTT
testation
AEINPPSSS
sappiness
AEINPPSST
snappiest
AEINPRRST
transpire
AEINPRTTY
paternity
AEINQSTTU
quaintest
AEINRRSTT
restraint
AEINRSSTT
resistant
AEINSSSTT
tastiness
AEIOORRST
oratories
AEIOPRRVZ
vaporizer
AEIOPSSTU
autopsies
AEIORSSSU
ossuaries
AEIORSSTV
savoriest
AEIQRTTUZ
quartzite
AEIRSTTUY
austerity
AEJLLOSUY
jealously
AEJOPSTUX
juxtapose
AEKLMOORT
toolmaker
AEKMNOPSS
spokesman
AEKMPRRSS
pressmark
AEKNOORST
snakeroot
AEKNPRRST
prankster
AEKNRSSST
starkness
AEKOPPRRW
paperwork
AELLLMOSU
malleolus
AELLLPTUU
pullulate

AELLLSSWY
lawlessly
AELLMNOTT
allotment
AELLMNSSS
smallness
AELLNOSTW
stonewall
AELLNRTUY
neutrally
AELLNSSUY
sensually
AELLOOPRT
allotrope
AELLRSSTY
artlessly
AELMMORST
maelstrom
AELMMOSUU
mausoleum
AELMNNNTU
annulment
AELMNNOOP
monoplane
AELMNRSTU
menstrual
AELMOORSS
salesroom
AELMORSUV
marvelous
AELNNSSUU
annuluses
AELNRRUVY
vulnerary
AELNRSTTU
resultant
AELNSSSUU
usualness
AELOORRTT
tolerator
AELOPRRTY
proletary
AELOPSTTU
postulate
AELPRSSST
psaltress
AELQRRTUY
quarterly
AEMMNNORY
momentary
AEMMNRSTU
sarmentum
AEMMRSTYY
asymmetry
AEMNORRTU
numerator
AEMNORSTY
monastery
AEMNPRTUY
prytaneum
AEMNQRRUY
quarrymen
AEMNRSTTU
transmute

AEMNRSTVY
vestryman
AEMOORSTT
stateroom
AEMOPRRTY
temporary
AEMOPRSTU
mousetrap
AEMOPSTTY
asymptote
AEMQRRTUY
marquetry
AENOOPSST
soapstone
AENOPRSST
patroness
AENOPRSTU
transpose
AENOPRSUV
supernova
AENORRSTW
narrowest
AEOPRRRTY
portrayer
AEOPRRSTT
prostrate
AEOQRRSSU
squarrose
AEOQRSTUZ
quatorzes
AEORSSTUU
trousseau
AEPPRSTUU
suppurate
AEPQRRTUY
parquetry
AEPRRSSTU
superstar
AFFGIIMNR
affirming
AFFGILNNS
snaffling
AFFIILNPT
plaintiff
AFFLLORUV
flavorful
AFGGIINSY
gasifying
AFGGIINTU
fatiguing
AFGGINNTU
fungating
AFGHIIMNS
famishing
AFGHILLNT
nightfall
AFGHIMNOT
fathoming
AFGIIILNT
filiating
AFGIILMNN
inflaming
AFGIILNNT
inflating
AFGIILNNU

unfailing
AFGIILNOT
foliating
AFGIILNSY
salifying
AFGIILRTY
fragility
AFGIIMNRY
ramifying
AFGIINRTY
ratifying
AFGIKNORS
forsaking
AFGILLNUY
gainfully
AFGILNNTU
flaunting
AFGILNORV
flavoring
AFGILRTUY
frugality
AFGIMORTU
fumigator
AFGINNOPR
profaning
AFHIILNTU
hifalutin
AFHIORSTY
forsythia
AFHLLMRUY
harmfully
AFHLLORST
shortfall
AFHOORRST
hoarfrost
AFIIILNOT
filiation
AFIILNNOT
inflation
AFIILNOOT
foliation
AFIILRSTT
tailfirst
AFIIMNRRY
infirmary
AFILLLUWY
wailfully
AFILLNPUY
painfully
AFILMMORS
formalism
AFILMNNTU
fulminant
AFILMORST
formalist
AFILMORTY
formality
AFILNOOTT
flotation
AFIMMMMOR
mammiform
AFIMNNORT
informant
AFIMNOORT

formation
AFINOPRTY
profanity
AFLMORRUY
formulary
AFMNORRST
transform
AGGHHILSY
haggishly
AGGHIILNT
alighting
AGGHILOOY
hagiology
AGGIIIMNN
imagining
AGGIIJNSW
jigsawing
AGGIILLNP
pillaging
AGGIILMNN
maligning
AGGIILNNS
signaling
AGGIIMNRT
migrating
AGGIINNOZ
agonizing
AGGIINNSS
assigning
AGGILLLNY
gallingly
AGGILLNOP
galloping
AGGILNNPS
spangling
AGGILNNRW
wrangling
AGGILNPPR
grappling
AGGIMMNRU
rummaging
AGGINOPRT
portaging
AGGINORRT
garroting
AGGINORTT
garotting
AGGINORTU
outraging
AGHHILTUY
haughtily
AGHHINRST
thrashing
AGHHLOOPR
holograph
AGHIILLTT
taillight
AGHIINNSV
vanishing
AGHIINRSV
ravishing
AGHILLMPT
lamplight
AGHILLNOW

hallowing
AGHILLNTY
haltingly
AGHILMORT
algorithm
logarithm
AGHILNPSS
splashing
AGHILNPTY
plaything
AGHILRSTT
starlight
AGHIMMNSY
shammying
AGHIMNRST
hamstring
AGHIMOPRY
amphigory
AGHINNOPR
orphaning
AGHINNOPT
phonating
AGHINORRW
harrowing
AGHINQSSU
squashing
AGHINRTTW
thwarting
AGHLNOOTY
anthology
AGHLNOSTU
onslaught
AGHLOOPTY
pathology
AGHLOPPRY
polygraph
AGHLOPRXY
xylograph
AGHLORSSU
hourglass
AGHMNOOPR
monograph
phonogram
AGHMNRSTU
hamstrung
AGHOOPRRY
orography
AGHOOPRYZ
zoography
AGIIIMNPR
impairing
AGIIIMNTT
imitating
AGIIINSTV
vaginitis
AGIIINTTV
vitiating
AGIIKLMNR
grimalkin
AGIIKMNST
mistaking
AGIILLNPR
pillaring
AGIILMNSY

mislaying
AGIILNORT
tailoring
AGIILNOST
isolating
AGIILNOTV
violating
AGIILNPRS
spiraling
AGIILNQTU
liquating
AGIILNSSS
isinglass
AGIILORTT
litigator
AGIIMMNRT
immigrant
AGIIMNORT
migration
AGIIMNOTZ
atomizing
AGIIMNPRT
imparting
AGIIMORTT
mitigator
AGIINNNOT
anointing
AGIINNORS
signorina
AGIINNORT
rationing
AGIINNPRS
spraining
AGIINNQTU
antiquing
AGIINNRST
straining
AGIINNRTT
nitrating
AGIINNRTU
ruinating
urinating
AGIINNSTU
sinuating
AGIINOTZZ
azotizing
AGIINPPRS
apprising
AGIINPRST
traipsing
AGIINPRSU
upraising
AGIINRSTT
striating
AGIINSSST
assisting
AGIINSTTU
situating
AGIIRSSTT
gastritis
AGIIRSTTU
guitarist
AGIJLNRRY
jarringly

AGIKLNPRS
sparkling
AGIKMNNSU
unmasking
AGIKNQSUW
squawking
AGILLNNNU
annulling
AGILLNOTT
allotting
AGILLNOTW
tallowing
AGILLNOWW
wallowing
AGILLNQSU
squalling
AGILLNTUU
ululating
AGILMNPRT
trampling
AGILMNSUY
amusingly
AGILMOORS
lagrimoso
AGILNNPTY
pantingly
AGILNORVY
vainglory
AGILNOTUV
ovulating
AGILNPRSW
sprawling
AGILNPRSY
raspingly
sparingly
AGILNPRTT
prattling
AGILNPSTU
pulsating
AGILNRSTT
startling
AGILNTTTW
twattling
AGILOOPST
apologist
AGILRRTUY
garrulity
AGILRTUVY
vulgarity
AGIMMNSUY
gymnasium
AGIMNNNNU
unmanning
AGIMNNOOR
marooning
AGIMNNORS
ransoming
AGIMNNOTU
amounting
AGIMNNSUU
unamusing
AGIMNOOSV
vamoosing
AGIMNORRT

mortaring
AGIMNORSU
ignoramus
AGIMNRRTY
martyring
AGIMORRTY
migratory
AGINNOORT
ratooning
AGINNORRW
narrowing
AGINNORTT
attorning
AGINNPRSU
unsparing
AGINNRUVY
unvarying
AGINOOSTT
goniostat
AGINOOTTT
tattooing
AGINOPPRV
approving
AGINOPRRT
parroting
AGINOPRTU
purgation
AGINORSST
assorting
AGINORSTY
signatory
AGINORSUV
savouring
AGINPPRST
strapping
AGINPRRTU
rapturing
AGINPRSTU
pasturing
AGINQRRUY
quarrying
AGINQSTTU
squatting
AGINRSTUX
surtaxing
AGIOPRRSY
spirogyra
AGKLPPRSU
sparkplug
AGLMOORSU
glamorous
AGLMPRSUU
sugarplum
AGLOORSTY
astrology
AGLOOTTUY
tautology
AGLORRSUU
garrulous
AGOPRRTUY
purgatory
AHHILMOPT
philomath
AHHMOSTUW

mouthwash
AHHNORRST
hartshorn
AHIILORSU
hilarious
AHIILOSST
halitosis
AHIILRSTT
shirttail
AHIINORST
historian
AHIINPSST
saintship
AHIIRRSTT
arthritis
AHIJMOPRS
majorship
AHIKKNRSS
sharkskin
AHIKLMSWY
mawkishly
AHILLSSVY
slavishly
AHILMNNSY
mannishly
AHILMORST
hailstorm
AHILMPRTU
triumphal
AHILNPPUY
unhappily
AHIMMMNOS
mammonish
AHIMOOSTX
homotaxis
AHINNOPTY
antiphony
AHIOPSTXY
hypotaxis
AHIORTTUY
authority
AHLOOPPTY
photoplay
AHMOOPRSU
amorphous
AHOORRTTY
hortatory
AIIILLNTY
initially
AIIIMNOTT
imitation
AIIINNSTY
asininity
AIIINORTT
initiator
AIIJLOTVY
joviality
AIILLMRSY
similarly
AIILLMTTW
milliwatt
AIILMOSST
altissimo
AIILMPRRY

primarily
AIILMRSTU
ritualism
AIILLNOOST
isolation
AIILNOOTV
violation
AIILNRSST
sinistral
AIILPRSST
spritsail
AIILPRSTU
spiritual
AIILRSTTU
ritualist
AIIMNNTUY
unanimity
AIIMNNOPSS
impassion
AIIMNOSTY
animosity
AIIMNPSTT
timpanist
AIIMPSSSV
passivism
AIINNORTU
ruination
AIINNORTT
urination
AIINNOTTX
antitoxin
AIINOPRTT
partition
AIINOPRTV
privation
AIINORSTT
striation
AIINORSVY
visionary
AIINORTTT
attrition
AIINOSTTU
situation
AIINQTTUY
antiquity
AIIOPRSSS
psoriasis
AIIPRTTUY
pituitary
AIIPSSTVY
passivity
AILLMMORY
immorally
AILLMNNOY
nominally
AILLNOTUU
ululation
AILLPRTUY
plurality
AILLRTUVY
virtually
AILMMOORT
immolator
AILMMRSUY
summarily

AILMMSTUU
mutualism
AILMMTTUU
ultimatum
AILMNOPSS
spoilsman
AILMNORTY
normality
AILMNSTTU
stimulant
AILMORSTU
simulator
AILMORTTY
mortality
AILMOSSTY
atmolysis
AILMPRSTY
palmistry
AILMTTUUY
mutuality
AILNNSTTY
instantly
AILNOORST
tonsorial
AILNOOSST
saloonist
AILNOPSTU
pulsation
AILNORSTU
insulator
AILNOSUXY
anxiously
AILNPPSTU
suppliant
AILNRTUUX
luxuriant
AILORSUVY
variously
AILPRRSSU
surprisal
AIMMMMNOS
mammonism
AIMMMNOST
mammonist
AIMMNORTY
matrimony
AIMMNOSTU
summation
AIMMPRSUU
marsupium
AIMNNOORT
nominator
AIMNNOSUU
unanimous
AIMNNOTYY
anonymity
AIMNOPRSY
parsimony
AIMNOPRTT
important
AIMNOPRTY
patrimony
AIMNORRST
rainstorm

AIMOPSSTU
potassium
AIMPSSSTU
assumpsit
AINNOORTV
innovator
AINOOPPRT
apportion
AINOOQTTU
quotation
AINRSTTTU
antitrust
AIORRSSTU
sartorious
AKLORSSTW
saltworks
ALLNOPTTU
pollutant
ALMNNOUWY
unwomanly
ALMNNOPST
monoplast
ALMNOORTY
monolatry
ALMNOPRUY
pulmonary
ALMOORSUY
amorously
ALNOPPRUU
unpopular
ALNOPSTTU
postulant
ALNORTUVY
voluntary
ALOPRRTYY
pyrolatry
AMNNOOSUY
anonymous
AMNOORSTY
astronomy
AMNOPRSST
sportsman
ANOOOPRTZ
protozoan
ANOPRRSTT
transport
AOOOORRTW
arrowroot
AOOQRSTUW
squawroot
AOPRRSTUU
rapturous
AORSTTTUY
statutory
BBBDEHNOD
hobnobbed
BBBEEELMU
bumblebee
BBBEEILSTU
bubbliest
BBCDEILRS
scribbled
BBCEHISTU
chubbiest

BBCEHLOUY
cubbyhole
BBCEILRRS
scribbler
BBCEIRRSU
scrubbier
BBCEIRSSU
subscribe
BBCGIILNR
cribbling
BBCGINRSU
scrubbing
BBDEELORS
slobbered
BBDEGIMNO
demobbing
BBDGIILNR
dribbling
BBEEELRYY
beylerbey
BBEEIIRRS
briberies
BBEELRRUY
blueberry
BBEGGIINR
gibbering
BBEGGIINT
gibbeting
BBEGHIIRS
gibberish
BBEGIMNNU
benumbing
BBEGIRSTU
grubbiest
BBEHIRRSU
shrubbier
BBEHLLMOS
bombshell
BBEHRRSUY
shrubbery
BBEIKNOST
knobbiest
BBEILNSTU
nubbliest
BBEILOSTW
wobbliest
BBEINOSST
snobbiest
BBEISSTTU
stubbiest
BBFGIILNR
fribbling
BBGHILNOO
hobgoblin
BBGHINORT
throbbing
BBGHINRSU
shrubbing
BBGIILNQU
quibbling
BBGIINNOR
ribboning
BBGIINQSU
squibbing

BCCCKMOOS
cockscomb
BCCDEMSUU
succumbed
BCCEHKKOO
checkbook
BCCEINNOU
concubine
BCCEKLLLO
cellblock
BCCGIILNY
bicycling
BCCIILSTY
bicyclist
BCCIKLLOY
billycock
BCCIORSTU
scorbutic
BCCMOORXY
coxcombry
BCCMORRUY
currycomb
BCDDEEHOU
debouched
BCDDEEILU
deducible
BCDDEEIRS
described
BCDDEELOU
beclouded
BCDDESTUU
subducted
BCDEEHOSU
debouches
BCDEEEINO
obedience
BCDEEGIKN
bedecking
BCDEEHIIR
herbicide
BCDEEHITW
bewitched
BCDEEILRU
reducible
BCDEEJSTU
subjected
BCDEEMNTU
decumbent
BCDEIINRS
inscribed
BCDEKLNUU
unbuckled
BCDEMOSTU
combusted
BCDEOOTTY
boycotted
BCDGIKLOR
goldbrick
BCDGINSUU
subducing
BCDKNOOOS
boondocks
BCEEEEHRS
beseecher

BCEEEEHSS	**BCEILMNOU**	**BDDDEEINR**	**BDEEELMZZ**
beseeches	columbine	bedridden	embezzled
BCEEEHKNO	**BCEIMNNTU**	**BDDEEEFIR**	**BDEEELNOS**
cheekbone	incumbent	debriefed	nosebleed
BCEEEIRRZ	**BCEIMNORY**	**BDDEEEFIR**	**BDEEENRTU**
cerebrize	embryonic	bedeviled	debenture
BCEEGHINR	**BCEINOSTU**	**BDDEEEILV**	**BDEEERTTV**
breeching	bounciest	bedizened	brevetted
BCEEHIRTW	**BCEINOSTY**	**BDDEEEINZ**	**BDEEFIILS**
bewitcher	obscenity	bedizened	disbelief
BCEEHORTT	**BCEINSSUU**	**BDDEEFOOR**	**BDEEFIIRV**
brochette	incubuses	foreboded	verbified
BCEEHRRTU	**BCEIOPRRS**	**BDDEEGGRU**	**BDEEFLLOW**
butcherer	proscribe	begrudged	bedfellow
BCEEIILNV	**BCEIORSTT**	**BDDEEGIMN**	**BDEEGGLOW**
envincible	obstetric	embedding	bowlegged
BCEEIJOTV	**BCELORSUY**	**BDDEEIOSY**	**BDEEGMRSU**
objective	obscurely	disobeyed	submerged
BCEEILLOS	**BCENORSTU**	**BDDEEIRSU**	**BDEEGNORU**
bellicose	curbstone	debruised	burgeoned
BCEEILRTY	**BCEOORTTY**	**BDDEELNRU**	**BDEEHIITX**
celebrity	boycotter	blundered	exhibited
BCEEIPRRS	**BCEOORSSTU**	**BDDEELORU**	**BDEEHILMS**
prescribe	obscurest	redoubled	blemished
BCEELNOSY	**BCEPRTTUU**	**BDDEENORU**	**BDEEHORTT**
obscenely	buttercup	rebounded	betrothed
BCEENPSTU	**BCFHILLNU**	**BDDEFINOR**	**BDEEIILLN**
pubescent	bullfinch	forbidden	indelible
BCEFIIKRR	**BCGHILNOT**	**BDDEFIORR**	**BDEEIILRS**
firebrick	blotching	forbidder	derisible
BCEFKLTUU	**BCGIIMNNO**	**BDDEGIIMN**	**BDEEIINRS**
bucketful	combining	imbedding	binderies
BCEGIIKNR	**BCGILMNRU**	**BDDEHINOU**	**BDEEIISTU**
bickering	crumbling	hidebound	dubieties
BCEGIIJNOT	**BCGINORSU**	**BDDEHLOOS**	**BDEEILLTT**
objecting	obscuring	bloodshed	belittled
BCEGIKNNO	**BCHIIOPRS**	**BDDEIISUV**	**BDEEILMOR**
beckoning	bishopric	subdivide	embroiled
BCEGIKNTU	**BCHKOOTTU**	**BDDEILNRU**	**BDEEILMSS**
bucketing	bucktooth	unbridled	dissemble
BCEGILNOR	**BCHLOOOSY**	**BDDEIMOSY**	**BDEEILNUZ**
corbeling	schoolboy	disembody	nebulized
BCEGIMNRU	**BCHLOORTW**	**BDDEIRSSU**	**BDEEILRST**
cumbering	blowtorch	disbursed	blistered
BCEHILORT	**BCIILMSUU**	**BDDEIRSTU**	**BDEEIMMRS**
blotchier	umbilicus	disturbed	dismember
BCEHINSTU	**BCIILPSTU**	**BDDELLOUZ**	**BDEEIMORR**
bunchiest	publicist	bulldozed	embroider
BCEHIOSTT	**BCIILPTUY**	**BDDENNOUU**	**BDEEIRRST**
botchiest	publicity	unbounded	bestirred
BCEHKNORW	**BCIIMOSTY**	**BDDENOTUU**	**BDEELLSSY**
workbench	symbiotic	undoubted	blessedly
BCEHLOSUU	**BCIKKNOST**	**BDDFILLNO**	**BDEELMRSU**
clubhouse	knobstick	blindfold	slumbered
BCEHMNOOY	**BCIKKORRW**	**BDDFMNOUU**	**BDEELNOUV**
honeycomb	brickwork	dumbfound	unbeloved
BCEIINOST	**BCIOOPRSS**	**BDEEEEFLN**	**BDEELNRRU**
bisection	proboscis	enfeebled	blunderer
BCEIINRRS	**BCIORSTUY**	**BDEEEEJLW**	**BDEELORST**
inscriber	obscurity	bejeweled	bolstered
BCEIJNOOT	**BCIPRSSTU**	**BDEEEELRV**	**BDEELRSTU**
objection	subscript	belvedere	blustered
BCEIKLOST	**BDDDEEFLU**	**BDEEEFINT**	**BDEEMMOOS**
blockiest	befuddled	benefited	embosomed
		BDEEEELMRS	
		resembled	

BDEEMRSSU
submersed
BDEEOPRRV
proverbed
BDEEOPSTT
bespotted
BDEEORVYY
everybody
BDEEPRRTU
perturbed
BDEERSSUV
subserved
BDEERSTUV
subverted
BDEFHIRSU
furbished
BDEFILLOO
lifeblood
BDEFINORY
boyfriend
BDEGGGINU
debugging
BDEGGHMUU
humbugged
BDEGGINTU
budgeting
BDEGHILNO
beholding
BDEGIIILR
dirigible
BDEGIIINR
birdieing
BDEGIIMMN
bedimming
BDEGIKOOU
guidebook
BDEGIMNOY
embodying
BDEGINNNU
unbending
BDEGINNRU
burdening
BDEGINORR
bordering
BDEHIIINT
inhibited
BDEHILPSU
published
BDEHIORSU
birdhouse
BDEIIILSV
divisible
BDEIIILTY
edibility
BDEIILMOZ
mobilized
BDEIISSSU
subsidies
BDEIISSUZ
subsidize
BDEIJNOSU
subjoined
BDEILLNOO
bloodline

BDEILLNPS
spellbind
BDEILLNRU
underbill
BDEILNNSS
blindness
BDEILOOST
bloodiest
BDEILOQTU
quodlibet
BDEILSTTU
subtitled
BDEIMSTTU
submitted
BDEINORTX
tinderbox
BDEINRSSU
sideburns
BDEIOORST
broodiest
BDEISSSTU
subsisted
BDELLOOSS
bloodless
BDELLORUZ
bulldozer
BDELMOOSS
blossomed
BDELNNOSS
blondness
BDELNOOTU
doubleton
BDELNOSSU
boundless
BDELOSSTU
doubtless
BDENNRSUU
sunburned
BDEORSSTU
sodbuster
BDFNOOSTU
softbound
BDGIINORS
disrobing
BDGIINSSU
subsiding
BDGILNOOY
bloodying
BDGINORTU
obtruding
BDHIIMRSY
hybridism
BDHIIRSTY
hybridist
BDHLOOOST
bloodshot
BDHOORSUW
brushwood
BDIIILSVY
divisibly
BDIIMORTY
morbidity
BDIIOSTUY
dubiosity

BDILOSUUY
dubiously
BDLMOOORW
bloodworm
BDLOOOORT
bloodroot
BDNNOOSUW
snowbound
BEEEFINSS
beefiness
BEEEGIMNS
beseeming
BEEEGNOOW
woebegone
BEEEHLLOR
hellebore
BEEEIRRSW
breweries
BEEEIRSTZ
breeziest
BEEEKRRRS
berserker
BEEELMRZZ
embezzler
BEEENORST
tenebrose
BEEFILRSS
fiberless
BEEFINRSS
briefness
BEEFOORTY
freebooty
BEEGGIINS
besieging
BEEGGINTT
begetting
BEEGIILLL
illegible
BEEGIILNV
believing
BEEGILLNR
rebelling
BEEGILMMN
embleming
BEEGINSST
beestings
BEEGINSTT
besetting
BEEHILLMS
embellish
BEEHIORRV
herbivore
BEEHLOPRY
hyperbole
BEEIILNRT
libertine
BEEIILRST
liberties
BEEILLNOR
rebellion
BEEILLNTU
ebullient
BEEILMORR
embroiler

BEEILNRUZ
nebulizer
BEEILORTT
briolette
BEEILOTTU
oubliette
BEEILSTUV
vestibule
BEEIMNRST
tribesmen
BEEIMRRSU
reimburse
BEEIOORST
booteries
BEEIOQSSU
obsequies
BEEIOSSSV
obsessive
BEEKNORSS
brokeness
BEELMMNRU
lumbermen
BEELNNOSS
nobleness
BEELORRTU
bourrelet
BEELORSVY
verbosely
BEELQRSUU
burlesque
BEENOORRV
overborne
BEENORSSS
soberness
BEENORSTU
tenebrous
BEENRSSTU
bruteness
BEEORSTTU
soubrette
BEEPRRSTY
presbyter
BEFFGINRU
buffering
rebuffing
BEFFGINTU
buffeting
BEFGGGINO
befogging
BEFGIINTT
befitting
BEFGILNOU
befouling
BEFGINSUU
subfeuing
BEFHIRRSU
furbisher
refurbish
BEFHKLOOS
bookshelf
BEFIORSTT
frostbite
BEFLRTTUY
butterfly

BEGGIILNU
beguiling
BEGGIINNN
beginning
BEGGILNNO
belonging
BEGGINNSU
bugginess
BEGHHINOT
thighbone
BEGHILNSU
busheling
BEGHINOOV
behooving
BEGHINORT
bothering
BEGHIRSTT
brightest
BEGIIILNT
ignitible
BEGIILLLN
libelling
BEGIILLLY
illegibly
BEGIILLNT
billeting
BEGIILMNR
limbering
BEGIILNOS
besoiling
obelising
BEGIILNOZ
obelizing
BEGIIMNRT
timbering
BEGIINNOZ
ebonizing
BEGIINNTY
benignity
BEGIINRTT
bittering
BEGIJRTTU
jitterbug
BEGILLNOW
bellowing
BEGILMNRT
trembling
BEGILMNRU
lumbering
BEGILNNNO
ennobling
BEGILRTTU
litterbug
BEGIMMNNOT
entombing
BEGIMNNRU
numbering
BEGIMNOSS
embossing
BEGIMNRTU
embruting
BEGINNSUV
subvening
BEGINORRS

resorbing
BEGINORSV
observing
BEGINOSSS
obsessing
BEGINOSTT
besotting
BEGINOSTW
bestowing
BEGINRTTU
buttering
rebutting
BEGIOORSU
bourgeois
BEHIILPST
phlebitis
BEHIIORTX
exhibitor
BEHIKLRSU
shrublike
BEHILOOSU
helobious
BEHILPRSU
publisher
BEHILPSSU
publishes
BEHINSSSU
bushiness
BEHIORRST
herborist
BEHKNOSUU
bunkhouse
BEHLORRTY
brotherly
BEHLRSSSU
shrubless
BEHMORSSU
rhombuses
BEIIILNSV
invisible
BEIILLNSY
sibylline
BEIIMNSSU
minibuses
BEIINORSU
inebrious
BEIKLNSSU
bulkiness
BEIKMOORT
motorbike
BEIKNRSSS
briskness
BEILLMSUY
sublimely
BEILLNOSU
insoluble
BEILLOQUY
obliquely
BEILMOOST
bloomiest
BEILMOSYZ
symbolize
BEILNOPTU
bluepoint

BEILNRSSU
burliness
BEILOOQSU
obloquies
BEILOSSTU
blousiest
BEILOSTTT
blottiest
BEILOSTWZ
blowziest
BEIMNORST
brimstone
BEIMNOSSU
omnibuses
BEINOOSSS
obsession
BEINOSSSS
bossiness
BEIOOPRRU
pourboire
BEIORSTUV
obtrusive
BEIORSTVY
verbosity
BEKNNNOUW
unbeknown
BEKOOORST
bookstore
BELMOOORW
elbowroom
BELNNSSTU
bluntness
BELNRTTUU
turbulent
BEMNOOSTT
tombstone
BEMNORTUU
outnumber
BEMNOSSUX
buxomness
BENNNOSTU
sunbonnet
BENNORSSW
brownness
BENOOSTUU
bounteous
BENORRSWY
snowberry
BENRTTTUU
butternut
BFGHILLTU
bullfight
BFGIINRUY
rubifying
BFILNOTUU
bountiful
BGGHIILNT
blighting
BGGILMNRU
grumbling
BGINOOOOO
boohooing
BGIIIKNTZ
kibitzing

BGIILLNOW
billowing
BGIILLNOY
boilingly
BGIILMNSU
subliming
BGIILMOOR
imbroglio
BGIILNRST
bristling
BGIILOOST
biologist
BGIKNOPRS
springbok
BGILMNSTU
stumbling
BGILNORTU
troubling
BGILNUYZZ
buzzingly
BGIMNOOTT
bottoming
BGINNORSU
suborning
BGINNOTTU
buttoning
BGINOORRW
borrowing
BGINORRUW
burrowing
BGINORSTW
bowstring
BGLMOOSYY
symbology
BGNOORSTX
strongbox
BHHIMORTY
biorhythm
BHIIINORT
inhibitor
BHIILLLLY
hillbilly
BHIKLOOSY
bookishly
BHILMNOTY
bimonthly
BHILOORSY
boorishly
BHILRSTUY
brutishly
BHLLOOOTT
tollbooth
BIIILNSVY
invisibly
BIILMSTUY
sublimity
BIILOOSUV
oblivious
BIIMOSSSY
symbiosis
BILLNCOPS
spoonbill
BILLNORST
stillborn

BILMMOSSY
symbolism
BILMOSSTY
symbolist
BILOOSUVY
obviously
BIMOPSTUU
bumptious
BINOOOSUX
obnoxious
BINOORSTU
obtrusion
BKLLMNSUU
numbskull
BKOOORSTY
storybook
BOOPPRRTU
turboprop
CCCCILNOY
concyclic
CCCDENOOT
concocted
CCCEEINRT
eccentric
CCDDEEESU
succeeded
CCDDEIINO
coincided
CCDDEKLOU
cuckolded
CCDDELNOU
concluded
CCDDENOTU
conducted
CCDEEEHKR
checkered
CCDEEEHRS
screeched
CCDEEEINS
decencies
CCDEEFNOT
confected
CCDEEHIKW
chickweed
CCDEEHKNU
unchecked
CCDEEHORT
crocheted
CCDEEIINN
incidence
CCDEEIKRT
cricketed
CCDEEILNR
encircled
CCDEEINOT
conceited
CCDEEINOV
conceived
CCDEELLOT
collected
CCDEEMMNO
commenced
CCDEEMMOR
commerced

CCDEENNOR
concerned
CCDEENNOS
ensconced
CCDEENNOT
connected
CCDEENORS
crescendo
CCDEENORT
concerted
concreted
CCDEENOTV
convected
CCDEEORRT
corrected
CCDEFIIRU
crucified
CCDEGINNO
conceding
CCDEGINOT
decocting
CCDEHIRST
scritched
CCDEHNRSU
scrunched
CCDEIIKNP
picnicked
CCDEILOOR
crocodile
CCDEINNOV
convinced
CCDEINOOT
decoction
CCDEINOTV
convicted
CCDEINOUV
conducive
CCDEINRTU
cinctured
CCDENORRU
concurred
CCDGILNOU
occluding
CCDGINNOU
conducing
CCDHIIMOR
dichromic
CCDHKOOUW
woodchuck
CCDIILNRY
cylindric
CCDNOORTU
conductor
CCDNOSTUU
conductus
CCEEEHNOR
coherence
CCEEEHRSS
screeches
CCEEEINNS
nescience
CCEEEIRSS
secrecies
CCEEGINOR

concierge
CCEEHIKLN
checkline
CCEEHILMY
hemicycle
CCEEHLORT
cerecloth
CCEEHLOTT
clochette
CCEEIIPPR
precipice
CCEEIILNOR
reconcile
CCEEINNNO
innocence
CCEEELLORT
recollect
CCEEENNORT
concenter
CCEFIIRRU
crucifier
CCEFIIRSU
crucifies
CCEGHILNN
clenching
CCEGIKNOR
cockering
CCEGILNRY
recycling
CCEGINORY
cryogenic
CCEHHIINR
chinchier
CCEHHKLOU
chuckhole
CCEHILNOR
chronicle
CCEHINRRU
crunchier
CCEHKLNOT
neckcloth
CCEHKMOOR
checkroom
CCEHKOORS
cockhorse
CCEHNNOOS
sconcheon
CCEHNOSTU
scutcheon
CCEHNRSSU
scrunches
CCEHORTTY
crotchety
CCEHOTTUZ
zucchetto
CCEIIIRTZ
criticize
CCEIIKNPR
picnicker
CCEIIMOSS
coseismic
CCEIKLLOY
kilocycle
CCEIKLOSW

clockwise
CCEILNOSY
concisely
CCEILORST
sclerotic
CCEINNORV
convincer
CCEINORRT
incorrect
CCEINRSTY
syncretic
CCEIOPRTY
precocity
CCEKORRSW
corkscrew
CCELLOORT
collector
CCELNSTUU
succulent
CCELOPRSU
corpuscle
CCELORRTY
correctly
CCENNNORU
unconcern
CCENNOORT
connector
CCENNOSTU
concentus
CCENDORSU
concourse
CCEOPPRUY
preoccupy
CCEORSSSU
successor
CCFGHIKOT
cockfight
CCFIILOOR
colorific
CCFIMORRU
cruciform
CCGHIIKLN
chickling
CCGHIILNN
clinching
CCGHIINPU
hiccuping
CCGHIKLNU
chuckling
CCGHILNTU
clutching
CCGHINNRU
crunching
CCGHINORS
scorching
CCGHINORU
crouching
CCGHINOST
scotching
CCGHINRTU
crutching
CCGIINNOR
cornicing
CCGIKNOOU

cuckooing
CCGILOOTY
cytologic
CCGINOPUY
occupying
CCGINORRU
occurring
CCGINORSU
succoring
CCHHOOPST
hopscotch
CCHIKOPST
chopstick
CCIIIMRST
criticism
CCIILMNOU
concilium
CCIINNOOS
concision
CCIIOPSST
scioptics
CCIIRRTUY
circuitry
CCILMOSTU
occultism
CCILNOOSU
occlusion
CCIMMOORS
microcosm
CCINOOSSU
conscious
CCINOPRST
conscript
CCINORSTT
constrict
CCKKLOORW
clockwork
CCKOOPPPY
poppycock
CCLNOORTY
cyclotron
CCNORSTTU
construct
CDDDEEENS
descended
CDDDEEILY
decidedly
CDDDEEINU
undecided
CDDDEIORS
discorded
CDDEEEFLT
deflected
CDDEEEINV
evidenced
CDDEEEOPR
proceeded
CDDEEHLSU
scheduled
CDDEEINRS
discerned
rescinded
CDDEEINSX
exscinded

CDDEEIPRT
predicted
CDDEEISST
dissected
CDDEEITUV
deductive
CDDEELOOR
decolored
CDDEEMMNO
commended
CDDEEMNNO
condemned
CDDEENNOS
condensed
CDDEENNOT
contended
CDDEENNOU
denounced
CDDEFIILU
dulcified
CDDEGINTU
deducting
CDDEIILMO
domiciled
CDDEIILPS
discipled
CDDEIILRU
ridiculed
CDDEIIRST
discredit
CDDEILOSS
disclosed
CDDEINOTU
deduction
CDDEIOSUU
deciduous
CDDEISSSU
discussed
CDDENORUW
uncrowded
CDDGINORS
scrodding
CDDHHILOO
childhood
CDEEEEFNR
deference
CDEEEELRT
reelected
CDEEEFITV
defective
CDEEEFLRT
reflected
CDEEEFPRT
perfected
CDEEEGINR
decreeing
CDEEEGINX
exceeding
CDEEEGLNT
neglected
CDEEEHKNP
henpecked
CDEEEHLNO
echeloned

CDEEEIMRT
decimeter
CDEEEINPT
centipede
CDEEEINRS
residence
CDEEEINRT
intercede
CDEEEIPRT
receipted
CDEEEIPRV
perceived
CDEEEIPTV
deceptive
CDEEEIRSX
exercised
CDEEEITTV
detective
CDEEELNOR
redolence
CDEEELNTU
unelected
CDEEELORT
electrode
CDEEELPRT
prelected
CDEEENNST
sentenced
CDEEENPRT
precedent
CDEEEORRV
recovered
CDEEEPRST
respected
CDEEEPRTX
excerpted
CDEEFGINT
defecting
CDEEFIINT
deficient
CDEEFIIPS
specified
CDEEFIIRT
certified
rectified
CDEEFIKLR
flickered
CDEEFILNT
inflected
CDEEFILTU
deceitful
CDEEFINOT
defection
CDEEFKLOT
fetlocked
CDEEFNORR
conferred
CDEEFNOSS
confessed
CDEEGIILN
ceilinged
CDEEGIIMR
germicide

CDEEGIINN
indigence
CDEEGIINV
deceiving
CDEEGIJNT
dejecting
CDEEGINPR
preceding
CDEEGINTT
detecting
CDEEGNORV
converged
CDEEGNOST
congested
decongest
CDEEHHIRS
cherished
CDEEHIKNT
thickened
CDEEHINRS
schneider
CDEEHIRTT
chittered
CDEEHKOSU
deckhouse
CDEEHLPPS
schlepped
CDEEHLQSU
squelched
CDEEHORTU
retouched
CDEEHRSTT
stretched
CDEEIILRT
deciliter
CDEEIIMPR
epidermic
CDEEIIPST
pesticide
CDEEIIRTV
directive
CDEEIJNOT
dejection
CDEEIJPRU
prejudice
CDEEIKNQU
quickened
CDEEIKNRS
snickered
CDEEILNNO
indolence
CDEEILNST
stenciled
CDEEILOSZ
solecized
CDEEILTXY
excitedly
CDEEIMNPU
impudence
CDEEINOPT
deception
CDEEINORT
recondite
CDEEINOST

sectioned
CDEEINPST
inspected
CDEEIORSX
exorcised
CDEEIOSTX
coexisted
CDEEIRRTU
recruited
CDEEIRSUV
decursive
CDEEIRTTU
certitude
rectitude
CDEEIRTUV
reductive
CDEEISTUV
seductive
CDEEJOPRT
projected
CDEEKORST
restocked
CDEELLMOP
compelled
CDEELMOPT
completed
CDEELNOSU
counseled
CDEELRSTU
clustered
CDEELRTTU
cluttered
CDEEMMNOR
recommend
CDEEMMNOT
commented
CDEEMNNOT
contemned
CDEEMOOPS
decompose
CDEENNORS
condenser
CDEENNORT
contender
CDEENNORU
renounced
CDEENNOST
consented
CDEENNOTT
contented
CDEENNRSU
scunnered
CDEENOQRU
conquered
CDEENORSV
conserved
conversed
CDEENORTU
countered
recounted
CDEENORTV
converted
CDEENORUV
uncovered

CDEENOSTT
contested
CDEENRSUU
unsecured
CDEENRSUW
unscrewed
CDEEOPRRT
porrected
CDEEOPRRU
procedure
reproduce
CDEEOPRSS
processed
CDEEOPRTT
protected
CDEEOQTTU
coquetted
CDEEPRSSU
percussed
CDEEPSSTU
suspected
CDEFGIINU
fungicide
CDEFGINOR
deforcing
CDEFIILNT
inflicted
CDEFIILSU
dulcifies
CDEFIINOR
cornified
CDEFIINST
disinfect
CDEFIKLOR
frolicked
CDEFIMNOR
confirmed
CDEFINNOT
confident
CDEFINTUY
fecundity
CDEFMNOOR
conformed
CDEFMOORT
comforted
CDEFNOORU
cofounder
CDEGGILNU
cudgeling
CDEGGILRS
scriggled
CDEGGLNOU
unclogged
CDEGHINNR
drenching
CDEGIIKNR
dickering
CDEGIILNN
declining
CDEGIINNR
cindering
CDEGIINPT
depicting
CDEGIINRT

crediting
directing
CDEGIKNOT
docketing
CDEGILNSU
secluding
CDEGILNUX
excluding
CDEGINNOS
consigned
seconding
CDEGINORR
recording
CDEGINRSY
descrying
CDEGNORSU
scrounged
CDEHIIKLL
childlike
CDEHIKOOY
doohickey
CDEHIKPSY
physicked
CDEHILPST
stepchild
CDEHINOSU
cushioned
CDEHIPRRU
chirruped
CDEHNOTUU
untouched
CDEIIILVZ
civilized
CDEIIKSST
sidestick
CDEIILLNO
decillion
CDEIILOST
solicited
CDEIILOSU
delicious
CDEIILTVY
declivity
CDEIIMNTY
mendicity
CDEIINOPT
depiction
CDEIINORT
direction
CDEIINRTT
interdict
CDEIINTUV
inductive
CDEIIRSTU
crudities
CDEIJNNOO
conjoined
CDEIKLLOR
rollicked
CDEILLLOU
celluloid
CDEILLTUY
ductilely
CDEILNOOZ

colonized
CDEILOSTU
cloudiest
CDEILRTUY
credulity
CDEIMMOTT
committed
CDEIMMNOT
condiment
CDEIMNOPR
princedom
CDEIMNORS
crimsoned
CDEIMOPRS
comprised
CDEINNOTU
continued
unnoticed
CDEINOPRS
conspired
CDEINORTT
contrited
CDEINORTU
introduce
reduction
CDEINORTV
contrived
CDEINOSST
consisted
CDEINOSTU
seduction
CDEINTTUV
ventiduct
CDEIORRTY
directory
CDEIORSSS
scissored
CDEIORSSU
discourse
CDEIORSVY
discovery
CDEIPPSTY
dyspeptic
CDELLOOPS
scolloped
CDELLOSSU
cloudless
CDELNOORT
decontrol
CDELNOOTY
cotyledon
CDELNOOVV
convolved
CDELNOPUU
uncoupled
CDELNORSU
scoundrel
CDELNOSTU
consulted
CDELNOSUV
convulsed
CDELORSUU
credulous
CDEMMOOOR

commodore
CDEMOOPRT
comported
CDEMOOPST
composted
CDENNOTUU
uncounted
CDENOORST
consorted
CDENOORTT
contorted
CDENOORTU
contoured
CDENORSTU
construed
CDENPRTUU
punctured
CDEOOPRRT
proctored
CDEOPRRTU
corrupted
CDFFIILTU
difficult
CDFGHILNO
goldfinch
CDFGIINNO
confiding
CDFGIINOY
codifying
CDFIIMOST
discomfit
CDGIIINNT
indicting
CDGIILLNO
colliding
CDGIILNNU
including
CDGIINNTU
inducting
CDGIINORV
divorcing
CDGILLNOU
colluding
CDGILNNOO
condoling
CDGILNNOY
condignly
CDGINNNOO
condoning
CDGINOORR
corroding
CDGINOORT
doctoring
CDGINOPRU
producing
CDHHIIOTY
ichthyoid
CDHHILOST
dishcloth
CDHIILLNW
windchill
CDHIMOOTY
dichotomy
CDHNOOORT

notochord
CDHNOOTUW
touchdown
CDIIJOSUU
judicious
CDIILPTUY
duplicity
CDIILTTUY
ductility
CDIINNOOT
condition
CDIINNOTU
induction
CDIKMRSTU
drumstick
CDILORSUU
ludicrous
CDIMMOOTY
commodity
CDIMNOORT
microdont
CDKKNNOOW
knockdown
CDMNNORUU
conundrum
CDNNOOTUW
countdown
CDOORRSSW
crossword
CEEEEFNRR
reference
CEEEEGMNR
emergence
CEEEEHMNV
vehemence
CEEEENRRV
reverence
CEEEFFITV
effective
CEEEFFLNU
effluence
CEEEFINNR
inference
CEEEFLNSS
fenceless
CEEEGINRS
regencies
CEEEGINRT
energetic
CEEEGLNRT
neglecter
CEEEGMNRY
emergency
CEEEHIKST
cheekiest
CEEEHIRST
cheeriest
CEEEHLRSS
cheerless
CEEEHMNVY
vehemency
CEEEHMORT
echometer
CEEEHQRUX

exchequer
CEEEHRTTV
chevrette
CEEEIIMPT
timepiece
CEEEIILLNT
clientele
CEEEILSTV
selective
CEEEINNNP
ninepence
CEEEINNPT
pentience
CEEEINNST
sentience
CEEEINOPS
nosepiece
CEEEINPRT
epicenter
CEEEINRSS
sceneries
CEEEINSTX
existence
CEEEIPRRV
perceiver
CEEEIPRST
creepiest
CEEEIPRTV
receptive
CEEEIRRSX
exerciser
CEEEIRSSV
recessive
CEEEIRSTV
secretive
CEEEISSVX
excessive
CEEEITUVX
executive
CEEEJMNTT
ejectment
CEEELLNTX
excellent
CEEELMNST
selectmen
CEEELNOQU
eloquence
CEEELOPST
telescope
CEEELPRST
preselect
CEEELRSST
electress
CEEELRSTV
cleverest
CEEEMNRTX
excrement
CEEENNSST
senescent
CEEEPRSTU
persecute
CEEFFGINT
effecting
CEEFFIINT

efficient
CEEFFOOPT
coffeepot
CEEFGLNTU
genuflect
CEEFIINTV
infective
CEEFIIRRT
certifier
rectifier
CEEFIIRST
certifies
rectifies
CEEFILNNU
influence
CEEFILRTY
electrify
CEEFIMPRT
imperfect
CEEFINORR
reinforce
CEEFINORT
refection
CEEFINORV
enforcive
CEEFKLLSS
fleckless
CEEFLOORS
foreclose
CEEFLORRT
reflector
CEEFLORSS
forceless
CEEFLORSU
fluoresce
CEEFLPRTY
perfectly
CEEFNOPRU
fourpence
CEEFNORRR
conferrer
CEEFNQRUY
frequency
CEEFORRTY
refectory
CEEGHILNR
lechering
CEEGHINSW
eschewing
CEEGIINRV
receiving
CEEGIJNRT
rejecting
CEEGILLNX
excelling
CEEGILNST
selecting
CEEGIMNNT
cementing
CEEGIMORT
geometric
CEEGINNOS
consignee
CEEGINNRS

screening	**CEEIIMMNN**	**CCEILSUVX**	**CEELMOPSX**
secerning	imminence	exclusive	complexes
CEEGINNRT	**CEEIIMPRS**	**CEEIMMOTT**	**CEELNORSU**
centering	imprecise	committee	enclosure
CEEGINORS	**CEEIINNRS**	**CEEIMNNRT**	**CEELNOSSS**
congeries	insincere	increment	closeness
CEEGINORZ	**CEEIINNTV**	**CEEIMNOOZ**	**CEELNSSST**
recognize	incentive	economize	scentless
CEEGINPTX	**CEEIINPRT**	**CEEIMNOPT**	**CEELNSSUU**
excepting	recipient	impotence	nucleuses
expecting	**CEEIINTVV**	**CEEIMNOST**	**CEEMNOPTT**
CEEGINRSS	invective	centesimo	competent
recessing	**CEEIIOSST**	**CEEIMNSTU**	**CEEMNSTTU**
CEEGINRST	societies	intumesce	tumescent
secreting	**CEEIIPRSV**	**CEEINOPRT**	**CEEMOSSTY**
CEEGINRTX	precisive	reception	ecosystem
excreting	**CEEIIPRUZ**	**CEEINOPST**	**CEENNORTU**
CEEGINTUX	epicurize	potencies	encounter
executing	**CEEIJLSSU**	**CEEINOPTX**	**CEENOOPST**
CEEGIORRS	juiceless	exception	copestone
groceries	**CEEIJNORT**	**CEEINORSS**	**CEENORRTV**
CEEGKNOOS	rejection	recession	converter
gooseneck	**CEEIJNRTT**	**CEEINORST**	reconvert
CEEGLMNRY	interject	secretion	**CEENOSSST**
clergymen	**CEEIKKSSZ**	**CEEINORTX**	contesses
CEEHHIRVW	skeezicks	excretion	**CEENRRRTU**
whichever	**CEEIKMORS**	**CEEINOSSS**	recurrent
CEEHIIPTT	mockeries	secession	**CEEOPPRRT**
epithetic	**CEEILLNTT**	**CEEINOTUX**	preceptor
CEEHIKNRT	intellect	execution	**CEEOPRSSS**
thickener	**CEEILMNNT**	**CEEINPRST**	processes
CEEHIKRST	inclement	prescient	**CEEOPRSTU**
sketchier	**CEEILMNOP**	**CEEINPRTT**	prosecute
CEEHILLMS	policemen	intercept	**CEEOQRTTU**
schlemiel	**CEEILMOST**	**CEEINQSTU**	croquette
CEEHINPRT	comeliest	quiescent	**CEEORRSSS**
phrenetic	**CEEILMRSS**	**CEEINRRSV**	sorceress
CEEHINQTU	merciless	scrivener	**CEEORRSST**
technique	**CEEILNNOS**	**CEEINRSST**	crosstree
CEEHIOPSW	insolence	sincerest	**CEEPRSSSY**
showpiece	**CEEILNOST**	**CEEINRSTT**	cypresses
CEEHIORTT	selection	intersect	**CEERRRSTU**
theoretic	**CEEILNPRT**	**CEEINRSTU**	resurrect
CEEHLORSU	princelet	centuries	**CEFFIRRSU**
lecherous	**CEEILNPST**	**CEEINRSTV**	scruffier
CEEHLPRSU	splenetic	virescent	**CEFGIINNT**
sepulcher	**CEEILNRTV**	**CEEINSSTY**	infecting
sepulchre	ventricle	necessity	**CEFGIKLNR**
CEEHLQSSU	**CEEILNRUV**	**CEEIOPPRS**	freckling
squelches	virulence	periscope	**CEFGINNOR**
CEEHOPRSU	**CEEILORSX**	**CEEIOPPRZ**	enforcing
proseuche	excelsior	copperize	**CEFGINORU**
CEEHORSTU	**CEEILOSSV**	**CEEIORRSS**	configure
retouches	voiceless	sorceries	**CEFIINNOT**
CEEHRRSTT	**CEEILPRSS**	**CEEIORRST**	infection
stretcher	priceless	rectories	**CEFIKORSS**
CEEHRSSTT	**CEEILPRSY**	**CEEIRSSTW**	fossicker
stretches	precisely	screwiest	**CEFIKORST**
CEEIIILVZ	**CEEILRSTU**	**CEEIRTUXX**	forestick
civilizee	cruelties	executrix	**CEFIMNORU**
CEEIILPPT	**CEEILRSUV**	**CEELLLOSU**	cuneiform
epileptic	reclusive	cellulose	**CEFIOORSU**
CEEIILPSS	**CEEILSSUV**	**CEELMNOUW**	ferocious
epiclesis	seclusive	unwelcome	**CEFKLOPTU**

pocketful
CEFKLORSS
frockless
CEFLNNOTU
confluent
CEFMOORRT
comforter
CEFNOORSS
confessor
CEFOORRSU
fourscore
CEFOORRTU
forecourt
CEGGILOST
cloggiest
CEGHIILNS
chiseling
CEGHIINNR
enriching
CEGHIINPR
ciphering
CEGHIKNST
sketching
CEGHILLOU
guilloche
CEGHILOOT
theologic
CEGHINNQU
quenching
CEGHINNRT
trenching
CEGHINNRW
wrenching
CEGHINORT
hectoring
CEGHINPRU
cheruping
CEGHIORRU
grouchier
CEGHKNORU
roughneck
CEGHLOOUY
euchology
CEGIIILNT
eliciting
CEGIIJNNT
injecting
CEGIIJNOR
rejoicing
CEGIIKLNN
nickeling
CEGIIKNNS
sickening
CEGIIKNPT
picketing
CEGIIKNTT
ticketing
CEGIILNNP
penciling
CEGIILNNR
reclining
CEGIILNNS
licensing
silencing

CEGIILNOR
recoiling
CEGIILNPS
eclipsing
CEGIILNST
clingiest
CEGIINNNS
incensing
CEGIINOTV
cognitive
CEGIINQSU
quiescing
CEGIINRSV
servicing
CEGIIOSTT
egotistic
CEGIJKNOY
jockeying
CEGIKLNPS
speckling
CEGIKNNOR
reckoning
CEGIKNOPT
pocketing
CEGIKNORT
rocketing
CEGIKNPRU
puckering
CEGILMMNO
commingle
CEGILMNOW
welcoming
CEGILNNOS
enclosing
CEGILNOST
closeting
CEGILNRSU
surcingle
CEGILNRTU
lecturing
CEGILOOST
ecologist
CEGIMNOPT
competing
CEGINNNOV
convening
CEGINNORR
cornering
CEGINNORS
necrosing
CEGINNOVY
conveying
CEGINNRSU
censuring
CEGINNSTY
encysting
CEGINOOPR
coopering
CEGINOPPR
coppering
CEGINOPRU
recouping
CEGINORRU
occurring

CEGINORST
corseting
escorting
CEGINOSST
cosseting
CEGINRRRU
recurring
CEGINSSUX
excussing
CEGIOOPRT
geotropic
CEGLNOORY
necrology
CEGNNORTU
congruent
CEGNORRSU
scrounger
CEGOOPRSY
gyroscope
CEHHHIIKT
hitchhike
CEHHIMSTT
hemstitch
CEHIIKNST
chinkiest
CEHIIKORS
hickories
CEHIILLST
chilliest
CEHIILMOT
homiletic
CEHIIMNST
ethnicism
CEHIINPRT
nephritic
CEHIINSST
itchiness
CEHIIPRST
chirpiest
CEHIIRSTU
heuristic
CEHIKLSTY
sketchily
CEHIKNSST
thickness
CEHIKNSTU
chunkiest
CEHIKPRSW
shipwreck
CEHILMNTU
lunchtime
CEHILMOTY
hemolytic
CEHILNSTZ
schnitzel
CEHILOPRT
plethoric
CEHIMMSTU
chummiest
CEHIMRSTY
chemistry
CEHINPRST
sphincter
CEHINSTTY

synthetic
CEHIOOSST
choosiest
CEHIOPPRT
prophetic
CEHIOPPST
choppiest
CEHIOPRTU
eutrophic
CEHIOPRTY
hypocrite
CEHIORRST
chorister
CEHIORRST
ostriches
CEHIORSST
touchiest
CEHIOSTTU
stitchery
CEHIRSTTY
cookhouse
CEHKOOOSU
preschool
CEHLOOPRS
splotches
CEHLOPSST
truncheon
CEHNNORTU
horoscope
CEHOOOPRS
psychoses
CEHOPSSSY
civilizer
CEIIILRVZ
victimize
CEIIIMTVZ
incipient
CEIIINNPT
epicrisis
CEIIIPRSS
injection
CEIIJNNOT
juiciness
CEIIJNSSU
injustice
CEIIJNSTU
quicklime
CEIIKLMQU
pricklier
CEIIKLPRR
sickliest
CEIIKLSST
princekin
CEIIKNNPR
nitpicker
CEIIKNPRT
trickiest
CEIIKRSTT
stickiest
CEIIKSSTT
crinoline
CEIILNNOR
principle
CEIILNPPR
CEIILNSUV

inclusive	**CEIKRRSTT**	convexity	prosector
CEIILOPST	trickster	**CEIOORRSV**	**CEOOPRRTT**
epistolic	**CEILLOSUV**	corrosive	protector
CEIIMNSST	collusive	**CEIOPRRTY**	**CEOOPSSTU**
scientism	**CEILMNOOS**	procerity	octopuses
CEIIMORST	cosmoline	**CEIORRTUU**	**CEOORRSSV**
eroticism	semicolon	couturier	crossover
isometric	**CEILMNSUU**	**CEIORSSSW**	**CEOORSTUU**
CEIIMPRRS	minuscule	crosswise	courteous
scrimpier	**CEILMSSTU**	**CEIPPRRST**	**CEOPRRRSU**
CEIIMPRSU	clumsiest	prescript	precursor
epicurism	**CEILNOORZ**	**CEIPRRSTU**	**CEOPRRSSU**
CEIINNOPT	colonizer	scripture	procuress
inception	**CEILNOOTU**	**CEIRRSTTU**	**CERRSTTUU**
CEIINOPRS	elocution	stricture	structure
precision	**CEILNOSSU**	**CEIRSSTTU**	**CFFFIISTU**
CEIINORRT	seclusion	crustiest	fisticuff
criterion	**CEILNOSUX**	**CEJOOPRRT**	**CFFGIINSU**
CEIINPPRS	exclusion	projector	sufficing
principes	**CEILOPRSV**	**CEKKORSTY**	**CFFGILNSU**
CEIINPSSS	slipcover	skyrocket	scuffling
spiciness	**CEILORSSS**	**CEKOOOSTV**	**CFFIIOOSU**
CEIINRSTX	sclerosis	cookstove	officious
extrinsic	**CEILOSSTT**	**CEKOORSTV**	**CFFIMORRU**
CEIINRSTY	costliest	overstock	furciform
sincerity	**CEIMMNOTU**	**CELLMOPXY**	**CFGHIILNN**
CEIINRTTY	comminute	complexly	flinching
intercity	**CEIMMRSTU**	**CELLNOSUU**	**CFGIINNNO**
CEIINRTYZ	crummiest	nucleolus	confining
citizenry	**CEIMMRSTY**	**CELLOORSS**	**CFGILNNOU**
CEIINSSTT	symmetric	colorless	flouncing
scientist	**CEIMMSSTU**	**CELMNOTUY**	**CFGINNORU**
CEIIOOPTZ	scummiest	contumely	frouncing
epizootic	**CEIMNOOST**	**CELNOORSU**	**CFGINNOSU**
CEIIORSTV	economist	counselor	confusing
victories	**CEIMOOPST**	**CELNOOTUV**	**CFGINNOTU**
CEIIPRSST	composite	convolute	confuting
crispiest	**CEIMOPSUU**	**CELNOPRTU**	**CFHIINOOR**
CEIIRSTUV	pumiceous	corpulent	honorific
curvities	**CEINNNOOX**	**CELNORSSW**	**CFHIKOPRT**
CEIKLNORT	connexion	crownless	pitchfork
interlock	**CEINNNOTT**	**CELNOSSTU**	**CFIILMMOR**
CEIKLNSSS	continent	countless	microfilm
slickness	**CEINNNOTV**	**CELNRRTUY**	**CFIIMOPRS**
CEIKLNSSU	connivent	currently	pisciform
luckiness	**CEINNOOTV**	**CELNRTTUU**	**CFIIOOPRS**
CEIKLOPST	connotive	truculent	soporific
stockpile	**CEINNORTU**	**CELPRSTUU**	**CFIKLLNOT**
CEIKLOSTV	centurion	sculpture	flintlock
livestock	**CEINNOTXY**	**CEMNNOOPT**	**CFILNSUUU**
CEIKLPSTU	connexity	component	funiculus
pluckiest	**CEINOORST**	**CEMOOPRSU**	**CFIMMOORR**
CEIKNORSS	cortisone	composure	microform
rockiness	**CEINOPPRU**	**CEMOOSTTY**	**CFINNOOSU**
CEIKNOSTT	porcupine	cystotome	confusion
stockinet	**CEINOPRST**	**CENNOOPRU**	**CGGIINNOZ**
CEIKNQSSU	inspector	pronounce	cognizing
quickness	**CEINORSTU**	**CENNOSSSU**	**CGGINORSU**
CEIKOSSTT	countries	consensus	scourging
stockiest	**CEINORSUX**	**CENOOQRRU**	**CGHIILLNS**
CEIKPPRSU	excursion	conqueror	schilling
pickpurse	**CEINOSTUV**	**CENORSSSS**	**CGHIILORR**
CEIKPQSTU	contusive	crossness	choirgirl
quickstep	**CEINOTVXY**	**CEOOPRRST**	**CGHIIMNRS**

smirching	**CGIKLMNOY**	**CGINRRSUY**	**CIILLNOOS**
CGHIINNST	mockingly	scurrying	collision
snitching	**CGIKLNNOU**	**CGINRSTUY**	**CIILLNOOT**
CGHIINSTT	unlocking	curtsying	cotillion
stitching	**CGIKLNRTU**	**CGLMOOOSY**	octillion
CGHIINSTW	truckling	cosmology	**CIILNNOSU**
switching	**CGIKNNOOV**	**CGMNOOOSY**	inclusion
CGHIINTTW	convoking	cosmogony	**CIILOORST**
twitching	**CGILLNORS**	**CGNNOOTTU**	solicitor
CGHILNOOS	scrolling	guncotton	**CIILOOSSS**
schooling	**CGILMNOPY**	**CGNOORSUU**	scoliosis
CGHILNOOY	complying	congruous	**CIILOSUVY**
ichnology	**CGILMNPRU**	**CHHKLLOOY**	viciously
CGHILNORT	crumpling	hollyhock	**CIILSSTTY**
chortling	**CGILNNNUY**	**CHIIKKNST**	stylistic
CGHILNOSU	cunningly	thickskin	**CIIMMSSTY**
slouching	**CGILNNOOS**	**CHIINOSTU**	mysticism
CGHILOOOR	consoling	chitinous	**CIIMNORUZ**
horologic	**CGILNNRUU**	**CHIIORRSS**	zirconium
CGHIMNOOS	uncurling	cirrhosis	**CIINNNOTU**
smooching	**CGILNOOOY**	**CHIIPSSTY**	inunction
CGHIMNOSU	iconology	physicist	**CIINNORSU**
smouching	**CGILNOPTU**	**CHIKLMOST**	incursion
CGHIMNSTU	octupling	locksmith	**CIINOPSSU**
smutching	**CGILNORSU**	**CHIKOOPTT**	suspicion
CGHINSSSU	closuring	toothpick	**CIIORSTUY**
schussing	**CGILNPRSU**	**CHILLNOOT**	curiosity
CGHIOPRTY	scrupling	loincloth	**CIIOSSTVY**
copyright	**CGILNPSTU**	**CHILLOSTY**	viscosity
CGIIIKMMN	sculpting	coltishly	**CIIRSTTUY**
mimicking	**CGILNRTUU**	**CHILPRSUU**	rusticity
CGIIILNNN	culturing	sulphuric	**CIKLORSTW**
inclining	**CGILNSTTU**	**CHIMNOPSY**	wristlock
CGIIKLNNR	scuttling	symphonic	**CILLMORUY**
crinkling	**CGILOOOSY**	**CHINOPSTU**	collyrium
CGIIKLNPR	sociology	countship	**CILLNOOSU**
prickling	**CGIMMNNOU**	**CHIOPRSTU**	collusion
CGIIKLNRT	communing	courtship	**CILMNOSTU**
trickling	**CGIMMNOTU**	**CHIOPRSYY**	columnist
CGIIKLNST	commuting	hypocrisy	**CILMOORTV**
stickling	**CGIMNNOSU**	**CHIOPSSSY**	microvolt
CGIILMNNY	consuming	psychosis	**CILOOPSUY**
mincingly	**CGIMNOOPS**	**CHLMNOORU**	copiously
CGIILMNOP	composing	lunchroom	**CILORRSUY**
compiling	**CGIMNOPTU**	**CHLNOTUUY**	cursorily
CGIILNPPR	computing	uncouthly	**CIMMMNOSU**
crippling	**CGIMNOSTU**	**CHNNORSYY**	communism
CGIIMNPRS	costuming	synchrony	**CIMMNNOOU**
scrimping	**CGINNNOOT**	**CHNORSTUU**	communion
CGIINNNOV	connoting	cothurnus	**CIMMNOOOT**
conniving	**CGINNOOTT**	**CHOOOPPTY**	commotion
CGIINNOOT	cottoning	photocopy	**CIMMNOSTU**
cognition	**CGINNOOVY**	**CHOOOPRSY**	communist
incognito	convoying	horoscopy	**CIMMNOTUY**
CGIINNRRU	**CGINNORTU**	**CIIILLLTY**	community
incurring	trouncing	illicitly	**CIMNOOORZ**
CGIINPRST	**CGINNOSTU**	**CIILMOPT**	microzoon
scripting	contusing	impolitic	**CINNOOSTU**
CGIINPRTU	**CGINOOPRS**	**CIIILORTV**	contusion
picturing	scrooping	vitriolic	**CINNOOSUU**
CGIJNNORU	**CGINOPRRU**	**CIIMSTTW**	innocuous
conjuring	procuring	witticism	**CINOOORRS**
CGIKKLNNU	**CGINORTUY**	**CIIINNRST**	corrosion
knuckling	outcrying	intrinsic	**CIOOOPRTZ**

protozoic
CIOPPRRST
proscript
CKKOORSTW
stockwork
CKMOOORST
stockroom
CLMOOOORT
locomotor
CLMOORSTU
colostrum
CLMOSSUUU
musculous
CLNOOPRSU
proconsul
CLNORTUUY
uncourtly
CMOOOORRTU
courtroom
CMOOORSST
motocross
CMOOSTTYY
cystotomy
CNOORSSTW
crosstown
DBEMMNOSU
ombudsmen
DDDEEHRSU
shuddered
DDDEEINST
distended
DDDEENOPS
desponded
DDDEENORU
redounded
DDDEGIINR
diddering
DDDEGILOS
dislodged
DDDEGINOR
doddering
DDDEIINUV
undivided
DDEEEFNRU
underfeed
DDEEEGIPR
pedigreed
DDEEEILRV
delivered
DDEEEIMRT
demerited
DDEEEIPTX
expedited
DDEEEELMOR
remodeled
DDEEEELOPV
developed
DDEEENNPT
dependent
DDEEENPRT
pretended
DDEEEORRR
reordered
DDEEEPRSS

depressed
DDEEERRSS
redressed
DDEEESTUU
desuetude
DDEEFGINN
defending
DDEEFNORU
foundered
DDEEGHILT
delighted
DDEEGILNR
engirdled
DDEEGINNP
depending
DDEEGIRSS
digressed
DDEEHIRRS
shreddier
DDEEHNORT
dethroned
DDEEHNRTU
thundered
DDEEIILMT
delimited
DDEEIILNS
sidelined
DDEEIILVZ
devilized
DDEEIIOXZ
deoxidize
DDEEIKLNR
rekindled
DDEEILLPS
dispelled
DDEEILMMN
middlemen
DDEEILMOZ
melodized
DDEEILOPS
despoiled
DDEEILORS
soldiered
DDEEIMNOZ
demonized
DDEEINORW
eiderdown
DDEEINPSS
dispensed
DDEEINRSU
underside
undesired
DDEEINSST
dissented
DDEEIOORZ
deodorize
DDEEIOPRX
peroxided
DDEEIOPST
deposited
DDEEIPRSS
dispersed
DDEEIPTUZ
deputized

DDEELMORS
smoldered
DDEELNPRU
plundered
DDEENNORU
underdone
DDEENOPRS
responded
DDEENOPRT
protended
DDEENOPUX
expounded
DDEENORSU
resounded
DDEENPSSU
suspended
DDEENRSSU
undressed
DDEEOOPRT
torpedoed
DDEEORSTY
destroyed
DDEFFIINT
diffident
DDEFGIIIN
dignified
DDEFGJORU
forjudged
DDEFIIMNU
mundified
DDEFNNOUU
unfounded
DDEGHINRS
shredding
DDEGIIMSU
misguided
DDEGIINSS
giddiness
DDEGIISSU
disguised
DDEGIJMSU
misjudged
DDEGINNOS
soddening
DDEGINRTU
detruding
DDEGLNOOR
goldenrod
DDEHHNRTU
hundredth
DDEHIOSST
shoddiest
DDEIIINVZ
divinized
DDEIIJNOS
disjoined
DDEIILLST
distilled
DDEIIMSSS
dismissed
DDEIIMTTW
dimwitted
DDEIINSST
dissident

DDEIINSTU
disunited
DDEILOSSV
dissolved
DDEIMNNOPU
impounded
DDEIMNSSU
muddiness
DDEINORTU
outridden
DDEINORWW
windrowed
DDEINRSSU
ruddiness
DDEINSTUU
unstudied
DDEIOPRSV
disproved
DDEIORSTT
distorted
DDEIPRSTU
disrupted
DDELNORSU
undersold
DDEOOPSUX
pseudodox
DDEOPRRTU
protruded
DDFIOORTW
driftwood
DDGIILNNW
dwindling
DDGIILNTW
twiddling
DDGILNNOY
noddingly
DDHIOOOWW
widowhood
DEEEEKNRW
weekender
DEEEENPST
steepened
DEEEENRRT
reentered
DEEEENSTW
sweetened
DEEEFHNRS
freshened
DEEEFHRRS
refreshed
DEEEFINSV
defensive
DEEEFMNRT
deferment
fermented
DEEEFPRRR
preferred
DEEEGIMNR
redeeming
DEEEGINRS
energised
DEEEGINRZ
energized
DEEEGIRST

greediest
DEEEGMNST
segmented
DEEEGNRTT
detergent
DEEEGRRSS
regressed
DEEEGRRTT
regretted
DEEEHILPS
ephelides
DEEEHLRST
sheltered
DEEEHNPRR
reprehend
DEEEHNRRU
hereunder
DEEEHORSW
horseweed
DEEEILNNV
enlivened
DEEEILNRT
treelined
DEEEILPTV
depletive
DEEEILSSW
edelweiss
DEEEILSTV
televised
DEEEIMNRT
determine
DEEEIMPRR
premiered
DEEEINNSS
neediness
DEEEINOPR
pioneered
DEEEINPTX
expedient
DEEEINRTZ
tenderize
DEEEINSSS
seediness
DEEEINSSW
weediness
DEEEIPRRV
reprieved
DEEEIPRVW
previewed
DEEEIPSST
speediest
DEEEIRRTV
retrieved
DEEEIRSTV
detersive
DEEELLPSW
speedwell
DEEELNOPV
enveloped
DEEELOPRV
redevelop
DEEELPPRX
perplexed
DEEELRSTW

sweltered
DEEEMNNOV
envenomed
DEEEMNRTT
determent
DEEEMOPRT
pedometer
DEEEMOPRW
empowered
DEEEMPPRT
preempted
DEEENPRRT
pretender
DEEENPRST
presented
serpented
DEEENPRTV
prevented
DEEENRRTT
deterrent
DEEEORSTV
stevedore
DEEEPRRSS
repressed
DEEEPRRSV
preserved
DEEEPRRTV
perverted
DEEEPRSSS
depresses
DEEEPRSSU
supersede
DEEEPRSSX
expressed
DEEEQRSTU
requested
DEEERRRSS
redresser
DEEFFINRT
different
DEEFFINST
stiffened
DEEFFIORT
forfeited
DEEFFOPRR
proffered
DEEFGHIRT
freighted
DEEFGIILR
filigreed
DEEFGILNY
feignedly
DEEFHLORT
threefold
DEEFHRRTU
furthered
DEEFIILNR
infielder
DEEFIILQU
liquefied
DEEFIIMNZ
feminized
DEEFIIMRT
metrified

DEEFIINRU
reunified
DEEFIIPRT
petrified
DEEFIIRRT
terrified
DEEFIISTT
testified
DEEFILNOX
deflexion
DEEFINNRU
unrefined
DEEFIORRT
torrefied
DEEFIPRTU
putrefied
DEEFIRRTT
frittered
DEEFIRSTU
surfeited
DEEFLLNUY
needfully
DEEFLNOSV
sevenfold
DEEFLRSTU
flustered
DEEFLRTTU
fluttered
DEEFMOPRR
performed
preformed
DEEFNOOST
festooned
DEEFOPRSS
professed
DEEFORRST
defroster
DEEGGINNR
gendering
DEEGGINRS
sniggered
DEEGGINRT
deterging
DEEGGIORS
doggeries
DEEGGIRRT
triggered
DEEGGSSTU
suggested
DEEGHIINV
inveighed
DEEGHILNT
lightened
DEEGHILNW
wheedling
DEEGHINNU
unheeding
DEEGHINRT
rightened
DEEGHINTT
tightened
DEEGHNORU
roughened
DEEGHNOTU

toughened
DEEGIILNU
guideline
DEEGIILNV
inveigled
DEEGIISTV
digestive
DEEGILMMR
glimmered
DEEGILNPT
depleting
DEEGILNST
glistened
DEEGILNTW
tweedling
DEEGILOOU
ideologue
DEEGILOUZ
eulogized
DEEGILRTT
glittered
DEEGIMNNT
dementing
DEEGIMNRY
remedying
DEEGINNPX
expending
DEEGINNRR
rendering
DEEGINNRT
tendering
DEEGINNTX
extending
DEEGINRRR
dererring
DEEGINRRT
deterring
DEEGINRST
deserting
DEEGINRSV
deserving
DEEGINRTV
divergent
DEEGINSTT
detesting
DEEGINSTV
devesting
DEEGINTTV
vignetted
DEEGIPRST
predigest
DEEGIRSSS
digresses
DEEGKLNOW
knowledge
DEEGLLORV
grovelled
DEEGNNORU
undergone
DEEGNOORW
greenwood
DEEGNORSS
engrossed

DEEHHIRTW
whithered
DEEHIINRT
inherited
DEEHIKRSW
whiskered
DEEHILNPS
plenished
DEEHILPRT
philtered
DEEHILRSV
shriveled
DEEHIMMRS
shimmered
DEEHIMPRW
whimpered
DEEHINNRS
enshrined
DEEHINRSW
swineherd
DEEHIORTZ
theorized
DEEHIPRSW
whispered
DEEHIPUUZ
euphuized
DEEHLNOPR
penholder
DEEHLORST
holstered
DEEHMORST
smothered
DEEHNNORT
enthroned
DEEHNORST
shortened
DEEHOORTX
heterodox
DEEHRSSTW
shrewdest
DEEHRSTTU
shuttered
DEEIILLMP
millipede
DEEIILMPR
imperiled
DEEIILRSV
devilries
DEEIILSTW
wieldiest
DEEIIMPRS
epidermis
DEEIINSST
densities
destinies
DEEIIPSSW
sideswipe
DEEIIRRSV
riverside
DEEIIRSTV
revisited
DEEIKRSTT
skittered
DEEILLNRW

indweller
DEEILNNRU
underline
DEEILNOPT
depletion
DEEILNOVZ
novelized
DEEILNPTU
plenitude
DEEILNRTU
interlude
DEEILNTVY
evidently
DEEILOPTX
exploited
DEEILORRS
orderlies
DEEILRTUY
eruditely
DEEIMMORZ
memorized
DEEIMNNOT
mentioned
DEEIMNNPT
impendent
DEEIMNNRU
undermine
DEEIMNNRV
nevermind
DEEIMNORZ
modernize
DEEIMNOST
moistened
DEEIMNRTT
detriment
DEEIMOORT
meteoroid
DEEIMOSST
modesties
DEEIMPRSS
impressed
DEEIMPRST
distemper
DEEIMPRTT
permitted
DEEIMRTUU
deuterium
DEEINNOPS
pensioned
DEEINNORV
environed
DEEINNOTT
detention
DEEINNPRU
unripened
DEEINNRTU
indenture
DEEINORST
desertion
DEEINPRRT
reprinted
DEEINPRRU
underripe
DEEINPRST

president
DEEINRSST
tiredness
DEEINRSTT
trendiest
DEEINSSTW
witnessed
DEEIOPPRW
piepowder
DEEIOPSTZ
despotize
DEEIORRVV
overdrive
DEEIPPRRS
perspired
DEEIPRSST
persisted
DEEIPRSTU
disrepute
DEEIRSSST
dressiest
DEEIRSTUV
servitude
DEEIRTTXY
dexterity
DEEISTTTU
destitute
DEEJNORUY
journeyed
DEEJOORVY
overjoyed
DEEKKNSUW
skunkweed
DEELLNRSU
undersell
DEELLNSSY
endlessly
DEELLOPPR
propelled
DEELMMPTU
plummeted
DEELNNPST
splendent
DEELNOOST
lodestone
DEELNSTTU
unsettled
DEELPPSTU
septupled
DEELPSTUX
sextupled
DEEMNNOTW
endowment
DEEMNOPRS
endosperm
DEEMNORTT
tormented
DEEMNORTU
remounted
DEEMPRTTU
trumpeted
DEENNRTUW
underwent
DEENOPRRV

provender
DEENOPRSV
overspend
DEENORTUY
tourneyed
DEENPRSSU
suspender
unpressed
DEENRRRSU
surrender
DEENRSTTU
entrusted
DEENRSTYY
dysentery
DEEOOPRST
torpedoes
DEEOPPRRS
prospered
DEEOPPRSS
oppressed
DEEOPRRSS
depressor
DEEOPRSTT
protested
DEEOPSSSS
possessed
DEEORRSTY
destroyer
DEEORSTUX
dexterous
DEEPRRSSU
pressured
DEEPRSTTU
sputtered
DEERSTTTU
stuttered
DEFFGIINR
differing
DEFFGINNO
offending
DEFFIIORT
fortified
DEFFIISUV
diffusive
DEFFILLLU
fulfilled
DEFFILNTU
diffluent
DEFFILSUY
diffusely
DEFFNSTUU
unstuffed
DEFGGGINO
defogging
DEFGGIINT
fidgeting
DEFGGILLN
fledgling
DEFGHILOT
eightfold
DEFGIIILN
lignified
DEFGIIINS
dignifies

signified
DEFGIILOR
glorified
DEFGIINNR
infringed
DEFGIIRSU
disfigure
DEFGIMNOR
deforming
DEFGINNRU
refunding
DEFHIIORR
horrified
DEFHIIRTU
thurified
DEFHINRSU
furnished
DEFIIINRT
nitrified
DEFIIIRTV
vitrified
DEFIIJLLO
jollified
DEFIIJSTU
justified
DEFIILLMO
mollified
DEFIILLNU
nullified
DEFIILMSU
semifluid
DEFIILPPU
pulpified
DEFIIMMMU
mummified
DEFIIMNNY
indemnify
DEFIIMORT
mortified
DEFIIMRWY
midwifery
DEFIIMSTY
mystified
DEFIINRTU
nutrified
DEFIIOPRT
torpified
DEFIIRSTT
driftiest
DEFIIRSVY
diversify
DEFILMNRU
remindful
DEFILNOUX
defluxion
DEFIMORTY
deformity
DEFINORSU
foundries
DEFIOPSTX
postfixed
DEFIORTTU
fortitude
DEFIOTTTU

outfitted
DEFLLLOUY
dolefully
DEFLNORUW
wonderful
DEFNOORTU
underfoot
DEGGIINNR
engirding
DEGGIINNS
designing
DEGGIINRV
diverging
DEGGIINST
digesting
DEGGILQSU
squiggled
DEGGINSTU
degusting
DEGGLNPUU
unplugged
DEGGLRSTU
struggled
DEGHIILNS
shielding
DEGHIINNR
hindering
DEGHIJPSU
judgeship
DEGHILNTU
unlighted
DEGHIMNRU
humdinger
DEGHIORTU
doughtier
DEGHIOSTU
doughiest
DEGHMOORT
godmother
DEGHNORUY
greyhound
DEGIIINST
dignities
DEGIILMNW
mildewing
DEGIILMPR
pilgrimed
DEGIILNRV
driveling
DEGIILNRW
wildering
DEGIIMNNP
impending
DEGIIMNNR
reminding
DEGIIMNOR
moidering
DEGIIMNTT
demitting
DEGIINNNT
indenting
DEGIINNST
destining

rewording
DEGINORTU
detouring
DEGINORUV
devouring
DEGINPRRU
perduring
DEGINRTUX
extruding
DEGIOOSVW
goodwives
DEGIOPRTY
pterygoid
DEGIOPSTU
guidepost
DEGLLLOOR
logrolled
DEGLMOPRU
promulged
DEGLNOOPR
prolonged
DEGLOOPRU
prologued
DEGNOPRUW
gunpowder
DEGORRSTU
drugstore
DEHHLOOSU
household
DEHHLORST
threshold
DEHIIMOPP
hippiedom
DEHIIORST
historied
DEHIISTWW
widthwise
DEHIKORSS
droshkies
DEHILNNOR
innholder
DEHILOSTW
dishtowel
DEHILOSUY
hideously
DEHILRRUY
hurriedly
DEHIMPRTU
triumphed
DEHINORSU
nourished
DEHINOSST
dishonest
DEHINRRUU
unhurried
DEHIOPRSW
worshiped
DEHIORRTY
erythroid
DEHLLOOSU
dollhouse
DEHLOOPRT
potholder
DEHLORTTT

DEGIINOST
digestion
DEGIINPRS
presiding
DEGIINPRV
depriving
DEGIINPSS
despising
DEGIINPST
despiting
DEGIINRTU
intrigued
DEGIINRTV
diverting
DEGIINSST
desisting
DEGIINSTV
divesting
DEGIIOPRS
prodigies
DEGILLNOY
yodelling
DEGILNNRU
underling
DEGILNNTU
indulgent
DEGILNOOR
gondolier
DEGILNOPR
deploring
DEGILNOPX
exploding
DEGILNOPY
deploying
DEGILNORS
soldering
DEGILNORU
ungodlier
DEGILNOSS
godliness
DEGILNOSU
delousing
DEGILNOTU
longitude
DEGILNPRU
preluding
DEGILOSTT
glottides
DEGIMNRRU
demurring
DEGIMNRRU
murdering
DEGINNOPR
pondering
DEGINNORS
endorsing
DEGINNORW
wondering
DEGINNRSU
sundering
DEGINOPRT
deporting
DEGINOPRW
powdering
DEGINORRW

throttled
DEHLOSSTU
shouldest
DEIIIMMNZ
minimized
DEIIINNQU
quinidine
DEIIKLNST
kindliest
DEIILLMNU
illumined
DEIILLNST
instilled
DEIILLOPR
pilloried
DEIILLOPS
ellipsoid
DEIILLRST
distiller
DEIILMNTU
unlimited
DEIILMOSS
semisolid
DEIILNSSV
lividness
DEIILORSU
delirious
DEIILPPUZ
pupilized
DEIIMMNUZ
immunized
DEIIMNNOS
dimension
DEIIMNNTY
indemnity
DEIIMNOSS
demission
DEIIMNPRT
imprinted
DEIIMNRTW
midwinter
DEIIMNSST
timidness
DEIIMOPTZ
optimized
DEIIMORTV
dormitive
DEIIMSSSS
dismisses
DEIINNOOP
opinioned
DEIINNORT
rendition
DEIINNOTT
dentition
DEIINNOUZ
unionized
DEIINNSSW
windiness
DEIINNTUV
uninvited
DEIINOPRT
perdition
DEIINOPSS

indispose
DEIIINORST
disorient
DEIINORSV
diversion
DEIINORTT
detrition
DEIINORTU
erudition
DEIINSSVV
vividness
DEIINSTTU
untidiest
DEIIOSSTU
seditious
DEIIPPRST
drippiest
DEIIRSTVY
diversity
DEIJLNOTY
jointedly
DEIJNNRUU
uninjured
DEIKLLNSU
unskilled
DEIKLNPRS
sprinkled
DEIKNSSSU
duskiness
DEILLORRW
worldlier
DEILMNOSS
moldiness
DEILMOOSU
melodious
DEILMTTUU
multitude
DEILNOPRU
purloined
DEILNOPSU
unspoiled
DEILNOSSS
solidness
DEILOSTUY
tediously
DEILOSUVY
deviously
DEIMMMRSU
midsummer
DEIMMNORS
modernism
DEIMMOSTY
immodesty
DEIMNOOSS
moodiness
DEIMNORST
modernist
DEIMNORTY
modernity
DEIMNPRTU
imprudent
DEIMOPSST
despotism
DEIMOQSTU

misquoted
DEINNRSUU
uninsured
DEINOOPRT
portioned
DEINOPRST
dripstone
DEIONPRTV
provident
DEINORSSW
wordiness
DEINRSTTY
dentistry
DEIOOPRST
depositor
DEIOOPRST
droopiest
DEIOOSSTW
woodsiest
DEIORSSST
drossiest
DEIORSSTW
drowsiest
DEIPRRSSU
surprised
DEIPRTTUU
turpitude
DEIRSSTTU
sturdiest
DEJNOORSU
sojourned
DEKLNNRUY
drunkenly
DEKNOORTU
undertook
DELNOPSUU
pendulous
DELNPRTUY
prudently
DELORSSSW
swordless
DELORSTUY
desultory
DELOSTUUY
duteously
DEMNNORSU
roundsmen
DEMNOPSUY
pseudonym
DEMNORSSW
swordsmen
DEMNORSTU
undermost
DEMORRSUU
murderous
DENNOSSSU
soundness
DENOOPPST
postponed
DENOOPPSU
unopposed
DENOOPRSS
sponsored
DENOOPRSU
ponderous

DENOPRSSU
proudness
DEOPPRRTU
purported
DEOPPRSTU
supported
DFFFOOSTU
foodstuff
DFFGIINSU
diffusing
DFFIINOSU
diffusion
DFGIIIMNW
midwifing
DFGIIINNY
nidifying
DFGIIIRTY
frigidity
DFGIIMNOY
modifying
DFGIINNUY
undignify
DFGILNNOU
foundling
DFGILNNOU
unfolding
DFHILOORY
hydrofoil
DFHINORSU
roundfish
DFHINOSTW
downshift
DFHIORSSW
swordfish
DFHLNOOUW
wolfhound
DFIINPRST
spindrift
DFIKOOPRS
skidproof
DFILLMNUY
mindfully
DFILLTUUY
dutifully
DFILMNNUU
unmindful
DFINOOPRW
windproof
DFINORSTW
snowdrift
DGGGINNOO
doggongin
DGGHILOSY
doggishly
DGGIILNNU
indulging
DGGIILNUV
divulging
DGGINNORU
·grounding
DGHHIINST
hindsight
DGHHINOPT
diphthong
DGHHOORSU

roughshod
DGHILMOST
goldsmith
DGHILNOPU
upholding
DGHILOPRT
droplight
DGHINORSU
shrouding
DGHINORTW
downright
DGHLOORYY
hydrology
DGHOORSUU
sourdough
DGIIIINRZ
iridizing
DGIIIKLNS
disliking
DGIIILNOZ
idolizing
DGIIIMNTT
dimitting
DGIIIMNVW
midwiving
DGIIINNNW
inwinding
DGIIINNTY
indignity
DGIIINOXZ
oxidizing
DGIIKNOSY
disyoking
DGIIKNSVY
skydiving
DGIILMNOP
imploding
DGIILNNPS
spindling
DGIILNNSW
swindling
DGIILNNWY
windingly
DGIILNPRY
pridingly
DGIILNRZZ
drizzling
DGIINNNUW
unwinding
DGIINNORS
indorsing
DGIINNOSW
disowning
DGIINNRTU
intruding
DGIINNTUY
untidying
DGIINOPRV
providing
DGIINOPSS
disposing
DGIINORTU
outriding
DGIINPSTU

disputing
DGILNNRTU
trundling
DGILNNUYY
undyingly
DHIILNRWW
whirlwind
DHIINOORT
ornithoid
DHIINOORT
withstood
DHLMOOTUU
loudmouth
DHOOORTXY
orthodoxy
DHOOPPPUY
puppyhood
DHOPRSTYY
dystrophy
DIIILQTUY
liquidity
DIIINOSSU
insidious
DIIINOSUV
invidious
DIILLMNOO
modillion
DIIPSTTUY
stupidity
DIMNORSTW
windstorm
DIMOORRTY
dormitory
DINORTTUY
rotundity
DLLNORUWY
unworldly
DMNOORRUW
roundworm
EEEEGNRRV
evergreen
EEEEHLRSW
elsewhere
EEEELMRTT
telemeter
EEEELNTVV
velveteen
EEEENNSTV
seventeen
EEEENOPRY
eyeopener
EEEENRSTW
sweetener
EEEEPRRSV
persevere
EEEFHNRRS
freshener
EEEFHORRT
therefore
EEEFHORRW
wherefore
EEEFHRRSS
refreshes
EEEFILRVX

reflexive
EEEFINRRS
ferneries
EEEFINRRT
interfere
EEEGIMNST
esteeming
EEEGINPRR
peregrine
EEEGINRRS
energiser
EEEGINRTT
teetering
EEEGLMNNT
gentlemen
EEEGMNRSS
messenger
EEEGNNRSS
greenness
EEEHIMPRS
ephemeris
EEEHIMPUZ
euphemize
EEEHISTWZ
wheeziest
EEEHLMNTY
methylene
EEEHLNOPT
telephone
EEEHLRRST
shelterer
EEEHMORST
threesome
EEEHMORSW
somewhere
EEEHNRSSS
sheerness
EEEHORSTU
ethereous
EEEHRSTTU
usherette
EEEIJKLLW
jewellike
EEEIKLNQU
queenlike
EEEIKNNPR
innkeeper
EEEILMSST
seemliest
EEEILNQRU
queenlier
EEEILPSST
sleepiest
EEEILPTVX
expletive
EEEILSSTT
steeliest
EEEIMMRSZ
mesmerize
EEEIMORTT
meteorite
EEEIMPRRT
perimeter
EEEINNRTV

intervene
EEEINPSVX
expensive
EEEINRTTV
retentive
EEEINSSTV
seventies
EEEINSTVX
extensive
EEEIPRSTX
expertise
EEEIQRRSU
equerries
EEEIQTTTU
etiquette
EEEIRRRTV
retriever
EEEIRSTTV
serviette
EEEKLNSSS
sleekness
EEEKMRSTU
musketeer
EEELLNPRT
repellent
EEELLNSSV
levelness
EEELLPSSS
sleepless
EEELMNOPT
elopement
EEELMNRTT
lettermen
EEELMRTTY
telemetry
EEELMRTXY
extremely
EEELNOTTV
novelette
EEELNRSSV
nerveless
EEELNSSSS
senseless
EEELPPRSX
perplexes
EEEMMNOST
mementoes
EEEMNORRV
nevermore
EEEMNRSTT
entremets
EEEMOPRTX
extempore
EEEMRSTTX
extremest
EEENNSSST
tenseness
EEENPRRST
represent
EEENPSSST
steepness
EEENQRSSU
queerness
EEENRSSST

terseness
EEENSSSTW
sweetness
EEEOPRRTV
portreeve
EEEORRTVX
overexert
EEEPPPRTU
puppeteer
EEEPRRSSS
represses
EEEQRSSTU
sequester
EEFFGLNTU
effulgent
EEFFHINTT
fifteenth
EEFFIILRS
fireflies
EEFFINOSV
offensive
EEFFIORRT
forfeiter
EEFFIPRSU
pufferies
EEFGHIRRT
freighter
EEFGILNNU
unfeeling
EEFGILNRU
refueling
EEFGILNRX
reflexing
EEFGINORR
foreigner
EEFGINRRR
referring
EEFGINRRT
ferreting
EEFGINRST
festering
EEFGINRTT
fettering
EEFGIORRS
forgeries
EEFHIIRSS
fisheries
EEFHILLRS
shellfire
EEFHIMNRS
fishermen
EEFHINQSU
queenfish
EEFHIORSU
firehouse
EEFHIOSUW
housewife
EEFHLLSSS
fleshless
EEFHMORRT
therefrom
EEFHNRSSS
freshness
EEFHRRRTU

furtherer
EEFIILNRT
infertile
EEFIILRTZ
fertilize
EEFIILSTW
wifeliest
EEFIIMRST
metrifies
EEFIINRSU
reunifies
EEFIIPRST
petrifies
EEFIIRRST
terrifies
EEFIIRSTT
testifier
EEFIISSTT
testifies
EEFILMPXY
exemplify
EEFILOORS
fooleries
EEFILSTVY
festively
EEFIOPPRS
fopperies
EEFIOPRRT
profiteer
EEFIPRSTU
putrefies
EEFIPSSTU
stupefies
EEFKNOORT
foretoken
EEFLNRTVY
fervently
EEFLRRTTU
flutterer
EEFMNOORW
forewomen
EEFMOPRRR
performer
EEFMPRRUY
perfumery
EEFOPRSSS
professes
EEGGIILNS
elegising
EEGGIILNZ
elegizing
EEGGILNNT
negligent
EEGGILOOS
geologies
EEGGINNRV
revenging
EEGGIORSU
egregious
EEGHHIITT
eightieth
EEGHIIRTW
weightier
EEGHILMPR

phlegmier
EEGHILNNT
enlighten
EEGHILNRT
lengthier
EEGHINRTT
tethering
EEGHIRSST
sightseer
EEGHLOOTT
logothete
EEGHNNORR
greenhorn
EEGHNNOTY
ethnogeny
EEGHNOOPT
photogene
EEGIIKLRT
tigerlike
EEGIILNRV
relieving
EEGIILPRV
privilege
EEGIINRVW
reviewing
EEGIISTTZ
zeitgeist
EEGIJLNRR
jerringlr
EEGIKLNNN
kenneling
EEGIKLNNR
kerneling
EEGILLLNV
levelling
EEGILLNPR
repelling
EEGILLNPT
pelleting
EEGILLNPX
expelling
EEGILLNRT
retelling
EEGILLSSU
guileless
EEGILNNRT
relenting
EEGILNNSS
lessening
EEGILNNUY
genuinely
EEGILNOOS
neologies
EEGILNRTT
lettering
EEGILORST
sortilege
EEGIMNPRT
tempering
EEGIMNPTX
exempting
EEGINNOPR
reopening
EEGINNPRT

repenting
EEGINNRST
resenting
EEGINOPRS
progenies
EEGINOPSU
epigenous
EEGINORSS
egression
EEGINORSV
sovereign
EEGINPPPR
peppering
EEGINPRST
estreping
pestering
EEGINQSUZ
squeezing
EEGINRRSV
reserving
reversing
EEGINRRTV
reverting
EEGINRSTT
resetting
EEGIORRSU
rogueries
EEGIORSTV
vertigoes
EEGIRRSSU
surgeries
EEGLLOOTY
teleology
EEGLNORTT
lorgnette
EEGLRSSSU
surgeless
EEGNOORSU
erogenous
EEGNORSSV
governess
EEGNRRSTU
resurgent
EEGOQRSTU
grotesque
EEHHINOSS
shoeshine
EEHHIRTTW
therewith
EEHHOORSS
horseshoe
EEHIINNTT
ninetieth
EEHIKLRSW
shrewlike
EEHIKNPSS
sheepskin
EEHILLSST
shelliest
EEHILMOST
homeliest
lithesome
EEHILNORS
shoreline

EEHILNPRS
replenish

EEHILNPSS
spleenish

EEHILNSST
litheness

EEHILPSVY
peevishly

EEHILRSTW
erstwhile

EEHIMMPSU
euphemism

EEHIMOPRT
hemitrope

EEHIMPSTU
euphemist

EEHINOPSU
euphonies

EEHINOPUZ
euphonize

EEHINORTT
thereinto

EEHINSSTW
whiteness

EEHINSTTX
sixteenth

EEHINTTTW
twentieth

EEHIORSTW
otherwise

EEHIPPRRY
periphery

EEHLMOOSW
wholesome

EEHLMORVW
overwhelm

EEHLNOSSW
wholeness

EEHLNOSSY
honeyless

EEHLORSSS
shoreless

EEHLOSSSU
houseless

EEHMNORTY
heteronym

EEHMNPTTU
umpteenth

EEHNOPRTU
thereupon

EEHNOPRUW
whereupon

EEHNOPSTU
penthouse

EEHNOPTTY
entophyte

EEHNORRST
shortener

EEHNOSTTW
whetstone

EEHOORSVW
howsoever
whosoever

EEHORRTVW
overthrew

EEIIIMNST
nimieties

EEIIIMPST
impieties

EEIIKLLST
likeliest

EEIIILLSTV
liveliest

EEIILNRST
resilient

EEIILRSTZ
sterilize

EEIIMOPTZ
epitomize

EEIIMRSSV
remissive

EEIINNSTT
intestine

EEIINNSTV
intensive

EEIINNTVV
inventive

EEIINRSSW
swineries

EEIINRSTT
enteritis

EEIINRTVW
interview

EEIINRTWZ
winterize

EEIINSSTV
sensitive

EEIINSSTZ
sensitize

EEIIOPQSU
equipoise

EEIIQRSTU
requisite

EEIIQSTUX
exquisite

EEIJKNRSS
jerkiness

EEIJPRRSU
perjuries

EEIKLMORT
kilometer

EEIKLNOST
stonelike

EEIKNPRSS
perkiness

EEIKOORRS
rookeries

EEILLMNOT
emollient

EEILLMSST
smelliest

EEILLNNTY
leniently

EEILLNOST
loneliest

EEILLOSTV
loveliest

EEILLRSUY
leisurely

EEILLRSVY
servilely

EEILLSUVY
elusively

EEILMMNPT
implement

EEILMMNSY
immensely

EEILMNNTY
eminently

EEILMNOST
limestone
milestone

EEILMNOSZ
solemnize

EEILMNPPR
pimpernel

EEILMNRVY
liverymen

EEILMOSTT
mistletoe

EEILMOTVY
emotively

EEILNNPSS
penniless

EEILNNSTY
intensely

EEILNOPRT
interlope

EEILNORVW
wolverine

EEILNOSSS
noiseless

EEILNOSTV
novelties

EEILNPSSS
spineless

EEILNPSTT
pestilent

EEILNPSVY
pensively

EEILNRSVY
inversely

EEILOPRTX
exploiter

EEILOPSST
politesse

EEILOPSSW
slopewise

EEILOPSVX
explosive

EEILORSTT
lotteries

EEILPPRTU
pulpiteer

EEILPRSTY
peristyle

EEILPRSUV
repulsive

EEILPRUVZ
pulverize

EEILPSSTW
sweetlips

EEILSSSSU
issueless

EEIMMMRSS
mesmerism

EEIMMNRRT
merriment

EEIMMRSST
mesmerist

EEIMMRSTW
swimmeret

EEIMMRSTX
extremism

EEIMNNRTT
interment

EEIMNNSTT
sentiment

EEIMNOPTX
exemption

EEIMNORSZ
sermonize

EEIMNPQTU
equipment

EEIMNPSST
emptiness

EEIMNRRSS
merriness

EEIMNRTTT
remittent

EEIMOPRTZ
temporize

EEIMORSSU
mouseries

EEIMPRRSS
impresser

EEIMPRRTT
pretermit

EEIMPRSTV
septemvir

EEIMPSSTU
impetuses

EEIMRRSTT
trimester

EEIMRSSSU
messieurs

EEIMRSSTY
mysteries

EEIMRSTTX
extremist

EEIMRTTXY
extremity

EEIMSSTYZ
systemize

EEINNNRSU
nunneries

EEINNOPRS
pensioner

EEINNORTT
retention

EEINNOSTV
veinstone

EEINNOSTX
extension

EEINNPRST
spinneret

EEINNPRTT
pertinent
EEINNPSST
ineptness
EEINNRSST
inertness
EEINOPRST
interpose
EEINOPTTZ
potentize
EEINORRSV
reversion
EEINOSSTV
ostensive
EEINPRRTT
interpret
EEINPRSTT
pinsetter
EEINPSSTT
pettiness
EEINNQSSTU
quietness
EEINRRSSU
nurseries
EEINRRTTW
rewritten
EEINRSSTT
triteness
EEINSSSTT
testiness
EEIOPPSTV
stovepipe
EEIOPRSTT
potteries
EEIOPRTTU
pirouette
EEIORRRSV
reservoir
EEIORRRTZ
terrorize
EEIPRRSTT
preterist
EEIPRSSST
priestess
EEIPRSSUV
supervise
EEIPRSTTT
prettiest
EEIQSSTUU
quietuses
EEIRRSSTV
reservist
EEIRSSSTT
tristesse
EEIRSTTUV
vestiture
EEJMNNOTY
enjoyment
EEKKORSTY
keystroke
EEKLMOSSS
smokeless
EEKLNPRSU
spelunker

EEKLORSTW
steelwork
EEKMNOPSS
spokesmen
EELLOPPRR
propeller
EELLOSTWY
yellowest
EELLPSSSU
pulseless
EELLSSSUY
uselessly
EELMNOSSY
moneyless
EELMOOPRT
melotrope
EELMOPRTU
petroleum
EELMORTTV
voltmeter
EELNNUPRS
personnel
EELNOOSSS
looseness
EELNOPSTU
plenteous
EELNORSSW
ownerless
EELNORTUV
volunteer
EELNPRSTY
presently
EELOPRSSW
powerless
EELOPRSTY
polyester
proselyte
EELORSSUV
ourselves
EELORSVWW
werwolves
EELPPSTTU
septuplet
EELPPSTUX
septuplex
EELPRSSXY
expressly
EELPRSTUU
sepulture
EELPSTTUX
sextuplet
EEMMNOORT
metronome
EEMMORTYZ
zymometer
EEMOOPRTT
optometer
EEMPRRTTU
trumpeter
EEMPRSSTT
temptress
EENNRSSST
sternness
EENOORRSU

erroneous
EENOPRSTV
overspent
EENOPSTTY
stenotype
EENORSTTT
rottenest
EENPRRSTY
serpentry
EEOOPRRVW
overpower
EEOOPRRRTY
repertory
EEOPRSSSS
repossess
EEOPSSTTU
poussette
EEORRTTVX
extrovert
EEORSSTTU
roussette
EERRSTTTU
stutterer
EFFFILSTU
fluffiest
EFFGGILNU
effulging
EFFGGINOR
goffering
EFFGIINNR
niffering
EFFGINRSU
suffering
EFFGLORTU
forgetful
EFFHINSSU
huffiness
EFFIIORRT
fortifier
EFFIIORST
fortifies
EFFIIPSST
spiffiest
EFFINPSSU
puffiness
EFFINSSST
stiffness
EFFIOOPRR
fireproof
EFFISSTTU
stuffiest
EFFNOORRT
forefront
EFFOOORRTY
offertory
EFGGIINNR
fingering
EFGGILNNU
engulfing
EFGGILOOS
solfeggio
EFGGINOOR
foregoing
EFGGINOSS

fogginess
EFGHIILRT
firelight
flightier
EFGHINORT
fothering
EFGHIORST
foresight
EFGIIINSS
signifies
EFGIILLNR
refilling
EFGIILLNT
filleting
EFGIILNRT
filtering
EFGIILORS
glorifies
EFGIINNRR
inferring
EFGIINNSS
finessing
EFGIINNST
infesting
EFGIINPRT
fingertip
EFGIINPRX
prefixing
EFGIINRVY
verifying
EFGILNNNU
funneling
EFGILNORW
flowering
EFGIMNNOT
fomenting
EFGIMNORR
reforming
EFGIMNPRU
perfuming
EFGIMNTUY
tumefying
EFGINNOST
softening
EFGINORST
foresting
fostering
EFGINPRSU
perfusing
EFGNOORTT
forgotten
EFHHIISTW
whitefish
EFHHILLSS
shellfish
EFHIILSTT
filthiest
EFHIIMSST
fetishism
EFHIINSSS
fishiness
EFHIIRRTT
thriftier
EFHIISSTT

shiftiest
EFHIJLLSY
jellyfish
EFHIKNORT
forethink
EFHILLSSY
selfishly
EFHILNSSU
unselfish
EFHILOOSS
shooflies
EFHILSSST
shiftless
EFHINRRSU
furnisher
EFHINRSSU
furnishes
EFHLLLPUY
helpfully
EFHLLOPUY
hopefully
EFHLLOSUV
shovelful
EFHLNSSSU
flushness
EFHLOOPSU
flophouse
EFIIINRST
nitrifies
EFIIIRSTV
vitrifies
EFIIJRSTU
justifier
EFIIJSSTU
justifies
EFIILLMOS
mollifies
EFIILLNRU
nullifier
EFIILLNSU
nullifies
EFIILLRST
fillister
EFIILMOTT
leitmotif
EFIILMSST
flimsiest
EFIILOSSZ
fossilize
EFIILRTTY
fertility
EFIIMMMSU
mummifies
EFIIMORST
mortifies
EFIIMSSTY
mystifies
EFIINNSTY
intensify
EFIINRSTU
nutrifies
EFIIRSTTU
fruitiest
EFIISTTVY

festivity
EFILLNPTU
plentiful
EFILMOPRX
plexiform
EFILMORUZ
formulize
EFILNOOSU
felonious
EFILNOSST
loftiness
EFILOPPST
floppiest
EFILRSSTU
fruitless
EFILRTUVY
furtively
EFINNNSSU
funniness
EFINOPRSU
perfusion
EFINOPRSY
personify
EFINRRTUU
furniture
EFINSSSTW
swiftness
EFINSSUZZ
fuzziness
EFIORSSTT
frostiest
EFKLMNOOW
womenfolk
EFLLMOSUY
fulsomely
EFLLSTUYZ
zestfully
EFLNOORVW
overflown
EFLNORSST
frontless
EFLNORSUW
sunflower
EFLNRSTUU
unrestful
EFLOOPRSS
proofless
EFLOOPRTW
flowerpot
EFLORSSST
frostless
EFNNOPRUY
fourpenny
EFOOPRRSS
professor
EGGGIIJNT
jiggeting
EGGGIILST
giggliest
EGGGINNOR
engorging
EGGHIILNS
sleighing
EGGHINNRU

hungering
EGGHINOPR
gophering
EGGIILLNNR
lingering
EGGIILRRW
wrigglier
EGGIILSTW
wiggliest
EGGIINNRS
resigning
EGGIINNST
ingesting
EGGIINNSW
swingeing
EGGIINOTZ
egotizing
EGGILLNTU
gulleting
EGGILNOPS
gospeling
EGGILNORV
groveling
EGGILOOST
geologist
EGGIMNNOR
mongering
EGGIMNSSU
mugginess
EGGINNORV
governing
EGGINNPUX
expunging
EGGINOSSS
sogginess
EGGINRSTU
gesturing
EGGINRSTU
grungiest
EGGINRTTU
guttering
EGGINSSTU
gusseting
EGGIORRTU
outrigger
EGHHINRST
threshing
EGHIIKNRS
shrieking
EGHIILLMT
limelight
EGHIILNRS
hirseling
EGHIIMNNS
inmeshing
EGHIIMNTT
nighttime
EGHIIMSTT
mightiest
EGHIINNTW
whitening
EGHIINPRS
perishing
EGHIINRSV

shivering
EGHIINRTW
withering
EGHIINSTY
hygienist
EGHIKLOST
ghostlike
EGHIKNNRU
hunkering
EGHILLNOR
hollering
EGHILNOSV
shoveling
EGHILNSST
lightness
EGHILNTSS
nightless
EGHILNSTU
sleuthing
EGHILSSST
sightless
EGHILSSTT
slightest
EGHIMNORT
mothering
EGHIMNOST
something
EGHINORSW
showering
EGHINORTV
overnight
EGHINORTX
exhorting
EGHINRRWY
wherrying
EGHINRSST
rightness
EGHINRSTU
hungriest
EGHINSSTT
tightness
EGHIOPRTT
tightrope
EGHIORSTU
righteous
EGHIORSTV
oversight
EGHLMOOOU
homologue
EGHLNOOPY
nephology
EGHLNOOPY
phenology
EGHLNOOTY
ethnology
EGHLNOPYY
phylogeny
EGHNORSSU
roughness
EGHNOSSTU
toughness
EGIIIMNTZ
itemizing
EGIIJNNOR
rejoining
EGIIJNRTT

jittering
EGIIKNNRT
tinkering
EGIIKNPPR
kippering
EGIILLMNP
impelling
EGIILLNNO
nielloing
EGIILNNST
enlisting
listening
EGIILNNSV
sniveling
EGIILNNTT
entitling
inletting
EGIILNNUV
unveiling
EGIILNORT
loitering
EGIILNPSS
singspiel
EGIILNRSV
silvering
slivering
EGIILNRTT
littering
EGIILNSVW
swiveling
EGIILNTTY
gentility
EGIILORST
trilogies
EGIILORSU
religious
EGIILRSST
grisliest
EGIILRSTU
liturgies
EGIILSTTU
guiltiest
EGIIMMNRS
immersing
simmering
EGIIMNNPT
impingent
EGIIMNPRS
simpering
EGIIMNRTT
remitting
EGIINNNRT
interning
EGIINNNTV
inventing
EGIINNNTW
entwining
EGIINNORS
signorine
EGIINNORT
orienting
EGIINNOST
ingestion
EGIINNOSU

ingenious
EGIINNRRT
interring
EGIINNRST
inserting
sintering
EGIINNRTU
reuniting
EGIINNRTV
inverting
EGIINNRTW
wintering
EGIINNSTT
insetting
EGIINNSTV
investing
EGIINNTUY
ingenuity
EGIINOPTZ
poetizing
EGIINPPQU
equipping
EGIINPRRS
respiring
springier
EGIINPRST
respiting
EGIINPRSV
prevising
EGIINQRRU
requiring
EGIINQRUV
quivering
EGIINRRST
stringier
EGIINRRTU
intriguer
EGIINRRTW
rewriting
EGIINRSST
resisting
EGIINRSSU
reissuing
EGIINRTTT
tittering
EGIINRTTY
integrity
EGIINSSTT
stingiest
EGIJKNNTU
junketing
EGIJLNSTY
jestingly
EGIJNPRRU
perjuring
EGIKLNNOO
inglenook
EGIKMNNOY
monkeying
EGIKNNOTY
keynoting
EGILLLNTY
tellingly
EGILLMNOW

mellowing
EGILLMNTY
meltingly
EGILLNNOR
enrolling
EGILLNOTX
extolling
EGILLNOWY
yellowing
EGILLOSYZ
syllogize
EGILLSSTU
guiltless
EGILMMNOP
pommeling
EGILMNOOS
neologism
EGILMNOPY
employing
EGILMNOST
molesting
EGILMOOSY
semiology
EGILNNNTU
tunneling
EGILNNOOS
loosening
EGILNNOST
singleton
EGILNOOST
neologist
EGILNOPRX
exploring
EGILNORSV
resolving
EGILNORTV
revolting
EGILNORTW
troweling
EGILNORVV
revolving
EGILNOTVY
longevity
EGILNPRST
springlet
EGILNPRSU
repulsing
EGILNRSTU
resulting
EGILNRSTW
wrestling
EGIMMNRSU
summering
EGIMNPRSU
presuming
EGIMNPRTU
permuting
EGIMNRSSY
synergism
EGIMNRSTU
mustering
EGIMNRTTU
muttering
EGINNNRRU

rerunning
EGINNNRUV
unnerving
EGINNORSW
worsening
EGINNOSUU
ingenuous
EGINNRRTU
returning
EGINNRSTT
stringent
EGINNRSTU
insurgent
EGINNRTUV
venturing
EGINOPPRS
preposing
EGINOPPST
estopping
EGINOPRRR
porringer
EGINOPRRT
reporting
EGINOPRRV
reproving
EGINOPRTX
exporting
EGINOPSST
spongiest
EGINOPSSU
espousing
EGINORRST
resorting
restoring
EGINORRTT
retorting
EGINORRTU
rerouting
EGINORSTY
oystering
EGINORTTT
tottering
EGINORTTX
extorting
EGINPPRSU
suppering
EGINPRTTU
puttering
EGINPRTTY
prettying
EGINPRUVY
purveying
EGINPSTTU
upsetting
EGINPSTWW
sweptwing
EGINRSSST
stressing
EGINRSSTY
synergist
EGINRSUVY
surveying
EGINRTTUX
texturing

EGKORSSUW
guesswork
EGLMNOOOU
monologue
EGLMOORTY
metrology
EGLMOOSUY
museology
EGLMOOTYY
etymology
EGLNNPTUY
pungently
EGLNOORUY
neurology
EGNNOSSUY
youngness
EGNOORRVW
overgrown
EGNORSSSS
grossness
EGNORSSTT
strongest
EGNORSTUY
youngster
EHHIIRTTT
thirtieth
EHHILLLSY
hellishly
EHHIMRTYZ
rhythmize
EHHIOPRSW
horsewhip
EHHIOSTVY
yeshivoth
EHHMNOOOP
homophone
EHHOOPSTY
theosophy
EHIIKNSTT
kittenish
EHIILLNSS
hilliness
EHIINNSSS
shininess
EHIINORRT
inheritor
EHIINPRST
nephritis
phrenitis
EHIINRSTW
winterish
EHIIORSST
histories
EHIIRRSTT
thirstier
EHIKLLPSY
sylphlike
EHIKLORTZ
kilohertz
EHIKNSSSU
huskiness
EHILLOSWY
yellowish
EHILMNOST

monthlies
EHILNNOOP
phelonion
EHILNOSTU
unholiest
EHILNOSUY
heinously
EHILOSSST
sloshiest
EHILPRRSU
rulership
EHILRSSST
shirtless
EHILSSSTU
slushiest
EHIMNNOOS
moonshine
EHIMNOPRS
premonish
EHIMNOPST
phonetism
EHIMNORST
horsemint
EHIMNSSSU
mushiness
EHIMOSTTU
mouthiest
EHIMSSSTU
isthmuses
EHINNORSS
horniness
EHINOPRSW
ownership
EHINOPSTT
phonetist
EHINOPTYZ
hypnotize
EHINORSSU
nourishes
EHINORSTT
thorniest
EHINOSSSW
showiness
EHINPSSSU
pushiness
EHINSSSTY
synthesis
EHIOPRSST
prothesis
EHIORRSTV
overshirt
EHIORSTTW
worthiest
EHKOORSUW
housework
workhouse
EHLLOOSTU
tollhouse
EHLMORSSU
humorless
EHLNOOPXY
xylophone
EHLNOORSS
honorless

EHLNOOSTY
holystone
EHLNORRTY
northerly
EHLOOSSTT
toothless
EHLOPRSTU
upholster
EHLOPSTYY
hypostyle
EHLORSSTW
worthless
EHLORSTUY
southerly
EHLRSSTTU
truthless
EHMNNOOOY
honeymoon
EHMOOOPRS
sophomore
EHMOOOSTT
toothsome
EHMOOSSTT
smoothest
EHNNOORST
hornstone
EHNOOPPTY
phonotype
EHNOOPSUU
euphonous
EHNOPSSTY
pythoness
EHNORSSST
shortness
EHNORSTTW
northwest
EHOOOPRSU
poorhouse
EHOOORSTV
overshoot
EHOOPPTTY
phototype
EHOORRTVW
overthrow
EHOSSTTUW
southwest
EIIILSTTU
utilities
EIIIMPRTV
primitive
EIIINQRSU
inquiries
EIIINRSTT
trinities
EIIINTTUV
intuitive
EIIKLLORT
kiloliter
EIIKLMNSS
milkiness
EIIKMPSST
skimpiest
EIIKNNPPR
nipperkin

EIIKNNPSS
pinkiness
EIIKNNSST
skinniest
EIILLLMMO
millimole
EIILLMNRY
millinery
EIILLMSST
limitless
EIILLNSSS
silliness
EIILLNSTU
nullities
EIILLOPRS
pillories
EIILMNORV
vermilion
EIILMNOSU
limousine
EIILMNSSS
sliminess
EIILMPPST
pimpliest
EIILMPSUV
impulsive
EIILOORST
olitories
EIILPRTUY
puerility
EIILRSTTY
sterility
EIILRSTVY
servility
EIIMMNORS
immersion
EIIMMNOSS
misoneism
EIIMMNSTY
immensity
EIIMMORST
memoirist
EIIMMPSSS
pessimism
EIIMNORSS
remission
EIIMOPRSU
imperious
EIIMOPRSV
improvise
EIIMPSSST
pessimist
EIINNNOTT
intention
EIINNNOTV
invention
EIINNNSST
tinniness
EIINNORST
insertion
EIINNORSV
inversion
EIINNOSSS
noisiness

EIINNRSTT
internist
EIINNSSTT
insistent
EIINNSTTY
intensity
EIINOPRSV
prevision
EIINOPSTT
pointiest
EIINOPTVW
viewpoint
EIINORSTY
seniority
EIINPSSST
tipsiness
EIINRSTTW
wintriest
EIINSSSSS
sissiness
EIINSSTTW
wittiness
EIINSTTTU
institute
EIIPRSSST
prissiest
EIJLLNOSS
jolliness
EIJLNOSST
jointless
EIKLMNOST
milkstone
EIKLNPRRS
sprinkler
EIKLNRSTU
knurliest
EIKMNRSSU
murkiness
EIKMNSSSU
muskiness
EIKNOSTTT
knottiest
EIKNPSSTU
spunkiest
EIKNRRSTU
knurriest
EIKOOPSST
spookiest
EILLMNOST
millstone
EILLMRTUU
tellurium
EILLNOSSW
lowliness
EILLNOTVY
violently
EILLNSSST
stillness
EILLOOSTW
woolliest
EILLSSTWY
witlessly
EILMNOPST
simpleton

EILMNOSTY
solemnity
EILMNOSWY
winsomely
EILNNOSTV
insolvent
EILNOOPSX
explosion
EILNOOTUV
evolution
EILNOPRSU
repulsion
EILNOPSST
pointless
EILNOPSUX
expulsion
EILNORSUV
revulsion
EILNORTUY
routinely
EILNOSUVY
enviously
EILNPPSSU
pulpiness
EILNPQTUU
quintuple
EILNPRSST
printless
EILNPRSTY
splintery
EILNRSSSU
surliness
EILNRSTTU
turnstile
EILNRTUUV
vulturine
EILNSSSTT
stintless
EILNSSSTU
lustiness
EILOPPSST
sloppiest
EILOPRSTT
portliest
EILOPSTUY
piteously
EILORRTVW
liverwort
EILORSSUY
seriously
EIMMNOPRS
persimmon
EIMNNOPRT
prominent
EIMNNORST
innermost
EIMNNPTUU
neptunium
EIMNNRTTU
nutriment
EIMNOORSS
roominess
EIMNOPRTU
importune

EIMNORSST
sermonist
EIMNORSSU
sensorium
EIMNOSSST
moistness
EIMNOSTTY
testimony
EIMNOTTZZ
mezzotint
EIMNSSSSU
mussiness
EIMNSSSTU
mustiness
EIMOOPSTU
impetuoso
EIMOPRSUV
primevous
EIMOPSTUU
impetuous
EIMORRRST
terrorism
EIMORSSTT
stormiest
EIMORSUVY
voyeurism
EIMOSSTUV
vomituses
EINNNOTTY
nonentity
EINNNSSSU
sunniness
EINNOOPRT
prenotion
EINNORTVY
inventory
EINNOSSST
stoniness
EINNPRSTW
newsprint
EINNRTTUW
unwritten
EINNSSTTU
nuttiness
EINOOPRRT
portioner
EINOORTTX
extortion
EINOORTTY
notoriety
EINOOSSST
sootiness
EINOOSSWZ
wooziness
EINOPRSUU
penurious
EINORRTTV
introvert
EINPRRTTU
interrupt
EIOOPRRST
posterior
EIOOPRSTX
expositor

EIOPPRRTY
propriety
EIOPRSSTT
sportiest
EIOPRSTTY
posterity
EIOPSSTTT
spottiest
EIOQRSTUU
turquoise
EIORRRSTT
terrorist
EIORRRTTY
territory
EIPRSSSTU
pertussis
EKLMMNOSU
muskmelon
EKMNNOORS
nonsmoker
EKNOOPSTU
outspoken
EKNORSSTU
sunstroke
ELLNOORST
stornello
ELMNNOOST
somnolent
ELMNPPSSU
plumpness
ELMORSSST
stormless
ELMORSTUU
tremulous
ELNOOOPRV
provolone
ELNOORSUY
onerously
ELNORSUVY
nervously
ELOPPRSUY
purposely
ELOPRSUUV
pulverous
ELOQRSUUU
querulous
ELPRSSSUU
surpluses
EMMNOOSTU
momentous
EMNNOOOST
moonstone
EMNNRRRUU
rumrunner
EMNOOPSUY
eponymous
EMNOORRTT
tormentor
EMNORSSTT
sternmost
EMOOORRST
storeroom
EMOOPRRSS
pressroom

EMOOPRTTY
optometry
EMOORRSTU
tremorous
EMOPPRSTU
uppermost
EMORSTTTU
uttermost
ENNOOPPRT
proponent
ENNOPRTWY
pennywort
ENOOPPRTU
opportune
ENORSSTUU
strenuous
ENORSTUUV
venturous
ENOSSSTTU
stoutness
EOOPPRRSS
oppressor
EOOPPRTTY
prototype
EOOPRSSSS
possessor
EOPPRRSTU
supporter
FFGHIILNW
whiffling
FFGHILNSU
shuffling
FFGHILRTU
frightful
FFGIILNNS
sniffling
FFGIINSUX
suffixing
FFGILNNSU
snuffling
FFGIMNORU
fungiform
FFGINOPRS
offspring
FFGINSSUU
suffusing
FFHHILSUY
huffishly
FFIILMOOR
foliiform
FFILMOORR
floriform
FFINOSSUU
suffusion
FFLOOOOPR
foolproof
FFORRSUUU
furfurous
FGGIILNNU
ingulfing
FGGIILNUY
uglifying
FGGIINORV
forgiving

FGHIIINNS
finishing
FGHILOPTT
topflight
FGHINORTT
fortnight
FGIIILLMNS
misfiling
FGIIILNVY
vilifying
FGIIIMNNY
minifying
FGIIIMNRS
misfiring
FGIIINVVY
vivifying
FGIILNOPR
profiling
FGIILNPTU
uplifting
FGIILNRZZ
frizzling
FGIILNTTY
fittingly
FGIIMNNOR
informing
FGIINNOTY
notifying
FGIINNTTU
unfitting
FGIINOPRT
profiting
FGIINOSSY
ossifying
FGIINPRUY
purifying
FGIINPTYY
typifying
FGIINRSSU
fissuring
FGILLNOOW
following
FGILLNOWY
flowingly
FGILNNRUU
unfurling
FGILNRRUY
flurrying
FGINORRUW
furrowing
FHHIORTTW
forthwith
FHIILOPST
pilotfish
FHILLOOSY
foolishly
FHILLSUWY
wishfully
FHINOOPRT
hoofprint
FHLLRTUUY
ruthfully

FHMOOOPRT
mothproof
FIIIMNRTY
infirmity
FIIKLNNST
skinflint
FIILMPRST
filmstrip
FIILORTVY
frivolity
FIILPRSTU
spiritful
FIIMMNORS
misinform
FILLSTUWY
wistfully
FILMNORUY
uniformly
FILMORSTY
styliform
FILOOOPRT
portfolio
FILOORSUV
frivolous
FILORSUUY
furiously
FINNOOPRT
nonprofit
FINOOPRSU
profusion
FINOOPRTT
footprint
FKLNOOSTW
townsfolk
FLLLOSUUY
soulfully
FLLNOORRY
forlornly
FLOOOOSTT
footstool
FLOORRSUW
sorrowful
FOOPSSTUY
pussyfoot
GGGHINRSU
shrugging
GGGIILNRW
wriggling
GGGILMNSU
smuggling
GGGILNNSU
snuggling
GGHHHIILT
highlight
GGHHILOSY
hoggishly
GGHIIILRW
whirligig
GGHIIKNNT
knighting
GGHIILNNS
shingling
GGHIILNNT
lightning

GGHIILNPT
plighting
GGHIILNST
slighting
GGHILNNOT
nightlong
GGHINNORT
thronging
GGHINNOTW
nightgown
GGIIIMNNP
impinging
GGIILMNPS
glimpsing
GGIILNNRY
ringingly
GGIILNNSS
singlings
GGIILNNSW
swingling
GGIIMNNPU
impugning
GGIINNPRS
springing
GGIINNRST
stringing
GGIINOPSS
gossiping
GGILNNOUY
youngling
GGILNPRSU
splurging
GGINNOPPU
oppugning
GGINPRSUU
upsurging
GHHIILPST
lightship
GHHILRSTU
rushlight
GHIIIMNNS
minishing
GHIIKNNRS
shrinking
GHIIKNSTT
skintight
GHIILLNRS
shrilling
GHIILLNRT
thrilling
GHIILNNTY
hintingly
GHIILNOPS
polishing
GHIILNSTW
whistling
GHIILNTTW
whittling
GHIIMMNSY
shimmying
GHIIMNPRS
shrimping
GHIINNNSY
shinnying

GHIINNNWY
whinnying
GHIINNPSU
punishing
GHIINRSTT
thirsting
GHILLNOOW
hollowing
GHILLOOPY
philology
GHILMNOOT
moonlight
GHILNOPYY
philogyny
GHILNOSST
slingshot
GHILNSTTU
shuttling
GHILNSTUY
unsightly
GHILOOSTY
histology
GHILOPSTT
spotlight
stoplight
GHILPRSTY
sprightly
GHINOOSSW
swooshing
GHINOPSTT
nightspot
GHINORTUW
inwrought
GHINRSTTU
thrusting
GHLMNOOYY
hymnology
GHLMOOTYY
mythology
GHLNOOOPY
phonology
GIIILLNNOZ
lionizing
GIIILNTUZ
utilizing
GIIILOSTU
litigious
GIIIMMNTT
immitting
GIIIMRSST
mistigris
GIIINNORZ
ionizing
GIIINNPRS
inspiring
GIIINNQRU
inquiring
GIIINNSST
insisting
GIIINNTTU
intuiting
GIIINNTUZ
unitizing
GIIINPRST

spiriting
GIIINRTVY
virginity
GIIKLLLNY
killingly
GIIKLNNRW
wrinkling
GIIKLNNTW
twinkling
GIIKLNSTT
skittling
GIILLLNWY
willingly
GIILLNNUW
unwilling
GIILLNOPW
pillowing
GIILMNOPR
imploring
GIILMNRSU
misruling
GIILNNNWY
winningly
GIILNNOVV
involving
GIILNNPST
splinting
GIILNNSTU
insulting
GIILNOPST
pistoling
GIILNPPST
stippling
GIILNPSTT
splitting
GIILNSTYZ
stylizing
GIILNTTWY
wittingly
GIILRSTTU
liturgist
GIIMNNOOT
motioning
GIIMNNTUY
mutinying
GIIMNOPRS
promising
GIIMNOPRT
importing
GIIMNOPRV
improving
GIIMNORRR
mirroring
GIIMNORST
mortising
GIIMNQRSU
squirming
GIIMNRSSU
surmising
GIINNNNPU
unpinning
GIINNNOWW
winnowing
GIINNOOPS

poisoning
GIINNOPPR
propining
GIINNOPRS
prisoning
GIINNOPRU
inpouring
GIINNPPUZ
unzipping
GIINNPRST
sprinting
GIINNQSTU
squinting
GIINNTTUW
unwitting
GIINPPRST
stripping
GIINPRRTU
irrupting
GIINPRSSU
suspiring
GIINQRSTU
squirting
GIINRSUVV
surviving
GIJLLNOTY
joltingly
GIKLNNOOO
onlooking
GIKLNNOWY
knowingly
GIKNOOPRV
provoking
GIKNOOTWW
kowtowing
GILLMOSSY
syllogism
GILLNOPTU
polluting
GILLNORST
strolling
GILLOOOPY
oligopoly
GILNOPTUY
poutingly
GILNOSTUU
glutinous
GILNPPSUY
supplying
GILOOOSTZ
zoologist
GILOORSTU
urologist
GIMMNNOSU
summoning
GIMMNRRUU
murmuring
GIMMNRSTU
strumming
GIMNNOORS
monsignor
GIMNOOPRT
promoting
GIMNOPPRT

prompting
GINNOOPPR
proponing
GINNORSTU
tonsuring
GINNRRTUU
nurturing
GINOOPPRS
proposing
GINOOPRSS
prognosis
GINOOPRTU
uprooting
GINOPPRST
stropping
GINOPPRSU
purposing
GINOPPSSU
supposing
GINOPRSTU
posturing
GINORRTTU
torturing
GINPRRTUU
rupturing
GINRSTTTU
strutting
HHILOOPPS
philosoph
HHMNOOOPY
homophony
HIILLMNOT
millionth
HIILOSTTY
hostility
HIILRSTTY
thirstily
HIIOPPRRS
priorship
HIKNNORST
stinkhorn
HILLOOPRW
whirlpool
HILLOSTUY
loutishly
HILLSSTYY
stylishly
HILMOOSYZ
hylozoism
HIMNOPSTY
hypnotism
HIMOOPRSS
morphosis
HINOPSTTY
hypnotist
HIOOPPRST
troopship
HIOPRSSTY
sophistry
HMNOOOPRY
phoronomy
HMOOSSTTU
southmost

HNOOPPTYY
phonotypy
HOOPRSSTT
shortstop
IIIKLLNPS
spillikin
IIIKMNRST
miniskirt
IIILNOSTV
violinist
IIIMMNOSS
immission
IIINNOTTU
intuition
IIJNORSUU
injurious
IIKNNNOOS
onionskin
IILLLMOTV
millivolt
IILMNOOPS
implosion

IILMOPSSS
solipsism
IILMOPSUY
impiously
IILOPSSST
solipsist
IIMOPRTXY
proximity
IIMOQSTUX
quixotism
IINNORSTU
intrusion
IINNORTTU
nutrition
IINOOPRSV
provision
IINOORSTT
sortition
IIOPRSSTU
spiritous
ILLNOOPTU
pollution

ILLOOQSUY
soliloquy
ILLOQRTUW
quillwort
ILMNOOSUY
ominously
ILMNOPTUU
plutonium
ILNOOSUXY
noxiously
ILORSUUUX
luxurious
IMMOPPRTU
impromptu
IMMOPSSUY
symposium
IMNOOOPRT
promotion
IMNORSTTU
strontium
INOOOPSSU
poisonous

INOOOORSTU
notorious
INOOPPRTU
pourpoint
INOPSSTTY
synoptist
IOOPPRRTU
potpourri
IOOPRRSVY
provisory
MNOORSSTU
monstrous
MNOORSSTW
snowstorm
MOPSSTUUU
sumptuous
NOOOPPSSU
soupspoon
OOPRSSTUU
stuporous
OORRSTTUU
torturous

10-LETTER WORDS

AAAAEGLMMT
amalgamate
AAAABBCILST
sabbatical
AAAABCCKNSV
canvasback
AAABCDELNR
candelabra
AAAABDMORSS
ambassador
AAAABEEGLMN
manageable
AAAABEELLPP
appealable
AAAABEELPPS
appeasable
AAAABEGGGMN
baggageman
AAAABEGLMNY
manageably
AAAABEILNTT
attainable
AAAABELMSTT
blastemata
AAACDEIMMZ
macadamize
AAACEENPPR
appearance
AAAACEFLQTU
catafalque
AAAACEJKNPS
jackanapes
AAACILLNTY
analytical
AAAACILNRST
scarlatina
AAACLMNRVY
cavalryman
AAADEGGRTV
aggravated
AAADEIMSTT
diastemata
AAAADELMNRS
salamander
AAADGNOPPR
propaganda
AAADINOPTT
adaptation
AAAEELPRST
palaestrae
AAAEGILMNR
managerial
AAAEGPSSWY
passageway

AAAAEHINSTU
euthanasia
AAAAEHPPRRS
paraphrase
AAAAEIMNQRU
aquamarine
AAAELLNRTT
tarantella
AAAAELMRSTT
metatarsal
AAAAGGNNRTU
gargantuan
AAAGIIMNPR
parmigiana
AAAAGILMNTX
malaxating
AAAAIINNRST
sanitarian
AAAAILMNOTX
malaxation
AABBCDKLOR
blackboard
AABBDDEORR
breadboard
AABBDEOORV
aboveboard
AABBEEIRTV
abbreviate
AABBEELNRU
unbearable
AABBEILMNO
abominable
AABBEILNOT
obtainable
AABBEKLLST
basketball
AABBELNRUY
unbearably
AABBILMNOY
abominably
AABCCEELPT
acceptable
AABCCELPTY
acceptably
AABCCELLLU
calculable
AABCCIILST
cabalistic
AABCDDEHKN
backhanded
AABCDDEIRR
barricaded
AABCDDEKLS
saddleback

AABCDEEHLT
detachable
AABCDEEILR
eradicable
AABCDEEELTU
educatable
AABCDEFIRT
fabricated
AABCDEIJTU
abjudicate
AABCDEILRT
calibrated
AABCDELNNU
unbalanced
AABCDENORT
carbonated
AABCDERSTT
abstracted
AABCDGIINT
abdicating
AABCDGKLRU
blackguard
AABCDIILLO
diabolical
AABCDIINOT
abdication
AABCDNNORT
contraband
AABCEEERTX
exacerbate
AABCEEGHLN
changeable
AABCEEGHLR
chargeable
AABCEEHILV
achievable
AABCEEELLNS
cleansable
AABCEELNRT
tabernacle
AABCEFIILP
pacifiable
AABCEGHLNY
changeably
AABCEGINRT
acerbating
AABCEGLMNN
blancmange
AABCEHILPT
alphabetic
AABCEHILRT
charitable
AABCEIINTU
beautician

AABCEILLMP
implacable
AABCEILLPP
applicable
AABCEILNOT
actionable
AABCELNOTU
outbalance
AABCERRTUU
bureaucrat
AABCGILNNR
barnacling
AABCGKMMNO
backgammon
AABCHILRTY
charitably
AABCHIOOPR
acrophobia
AABCIILLMY
iambically
AABCIILPTY
capability
AABCILLMPY
implacably
AABCILNOTY
actionably
AABCLLNNNO
cannonball
AABCLMMRUU
ambulacrum
AABCLORUVY
vocabulary
AABCLRSTTY
abstractly
AABDDEEEHR
bareheaded
AABDDEEHNR
barehanded
AABDDEGGNS
sandbagged
AABDDEHLMO
hebdomadal
AABDDEHLRS
balderdash
AABDDINORR
drainboard
AABDEEHLLN
handleable
AABDEEHRRT
threadbare
AABDEELNRU
unreadable
AABDEELORT
elaborated

AABDEFFLOR
affordable
AABDEHITTU
habituated
AABDEILLNR
banderilla
AABDEINRTZ
bartizaned
AABDEIRRTT
arbitrated
AABDEIRSTZ
bastardize
AABDEJLSTU
adjustable
AABDEKORST
skateboard
AABDELLNNO
belladonna
AABDELNOPR
pardonable
AABDELRSTU
balustrade
AABDEOPRST
pasteboard
AABDGINNNO
abandoning
AABDHMNNSU
husbandman
AABDLNNTUY
abundantly
AABDORRSTW
strawboard
AABEEGLMSS
assemblage
AABEEHKRRT
heartbreak
AABEEILLRZ
realizable
AABEEJKRRW
jawbreaker
AABEEKLMRT
marketable
AABEEKLRRW
lawbreaker
AABEEKRRTW
breakwater
AABEELLMNT
lamentable
AABEELLPRR
pallbearer
AABEELMRSU
measurable
AABEELNOSS
seasonable
AABEELNPTT
patentable
AABEELNRSW
answerable
AABEELSSSS
assessable
AABEFHLMOT
fathomable
AABEGIILMN
imaginable

AABEGILNOZ
zabaglione
AABEGILNSS
assignable
AABEGINNOT
abnegation
AABEGINRRT
aberrating
AABEHIILTT
habilitate
AABEIILNST
banalities
insatiable
AABEILLMPP
impalpable
AABEILLNUV
invaluable
AABEILMPSS
impassable
AABEILNRST
strainable
AABEILQRRU
quarriable
AABEILRRST
arbalister
AABEINORRT
aberration
AABELLMNTY
lamentably
AABELMRSUY
measurably
AABELNNOTX
nontaxable
AABELNORSY
reasonably
AABELNOSSY
seasonably
AABELOORRT
elaborator
AABEMRSTTU
masturbate
AABFFIILTY
affability
AABFLMNOTY
flamboyant
AABGGIINNR
bargaining
AABGGINORT
abrogating
AABGIILMNY
imaginably
AABGIILNOR
aboriginal
AABGIINNST
abstaining
AABGILMNST
lambasting
AABGILMNTU
ambulating
AABGILNTTU
tabulating
AABGINOORT
abrogation
AABHIINNTT

inhabitant
AABHIINOTT
habitation
AABHILLTUY
habitually
AABHLLLOOU
hullabaloo
AABIILMTY
amiability
AABIILNRVY
invariably
AABIILNSTY
insatiably
AABIJNORTU
abjuration
AABILLMPPY
impalpably
AABILLNNUY
biannually
AABILMPSSY
impassably
AABILNOTTU
tabulation
AABIORRRTT
arbitrator
AABLLMNORY
abnormally
AABLMORTUY
ambulatory
AABLOORRTY
laboratory
AACCCDENOR
accordance
AACCCEENPT
acceptance
AACCCEIRSU
accuracies
AACCCINRUY
inaccuracy
AACCDEENNS
ascendance
AACCDEHNOR
archdeacon
AACCDEILNT
accidental
AACCDEINTV
vaccinated
AACCDELLTU
calculated
AACCDENNSY
ascendancy
AACCEEELRT
accelerate
AACCEEGPRS
scapegrace
AACCEENTTU
accentuate
AACCEFPRST
spacecraft
AACCEGHOST
stagecoach
AACCEHILMN
mechanical
AACCEHINRS

saccharine
AACCEIIPST
capacities
AACCEILSTT
ecstatical
AACCEINNRT
anticancer
AACCEINPRT
pancreatic
AACCEINRTU
inaccurate
AACCEIRRTU
caricature
AACCEISTUV
accusative
AACCELMTUU
accumulate
AACCELRTUY
accurately
AACCENRSTU
crustacean
AACCGHIORY
hagiocracy
AACCGIILMN
acclaiming
AACCGILLNT
catcalling
AACCIINPRT
practician
AACCILLTTY
tactically
AACCILNOOS
occasional
AACCILOSTU
acoustical
AACCIMNORS
macroscian
AACCINOSTU
accusation
AACCINSTTY
asyntactic
AACCIORTTU
autocratic
AACCLLORTU
calculator
AACCMMNORY
cartomancy
AACCNNOTTU
accountant
AACCNORSST
sacrosanct
AACDDEEIRT
eradicated
AACDDEELNR
calendared
AACDDEEMRT
demarcated
AACDDEGNOS
gasconaded
AACDDELNPS
landscaped
AACDDEMNTU
manducated
AACDDHKPWY

paddywhack
AACDEEFHMS
shamefaced
AACDEEIPTT
decapitate
AACDEEEJLTU
ejaculated
AACDEEENNTT
attendance
AACDEFINST
fascinated
AACDEGILNS
escalading
AACDEGIMNP
campaigned
AACDEGISTT
castigated
AACDEGLOTU
catalogued
coagulated
AACDEGNORS
gasconader
AACDEHIMNT
machinated
AACDEHNTTU
unattached
AACDEHOPPR
approached
AACDEHPRTU
parachuted
AACDEIILRZ
radicalize
AACDEIJLTV
adjectival
AACDEILLTV
vacillated
AACDEILMNR
aldermanic
AACDEILNNT
lancinated
AACDEILNSZ
scandalize
AACDEILTUZ
actualized
AACDEIMNTT
admittance
AACDEIMSTT
masticated
AACDEINQTU
acquainted
AACDEINQUY
inadequacy
AACDEIORRT
corradiate
AACDEIOSST
associated
AACDEIPSTU
auspicated
AACDEIPTTV
captivated
AACDEJLNTY
adjacently
AACDELPTTU
catapulted

AACDENRSTT
transacted
AACDEORSUV
cadaverous
AACDFHINRT
handicraft
AACDFIINOO
aficionado
AACDFIMORR
microfarad
AACDGIINRT
radicating
AACDGILNNS
scandaling
AACDGIMORR
cardiogram
AACDGINOTV
advocating
AACDINOOTV
advocation
AACDJNOTTU
coadjutant
AACDLNOSSU
scandalous
AACDMMNNOT
commandant
AACEEEKMPR
peacemaker
AACEEGILLN
allegiance
AACEEHKPST
cheapskate
AACEEILMRZ
caramelize
AACEEILPRT
altarpiece
AACEEIMNPT
emancipate
AACEEIPPRT
appreciate
AACEEIRTTV
reactivate
AACEELMSTU
emasculate
AACEELPPSU
applesauce
AACEFGLMOU
camouflage
AACEFIILTT
facilitate
AACEFLMORT
malefactor
AACEFMNNRU
furnaceman
AACEGHMOPR
macrophage
AACEGIIMNT
emaciating
AACEGILMNN
malignance
AACEGILNRT
lacerating
AACEGILNST
escalating

AACEGILPPR
paraplegic
AACEGIMNPR
campaigner
AACEGIMNRT
macerating
AACEGINRSV
vagrancies
AACEGINTUV
evacuating
AACEGINTVX
excavating
AACEGLORTU
cataloguer
AACEHHILRR
hierarchal
AACEHIIMNR
hemicrania
AACEHILRTT
theatrical
AACEHIMMTT
mathematic
AACEHIMPRS
pharmacies
AACEHINRTT
anthracite
AACEHIPPRS
paparchies
AACEHIRSTU
autarchies
AACEHJKMMR
jackhammer
AACEHKLMRS
ramshackle
AACEHKMMRT
matchmaker
AACEHKMRTW
watchmaker
AACEHMNTTT
attachment
AACEHMOPRT
camphorate
AACEHOPRTY
apothecary
AACEIILMST
calamities
AACEIILPTZ
capitalize
AACEIIMNOT
emaciation
AACEIINPTT
anticipate
AACEIIPRRS
persicaria
AACEILLRVY
cavalierly
AACEILMMTU
immaculate
AACEILMNRU
unicameral
ACCEILMNTU
calumniate
AACEILNORT
laceration

AACEILPTTU
capitulate
AACEILRTTU
articulate
AACEILSSTU
casualties
AACEILSTTT
stalactite
AACEIMNORT
maceration
AACEINNNTU
annunciate
AACEINORTU
aeronautic
AACEINOTUV
evacuation
AACEINOTVX
excavation
AACEINRSST
incrassate
AACEINSSST
assistance
AACEIRTTTV
attractive
AACEJLORTU
ejaculator
AACELLLORT
collateral
AACELMNRVY
cavalrymen
AACELNOPTU
cantaloupe
AACELNRRUV
vernacular
AACELNSSSU
casualness
AACELOPPSY
apocalypse
AACFFGIINN
affiancing
AACFHKNRST
crankshaft
AACFIIILRT
artificial
AACFIIMNST
fanaticism
AACFILLOSU
fallacious
AACFILNORT
fractional
AACFINORST
fascinator
AACGGIILNT
glaciating
AACGGILNOT
cataloging
AACGHILNPY
anaglyphic
AACGHIOPRS
sarcophagi
AACGHOPRSY
sarcophagy
AACGIILNNZ
canalizing

AACGIINNPT
captaining
AACGIINTTV
activating
AACGIKNNRS
ransacking
AACGILLNOT
allocating
AACGILLRTY
tragically
AACGILMNNY
malignancy
AACGILMNTU
maculating
AACGIMNORT
morganatic
AACGIMNRSS
massacring
AACGINNPPT
catnapping
AACGINNSSV
canvassing
AACGINRSTT
castrating
AACGINRTTT
attracting
AACGIORSTT
castigator
AACHILMNOR
monarchial
AACHIMNORS
maraschino
AACHIMNORW
chairwoman
AACHIMPRST
pharmacist
AACHIMRRTY
matriarchy
AACHLNNNOT
nonchalant
AACHLOPPRY
apocryphal
AACIILLNNT
anticlinal
AACIILLOPT
apolitical
AACIILMNTX
anticlimax
AACIILMPST
capitalism
AACIILNNST
annalistic
AACIILNOST
antisocial
AACIILPSTT
capitalist
AACIIORSUV
avaricious
AACILLNOOT
allocation
AACILLNTUY
nautically
AACILLPTYY
atypically

AACILMOSTU
calamitous
AACILNNRTY
tyrannical
AACILNOOTV
vocational
AACILOORRT
oratorical
AACILOPPRT
applicator
AACILPRRTU
particular
AACIMNOPRY
pyromaniac
AACINORTTT
attraction
AACINORTUY
cautionary
AACIORRSTT
aristocrat
AACLOORRTU
coloratura
AADDDEENNP
deadpanned
AADDEEHIMN
maidenhead
AADDEELTUV
devaluated
AADDEESTTV
devastated
AADDEGIPRS
disparaged
AADDEHIMNN
handmaiden
AADDEHLNNP
panhandled
AADDEHNRTY
anhydrated
AADDEIILPT
dilapidated
AADDEIILLNS
landladies
AADDEILNVZ
vandalized
AADDEIMRTZ
dramatized
AADDEIRRSY
disarrayed
AADDGNNRST
grandstand
AADDIILNOT
additional
AADDLNOOSW
sandalwood
AADEEEPPRR
reappeared
AADEEFGLRT
deflagrate
AADEEGGGRT
aggregated
AADEEGIRTV
variegated
AADEEGNRRR
rearranged

AADEEGNRTU
guaranteed
AADEEHHLRX
hexahedral
AADEEHHMMR
hammerhead
AADEEHMRST
headmaster
AADEEHNRVW
heavenward
AADEEHQRSU
squarehead
AADEEILLTV
alleviated
AADEEILRTT
retaliated
AADEEINQTU
inadequate
AADEEIPRST
deaspirate
AADEEIRSTT
asteriated
AADEELLLPR
paralleled
AADEELLOTV
alveolated
AADEELLPPR
apparelled
AADEELMRTT
maltreated
AADEELNRTT
alternated
AADEELQTUY
adequately
AADEELRTTU
adulterate
AADEEMQRSU
masquerade
AADEENTTTU
attenuated
AADEEOPRTV
evaporated
AADEFFIILT
affiliated
AADEFHLNRT
fatherland
AADEFIMNOT
defamation
AADEFINSTZ
fantasized
AADEFINTTU
infatuated
AADEFMORTY
defamatory
AADEGGINRZ
aggrandize
AADEGHHINS
shanghaied
AADEGIINRT
eradiating
AADEGILNOZ
analogized
AADEGILNVZ
galvanized

AADEGIMMNS
mismanaged
AADEGINNTT
antedating
AADEGIRTTV
gravitated
AADEGLNQRU
quadrangle
AADEGLNRTU
granulated
AADEGLRTTU
gratulated
AADEGOPPRT
propagated
AADEHIIMNR
maidenhair
AADEHLLMRS
marshalled
AADEIILMNZ
animalized
AADEIILNTV
invalidate
AADEIIMNNT
maintained
AADEIINORT
eradiation
AADEILMNNR
mainlander
AADEILNRSU
unsalaried
AADEILNTTZ
tantalized
AADEILORRR
railroader
AADEILPPTT
palpitated
AADEIMMNOT
ammoniated
AADEIMNRTV
animadvert
AADEINNTTU
unattained
AADEINPQSU
pasquinade
AADEINQRSU
quandaries
AADEINQTTU
antiquated
AADEIPPTTT
pitapatted
AADEKLMORW
meadowlark
AADELNRSTT
translated
AADEMMNSSU
mandamuses
AADEMRRSTY
yardmaster
AADENQRSTU
quadrantes
AADEQRRTUU
quadrature
AADFGLNOPR
flapdragon

AADGGIIMNR
diagraming
AADGGILLNNR
garlanding
AADGGINNRTU
graduating
AADGHIOPRR
radiograph
AADGIILLNPS
palisading
AADGIILNTV
validating
AADGIIMMNNR
marinading
AADGILLNOY
diagonally
AADGILMNSU
salmagundi
AADGINNRTU
danaturing
AADGINORTU
graduation
AADGINQRTU
quadrating
AADGNNOPRS
snapdragon
AADHILRTWW
withdrawal
AADIILNOPT
lapidation
AADIILQRUV
quadrivial
AADIIMNOPS
dipsomania
AADIIMNORT
admiration
AADILMOPRR
parlormaid
AADLMNNRUY
laundryman
AADNOPRRUW
wraparound
AAEEEGGRTX
exaggerate
AAEEEHRSST
heartsease
AAEEELMNRW
enamelware
AAEEEPRSTX
exasperate
AAEEEPRTTX
praetextae
AAEEFGLLLT
flagellate
AAEEFRSTTT
aftertaste
AAEEGINRTV
vegetarian
AAEEGMMNNT
management
AAEEGMNRSS
manageress
AAEEGNPRRR
prearrange

AAEEGNRSXY
sexagenary
AAEEGNSSSV
savageness
AAEEGQRRTU
quarterage
AAEEHILRTX
exhilarate
AAEEHINSST
anesthesia
AAEEHKQRTU
earthquake
AAEEHLNTVX
hexavalent
AAEEHMNRTW
weatherman
AAEEHMPRST
metaphrase
AAEEIILLRTT
alliterate
AAEEILMORT
ameliorate
AAEEILRTTV
alterative
AAEEIPRSTV
separative
AAEEIPRTTX
expatriate
AAEELLTTTT
tattletale
AAEELPRSTY
separately
AAEEPPRSTW
wastepaper
AAEFGINNPR
frangipane
AAEFGLMNRT
fragmental
AAEFIILSTT
fatalities
AAEGHINNNS
shenanigan
AAEGHMPRTY
metagraphy
AAEGIILNNT
alienating
AAEGIILPRS
plagiaries
AAEGIILPRZ
plagiarize
AAEGIINRTT
ingratiate
AAEGILLMNT
malleating
AAEGILLNOT
allegation
AAEGILMSTT
stalagmite
AAEGILNNTT
tangential
AAEGILNPPR
appareling
AAEGILNPRV
palavering

AAEGILNTUV
evaluating
AAEGIMRSTT
magistrate
AAEGINNOTZ
antagonize
AAEGINNSTU
nauseating
AAEGINPRST
separating
AAEGINRSTU
guaranties
AAEGINRTUU
inaugurate
AAEGLLPSST
plateglass
AAEGLNNOPT
pentagonal
AAEHHILLLU
halleluiah
AAEHHJLLLU
hallelujah
AAEHIILLNNT
annihilate
AAEHIKRRST
hairstreak
AAEHILNOTX
exhalation
AAEHIMNPSS
seamanship
AAEHIMNSTY
myasthenia
AAEHIMRSTU
amateurish
AAEHIPSTXY
asphyxiate
AAEHMNRSST
harassment
AAEIIILLPTV
palliative
AAEIILMMRT
immaterial
AAEIILMSST
assimilate
AAEIILNNOT
alienation
AAEIILPRTZ
partialize
AAEIIMNNRS
seminarian
AAEIIMNNRT
maintainer
AAEIILLLLNV
villanella
AAEIILLMRTY
materially
AAEIILLNRTU
unilateral
AAEIILMNNSU
semiannual
AAEIILMNNSV
manavelins
AAEIILMNPRT
parliament

AAEIILMNPTU
manipulate
AAEIILMNRTY
alimentary
AAEIILNORST
senatorial
AAEIILNORTT
alteration
AAEIILNORTX
relaxation
AAEIILNOTTX
exaltation
AAEIILNOTUV
evaluation
AAEIILNRTUZ
naturalize
AAEIILOQRTU
equatorial
AAEIILORSTV
lavatories
AAEIIMMNORT
metromania
AAEIIMMNRST
mainstream
AAEIIMMRSTU
amateurism
AAEIIMNNOSY
mayonnaise
AAEIIMNRTTT
antimatter
AAEIIMPRSST
separatism
AAEIIMSSSTT
metastasis
AAEIINNNOTX
annexation
AAEIINNQRTU
quarantine
AAEIINOPRST
separation
AAEIINOPSST
passionate
AAEIINRRSTW
warranties
AAEIINRSTTT
intrastate
AAEIIOPSSST
apostasies
AAEIIPRSSTT
separatist
AAEKMRSSTT
taskmaster
AAEKRRSTUU
sauerkraut
AAELLLMNOS
salmonella
AAELLMNRTY
maternally
AAELLMORZZ
mozzarella
AAELLNOSSY
seasonally
AAELMNNORT
ornamental

AAELMNOSSW	**AAGIILNRTV**	**AAIIKLLNTY**	translator
saleswoman	travailing	alkalinity	**AALORSTTUY**
AAELNNPSTU	**AAGIILNSTV**	**AAIILMNNOT**	salutatory
unpleasant	salivating	lamination	**AAMNNOTTTU**
AAELNORRTT	**AAGIIMMNNRT**	**AAIILNORRT**	tantamount
alternator	marinating	irrational	**ABBCDEEHMR**
AAELNPPRTY	**AAGIINNOPT**	**AAIILNOSTV**	bedchamber
apparently	pagination	salivation	**ABBCEEIRRS**
AAELOOPSTT	**AAGIINNOTV**	**AAIILPRTTY**	crabberies
apostolate	navigation	partiality	**ABBCEEGINRU**
AAELPRRTTT	**AAGIINNTTT**	**AAIIMNRSTU**	barbecuing
rattletrap	attainting	sanitarium	**ABBCEIKNTT**
AAEMNNRSTV	**AAGIINNPPRS**	**AAIIMPRSST**	backbitten
manservant	appraising	parasitism	**ABBCEILMNO**
AAEMNQRRTU	**AAGIJKLNWY**	**AAIINNOSTT**	combinable
quarterman	jaywalking	sanitation	**ABBCEKLRRY**
AAENRRSTTU	**AAGILLMNRY**	**AAIINOPPRT**	blackberry
restaurant	alarmingly	apparition	**ABBCENORSY**
AAEOOPRRTV	**AAGILMNRY**	**AAIINOPRST**	absorbency
evaporator	marginally	aspiration	**ABBCFGINNO**
AAEQRRSTUW	**AAGILNPRYZ**	**AAIIRSSSTY**	confabbing
quartersaw	paralyzing	satyriasis	**ABBCGILNRS**
AAFFGIMNRU	**AAGILNRRTU**	**AAILLNNOTY**	scrabbling
ragamuffin	triangular	nationally	**ABBCIILLLY**
AAFGINNSTY	**AAGILNRTUY**	**AAILLNORTY**	biblically
fantasying	angularity	rationally	**ABBDEELNNU**
AAFGLLNRTY	**AAGILNSSTU**	**AAILMNRRTU**	unbendable
flagrantly	assaulting	intramural	**ABBDEFIORR**
AAFGLNRRTY	**AAGIMMPRST**	**AAILMNRSTU**	fiberboard
fragrantly	pragmatism	naturalism	**ABBDEIMORR**
AAFIILLMRY	**AAGIMNNOST**	**AAILNNOPTT**	bombardier
familiarly	antagonism	plantation	**ABBDELLNRU**
AAFIILMNRU	**AAGIMNOTTU**	**AAILNOSTTU**	landlubber
unfamiliar	automating	salutation	**ABBDELMOOZ**
AAGGHINNRU	**AAGIMNPRRT**	**AAILNRSTTU**	bamboozled
haranguing	ramparting	naturalist	**ABBDGIMNOR**
AAGGIILNTT	**AAGIMNPTTU**	**AAIMNNOOTTU**	bombarding
tailgating	amputating	automation	**ABBEEEILLV**
AAGGIINNPT	**AAGIMNRTTU**	**AAIMNOPTTU**	believable
paginating	maturating	amputation	**ABBEEIRRSY**
AAGGIINNRR	**AAGIMPRSTT**	**AAIMNORSTU**	bayberries
arraigning	pragmatist	sanatorium	**ABBEELORSV**
AAGGIINNTV	**AAGINNNOTT**	**AAIMNORTTU**	observable
navigating	annotating	maturation	**ABBEENORST**
AAGGINNSTT	**AAGINNOSTT**	**AAIMNORTTU**	breastbone
stagnating	antagonist	natatorium	**ABBEENORTW**
AAGGINORRT	**AAGINNOSTT**	**AAINNNOOOTT**	browbeaten
arrogating	stagnation	annotation	**ABBEEORRTW**
AAGHHIMNWY	**AAGINNRRTW**	**AAINNRSTUY**	browbeater
highwayman	warranting	unsanitary	**ABBEGILNOR**
AAGHILMNRS	**AAGINNRSUY**	**AAINORSTTU**	belaboring
marshaling	sanguinary	saturation	**ABBEGILNRS**
AAGIIKLLNZ	**AAGINRSTTU**	**AAINORSTTV**	slabbering
alkalizing	saturating	starvation	**ABBEHINSSS**
AAGIILLNPT	**AAGLNORRTY**	**AAINORSTTY**	shabbiness
palliating	arrogantly	stationary	**ABBEHOPRRS**
AAGIILMNNT	**AGOOPPRRT**	**AAKMMNORSW**	barbershop
laminating	propagator	markswoman	**ABBEILMOPR**
AAGIILNNSZ	**AAHIILNNOT**	**AALLOPRSTY**	improbable
nasalizing	inhalation	pastorally	**ABBELLRTTU**
AAGIILNNUV	**AAHIMNNOOP**	**AALMOOPPRS**	butterball
unavilaing	phonomania	malapropos	**ABBGILNQSU**
AAGIILNPPZ	**AAIIILMMNT**	**AALNNPRSTT**	squabbling
papalizing	militiaman	transplant	**ABBHIILOPT**
	AAIIJLNORT	**AALNORRSTT**	
	janitorial		

bibliotaph
ABBILMOPRY
improbably
ABCCEEILMP
impeccable
ABCCEEILSS
accessible
ABCCHIKSTW
switchback
ABCCIILRRU
bicircular
ABCCILNNOU
concubinal
ABCCMOPSTU
subcompact
ABCDEEEILV
deceivable
ABCDEEELLT
delectable
ABCDEEELRT
celebrated
ABCDEEELTT
detectable
ABCDEEERRT
cerebrated
ABCDEEHRUY
debauchery
ABCDEEILPS
despicable
ABCDEEILVY
deceivably
ABCDEELLTY
delectably
ABCDEFIRTU
bifurcated
ABCDEFOSTU
obfuscated
ABCDEGHINU
debauching
ABCDEHORSS
chessboard
ABCDEIIMRT
imbricated
ABCDEIKLRS
backslider
ABCDEIKOUV
bivouacked
ABCDEILPSY
despicably
ABCDEILRTU
lubricated
ABCDEINORZ
carbonized
ABCDEIRRTU
rubricated
ABCDELRTUU
lucubrated
ABCDEOORRS
scoreboard
ABCDERSTTU
subtracted
ABCDGIKLNO

blockading
ABCDGINNOS
absconding
ABCDGKNORU
background
ABCDHIILNR
brainchild
ABCDHLOORT
broadcloth
ABCEEEIKRR
icebreaker
ABCEEENRUX
exuberance
ABCEEFIILN
beneficial
ABCEEFNORT
benefactor
ABCEEHLNQU
quenchable
ABCEEHNORR
abhorrence
ABCEEHORSU
herbaceous
ABCEEIKLNR
linebacker
ABCEEILMMT
emblematic
ABCEEILNOT
noticeable
ABCEEINNST
abstinence
ABCEEJNSST
abjectness
ABCEELLNOS
enclosable
ABCEELNNOV
convenable
ABCEELNOVY
conveyable
ABCEELORRT
celebrator
ABCEENORSV
observance
ABCEFILNNO
confinable
ABCEFLNOSU
confusable
ABCEFLNOTU
confutable
ABCEGHIMNR
chambering
ABCEGIKLNN
blackening
ABCEGIKNRT
bracketing
ABCEGILMNR
clambering
ABCEGILNOZ
cognizable
ABCEGLNOOT
conglobate
ABCEHILPRT
birthplace
ABCEHLLOOS

schoolable
ABCEHLLOTT
tablecloth
ABCEHLNRSS
branchless
ABCEHORTTX
chatterbox
ABCEIILLNR
brilliance
ABCEIILMTU
umbilicate
ABCEIIMRST
bicamerist
ABCEIKKMRR
brickmaker
ABCEIKLRRY
bricklayer
ABCEILMOPT
compatible
ABCEILNOSU
unsociable
ABCEILNOTY
noticeably
ABCEILNPRU
republican
ABCEIMORRT
barometric
ABCEINRRST
transcribe
ABCEJKLMRU
lumberjack
ABCEKKORST
backstroke
ABCELLNOOR
collarbone
ABCELLNOOS
consolable
ABCELMNOSU
consumable
ABCELMOPTU
computable
ABCEORRRTU
carburetor
ABCGHIINOT
cohabiting
ABCGHIIOPR
biographic
ABCGIILLOO
biological
ABCGIINNTU
incubating
ABCGILMNRS
scrambling
ABCHHIOPRS
archbishop
ABCHIKLMST
blacksmith
ABCIIINOTT
antibiotic
ABCIILLNRY
brilliancy
ABCIINNOTU
incubation
ABCILLMOSY

symbolical
ABCKNPRTUY
bankruptcy
ABCLOSSTTY
cystoblast
ABCMNORSUW
scrubwoman
ABDDDEIORS
broadsided
ABDDEEELNP
dependable
ABDDEGINRU
unabridged
ABDDEGIRRW
drawbridge
ABDDEHILNS
blandished
ABDDEHINRS
brandished
ABDDEIIMRS
bridesmaid
ABDDGIINNS
disbanding
ABDDOOORRSW
broadsword
ABDEEEHQTU
bequeathed
ABDEEEILRT
deliberate
ABDEEEKMRR
reembarked
ABDEEELNPX
expendable
ABDEEELSTT
detestable
ABDEEEMNST
debasement
ABDEEERSTW
sweetbread
ABDEEFHNOR
beforehand
ABDEEFIITU
beautified
ABDEEHILRR
halberdier
ABDEEHIMSV
misbehaved
ABDEEHINRT
hibernated
ABDEEIILTT
debilitate
ABDEEIINRT
inebriated
ABDEEILMRZ
marbelized
ABDEEILNNU
undeniable
ABDEEILRVZ
verbalized
ABDEELLOPR
deplorable
ABDEENOPSU
subpoenaed
ABDEFIILMO

.modifiable
ABDEFIIMRT
fimbriated
ABDEFILMOR
formidable
ABDEFIRRTU
breadfruit
ABDEGGNOOT
tobogganed
ABDEGIINNR
brigandine
ABDEGIMNRT
abridgment
ABDEGJORTU
objurgated
ABDEGJSTUU
subjugated
ABDEGORSTU
subrogated
ABDEHIILLS
dishabille
ABDEHILNRS
blandisher
ABDEHNORTU
earthbound
ABDEHORRST
shortbread
ABDEIILMSS
admissible
ABDEIILSTZ
stabilized
ABDEIINOST
antibodies
ABDEILLSYZ
syllabized
ABDEILMNRT
timberland
ABDEILMSTU
sublimated
ABDEILNNUY
undeniably
ABDEILOPSS
disposable
ABDEILPSTU
disputable
ABDEILRTUZ
brutalized
ABDEIMRTUW
dumbwaiter
ABDEINORSU
boundaries
ABDEIRTTTU
attributed
ABDELLOPRY
deplorably
ABDELMRRUY
lumberyard
ABDENOPPRU
paperbound
ABDENRSSSU
absurdness
ABDFILMORY
formidably
ABDFLOOORR

floorboard
ABDGHINNSU
husbanding
ABDGIIINPRU
upbraiding
ABDGIIINRRS
disbarring
ABDGIINSSU
disabusing
ABDGINORTU
obdurating
ABDIIILSTY
disability
ABDIIILTUY
audibility
ABDIILRTUY
durability
ABDIIRSSUY
subsidiary
ABDILNOOST
bloodstain
ABDNOORTUU
roundabout
ABDOORRTUU
troubadour
ABDEEEELMST
esteemable
ABEEEFLPRR
preferable
ABEEEHRSTT
hartebeest
ABEEEELMNRU
enumerable
ABEEEELMRSS
reassemble
ABEEEELNPRT
penetrable
ABEEEELQSUZ
squeezable
ABEEEERRTTV
vertebrate
ABEEFFLMNT
bafflement
ABEEFFLRSU
sufferable
ABEEFIILRV
verifiable
ABEEFIIRTU
beautifier
ABEEFIISTU
beautifies
ABEEFILNSU
unfeasible
ABEEFILNTT
fleabitten
ABEEFLPRRY
preferably
ABEEGIKNPS
bespeaking
ABEEGILNOT
negotiable
ABEEGIMNRS
besmearing
ABEEGLNORV

governable
ABEEHHRRTY
heathberry
ABEEHILPRS
perishable
ABEEHLMPRS
blasphemer
ABEEHLRSST
breathless
ABEEHORTTU
thereabout
ABEEHORTUW
whereabout
ABEEIILLRZ
liberalize
ABEEIILNTV
inevitable
ABEEIIRRSV
breviaries
ABEEIIRSST
bestiaries
ABEEILLMNR
bellarmine
ABEEILLNRU
unreliable
ABEEILMOTZ
metabolize
ABEEILMSSS
assemblies
ABEEILNOPR
inoperable
ABEEILNORX
inexorable
ABEEILORTT
obliterate
ABEEILSSTT
beastliest
ABEEKMMNNT
embankment
ABEEKMMNRT
embarkment
ABEELLMOPY
employable
ABEELLNRUV
vulnerable
ABEELMNRSU
mensurable
ABEELMNTTT
battlement
ABEELMPRSU
presumable
ABEELNOPRS
personable
ABEENNRRSS
barrenness
ABEENNRRSTU
subterrane
ABEFFLRSUY
sufferably
ABEFGIINTY
beatifying
ABEFGILORV
forgivable
ABEFGILRSS

fiberglass
ABEFGINORR
forbearing
ABEFHIRRTT
afterbirth
ABEFIILLLN
infallible
ABEFILOPRT
profitable
ABEFKNORRT
breakfront
ABEGGIMNOR
embargoing
ABEGHILNRT
blathering
ABEGHIOPRR
biographer
ABEGIILNNT
intangible
ABEGIILNRT
liberating
ABEGIINNRT
brigantine
ABEGIKLNNT
blanketing
ABEGILMNPR
preambling
ABEGILMNSS
assembling
ABEGILMNTT
embattling
ABEGILNSSU
subleasing
ABEGILRRSU
burglaries
ABEGILRRUZ
burglarize
ABEGINNOTY
bayoneting
ABEGINNQTU
banqueting
ABEGLNORRY
loganberry
ABEHHORRTT
heartthrob
ABEHIILMNT
habiliment
ABEHILMNOR
hambroline
ABEHILNPSU
punishable
ABEHILOPST
hospitable
ABEHILPSTT
battleship
ABEHIMNNST
banishment
ABEHLORRSS
harborless
ABEIIILMNT
inimitable
ABEIILLMRS
liberalism
ABEIILLNNY

biennially
ABEIILLNOV
inviolable
ABEIILLRTY
liberality
ABEIILMRST
bimestrial
ABEIILNORT
liberation
ABEIILNTVY
inevitably
ABEIILQTUY
equability
ABEIILRSTZ
stabilizer
ABEIILSTTY
bestiality
ABEIIORSTU
obituaries
ABEILMMOST
metabolism
ABEILMNQRU
lambrequin
ABEILMOOTU
automobile
ABEILMOPRV
improvable
ABEILNORXY
inexorably
ABEILOPRRV
proverbial
ABEILORTVY
abortively
ABEIMNORTU
tambourine
ABEIMOSSTU
abstemious
ABEINNOSTT
abstention
ABEINNRSSW
brawniness
ABEIPRSTTY
baptistery
ABEKKORSTW
basketwork
ABEKLNNOUW
unknowable
ABEKLNORUW
unworkable
ABEKMNNOTU
mountebank
ABEKNOPRRW
pawnbroker
ABEKORRSTW
breastwork
ABELLLLOVY
volleyball
ABELLOSTUY
absolutely
ABELMNNOOW
noblewoman
ABELMPRSUY
presumably
ABELNOOPST

tablespoon
ABELNOPRUV
unprovable
ABELRSSTUY
abstrusely
ABEMMNNORSU
membranous
ABENPRSSTU
abruptness
ABERRRSTWY
strawberry
ABFIILLLNY
infallibly
ABFLLOSTUY
boastfully
ABFLLOSUUY
fabulously
ABGGGGILNRY
braggingly
ABGGIILNOT
obligating
ABGHIIINNT
inhabiting
ABGHIILNOS
abolishing
ABGHINNSTU
sunbathing
ABGHIRRSTT
starbright
ABGIIILNST
sibilating
ABGIIJLNTU
jubilating
ABGIILNOOT
obligation
ABGIILNOPR
parboiling
ABGIINNRUZ
urbanizing
ABGIINNSTU
antibusing
ABGILLLNSY
syllabling
ABGILLNNOO
ballooning
ABGILOORTY
obligatory
ABGIMNORTU
tambouring
ABGINORTTU
obturating
ABHIIMOPSU
amphibious
ABHILOPSTY
hospitably
ABHINPRSTU
paintbrush
ABIIILLPTY
pliability
ABIIILMNTY
inimitably
ABIIJLNOTU
jubilation
ABIILLMNSU

subliminal
ABIILMTTUY
mutability
ABIILNOTTY
notability
ABIIMORSSV
bravissimo
ABILLNOOST
balloonist
ABILMOSSTU
absolutism
ABILNOOSTU
absolution
ABILOSSTTU
absolutist
ABIMNORRST
brainstorm
ABINOOPRST
absorption
ABINOOSSST
bassoonist
ABNOORRSTU
brontosaur
ABOORSTTUU
roustabout
ACCCEEHITT
catechetic
ACCCEILLNY
encyclical
ACCCEILMOP
accomplice
ACCCINOPPU
cappuccino
ACCDDEEIST
desiccated
ACCDEEHKMT
checkmated
ACCDEEHNOR
encroached
ACCDEEINNS
incandesce
ACCDEEIQSU
acquiesced
ACCDEELPST
spectacled
ACCDEFIIRS
sacrificed
ACCDEIIRTZ
cicatrized
ACCDEILLOP
peccadillo
ACCDEILNTU
inculcated
ACCDEILRTU
circulated
ACCDEIMORT
democratic
ACCDEINOOS
occasioned
ACCDELLOOT
collocated
ACCDEMOSTU
accustomed
ACCDENORTT

contracted
ACCDHHRRUY
churchyard
ACCDHILORV
clavichord
ACCDIIIORT
idiocratic
ACCDINORTT
contradict
ACCDNNOORT
concordant
ACCEEEEHKS
cheesecake
ACCEEEFFKO
coffeecake
ACCEEELPRT
receptacle
ACCEEHINRS
chanceries
ACCEEILLRT
electrical
ACCEEILMNU
ecumenical
ACCEEILSST
ecclesiast
ACCEEIRTUX
excruciate
ACCEELNOSV
convalesce
ACCEELNRTU
reluctance
ACCEEMNRST
marcescent
ACCEENNOVY
conveyance
ACCEENORST
consecrate
ACCEENRSSS
scarceness
ACCEFFIINY
inefficacy
ACCEFHLRTY
flycatcher
ACCEFINOST
confiscate
ACCEGIKNOP
peacocking
ACCEGILLNN
cancelling
ACCEGILLOO
ecological
ACCEGILNNO
concealing
ACCEGILNOS
coalescing
ACCEGIMOPS
megascopic
ACCEGINNOR
carcinogen
ACCEGINNOZ
cognizance
ACCEHIILMR
chimerical
ACCEHIINNT

technician
ACCEHILLTY
hectically
ACCEHIORRY
hierocracy
ACCEHIORTT
theocratic
ACCEHIRRST
scratchier
ACCELLNOR
chancellor
ACCEHLMOOR
homocercal
ACCEIILNOT
conciliate
ACCEIILSSZ
classicize
ACCEIIMSST
asceticism
ACCEIIRSST
scarcities
ACCEIKLRST
crackliest
ACCEILMMOR
commercial
ACCEILMNOO
economical
ACCEILMNOP
compliance
ACCEILMOPT
complicate
ACCEILNOSS
neoclassic
ACCEILOPRR
reciprocal
ACCEINNNOV
connivance
ACCEINNORT
concertina
ACCEIOPPSY
episcopacy
ACCEKNRRTU
nutcracker
ACCELMNOPT
complacent
ACCELNOPTU
conceptual
ACCEMNNORY
necromancy
ACCENORTTU
counteract
ACCEORSUUV
curvaceous
ACCFGIILNY
calcifying
ACCFHIRTTW
witchcraft
ACCGHINRST
scratching
ACCGIIMORT
tragicomic
ACCGIINPRT
practicing
ACCGILNSUY

accusingly
ACCGIMNOPT
compacting
ACCGINNOTT
contacting
ACCGINNOTU
accounting
ACCHHIILLN
chinchilla
ACCHHORSST
crosshatch
ACCHIIMSST
schismatic
ACCHILLOTY
catholicly
ACCHILMOPS
accomplish
ACCHILOSST
scholastic
ACCHNORRST
cornstarch
ACCHOPRSST
crosspatch
ACCIIILLLP
piccalilli
ACCIILLLNY
clinically
ACCIILMSSS
classicism
ACCIILNRTU
uncritical
ACCIILSSST
classicist
ACCIINNNPY
piccaninny
ACCIIOPRSU
capricious
ACCIKKKKNN
knickknack
ACCILLRRUY
circularly
ACCILMNOOS
iconoclasm
ACCILNOOST
iconoclast
ACCILORRTU
circulator
ACCINOOPRU
cornucopia
ACCINOOPTU
occupation
ACCINOPRSY
conspiracy
ACCIOOPRSU
procacious
ACCLOPRTUY
plutocracy
ACCNOORRTT
contractor
ACDDEEELTT
delectated
ACDDEEEPRT
deprecated
ACDDEEERST

desecrated
ACDDEEILMT
maledicted
ACDDEEILTU
elucidated
ACDDEEIPRT
predicated
ACDDEELLOT
decollated
ACDDEENNST
descendant
ACDDEENTUU
uneducated
ACDDEESSTU
decussated
ACDDEFFHNU
handcuffed
ACDDEFFIRT
diffracted
ACDDEFFLOS
scaffolded
ACDDEGHIRS
discharged
ACDDEGIINT
dedicating
ACDDEHINSW
sandwiched
ACDDEHIPST
dispatched
ACDDEHNNOS
secondhand
ACDDEIILMS
disclaimed
ACDDEIINOT
dedication
ACDDEIINTV
vindicated
ACDDEILOST
dislocated
ACDDEILPTU
duplicated
ACDDEINNSS
candidness
ACDDEINSTY
syndicated
ACDDEIRSTT
distracted
ACDDEKLLNO
landlocked
ACDDELNNOO
colonnaded
ACDDGHILNR
grandchild
ACDDGIINRS
discarding
ACDDGIKNOP
paddocking
ACDDINORST
discordant
ACDEEEEHHS
headcheese
ACDEEEEELRT
decelerate
ACDEEEHRRS

researched
ACDEEEIPRT
depreciate
ACDEEENNTT
antecedent
ACDEEFFLTY
affectedly
ACDEEFFNTU
unaffected
ACDEEFGINT
defecating
ACDEEFINNR
refinanced
ACDEEGHLLN
challenged
ACDEEGINNR
grandniece
ACDEEGINRS
decreasing
ACDEEGINRT
centigrade
ACDEEGNORU
encouraged
ACDEEHILNR
chandelier
ACDEEHIMNZ
mechanized
ACDEEHKLLS
shellacked
ACDEEHMNTT
detachment
ACDEEHNOPR
chaperoned
ACDEEHOPPR
copperhead
ACDEEHOPRR
reproached
ACDEEIILMP
epidemical
ACDEEIILNT
indelicate
ACDEEILLRS
escadrille
ACDEEILLTY
delicately
ACDEEILNRT
interlaced
ACDEEILPTX
explicated
ACDEEIMPRT
imprecated
ACDEEINNTU
denunciate
enunciated
ACDEEINPPS
appendices
ACDEEINRTT
interacted
ACDEEIORTV
decorative
ACDEEIORTX
excoriated
ACDEEIOTTX
detoxicate

ACDEEIRTTX
extricated
ACDEEISSTZ
ecstasized
ACDEEITTUX
exactitude
ACDEELLOPS
escalloped
ACDEELNOST
adolescent
ACDEELOPRT
percolated
ACDEELORRT
correlated
ACDEELPSTU
speculated
ACDEEMMNNOR
commandeer
ACDEEOOPRT
cooperated
ACDEEOPRRT
procreated
ACDEEORRTT
retroacted
ACDEFFIIOT
officiated
ACDEFFIKRT
trafficked
ACDEFFOSTU
suffocated
ACDEFHINRS
franchised
ACDEFIILSS
classified
ACDEFIINST
sanctified
ACDEFIIRRT
fratricide
ACDEFINORT
fornicated
ACDEFLTTUU
fluctuated
ACDEGHRRSU
surcharged
ACDEGIILMN
declaiming
ACDEGIIMNT
decimating
medicating
ACDEGIMMRS
scrimmaged
ACDEGINORT
decorating
ACDEGINRTT
detracting
ACDEGIORSU
discourage
ACDEGJNOTU
conjugated
ACDEGLNNRU
granduncle
ACDEGORRTU
corrugated
ACDEHHOPRT

heptachord
ACDEHILMOT
methodical
ACDEHILOPR
epichordal
ACDEHIMMST
mismatched
ACDEHIMNOP
championed
ACDEHINNST
disenchant
ACDEHIPRST
dispatcher
ACDEHIPSST
dispatches
ACDEHNOORT
octahedron
ACDEIIILST
idealistic
ACDEIIILTZ
italicized
ACDEIIINTV
indicative
ACDEIILMPT
implicated
ACDEIILMRS
disclaimer
ACDEIILNNT
incidental
ACDEIILOPR
periodical
ACDEIILOSZ
socialized
ACDEIIMNOT
decimation
medication
ACDEIIMRRS
miscarried
ACDEIINNRY
incendiary
ACDEIIOSST
dissociate
ACDEILLORR
cordillera
ACDEILLOST
oscillated
ACDEILMNOP
complained
ACDEILMNTU
culminated
ACDEILMOPR
proclaimed
ACDEILNOTU
inoculated
ACDEILNUVZ
vulcanized
ACDEILTTUV
cultivated
ACDEIMNOSU
mendacious
ACDEIMRTTU
micturated
ACDEINNOSS
dissonance

ACDEINOORT
coordinate
ACDEINORTT
detraction
ACDEINOSTT
anecdotist
ACDEINPRST
discrepant
ACDEINSTTU
sanctitude
ACDEIORSTZ
ostracized
ACDEIPQRSU
quadriceps
ACDEIRSSTT
dictatress
ACDELNOORT
decolorant
ACDEMMNOOS
commandos
ACDEMMNORY
commandery
ACDENOPSTY
syncopated
ACDENORSTT
contrasted
ACDENPTTUU
punctuated
ACDEOPRRTT
protracted
ACDFGIIINY
acidifying
ACDGGIINRS
disgracing
ACDGIIINNT
indicating
ACDGIILNPS
displacing
ACDGIINNST
distancing
ACDGIINOST
diagnostic
ACDGIKLNOP
padlocking
ACDGIKNOST
stockading
ACDGILOORY
cardiology
ACDGIMMNNO
commanding
ACDGMNOPRU
campground
ACDHIIIOPT
idiopathic
ACDHLOORSY
schoolyard
ACDHMNORYY
hydromancy
ACDIIINNOT
indication
ACDIIJLLUY
judicially
ACDIILMOPT
diplomatic

ACDIIINORTY
dictionary
ACDILOPRTU
duplicator
ACDLLOPTYY
polydactyl
ACEEEFFTTU
effectuate
ACEEEGNPRT
percentage
ACEEEHRRSS
researches
ACEEEIMRRS
creameries
ACEEEIRSTV
eviscerate
ACEEELNPRV
prevalence
ACEEELORTT
electorate
ACEEEMNNPR
permanence
ACEEEMNNST
encasement
ACEEEMNPRT
temperance
ACEEEMNPST
escapement
ACEEENNSTV
evanescent
ACEEEPRRTU
recuperate
ACEEFFIMNY
effeminacy
ACEEFIILTT
felicitate
ACEEFILMNT
maleficent
ACEEFIRRTV
refractive
ACEEFLLNTU
flatulence
ACEEFLLORV
cloverleaf
ACEEFLLPUY
peacefully
ACEEFLORST
forecastle
ACEEFMNNRU
furnacemen
ACEEFORRST
forecaster
ACEEGGNORT
congregate
ACCEGHILNT
genethliac
ACEEGHINNP
cheapening
ACEEGHINST
escheating
ACEEGHLLNR
challenger
ACEEGHLNSS
changeless

ACEEGHNORV	**ACEEILNNNT**	**ACEENPRUVY**	**ACEGHILNNN**
changeover	centennial	purveyance	channeling
ACEEGHORRV	**ACEEILNPRT**	**ACEEÓSSTTU**	**ACEGHINNNR**
overcharge	epicentral	testaceous	channering
ACEEGILLOT	**ACEEILNRTV**	**ACEERRSSTW**	**ACEGHINNNT**
collegiate	cantilever	watercress	enchanting
ACEEGILNTU	**ACEEILNRTZ**	**ACEFFGHINR**	**ACEGHINNST**
geniculate	centralize	chaffering	chastening
ACEEGINNRT	**ACEEILORST**	**ACEFFIILTV**	**ACEGHINPRT**
reenacting	esoterical	afflictive	chaptering
ACEEGINNSV	**ACEEILRSUZ**	**ACEFFIKRRT**	**ACEGHINRRT**
evanescing	secularize	trafficker	chartering
ACEEGINRRT	**ACEEIMNRSV**	**ACEFGHIMNR**	**ACEGHINRTT**
recreating	serviceman	chamfering	chattering
ACEEGIORST	**ACEEIMNRTT**	**ACEFGIINTY**	**ACEGHLOORY**
categories	remittance	acetifying	archeology
ACEEGNNORV	**ACEEIMPRST**	**ACEFGINRRT**	**ACEGIILMNR**
governance	spermaceti	refracting	reclaiming
ACEEGNORRU	**ACEEINNRST**	**ACEFGLLRUY**	**ACEGIILMNX**
encourager	transience	gracefully	exclaiming
ACEEHHILRW	**ACEEINORRT**	**ACEFHINRRS**	**ACEGIILMTY**
wheelchair	recreation	franchiser	legitimacy
ACEEHHIRRS	**ACEEINORTU**	**ACEFHIRSSY**	**ACEGIILOST**
heresiarch	auctioneer	crayfishes	egoistical
ACEEHHIRST	**ACEEINPPRT**	**ACEFIIILST**	**ACEGIINNRS**
hatcheries	apprentice	facilities	increasing
ACEEHILPTT	**ACEEINPRST**	**ACEFIILRSS**	**ACEGIINORS**
telepathic	interspace	classifier	congiaries
ACEEHIMNPZ	**ACEEINRSST**	**ACEFIILSSS**	**ACEGIIOTTV**
chimpanzee	resistance	classifies	cogitative
ACEEHINSTT	**ACEEIOPPST**	**ACEFIINSST**	**ACEGIKLNNS**
anesthetic	episcopate	sanctifies	slackening
ACEEHIORRT	**ACEEIOQTUV**	**ACEFKLNORS**	**ACEGILLMNR**
charioteer	equivocate	cornflakes	marcelling
ACEEHLLNOP	**ACEEIORTVV**	**ACEFNNOORT**	**ACEGILLOQU**
cellophane	overactive	oceanfront	coquillage
ACEEHILNPTT	**ACEEIPQRSU**	**ACEFORRRTY**	**ACEGILMNNY**
planchette	picaresque	refractory	menacingly
ACEEHLSSST	**ACEEKLLRSS**	**ACEGGHILNN**	**ACEGILNNUT**
scatheless	salesclerk	changeling	congenital
ACEEHMORTT	**ACEEKORRSW**	**ACEGGHINNX**	**ACEGILNNPS**
tachometer	caseworker	exchanging	enclasping
ACEEHOPRRS	**ACEELLRSSY**	**ACEGGHIOPR**	**ACEGILNNTU**
reproaches	carelessly	geographic	nucleating
ACEEHPPRSY	**ACEELNOPST**	**ACEGGILNNO**	**ACEGILNOPS**
hyperspace	opalescent	congealing	opalescing
ACEEHRRSTU	**ACEELNPRSY**	**ACEGGILRRS**	**ACEGILNORT**
chartreuse	screenplay	scragglier	relocating
ACEEIILPSZ	**ACEELOSSTT**	**ACEGGINNSV**	**ACEGILNPTU**
specialize	cassolette	scavenging	peculating
ACEEIIMNPT	**ACEELPPRTU**	**ACEGGIRSST**	**ACEGILNQRU**
impatience	perceptual	scraggiest	lacquering
ACEEIINNRT	**ACEEMMNNPT**	**ACEGHHINTT**	**ACEGILNRTT**
incinerate	encampment	hatcheting	clattering
ACEEIIJLORS	**ACEEMMNOPST**	**ACEGHIILMT**	**ACEGILNRTU**
cajoleries	compensate	megalithic	ulcerating
ACEEILLORT	**ACEEMNPRST**	**ACEGHIIMNP**	**ACEGILOOPT**
electorial	escarpment	impeaching	apologetic
ACEEILLPSY	**ACEENNORTV**	**ACEGHIINRS**	**ACEGIMNPRS**
especially	contravene	cashiering	scampering
ACEEILMNOR	**ACEENNSSTU**	**ACEGHIIPPR**	**ACEGINNNRT**
ceremonial	sustenance	epigraphic	entrancing
ACEEILMNRT	**ACEENORSSS**	**ACEGHILMPT**	**ACEGINNORS**
mercantile	coarseness	phlegmatic	coarsening

ACEGINRRTT
retracting
ACEGINRSTT
scattering
ACEGINRTTU
eructating
ACEGINRTTX
extracting
ACEGINSSTY
ecstasying
ACEGLNOOOY
oceanology
ACEGOORSUU
courageous
ACEGOPRRSU
supercargo
ACEHIILPST
cephalitis
ACEHIIMRTT
arithmetic
ACEHILLOOZ
alcoholize
ACEHILLORY
heroically
ACEHILNORT
chlorinate
ACEHILORRT
rhetorical
ACEHILRSTY
hysterical
ACEHIMMSST
mismatches
ACEHIMNORS
monarchies
nomarchies
ACEHIMNORW
chairwomen
ACEHIMOPRT
metaphoric
ACEHIMOSTT
hemostatic
ACEHINPSST
patchiness
ACEHINPSTU
paunchiest
ACEHIOPRST
toparchies
ACEHIPRRST
archpriest
ACEHIPRSSU
haruspices
ACEHKLMMOR
hammerlock
ACEHKLNOST
chalkstone
ACEHLLMNOY
melancholy
ACEHLLPRSU
sepulchral
ACEHLMOOST
schoolmate
ACEHLNORSS
anchorless
ACEHLORRST

orchestral
ACEHLPRTYY
phylactery
ACEHORTTWW
watchtower
ACEIIIMNST
intimacies
ACEIIISTTV
activities
ACEIILLLPT
elliptical
ACEIILLOST
localities
ACEIILLRTY
illiteracy
ACEIILORSZ
socializer
ACEIILPPRT
participle
ACEIILPSST
specialist
ACEIILPSTY
speciality
ACEIILSTTY
elasticity
ACEIINNORT
cineration
ACEIINOTTX
intoxicate
ACEIINPPRT
principate
ACEIINPSTT
antiseptic
ACEIINSSTT
sanctities
ACEIIORSTT
atrocities
ACEIIRSSST
sacristies
ACEIIRTTVY
creativity
ACEIJKKNSV
jackknives
ACEILLMNSY
miscellany
ACEILLMRTY
metrically
ACEILLOPSW
pillowcase
ACEILLPRUY
peculiarly
ACEILLPSTY
septically
ACEILLRTVY
vertically
ACEILMMNSS
clamminess
ACEILMNRUW
lawrencium
ACEILMOPRR
proclaimer
ACEILMRSSU
secularism
ACEILMTUUV

cumulative
ACEILNOPPS
scaloppine
ACEILNORTU
ulceration
ACEILNSSSS
classiness
ACEILPPSTU
supplicate
ACEILRSSTU
secularist
ACEIMMRSTY
asymmetric
ACEIMNOPRT
importance
ACEIMSSTTY
systematic
ACEINNORTU
enunciator
ACEINNSSST
scantiness
ACEINOORTV
revocation
ACEINOPRTU
precaution
ACEINOPSTT
constipate
ACEINORRST
contraries
ACEINORRTT
retraction
ACEINORSSY
cessionary
ACEINORTTU
eructation
ACEINORTTX
extraction
ACEINRSSTW
scrawniest
ACEIOPRRSU
precarious
ACEIPPRSST
scrappiest
ACEJORRTTY
trajectory
ACEKKMOSST
smokestack
ACEKLLRSTU
lackluster
ACEKPRRSSY
skyscraper
ACELLLORSS
collarless
ACELMNNOTT
malcontent
ACELNNOSSU
consensual
ACELNNOTUV
conventual
ACELNOPRSY
narcolepsy
ACELNOTTUX
contextual
ACELOOPRRT

percolator
ACELOORRTW
watercolor
ACELOPRSSU
processual
ACELOPRSTU
speculator
ACELOPSTUU
pultaceous
ACELORRSTY
clearstory
ACEMMNNORTY
commentary
ACEMMNOSTU
consummate
ACEMMNORST
monstrance
ACEMMNNORTU
counterman
ACENNORSTV
conservant
conversant
ACENNOSTTT
contestant
ACEOOPRRRT
procreator
ACFFGIILNT
afflicting
ACFFIILLOY
officially
ACFFIILNOT
affliction
ACFFIIOORT
officiator
ACFGIILNRY
clarifying
ACFGIINNRT
infracting
ACFGIINRSY
scarifying
ACFGILNNOT
conflating
ACFGINRRTU
fracturing
ACFHLLTUWY
watchfully
ACFIILNOPT
pontifical
ACFIINNORT
infarction
infraction
ACFILNNOOT
conflation
ACFINOORRT
fornicator
ACGGHIINNR
chagrining
ACGGHINNNU
unchanging
ACGGIINOTT
cogitating
ACGHIINNNU
unchaining
ACGHIINSST

chastising
ACGHILOOPT
pathologic
ACGHIMNNOP
champignon
ACGHIMNOST
stomaching
ACGHINPRSU
purchasing
ACGHIOPPRT
pictograph
ACGHMNOORR
chronogram
ACGIIILLRT
argillitic
ACGIIKMNNN
nicknaming
ACGIILLNOZ
localizing
ACGIILLRTU
liturgical
ACGIILMNPS
misplacing
ACGIILMORS
algorismic
ACGIILNNNP
pinnacling
ACGIILNOPR
caprioling
ACGIILNORT
loricating
ACGIILNOVZ
vocalizing
ACGIILNRTU
curtailing
ACGIILNTUV
victualing
ACGIIMNNRU
manicuring
ACGIINNNOT
containing
ACGIINNNOZ
canonizing
ACGIINNOPT
captioning
ACGIINNOTU
auctioning
cautioning
ACGIINNRTU
curtaining
ACGIINOOTT
cogitation
ACGIINPRST
practising
ACGIINRSTT
astricting
ACGIJKKNSY
skyjacking
ACGIKMMMNO
mammocking
ACGILLNOPS
collapsing
scalloping
ACGILLNORR

corralling
ACGILLNOSU
callousing
ACGILMNTUU
cumulating
ACGILNOORY
craniology
ACGILNOPTU
copulating
ACGILNOSTU
osculating
ACGILORSUY
graciously
ACGIMNNOPY
companying
ACGIMNOPSS
compassing
ACGINNNNOU
announcing
ACGINNOORT
cartooning
ACGINNRTTU
truncating
ACGINOOSTU
contagious
ACGINOPSUU
pugnacious
ACGINORSUU
ungracious
ACGLNOORSU
clangorous
ACGMOPRRTY
cryptogram
ACHHILMOPT
ophthalmic
ACHHILMRTY
rhythmical
ACHHOPPSTY
psychopath
ACHIILORST
historical
ACHIIMNSTU
humanistic
ACHIIMNSUV
chauvinism
ACHIINSTUV
chauvinist
ACHIIOPRST
aphoristic
ACHIKLOORW
workaholic
ACHIKLQSUY
quackishly
ACHIKMNOST
mackintosh
ACHILLMOOS
alcoholism
ACHILLMTYY
mythically
ACHILORSUV
chivalrous
ACHIMMNORS
monarchism
ACHIMNORST

monarchist
ACHIOPRSTY
physiocrat
ACHIOPSTTY
hypostatic
ACHIPRSTYY
psychiatry
ACHLMMOORS
schoolmarm
ACIIILLMNY
inimically
ACIIILNOPT
politician
ACIIINTTVY
inactivity
ACIIJRSTUY
justiciary
ACIILLNORY
ironically
ACIILNOPRV
provincial
ACIILOQTUX
quixotical
ACIILOSSUV
lascivious
ACIILPSTTY
plasticity
ACIILRSTTU
altruistic
ACIIMMNSTU
numismatic
ACIIMNRSSS
narcissism
ACIIMNRSTU
manicurist
ACIINNOOTV
invocation
ACIINNOTTX
intoxicant
ACIIOPSSUU
auspicious
ACIIORSTVY
varicosity
ACILLLNOOY
colonially
ACILLLOOQU
colloquial
ACILLMSTYY
mystically
ACILLOOPRT
allotropic
ACILLOORST
oscillator
ACILMMRSUU
simulacrum
ACILMNOSUU
calumnious
ACILMORSUU
miraculous
ACILNOOORT
coloration
ACILNOOPTU
copulation
ACILNOOSTU

osculation
ACILNOOTTT
cottontail
ACILNORRTY
contrarily
ACILNORSTU
ultrasonic
ACILNPPSTU
supplicant
ACILNRTTUY
taciturnly
ACILOCQSUU
loquacious
ACILOPSTUY
captiously
ACILPRRSTU
scriptural
ACIMMORSSY
commissary
ACIMNNOSTY
sanctimony
ACIMNOOPRS
comparison
ACIMNOOPSS
compassion
ACIMNPRSTU
manuscript
ACIMOOPRTT
compatriot
ACINNNOSTT
inconstant
ACINNOOORT
coronation
ACINNOPRST
conspirant
ACINNORSTT
constraint
ACINNORTTU
truncation
ACINOOORST
cartoonist
ACINPRRSTT
ACKKNRSTUW
knackwurst
ACLLNPTUUY
punctually
ACLNNOSTTU
consultant
ACLNNOSTTY
constantly
ACLRRSTTUU
structural
ACMNNORTUY
countryman
ACOOPRRRTT
protractor
ACOPRSSSTT
sportscast
ADDDDEEKLS
skedaddled
ADDDEEHNRU
dunderhead
ADDDEEHRTY

dehydrated
ADDDEEILSS
sidesaddle
ADDEEEEFLOR
freeloaded
ADDEEEGNNR
endangered
ADDEEEILNT
delineated
ADDEEELRST
saddletree
ADDEEEENORV
endeavored
ADDEEFILOT
defoliated
ADDEEGGINS
disengaged
ADDEGINRSS
addressing
ADDEEGINRT
denigrated
ADDEEGINST
designated
ADDEEHNRTU
unthreaded
ADDEEILOTV
dovetailed
ADDEEILPSS
displeased
ADDEEIMRTT
readmitted
ADDEEIPRSW
widespread
ADDEEIPRTU
repudiated
ADDEEIRSTV
advertised
ADDEEIRTTX
extradited
ADDEEJRSTU
readjusted
ADDEELOORV
overloaded
ADDEELORSS
saddlesore
ADDEELPRST
stepladder
ADDEEMNNRU
undernamed
ADDEENNTTU
unattended
ADDEENQRSU
squandered
ADDEENRRTU
underrated
ADDEENRTUV
adventured
ADDEEPRSTU
depastured
ADDEFGINRU
defrauding
ADDEFILLSU
fusilladed
ADDEFIORSV

disfavored
ADDEFLLOOP
flapdoodle
ADDEGGILNN
gladdening
ADDEGIMOTZ
dogmatized
ADDEHILMNS
mishandled
ADDEHIMNOO
maidenhood
ADDEHIMNOS
admonished
ADDEIILQTU
liquidated
ADDEIIPSST
dissipated
ADDEILMNST
dismantled
ADDEILMOPS
psalmodied
ADDEILMTTY
admittedly
ADDEINOPSW
pandowdies
ADDELNNORW
wonderland
ADDELPQRUU
quadrupled
ADDENNRSTU
understand
ADDFGIINNY
dandifying
ADDFIILNSU
disdainful
ADDGIIINNS
disdaining
ADDGIINSSU
dissuading
ADDGILNNSU
unsaddling
ADDGILNRST
straddling
ADDIIILNUV
individual
ADDILLLLYY
dillydally
ADEEEEGNRT
degenerate
ADEEEFILRZ
federalize
ADEEEGGRST
segregated
ADEEEGLRTU
deregulate
ADEEEHLPSY
sleepyhead
ADEEEHLRTT
letterhead
ADEEEHLRTW
treadwheel
ADEEEHNRTT
threatened
ADEEEIMNRX

reexamined
ADEEEIRRTT
reiterated
ADEEELNNUV
unleavened
ADEEELNRSW
newsdealer
ADEEELNSST
elatedness
ADEEEMNNRT
endearment
ADEEEMNRTU
enumerated
ADEEEMNRUV
maneuvered
ADEEENORTX
exonerated
ADEEENPRTT
penetrated
ADEEENRTTV
anteverted
ADEEENSSST
sedateness
ADEEENTTUX
extenuated
ADEEERRSST
reasserted
ADEEERRSST
reafffirmed
ADEEFGHIRU
figurehead
ADEEFGINRT
federating
ADEEFGLNNW
newfangled
ADEEFGMNRT
fragmented
ADEEFILOTX
exfoliated
ADEEFILRST
federalist
ADEEFMINST
manifested
ADEEFINORT
federation
ADEEFNNSTU
unfastened
ADEEFNORRW
forewarned
ADEEFOPRRT
perforated
ADEEFORSTT
foretasted
ADEEGGHLOR
loggerhead
ADEEGGILNT
delegating
ADEEGGINRS
degreasing
ADEEGGJNSS
jaggedness
ADEEGHINRS
garnisheed
ADEEGILLST

legislated
ADEEGILMNR
malingered
ADEEGILNOT
delegation
ADEEGILNRR
ringleader
ADEEGIMNNR
meandering
ADEEGIMNRT
germinated
ADEEGIMNTZ
magnetized
ADEEGINNRS
serenading
ADEEGINORT
negotiated
ADEEGINRTT
integrated
ADEEGIORTV
derogative
ADEEGLRRSS
regardless
ADEEGNOTXY
oxygenated
ADEEHHMNOT
heathendom
ADEEHHNORX
hexahedron
ADEEHHNPTY
hyphenated
ADEEHHNRTU
headhunter
ADEEHILPRS
dealership
ADEEHIMPSZ
emphasized
ADEEHIMPTZ
empathized
ADEEHINRST
dishearten
ADEEHIRRTY
hereditary
ADEEHLLNRT
enthralled
ADEEHLLOSW
wholesaled
ADEEHNNRTU
underneath
ADEEHNRRTW
netherward
ADEEHORSUW
warehoused
ADEEIIJNRR
jardiniere
ADEEIILMNT
eliminated
ADEEIILRSZ
serialized
ADEEIIMTTV
meditative
ADEEIIRTVV
derivative

ADEEIJOPRZ
jeopardize
ADEEILLPRS
espadrille
ADEEILLUVV
vaudeville
ADEEILMORT
meliorated
ADEEILMORZ
demoralize
ADEEILNRUZ
unrealized
ADEEILNTTT
dilettante
ADEEILNTTV
ventilated
ADEEILSUXZ
sexualized
ADEEIMMORT
immoderate
ADEEIMNNOT
emendation
ADEEIMNRTT
terminated
ADEEIMORRT
radiometer
ADEEIMQRRU
quadrireme
ADEEIMRSTT
mistreated
ADEEINNRRW
dinnerware
ADEEINORTT
orientated
ADEEINPRST
pedantries
pedestrian
ADEIINRRST
restrained
ADEEINRSTT
reinstated
ADEEINSSST
steadiness
ADEEIPPRTW
wiretapped
ADEEIPRTTX
extirpated
ADEEIRRSTV
advertiser
ADEEJRRSTU
readjuster
ADEEKNNRTU
undertaken
ADEEKNRRTU
undertaker
ADEELLOSTY
desolately
ADEELMNNTU
unlamented
ADEELMNTZZ
dazzlement
ADEELMORTY
moderately
ADEEONNTTU

untalented
ADEELNRTUV
untraveled
ADEELNRUUV
undervalue
ADEELOPPRV
overlapped
ACEELPRSTT
splattered
ADEELRSSTU
adulteress
ADEEMNNORT
ornamented
ADEEMNPRTT
department
ADEENNOSSU
unseasoned
ADEENNRSUW
unanswered
ADEENPPRRU
unprepared
ADEENPRRTU
enraptured
ADEENPRSST
depressant
ADEENRRTUV
adventurer
ADEENRRTUW
underwater
ADEENRSTTU
understate
ADEEPRSSST
trespassed
ADEERSSSTW
stewardess
ADEFGHIRST
farsighted
ADEFGILNRY
ladyfinger
ADEFGILNTU
defaulting
ADEFGINORT
foredating
ADEFGISTTU
fustigated
ADEFGLRTUU
fulgurated
ADEFHHOORT
fatherhood
ADEFHINPRT
pathfinder
ADEFHOORSW
foreshadow
ADEFIINQTU
quantified
ADEFIINRTU
infuriated
ADEFIIRSTT
stratified
ADEFILMNTU
fulminated
ADEFILMORZ
formalized
ADEFILSTTU

fistulated
ADEFINOORR
foreordain
ADEFINRSTX
transfixed
ADEFLMOPRT
platformed
ADEFLMORTU
formulated
ADEFLNRTUU
fraudulent
ADEFLORRTW
afterworld
ADEFLRSTTU
flustrated
ADEFNRSSTU
transfused
ADEFRRSTTU
frustrated
ADEGGINORT
derogating
ADEGHHIILT
hightailed
ADEGHHILNR
highlander
ADEGHHINST
nightshade
ADEGHIILNN
headlining
ADEGHILNSU
languished
ADEGHINPRS
headspring
ADEGHMOPRY
demography
ADEGHNORST
headstrong
ADEGHORSUU
guardhouse
ADEGIIILNZ
idealizing
ADEGIIMNNU
unimagined
ADEGIILMNP
impleading
ADEGIILMNS
misdealing
misleading
ADEGIILNPT
depilating
ADEGIILNSZ
signalized
ADEGIIMMRT
immigrated
ADEGIIMNRS
misreading
ADEGIIMNTT
meditating
ADEGIINNPT
depainting
ADEGGINORT
originated
ADEGIINPRS
despairing

ADEGIINSTT
instigated
ADEGIJNNRU
jaundering
ADEGILNNNO
nonaligned
ADEGILNNRS
slandering
ADEGILNNRU
laundering
ADEGILNOST
desolating
ADEGILOOPZ
apologized
ADEGILRUVZ
vulgarized
ADEGIMNNRU
maundering
ADEGIMNORT
moderating
ADEGIMNORZ
gormandize
ADEGIMNPST
stampeding
ADEGINNOTT
detonating
ADEGINNSSU
unassigned
ADEGINORRS
garrisoned
ADEGINPRSU
persuading
ADEGINPRSW
wingspread
ADEGINPRTU
depurating
ADEGINRSTW
stewarding
ADEHHIIPRT
diphtheria
ADEHHMPRRU
harrumphed
ADEHHNOPRY
hydrophane
ADEHIILMTU
humiliated
ADEHILNNRT
hinterland
ADEHIMNNORZ
harmonized
ADEHIMORTU
rheumatoid
ADEHIMOOPR
radiophone
ADEHINOSST
astonished
ADEHINQSUV
vanquished
ADEHIOPRSS
rhapsodies
ADEHIORTUZ
authorized
ADEHIOSSTW
shadowiest

ADEHLMNOSY
handsomely
ADEHMNOSST
handsomest
ADEHMOOPRT
parenthood
ADEHOORSVW
overshadow
ADEIIIMNTT
intimidate
ADEIILLSTT
distillate
ADEIILLTTT
titillated
ADEIILMMTU
multimedia
ADEIILMNOST
modalities
ADEIILNOPT
depilation
ADEIILNPTZ
platinized
ADEIILNTTT
dilettanti
ADEIILSUVZ
visualized
ADEIIMNOTT
meditation
ADEIIMNPRU
unimpaired
ADEIIMNRST
administer
ADEIIMRSTT
dermatitis
ADEIINNORT
inordinate
ADEIINNOTW
nationwide
ADEIINNSTU
insinuated
ADEIINORRS
ordinaries
ADEIINORTV
derivation
ADEIIPRRSY
presidiary
ADEILLNPSS
pallidness
ADEILMNOPR
palindrome
ADEILMNORS
normalised
ADEILMORTZ
mortalized
ADEILMSTTU
stimulated
ADEILNOOST
desolation
ADEILNOOTV
devotional
ADEILNPRTU
prudential
ADEILOPRTY
depilatory

ADEILPSTTU
stipulated
ADEILRTUUX
luxuriated
ADEIMMNTTU
manumitted
ADEIMMRSUZ
summarized
ADEIMNOORT
moderation
ADEINNOOTT
detonation
ADEINNOPWW
windowpane
ADEINNRTYZ
tyrannized
ADEINOPRTU
depuration
ADEINOPRTZ
patronized
ADEINOPTTU
deputation
ADEINORSST
adroitness
intradoses
ADEINPRRST
transpired
ADEINPRSSY
dispensary
ADEINRSSTW
tawdriness
ADEINSSSTU
unassisted
ADEIOPPRSV
disapprove
ADEIOPRSTY
depositary
ADEJMNSTTU
adjustment
ADEJOPSTUX
juxtaposed
ADELLLPTUU
pullulated
ADELNORSSU
slanderous
ADELNPPSTU
supplanted
ADELNRSTUW
wanderlust
ADELOPSTTU
postulated
ADELORSTUU
adulterous
ADELPQRTUU
quadruplet
ADELPQRUUX
quadruplex
ADELRSTWWY
westwardly
ADEMMMNORU
memorandum
ADEMNORSTW
downstream
ADEMNRSTTU

transmuted
ADENNPRSTU
underpants
ADENOPRSST
transposed
ADEOPPRSST
passported
ADEOPRRSTT
prostrated
ADEPPRSTUU
suppurated
ADFGINORRU
fairground
ADFGINORRW
forwarding
ADFHILRSWY
dwarfishly
ADFIILQSUY
disqualify
ADFIIOSSTU
fastidious
ADFIISSSTY
dissatisfy
ADFILLMNOY
manifoldly
ADFIMOQRRU
quadriform
ADFINNOOTU
foundation
ADFMNNORUY
foundryman
ADGGIINNOS
diagnosing
ADGGINNOOR
dragooning
ADGHINNPRS
handspring
ADGHIRSTTU
distraught
ADGIIINNST
distaining
ADGIIKNNPP
kidnapping
ADGIILLNSY
disallying
ADGIILMNOP
diplomaing
ADGIILMNRY
admiringly
ADGIILNPSY
displaying
ADGIIMNNOT
dominating
ADGIIMNNTY
dynamiting
ADGIINNNTU
inundating
ADGIINNORT
ordinating
ADGIINNRTU
indurating
ADGIINOSVW
disavowing
ADGIINSSTT

distasting
ADGIJNNORU
adjourning
ADGILMNOTU
modulating
ADGILNNTUU
undulating
ADGINNNOTU
dauntoning
ADGINNOSTU
astounding
ADGINNPSTU
upstanding
ADGINOPSTT
postdating
ADGINRRSTW
drawstring
ADGLNOPRUY
playground
ADHHNOSTTU
thousandth
ADHHOPRTYY
hydropathy
ADHIIMMNPS
midshipman
ADHILNOSTU
outlandish
ADHILOOPRS
drosophila
ADHINNOOOT
nationhood
ADHINOOPRT
anthropoid
ADHLNOPSSW
splashdown
ADIIILMRSS
dissimilar
ADIILMOPRR
primordial
ADIILMOPRS
prismoidal
ADIILNORRY
ordinarily
ADIILNRSTU
industrial
ADIILOQRTU
liquidator
ADIILORSTY
solidarity
ADIIMNNOOT
admonition
domination
ADIIMOPRST
prismatoid
ADIIMORTUU
auditorium
ADIIMQRUUV
quadrivium
ADIINNNOTU
inundation
ADIINNOORT
ordination
ADIINOPPST
disappoint

ADIINOSSSU
dissuasion
ADILLNSSTT
standstill
ADILLOSTYY
disloyalty
ADILMNOOTU
modulation
ADILNNOTUU
undulation
ADILOOPRRT
dripolator
ADILOORSTU
idolatrous
ADINNOPSTT
standpoint
ADINOOPRST
adsorption
ADINOPRSTU
drainspout
ADINORSSTW
downstairs
ADIORSSSTU
disastrous
ADLMOOORSU
malodorous
ADNNORRTUU
turnaround
AEEEEGKMPR
gamekeeper
AEEEEGNRRT
regenerate
AEEEFFIMNT
effeminate
AEEEFHRRTT
thereafter
AEEEFINRTZ
antifreeze
AEEEFNRRST
transferee
AEEEGGMNNT
engagement
AEEEGILNRZ
generalize
AEEEGILNVZ
evangelize
AEEEGLSSSY
eyeglasses
AEEEHHINTZ
heathenize
AEEEHLLRTY
ethereally
AEEEHMNRTW
weathermen
AEEEHRSTTW
sweetheart
AEEEILNRTZ
eternalize
AEEEILRSST
easterlies
AEEEINRSTT
entreaties
AEEEINRTTV
inveterate

AEEEINRTVW
interweave
AEEEJNRTUV
rejuvenate
AEEEKPSSTW
sweepstake
AEEELMNRTY
elementary
AEEELORTTT
teetotaler
AEEEMMNNORT
anemometer
AEEEMNPRTT
pentameter
AEEEMNRRTU
remunerate
AEEEPPRRTT
perpetrate
AEEEPPRTTU
perpetuate
AEEERRSTYY
yesteryear
AEEFFHORRT
forefather
AEEFGHINRT
feathering
AEEFGILPRS
persiflage
AEEFHIKSSW
weakfishes
AEEFHLRSST
fatherless
AEEFHPRSTT
stepfather
AEEFIKNRSS
freakiness
AEEFILRSTT
flatteries
AEEFINRRTZ
fraternize
AEEGGHOPRR
geographer
AEEGGILNRT
relegating
AEEGGINNRT
generating
AEEGGINTTV
vegetating
AEEGGIRSSV
aggressive
AEEGHHMORR
hemorrhage
AEEGHILNRT
leathering
AEEGHINNRT
heartening
AEEGHINRRS
rehearsing
AEEGHINRTW
weathering
AEEGHIPPRR
epigrapher
AEEGHLNTVW
wavelength

AEEGHLORTT
altogether
AEEGIILLST
legalities
AEEGIILMTT
legitimate
AEEGIILNTX
gelatinize
AEEGIILNTX
gelatinize
AEEGILLORS
allegories
AEEGILLORZ
allegorize
AEEGILMNNP
empaneling
AEEGILMNRR
malingerer
AEEGILNRST
easterling
generalist
AEEGILNRTY
generality
AEEGILNSTV
evangelist
AEEGILNTVY
negatively
AEEGIMNPRT
impregnate
permeating
AEEGINNNRX
reannexing
AEEGINNORT
generation
AEEGINNRTT
entreating
AEEGINNRTV
enervating
venerating
AEEGINORRZ
reorganize
AEEGINORTV
overeating
AEEGINOTTV
vegetation
AEEGINRRTT
retreating
AEEGINRSTT
estreating
AEEGIRSSTT
strategies
AEEGLLORTT
allegretto
AEEGLMRRTT
lettergram
AEEGLORTUV
travelogue
AEEGMNRSTY
segmentary
AEEGNORSTV
gravestone
AEEHHHINST
heathenish
AEEHHILSTT
healthiest
AEEHHIMNST

heathenism
AEEHHKNPSS
sheepshank
AEEHHLSSST
sheathless
AEEHIINPPS
epiphanies
AEEHIKLLRT
halterlike
AEEHIKLMMR
hammerlike
AEEHIKLPRS
seraphlike
AEEHILPPPR
peripheral
AEEHILPSST
shapeliest
AEEHILRSTT
earthliest
AEEHILSTTW
wealthiest
AEEHINORST
antiheroes
AEEHINRSST
earthiness
heartiness
AEEHINSSTT
antitheses
AEEHKORSTT
heatstroke
AEEHLLORSW
wholesaler
AEEHLMNNOP
phenomenal
AEEHMNNSSU
humaneness
AEEHMOPRST
atmosphere
AEEHNORSSS
hoarseness
AEEHOOPRST
peashooter
AEEHORSSUW
housewares
AEEHORSTVW
whatsoever
AEEHOSSTTU
statehouse
AEEIILLRTT
illiterate
AEEIILMNRZ
mineralize
AEEIILQSTU
equalities
AEEIILRRTV
irrelative
AEEIILRTVZ
revitalize
AEEIIMNRSS
seminaries
AEEIIMPRTV
imperative
AEEIIMRSSS
emissaries

AEEIIPRSST
asperities
AEEIIPRSSV
vespiaries
AEEIJLOSSU
jealousies
AEEIJOPRTV
pejorative
AEEIKMNORS
noisemaker
AEEIKQSSTU
squeakiest
AEEIKRSSTT
streakiest
AEEILLLLNV
villanelle
AEEILMNPRT
planimeter
AEEILMNRST
streamline
AEEILMRSYY
semiyearly
AEEILNNPST
septennial
AEEILNNTTU
lieutenant
AEEILNORTV
revelation
AEEILNPRSS
pearliness
AEEILNQSTU
sequential
AEEILNQTUV
equivalent
AEEILNRRTV
irrelevant
AEEILNRTUZ
neutralize
AEEILNSSUZ
sensualize
AEEILPRSSS
praiseless
AEEILRRSVW
silverware
AEEILRRTTU
literature
AEEILSSTTT
stateliest
AEEIMMORTV
memorative
AEEIMNNORT
renominate
AEEIMNORTT
marionette
AEEIMQRSUV
semiquaver
AEEINNORTV
veneration
AEEINNSSSU
uneasiness
AEEINOPTTT
potentiate
AEEINQRSTU
equestrian

AEEINQSSSU
queasiness
AEEINRRTVY
veterinary
AEEINRSTTT
interstate
AEEINSSSTW
sweatiness
AEEIPPRRTW
wiretapper
AEEIPRSSTT
striptease
tapestries
AEEIPRSSUV
persuasive
AEEIPRSTTX
sexpartite
AEEIPRSTUZ
pasteurize
AEEIPRTTUV
vituperate
AEEIRRSSTU
treasuries
AEEIRSSTTV
travesties
AEEKMMRRRY
merrymaker
AEEKNNOSST
snakestone
AEELLMNOTV
malevolent
AEELLMNRTU
allurement
AEELLMNSSY
namelessly
AEELLNTUVY
eventually
AEELMNNRSS
mannerless
AEELMNORTW
watermelon
AEELMNOSSW
saleswomen
AEELNOPSSW
weaponless
AEELNOSSSS
seasonless
AEELOPPRTU
repopulate
AEEMNNPRTT
entrapment
AEEMNORRTU
enumerator
AEEMNRSTTU
menstruate
AEEMNSSSST
assessment
AEEMRSSSST
seamstress
AEENORSTUX
extraneous
AEENQRSSSU
squareness
AEENRRSSTV

transverse
AEENSSSTTU
astuteness
AEEOPRSSSV
overpasses
AEEPRRSSST
trespasser
AEEPRSSWXY
expressway
AEEQSSTTUU
statuesque
AEFFIIINST
affinities
AEFFLLNTUY
affluently
AEFGIILNNR
fingernail
AEFGIINNRR
refraining
AEFGILMNNU
meaningful
AEFGILNNTT
flattening
AEFGILNRTT
flattering
AEFGILOPRT
profligate
AEFGIMNORR
forearming
AEFGINORSY
foresaying
AEFGIPRRTU
grapefruit
AEFGLNRTUU
ungrateful
AEFHLLMSUY
shamefully
AEFHLMOSST
fathomless
AEFIIILNST
finalities
AEFIILNRTT
infiltrate
AEFIINNRST
infantries
AEFIINQRTU
quantifier
AEFIINQSTU
quantifies
AEFIIRSSTT
stratifies
AEFILMMORS
semiformal
AEFILMNSTY
manifestly
AEFILOQRTU
quatrefoil
AEFINNRSSU
unfairness
AEFINRRTTY
fraternity
AEFINRSSTX
transfixes
AEFLLLOPWY

playfellow
AEFLLLORWW
wallflower
AEFLLNOSSW
fallowness
AEFLLORSSV
flavorless
AEFLLSTTUY
tastefully
AEFLLSTUWY
wastefully
AEFLNRSSTU
artfulness
AEFMOPRRST
permafrost
AEFNORRTTW
waterfront
AEFOOPRRTW
waterproof
AEFOQRRSUU
foursquare
AEGGGIINRW
earwigging
AEGGGINNNR
gangrening
AEGGGINNRST
staggering
AEGGGINRSW
swaggering
AEGGIILLNZ
legalizing
AEGGIILMPR
pilgrimage
AEGGIILNNR
realigning
AEGGIILNTV
levigating
AEGGIIMNRT
emigrating
AEGGIINNSV
envisaging
AEGGIINNTV
negativing
AEGGILNNNT
entangling
AEGGILNNOT
elongating
AEGGILNRTU
regulating
AEGGIMNNRT
garmenting
AEGGIMNNTU
augmenting
AEGGINNRST
estranging
AEGGINORSS
aggression
AEGGIORRSU
gregarious
AEGGNNORSU
gangrenous
AEGHHILOPR
heliograph
AEGHHIMNWY

highwaymen	**AEGIILNTTV**	glassiness	astrologer
AEGHHINNRS	levitating	**AEGILORSSS**	**AEGLPRSSUU**
harshening	**AEGIIMNNST**	glossaries	surplusage
AEGHHISTTU	seminating	**AEGIMMNRST**	**AEGMMOPRRR**
haughtiest	**AEGIIMNORT**	stammering	programmer
AEGHHOPRTY	emigration	**AEGIMNNRST**	**AEGNRRSSST**
ethography	**AEGIIMNSTT**	smartening	transgress
AEGHIINSTT	estimating	**AEGIMNNSST**	**AEGOORSTUU**
hesitating	**AEGIIMNSTV**	assignment	outrageous
AEGHILNNSU	negativism	**AEGIMNOPRS**	**AEHHIILNNT**
unleashing	timesaving	angiosperm	helianthin
AEGHILNOOT	**AEGIIMSTTZ**	**AEGIMNPTTT**	**AEHHMMOOPTY**
theologian	stigmatize	attempting	homeopathy
AEGHILNRST	**AEGIINNPRT**	**AEGIMNRRRY**	**AEHIILMNSTU**
slathering	pertaining	remarrying	humanities
AEGHILNSSU	**AEGIINORTV**	**AEGIMNRSTT**	**AEHIINOSTT**
languishes	invigorate	smattering	hesitation
AEGHIMMOPR	**AEGIINPPTZ**	**AEGINNORST**	**AEHIINSSTT**
mimeograph	appetizing	resonating	antithesis
AEGHINNPRS	**AEGIINTTVY**	**AEGINNORTV**	**AEHILMMSTT**
sharpening	negativity	renovating	metalsmith
AEGHINNRSS	**AEGIIRSTTU**	**AEGINNPPRT**	**AEHILMORST**
harnessing	gratuities	entrapping	isothermal
AEGHINNRTU	**AEGIKNORTV**	**AEGINNPRRW**	**AEHILNOSSS**
unearthing	overtaking	prewarning	shoaliness
AEGHINNRSTT	**AEGILLMNRV**	**AEGINNPRTT**	**AEHILNSSSV**
shattering	marvelling	patterning	lavishness
straighten	**AEFILLORST**	**AEGINNRSTT**	**AEHILNSTTY**
AEGHINRSTV	legislator	astringent	hesitantly
harvesting	**AEGILLPSSX**	**AEGINNRSTU**	**AEHILOPRST**
AEGHINSTTU	plexiglass	sauntering	hospitaler
naughtiest	**AEGILMNORY**	**AEGINNRUVW**	**AEHIMMRSTU**
AEGHINSTUX	mineralogy	unwavering	rheumatism
exhausting	**AEGILMSTTU**	**AEGINOORTT**	**AEHIMNNPPS**
AEGHIRRSTT	multistage	negotiator	penmanship
straighter	**AEGILNNNRU**	**AEGINORRTV**	**AEHIMNORRZ**
AEGHIRTTTW	unlearning	overrating	harmonizer
watertight	**AEGILNNOOT**	**AEGINORTUW**	**AEHIMNSSTU**
AEGHNOPRST	elongation	outwearing	enthusiasm
stenograph	**AEGILNNPSU**	**AEGINORTVX**	**AEHIMPRSST**
AEGHOPPRTY	unpleasing	overtaxing	shipmaster
graphotype	**AEGILNNRUV**	**AEGINPQRTU**	**AEHIMPSSTY**
AEGHOPRRXY	unraveling	parqueting	sympathies
xerography	**AEGILNNSUY**	**AEGINPRSTT**	**AEHIMPSTYZ**
AEGIIILLLTY	sanguinely	spattering	sympathize
illegality	**AEGILNORTT**	**AEGINQRRTU**	**AEHINOSSST**
AEGIILMNNP	tolerating	quartering	astonishes
impaneling	**AEGILNORTU**	**AEGINRRSSU**	**AEHINOSTUX**
AEGIILMNTZ	regulation	reassuring	exhaustion
metalizing	**AEGILNORVY**	**AEGINRRSTU**	**AEHINPPSTU**
AEGIILNNPX	overlaying	treasuring	unhappiest
explaining	**AEGILNOSTU**	**AEGINRRSTV**	**AEHINQSSUV**
AEGIILNNPZ	gelatinous	traversing	vanquishes
penalizing	**AEGILNPPRY**	**AEGINRSSSS**	**AEHINSSTTU**
AEGIILNOST	reapplying	grassiness	enthusiast
antilogies	**AEGILNPRST**	**AEGIRSSTTT**	**AEHIRSSTTW**
AEGIILNOTV	plastering	strategist	swarthiest
levigation	**AEGILNPRSU**	**AEGLLMRTUY**	**AEHHLMRSSY**
AEGIILNPRV	pleasuring	metallurgy	harmlessly
prevailing	**AEGILNQRRU**	**AEGLMOOSTY**	**AEHLLOSSTW**
AEGIILNQTU	quarreling	sematology	shallowest
eliquating	**AEGILNRVWY**	**AEGLNOOPRT**	**AEHLMOOSUX**
AEGIILNQUZ	waveringly	protogenal	homosexual
equalizing	**AEGILNSSSS**	**AEGLOORRST**	**AEHMNPRSUU**

superhuman	**AEIIMNOSTT**	**AEILNORRTT**	**AEKMMNORSW**
AEHMORSTTT	estimation	torrential	markswomen
thermostat	**AEIIMNQTUY**	**AEILNORTTV**	**AEKMORRSTW**
AEHNNNOOTY	equanimity	ventilator	masterwork
hootenanny	**AEIIMOPRRS**	**AEILNRSTTU**	**AEKORRSTWW**
AEHNOOPSSU	impresario	neutralist	waterworks
sousaphone	**AEIINOPPTV**	**AEILNRTTUY**	**AELLNOPPRT**
AEHOOPPRST	appointive	neutrality	propellant
apostrophe	**AEIINOPSTT**	**AEILNSSSTU**	**AELLNOPRSY**
AEHOOPSTTT	poinsettia	sensualist	personally
toothpaste	**AEIINOQTTU**	**AEILNSSTUU**	**AELLPRSTUU**
AEHOOPSTTY	equitation	nautiluses	sepultural
osteopathy	**AEIINOSTTV**	**AELINSSTUY**	**AELMMMNNOTU**
AEHOORSSTY	estivation	sensuality	monumental
soothsayer	**AEIINQSTTU**	**AEILOPRSTY**	**AELMNNNRUY**
AEIIIINTTV	quantities	epistolary	unmannerly
initiative	**AEIINRSTTV**	**AEIMMNPRTT**	**AELMNNORSS**
AEIIILLNSV	transitive	impartment	normalness
villainies	**AEIIOPPRTT**	**AEIMNNNOTT**	**AELMORSSTU**
AEIIILMRST	propitiate	anointment	somersault
militaries	**AEIIPRRTTT**	**AEIMNOPTTT**	**AELNNOPRYY**
AEIIINSTTV	tripartite	temptation	pennyroyal
nativities	**AEIJLNOSSV**	**AEIMNRRRTY**	**AELOPPRRRU**
AEIIJMORST	jovialness	intermarry	pourparler
majorities	**AEIJNNSSTU**	**AEIMORRSTU**	**AELPPSSTUY**
AEIIKLLNPR	jauntiness	mortuaries	platypuses
painkiller	**AEIKLMNSTY**	**AEIMQRSTUZ**	**AEMNNNOPTY**
AEIILLLMNN	mistakenly	quizmaster	nonpayment
millennial	**AEIKMNNSTU**	**AEINNORRTV**	**AEMNNORTTU**
AEIILLMNTU	unmistaken	renovation	tournament
illuminate	**AEILLMMRST**	**AEINNOPRSY**	**AEMNNRRSUY**
AEIILLNSSV	millstream	pensionary	nurseryman
villainess	**AEILLMNRTY**	**AEINNOQRTU**	**AEMNOORRST**
AEIILMMMOR	terminally	quaternion	astronomer
immemorial	**AEILLMTTUY**	**AEINNOQSTU**	**AEMNNORSSTT**
AEIILMNORT	ultimately	equisonant	assortment
eliminator	**AEILLNNRTY**	**AEINNORSTT**	**AEMOPRSSTT**
AEIILMNRSU	internally	stentorian	postmaster
luminaries	**AEILLNPSSY**	**AEINNQSSTU**	**AENNORRSSW**
AEIILMNTTY	painlessly	quaintness	narrowness
intimately	**AEILLORWWW**	**AEINOORRTT**	**AENOOQRRTU**
AEIILMORST	willowware	orientator	quarteroon
moralities	**AEILLRSTTU**	**AEINOPRRTZ**	**AENOORSSTU**
AEIILNOQTU	illustrate	patronizer	treasonous
eliquation	**AEILMMRTUY**	**AEINOPRSSU**	**AENOPRSTTT**
AEIILNORTT	immaturely	persuasion	protestant
literation	**AEILMNOPRS**	**AEINOPRTTU**	**AEOPRRSSTW**
AEIILNOTTV	impersonal	reputation	sportswear
levitation	**AEILMNOPRT**	**AEINOPTTTU**	**AEOPRSTTUW**
AEIILNQTUY	trampoline	outpatient	waterspout
inequality	**AEILMNRRTU**	**AEINORRSTU**	**AFFGIILNSY**
AEIILNSSTT	intermural	souterrain	falsifying
saintliest	**AEILMNSSSU**	**AEINORSSSV**	**AFFGINNORT**
AEIILOPRST	sensualism	savoriness	affronting
polarities	**AEILMPRSST**	**AEINORSTTY**	**AFFGIRSSTU**
AEIILRTTVY	slipstream	stationery	suffragist
relativity	**AEILMPRTUU**	**AEINQRTTUY**	**AFFGNOORST**
AEIIMMNPRT	parimutuel	quaternity	stroganoff
impairment	**AEILNNORTT**	**AEINRSSSTT**	**AFFHILLTUY**
AEIIMNNOST	intolerant	straitness	faithfully
semination	**AEILNNPRSU**	**AEIOPRRRST**	**AFFHILNTUU**
AEIIMNNOTV	peninsular	respirator	unfaithful
nominative	**AEILNOORTT**	**AEJMNNORUY**	**AFGGGILNNU**
	toleration	journeyman	unflagging

AFGGIIMNNY
magnifying
AFGGIIMNTU
fumigating
AFGGIINRTY
gratifying
AFGHHILLST
flashlight
AFGHIINNOS
fashioning
AFGIIILNNZ
finalizing
AFGIIILNRT
airlifting .
AFGIILMNPY
amplifying
AFGIILNQUY
qualifying
AFGIILNRTT
filtrating
AFGIIMNOTU
fumigation
AFGIINSSTY
satisfying
AFHHLLORUY
halfhourly
AFHKLLNTUY
thankfully
AFIILNORTT
filtration
flirtation
AFILLMNORY
informally
AFILLNPPTY
flippantly
AFILMNOSUY
infamously
AFLLLNUUWY
unlawfully
AFLMOORRTU
formulator
AGGGGIINZZ
zigazgging
AGGGILNRST
straggling
AGGGIMNORT
mortgaging
AGGHIINNRS
garnishing
AGGHIINNSU
anguishing
AGGIIILNTT
litigating
AGGIIIMNTT
mitigating
AGGIIINNNR
ingraining
AGGIIINRRT
irrigating
AGGIINNORZ
organizing
AGGILNNNTU
untangling
AGGILNNRST

strangling
AGGIMNOPRR
programing
AGHHILOPRT
lithograph
AGHHNOOPPR
phonograph
AGHHOOPPRT
photograph
AGHIIMNPSS
misshaping
AGHIINNRST
tarnishing
AGHIINNRSV
varnishing
AGHIINOPRZ
aphorizing
AGHIINPRRS
hairspring
AGHIINPSWW
whipsawing
AGHIINRTWW
wainwright
AGHILLNOSW
shallowing
AGHILPRTWY
playwright
AGHILRSTTY
straightly
AGHIMNOOPS
shampooing
AGHINNOOPR
harpooning
AGHINOPRTY
atrophying
AGHLNOOORT
orthogonal
AGHLOPRXYY
xylography
AGHOOPPRTY
topography
AGHOPPRTYY
typography
AGIIIILNNT
initialing
AGIIIINNTT
initiating
AGIIILMNTT
militating
AGIIILNOTT
litigation
AGIIILNTVZ
vitalizing
AGIIIMMNXZ
maximizing
AGIIIMNNTT
intimating
AGIIIMNOTT
mitigation
AGIIINSTZ
sanitizing
AGIIINORRT
irrigation
AGIIINRRTT

irritating
AGIIINRSTZ
satirizing
AGIIILLNNST
installing
AGIILLNORY
originally
AGIILMMNOT
immolating
AGIILMNNPT
implanting
AGIILMNORZ
moralizing
AGIILMNSTU
simulating
AGIILMNTTU
mutilating
AGIILNNORU
unoriginal
AGIILNNSTU
insulating
AGIILNOPPT
oppilating
AGGILNOPRZ
polarizing
AGIILNOPST
spoliating
AGIILNORSZ
solarizing
AGIILNRRUZ
ruralizing
AGIILNRSTY
laryngitis
AGIIMMNNOT
nominating
AGIIMMNNPRS
mainspring
AGIIMMNNRTU
ruminating
AGIIMNORTZ
amortizing
AGIIMNOTTV
motivating
AGIIMNSSTT
misstating
AGIIMMNNOTT
intonating
AGIINNNOTV
innovating
AGIINNOPPT
appointing
AGIINNORTZ
notarizing
AGIINNOSTT
stationing
AGIINNPRSU
unaspiring
AGIINNQTUZ
quantizing
AGIINNRSTT
transiting
AGIINNSSTU
sustaining
AGIINOORRT

originator
AGIINOPRVZ
vaporizing
AGIINORSTT
instigator
AGIJLNNORU
journaling
AGIKMNNORW
workingman
AGILLLNRUY
alluringly
AGILLNOPRT
patrolling
AGILLNOSWW
swallowing
AGILLNRSUY
singularly
AGILMNNOOP
lampooning
AGILNNNOYY
annoyingly
AGILNNORTY
ignorantly
AGILNNTTUY
tauntingly
AGILNOPPTU
populating
AGILNRSTTU
lustrating
AGIMNNSSUU
unassuming
AGINOPRRTY
portraying
AGINPRSSSU
surpassing
AGMMNOOOSU
monogamous
AGMNOORSTY
gastronomy
AHHIOPRSTU
authorship
AHIIIJKNRS
jinrikisha
AHIIMNNTUY
inhumanity
AHIIRSSTTW
shirtwaist
AHILNOORTZ
horizontal
AHIMNOORRU
honorarium
AHIMNOORSU
harmonious
AHIMNPRTTU
triumphant
AHIOPSSSTY
hypostasis
AHNNOSTTWY
shantytown
AIIIINNOTT
initiation
AIIILLMNTU
illuminati
AIIILMMRST

militarism
AIIILMNOTT
limitation
AIIILMRSTT
militarist
AIIILMRSTY
similarity
AIIILRTTVY
triviality
AIIIMNNOTT
intimation
AIIIMNOPSS
pianissimo
AIIINNOTTV
invitation
AIIINORRTT
irritation
AIIINOSTTV
visitation
AIIILMNNTU
illuminant
AIIILLNOSUV
villainous
AIILMMNNOS
nominalism
AIILMMNNOOT
immolation
AIILMMORTY
immorality
AIILMNNOTU
lumination
AIILMNOSTU
simulation
AIILMNOTTU
mutilation
AIILNNOOST
insolation
AIILNNOSTU
insulation
AIILNOOPST
spoliation
AIILNRSSUY
urinalysis
AIIMMNNOTU
ammunition
AIIMMPRRTU
imprimatur
AIIMMRTTUY
immaturity
AIIMNNNOOT
nomination
AIIMNNOORT
minoration
AIIMNNRSTT
ministrant
AIIMNOOTTV
motivation
AIIMNOPSTU
utopianism
AIIMNOPTTU
inputation
AIIMNORSSY
missionary
AIIMOPRSTT

patriotism
AIINNNOOTT
intonation
AIINNNOOTV
innovation
AIINNORSTT
transition
AIINOOPPST
apposition
AIJLMNORSU
journalism
AIJLNORSTU
journalist
AILLMMORTY
immortally
AILLNQRTUY
tranquilly
AILNOOPPTU
population
AILNORSTTU
lustration
AIMMOORRTU
moratorium
AIMNOPSSTU
assumption
AIMNRSTTUU
nasturtium
AINORRSSTT
transistor
AINORRSTTY
transitory
AIOOPRRSUU
uproarious
AIOORRSTTU
traitorous
ALLOORSUVY
valorously
ALMOOPPRST
protoplasm
ALOOPPRSTT
protoplast
ALOPRTUUVY
voluptuary
AMNOOOSTUU
autonomous
BBBEEIINRW
winebibber
BBBGHINNOO
hobnobbing
BBCDEIRSSU
subscribed
BBCEEKNRRU
rubberneck
BBCEIRRSSU
subscriber
BBCEIRSSTU
scrubbiest
BBCGIILNRS
scribbling
BBDEIKNOOR
bookbinder
BBDEIOSSUY
busybodies
BBEEIILRRS

bilberries
BBEEIORRSX
boxberries
BBEELLOTTU
bluebottle
BBEGILNORS
slobbering
BBEHHILOST
shibboleth
BBEHIRSSTU
shrubbiest
BBEIKLMOOO
bookmobile
BBEINSSSTU
stubbiness
BBGHIMNOTU
thingumbob
BBLNORSTUY
stubbornly
BCCDEILNOU
conducible
BCCEEENPSU
pubescence
BCCEEINRTY
cybernetic
BCCEIINORT
biocentric
BCCEIMNNUY
incumbency
BCCGIMNSUU
succumbing
BCDEEEMNRU
encumbered
BCDEEHIMRS
besmirched
BCDEEHLOST
bedclothes
BCDEEIILNR
incredible
BCDEEIPRRS
prescribed
BCDEFLOOTU
clubfooted
BCDEGHINOU
debouching
BCDEGIINRS
describing
BCDEGILNOU
beclouding
BCDEIILNRY
incredibly
BCDEILMNOY
combinedly
BCDEIOPRRS
proscribed
BCDELORRUY
cloudberry
BCDEMMNRUU
cummerbund
BCDEORSTTU
obstructed
BCDGINSTUU
subducting
BCDHHILLRT

childbirth
BCDILLOSSU
discobolus
BCDKMRSTUU
dumbstruck
BCDLORSTUU
cloudburst
BCEEEFFILT
effectible
BCEEEFINNT
beneficent
BCEEEGHINS
beseeching
BCEEELLMRU
cerebellum
BCEEENOQSU
obsequence
BCEEENRSTU
erubescent
BCEEHKORRY
chokeberry
BCEEIILPST
plebiscite
BCEEIJSTUV
subjective
BCEEILMOST
comestible
BCEEIPSSSU
subspecies
BCEEJLOSST
objectless
BCEEKLNOTT
bottleneck
BCEELNOTTU
cuttlebone
BCEELNRTUU
turbulence
BCEEMMORSU
cumbersome
BCEGHIINTW
bewitching
BCEGIILORR
corrigible
BCEGIJNSTU
subjecting
BCEGILMNOY
becomingly
BCEGIMNNOU
unbecoming
BCEHHNNOUY
honeybunch
BCEHILOPRY
hyperbolic
BCEHILOSTT
blotchiest
BCEHKKOOST
sketchbook
BCEHKLOOSU
blockhouse
BCEHMRSTUW
thumbscrew
BCEIIILMMS
immiscible
BCEIIILMTY

imbecility
BCEIIILNNV
invincible
BCEIIMORST
biometrics
BCEIJNOSTU
subjection
BCEILNPSSU
publicness
BCEILNRTUU
tuberculin
BCEIMOSTUV
combustive
BCEINORTTU
contribute
BCEKKOOOPT
pocketbook
BCEKLNRTUU
turnbuckle
BCELRSTUUU
subculture
BCENOORSSS
crossbones
BCGIIINNRS
inscribing
BCGIKLNNUU
unbuckling
BCGIMNOSTU
combusting
BCGINOOTTY
boycotting
BCHIINORST
bronchitis
BCHIKLLOSY
blockishly
BCHKLOOOOS
schoolbook
BCIKMOORST
broomstick
BCIMNOOSTU
combustion
BCOORRSTTU
obstructor
BDDDEIISUV
subdivided
BDDEEEEFINR
befriended
BDDEEEEILRW
bewildered
BDDEEEELMNO
emboldened
BDDEEIILMSS
dissembled
BDDEENNRUU
unburdened
BDDEFGILNU
befuddling
BDDEGGLLOU
bulldogged
BDDEHLNOOR
bondholder
BDDEIIRSUV
subdivider
BDDEIISSUZ

subsidized
BDDFGIINOR
forbidding
BDDHLNOOOU
bloodhound
BDEEEEMMRR
remembered
BDEEEFILNS
defensible
BDEEEHLLNR
hellbender
BDEEEIILSV
disbelieve
BDEEEEILNSS
edibleness
BDEEEILSTW
wildebeest
BDEEEIMRTT
embittered
BDEEEELMTUW
tumbleweed
BDEEEELRRRY
elderberry
BDEEFGIINR
debriefing
BDEEGHINOR
neighbored
BDEEGHINRT
brightened
BDEEGIILNV
bedeviling
BDEEGIILST
digestible
BDEEGIINNZ
bedizening
BDEEGIORRS
dogberries
BDEEHLNNOR
hornblende
BDEEIIILST
debilities
BDEEIILMOZ
demobilize
BDEEIILNOTY
obediently
BDEEILSTUV
vestibuled
BDEEIMMNOT
embodiment
BDEEIMORRY
embroidery
BDEEIMRRSU
reimbursed
BDEELLNRUY
underbelly
BDEEMNOSRU
burdensome
BDEERSSTTU
buttressed
BDEFGINOOR
foreboding
BDEGGGINRU
begrudging
BDEGGLNOOO

boondoggle
BDEGIILNRU
rebuilding
BDEGIINOSY
disobeying
BDEGIINRSU
debruising
BDEGIKORRW
bridgework
BDEGILNNRU
blundering
BDEGILNORU
redoubling
BDEGINNORU
rebounding
BDEHIIOPRT
prohibited
BDEHNRRSUU
underbrush
BDEIIRSSUZ
subsidizer
BDEIIRSTTU
distribute
BDEILLORWY
yellowbird
BDEILMOSYZ
symbolized
BDELLNOPSU
spellbound
BDELNORTUU
untroubled
BDENNOTTUU
unbuttoned
BDFLLOTUUY
doubtfully
BDGIILNNRU
unbridling
BDGIINRSSU
disbursing
BDGIINRSTU
disturbing
BDGIKMNOSU
subkingdom
BDGILLNOUZ
bulldozing
BDGINNOTUU
undoubting
BDHIILRRWY
whirlybird
BDHNOOSTUU
southbound
BDIIILNOSU
libidinous
BDILLNPRUY
purblindly
BDNOOOTTUW
buttonwood
BEEEEFLNSS
feebleness
BEEEFGILNN
enfeebling
BEEEFIMORT

beforetime
BEEEEFOORRT
freebooter
BEEEGIILLR
reeligible
BEEEGIJLNW
bejeweling
BEEEGINRRR
greenbrier
BEEEILNRUV
unbeliever
BEEEILRRSV
reversible
BEEEIRRSTW
sweetbrier
BEEELNNOTV
benevolent
BEEEMNRTTT
betterment
BEEENRSSTT
betterness
BEEFGIINNT
benefiting
BEEFGRSTUU
subterfuge
BEEFIILLNX
inflexible
BEEGGIILLN
negligible
BEEGIIILLN
ineligible
BEEGIINOSS
biogenesis
BEEGILMNRS
resembling
BEEGILMNZZ
embezzling
BEEGINRTTV
brevetting
BEEGNNOTTU
unbegotten
BEEGOORRSY
gooseberry
BEEHILNSST
blitheness
BEEHIMMPRS
membership
BEEHLMNSSU
humbleness
BEEHMOORST
bothersome
BEEIILMRSS
remissible
BEEIILNNSS
insensible
BEEIILSSTX
bissextile
BEEILLORSU
rebellious
BEEILMNNSS
nimbleness
BEEILMRRSU
mulberries
BEEILNOSST

ostensible
BEEILSSTTU
subtleties
BEEINRSSTT
bitterness
BEEIRSSUVV
subversive
BEEKLLOORS
bookseller
BEELLOOSTY
obsoletely
BEELMNNOOW
noblewomen
BEELMNRSSU
numberless
BEEMMNNNOTT
entombment
BEENOSSSTU
obtuseness
BEENQSSTUU
subsequent
BEEPRRSTYY
presbytery
BEFFNOORUY
buffoonery
BEFGIINRVY
verbifying
BEFIILRSTU
filibuster
BEGGIILLNY
negligibly
BEGGIMNRSU
submerging
BEGGINNORU
burgeoning
BEGHIIINTX
exhibiting
BEGHIILMNS
blemishing
BEGHILMNOO
hemoglobin
BEGHILNORY
neighborly
BEGHINORTT
betrothing
BEGHINRSST
brightness
BEGHOORTUV
overbought
BEGHRSTTUU
shutterbug
BEGIILLNTT
belittling
BEGIILMNOR
embroiling
BEGIILNNUZ
nebulizing
BEGIILNRST
blistering
BEGIINRRST
bestirring
BEGILMNRSU
slumbering
BEGILNORST

bolstering
BEGILNRSTU
blustering
BEGILNSTTU
subletting
BEGIMMNNOOS
embosoming
BEGIMNRSSU
submersing
BEGINOPRRV
proverbing
BEGINOPSTT
bespotting
BEGINORUVY
overbuying
BEGINPRRTU
perturbing
BEGINRSSUV
subserving
BEGINRSTUV
subverting
BEGLMOORYY
embryology
BEHIIINOTX
exhibition
BEHINOSSSY
boyishness
BEHLMOOPTY
phlebotomy
BEHLNOOTTU
buttonhole
BEIIILMMOZ
immobilize
BEIIILNOST
nobilities
BEIILLNOTU
ebullition
BEIILMOPSS
impossible
BEIILMRTUY
muliebrity
BEIIMSSSUV
submissive
BEIIORSSTU
bistouries
BEIKLMRTTU
buttermilk
BEILMNOOSW
snowmobile
BEILNOSSTY
ostensibly
BEIMNORSSU
submersion
BEINORSSUV
subversion
BEINSSSTTU
subsistent
BEIOOQSSUU
obsequious
BEIOORSSTU
boisterous
BEISSTTTUU
substitute
BEKLNNORUY

unbrokenly
BELLNOSUUY
nebulously
BELMOOSSTT
bottomless
BENNOORSTW
brownstone
BEORRTTTUW
butterwort
BFFHINOOOS
boffoonish
BFGHIINRSU
furbishing
BFILLLSSUY
blissfully
BGGGHIMNUU
humbugging
BGGIILLNOY
obligingly
BGGIINNPRU
upbringing
BGHHIIRRTT
birthright
BGHIIIINNT
inhibiting
BGHIILNPSU
publishing
BGHIILNSUY
blushingly
BGHILNNSUU
unblushing
BGIIILMNOZ
mobilizing
BGIIILNOTY
ignobility
BGIIJNNOSU
subjoining
BGIIKLLNNY
blinkingly
BGIILNSTTU
subtitling
BGIIMNSTTU
submitting
BGIINSSSTU
subsisting
BGILMNOOSS
blossoming
BGILORSUUU
lugubrious
BHHOORSTTU
toothbrush
BHIIINNOT
inhibition
BHIMOORSST
thrombosis
BIIIILSTVY
visibility
BIIILMMOTY
immobility
BIILLOSTUY
solubility
BIILLOTUVY
volubility
BIILMOPSSY

impossibly
BIIMNOSSSU
submission
BIIMNOSTUU
bituminous
BIIOQSTUUU
ubiquitous
BILLMNORUU
rumbullion
CCCEEIINNOS
conscience
CCCEEENORRU
occurrence
CCCEIIMRSU
circumcise
CCCEIINNORT
concentric
CCCGINNOOT
concocting
CCCHIKOPST
spitchcock
CCCILNSTUY
succinctly
CCCINNOOOT
concoction
CCDEEFIINY
deficiency
CCDEEFINNO
confidence
CCDEEGINSU
succeeding
CCDEEHIORT
ricocheted
CCDEEHORTT
crotcheted
CCDEEIILRT
dielectric
CCDEEILNOR
reconciled
CCDEFILNOT
conflicted
CCDEHILNOR
chronicled
CCDEIIIRTZ
criticized
CCDEIINNOT
coincident
CCDEINNOST
disconnect
CCDEINOPUU
unoccupied
CCDEINORST
disconcert
CCDEINOTUV
conductive
CCDGIIINNO
coinciding
CCDIKLNOU
cuckolding
CCDGILNNOU
concluding
CCDGINNOTU
conducting
CCGIMNOSTU

misconduct

CCDINNOOTU
conduction

CCEEEELLNX
excellence

CCEEEENNSS
senescence

CCEEEFNNOR
conference

CCEEEINPRS
prescience

CCEEEINQSU
quiescence

CCEEELLNXY
excellency

CCEEEMNOPT
competence

CCEEFFIINY
efficiency

CCEEFLNNOU
confluence

CCEEGHIKNR
checkering

CCEEGHINRS
screeching

CCEEGINORT
egocentric
geocentric

CCEEGNNORU
congruence

CCEEHILOSS
choiceless

CCEEHNOSTU
escutcheon

CCEEIILMRS
semicircle

CCEEILLOTV
collective

CCEEILNORT
electronic

CCEEILOPST
telescopic

CCEEINNNOT
continence

CCEEINNOTV
connective

CCEEINORTV
concretive

CCEEINOTVV
convective

CCEEIOPRSS
crosspiece

CCEEISSSUV
successive

CCEEJNORTU
conjecture

CCEELNOPRU
corpulence

CCEEMNOPTY
competency

CCEFGINNOT
confecting

CCEFHIIMOR
microfiche

CCEFIIINST
scientific

CCEFIIRSUX
crucifixes

CCEFILMRUX
circumflex

CCEFIMRSUU
circumfuse

CCEFINNOOT
confection

CCEFLLNOTU
flocculent

CCEFLSSSUU
successful

CCEGHHORRU
churchgoer

CCEGHINORT
crocheting

CCEGIIKNRT
cricketing

CCEGIILNNR
encircling

CCEGIINNOV
conceiving

CCEGILLNOT
collecting

CCEGIMMNNO
commencing

CCEGIMMNNOR
commercing

CCEGINNNOR
concerning

CCEGINNNOS
ensconcing

CCEGINNNOT
connecting

CCEGINNNORT
concreting

CCEGINNOTV
convecting

CCEGINORRT
correcting

CCEHHIINST
chinchiest

CCEHIKNOPT
checkpoint

CCEHINRSTU
crunchiest

CCEIIIRSTV
cervicitis

CCEIKKOPPT
pickpocket

CCEILLNOOT
collection

CCEILNOSUV
conclusive

CCEILOOQTU
coquelicot

CCEIMNORST
concretism

CCEIMNRTUV
circumvent

CCEIMOOPRS
microscope

CCEINNNOOT
connection

CCEINNNOTY
continency

CCEINNOOPT
conception

CCEINNOORT
concertino

CCEINNOORT
concretion

CCEINNOOSS
concession

CCEINNOOTV
convection

CCEINOOORRT
correction

CCEINOSSSU
succession

CCEINOSSUV
concussive

CCEIOOPRSU
precocious

CCELMOORTY
motorcycle

CCENNORRTU
concurrent

CCEOOPSSTY
cystoscope

CCFGIINRUY
crucifying

CCGHIIINRST
scritching

CCGHINNRSU
scrunching

CCGIIIKNNP
picnicking

CCGIINNNOV
convincing

CCGIINNOTV
convicting

CCGINNORRU
concurring

CCHHHOOPTT
hotchpotch

CCHIMNOOOR
monochroic

CCIILMOPTY
complicity

CCIINNOOTV
conviction

CCIIORSTUU
circuitous

CCILMRRUUU
curriculum

CCILNNOOSU
conclusion

CCINNOOSSU
concussion

CCIORRSSSS
crisscross

CCJLNNOTUY
conjunctly

CDDEEEENNP
dependence

CDDEEEHIPR
deciphered

CDDEEEINRT
interceded

CDDEEEIRRT
redirected

CDDEEENNPY
dependency

CDDEEENNST
descendent

CDDEEFFIIN
diffidence

CDDEEGINNS
descending

CDDEEIINSS
dissidence

CDDEEIJPRU
prejudiced

CDDEEINORS
considered

CDDEEINPRS
prescinded

CDDEEINRTU
undirected

CDDEEIORSV
discovered

CDDEEMNOTU
documented

CDDEEMOOPS
decomposed

CDDEEOPRRU
reproduced

CDDEFNNOOU
confounded

CDDEIIRSTT
districted

CDDEILOORS
discolored

CDDEINORTU
introduced

CDDEINOSTU
discounted

CDDEIORSSU
discoursed

CDDEMNOOPU
compounded

CDDGIINORS
discording

CDEEEFFINR
difference

CDEEEGINRV
divergence

CDEEEHNRRT
retrenched

CDEEEILOPV
velocipede

CDEEEILQSU
deliquesce

CDEEEIMNNO
comedienne

CDEEEINNST
tendencies

CDEEEINPXY
expediency

CDEEELLNUX

unexcelled
CDEEELOPST
telescoped
CDEEENPTUX
unexpected
CDEEEPRSTU
persecuted
CDEEFGILNT
deflecting
CDEEFIINRT
dentifrice
CDEEFILNNU
influenced
CDEEFILNOT
deflection
CDEEFINORR
reinforced
CDEEFLNORT
centerfold
CDEEFLNORY
enforcedly
CDEEFLOORS
foreclosed
CDEEFLORSU
fluoresced
CDEEGIINNV
evidencing
CDEEGILNNU
indulgence
CDEEGINOPR
proceeding
CDEEGINORZ
recognized
CDEEHIMNOR
echinoderm
CDEEHINNRT
intrenched
CDEEHINRST
christened
CDEEHLRTWY
wretchedly
CDEEHMNOPR
comprehend
CDEEIIINSV
indecisive
CDEEIILSVY
decisively
CDEEIINRST
indiscreet
iridescent
CDEEIIPRTV
predictive
CDEEIKNSSW
wickedness
CDEEILNNOS
declension
CDEEILNNSU
unlicensed
CDEEILORST
cloistered
CDEEIMNNTU
inducement
CDEEIMNNOZ
economized

CDEEIMNPRU
imprudence
CDEEIMNSTU
intumesced
CDEEINNOSS
descension
CDEEINOPRV
providence
CDEEINORRS
reconsider
CDEEINPRSY
presidency
CDEEIORRSV
discoverer
rediscover
CDEEIORSTU
courtesied
CDEEIPRSST
disrespect
CDEEIRRSTT
restricted
CDEEKOOPRW
woodpecker
CDEEMOPRSS
compressed
CDEENOOSTT
cottonseed
CDEENOOTTW
cottonweed
CDEENORRSU
underscore
CDEENORRUV
undercover
CDEENOSTUU
consuetude
CDEEOPPRST
prospected
CDEEOPRSTU
prosecuted
CDEERSSSTU
seductress
CDEFFIIRTU
fructified
CDEFGINORU
configured
CDEFINNOTU
functioned
CDEFLNOSUY
confusedly
CDEFNNOORT
confronted
CDEGHILNSU
scheduling
CDEGIINNRS
discerning
rescinding
CDEGIINNSX
exscinding
CDEGIINPRT
predicting
CDEGIINSST
dissecting
CDEGILMMNO
commingled

CDEGILNOOR
decoloring
CDEGIMMNNO
commending
CDEGIMNNNO
condemning
CDEGINNNOS
condensing
CDEGINNNOT
contending
CDEGINNNOU
denouncing
CDEGMNORUU
curmudgeon
CDEHHHIIKT
hitchhiked
CDEHIINOST
hedonistic
CDEHIMOPRY
hypodermic
CDEHIOOPRT
orthopedic
CDEHLOOPPR
clodhopper
CDEHOOPRSY
hydroscope
CDEIIILNPS
discipline
CDEIIIMRSV
recidivism
CDEIIIMTVZ
victimized
CDEIIINNOS
indecision
CDEIIINTVV
vindictive
CDEIILNPPR
principled
CDEIILNRTY
indirectly
CDEIILOSTU
solicitude
CDEIIMNNTT
indictment
CDEIIMORTY
mediocrity
CDEIINOPRT
prediction
CDEIINORST
discretion
CDEIINOSST
dissection
CDEIIRRSTT
redistrict
CDEIIRSSUV
discursive
CDEIKLOPST
stockpiled
CDEILNOSSU
cloudiness
CDEILOPSUU
pediculous
CDEILORSSU
disclosure

CDEIMMNOPU
compendium
CDEIMNOSTU
miscounted
CDEIMNOSUU
mucedinous
CDEINNOSTT
discontent
CDEINRSTTU
instructed
CDEIOPRTUV
productive
CDEKNORSTU
understock
CDELLNOORT
controlled
CDELNNOOSU
unconsoled
CDELOORSUY
decorously
CDELPRSTUU
sculptured
CDENNOOPRU
pronounced
CDENOOPRRS
correspond
CDEOOPPRTU
outcropped
CDEOOORTTUW
woodcutter
CDERRSTTUU
structured
CDFFIILTUY
difficulty
CDFGIILNUY
dulcifying
CDFHILOOPR
childproof
CDFIMOORST
discomfort
CDGIILMNO
domiciling
CDGIIILNPS
discipling
CDGIIILNRU
ridiculing
CDGIILNOSS
disclosing
CDGIINNOTY
condignity
CDGIINSSSU
discussing
CDGIKLLOOS
goldilocks
CDIIINNSTT
indistinct
CDIILNSTTY
distinctly
CDIILORSUU
ridiculous
CDIINOSSSU
discussion
CDINOOPRTU
production

CDNOOOOTTW
cottonwood
CEEEEFFRSV
effervesce
CEEEEFNPRR
preference
CEEEEGILNS
elegencies
CEEEEHNPRT
threepence
CEEEEIMRST
cemeteries
CEEEEINPRX
experience
CEEEFFGLNU
effulgence
CEEEFFLORS
effloresce
CEEEFFLSST
effectless
CEEEFILRTV
reflective
CEEEFINRSS
fierceness
CEEEFINRSV
fervencies
CEEEGGILNN
negligence
CEEEGIINSX
exigencies
CEEEGILNRT
reelecting
CEEEGINRST
energetics
CEEEHLPSSS
speechless
CEEEHMORTT
hectometer
CEEEHNRRST
retrenches
CEEEIJLTVY
ejectively
CEEEIKLNRS
screenlike
CEEEILLTVY
electively
CEEEILNPRT
percentile
CEEEILNPST
pestilence
CEEEIMNNTT
enticement
CEEEIMNORS
ceremonies
CEEEIMNRSV
servicemen
CEEEIMNRTT
centimeter
CEEEIMNTTX
excitement
CEEEINNPRT
pertinence
CEEEIORRSV
recoveries

CEEEIPPRTV
perceptive
CEEEJLORTT
electrojet
CEEEKRRSSU
seersucker
CEEELNRSSV
cleverness
CEEFGILNRT
reflecting
CEEFGINPRT
perfecting
CEEFGINRTU
centrifuge
CEEFGLLNTU
neglectful
CEEFHHNORT
henceforth
CEEFHLLRUY
cheerfully
CEEFHORTTU
fourchette
CEEFIILLST
felicities
CEEFIILNTV
inflective
CEEFILNORT
reflection
CEEFINOPRT
perfection
CEEFLNORST
florescent
CEEFLNSTUV
fulvescent
CEEFLPPRTU
pluperfect
CEEGGILNNT
neglecting
CEEGHIKNNP
henpecking
CEEGHILNNO
echeloning
CEEGHIMORT
geothermic
CEEGIINPRT
receipting
CEEGIINPRV
perceiving
CEEGIINRSX
exercising
CEEGILNPRT
prelecting
CEEGINNNST
sentencing
CEEGINORRV
recovering
CEEGINOSTV
congestive
CEEGINPRST
respecting
CEEGINPRTX
excerpting
CEEGNNORTV
convergent

CEEGNOOSTU
ectogenous
CEEGNORSSS
congresses
CEEHIIRSTW
witcheries
CEEHIKSSTT
sketchiest
CEEHILNOPT
telephonic
CEEHILOPRT
helicopter
CEEHIMNNRT
enrichment
CEEHIMOPTU
mouthpiece
CEEHINNORT
incoherent
CEEHINNRST
intrenches
CEEHIOPPRS
prophecies
CEEIILLMRV
vermicelli
CEEIILOSTV
velocities
CEEIIMNNTT
incitement
CEEIINNSST
insistence
CEEIINPPRT
percipient
CEEIINRSTT
interstice
CEEIINSSTZ
citizeness
CEEIIRSSTU
securities
CEEIJLOPRT
projectile
CEEIKLNRSS
silkscreen
CEEILLORSS
recoilless
CEEILLRSSU
sculleries
CEEILMNOPT
incomplete
CEEILMNOSS
comeliness
CEEILNQSTU
liquescent
CEEILNRSUY
insecurely
CEEILPRSUV
preclusive
CEEIMMORRT
micrometer
CEEIMNNOPR
prominence
CEEIMNOORZ
economizer
CEEINNNOTV
convenient

CEEINOPPRT
perception
CEEINOPRSS
necropsies
CEEINORRSW
cornerwise
CEEINOSTTX
coexistent
CEEIOPRTTV
protective
CEEIOQRSTU
coquetries
CEEIORSSTU
courtesies
CEEIPSSTUV
susceptive
CEEKLNRTTU
turtleneck
CEELMMNOPT
complement
CEELMNNOOS
somnolence
CEELNORSVY
conversely
CEEMNNORTU
countermen
CEENNOQSTU
consequent
CEENNOSSVX
convexness
CEENOPPPRR
peppercorn
CEENPRSTTU
putrescent
CEEOPRRSTT
retrospect
CEEOPRRSTU
persecutor
CEFFIINSTU
sufficient
CEFFIRSSTU
scruffiest
CEFFLLORUY
forcefully
CEFGIIKLNR
flickering
CEFGIILNNT
inflecting
CEFGIINPSY
specifying
CEFGIINRTY
certifying
rectifying
CEFGINNORR
conferring
CEFGINNOSS
confessing
CEFHILSTTU
cuttlefish
CEFIILNNOT
inflection
CEFIILOSTU
felicitous
CEFIIMNNTU

munificent
CEFIINOPRT
proficient
CEFIINOPST
pontifices
CEFIINOSTU
infectious
CEFILLMRUY
mercifully
CEFILMNRUU
unmerciful
CEFILMOORS
frolicsome
CEFINNOOSS
confession
CEFINOORSU
coniferous
CEFIOORSUV
vociferous
CEFKLOOORT
footlocker
CEGGILNOSS
clogginess
CEGGINNORV
converging
CEGGINNOST
congesting
CEGGLNOOYY
gynecology
CEGHHIINRS
cherishing
CEGHIIKNNT
thickening
CEGHIINRTT
chittering
CEGHILNPPS
schlepping
CEGHILNQSU
squelching
CEGHINOOPT
photogenic
CEGHINRSTT
stretching
CEGHIOPSSY
geophysics
CEGHIORSTU
grouchiest
CEGHLNOOTY
technology
CEGHNOPSYY
psychogeny
CEGHOOPRSY
hygroscope
CEGIIKNNQU
quickening
CEGIIKNNRS
snickering
CEGIILLNNST
stenciling
CEGIILNNTY
enticingly
CEGIILNOSZ
solecizing
CEGIINNOST

sectioning
CEGIINNPST
inspecting
CEGIINORSX
exorcising
CEGIINOSTX
coexisting
CEGIINRRTU
recruiting
CEGIJNOPRT
projecting
CEGIKNORST
restocking
CEGILLMNOP
compelling
CEGILMNOPT
completing
CEGILMOOTY
etymologic
CEGILNNOSU
counseling
CEGILNRSTU
clustering
CEGILNRTTU
cluttering
CEGIMMMNNOT
commenting
CEGIMMNNNOT
contemning
CEGIMNOORV
overcoming
CEGINNNORU
renouncing
CEGINNNOST
consenting
CEGINNNOTT
contenting
contingent
CEGINNNRSU
scunnering
CEGINNOOST
congestion
CEGINNOQRU
conquering
CEGINNORSV
conserving
conversing
CEGINNORTU
countering
recounting
CEGINNORTV
converting
CEGINNORUV
uncovering
CEGINNOSTT
contesting
CEGINNRSUW
unscrewing
CEGINNRSUY
insurgency
CEGINOPRRT
porrecting
CEGINOPRSS
processing

CEGINOPRTT
protecting
CEGINOQTTU
coquetting
CEGINPRSSU
percussing
CEGINPSSTU
suspecting
CEHHHIIKRT
hitchhiker
CEHHIILMNT
helminthic
CEHIILLNSS
chilliness
CEHIINPSST
pitchiness
CEHILMNOOP
melophonic
CEHILNOPST
clothespin
CEHIMNOOPR
microphone
CEHINNRSTY
strychnine
CEHINOORRS
rhinoceros
CEHINOPRSS
censorship
CEHINOPSTT
pitchstone
CEHINOSSTU
touchiness
CEHIOQSTTU
coquettish
CEHMMNOOOR
monochrome
CEHMMOOORS
chromosome
CEHNOOSTTU
touchstone
CEHOORSTUU
courthouse
CEHORSTTTU
outstretch
CEIIILSTV
civilities
CEIIIINSTV
vicinities
CEIIILLNNP
penicillin
CEIIILNSVY
incisively
CEIIILOPTZ
politicize
CEIIIMMPRS
empiricism
CEIIIMPRST
empiricist
CEIIJOOSST
jocosities
CEIIKLPRST
prickliest
CEIIKMPSST
skepticism

CEIIKNRSST
trickiness
CEIILMSSTV
victimless
CEIILNOSTU
licentious
CEIILNOSTV
novelistic
CEIIMMNNOST
omniscient
CEIIMPRSST
scrimpiest
CEIINNOPST
inspection
CEIINNOTTX
extinction
CEIINOPRSU
pernicious
CEIINOPRTV
voiceprint
CEIINRSSTU
scrutinies
CEIINRSTUY
insecurity
CEIINRSTUZ
scrutinize
CEIJNOOPRT
projection
CEIKKORRWW
wickerwork
CEIKNOSSST
stockiness
CEILMMNOPT
compliment
CEILMNOOPT
completion
CEILMNOOPX
complexion
CEILMNSSSU
clumsiness
CEILMOOOTV
locomotive
CEILMOPSUV
compulsive
CEILMOPTXY
complexity
CEILMORTUV
volumetric
CEILMOSTUU
meticulous
CEILNNNOTY
innocently
CEILNOOPRS
necropolis
CEILNOPRSU
preclusion
CEILNOSUVV
convulsive
CEILOPRSUY
preciously
CEIMMMNOTT
commitment
CEIMMNOORT
metronomic

CEIMMOOPRS
compromise
CEIMNOPRSU
proscenium
CEIMNRSSTY
syncretism
CEIMOOPRTT
competitor
CEINNNOOTT
contention
CEINNNOOTV
convection
CEINNOORSV
conversion
CEINNOSSTT
consistent
CEINOOPRSS
procession
CEINOOPRTT
protection
CEINOPRSSU
percussion
supersonic
CEINOSSTUU
incestuous
CEINOSTTTU
constitute
CEINRSSTTY
syncretist
CEIOOPRRTY
corporeity
CEIOPRRTWY
copywriter
CELLNOORRT
controller
CELPRSSSTU
sculptress
CEMNNORTUY
countrymen
CEMOOPRRSS
compressor
CENOORRTTV
controvert
CENOPRSTUY
counterspy
CEOOPPRRST
prospector
CEOOPRRSTU
prosecutor
CEOOPRRTTY
protectory
CEOPPRSSTU
prospectus
CEOPRRRSUY
precursory
CFFGILNOSY
scoffingly
CFFIIILMOR
filiciform
CFGIIILNNT
inflicting
CFGIIKLNOR
frolicking
CFGIIMNNOR

confirming
CFGIINNORY
cornifying
CFGIMNNOOR
conforming
CFGIMNOORT
comforting
CFHKOOOPRS
shockproof
CFHLMOOORR
chloroform
CFIIIOSTTU
fictitious
CFIINNNOOT
nonfiction
CFIMNOORST
conformist
CFIMNOORTY
conformity
CGGGIILNRS
scriggling
CGGGILNNOU
unclogging
CGGIINNNOS
consigning
CGGINNORSU
scrounging
CGHHILORTT
torchlight
CGHIIKNPSY
physicking
CGHIILLOOP
philologic
CGHIINNOSU
cushioning
CGHIINPRRU
chirruping
CGHILLOORS
schoolgirl
CGHILMOOTY
mythologic
CGHILNOTUY
touchingly
CGHLNOOORY
chronology
CGHLOOPSYY
psychology
CGIIIILNVZ
civilizing
CGIIILNOST
soliciting
CGIIILNSTU
linguistic
CGIIJNNNOO
conjoining
CGIIKLLNOR
rollicking
CGIIKNNSTU
unsticking
CGIILNNOOZ
colonizing
CGIIMMNOTT
committing
CGIIMMNNORS

crimsoning
CGIIMNOPRS
comprising
CGIINNNOTU
continuing
CGIINNOPRS
conspiring
CGIINNORTV
contriving
CGIINNOSST
consisting
CGIINORSSS
scissoring
CGIINOTTUY
contiguity
CGILLNOOPS
scolloping
CGILNNOOVV
convolving
CGILNNOPUU
uncoupling
CGILNNOSTU
consulting
CGILNNOSUV
convulsing
CGILOOOTXY
toxicology
CGIMNOOPRT
comporting
CGIMNOOPST
composting
CGINNOORST
consorting
CGINNOORTT
contorting
CGINNOORTU
contouring
CGINNORSTU
construing
CGINNPRTUU
puncturing
CGINOOPRRT
proctoring
CGINOOSTUU
contiguous
CGINOPRRTU
corrupting
CHHIOOPPRS
phosphoric
CHIIIILNST
nihilistic
CHIIILPSTY
syphilitic
CHIIINORST
histrionic
CHIILMNOOT
monolithic
CHIINNOPSU
pincushion
CHILNOPSSU
consulship
CHIMNNOOOP
monophonic
CHIORSTTTW

stitchwort
CHKLOOORSW
schoolwork
CHLMNOSUUU
homunculus
CHLMOOOORS
schoolroom
CIIILLMPTY
implicitly
CIIILMPSST
simplistic
CIIILMPSTY
simplicity
CIIIMNNPPRU
principium
CIIIMOPSTT
optimistic
CIIJNNNOTU
injunction
CIILOOSSTU
solicitous
CIILOPRTVY
proclivity
CIIMMNOOSS
commission
CIIMMNOOTX
commixtion
CIIINNNOOPT
conniption
CIINNOORTT
contrition
CIINNOTTUY
continuity
CIIOORSTUV
victorious
CIIOPSSSUU
suspicious
CILLMOOQUU
colloquium
CILLOOQSTU
colloquist
CILLOPRSTU
portcullis
CILLOSSUUY
lusciously
CILMNOOOOT
locomotion
CILMNOOPSU
compulsion
CILNNOOSUV
convulsion
CILORRSSUU
scurrilous
CIMNNOOOPP
nincompoop
CIMNOORSTU
consortium
CIMOOOPRST
compositor
CINNOOORTT
contortion
CINNOOSTUU
continuous
CINOOPRRTU

corruption
CINOORSSTY
cinsistory
CINORRSTTU
instructor
CIOOPRSTTU
prosciutto
CIOPPRSSTT
postscript
CKLLOORRSW
scrollwork
CKMNOORSTU
moonstruck
CLMMNNOOUY
uncommonly
CLMOOPRSUY
compulsory
CLNOSTUUUY
unctuously
CLOPRSSUUU
scrupulous
DDDEEFIOST
eisteddfod
DDDEEIIOXZ
deoxidized
DDDEEIOORZ
deodorized
DDDEEIORRS
disordered
DDEEEEGNNR
engendered
DDEEEFLORW
deflowered
DDEEEGINRS
redesigned
DDEEEHHPRS
shepherded
DDEEEHILSV
disheveled
DDEEEIMNRT
determined
DDEEEINRTZ
tenderized
DDEEELMMOS
meddlesome
DDEEENRSUV
undeserved
DDEEEPRSSU
superseded
DDEEFIIINT
identified
DDEEFIIOTX
detoxified
DDEEFLNORU
floundered
DDEEGGHOOP
hodgepodge
DDEEGINSTU
undigested
DDEEGIRRSU
drudgeries
DDEEHILMOS
demolished
DDEEHIRSST

shreddiest
DDEEHLORSU
shouldered
DDEEHNORSU
enshrouded
DDEEIINRST
disintered
DDEEIINRSW
sidewinder
DDEEIIPSSW
sideswiped
DDEEIIQSTU
disquieted
DDEEILNNRU
underlined
DDEEIMNNRU
undermined
DDEEIMNNSS
mindedness
DDEEIMNORZ
modernized
DDEEINNRTU
indentured
DDEEIOORRZ
deodorizer
DDEEIOPSTZ
despotized
DDEEIPRSTU
disreputed
DDEEIRSSST
distressed
DDEELRRSSU
rudderless
DDEENNOPST
despondent
DDEENNSSSU
suddenness
DDEENRRSSU
underdress
DDEFGIIRSU
disfigured
DDEFHIIIMU
humidified
DDEFIIILOS
solidified
DDEGHINRSU
shuddering
DDEGIINNST
distending
DDEGINNOPS
desponding
DDEGINNORU
redounding
DDEGNNORUU
ungrounded
DDEHIIIMNS
diminished
DDEHIILNSW
windshield
DDEHIKNOOW
hoodwinked
DDEHINOORS
dishonored

DDEHINOSSS
shoddiness
DDEIIIPRST
dispirited
DDEIIIQSTU
quiddities
DDEIIJNOST
disjointed
DDEIIMNNOU
diminuendo
DDEIINOPSS
indisposed
DDEILLNPSY
splendidly
DDEILMMOST
middlemost
DDEILORRSY
disorderly
DDEIMNOSTU
dismounted
DDEINPSTUU
undisputed
DDEIRSSTTU
distrusted
DDELNORRUW
underworld
DDENOOPPRU
propounded
DDENOORSTU
understood
DDENORRSUU
surrounded
DDENRSTUUY
understudy
DDGGIILNOS
dislodging
DDGGILNRUY
drudgingly
DEEEEGINNR
engineered
DEEEEPRRSV
persevered
DEEEFHLORR
freeholder
DEEEFINRRT
interfered
DEEEFMNRRU
referendum
DEEEFNRTTU
unfettered
DEEEFORRST
reforested
DEEEGHHINT
heightened
DEEEGHLNNT
lengthened
DEEEGIRRST
registered
DEEEHIMPUZ
euphemized
DEEEHLLSSY
heedlessly
DEEEHLNOPT
telephoned

DEEEEHLNORS
lederhosen
DEEEIILRSV
deliveries
DEEEILLMOS
demoiselle
DEEEILNNST
sentineled
DEEEILNRST
reenlisted
DEEEILRSVW
silverweed
DEEEIMMRSZ
mesmerized
DEEEIMPRTV
redemptive
DEEEINNRTV
intervened
DEEEINRRTZ
tenderizer
DEEEINRSTT
interested
DEEEINRSTV
reinvested
DEEEIPRSSV
depressive
DEEEKLNORW
needlework
DEEELLNSSY
needlessly
DEEELLOWWY
yellowweed
DEEELNRTTU
unlettered
DEEENNRSST
tenderness
DEEEOPPRRY
eyedropper
DEEFGHINRT
frightened
DEEFHIILLT
helilifted
DEEFHIINRS
refinished
DEEFIIILST
fidelities
DEEFIIINNT
indefinite
DEEFIINST
identifies
DEEFIIINTV
definitive
DEEFIILMSU
emulsified
DEEFIILNTY
definitely
DEEFIILRTZ
fertilized
DEEFIINRVW
viewfinder
DEEFIIPRTT
prettified
DEEFILNOST
fieldstone

DEEFILNRSS
friendless
DEEFLOORVW
overflowed
DEEFNOORTT
tenderfoot
DEEGHINSTU
gesundheit
DEEGHIOTUW
outweighed
DEEGIILNRV
delivering
DEEGIILOOS
ideologies
DEEGIILPRV
privileged
DEEGIIMNRT
demeriting
DEEGIINNRT
ingredient
DEEGIINPTX
expediting
DEEGIIRSSV
digressive
DEEGILMNOR
remodeling
DEEGILNOPV
developing
DEEGINNPRT
pretending
DEEGINORRR
reordering
DEEGINPRSS
depressing
DEEGINRRSS
redressing
DEEGOPRRSS
progressed
DEEHIIKLLS
shieldlike
DEEHIINPRS
hesperidin
DEEHILLSSS
shieldless
DEEHILMOSS
demolishes
DEEHINOPUZ
euphonized
DEEHINORST
threnodies
DEEHIOPPRS
prophesied
DEEHMORRTY
hydrometer
DEEHNRSSSW
shrewdness
DEEHOORTXY
heterodoxy
DEEIIINSTT
identities
DEEIILRSTV
deviltries
DEEIILRSTZ
sterilized

DEEIIMMNPT
impediment
DEEIIMNRST
ministered
DEEIIMNRTX
intermixed
DEEIIMOPTZ
epitomized
DEEIINOPTT
petitioned
DEEIINOPTX
expedition
DEEIINRTWZ
winterized
DEEIINSSTZ
sensitized
DEEIJNOSTT
jettisoned
DEEIKORSST
sidestroke
DEEILLMPSS
misspelled
DEEILLORRS
drolleries
DEEILMNOSZ
solemnized
DEEILNNORT
tenderloin
DEEILNNQTU
delinquent
DEEILNOPRT
interloped
DEEILNPRST
splintered
DEEILNRSSW
wilderness
DEEILPRUVZ
pulverized
DEEIMNOPRT
redemption
DEEIMMNORRZ
modernizer
DEEIMNORSZ
sermonized
DEEIMNSTTV
divestment
DEEIMOPRTZ
temporized
DEEIMSSTYZ
systemized
DEEINNNOSU
innuendoes
DEEINNOPRSS
depression
DEEINOPRST
interposed
DEEINOPTTZ
potentized
DEEINOQSTU
questioned
DEEINQRTUU
unrequited
DEEINRRTUW
underwrite

DEEIOPPRSS
predispose
DEEIOPRTTU
pirouetted
DEEIORRRTZ
terrorized
DEEIPRSSUV
supervised
DEEIRSSSST
distresses
DEEKLMRTTU
kettledrum
DEEKOORRVW
overworked
DEELMNOPUY
unemployed
DEELMPRSUY
presumedly
DEELNORSUV
unresolved
DEELORTTUV
turtledove
DEELPRSTTU
spluttered
DEELPRSTUU
sepultured
DEEMNNORTW
wonderment
DEEMNOPRTT
deportment
DEEMNORSTU
tremendous
DEEMOPRRTY
redemptory
DEENOQRTUU
underquote
DEENORRTUW
underwrote
DEENORSUVZ
rendezvous
DEEPPRSSSU
suppressed
DEFGHILLTU
delightful
DEFGHLORUU
furloughed
DEFGIILNYY
edifyingly
DEFGIINNUY
unedifying
DEFGINNORU
foundering
DEFGNOOORRU
foreground
DEFHIIIMSU
humidifies
DEFHIIIMRU
humidifier
DEFHIILNSY
fiendishly
DEFHIINNSU
unfinished
DEFHIINPRS
friendship

DEFHILORSU
flourished
DEFIIILMPS
simplified
DEFIIILNTY
infidelity
DEFIIINNOT
definition
DEFIIINNTU
infinitude
DEFIILOSSZ
fossilized
DEFIILSTTU
stultified
DEFILMORUZ
formulized
DEFILNNRUY
unfriendly
DEFILNORWW
windflower
DEFIMNNORU
uninformed
DEFMNNORUY
foundrymen
DEGGHIILNT
delighting
DEGGIILNNR
engirdling
DEGGIINRSS
digressing
DEGGINNORU
undergoing
DEGHIINRRT
nightrider
DEGHINNORT
dethroning
DEGHINNRTU
thundering
DEGHINOSSU
doughiness
DEGHIORRRU
roughrider
DEGHIOSTTU
doughtiest
DEGHNNOSTU
shotgunned
DEGIIILMNT
delimiting
DEGIIILNVZ
devilizing
DEGIIKLNNR
rekindling
DEGIILLNNW
indwelling
DEGIILLNPS
dispelling
DEGIILMNOZ
melodizing
DEGIILNNUY
unyielding
DEGIILNOPS
despoiling
DEGIILNORS
soldiering

DEGIIMNNOZ
demonizing
DEGIINNOSU
indigenous
DEGIINNPSS
dispensing
DEGIINNSST
dissenting
DEGIINOPRX
peroxiding
DEGIINOPST
depositing
DEGIINORRV
overriding
DEGIINORSS
digression
DEGIINPRSS
dispersing
DEGIINPRST
springtide
DEGIINPTUZ
deputizing
DEGILLOSYZ
syllogized
DEGILMNORS
smoldering
DEGILNNPRU
plundering
DEGILNNRUY
underlying
DEGILNOSTU
ungodliest
DEGILNRSTU
disgruntle
DEGINNOPRS
responding
DEGINNOPRT
protending
DEGINNOPUX
expounding
DEGINNORST
grindstone
DEGINNORSU
resounding
DEGINNPSSU
suspending
DEGINNRSSU
undressing
DEGINOOPRT
torpedoing
DEGINORSTY
destroying
DEGLNORSSU
groundless
DEGLOORTTY
troglodyte
DEHHIMOORR
hemorrhoid
DEHHIMRTYZ
rhythmized
DEHHMOOORT
motherhood
DEHIIIMNSS
diminishes

DEHIIINRST
disinherit
DEHIIKLLOO
likelihood
DEHIIKMRSS
skirmished
DEHIILLOOV
livelihood
DEHIILMNPU
delphinium
DEHIIMMNPS
midshipmen
DEHIIOPRST
editorship
DEHIKLORSU
shroudlike
DEHILNOPSU
unpolished
DEHIMOOPPR
hippodrome
DEHIMOPRSY
hypodermis
DEHINNPSUU
unpunished
DEHINOPTYZ
hypnotized
DEHINORRSS
horridness
DEHINOSSTY
dishonesty
DEHINRRSTU
undershirt
DEHIOOPRST
priesthood
DEHIOORSST
sisterhood
DEHLNOOPRY
polyhedron
DEHMORRTYY
hydrometry
DEHNOORRSU
horrendous
DEHNOORSUU
roundhouse
DEHNORSTUU
thunderous
DEIIINNSTV
divinities
DEIIILMQSU
semiliquid
DEIIILMSTU
similitude
DEIIIMNTUV
diminutive
DEIIINSSTU
disunities
DEIIKLNNSS
kindliness
DEIILLMPTU
multiplied
DEIILLNUWY
unwieldily
DEIILLRSTY
distillery

DEIILMNOOT
demolition
DEIILNPRTY
intrepidly
DEIIMNOPRS
imprisoned
DEIIMNPRST
misprinted
DEIIMOPRSV
improvised
DEIINNOSSS
dissension
DEIINNOSTT
distention
DEIINNPRSU
uninspired
DEIINOOPST
deposition
DEIINOPRSS
dispersion
DEIINRSSTU
industries
DEIINSTTTU
instituted
DEIIPRSTUV
disruptive
DEIKNNNORR
nondrinker
DEILLLLSUV
dullsville
DEILLNNOTY
indolently
DEILLNORSS
lordliness
DEILLORSTW
worldliest
DEILMMOSTY
immodestly
DEILMNPTUY
impudently
DEILNOSSWW
windowless
DEILNPQTUU
quintupled
DEIMNOPRTU
importuned
DEIMNOPRVU
unimproved
DEIMRSSTTU
mistrusted
DEINOOSSSU
odiousness
DEINORSSSW
drowsiness
DEINORSSUU
undesirous
DEIOOPRSTY
depository
DEIOPRRSTW
spiderwort
DEIOPSSSSS
dispossess
DEKNOOPRUV
unprovoked

DEKNOORRWW
wonderwork
DEKOOOORRWW
woodworker
DELNNOPSSU
nonplussed
DEMNORSTUU
surmounted
DENNOORSTU
roundstone
DENOPSSTUU
stupendous
DFGGIIINNY
dignifying
DFGHILLOOT
floodlight
DFGIIMNNUY
mundifying
DFNOOOPRSU
soundproof
DGGIIINNSU
disguising
DGGIIJMNSU
misjudging
DGHHIKNOOT
knighthood
DGHLNOORST
stronghold
DGIIIINNVZ
divinizing
DGIIIJNNOS
disjoining
DGIIILLNST
distilling
DGIIIMNSSS
dismissing
DGIIINNSTU
disuniting
DGIILNOSSV
dissolving
DGIIMNNOPU
impounding
DGIINNORWW
windrowing
DGIINOPRSV
disproving
DGIINORSTT
distorting
DGIINPRSTU
disrupting
DGIIOOPRSU
prodigious
DGILNOOPRY
droopingly
DGINOPRRTU
protruding
DGKNOORRUW
groundwork
DGLNOOOOTY
odontology
DHILORSSYY
hydrolysis
DHNOOORTUX
unorthodox**

DIINOORSTT
distortion
DIINOPRSTU
disruption
DILOSSTUUY
studiously
DLNOORSUWY
wondrously
EEEEFFNSST
effeteness
EEEEGINRRS
greeneries
EEEEHIMRUZ
euhemerism
EEEEHRRVWY
everywhere
EEEEIKMPRT
timekeeper
EEEELLSSSV
sleeveless
EEEEENNRSSS
sereneness
EEEENRSSSV
severeness
EEEEFFLNRTY
efferently
EEEFGINORS
foreseeing
EEEFHOOORRT
heretofore
EEEEFIINRRS
refineries
EEEFIMNNRT
refinement
EEEFLLORRT
foreteller
EEEFNNORSU
unforeseen
EEEFNQRRTU
frequenter
EEEGHHINTT
eighteenth
EEEGHNORSU
greenhouse
EEEGIINPSS
epigenesis
EEEGIMORST
geometries
EEEGINNPST
steepening
EEEGINNRRT
reentering
EEEGINNSTW
sweetening
EEEGINORSV
overseeing
EEEGIRRSSV
regressive
EEEGLNNSST
gentleness
EEEHHIMPRS
hemisphere
EEEHHLOSUW
wheelhouse

EEEEHIIRSTV
thieveries
EEEEHILNPRS
prehensile
EEEEHIMMRSU
euhemerism
EEEEHINNNTT
nineteenth
EEEEHINSTTV
seventieth
EEEEHKOPPRS
shopkeeper
EEEEHLMNTVY
vehemently
EEEEHLMSSTV
themselves
EEEEHLPRSSS
sphereless
EEEEHMPRRTY
hypermeter
EEEEHNORSVW
whensoever
EEEEIINRSST
serenities
EEEEIINRSTT
entireties
eternities
EEEEIKLMSWY
semiweekly
EEEEILMRSST
smelteries
EEEEILNQSTU
queenliest
EEEEILRSSTW
westerlies
EEEEIMNNPRT
preeminent
EEEEIMNPRTX
experiment
EEEEIMNRRTT
retirement
EEEEINNPRST
serpentine
EEEEINNPRST
enterprise
EEEEINNPRTZ
serpentize
EEEEINNPRTVV
preventive
EEEEINNRRTV
irreverent
EEEEINNRSTWZ
westernize
EEEEINSSTWY
eyewitness
EEEEIOPRRRT
repertoire
EEEEIPRSSVX
expressive
EEEEJJNNSSU
jejuneness
EEEELLNRSST
relentless
EEEELMMOSTT

mettlesome
EEEELMNOSTT
nettlesome
EEEELMNSTTT
settlement
EEEELNRSTTW
newsletter
EEEELOPPSTT
steepletop
EEEELORSVWW
werewolves
EEEELPRRSVY
perversely
EEEEOPRSTTY
stereotype
EEEEPRSTTTY
typesetter
EEEFFGINORR
forefinger
EEEFFILSUVY
effusively
EEEFFIIORRTU
forfeiture
EEEFFLORSST
effortless
EEEFFNORRTY
effrontery
EEEFGHINNRS
freshening
EEEFGHINRRS
refreshing
EEEFGIINORZ
foreignize
EEEFGILNRSS
fringeless
EEEFGIMNNRT
fermenting
EEEFGINPRRR
preferring
EEEFGKLLNOT
gentlefolk
EEEFHIINRSS
refinishes
EEEFHILNSSS
elfishness
fleshiness
EEEFHNORTTU
fourteenth
EEEFIILRRTZ
fertilizer
EEEFIIPRSTT
prettifies
EEEFIIRRRSU
furrieries
EEEFILLLSSY
lifelessly
EEEFIMNOSTT
oftentimes
EEEFINNQRTU
infrequent
EEEFLMORRSU
remorseful
EEEFLNNTUUV
uneventful

EEEFLNQRTUY
frequently
EEEFNNORRRU
forerunner
EEEFORRSSST
fortresses
EEEGGIINNRS
energising
EEEGGIINNRZ
energizing
EEEGGIMNNST
segmenting
EEEGGINRRSS
regressing
EEEGGINRRTT
regretting
EEEGGISSTUV
suggestive
EEEGHIISTTW
weightiest
EEEGHILMPST
phlegmiest
EEEGHILNOOP
pigeonhole
EEEGHILNRST
sheltering
EEEGHILNSTT
lengthiest
EEEGHILNSTW
lengthwise
EEEGHILOOST
ethologies
theologies
EEEGHILOOTZ
theologize
EEEGHILSSTW
weightless
EEEGHIMNOOZ
homogenize
EEEGHINNPTY
eightpenny
EEEGHINRTVY
everything
EEEGHIORTVW
overweight
EEEGHMORRTY
hygrometer
EEEGHNNRSTT
strengthen
EEEGIILNNNV
enlivening
EEEGIILNNST
lentigines
EEEGIILNSTV
televising
EEEGIIMNPRR
premiering
EEEGIINNOPR
pioneering
EEEGIINPRRV
reprieving
EEEGIINPRVW
previewing
EEEGIINRRTV

retrieving
EEGIIRRSST
registries
EEGILMNOOS
menologies
EEGILMNORZ
mongrelize
EEGILNNOPV
enveloping
EEGILNPPRX
perplexing
EEGILNRSTW
sweltering
EEGIMNNNOV
envenoming
EEGIMNOPRW
empowering
EEGIMNPPRT
preempting
EEGINNPRST
presenting
serpenting
EEGINNPRTV
preventing
EEGINORRSS
regression
EEGINORRWW
winegrower
EEGINORSTY
generosity
EEGINPRRSS
repressing
EEGINPRRSV
preserving
EEGINPRRTV
perverting
EEGINPRSSX
expressing
EEGINQRSTU
requesting
EEGLNORSUY
generously
EEGLNOSSTU
tongueless
EEGMNNORSW
newsmonger
EEGMNNORTV
government
EEGNNORSUU
ungenerous
EEGOPRRSSS
progresses
EEGORRRSST
retrogress
EEHHILPSSY
sheepishly
EEHHINRTTT
thirteenth
EEHHOORSUW
whorehouse
EEHHOPSSTY
hypotheses
EEHIIKLMRT
hermitlike

EEHILMNOSS
homeliness
EEHILNNRTY
inherently
EEHILOOPRT
heliotrope
EEHILOSTTU
silhouette
EEHINNORST
rhinestone
EEHINOOPRS
ionosphere
EEHINSSTYZ
synthesize
EEHINSTTYZ
synthetize
EEHIOPPRSS
prophesies
EEHIOPPRST
epistrophe
EEHIOPPSSU
eohippuses
EEHIOSSUVW
housewives
EEHKMOOSSU
smokehouse
EEHLLLPSSY
helplessly
EEHLLOPSSY
hopelessly
EEHLMORSST
motherless
EEHLNOOSSV
shovelnose
EEHMNNNNOOP
phenomenon
EEHMNORSTT
nethermost
EEHMOOPRTT
photometer
EEHMOORSVW
whomsoever
EEHMOPRSTT
stepmother
EEHNOPSTUY
hypotenuse
EEHNORRSTU
southerner
EEHOOPRRSW
horsepower
EEHOOPRSUW
powerhouse
EEHOORSSTU
storehouse
EEIIINQSTU
inequities
EEIIKLLNSS
likeliness
EEIIKLNPRW
periwinkle
EEIIILLMMRT
millimeter
EEIIILLNSSV
liveliness

EEIILMNSST
timeliness
EEIILNOSTV
television
EEIILOPSTZ
epistolize
EEIILPPRRS
slipperier
EEIILPRRST
priestlier
EEIILRRSTZ
sterilizer
EEIIMNNPTT
impenitent
EEIIMNORST
enormities
EEIIMNRTTW
wintertime
EEIIMNRTZZ
intermezzi
EEIIMOPRTZ
epitomizer
EEIIMPRSSV
impressive
permissive
EEIINNRTTW
intertwine
EEIINOPRTT
petitioner
repetition
EEIINPRRST
printeries
EEIIORRSST
rotisserie
EEIIPQRSTU
perquisite
EEIILLNNOSS
loneliness
EEIILLNOSSV
loveliness
EEIILLNSSTT
littleness
EEIILLRSSTY
tirelessly
EEIILMNNSTT
enlistment
EEIILMNOSSU
mousseline
EEIILNOPRRT
interloper
EEIILORRSTU
irresolute
EEIILPPRTXY
perplexity
EEIILPSTTTY
teletypist
EEIMMMRRSTU
summertime
EEIMMRSSTY
symmetries
EEIMNNORST
minestrone

EEIMNNNSSTU
minuteness
EEIMNNSTTV
investment
EEIMNOPRTU
peritoneum
EEIMNORRSZ
sermonizer
EEIMNORTZZ
intermezzo
EEIMNPPPRT
peppermint
EEIMNPRSTU
episternum
EEIMRSSTYZ
systemizer
EEINNOPRSS
presension
EEINNOPRST
pretension
EEINNOPRTV
prevention
EEINNORTVW
interwoven
EEINNPRTTU
turpentine
EEINNRRTUV
turnverein
EEINOPRRSS
repression
EEINOPRRSV
perversion
EEINOPRSSV
responsive
EEINOPRSSX
expression
EEINOPRSTV
protensive
EEINPRSSTT
persistent
prettiness
EEINPSSSUV
suspensive
EEIOPPRRST
properties
EEIOPPRSSV
oppressive
EEIPPRRTTUY
perpetuity
EEIPPRRSTVY
perversity
EEIPRRTTWY
typewriter
EEIPRSSSTT
stepsister
EEJMNNORUY
journeymen
EELLMNNORT
enrollment
EELLMNOOSY
lonesomely
EELLMNOSSW
mellowness
EELLNOPPRT

propellent	frittering	EFIMNORSTU	EGHHOORSUU
EELLNOQTUY	EFGIINRRTY	misfortune	roughhouse
eloquently	terrifying	EFINOOOPRS	EGHIIINNRT
EELLNOSSWY	EFGIINRSTU	noiseproof	inheriting
yellowness	surfeiting	EFINOOPRSS	EGHIILNNPS
EELMMNOPTY	EFGIINSTTY	profession	plenishing
employment	testifying	EFINORSSST	EGHIILNPRT
EELMNPPSTU	EFGILNRSTU	frostiness	philtering
supplement	flustering	EFLMOOORTY	EGHIILNRSV
EELMNPTUZZ	EFGILNRTTU	tomfoolery	shriveling
puzzlement	fluttering	EFLOPPRSUU	EGHIIMMNRS
EELNPPSSSU	EFGIMNOPRR	purposeful	shimmering
suppleness	performing	EFNOORRSTT	EGHIIMNPRW
EELORSSUVY	preforming	storefront	whimpering
yourselves	EFGINOPRSS	EGGGIINNRS	EGHIIINNNRS
EEMNNRRSUY	professing	sniggering	enshrining
nurserymen	EFGINORRTY	EGGGIINNRT	EGHIINORTZ
EEMOPPRRTY	torrefying	triggering	theorizing
peremptory	EFGINPRTUY	EGGGINSSTU	EGHIINPRSW
EEOPPPRSSU	putrefying	suggesting	whispering
presuppose	EFHIILRSSV	EGGHHIPRSU	EGHIINPUUZ
EEOPPRRSUW	silverfish	hiphuggers	euphuizing
superpower	EFHIINSSST	EGGHIIINNV	EGHIINSTUX
EFFGIINNST	shiftiness	inveighing	extinguish
stiffening	EFHIIRSTTT	EGGHIILNNT	EGHILLOOPU
EFFGIINORT	thriftiest	lightening	philologue
forfeiting	EFHILLOPSW	EGGHIINNRT	EGHILMOOOS
EFFGINOPRR	fellowship	rightening	homologies
proffering	EFHILLOSWY	EGGHIINNTT	EGHILNORVY
EFFGINOSTT	yellowfish	tightening	hoveringly
offsetting	EFHILOPRST	EGGHINNORU	EGHILOOSTT
EFFINSSSTU	shoplifter	roughening	theologist
stuffiness	EFHILORRSU	EGGHINNOTU	EGHIMNORST
EFFLMNNORU	flourisher	toughening	smothering
funnelform	EFHILORSSU	EGGIIILNNV	EGHINNNORT
EFGGHINRTU	flourishes	inveigling	enthroning
gunfighter	EFHILRSSTT	EGGIILMMNR	EGHINNORST
EFGGINORTT	thriftless	glimmering	shortening
forgetting	EFHINORSST	EGGIILNNST	EGHINNRSSU
EFGHIIKNRS	frothiness	glistening	hungriness
kingfisher	EFIIIINNTV	EGGIILNOUZ	EGHINORSST
EFGHIILSTT	infinitive	eulogizing	shoestring
flightiest	EFIIILMPRS	EGGIILNRTT	EGHINRSTTU
EFGHILLSST	simplifier	glittering	shuttering
flightless	EFIIILMPSS	EGGIILRSTW	EGHIORSTTW
EFGHIMNORS	simplifies	wriggliest	ghostwrite
fishmonger	EFIIILNNTY	EGGIINNTTV	EGHLNOOPRY
EFGHINRRTU	infinitely	vignetting	phrenology
furthering	EFIIILSTTU	EGGILLNORV	EGHLOPPRTY
EFGHLLNORU	futilities	grovelling	petroglyph
flugelhorn	EFIIIMNNTY	EGGILNNRSU	EGHMNOOOSU
EFGIIIMNNZ	femininity	gunslinger	homogenous
feminizing	EFIILMNSSS	EGGINNORSS	EGHMORRTYY
EFGIILNQUY	flimsiness	engrossing	hygrometry
liquefying	EFIILNNSST	EGGINOSSTU	EGHOORRTVW
EFGIIMNRTY	flintiness	suggestion	overgrowth
metrifying	EFIILSSTTU	EGGLOORSUY	EGIIILMNPR
EFGIINNRUY	stultifies	gorgeously	imperiling
reunifying	EFIIORSTTU	EGHHIINRTW	EGIIIMNNST
EFGIINPRSY	fortuities	whithering	meningitis
presignify	EFIIRSTTUU	EGHHILOPRY	EGIIINRSTV
EFGIINPRTY	futurities	hieroglyph	revisiting
petrifying	EFILNOSSSU	EGHHILOSTU	EGIIKNRSTT
EFGIINRRTT	fusionless	lighthouse	skittering

EGIILLNOTU
guillotine
EGIILNNOVZ
novelizing
EGIILNOPTX
exploiting
EGIILOPSTT
epiglottis
EGIIMMNORZ
memorizing
EGIIMNNNOT
mentioning
EGIIMNNOST
moistening
EGIIMNPRSS
impressing
EGIIMNPRST
springtime
EGIIMNPRTT
permitting
EGIINNNOPS
pensioning
EGIINNNORV
environing
EGIINNPRRT
reprinting
EGIINNSSST
stinginess
EGIINNSSTW
witnessing
EGIINPPRRS
perspiring
EGIINPRSST
persisting
EGIINRSSTT
stringiest
EGIJNNORUY
journeying
EGIKMNNORW
workingmen
EGILLNOPPR
propelling
EGILLNOSTU
outselling
EGILLNPRSW
wellspring
EGILMMNPTU
plummeting
EGILMNOOOS
monologies
EGILMNPTTY
temptingly
EGILNNRRUY
unerringly
EGILNNSTTU
unsettling
EGILNOSTTU
gluttonies
EGILNOTTUZ
gluttonize
EGILNPPSTU
septupling
EGILNPRSSY

pressingly
EGILNPSTUX
sextupling
EGIMNNORTT
tormenting
EGIMNNORTU
remounting
EGIMNPRTTU
trumpeting
EGINNOPSSS
sponginess
EGINNORTUY
tourneying
EGINNRSTTU
entrusting
EGINOOPRRT
progenitor
EGINOPPRRS
prospering
EGINOPPRSS
oppressing
EGINOPRSTT
protesting
EGINOPSSSS
possessing
EGINORRSTW
songwriter
EGINPRRSSU
pressuring
EGINPRSTTU
sputtering
EGINRSTTTU
stuttering
EGLMNOOOTY
entomology
EGLMNOORUY
numerology
EGNORSSSST
songstress
EHHIILSTVY
thievishly
EHHIOPSSTY
hypothesis
EHIIILNPST
philistine
EHIIKMRRSS
skirmisher
EHIIKMRSSS
skirmishes
EHIILNQRSU
relinquish
EHIIMOPRSV
impoverish
EHIINNPRST
internship
EHIIRRSTTU
urethritis
EHIIRSSTTT
thirstiest
EHILLNRSSS
shrillness
EHILMOPSTY
polytheism
EHILOPSTTY

polytheist
EHIMMNOOST
monotheism
EHIMNNPSTU
punishment
EHIMNOOSTT
monotheist
EHIMNOPSSY
symphonies
EHINNORSST
thorniness
EHINOOPSUU
euphonious
EHINORSSTW
worthiness
EHINSSTTTY
synthetist
EHIOPRRSTY
prehistory
EHLLNOOSSW
hollowness
EHLOPRSTUY
upholstery
EHMNOOSSST
smoothness
EHMOOPRTTY
photometry
EHNOORRTVW
overthrown
EHNOORTTWY
noteworthy
EHNORSTWWY
newsworthy
EIIIINQSTU
iniquities
EIIILLLMRT
milliliter
EIIIMMNSTU
immunities
EIIIMNORST
minorities
EIIIMNPSTU
impunities
EIIIMNNRSST
ministries
EIIIMPRSTU
impurities
EIIIOPRRST
priorities
EIIJLNTUVY
juvenility
EIIKLLNRTW
winterkill
EIIKNQRSSU
quirkiness
EIILLLSUVY
illusively
EIILLMMNNU
millennium
EIILLMOPTY
impolitely
EIILLMPRTU
multiplier
EIILLMPSTU

multiplies
EIILLNOPST
septillion
EIILLNOSTX
sextillion
EIILMMNNTY
imminently
EIILOPSTVY
positively
EIILPRSSST
spiritless
EIIMMSSTTU
mittimuses
EIIMNOPRSS
impression
EIIMNOPRSS
permission
EIIMOPRRSV
improviser
EIIMOPRSUV
impervious
EIINOOPSTX
exposition
EIINPRSSSS
prissiness
EIINRSTUVY
university
EIIOORRSST
sororities
EILLLSSSTY
listlessly
EILLOPRSUY
perilously
EILMNOOOPS
monopolies
EILMNOOOPZ
monopolize
EILMNOOSST
motionless
EILMNOPTTY
impotently
EILMOOPRST
metropolis
EILMOPPRRY
improperly
EILNOORSTU
resolution
EILNOORTUV
revolution
EILNOPPSSS
sloppiness
EILNOPRSST
portliness
EILNPQTTUU
quintuplet
EILNPQTUUX
quintuplex
EILNPRSTUY
unpriestly
EILNRSSTUY
unsisterly
EILOPRSUVY
previously
EILRRSTUVW
liverwurst

EIMNNOOPTT omnipotent	**FFILNRTUUU** unfruitful	**FHILOPRSUW** worshipful	**GIIIIMMNNZ** minimizing
EIMNNRSTTU instrument	**FGGIILNNNY** lignifying	**FHLLRTTUUY** truthfully	**GIIILLMMNNU** illumining
EIMOOQSSTU mosquitoes	**FGGIIINNNR** infringing	**FHLNRTTUUU** untruthful	**GIIILLNNST** instilling
EIMORSSTUY mysterious	**FGGIIINNSY** signifying	**FIIMNORTUY** uniformity	**GIIILNPPUZ** pupilizing
EINNOPSSSU suspension	**FGGIILNORY** glorifying	**FIIMOORSST** fortissimo	**GIIIMMMNNUZ** immunizing
EINOOPPRSS oppression	**FGHHIORRTT** forthright	**FIKLLLLSUY** skillfully	**GIIIMNNPRT** imprinting
EINOOPRRST resorption	**FGHHLOTTUU** thoughtful	**FIOORSTTUU** fortuitous	**GIIIMNOPTZ** optimizing
EINOOPSSSS possession	**FGHIINNRSU** furnishing	**GGGIILNQSU** squiggling	**GIIINNNOOP** opinioning
EINOPPRSTY propensity	**FGHIINORRY** horrifying	**GGGILNNPUU** unplugging	**GIIINNNOUZ** unionizing
EINOPRSSST sportiness	**FGHIINRTUY** thurifying	**GGGILNRSTU** struggling	**GIIKLNNPRS** sprinkling
EINOQRTTUU tourniquet	**FGHILLNSUY** flushingly	**GGIIILMNPR** pilgriming	**GIIKLNRSTY** strikingly
EINPRSSSST spinstress	**FGHILLRTUY** rightfully	**GGIIINNRTU** intriguing	**GIIKNRSTWY** skywriting
EINRSSSTTU trustiness	**FGHILOOSTT** footlights	**GGILLLNOOR** logrolling	**GIILLNOPRY** pillorying
EIOOPPRRRT proprietor	**FGIIINNRTY** nitrifying	**GGILNOPRU** promulging	**GIILMNOPSY** imposingly
EIOOPRRSTY repository	**FGIIINRTVY** vitrifying	**GGILNNOOPR** prolonging	**GIILNNOPRU** purloining
EIOPPRRSTY prosperity	**FGIIJLLNOY** jollifying	**GGILNOOPRU** prologuing	**GIIMNOQSTU** misquoting
EIOPPRSTUV supportive	**FGIIJNSTUY** justifying	**GHHIINRSTT** nightshirt	**GIIMNOSSTY** misogynist
EIOPRRSSUV supervisor	**FGIILLMNOY** mollifying	**GHHIIPRSTW** shipwright	**GIINNOOPRT** portioning
EIOPRRSTUV protrusive	**FGIILLNNUY** nullifying	**GHHLOORTUY** thoroughly	**GIINPRRSSU** surprising
EIOPRSTTTU prostitute	**FGIILMNORU** linguiform	**GHHOORTTUU** throughout	**GIJNNOORSU** sojourning
ELLOOORTWY yellowroot	**FGIILNOSUU** fuliginous	**GHHOOTTTUU** outthought	**GILMMNOOUY** immunology
ELLOPSSSTY spotlessly	**FGIILNPPUY** pulpifying	**GHIIKNNNTU** unthinking	**GILMNOOOST** monologist
ELMNOORSUY enormously	**FGIIMMMNUY** mummifying	**GHIIMNPRTU** triumphing	**GILOORSUVY** vigorously
ELNOORSTUU ultroneous	**FGIIMNORTY** mortifying	**GHIIINNORSU** nourishing	**GINNOOPPST** postponing
ELNOSSSUUY sensuously	**FGIIMNSTYY** mystifying	**GHIIINOPRSW** worshiping	**GINNOOPRSS** sponsoring
EMNNOOOPRT monopteron	**FGIINNRTUY** nutrifying	**GHILNOOSTY** soothingly	**GINOPPRRTU** purporting
ENOOPRSTTU portentous	**FGIINOPRTY** torpidfying	**GHILNORTTT** throttling	**GINOPPRSTU** supporting
ENOPRSSSUY suspensory	**FGIINOPSTX** postfixing	**GHILOOORST** horologist	**GINOPRRSTW** springwort
EOPPRRSSSU suppressor	**FGIINOTTTU** outfitting	**GHILOOPSYY** physiology	**HHILOOPPSY** philosophy
FFGHIIOPPR hippogriff	**FGILLNOTUY** floutingly	**GHINOOPSYY** physiogony	**HHOOPPRSSU** phosphorus
FFGIILLLNU fulfilling	**FGLLNORUWY** wrongfully	**GHLMOOOOSU** homologous	**HIIKLSSTTY** skittishly
FFGIINORTY fortifying	**FHHIOPRSTT** thriftshop	**GHLMOOOPRY** morphology	**HILOOPSSTY** photolysis

HLMOORSUUY
humorously
HLOPRSSUUU
sulphurous
HMOOPSSTUU
posthumous
IIIMNOOPST
imposition
IIIMOPSSTV
positivism
IIINOQRSTU
inquisitor
IILLNOOPST
postillion

IILMMNOOSU
moliminous
IINOOOPPST
opposition
IINORSTTUU
nutritious
IIOOPPRSTU
propitious
IIORSTTUVY
virtuosity
ILLMNOSUUY
luminously
ILMNOOOPST
monopolist

ILMNOOSUUV
voluminous
ILNOOPPRSU
propulsion
ILOOPPRSST
spoilsport
ILOPRSSUUY
spuriously
ILORSTUUVY
virtuously
IMNOOORSUV
omnivorous
INOOOPPRRT
proportion

INOOPPRRSTU
protrusion
LMOSTTUUUU
tumultuous
LOOPSTUUUV
voluptuous
MNNOOOOSTU
monotonous
MNNOOSSUYY
synonymous
NNOOPPRSTU
nonsupport

11-LETTER WORDS

AAAAABBCDRR
abracadabra
AAABCDEEINR
abecedarian
AAABEHIMNPS
amphisbaena
AAABEILLNUV
unavailable
AAABGHIOOPR
agoraphobia
AAACCDEIIMN
academician
AAACCILMNOT
acclamation
AAACCIMNORT
carcinomata
AAACDILOPRX
paradoxical
AAACEEFLMNS
malfeasance
AAACEHIMNTT
anathematic
AAACELMNRST
sacramental
AAACGILMMRT
grammatical
AAACHILMRRT
matriarchal
AAACILLNSTY
satanically
AAADEGHPPRR
paragraphed
AAADHHLPRYZ
haphazardly
AAAEGIILNRT
egalitarian
AAAEGNRTTVX
extravagant
AAAEINSSSST
assassinate
AAAELMNPRTT
apartmental
AAAGGGINRTV
aggravating
AAAGGINORTV
aggravation
AAAGIIMNRRS
agrarianism
AAAIINNQRTU
antiquarian
AABBCDEKLLL
blackballed
AABBCEINORT
bicarbonate

AABBDEEIRTV
abbreviated
AABBEFGLRST
flabbergast
AABBEHIILNT
inhabitable
AABBIIILMNO
bibliomania
AABBLORRSUY
barbarously
AABCCEELLNO
concealable
AABCCELNOTU
accountable
AABCCERRUUY
bureaucracy
AABCDDEORST
broadcasted
AABCDEEERTX
exacerbated
AABCDEHIMMR
chambermaid
AABCDEIKLLM
blackmailed
AABCDELMNRU
candelabrum
AABCDGGIOOR
braggadocio
AABCDGIINRR
barricading
AABCEEHILMP
impeachable
AABCEEHMNRT
antechamber
AABCEEIILMNV
ambivalence
AABCEEILNPS
inescapable
AABCEEILPPR
appreciable
AABCEELNPSS
capableness
AABCEHILMNR
chamberlain
AABCEHLPRSU
purchasable
AABCEIILNNZ
cannibalize
AABCEILNRTT
intractable
AABCEIMNORT
embarcation
AABCEKQRRTU
quarterback

AABCELLOORT
collaborate
AABCFGIINRT
fabricating
AABCFIINORT
fabrication
AABCGIILNRT
calibrating
AABCGILNNNU
unbalancing
AABCGINNORT
carbonating
AABCGINRSTT
abstracting
AABCIILMNNS
cannibalism
AABCIILNORT
calibration
AABCINNOORT
carbonation
AABCINORSTT
abstraction
AABDDNRSSTU
substandard
AABDEEFKRST
breakfasted
AABDEEHHRRS
haberdasher
AABDEEHINRR
harebrained
AABDEEMRSS
embarrassed
AABDEHHIRRT
hairbreadth
AABDEHIILTT
habilitated
AABDEILNOUV
unavoidable
AABDEMNNNOT
abandonment
AABDGGGINNS
sandbagging
AABDILLMNOY
abdominally
AABDILMNRUY
mandibulary
AABDILNOUVY
unavoidably
AABDMOORRRT
mortarboard
AABEEHILPTZ
alphabetize
AABEEIILLNN
inalienable

AABEEIILNPRS
inseparable
AABEEIILPRRR
irreparable
AABEEKLNPSU
unspeakable
AABEEKSSTTW
wastebasket
AABEELLNRTU
unalterable
AABEELLORTY
elaborately
AABEELMPRTU
perambulate
AABEELNORST
treasonable
AABEELNRTTU
untreatable
AABEELPRSTT
breastplate
AABEENRRSTU
sauerbraten
AABEFGIILMN
magnifiable
AABEGHILNOS
fashionable
AABEFIILLQU
qualifiable
AABEFILLMMN
inflammable
AABEFLNORUV
unfavorable
AABEGILNORT
elaborating
AABEIILMMOR
memorabilia
AABEIKMNORT
embarkation
AABEILLRRTZ
trailblazer
AABEILNOORT
elaboration
AABEILNPRSY
inseparably
AABEILPRRRY
irreparably
AABEKLNPSUY
unspeakably
AABELLNRTUY
unalterably
AABELMMNSSY
assemblyman
AABELPRSSSU
surpassable

AABFHILNOSY
fashionably
AABFLNORUVY
unfavorably
AABGHIINTTU
habituating
AABGIINRRTT
arbitrating
AABIIILRTVY
variability
AABIIMNNOOT
abomination
AABIINORRTT
arbitration
AABILMNORTY
abnormality
AABILNSSTTU
substantial
AACCCEJKKRR
crackerjack
AACCCILMSTY
cataclysmic
AACCCNNOTUY
accountancy
AACCDDEIINS
candidacies
AACCDEEEELRT
accelerated
AACCDEILMNU
unacclaimed
AACCDEIMNOP
accompained
AACCDELMTUU
accumulated
AACCDEMMOOT
accommodate
AACCEEINRRT
incarcerate
AACCEEELORRT
accelerator
AACCEFIKRRR
firacracker
AACCEGILORT
categorical
AACCEHLNNNO
nonchalance
AACCEHLRRST
clearstarch
AACCEIILMTZ
acclimatize
AACCEILMPRT
malpractice
AACCEIMNOPR
accompanier
AACCEIORSTU
autocracies
AACCELPRSTU
spectacular
AACCFIIILRS
sacrificial
AACCGIIINNTV
vaccinating
AACCGILLNTU
calculating

AACCHIINRST
anarchistic
AACCHILLOTY
chaotically
AACCIILMNOT
acclimation
AACCIILMPRT
impractical
AACCIINNOTV
vaccination
AACCILLLNOY
laconically
AACCILLNOTU
calculation
AACCILLPRTY
practically
AACCILLSTUY
caustically
AACCILOPPTY
apocalyptic
AACCILOPSUY
capaciously
AACCIMNOPST
accompanist
AACCIORRSTY
aristocracy
AACCLMORTUU
accumulator
AACDDEEIPTT
decapitated
AACDDEHINPP
handicapped
AACDDEIILRZ
radicalized
AACDDEILNSZ
scandalized
AACDEEILRTV
declarative
AACDEEIMNPT
emancipated
AACDEEINRST
ascertained
AACDEEIPPRT
appreciated
AACDEEIRRTTV
reactivated
AACDEELLNNT
cannellated
AACDEELMSTU
emasculated
AACDEEMNNTV
advancement
AACDEFGLMOU
camouflaged
AACDEFIILTT
facilitated
AACDEFILNOT
defalcation
AACDEGIINRT
eradicating
AACDEGILNNR
calendaring
AACDEGIMNRT
demarcating

AACDEHINPPR
handicapper
AACDEIILPTZ
capitalized
AACDEIINORT
eradication
AACDEIINPTT
anticipated
AACDEIIORTV
radioactive
AACDEILMNOT
declamation
AACDEILMNTU
calumniated
AACDEILNORT
declaration
AACDEILNOTU
educational
AACDEILPTTU
capitulated
AACDEILRTTU
articulated
AACDEIMNORY
aerodynamic
AACDEINNNTU
annunciated
AACDEINRSST
incrassated
AACDELMORTY
declamatory
AACDELORRTY
declaratory
AACDFIILRRT
fratricidal
AACDGGINNOS
gasconading
AACDGHIOPRR
cardiograph
AACDGILNNPS
landscaping
AACDGIMNNTU
manducating
AACDHIIOPRS
aphrodisiac
AACDHMOPRSY
psychodrama
AACDILLMNYY
dynamically
AACDIMNNOTU
manducation
AACEEFIMNSS
misfeasance
AACEEGILLNV
evangelical
AACEEILRRST
secretarial
AACEEIMNNNT
maintenance
AACEEINNRSS
renaissance
AACEEIRRSTT
secretariat
AACEEKLMPRT
marketplace

AACEELNPSTU
encapsulate
AACEFFINOTT
affectation
AACEFGLNORT
conflagrate
AACEFILMNOT
malefaction
AACEFMNRTUU
manufacture
AACEGHILOPR
archipelago
AACEGHLOORY
archaeology
AACEGIIMRRS
miscarriage
AACEGIJLNTU
ejaculating
AACEGILLLOR
allegorical
AACEHILLMNO
melancholia
AACEHILLNTU
hallucinate
AACEHMMNNRT
merchantman
AACEHOPRSTT
catastrophe
AACEIILLPRS
capillaries
AACEIILNRRT
interracial
AACEIILSTTU
actualities
AACEIINORTT
ratiocinate
AACEIIOSSTV
associative
AACEIIPPRTT
participate
AACEIJLNOTU
ejaculation
AACEILLPRRT
caterpillar
AACEILMNORT
reclamation
AACEILMNOTX
exclamation
AACEILMRTTU
matriculate
AACEILNORTT
altercation
AACEILNPSTU
incapsulate
AACEILPRTTU
particulate
AACEIMNNOTT
contaminate
AACEIMNOPRT
emancipator
AACEINRSSTU
sanctuaries
AACEKLQRSUV
quacksalver

AACELMORTXY
exclamatory

AACFGIINNST
fascinating

AACFGLNNORT
conflagrant

AACFIINNOST
fascination

AACFILLNRTY
frantically

AACGGIIMNNP
campaigning

AACGGIINSTT
castigating

AACGGILNOTU
cataloguing
coagulating

AACGHIIMNNT
machinating

AACGHILLPRY
calligraphy
graphically

AACGHINOPPR
approaching

AACGHINPRTU
parachuting

AACGHOPRSSU
sarcophagus

AACGIILLNTV
vacillating

AACGIILNNNT
lancinating

AACGIILNTUZ
actualizing

AACGIIMNSTT
masticating

AACGIINNQTU
acquainting

AACGIINOSST
associating

AACGIINOSTT
castigation

AACGIINPSTU
auspicating

AACGIINPTTV
captivating

AACGILLNORY
organically

AACGILNPTTU
catapulting

AACGINNRSTT
transacting

AACHIIMNNOT
machination

AACHIMNNORS
anachronism

AACHIPRSTTU
parachutist

AACIIILMNST
animalistic

AACIIILPPRT
participial

AACIILLNOTV
vacillation

AACIILLRSTY
satirically

AACIILLRSTY
application

AACIIMNNOPT
mancipation

AACIIMNOSTT
mastication

AACIINNNORT
incarnation

AACIINNNOTT
incantation

AACIINOOSST
association

AACIINOPTTV
captivation

AACIINPPRTT
participant

AACILMNOPST
complaisant

AACILNORTVY
clairvoyant

AACINNORSTT
transaction

AADDDEIILPT
dilapidated

AADDEEFGLRT
deflagrated

AADDEEIPPRS
disappeared

AADDEEIPRST
deaspirated

AADDEEMQRSU
masqueraded

AADDEENPPRS
sandpapered

AADDEGGINRZ
aggrandized

AADDEGINNNP
deadpanning

AADDEGINORT
degradation

AADDEIILNTV
invalidated

AADDEINRSTZ
standardize

AADDEJLMSTU
maladjusted

AADEEEGGRTX
exaggerated

AADEEEPRSTX
exasperated

AADEEFGLLLT
flagellated

AADEEGNPRRR
prearranged

AADEEHILRTX
exhilarated

AADEEHMPRST
metaphrased

AADEEILLSSS
salesladies

AADEEILMORT
ameliorated

AADEEINPPRT
appertained

AADEEIRRSSV
adversaries

AADEEMQRRSU
masquerader

AADEFGHNRRT
grandfather

AADEFLMNNTU
fundamental

AADEFLSSTTY
steadfastly

AADEGIILPRZ
plagiarized

AADEGIINRTT
ingratiated

AADEGILLNTV
gallivanted

AADEGILNTUV
devaluating

AADEGINNOTZ
antagonized

AADEGINRTUU
inaugurated

AADEGINSTTV
devastating

AADEGLNRSSU
gradualness

AADEGNNPRRT
grandparent

AADEHIILNNT
annihilated

AADEHIPSTXY
asphyxiated

AADEIILMRST
admiralties

AADEIILMSST
assimilated

AADEIILPRTZ
partialized

AADEILMNPTU
manipulated

AADEILNNQRU
quadrennial

AADEILNOTUV
devaluation

AADEILNRTUZ
naturalized

AADEILOPRTZ
trapezoidal

AADEIMNRSTV
maidservant

AADEINNQRTU
quarantined

AADEINOPRTV
depravation

AADEINORRTT
retardation

AADEINOSTTV
devastation

AADEKNRSSWW
awkwardness

AADENNRRTUW
unwarranted

AADENRSSWWY
waywardness

AADENRSTTUU
unsaturated

AADGGIINPRS
disparaging

AADGHILNNNP
panhandling

AADGHINNRTY
anhydrating

AADGIILNNVZ
vandalizing

AADGIIMNRTZ
dramatizing

AADGIINRRSY
disarraying

AADIINORRT
irradiation

AADIILLNTTU
latitudinal

AADIILNORTT
traditional

AADIILOSUUV
audiovisual

AADILLMNOOT
amontillado

AADILLMORTY
maladroitly

AAEEEHNRRTW
earthenware

AAEEGINPPRR
reappearing

AAEEGINPRST
pageantries

AAEEGMNNRRT
arrangement

AAEEGMNOPRT
pomegranate

AAEEIILMRTZ
materialize

AAEEILLQRTU
equilateral

AAEEILNPRST
planetaries

AAEEKLNRSTT
rattlesnake

AAEELLNRTTY
alternately

AAEFFIIMRTV
affirmative

AAEFGMNRRTY
fragmentary

AAEFIIILMRZ
familiarize

AAEEGGGGINRT
aggregating

AAEGGGINORT
aggregation

AAEGGIINRTV
variegating

AAEGGILNTTU
agglutinate

AAEGGINNRRR
rearranging

AAEGHIMNPRS
managership
AAEGHLLNOXY
hexagonally
AAEGHNPRRST
straphanger
AAEGIIIMNTV
imaginative
AAEGIILLNTV
alleviating
AAEGIILMRST
magisterial
AAEGIILNRTT
retaliating
AAEGILLLNPR
paralleling
AAEGILLNPPR
apparelling
AAEGILLNRST
gallantries
AAEGILMNRTT
maltreating
AAEGIILNNRTT
alternating
AAEGILNQRUU
equiangular
AAEGILNRTTU
triangulate
AAEGIMNNNRRT
arraignment
AAEGINNTTTU
attenuating
AAEGINOPRTV
evaporating
AAEGLLNNTTY
tangentially
AAEGLNRSTTU
strangulate
AAEHIINPSTT
antipathies
AAEHMNORSWW
washerwoman
AAEIIILRSUX
auxiliaries
AAEIILLNOTV
alleviation
AAEIILMMRST
materialism
AAEIILMRSTT
materialist
AAEIILNNOTZ
nationalize
AAEIILNORTZ
rationalize
realization
AAEIILQTTUV
qualitative
AAEIIMNNOTX
examination
AAEIINQRSTU
antiquaries
AAEIKLLTTVY
talkatively
AAEILLNOPPT

appellation
AAEILMNNOTT
lamentation
AAEILMNPRST
paternalism
AAEILMNPRTU
planetarium
AAEILMNRRTU
ultramarine
AAEILNNOPTX
explanation
AAEILNNORTT
alternation
AAEILNNOSST
sensational
AAEILNOPRRT
proletarian
AAEILOPRRTT
proletariat
AAEIMOPPRTX
approximate
AAEINNRRSVY
anniversary
AAEINOOPRTV
evaporation
AAEINOPPRRT
preparation
AAEIOPPPRRT
appropriate
AAELNNRSSTU
naturalness
AAELNRRSSTV
transversal
AAELNRSSTUX
transsexual
AAENNPRRSTT
transparent
AAENQRRSTUW
quartersawn
AAEOOPPRRRT
paratrooper
AAEOPPRRRTY
preparatory
AAFFGIIILNT
affiliating
AAFFIIILNOT
affiliation
AAFFIIMNORT
affirmation
AAFGIINNSTZ
fantasizing
AAFGIINNTTU
infatuating
AAFGILLMRUY
gallimaufry
AAFGILNOSTT
stagflation
AAFIIILMRTY
familiarity
AAFIINNOTTU
infatuation
AAFIMNNNRTY
infantryman
AAGGIILNNOZ

analogizing
AAGGIILNNVZ
galvanizing
AAGGIIMMNNS
mismanaging
AAGGIINRTTV
gravitating
AAGGILNNRTU
granulating
AAGGILNRTTU
gratulating
AAGGINOPPRT
propagating
AAGHILLMNRS
marshalling
AAGHIRSTTWY
straightway
AAGIIILMNNZ
animalizing
AAGIIIMNNNT
maintaining
AAGIIIMNNOT
imagination
AAGIIKNNPST
painstaking
AAGIILNNTTZ
tantalizing
AAGIILNPPTT
palpitating
AAGIIMMNNTY
magnanimity
AAGIIMMSSTT
astigmatism
AAGIINNOSST
assignation
AAGIINNQTTU
antiquating
AAGIINPPTTT
pitapatting
AAGIINRTTVY
antigravity
AAGILNNRSTT
translating
AAGIMMNNOSU
magnanimous
AAGINOOPPRT
propagation
AAHIILNNORT
annihilator
AAHIINPRSST
antiphrasis
AAHIMMNNOPY
nymphomania
AAHINNOPRTY
antiphonary
AAHLLMMORSW
marshmallow
AAIIILNRTTU
utilitarian
AAIILLMPRTY
impartially
AAIILMMNORT
matrimonial
AAIILMNNOST

nationalism
AAIILMNORST
rationalism
AAIILNNOSTT
nationalist
AAIILNNOTTY
nationality
AAIILNOPPTT
palpitation
AAIILNORTTY
rationality
AAILLLOSTWW
swallowtail
AAILMMOPPRS
malapropism
AAILMNOPRTU
manipulator
AAILNNORSTT
translation
AAINNNOPRST
nonpartisan
AALLMNOOSUY
anomalously
AALLNNRTUUY
unnaturally
ABBCCEEHMOR
beachcomber
ABBCDEEFIKO
biofeedback
ABBCEEJLSTU
subjectable
ABBCEHIILOT
bibliotheca
ABBCIILMNOY
bibliomancy
ABBDEIILNTU
indubitable
ABBDEMMNORT
bombardment
ABBDIILNTUY
indubitably
ABBEGINORTW
browbeating
ABBEHINSSSY
babyishness
ABBGILMNOOZ
bamboozling
ABBIILLORTY
bibliolatry
ABBILLOPRTY
probability
ABCCDEHHKNU
hunchbacked
ABCCEEILNOV
conceivable
ABCCEELLLOT
collectable
ABCCEEMNNRU
encumbrance
ABCCEGINNOU
concubinage
ABCCIIMOORT
macrobiotic
ABCCINOOSTT

tobacconist
ABCDEEILPRT
predictable
ABCDEELMMNO
commendable
ABCDEELNNOS
condensable
ABCDEENORRT
centerboard
ABCDEHILSTW
switchblade
ABCDEIILTUY
educability
ABCDEIKLLST
blacklisted
ABCDEINRRST
transcribed
ABCDEINRSTU
disturbance
ABCDGIIKLNS
backsliding
ABCDHINOOPR
branchiopod
ABCDHIORSTW
switchboard
ABCDHNOORRY
hydrocarbon
ABCEEEFLNOR
enforceable
ABCEEEGLLNT
neglectable
ABCEEEILRSV
serviceable
ABCEEEELPRST
respectable
ABCEEFIINRY
beneficiary
ABCEEFINNOT
benefaction
ABCEEGIINOT
abiogenetic
ABCEEGILNRT
celebrating
ABCEEGINRRT
cerebrating
ABCEEHIKRRS
hackberries
ABCEEIILLNTU
ineluctable
ABCEEILNORT
celebration
ABCEEILNSUX
inexcusable
ABCEEILORRV
irrevocable
ABCEEINORRT
cerebration
ABCEEINRRRS
cranberries
ABCEELNORSV
conservable
conversable
ABCEELNOSTT
contestable

ABCEFLMOORT
comfortable
ABCEGIILLOT
bicolligate
ABCEHHKRSUW
bushwhacker
ABCEHLNOTUU
untouchable
ABCEIINOSST
obstinacies
ABCEIKNORTW
cabinetwork
ABCEILLLOPS
collapsible
ABCEILNRSTU
inscrutable
ABCEILNSUXY
inexcusably
ABCEILORRVY
irrevocably
ABCEILORSTT
obstetrical
ABCEINORRTU
carburetion
ABCEINRRRST
transcriber
ABCELNNOTUU
uncountable
ABCEOOOORRRT
corroborate
ABCFGINOSTU
obfuscating
ABCFLMNOORY
conformably
ABCGIIIMNRT
imbricating
ABCGIIKLNRY
bricklaying
ABCGIIKNOUV
bivouacking
ABCGIILNRTU
lubricating
ABCGIINRRTU
rubricating
ABCGILNRTUU
lucubrating
ABCGINRSTTU
subtracting
ABCIIILOSTY
sociability
ABCIILLPTUY
culpability
ABCIILNOPTU
publication
ABCIILNORTU
lubrication
ABCIIMNNOOT
combination
ABCILNRSTUY
inscrutably
ABCILOPRSTU
subtropical
ABCINORSTTU
subtraction

ABDDEEEILRT
deliberated
ABDDEEIILTT
debilitated
ABDDEEIKMRS
disembarked
ABDDEHOOSWX
shadowboxed
ABDDEIILNUV
undividable
ABDDEILORRTW
bladderwort
ABDEEEEGLRU
beleaguered
ABDEEEELMRSS
reassembled
ABDEEELNSST
belatedness
ABDEEEPRSTT
bespattered
ABDEEFIILNN
indefinable
ABDEEGGINRR
gingerbread
ABDEEHILSST
established
ABDEEHIRSTW
breadthwise
ABDEEIILLRZ
liberalized
ABDEEIILMOTZ
metabolized
ABDEEIILNPSS
dispensable
ABDEEIILNRSU
undesirable
ABDEEILORTT
obliterated
ABDEEINNRRW
breadwinner
ABDEEKLOPSU
doublespeak
ABDEEELNNRUU
unendurable
ABDEFIILNNY
indefinably
ABDEGILRRUZ
burglarized
ABDEGNOORUV
aboveground
ABDEHIINNTU
uninhabited
ABDEHLNSSSU
husbandless
ABDEIILMNOT
indomitable
ABDEIIRSSTU
absurdities
ABDEILNRSUY
undesirably
ABDEINORSTU
subordinate
ABDGHIILNNS
blandishing

ABDGHIINNRS
brandishing
ABDGINOPRRS
springboard
ABDGMOORRSS
smorgasbord
ABDHHIOOPRY
hydrophobia
ABDIILMNOTY
indomitably
ABEEEEMNRTV
bereavement
ABEEEERRRTV
reverberate
ABEEEILMMPR
impermeable
ABEEEIMNSST
absenteeism
ABEEEELPRRSV
preservable
ABEEEELNPRST
presentable
ABEEEELNPRTV
preventable
ABEEFGLORTT
forgettable
ABEEFHIRSSZ
zebrafishes
ABEEFILRRTU
irrefutable
ABEEFLLNSSU
balefulness
ABEEFNRRRTU
afterburner
ABEEGHINQTU
bequeathing
ABEEGIINOSS
abiogenesis
ABEEGIKMNRR
reembarking
ABEEGILMNPR
impregnable
ABEEGINORRV
overbearing
ABEEHILMPSS
blasphemies
ABEEHILRSST
reestablish
ABEEHILSSST
establishes
ABEEHILSTUX
exhaustible
ABEEHKNORRT
heartbroken
ABEEHLORRWW
wheelbarrow
ABEEIILMNST
inestimable
ABEEIILNQTU
inequitable
ABEEIILQRTU
equilibrate
ABEEIILNORT
intolerable

ABEEILMNNOT
mentionable
ABEEILNPRSU
insuperable
ABEEILNSSST
beastliness
ABEEINSSSUV
abusiveness
ABEEIPRRRSS
raspberries
ABEELMMNSSY
assemblymen
ABEELNRTTUU
unutterable
ABEFGIINTUY
beautifying
ABEFHLNSSSU
bashfulness
ABEFIIJLSTU
justifiable
ABEFILRRTUY
irrefutably
ABEGHIIMNSV
misbehaving
ABEGHIINNRT
hibernating
ABEGHIIOPRS
biographies
ABEGIIILMMT
immitigable
ABEGIIMSTU
ambiguities
ABEGIIINNRT
inebriating
ABEGIILMNRZ
marbleizing
ABEGIILNRVZ
verbalizing
ABEGINNOPSU
subpoenaing
ABEGMORRSTU
burgomaster
ABEHHIRRSSU
hairbrushes
ABEHIIMORSV
misbehavior
ABEHIINNORT
hibernation
ABEHIKLNNTU
unthinkable
ABEHLMORTWY
blameworthy
ABEHLNORRTY
abhorrently
ABEIIIILLST
liabilities
ABEIIILLNOR
billionaire
ABEIILLMPSU
implausible
ABEIIILMNSTY
inestimably
ABEIIILNQTUY
inequitably

ABEIIRRSTTU
tributaries
ABEIILNORTY
intolerably
ABEILNNPRTU
unprintable
ABEILNOSTTY
obstinately
ABEIMNNSSSU
businessman
ABEINOORSTV
observation
ABEINSSTTUV
substantive
ABELNRTTUUY
unutterably
ABELOPPRSTU
supportable
ABENOPRRTTU
protuberant
ABEOORRSTVY
observatory
ABFGIIIMNRT
fimbriating
ABFIIJLSTUY
justifiably
ABFILMNSTUU
funambulist
ABGGGINNOOT
tobogganing
ABGGIJNORTU
objurgating
ABGGIJNSTUU
subjugating
ABGGINORSTU
subrogating
ABGIIILMMTY
immitigably
ABGIIILNSTZ
stabilizing
ABGIILLNSYZ
syllabizing
ABGIILMNSTU
sublimating
ABGIILNRTUZ
brutalizing
ABGIINRTTTU
attributing
ABGIJNOORTU
objurgation
ABGIJNOSTUU
subjugation
ABGILMOSUUY
ambiguously
ABGIMNOSUUU
unambiguous
ABGINOORSTU
subrogation
ABHHIOOOPPT
photophobia
ABIIILNSTTY
instability
ABIIILSTTUY
suitability

ABIIKLORTWY
workability
ABIILLLNRTY
brilliantly
ABIILLMPSUY
implausibly
ABIILMOSTUY
ambitiously
ABIILNORTTU
tribulation
ABIINOORSTT
abortionist
ABIINORTTTU
attribution
ABILLOORSUY
laboriously
ACCCDENNOOR
concordance
ACCCEHKOORS
cockroaches
ACCCEINOPSU
occupancies
ACCCIMMOORS
macrocosmic
ACCDDEEFIIL
decalcified
ACCDDEEINNS
incandesced
ACCDEEELNOS
adolescence
ACCDEEFNORY
confederacy
ACCDEEHIORS
archdiocese
ACCDEEIMORS
democracies
ACCDEEIRTUX
excruciated
ACCDEELNOSV
convalesced
ACCDEENORST
consecrated
ACCDEFINOST
confiscated
ACCDEGIINST
desiccating
ACCDEHHITTT
chitchatted
ACCDEHHRSSU
archduchess
ACCDEIILNOT
conciliated
ACCDEIKLNST
candlestick
ACCDEILMOPT
complicated
ACCDEILQRUY
quadricycle
ACCDEINOOTU
coeducation
ACCDEINPRSY
discrepancy
ACCDGILNORY
accordingly

ACCEEEENNSV
evanescence
ACCEEEFILMN
maleficence
ACCEEFIIRTT
certificate
ACCEEFIKRRR
firecracker
ACCEEHILNRT
chanticleer
ACCEEHIORST
theocracies
ACCEEHLLNRY
chancellery
ACCEEIILNRT
electrician
ACCEEIILNNST
incalescent
ACCEEINQSTU
acquiescent
ACCEEIOPRRT
reciprocate
ACCEEIORSSS
accessories
ACCEENNNOTU
countenance
ACCEENNORTT
concentrate
ACCEFFIIOSU
efficacious
ACCEFILORSU
calciferous
ACCEGHIKMNT
checkmating
ACCEGHINNOR
encroaching
ACCEGIINQSU
acquiescing
ACCEHIIMNST
mechanistic
ACCEHIIRSTU
eucharistic
ACCEHILLMNO
melancholic
ACCEHILLNTY
technically
ACCEHIRSSTT
scratchiest
ACCEIIILSTV
acclivities
ACCEIIINRST
intricacies
ACCEIILPRRT
precritical
ACCEIINNOSU
insouciance
ACCEIINOSTV
concavities
ACCEIKNRSSS
carsickness
ACCEILNNOTY
anticyclone
ACCEILNORTT
contractile

ACCEIMMNOTU
communicate

ACCEIMNOORS
monocracies

ACCEINNORTV
contrivance

ACCELMMNOOP
commonplace

ACCENOORRST
consecrator

ACCENPRTUUU
acupuncture

ACCFGIIINRS
sacrificing

ACCFINNOORT
confraction

ACCGIIINRTZ
cicatrizing

ACCGIILNNTU
inculcating

ACCGIILNRTU
circulating

ACCGIINNOOS
occasioning

ACCGILLNOOT
collocating

ACCGINNORTT
contracting

ACCHIIPRSTY
psychiatric

ACCHILLNORY
chronically

ACCHILLPSYY
psychically

ACCIIILOSST
socialistic

ACCIILNOORT
conciliator

ACCILORRTUY
circulatory

ACCIMMNNOOTT
concomitant

ACCINNOOOTV
convocation

ACCINNOORTT
contraction

ACDDEEEELRT
decelerated

ACDDEEEIPRT
depreciated

ACDDEEFNNOT
codefendant

ACDDEEIKRST
sidetracked

ACDDEEIOTTX
detoxicated

ACDDEGIORSU
discouraged

ACDDEIIOSST
dissociated

ACDDEINOORT
coordinated

ACDEEEEHLRR
cheerleader

ACDEEEFFTTU
effectuated

ACDEEEFLNRT
needlecraft

ACDEEEFNORT
confederate

ACDEEEILNRV
deliverance

ACDEEEIRSTV
eviscerated

ACDEEENPRRT
carpentered

ACDEEEPRRTU
recuperated

ACDEEFIILTT
felicitated

ACDEEGGNORT
congregated

ACDEEGHNRRU
undercharge

ACDEEGHORRV
overcharged

ACDEEGILNTT
delectating

ACDEEGINPRT
deprecating

ACDEEGINRST
desecrating

ACDEEGKLNOW
acknowledge

ACDEEHIMNRS
merchandise

ACDEEHNRRTU
unchartered

ACDEEIILPSZ
specialized

ACDEEIINNRT
incinerated

ACDEEILNNST
clandestine

ACDEEILNRTZ
centralized

ACDEEILRSUZ
secularized

ACDEEILRTTU
reticulated

ACDEEIMNPRT
predicament

ACDEEIMOSTT
domesticate

ACDEEINORSS
secondaries

ACDEEINORST
considerate

ACDEEIOOQTUV
equivocated

ACDEELNOPRW
candlepower

ACDEEMNOPSS
encompassed

ACDEEMNOPST
compensated

ACDEFGILRSU
disgraceful

ACDEFIIINOT
edification

ACDEFIIIRSU
fiduciaries

ACDEGHILLNT
candlelight

ACDEGIILLOO
ideological

ACDEGIILMNT
maledicting

ACDEGIILNTU
elucidating

ACDEGIINPRT
predicating

ACDEGILLNOT
decollating

ACDEGINSSTU
decussating

ACDEHIINORS
diachronies

ACDEHILNORT
chlorinated

ACDEHLNPRTU
thunderclap

ACDEIIJLPRU
prejudicial

ACDEIIILLMNY
medicinally

ACDEIILLNTY
identically

ACDEIILMNOT
malediction

ACDEIILMOPS
diplomacies

ACDEIILNNOT
declination

ACDEIILNOTU
elucidation

ACDEIILNOTV
valediction

ACDEIINORRT
doctrinaire

ACDEIINOTTX
intoxicated

ACDEILLLMOY
melodically

ACDEILMORTY
maledictory

ACDEILNOOST
consolidate

ACDEILORTVY
valedictory

ACDEINNORST
constrained

ACDEINNRTUU
uncurtained

ACDEINOPSTT
constipated

ACDEINOSTTW
wainscotted

ACDEMMNOORT
commendator

ACDEMNNORTU
countermand

ACDEMNORTUY
documentary

ACDEFIIIRSU
fiduciaries

ACDFFGHINNU
handcuffing

ACDFFGIINRT
diffracting

ACDFFGILNOS
scaffolding

ACDFFIILMOO
officialdom

ACDFFIINORT
diffraction

ACDGGHIINRS
discharging

ACDGHIINNSW
sandwiching

ACDGHIINPST
dispatching

ACDGIIILMNS
disclaiming

ACDGIIINNTV
vindicating

ACDGIILNOST
dislocating

ACDGIILNPTU
duplicating

ACDGIINNSTY
syndicating

ACDGIINRSTT
distracting

ACDHHIOPRRS
harpsichord

ACDHIORSTTY
hydrostatic

ACDIIILLOTY
idiotically

ACDIIINNOTV
vindication

ACDIILNNOOT
conditional

ACDIILNOOST
dislocation

ACDIILNOPTU
duplication

ACDIINORSTT
distraction

ACEEEFFFRTT
aftereffect

ACEEEHIMNRS
archenemies

ACEEEHIMNTV
achievement

ACEEEHIRRST
treacheries

ACEEEHIRTTZ
catheterize

ACEEEHKLNRT
leatherneck

ACEEEHLLNRT
chanterelle

ACEEEILMNPT
mantelpiece

ACEEEILNQUV
equivalence**

ACEEEILNRRV
irrelevance
ACEEEILRSTU
electuaries
ACEEEIMNRRS
mercenaries
ACEEEIMPRST
masterpiece
ACEEEINNRST
centenaries
ACEEEINRSSS
necessaries
ACEEEINSSTT
necessitate
ACEEEIRRSST
secretaries
ACEEEJKLPST
steeplejack
ACEEELLMNOV
malevolence
ACEEELLSSSY
ceaselessly
ACEEELMMNPT
emplacement
ACEEELMNPRT
replacement
ACEEELPRSTT
letterspace
ACEEFFILNTU
ineffectual
ACEEFFLLTUY
effectually
ACEEFHINNRS
enfranchise
ACEEFLLNRST
crestfallen
ACEEFLNRSSU
carefulness
ACEEFMNOPRR
performance
ACEEGHINNRT
interchange
ACEEGHINRRS
researching
ACEEGHPRRSU
supercharge
ACEEGILSTTU
gesticulate
ACEEHHIIRRS
hierarchies
ACEEHIILPTT
epithetical
ACEEHIINNRT
inheritance
ACEEHILORTT
theoretical
ACEEHIMMNPT
impeachment
ACEEHINPRST
pentarchies
ACEEHINPRTT
parenthetic
ACEEHIPRTTU
therapeutic

ACEEHIPRTVY
hyperactive
ACEEHMMNNRT
merchantmen
ACEEHMNNNTT
enchantment
ACEEHNNRSST
enchantress
ACEEHORRSTT
orchestrate
ACEEHORRSTU
treacherous
ACEEIILPSST
specialties
ACEEIIPPRTT
peripatetic
precipitate
ACEEIKNSSSS
seasickness
ACEEILLNNSS
cleanliness
ACEEILNNORT
intolerance
ACEEILNOPTX
exceptional
ACEEILNQUVY
equivalency
ACEEILNRSSY
necessarily
ACEEILPSTUV
speculative
ACEEIMMORST
commiserate
ACEEIMOSSTV
vasectomies
ACEEINNNSST
ancientness
ACEEINNRSST
certainness
ACEEINOPTTX
expectation
ACEEIORRTTV
retroactive
ACEEIRRSSTTU
resuscitate
ACEELLNOSTT
constellate
ACEELMNOPTT
contemplate
ACEELNORSTU
counterseal
ACEEMMMOORT
commemorate
ACEENNOPRTU
counterpane
ACEENNRSSUY
unnecessary
ACEFGIIMNNT
magnificent
ACEFGIIINNR
refinancing
ACEFGILNRTU
centrifugal
ACEFGINORST

forecasting
ACEFIILPRSU
superficial
ACEFIIMORRS
formicaries
ACEFILLORUW
cauliflower
ACEFILOORST
olfactories
ACEFILOSTUY
facetiously
ACEFIPRRSTT
priestcraft
ACEFLMOOORX
coxofemoral
ACEGGHILLNN
challenging
ACEGGILRSST
suraggliest
ACEGGINNORU
encouraging
ACEGHHILRST
searchlight
ACEGHHOOPRR
choreograph
ACEGHIILORS
oligarchies
ACEGHIIMMNZ
mechanizing
ACEGHIKLLNS
shellacking
ACEGHILLOOT
theological
ACEGHILOPSY
geophysical
ACEGHINNOPR
chaperoning
ACEGHINOPRR
reproaching
ACEGIILNNRT
interlacing
ACEGIILNPTX
explicating
ACEGIILOSTT
egotistical
ACEGIIMNPRT
imprecating
ACEGIINNNTU
enunciating
ACEGIINNRTT
interacting
ACEGIINORTX
excoriating
ACEGIINRTTX
extricating
ACEGIINSSTZ
ecstasizing
ACEGILNNSUY
unceasingly
ACEGILNOPRT
percolating
ACEGILNORRT
correlating
ACEGILNPSTU

speculating
ACEGILNRSSY
caressingly
ACEGILRRTUU
agriculture
ACEGINOOPRT
cooperating
ACEGINOPRRT
procreating
ACEGINORRTT
retroacting
ACEGMNNORSS
congressman
ACEHHIILMOP
hemophiliac
ACEHHOPRTYY
hypothecary
ACEHIMMNNOOS
monomachies
ACEHIMMOPRT
metamorphic
ACEHIMNORSS
marchioness
ACEHIMOPRST
atmospheric
ACEHIMPSSTY
metaphysics
ACEHIMPSTTY
sympathetic
ACEHINOPRRS
chairperson
ACEHIPRSSUY
hyperacusis
ACEHLLMSSTY
matchlessly
ACEIIMMNNRT
incriminate
ACEIIIQSTUV
acquisitive
ACEIILLMPRY
empirically
ACEIILLNSTT
scintillate
ACEIILNOORT
coalitioner
ACEIILNRTTY
intricately
ACEIILPRTUY
peculiarity
ACEIIMNORTZ
romanticize
ACEIINNNOTU
enunciation
ACEIINNORRT
incinerator
ACEIINNORTT
interaction
ACEIINPPRTT
precipitant
ACEILLLNRUU
unicellular
ACEILLNRSTY
crystalline
ACEILLOORRS

corollaries
ACEILLOPPSY
episcopally
ACEILLOQUVY
equivocally
ACEILLRSTYZ
crystallize
ACEILMNOOPW
policewoman
ACEILNNNOSS
nonsensical
ACEILNNNOTT
continental
ACEILNNSSTY
incessantly
ACEILNOPSTU
speculation
ACEILNOQUUV
unequivocal
ACEILNORTUV
countervail
ACEILORSUVY
veraciously
ACEIMMORRTU
crematorium
ACEINNNNSSU
uncanniness
ACEINNRTTUY
uncertainty
ACEINOOOOPRT
cooperation
ACEINOOPPRT
incorporate
ACEINPPRSSS
scrappiness
ACEINRSSSSU
narcissuses
ACEIOOPRTVV
provocative
ACEIOOQRTUV
equivocator
ACELLNOSSSU
callousness
ACELMRSTUUU
musculature
ACELNNRSTTU
translucent
ACELNORSUVY
cavernously
ACELNOSSTTU
sansculotte
ACELOPRSTUY
speculatory
ACEMMNOORTT
commentator
ACEMMNOPRTT
compartment
ACEMORSSTTU
scoutmaster
ACENOPRRTTU
counterpart
ACENOSSSUUV
vacuousness
ACFFGIIINOT

officiating
ACFFGIIKNRT
trafficking
ACFFGINOSTU
suffocating
ACFFINOOSTU
suffocation
ACFGHIINNRS
franchising
ACFGIIINNST
significant
ACFGIILNSSY
classifying
ACFGIINNORT
fornicating
ACFGIINNSTY
sanctifying
ACFGILNTTUU
fluctuating
ACFIIINNOTU
unification
ACFIINNOORT
fornication
ACFIIOPRRTU
purificator
ACFILNNOOSU
confusional
ACFILNOTTUU
fluctuation
ACGGHINRRSU
surcharging
ACGGIIMMNRS
scrimmaging
ACGGIJNNOTU
conjugating
ACGGINORRTU
corrugating
ACGHHILOOPR
holographic
ACGHHNOOPRR
chronograph
ACGHIIMMNNOP
championing
ACGHOPPRRTY
cryptograph
ACGIIIILNTZ
italicizing
ACGIIILMNPT
implicating
ACGIIILNOSZ
socializing
ACGIILLLLOY
illogically
ACGIILLNOST
oscillating
ACGIILMNNOP
complaining
ACGIILMNNTU
culminating
ACGIILMNOPR
proclaiming
ACGIILNNOTU
inoculating
ACGIILNNUUZ

vulcanizing
ACGIILNTTUV
cultivating
ACGIIMNOSST
agnosticism
ACGIIMNNRRSY
miscarrying
ACGIIMNRTTU
micturating
ACGIINNOSTW
wainscoting
ACGIINORSTZ
ostracizing
ACGIJNNOUTU
conjugation
ACGILNORSUY
carousingly
ACGINNOPSTY
syncopating
ACGINNORSTT
contrasting
ACGINNPTTUU
punctuating
ACGINOPRRTT
protracting
ACHHILOPRSS
scholarship
ACHHOPPSTYY
psychopathy
ACHIILLMSWY
whimsically
ACHIINNRSTU
unchristian
ACHIMNOPTYY
amphictyony
ACHIMOPPSSU
hippocampus
ACHLLOOPRST
chloroplast
ACIIILMNOPT
implication
ACIIILNNNOT
inclination
ACIIINOQSTU
acquisition
ACIILLMNOSS
colonialism
ACIILLMOSUY
maliciously
ACIILLNNSTT
scintillant
ACIILLNOOST
oscillation
ACIILLNPPRY
principally
ACIILMNNOTU
culmination
ACIILMNOOPT
compilation
ACIILMNSTUY
masculinity
ACIILNNOOTU
inoculation
ACIILNOTTUV

cultivation
ACIILOSUVVY
vivaciously
ACIIMMNOSST
monasticism
ACIIMNOORSU
acrimonious
ACIINRTTTUY
taciturnity
ACILMRSTUUY
muscularity
ACILNNOOOST
consolation
ACILNPTTUUY
punctuality
ACILOORSTUY
atrociously
ACILOORSUVY
voraciously
ACIMMOPSTTY
symptomatic
ACIMNOOPTTU
computation
ACINNNNOOST
inconsonant
ACINNOOPRTT
contraption
ACINNOOPSTY
syncopation
ACINNOPTTUU
punctuation
ACINOOOPRRT
corporation
ACINOOOPRTV
provocation
ACINOOPRRST
conspirator
ACINOOPRRTT
protraction
ACINOORRSUV
carnivorous
ADDDEEGIRRS
disregarded
ADDDEEHNNRU
underhanded
ADDDEGIKLNS
skedaddling
ADDEEEEGNRT
degenerated
ADDEEEFILRZ
federalized
ADDEEEEHNPPR
apprehended
ADDEEEOPRSS
desperadoes
ADDEEGHNORW
wrongheaded
ADDEEHHNRTU
thunderhead
ADDEEHILNPR
philandered
ADDEEIILNST
disentailed
ADDEEIJOPRZ

jeopardized
ADDEEILMORZ
demoralized
ADDEEIMORRS
dromedaries
ADDEEINOPRR
preordained
ADDEELNPRUY
underplayed
ADDEELNRUUV
undervalued
ADDEENRSTTU
understated
ADDEGHINRTY
dehydrating
ADDEGILMNNY
maddeningly
ADDEGIMNORZ
gormandized
ADDEIOPPRSV
disapproved
ADDELNNTUUY
undauntedly
ADEEEEGNRRT
regenerated
ADEEEFILNRT
deferential
ADEEEFNRSTT
fenestrated
ADEEEGHLPRT
telegraphed
ADEEEGILMNR
legerdemain
ADEEEGILNRZ
generalized
ADEEEGILNVZ
evangelized
ADEEEGIMNRR
gendarmerie
ADEEEGLMMRT
telegrammed
ADEEEHMORST
homesteader
ADEEEIMNRTT
determinate
ADEEEIMPRTT
premeditate
ADEEEINNRTT
entertained
ADEEEIORRTT
deteriorate
ADEEEJNRTUV
rejuvenated
ADEEELPRSTY
desperately
ADEEEMNRRTU
remunerated
ADEEENRSSSV
adverseness
ADEEEPPRRTT
perpetrated
ADEEEPPRTTU
perpetuated
ADEEFFIINRT

differentia
ADEEFGGLOPR
leapfrogged
ADEEFGHORRT
forgathered
ADEEFGILNOR
freeloading
ADEEFINRRTZ
fraternized
ADEEFLLORST
forestalled
ADEEFNRRRST
transferred
ADEEGGIINRS
disagreeing
ADEEGGINNNR
endangering
ADEEGGLORTW
waterlogged
ADEEGHLRSTU
slaughtered
ADEEGHNNPRW
grandnephew
ADEEGHNORTY
hydrogenate
ADEEGIILMTT
legitimated
ADEEGIILNNT
delineating
ADEEGIILNTZ
gelatinized
ADEEGILLORZ
allegorized
ADEEGIMNPRT
impregnated
ADEEGINNORV
endeavoring
ADEEGINORRZ
reorganized
ADEEGMNRRRY
gerrymander
ADEEHHISTWW
whitewashed
ADEEHHLORRS
shareholder
ADEEHILNSST
deathliness
ADEEHIRRRSS
hairdresser
ADEEHLLORSV
slaveholder
ADEEHLMNOTT
mentholated
ADEEHNNRSSU
unharnessed
ADEEIILMMTY
immediately
ADEEIILMNRZ
mineralized
ADEEIILMSTV
medievalist
ADEEIILNNOT
delineation
ADEEIILRTVZ

revitalized
ADEEIIMNSST
disseminate
ADEEIIPRSTV
depravities
ADEEIIRSSTV
adversities
ADEEILMNRST
streamlined
ADEEILNRTUZ
neutralized
ADEEILNSSUZ
sensualized
ADEEILPRSSU
displeasure
ADEEIMMNORS
misdemeanor
ADEEIMNNRTT
determinant
ADEEIMNRSTY
sedimentary
ADEEINNRTTV
inadvertent
ADEEINOPRST
desperation
ADEEINOPTTT
potentiated
ADEEIPRSTUZ
pasteurized
ADEEIPRTTUV
vituperated
ADEEELOPPRTU
repopulated
ADEEMNORSTT
demonstrate
ADEEMNPTTTU
unattempted
ADEEMNRSTTU
menstruated
ADEENRRSSTV
transversed
ADEENRSSTUV
adventuress
ADEFFILNRTU
faultfinder
ADEFGIILNOT
defoliating
ADEFGILNORS
dragonflies
ADEFIILNQUU
unqualified
ADEFIILNRTT
infiltrated
ADEFILSSTTU
distasteful
ADEFMNORRST
transformed
ADEFNORRSSW
forwardness
ADEGGGIINNS
disengaging
ADEGGIINNRT
denigrating
ADEGGIINNST

designating
ADEGGILNNOT
goaltending
ADEGHINNRTU
unthreading
ADEGHMNOOPR
monographed
ADEGHMNORRT
grandmother
ADEGIIINRST
dignitaries
ADEGIILNOTV
dovetailing
ADEGIIMNRTT
readmitting
ADEGIIMNTTU
unmitigated
ADEGIIMSTTZ
stigmatized
ADEGIINNOST
designation
ADEGIINNTUV
undeviating
ADEGIINORTV
invigorated
ADEGIINPRTU
repudiating
ADEGIINRSTV
advertising
ADEGIINRTTU
ingratitude
ADEGIINRTTX
extraditing
ADEGIJNRSTU
readjusting
ADEGIKNNRTU
undertaking
ADEGILNNRUY
underlaying
ADEGILNNRWY
wanderingly
ADEGINNQRSU
squandering
ADEGINNRRTU
underrating
ADEGINORRVW
overdrawing
ADEGINPRSTU
depasturing
ADEHHIORRSS
horseradish
ADEGINNRTUV
adventuring
ADEHIIIOPST
idiopathies
ADEHIMPSTYZ
sympathized
ADEHINNRTTW
handwritten
ADEHINQRRTU
hindquarter
ADEHIPRSSTW
stewardship
ADEIIIPRSST

disparities
ADEIIISSSTU
assiduities
ADEIILLMNTU
illuminated
ADEIILLORTY
editorially
ADEIIMNOPSS
impassioned
ADEIINNNOTT
indentation
ADEIINNOOPT
opinionated
ADEIINNOSTT
destination
ADEIINOPRTT
partitioned
trepidation
ADEIINOPRTV
deprivation
ADEIINORTTX
extradition
ADEIIOPPRTT
propitiated
ADEIILLRSTTU
illustrated
ADEIMMNNOPU
pandemonium
ADEIMNNOORT
denominator
ADEIMNNQRUU
quadrennium
ADEIMNRRTUY
rudimentary
ADEIMNRSTTT
transmitted
ADEIMNRSTUV
adventurism
ADEINNSSTUU
unsustained
ADEINOOPPRT
apportioned
ADEINOOPRTT
deportation
ADEJMNNORTU
adjournment
ADELMNORRTU
ultramodern
ADENOPRRSTT
transported
ADENORSSSUU
arduousness
ADENORSTUUV
adventurous
ADFGIILLNSU
fusillading
ADFGIINORSV
disfavoring
ADGGIIMNNOTZ
dogmatizing
ADGHHOPRRYY
hydrography
ADGHIILMNNS
mishandling

ADGHIIMNNOS
admonishing
ADGHIINNRTW
handwriting
ADGHIINRTWW
withdrawing
ADGIIILNQTU
liquidating
ADGIIINNNOT
indignation
ADGIIINPSST
dissipating
ADGIILMNNST
dismantling
ADGILMNOPSY
psalmodying
ADGILNPQRUU
quadrupling
ADGNNOORSUY
androgynous
ADIIILNOQTU
liquidation
ADIILLNOQRU
quadrillion
ADIIOOPRSUV
avoirdupois
AEEEEHILRTZ
etherealize
AEEEEFGIKNPS
safekeeping
AEEEFGIRRRT
refrigerate
AEEEFHINRRT
hereinafter
AEEEFHLRSST
featherless
AEEEGGILNOS
genealogies
AEEEGLMNNRT
enlargement
AEEEHILNNPT
elephantine
AEEEHINSTTZ
anesthetize
AEEEHLMPPRT
pamphleteer
AEEEHNPRSST
parentheses
AEEEIMNPRTT
intemperate
AEEEIMNRTTX
exterminate
AEEEINNRRTT
entertainer
AEEEINSSSVV
evasiveness
AEEEKLLPRSW
sleepwalker
AEEELMPRTTY
temperately
AEEELMRSSSU
measureless
AEEELPQRSTU
plateresque

AEEEMMNPRTT
temperament
AEEEMMNNRSTU
measurement
AEEEMPRRTTU
temperature
AEEEENNRSSST
earnestness
AEEFFGRSTTU
suffragette
AEEFHHORSTU
housefather
AEEFHLNSSTU
hatefulness
AEEFKLNSSUW
wakefulness
AEEFMNOPRTY
forepayment
AEEGGGINRST
segregating
AEEGGHIOPRS
geographies
AEEGGINORST
segregation
AEEGGIRRTTU
regurgitate
AEEGHINNRTT
threatening
AEEGHIPPRTW
paperweight
AEEGIIKLLLS
skilligalee
AEEGIILLSTV
legislative
AEEGIIMMNNRX
reexamining
AEEGIINRRTT
reiterating
AEEGIINRTTV
vinaigrette
AEEGIINSTTV
investigate
AEEGILLRSTU
legislature
AEEGILMNNSS
meaningless
AEEGILNRSTV
everlasting
AEEGIMNNRTU
enumerating
AEEGIMNNRUV
maneuvering
AEEGIMNOTTW
witenagemot
AEEGINNORTX
exonerating
AEEGINNPRTT
penetrating
AEEGINNRTTV
anteverting
AEEGINNTTUX
extenuating
AEEGINORRTT
interrogate

AEEGINRRSST
reasserting
AEEGIOPRRTV
prerogative
AEEGLLMNNTY
gentlemanly
AEEGLMNNOTW
gentlewoman
AEEGNNRSSST
strangeness
AEEHHILNRTU
unhealthier
AEEHHILNSST
healthiness
AEEHHILRTWW
wherewithal
AEEHHNORSTT
hearthstone
AEEHIKLNRSS
harnesslike
AEEHILNPSSS
shapeliness
AEEHILNRSST
earthliness
AEEHILNSSTW
wealthiness
AEEHINPRSST
parenthesis
AEEHINSSTTT
anesthetist
AEEHIORSTTX
heterotaxis
AEEHKLLRRST
rathskeller
AEEHLLMSSSY
shamelessly
AEEHLNPSSSS
haplessness
AEEHMNORSWW
washerwomen
AEEHNNORRSTT
northeaster
AEEHORSSTTU
southeaster
AEEIIILMPRZ
imperialize
AEEIILNRRST
itineraries
AEEIILMMORZ
memorialize
AEEIILMNSTT
mentalities
AEEIILMRRST
semitrailer
AEEIILNNRTZ
internalize
AEEIILNSTTX
existential
AEEIIMPRSTV
semiprivate
AEEIINNTTTV
inattentive
AEEIINOPRTV
inoperative

AEEIIRSSTTU
austerities
AEEIKLNRSTV
servantlike
AEEILLNNPRY
perennially
AEEILLNSSTY
essentially
AEEILMNNSTT
sentimental
AEEILNOPRSZ
personalize
AEEILNOPRTT
interpolate
AEEILNRRSUV
vulneraries
AEEILNRRTUZ
neutralizer
AEEILNTTTVY
tentatively
AEEILNTTUVY
eventuality
AEEILPRSTUV
superlative
AEEILQRRSTU
quarterlies
AEEILRRRSTT
terrestrial
AEEILRSSTVY
assertively
AEEIMMNNPRT
impermanent
AEEIMMRSSTY
asymmetries
AEEIMNNORTU
enumeration
mountaineer
AEEIMNOPRST
impersonate
AEEIMNORSST
monasteries
AEEIMNSSSSV
massiveness
AEEINNOPRTT
penetration
AEEINNTTTUV
unattentive
AEEINORRSTV
reservation
AEEINPSSSSV
passiveness
AEEIOPPRRTX
expropriate
AEEIORRSTTV
restorative
AEEKMPRRSTU
supermarket
AEEKNPRRSTU
supertanker
AEELLMORRST
steamroller
AEELLNSSSSW
lawlessness
AEELLPPRTUY
perpetually
AEELLSSSTTY
tastelessly
AEELMOQRRSU
quarrelsome
AEELNOPRSSS
salesperson
AEEMNORSSTT
easternmost
AEENOPRRSTT
paternoster
AEEOPPRRRTT
perpetrator
AEFFGIIMNRR
reaffirming
AEFFKNRRRTU
frankfurter
AEFGGIMNNRT
fragmenting
AEFGIILNOTX
exfoliating
AEFGIIMNNST
manifesting
AEFGILLLLNNN
flannelling
AEFGILNNRTU
unfaltering
AEFGINNNSTU
unfastening
AEFGINNORRW
forewarning
AEFGINOPRRT
perforating
AEFGINORRSW
forswearing
AEFGINORSTT
foretasting
AEFHHLLLTUY
healthfully
AEFHHLLNTUU
unhealthful
AEFHLMNRSSU
harmfulness
AEFIILLNNTU
influential
AEFIILMORST
formalities
AEFIIMNORTV
informative
AEFIINNOSTT
infestation
AEFIINOPRST
profanities
AEFILNORSUY
nefariously
AEFIMNNNRTY
infantrymen
AEFIMNOORRT
reformation
AEFINOOPRRT
perforation
AEFLLMRSTUY
masterfully
AEFLNOOPSTU

teaspoonful
AEFLNORTTUY
fortunately
AEFMNORRRST
transformer
AEFMOORRRTY
reformatory
AEFNNORTTUU
unfortunate
AEGGHIILNNT
nightingale
AEGGIILLNST
legislating
AEGGIILMNNR
malingering
AEGGIIMNNRT
germinating
AEGGIIMNNTZ
magnetizing
AEGGIINNOTT
negotiating
AEGGIINNRTT
integrating
AEGGINNOTXY
oxygenating
AEGHHINNPTY
hyphenating
AEGHHINSSTU
haughtiness
AEGHHNOPRTY
ethnography
AEGHIIMNPSZ
emphasizing
AEGHIIMNPTZ
empathizing
AEGHIKLNNRY
hankeringly
AEGHIKLNRTW
nightwalker
AEGHILLNNRT
enthralling
AEGHILLNOSW
wholesaling
AEGHILNOOST
anthologies
AEGHILOOPST
pathologies
AEGHIMOPRSS
seismograph
AEGHINNSSTU
naughtiness
AEGHINORSUW
warehousing
AEGHIRSSTTT
straightest
AEGHLOOPRSY
phraseology
AEGHOPPRRSS
grasshopper
AEGIIILMNNT
eliminating
AEGIIILMNPR
primigenial
AEGIIILNRSZ

serializing
AEGIILLNOST
legislation
AEGIILMNORT
meliorating
AEGIILNNTTV
ventilating
AEGIILNSUXZ
sexualizing
AEGIILRSTUV
vulgarities
AEGIIMNNORT
germination
AEGIIMNNRTT
terminating
AEGIIMNRSTT
mistreating
AEGIINNOOTT
negotiation
AEGIINNORST
resignation
AEGIINNORTT
integration
AEGIINNORTT
orientating
AEGIINNRRST
restraining
AEGIINNRSTT
reinstating
AEGIINPPRTW
wiretapping
AEGIINPRTTX
extirpating
AEGIKMMNRRY
merrymaking
AEGILLMOOPS
megalopolis
AEGILLRRRUY
irregularly
AEGILMOOSSY
semasiology
AEGILNOPPRV
overlapping
AEGILNPRSTT
splattering
AEGILNQRUVY
quaveringly
AEGIMNNNORT
ornamenting
AEGINNPRRTU
enrapturing
AEGINPRSSST
trespassing
AEHIILLPSTT
philatelist
AEHIILOPSTZ
hospitalize
AEHIINOPRRS
parishioner
AEHIIORSTTU
authorities
AEHILNPRSST
shinplaster
AEHIMNOPRST
misanthrope

AEHIMORSTTX thermotaxis	**AEIIMRRTTUV** triumvirate	**AFGGILNRTUU** fulgurating	**AGGIINNORRS** garrisoning
AEHINNPPSSU unhappiness	**AEIINNOORTT** orientation	**AFGHHIILNTU** highfalutin	**AGHHIIMNRST** nightmarish
AEHINOORTTX exhortation	**AEIINOPRRST** respiration	**AFGIIINNRTU** infuriating	**AGHHIMNPRRU** harrumphing
AEHINORSSTT throatiness	**AEIKKLMNORW** workmanlike	**AFGIILMNORZ** formalizing	**AGHHIOPRSTY** histography
AEHINPPRRST partnership	**AEILLMNNSTT** installment	**AFGIILLNNUY** unfailingly	**AGHHOOPPRTY** photography
AEHKLLNSSTY thanklessly	**AEILLNOPTTY** potentially	**AFGIILMNNTU** fulminating	**AGHHOOPRRTY** orthography
AEIIILLMNOR millionaire	**AEILLNRSUVY** universally	**AFGIINNQTUY** quantifying	**AGHIIILMNTU** humiliating
AEIIILMMPRS imperialism	**AEILLORTTUV** ultraviolet	**AFGIINNRSTX** transfixing	**AGHIIMNNURZ** harmonizing
AEIIILMNNOT elimination	**AEILMMNORTY** momentarily	**AFGIINOSTTU** fustigation	**AGHIINNOSST** astonishing
AEIIILMNRST ministerial	**AEILMNNOOTU** unemotional	**AFGIINRSTTY** stratifying	**AGHIINNQSUV** vanquishing
AEIIILMNSST antimissile	**AEILMNNOSSW** womanliness	**AFGILMNOPRT** platforming	**AGHIINORTUZ** authorizing
AEIIILMRRSV verisimilar	**AEILMNOOSTT** molestation	**AFGILMNORTU** formulating	**AGHIINPRSTY** pharyngitis
AEIIILMTTVY imitatively	**AEILNNRSTTY** transiently	**AFGILNRSTTU** flustrating	**AGHLLOOPSSY** hypoglossal
AEIIIMNOSST animosities	**AEILNOOPRTX** exploration	**AFGINNRSSTU** transfusing	**AGHNOOPPRRY** pornography
AEIIIMNNOTTZ itemization	**AEILNOPRSTY** personality	**AFGINRRSTTU** frustrating	**AGIIILLNTTT** titillating
AEIIINORSSV visionaries	**AEILNOPSSSS** passionless	**AFIILMNNOTU** fulmination	**AGIIILNNPTZ** platinizing
AEIIINQSTTU antiquities	**AEIMNNOPPTT** appointment	**AFIILMNORTY** informality	**AGIIILNORTY** originality
AEIIIPRSTTU pituitaries	**AEIMNOPRTTU** permutation	**AFIILNORRTT** infiltrator	**AGIIILNSUVZ** visualizing
AEIILLPRSTU pluralities	**AEIMNRRSTTT** transmitter	**AFIIMNNOORT** information	**AGIIMMNNORT** immigration
AEIILMMORTZ immortalize	**AEINNOOSTTT** ostentation	**AFILMNOORTU** formulation	**AGIIINNNSTU** insinuating
AEIILMNOSTT testimonial	**AEINNORSTUV** intravenous	**AFILNORSTTU** flustration	**AGIIINNOSTT** instigation
AEIILMNPRRY preliminary	**AEINNOSSSUX** anxiousness	**AFINNORSSTU** transfusion	**AGIILMNNORS** normalising
AEIILMNPTTY impatiently	**AEINOORRSTT** restoration	**AFINORRSTTU** frustration	**AGIILMNNORZ** normalizing
AEIILMPSSVY impassively	**AEINOPRTTVY** antipoverty	**AGGHHIIILNT** hightailing	**AGIILMNORTZ** mortalizing
AEIILNNNOTT intentional	**AEIOPPRRRTY** proprietary	**AGGHIIJMNTU** thingumajig	**AGIILMNSTTU** stimulating
AEIILNNOTTV ventilation	**AEIOPRRRTTU** portraiture	**AGGHIILNNSU** languishing	**AGIILNPSTTU** stipulating
AEIILNNSSST saintliness	**AELLMORSUVY** marvelously	**AGGIIILNNSZ** signalizing	**AGIILNRSTUY** singularity
AEIILNQRTUZ tranquilize	**AELMMRSSTUU** summersault	**AGGIIIMMNRT** immigrating	**AGIILNRTUUX** luxuriating
AEIILORRRTT territorial	**AELOOPRRTXY** exploratory	**AGGIIIINNORT** originating	**AGIIMMNNTTU** manumitting
AEIILRSTTVY versatility	**AENNOOPSSTU** spontaneous	**AGGIIINNSTT** instigating	**AGIIMMNRSUZ** summarizing
AEIIMMRRTTU termitarium	**AENOPRRRSTT** transporter	**AGGIILNOOPZ** apologizing	**AGIINNNRTYZ** tyrannizing
AEIIMNNORTT termination	**AFGGIINSTTU** fustigating	**AGGIILNRUVZ** vulgarizing	**AGIINNOPRTZ** patronizing

AGIINNPRRST
transpiring
AGIJNOPSTUX
juxtaposing
AGILLLNPTUU
pullulating
AGILNNPPSTU
supplanting
AGILNNPRSUY
unsparingly
AGILNOPSTTU
postulating
AGIMNNRSTTU
transmuting
AGINNOPRSST
transposing
AGINOOPRSTT
protagonist
AGINOORRSTU
surrogation
AGINOPPRSST
passporting
AGINOPPRRSTT
prostrating
AGINPPRSTUU
suppurating
AHIIILMNOTU
humiliation
AHIILLORSUY
hilariously
AHIILOPSTTY
hospitality
AHIKMNOPRSW
workmanship
AHILNOPRSTY
rhinoplasty
AHILOPRSTYY
physiolatry
AHIMNOPRSTY
misanthropy
AIIILLNOTTT
titillation
AIIIMNRSTTU
miniaturist
AIIINNNOSTU
insinuation
AIIINNOPRST
inspiration
AIILLMNORTU
illuminator
AIILLPRSTUY
spiritually
AIILMMORTTY
immortality
AIILMNOSTTU
stimulation
AIILNOOPRSV
provisional
AIILNOPSTTU
stipulation
AIILNQRTTUY
tranquility
AIIMMNNOSSU
manumission

AIIMMNSSTTU
numismatist
AILLORRSTTU
illustrator
AILMNNOSUUY
unanimously
AILMNOPRTTY
importantly
AILNNORTUVY
involuntary
AIMNNOPRTTU
unimportant
AIMNNOOSTUU
mountainous
AINOOPRRSTT
prostration
ALMNOOSUYY
anonymously
BBCEELNOOST
cobblestone
BBCEILMOSTU
combustible
BBCGIINRSSU
subscribing
BBDEIKNOORY
bookbindery
BBDEILLMOOO
bloodmobile
BBDELNRSSUU
blunderbuss
BBEEEILRRSU
blueberries
BBEEHIRRSSU
shrubberies
BBEEILMRSSU
submersible
BBEHIIILLOP
bibliophile
BBHIIILLOPY
bibliophily
BCCDEILNOTU
conductible
BCCEEEEFINN
beneficence
BCCEEEENRSU
erubescence
BCCEIILNNOV
convincible
BCDEEHILNPT
pitchblende
BCDEEHMNOOY
honeycombed
BCDEEIILNRS
discernible
BCDEEIINNOT
benediction
BCDEINORTTU
contributed
BCDELMNOSUU
musclebound
BCDGIIKMNOR
mockingbird
BCDHHIOOPRY
hydrophobic

BCEEEELNNOV
benevolence
BCEEEFILPRT
perfectible
BCEEEIILLRST
celebrities
BCEEEILPPRT
perceptible
BCEEGIMNNRU
encumbering
BCEEHKLRRUY
huckleberry
BCEEIINOSST
obscenities
BCEEIJLOTVY
objectively
BCEEIILLLOSY
bellicosely
BCEEIILNORTV
convertible
BCEEIILPSSTU
susceptible
BCEEINSSSTU
subsistence
BCEEJLSSSTU
subjectless
BCEELNOOSST
obsolescent
BCEFHILLNSU
bullfinches
BCEGHIIMNRS
besmirching
BCEGIIINPRRS
prescribing
BCEIIJMOSTV
objectivism
BCEIIJOTTVY
objectivity
BCEIIORSSTU
obscurities
BCEIJNSTUUV
subjunctive
BCEIORSTTUV
obstructive
BCEKKOORRST
stockbroker
BCELSTTTTUU
scuttlebutt
BCGIINOPRRS
proscribing
BCGINORSTTU
obstructing
BCHHIOOOPPT
photophobic
BCHIIOOOPTT
photobiotic
BCIIIILMSTY
miscibility
BCINOORRTTU
contributor
BCINOORSTTU
obstruction
BDDDEEIIMOS
disembodied

BDDDEFILLNO
blindfolded
BDDEEEIILSV
disbelieved
BDDEEEIMMRS
dismembered
BDDEEEIMORR
embroidered
BDDEEIILMOZ
demobilized
BDDEEIIMOSS
disembodies
BDDEEIINOST
disobedient
BDDEEIILLNRU
underbilled
BDDEHINRRTU
thunderbird
BDDEIIRSTTU
distributed
BDDEINRSTUU
undisturbed
BDDELNOTUUY
undoubtedly
BDDGIIINSUV
subdividing
BDEEEHILLMS
embellished
BDEEELNSSSS
blessedness
BDEEEFGIINNR
befriending
BDEEFHIRRSU
refurbished
BDEEGIILNRW
bewildering
BDEEGILMNNO
emboldening
BDEEIILLNPRS
spellbinder
BDEENPRRTUU
unperturbed
BDEGHNORTUU
underbought
BDEGIILMNSS
dissembling
BDEGILNNNUY
unbendingly
BDEGINNNRUU
unburdening
BDEGINNRUUY
underbuying
BDEHHOOOORRT
brotherhood
BDEHIILPRSU
shipbuilder
BDEHILNPSUU
unpublished
BDEHLNORTTU
thunderbolt
BDEIIILLNSV
indivisible
BDEIIILMMOZ
immobilized

BDEIIIOSSTU
dubiosities
BDEIKNORSTU
strikebound
BDEISSTTTUU
substituted
BDELLNOSSUY
boundlessly
BDGGGILLNOU
bulldogging
BDGHIIMMNRU
hummingbird
BDGIIINSSUZ
subsidizing
BDGIILNOTUU
outbuilding
BDIIIILNSVY
indivisibly
BDIIINOSSUV
subdivision
BEEEGILLNRT
belligerent
BEEEGIMMNRR
remembering
BEEEHILLMSS
embellishes
BEEEIRSTTTW
bittersweet
BEEEENOPPRTY
teenybopper
BEEFHIRRSSU
refurbishes
BEEGGILSSTU
suggestible
BEEGHINNORR
herringbone
BEEGIILNNUV
unbelieving
BEEGIIMNRTT
embittering
BEEGIIOORSU
bourgeoisie
BEEGIKKNOOP
bookkeeping
BEEGIMNOSTT
misbegotten
BEEHILOPRYZ
hyperbolize
BEEHKNOORSU
housebroken
BEEHOPRRSTT
stepbrother
BEEIILMPRSS
permissible
BEEILNOPRSS
responsible
BEEILNOQSSU
obliqueness
BEEILNRSSTT
brittleness
BEEINRSSTUV
subservient
BEELLLLOWYY
yellowbelly

BEELMOORSTU
troublesome
BEENQRSSSUU
brusqueness
BEFIIILLTXY
flexibility
BEGGHIINNOR
neighboring
BEGGHIINNRT
brightening
BEGIIIILLTY
eligibility
BEGIILNSTUV
vestibuling
BEGILLMNRTY
tremblingly
BEGINRSSTTU
buttressing
BEHIIILLLLS
hillbillies
BEHIIIOPRTV
prohibitive
BEHINOORSSS
boorishness
BEHINRSSSTU
brutishness
BEHIOORRSUV
herbivorous
BEHLNORRTUY
unbrotherly
BEIIILMQRUU
equilibrium
BEIIILMSSTU
sublimities
BEIIILNSSTY
sensibility
BEIINORRTTU
retribution
BEILORSTUVY
obtrusively
BEINORSTUUV
unobtrusive
BEKNNNOSTUW
unbeknownst
BELLNRTTUUY
turbulently
BELNOOSTUUY
bounteously
BFILLNOTUUY
bountifully
BGHIIINOPRT
prohibiting
BGIILMNOSYZ
symbolizing
BGINNNOTTUU
unbuttoning
BHIIINOOPRT
prohibition
BIIILOPSSTY
possibility
BIIILLOOSUVY
obliviously
BILNOOOSUXY
obnoxiously

CCCDEEIINNO
coincidence
CCCEEIILMST
eclecticism
CCCEEIMPRSTU
circumspect
CCCIIMOOPRS
microscopic
CCDEEELLORT
recollected
CCDEEHILPSY
psychedelic
CCDEEIIIINST
insecticide
CCDEEIOPPRU
preoccupied
CCDEEJNORTU
conjectured
CCDEELLNOTU
uncollected
CCDEENNNORU
unconcerned
CCDEENNNOTU
unconnected
CCDEIMNOORS
microsecond
CCDEINOPRST
conscripted
CCDEINORSTT
constricted
CCDENORSTTU
constructed
CCDHHILLOOS
schoolchild
CCEEEEINPRT
centerpiece
CCEEEFHIKNR
neckerchief
CCEEEFLNORS
florescence
CCEEEHHLOST
cheesecloth
CCEEEINNNOV
convenience
CCEEEINOPRV
preconceive
CCEEEINOSTX
coexistence
CCEEELORTTU
electrocute
CCEEENNOQSU
consequence
CCEEFFIINOT
coefficient
CCEEFIIMNNU
munificence
CCEEIILRTTY
electricity
CCEEIIOPRST
precocities
CCEEIMNOORT
econometric
CCEEINOSTUV
consecutive

CCEEIOPPRSU
preoccupies
CCEFFIINSUY
sufficiency
CCEFIILNOTV
conflictive
CCEGHIINORT
ricocheting
CCEGHILNOOT
technologic
CCEGHINORTT
crotcheting
CCEGIILNNOR
reconciling
CCEGINNNOTY
contingency
CCEHIIPRRTY
hypercritic
CCEHILNOPTY
polytechnic
CCEHIMNOORT
homocentric
CCEHKLOSTTU
shuttlecock
CCEIIOPRRTY
reciprocity
CCEIJNNOTUV
conjunctive
CCEILNORRTY
incorrectly
CCEJNNORTUU
conjuncture
CCENORRSTTU
reconstruct
CCFGIILNNOT
conflicting
CCFIIINORUX
crucifixion
CCFIILNNOOT
confliction
CCGHIILLNNOR
chronicling
CCGHILNOOOR
chronologic
CCGHILOOPSY
psychologic
CCGHIOOPRSY
hygroscopic
CCGIIIINRTZ
criticizing
CCHIIMNOOPR
microphonic
CCILNOOSSUY
consciously
CCIMNNOOPTU
compunction
CCINNOOSSUU
unconscious
CCINOOPSSUU
conspicuous
CDDDEEIIRST
discredited
CDDDEEILNUY
undecidedly

CDDEEEEILQSU
deliquesced
CDDEEEMMNOR
recommended
CDDEEFIINST
disinfected
CDDEEIINRTT
interdicted
CDDEENORRSU
underscored
CDDEFIIKLST
fiddlestick
CDDEFIIMOST
discomfited
CDDEIIILNPS
disciplined
CDDEIINNOOT
conditioned
CDDELLLMOOY
mollycoddle
CDEEEEINPRX
experienced
CDEEEFFLORS
effloresced
CDEEEFGLNTU
genuflected
CDEEEFIILRT
electrified
CDEEEIJNRTT
interjected
CDEEEINPRTT
intercepted
CDEEEINRSTT
intersected
CDEEENNORTU
encountered
CDEEEOPRRSS
predecessor
CDEEERRRSTU
resurrected
CDEEFIINPSU
unspecified
CDEEGHIIINPR
deciphering
CDEEGIINNRT
interceding
CDEEGIIINRRT
redirecting
CDEEHIKPRSW
shipwrecked
CDEEHIOQSTU
discotheque
CDEEIIILSTV
declivities
CDEEIIMORRS
misericorde
CDEEIIINRSTV
viridescent
CDEEIIORRST
directories
CDEEIIORRSSV
discoveries
CDEEIIPRSTV
descriptive

CDEEIKLNNOO
nickelodeon
CDEEIKLNORT
interlocked
CDEEILNNQUY
delinquency
CDEEIRRRSVW
screwdriver
CDEEIRSTTUV
destructive
CDEEKOORSTV
overstocked
CDEENNOQRUU
unconquered
CDEENOPRTTU
unprotected
CDEENPSSTUU
unsuspected
CDEEOOPPSSU
pseudoscope
CDEFIINORTU
countrified
CDEFIMNNORU
unconfirmed
CDEGIIJNPRU
prejudicing
CDEGIINNORS
considering
CDEGIINNPRS
prescinding
CDEGIINORSV
discovering
CDEGIMNNOTU
documenting
CDEGIMNNOOPS
decomposing
CDEGINOPRRU
reproducing
CDEHIIMOOST
dichotomies
CDEHIOOOPPT
photocopied
CDEHKLOORST
stockholder
CDEIIILNUVZ
uncivilized
CDEIIILLOPTZ
politicized
CDEIIILPSTU
duplicities
CDEIIINNORT
indirection
CDEIIINSTTV
distinctive
CDEIIIOPRTY
periodicity
CDEIIISSTUV
vicissitude
CDEIIJNSTUV
disjunctive
CDEIILLMNOS
millisecond
CDEIILLOSUY
deliciously

CDEIILNRTUY
incredulity
CDEIILNTUVY
inductively
CDEIIMMOOST
commodities
CDEIINNOSTU
discontinue
CDEIINOPRST
description
CDEIINRSTUZ
scrutinized
CDEIKRRRTUV
truckdriver
CDEILNORSUU
incredulous
CDEIMMNOTTU
uncommitted
CDEIMMOOPRS
compromised
CDEINNOPRST
nondescript
CDEINORSTTU
destruction
CDEINORSTUY
countryside
CDELLLOSSUY
cloudlessly
CDFGINNNOOU
confounding
CDGHILNOOPP
clodhopping
CDGIIINNRSTT
districting
CDGIILNOORS
discoloring
CDGIINNORTU
introducing
CDGIINNOSTU
discounting
CDGIINORSSU
discoursing
CDGIMNNOOPU
compounding
CDIIINNOSTT
distinction
CDIIJNNOSTU
disjunction
CDIIMMNNOOU
condominium
CDILLORSUUY
ludicrously
CEEEEGIMNRS
emergencies
CEEEEILNORT
electioneer
CEEEEINRRRV
irreverence
CEEEEKOPRRS
scorekeeper
CEEEFFHOOSU
coffeehouse
CEEEFFIINTV
ineffective

CEEEFFILTVY
effectively
CEEEFIILRST
electrifies
CEEEFINQRSU
frequencies
CEEEFMNNORT
enforcement
CEEEHILORTT
heteroclite
CEEEIINSSST
necessities
CEEEILLORRT
electrolier
CEEEILNOPRT
preelection
CEEEILSSVXY
excessively
CEEEINORTUX
executioner
CEEEINPRRTT
intercepter
CEEEINPRSSS
preciseness
CEEEIPPRSTV
perspective
CEEELLLNTXY
excellently
CEEELLORTTY
electrolyte
CEEEOOPRSST
stereoscope
CEEFFIIINNT
inefficient
CEEFFIILNTY
efficiently
CEEFIKKNOPT
pocketknife
CEEFILMPRTY
imperfectly
CEEFIMNNNOT
confinement
CEEFINORTTU
counterfeit
CEEFLNORSTU
fluorescent
CEEFLOORRSU
foreclosure
CEEGHILOOSU
euchologies
CEEGHINNRRT
retrenching
CEEGILNOORS
necrologies
CEEGILNOPST
telescoping
CEEGINPRSTU
persecuting
CEEHHIIMPRS
hemispheric
CEEHHMORSTT
homestretch
CEEHIIMPSTU
euphemistic

CEEHIIMSSTT
estheticism
CEEHIKNSSST
sketchiness
CEEHILLNOST
clothesline
CEEHKLNOSUY
honeysuckle
CEEHLLOORST
cholesterol
CEEHOOPSSTT
stethoscope
CEEIIMNNRST
reminiscent
CEEIIMOPTTV
competitive
CEEIIRRSTTV
restrictive
CEEIKNPRSTY
persnickety
CEEILLMRSSY
mercilessly
CEEILLSUVXY
exclusively
CEEILMNNSTU
luminescent
CEEILMNOOPW
policewomen
CEEILNNOOV
nonviolence
CEEIMNNOOPT
omnipotence
CEEIMNNOPTT
incompetent
CEEIMOPRTUZ
computerize
CEEINNOORRT
reconnoiter
CEEINOPRRTT
interceptor
CEEINOPRSTU
persecution
CEEINORRSTU
intercourse
CEEINORTUVW
counterview
CEEIOPPRSTV
prospective
CEEIPQRSTUU
picturesque
CEEKOORRRTT
retrorocket
CEEMNNNOTTT
contentment
CEFFFIIRSTU
fisticuffer
CEFGIILNNNU
influencing
CEFGIINNORR
reinforcing
CEFGILNOORS
foreclosing
CEFGILNORSU
fluorescing

CEFILNOORTU
counterfoil
CEFLOOOPRSU
fluoroscope
CEFNOORRTTU
counterfort
CEFNOPRRTUY
perfunctory
CEGGIINNORZ
recognizing
CEGHIILNRTT
chitterling
CEGHIINNNRT
intrenching
CEGHIINNRST
christening
CEGHINORSSU
grouchiness
CEGIILNORST
cloistering
CEGIIMNNOOZ
economizing
CEGIIMNNSTU
intumescing
CEGIINNOORT
recognition
CEGIINRRSTT
restricting
CEGILNOORST
necrologist
CEGIMNOPRSS
compressing
CEGINNORSTU
countersign
CEGINOPPRST
prospecting
CEGINOPRSTU
prosecuting
CEGINORSTUY
courtesying
CEHHLOOOSSU
schoolhouse
CEHIIINPSTZ
citizenship
CEHIILOOPRT
heliotropic
CEHIIMOSSUV
mischievous
CEHIIOPRRST
prehistoric
CEHIIOSSSVY
vichyssoise
CEHIMOPPRST
coppersmith
CEHINNORSYZ
synchronize
CEHIOOOPPRT
photocopier
CEHIOOOPPST
photocopies
CEHMOPRSTYY
psychometry
CEIIILLNNPTY
incipiently

CEIIIMNOPRS
imprecision
CEIIIMPSSST
pessimistic
CEIIINNRSTY
insincerity
CEIIINNSTTV
instinctive
CEIIINOSTVV
vivisection
CEIIIORSSTU
curiosities
CEIIIOSSSTV
viscosities
CEIIIRSSTTU
rusticities
CEIIKLQRSUV
quicksilver
CEIILNRTUUV
viniculture
CEIILSSTUVX
exclusivist
CEIIMMNOSTU
communities
CEIIMNOOPTT
competition
CEIIMNOPSUU
impecunious
CEIINNNOTT
incontinent
CEIINORRSTT
restriction
CEIINOSSSUV
viciousness
CEIINRSTTUV
instructive
CEIIOPPRSTU
precipitous
CEIIPPRSTUY
perspicuity
CEIKNNORSTU
countersink
CEILMOOOPST
cosmopolite
CEIMMNORSSU
consumerism
CEIMNOOPRSS
compression
CEIMNOPSTUV
consumptive
CEIMNORSSTU
misconstrue
CEINNOORSSU
connoisseur
CEINNOOSTTU
contentious
CEINNOSTTTU
constituent
CEINOOPRSTU
prosecution
CEINOOPSSSU
copiousness
CEKNNORSTUU
countersunk

CELLMOOPRRT
comptroller
CELNOOPRTTU
counterplot
CFFGIINRTUY
fructifying
CFGGIINNORU
configuring
CFGHIILNNNU
unflinching
CFGHIMNNOORT
forthcoming
CFGIINNNOTU
functioning
CFGINNNOORT
confronting
CGGILMMNNNO
commingling
CGHHHIIIKNT
hitchhiking
CGHIMNOORST
shortcoming
CGIIIMNTVZ
victimizing
CGIIKLNOPST
stockpiling
CGIILOOOSST
sociologist
CGIIMNNOSTU
miscounting
CGIINNORTUY
incongruity
CGIINNRSTTU
instructing
CGILLNNOORT
controlling
CGILNPRSTUU
sculpturing
CGINNNOOPRU
pronouncing
CGINNOORSUU
incongruous
CGINOOPPRTU
outcropping
CGINRRSTTUU
structuring
CHHIILOOPPS
philosophic
CHHIMMOOOPR
homomorphic
CHHMOOOPRTY
photochromy
CHIMNNORSSY
synchronism
CHMNOOOTTTU
cottonmouth
CHMOOOPRSTY
psychomotor
CIIINNOPRST
inscription
CIIMNOOOPST
composition
CIIMOPRSTUY
promiscuity

CIINNORSTTU
instruction
CILNNOOOTUV
convolution
CILNNOOSUUY
innocuously
CIMNNOOPSTU
consumption
CIMOOPRSSUU
promiscuous
CIMOPRSSTUU
scrumptious
DDDEFHLNORU
hundredfold
DDDENNOORTW
downtrodden
DDEEEEHNPRR
reprehended
DDEEEEELOPRV
redeveloped
DDEEEEGIPRST
predigested
DDEEEIMPRST
distempered
DDEEEEINNNPT
independent
DDEEEENOPRRV
provendered
DDEEENRRRSU
surrendered
DDEEFIIIMNN
indemnified
DDEEFIIIRSV
diversified
DDEEGNOPRSU
groundspeed
DDEEIILPPSS
sideslipped
DDEEIINORST
disoriented
DDEEINNNPRU
underpinned
DDEEIOPPRSS
predisposed
DDEFGIIINNU
undignified
DDEGIIINOXZ
deoxidizing
DDEGIINOORZ
deodorizing
DDEGIINORRS
disordering
DDEGILNRSTU
disgruntled
DDEGNNORRUU
underground
DDEILNOSSUV
undissolved
DDIIKLNSTWY
tiddlywinks
DEEEEFLNSSS
defenseless
DEEEEHIMPRS
ephemerides

DEEEEMOPRST
speedometer
DEEEENPRRST
represented
DEEEEQRSSTU
sequestered
DEEEFIIMPXY
exempyified
DEEEGGINNNR
engendering
DEEEGHHOPPR
hedgehopper
DEEEGHILNNT
enlightened
DEEEHILNPRS
replenished
DEEEHLMORVW
overwhelmed
DEEEIINRTVW
interviewed
DEEEILMMNPT
implemented
DEEEILNNOPT
needlepoint
DEEEINNPRST
serpentined
DEEEINPRRTT
interpreted
DEEEINPRSTZ
serpentized
DEEEINRSTWZ
westernized
DEEELMNOPTV
development
DEEELNNPRST
resplendent
DEEELNNSSSS
endlessness
DEEEELNORTUV
volunteered
DEEENQRSTUU
unrequested
DEEEOOPRRVW
overpowered
DEEEOPRSSSS
repossessed
DEEEOPRSTTY
stereotyped
DEEFFIINNRT
indifferent
DEEFFILNRTY
differently
DEEFFIOOPRR
fireproofed
DEEFFORSTUV
overstuffed
DEEFGGIOPTT
pettifogged
DEEFGHIORST
foresighted
DEEFGIINORZ
foreignized
DEEFGILNORW
deflowering

DEEFIIIMNNS
indemnifies
DEEFIIINNST
intensified
DEEFIIIRSSV
diversifies
DEEFIIMORST
deformities
DEEFIINOPRS
personified
DEEGGIINNRS
redesigning
DEEGHHINPRS
shepherding
DEEGHIILNSV
disheveling
DEEGHILNOOP
pigeonholed
DEEGHILOOTZ
theologized
DEEGHIMNOOZ
homogenized
DEEGHINRTUW
underweight
DEEGIIMNNRT
determining
DEEGIINNRTZ
tenderizing
DEEGILMNORZ
mongrelized
DEEGINNRSUV
undeserving
DEEGINPRSSU
superseding
DEEHHLOORSU
householder
DEEHILOSTTU
silhouetted
DEEHINOSSSU
hideousness
DEEHINSSSTYZ
synthesized
DEEHINSTTYZ
synthetized
DEEHLOPRSTU
upholstered
DEEHMNNOOOY
honeymooned
DEEIIIMNNST
indemnities
DEEIIIRSSTV
diversities
DEEIIKLLMSS
semiskilled
DEEIILOPSTZ
epistolized
DEEIIMMNRST
determinism
DEEIIMNORST
modernities
DEEIINNORTV
inventoried
DEEIINNRTTW
intertwined

DEEIINPRSTY
serendipity
DEEILNORRSS
orderliness
DEEIMNNORST
indorsement
DEEINNNORST
nonresident
DEEINNPRSTU
superintend
DEEINOSSSUV
deviousness
DEEINPRRTTU
interrupted
DEEINRRRTUW
underwriter
DEEKNNNRSSU
drunkenness
DEENOSSSTUU
duteousness
DEEOPPPRSSU
presupposed
DEFFILLLNUU
unfulfilled
DEFGIIINNTY
identifying
DEFGIILNORU
unglorified
DEFGIINOTXY
detoxifying
DEFGILNNORU
floundering
DEFHINPRSTT
spendthrift
DEFHLMOOTUU
foulmouthed
DEFIIMMNORS
misinformed
DEFILNSSTUU
dutifulness
DEFIOOOORRSU
odoriferous
DEFLLNORUWY
wonderfully
DEGGHHHIILT
highlighted
DEGGKLRSUUY
skulduggery
DEGHIILMNOS
demolishing
DEGHILNORSU
shouldering
DEGHINNORSU
enshrouding
DEGHLMOOOTY
methodology
DEGHNOORSUY
hydrogenous
DEGHNORRTUW
undergrowth
DEGIIIINNST
indignities
DEGIIINNOST
indigestion

DEGIIINNRST
disintering
DEGIIINQSTU
disquieting
DEGIILLNOTU
guillotined
DEGIILNNNRU
underlining
DEGIIMNNNRU
undermining
DEGIIMNNORZ
modernizing
DEGIIINNNRTU
indenturing
DEGIIINOPSTZ
despotizing
DEGIINPRSTU
disreputing
DEGIIINRSSST
distressing
DEGILLNNTUY
indulgently
DEGILNNORWY
wonderingly
DEGILNOTTUZ
gluttonized
DEHIIOOPRSTT
orthopedist
DEHNORRSSTU
undershorts
DEIIMNOPRTV
improvident
DEIINOOPRSV
provisioned
DEIINOSTTTU
destitution
DEILLNORSSW
worldliness
DEILLORSTUY
desultorily
DEILMNOOOPZ
monopolized
DEILMNPRTUY
imprudently
DEINOOPPRTU
pourpointed
DEIOPPRSTTU
outstripped
DEIOPRSTTTU
prostituted
DELMORRSUUY
murderously
DFGGIIINRSU
disfiguring
DFGHIIIMNUY
humidifying
DFGIIILNOSY
solidifying
DGHHIILNOTW
withholding
DGHIIIIMNNS
diminishing
DGHIIINSSTU
distinguish

DGHIIKNNOOW
hoodwinking
DGHIINNOORS
dishonoring
DGIIIJNNOST
disjointing
DGIIINNOPSS
indisposing
DGIIMNNOSTU
dismounting
DGIINRSSTTU
distrusting
DGINNOOPPRU
propounding
DGINNOORRSUU
surrounding
DIIILLNOSSU
disillusion
DIIILNOSSUY
insidiously
DIIINOOPSST
disposition
DIINORSSTUU
industrious
EEEEHKOPRSU
housekeeper
EEEEHNNSTTV
seventeenth
EEEEHORRSVW
wheresoever
EEEEIMNPRSW
minesweeper
EEEEKOPRRST
storekeeper
EEEFHMNRRST
refreshment
EEEFIILMPSX
exemplifies
EEEFIMPRRSU
perfumeries
EEEGGIIINNNR
engineering
EEEGGMNNORT
engorgement
EEEGIINNRRTW
wintergreen
EEEGINPRRSV
persevering
EEEGNORSSSV
governesses
EEEHHNPRSTY
hypersthene
EEEHIIPPRRS
peripheries
EEEHILNPRSS
replenishes
EEEHIIMNRSST
smithereens
EEEHILNNOSST
nonetheless
EEEHMMORRTT
thermometer
EEEIIMRSTTX
extremities

EEEEIINNPSVX
inexpensive
EEEIINRRTVW
interviewer
EEEIMNQRRTU
requirement
EEEIMOPRTXZ
extemporize
EEEINPRRRTT
interpreter
EEEINPRRSST
intersperse
EEEINPRSTTX
preexistent
EEEIOPRRRST
repertories
EEELLLPSSSY
sleeplessly
EEELLNSSSSY
senselessly
EEELMNNNOPTV
envelopment
EEELPRRSSTT
letterpress
EEEMNORSTUV
venturesome
EEEFFIINNOSV
inoffensive
EEEFFIOORRST
offertories
EEEFGGIOPRTT
pettifogger
EEEFGIIINNRRT
interfering
EEEFGILLNORT
foretelling
EEEFGILMOPRS
foreglimpse
EEEFGINNORSS
foreignness
EEEFGINORRST
reforesting
EEEFGINORSSV
forgiveness
EEEFHIJLLSSY
jellyfishes
EEEFHILNSSSS
selfishness
EEEFHILOSUWY
housewifely
EEEFHLLNPSSU
helpfulness
EEEFHLNOPSSU
hopefulness
EEEFHMORRRTU
furthermore
EEEFHNOORRST
foreshorten
EEEFIINNSST
intensifies
EEEFIIISSTTV
festivities
EEEFIINOPRSS
personifies

EEFILLLMNTU
mellifluent
EEFILLMORSU
melliferous
EEFLMNOSSSU
fulsomeness
EEGGHHIIINNT
heightening
EEGGHIINSST
sightseeing
EEGGHILNNNT
lengthening
EEGGIINRRST
registering
EEGGILLNNTY
negligently
EEGGILORSUY
egregiously
EEGHHILRTWW
wheelwright
EEGHIIMNPUZ
euphemizing
EEGHIINSSTW
weightiness
EEGHILNNOPT
telephoning
EEGHILRSTTT
streetlight
EEGHINNPTWY
pennyweight
EEGHINRSTTY
yesternight
EEGHMNOOOSU
homogeneous
EEGIILLNNTT
intelligent
EEGIILMNNRT
intermingle
EEGIILNNNST
sentineling
EEGIILNNRST
reenlisting
EEGIIMMNRSZ
mesmerizing
EEGIINNNRTV
intervening
EEGIINNRSTT
interesting
EEGIINNRSTV
reinvesting
EEGILMOOSTY
etymologies
EEGILNNNRTU
unrelenting
EEGILNORSVY
sovereignly
EEGIMNNORSU
monseigneur
EEGIMNNRRTU
interregnum
EEGINORSTVY
sovereignty
EEGINPRSTTU
guttersnipe**

EEGINPSTTTY
typesetting
EEGIOPRRSSV
progressive
EEGLMOOORTY
meteorology
EEGLOQRSTUY
grotesquely
EEHHILLNSSS
hellishness
EEHHIOPSTYZ
hypothesize
EEHHMOORSTU
housemother
EEHILNORRST
northerlies
EEHINNOSSSU
heinousness
EEHINRSSSTU
hirsuteness
EEHINRSSTYZ
synthesizer
EEHIPRSSTTU
trusteeship
EEHLMNOOSUW
unwholesome
EEHLOPRRSTU
upholsterer
EEHMNNOOOORY
honeymooner
EEHNORRSTTW
northwester
EEHOOPRRSTU
porterhouse
EEHORSSTTUW
southwester
EEIIILPRSTU
puerilities
EEIIIMMNSST
immensities
EEIIINNSSTV
insensitive
EEIIINORSST
seniorities
EEIILLPRSTU
spirituelle
EEIILMNOSST
solemnities
EEIILNSSTVY
sensitively
EEIILPPRSST
slipperiest
EEIILPRSSTT
priestliest
EEIIMNNPRTT
impertinent
EEIIMNOSSTT
testimonies
EEIINNNOSTT
nonentities
EEIINNORSTV
inventories
EEIINOORSTT
notorieties

EEIINOPRRTT
preterition
EEIIOPPRRST
proprieties
EEIIORRRSTT
territories
EEILLNOSSSY
noiselessly
EEILMNNOTVV
involvement
EEILOPRSTYZ
proselytize
EEIMMNNOPRTV
improvement
EEIMNNNORTV
environment
EEIMNNOPRST
omnipresent
EEIMPPRSTUV
presumptive
EEINNOSSTTU
sententious
EEINOPRSTTU
pretentious
EELLORRSTTY
storyteller
EELNOOPPSTW
townspeople
EELNOORRSUY
erroneously
EEMOPSSTTUU
tempestuous
EENNORSSSUV
nervousness
EFGGHIINNRT
frightening
EFGHHOORTTU
forethought
EFGHIIILLNT
helilifting
EFGHIIINNRS
refinishing
EFGIIILNRTZ
fertilizing
EFGIILMNSUY
emulsifying
EFGIINNPRRT
fingerprint
EFGIINPRTTY
prettifying
EFGILMNOORT
montgolfier
EFGILNOORVW
overflowing
EFGNNOOORTTU
unforgotten
EFHIINRSSTT
thriftiness
EFHILNOOSSS
foolishness
EFHIMNNRSTU
furnishment
EFHINOPPSSS
foppishness

EFHMORRSTTU
furthermost
EFIIIIMNRST
infirmities
EFIIILNRTTY
infertility
EFIIILORSTV
frivolities
EFIIINORRTY
inferiority
EFILLLMOSUU
mellifluous
EFILLLNSSUW
willfulness
EFILOOPRRSU
proliferous
EFILPRSTUUY
superfluity
EFLOPRSSUUU
superfluous
EGGHHIILTTW
lightweight
EGGHIINOTUW
outweighing
EGGIIILNPRV
privileging
EGGINOOORRVW
overgrowing
EGGINOPRRSS
progressing
EGHHILOSSTU
houselights
EGHHLOSSTTU
thoughtless
EGHIILLOOPZ
philologize
EGHIILPRRST
sprightlier
EGHIINNOPUZ
euphonizing
EGHILMNOOORT
moonlighter
EGHILMOOSTY
mythologies
EGHILMOOTYZ
mythologize
EGHILNOOSTT
ethnologist
EGHILORSTUY
righteously
EGHINNNOSST
nothingness
EGHINOPPRSY
prophesying
EGHINORSTUU
unrighteous
EGIIILNRSTZ
sterilizing
EGIIIMNNRST
ministering
EGIIIMNNRTX
intermixing
EGIIMNOPTZ
epitomizing

EGIIINNOPTT
petitioning
EGIIINNRTWZ
winterizing
EGIIINNSSTZ
sensitizing
EGIIJNNOSTT
jettisoning
EGIILLMNPSS
misspelling
EGIILMNNOSZ
solemnizing
EGIILNNOPRT
interloping
EGIILNNOSUY
ingeniously
EGIILNNPRST
splintering
EGIILNPRUVZ
pulverizing
EGIIMNNORSZ
sermonizing
EGIIMNNRTTU
unremitting
EGIIMNOPRTZ
temporizing
EGIIMNSSTYZ
systemizing
EGIINNOPRST
interposing
EGIINNOPTTZ
potentizing
EGIINNOQSTU
questioning
EGIINNPRSSS
springiness
EGIINOPRTTU
pirouetting
EGIINORRRTZ
terrorizing
EGIINPRSSUV
supervising
EGIIOPRSSTU
prestigious
EGIKNOORRVW
overworking
EGILMNOORTY
terminology
EGILNOORSTU
neurologist
EGILNPRSTTU
spluttering
EGILNPRSTUU
sepulturing
EGINNOORSTU
nitrogenous
EGINOOPRRSS
progression
EGINPPRSSSU
suppressing
EHHILOOPPRS
philosopher
EHIIILOSSTT
hostilities

EHIILMRSSTV silversmith	**EILMNOOOPRZ** monopolizer	**GHIIKNNOTTU** outthinking	**GILNNNOPSSU** nonplussing
EHIINPRSSST spinsterish	**EILMOPSTUUY** impetuously	**GHIILLOOPST** philologist	**GIMNNORSTUU** surmounting
EHIINRSSSTT thirstiness	**EIMNOPPRSTU** presumption	**GHIILNOPSTY** philogynist	**HORRSTTTUWY** trustworthy
EHILMMNOSTY semimonthly	**EINNOOPPRTU** inopportune	**GHIINNOPTYZ** hypnotizing	**IIIINNOQSTU** inquisition
EHIMNNORSTU nourishment	**EINOPPRSSSU** suppression	**GHILNOOORTY** ornithology	**IIILLNNOQTU** quintillion
EIIIINQSTUV inquisitive	**ELMMNOOSTUY** momentously	**GIIIMNNOOSU** ignominious	**IIILLNOSSTT** tonsillitis
EIIIMOPRSTX proximities	**FGGHILNORUU** furloughing	**GIIIMNNOPRS** imprisoning	**IIILLNOSSTU** illusionist
EIIINOPRSTT peritonitis	**FGGIINNORUV** unforgiving	**GIIIMNNPRST** misprinting	**IIINNOSTTTU** institution
EIIINOQRSTU requisition	**FGHIILNOPST** shoplifting	**GIIIMNOPRSV** improvising	**IILLORSSTUU** illustrious
EIIINSSTTVY sensitivity	**FGHIILNORSU** flourishing	**GIIINNSTTTU** instituting	**IINOOOOPPRST** proposition
EIILLOOQSSU soliloquies	**FGHILNORTTY** fortnightly	**GIIKMMNNOST** skimmington	**IINOOPPSSTU** supposition
EIILNNSSTTY insistently	**FGIIILMNPSY** simplifying	**GIILLMNPTUY** multiplying	**IINOPPQRTUY** propinquity
EIIMNNOOPRT premonition	**FGIIILNOSSZ** fossilizing	**GIILNNPQTUU** quintupling	**ILNOOORSTUY** notoriously
EIIMOORRSTU meritorious	**FGIILMNORUZ** formulizing	**GIILNNTTUWY** unwittingly	**IMNOOPPRSTU** opportunism
EIIMOPSTTUY impetuosity	**FGIILNSTTUY** stultifying	**GIIMNNOPRSU** unpromising	**IMNOORSSTTY** monstrosity
EIINOOPPRST preposition	**GGHINNNOSTU** shotgunning	**GIIMNNOPRTU** importuning	**INOOPPRSTTU** opportunist
EIINOPRSSUV supervision	**GGIILLNOSYZ** syllogizing	**GIIMNRSSTTU** mistrusting	**INOOPPRTTUY** opportunity
EIINORSTTTU restitution	**GHHIIMNRTYZ** rhythmizing	**GIKLNNNOUWY** unknowingly	**IOOPPRSSTUY** suppository
EIIOPRRSTUY superiority	**GHIIIKMNRSS** skirmishing	**GILLLMNOSUU** slumgullion	**LMNOORSSTUY** monstrously

12-LETTER WORDS

AAAAABCCHILNN
bacchanalian

AAAACGIMMNRT
anagrammatic

AAAAILLPRRSS
sarsaparilla

AAAABCEHILLPT
alphabetical

AAAABDIILPTTY
adaptability

AAAABEEGILMRR
marriageable

AAAABEEGLMNNU
unmanageable

AAABEIILMNNT
maintainable

AAAABEILNNTTU
unattainable

AAAABIIILLTVY
availability

AAACCDEILLMY
academically

AAACCEINNQTU
acquaintance

AAACCILORSTU
accusatorial

AAACDILNNOTV
vacationland

AAACEHILMMTT
mathematical

AAACIILNNOTZ
canalization

AAACILLLNTYY
analytically

AAADDEGINSTV
disadvantage

AAADEGNOSTUV
advantageous

AAADEINSSSST
assassinated

AAAEEGIMNNRSX
sexagenarian

AAAEIILNQRTU
equalitarian

AAAGGHINPPRR
paragraphing

AAAGIILNNOTV
navigational

AAAHIIMNNRTU
humanitarian

AAAIILMPRRTY
paramilitary

AABBCGIKLLLN
blackballing

AABBCIIILMNO
bibliomaniac

AABBEGIINRTV
abbreviating

AABBEIINORTV
abbreviation

AABCCEELNPTU
unaccpetable

AABCCEILLLNU
incalculable

AABCCEIRRTUU
bureaucratic

AABCDEHORRTY
carbohydrate

AABCDEIILNNZ
cannibalized

AABCDEKNRSSW
backwardness

AABCDELLOORT
collaborated

AABCDELRSTTY
abstractedly

AABCDGINORST
broadcasting

AABCDIIJNOTU
abjudication

AABCEEEGHLNX
exchangeable

AABCEEEGHLRR
rechargeable

AABCEEGGPRRT
carpetbagger

AABCEEGHLNNU
unchangeable

AABCEEGINRTX
exacerbating

AABCEEIKMNRT
cabinetmaker

AABCEHILLSXY
hexasyllabic

AABCEHILNRTU
uncharitable

AABCEIIILPST
capabilities

AABCEIILLNPP
inapplicable

AABCEILMNOPR
incomparable

AABCEILORSUV
vocabularies

AABCEINRRSTT
scatterbrain

AABCENRSSSTT
abstractness

AABCGHIILOPR
biographical

AABCGIIKLLMN
blackmailing

AABCHIINOOTT
cohabitation

AABCILMNOPRY
incomparably

AABCLLOOOORRT
collaborator

AABDDEHLLMOY
hebdomadally

AABDEEEGILRS
disagreeable

AABDEEHHRRSY
haberdashery

AABDELOPRRST
plasterboard

AABDIIILMRTY
admirability

AABEEEEHKRRRT
heartbreaker

AABEEEFHINRRT
featherbrain

AABEEFLNRRST
transferable

AABEEHIILRTT
rehabilitate

AABEEILMMRSU
immeasurable

AABEELNNORSU
unreasonable

AABEELNNOSSU
unseasonable

AABEELNNRSUW
unanswerable

AABEENNRRSTU
subterranean

AABEGIILMNNU
unimaginable

AABEGIMNNRSS
embarrassing

AABEIILLLMTY
malleability

AABEIKLMNSTU
unmistakable

AABEILMMRSUY
immeasurably

AABEILOORRST
laboratories

AABEINSSTTTU
substantiate

AABELMOPRRTU
perambulator

AABELNNORSUY
unreasonably
AABELNNRSUWY
unanswerably
AABGHIIILNTT
habilitating
AABGIIILNTVY
navigability
AABGIIILLNORY
aboriginally
AABIMNORSTTU
masturbation
AACCCEIINRSU
inaccuracies
AACCDDEMMOOT
accommodated
AACCDEIILLNTY
accidentally
AACCEEGILNRT
accelerating
AACCEEHIRRTZ
characterize
AACCEEILNORT
acceleration
AACCEENRSSTU
accurateness
AACCEHILLMNY
mechanically
AACCEHILPRTY
archetypical
AACCEILLMSTU
miscalculate
AACCEILLNNOT
cancellation
AACCEILLSTTY
ecstatically
AACCEILMNOPT
cleptomaniac
AACCEILNORVY
clairvoyance
AACCEINNOTTU
accentuation
AACCGILLMNTUU
accumulating
AACCGIMMNNOPY
accompanying
AACCHIOPRSTT
catastrophic
AACCIIILPSTT
capitalistic
AACCIIORRSTT
aristocratic
AACCIIRRSTTU
caricaturist
AACCILLOSTUY
acoustically
AACCILLNOOSY
occasionally
AACCILMNOTUU
accumulation
AACCILNOOPTU
occupational
AACDDIIJNOTU
adjudication

AACDEEEFFINT
decaffeinate
AACDEELNPSTU
encapsulated
AACDEFMNRTUU
manufactured
AACDEGIINPTT
decapitating
AACDEHILLNTU
hallucinated
AACDEIIINPRT
pediatrician
AACDEIINORTT
ratiocinated
AACDEIIOSSST
disassociate
AACDEIIPPRTT
participated
AACDEILMMORT
melodramatic
AACDEILMRTTU
matriculated
AACDGHIINNPP
handicapping
AACDGIIILNRZ
radicalizing
AACDGIILLNNSZ
scandalizing
AACDHINOPQRU
quadraphonic
AACDILLOPRSY
sporadically
AACDLLNOSSUY
scandalously
AACEEFFINOTT
affectionate
AACEEHIOPRST
apothecaries
AACEFIIINORT
aerification
AACEFMNRRTUU
manufacturer
AACEGHILLPRR
calligrapher
AACEGHNOOPRY
oceanography
AACEGIIMMNNPT
emancipating
AACEGIIINNRST
ascertaining
AACEGIINPPRT
appreciating
AACEGIINRTTV
reactivating
AACEGILLMNTY
magnetically
AACEGILMNSTU
emasculating
AACEGINNOORT
octogenarian
AACEGLNORTTU
congratulate
AACEHIILMRTT
arithmetical

AACEHILLLTTY
athletically
AACEHILLMPTY
emphatically
AACEHILLPTTY
pathetically
AACEHILRTTY
theatrically
AACEHILMPSTY
metaphysical
AACEIILLNOPPS
episcopalian
AACEIILNRTTU
inarticulate
AACEIIMMNNOPT
emancipation
AACEIINOPPRT
appreciation
AACEIKLMNOPT
kleptomaniac
AACEINNNORST
nonsectarian
AACEINRTTTUV
unattractive
AACEKNNORSTU
cantankerous
AACENNPRRSTY
transparency
AACFGIIILNTT
facilitating
AACFIIILLRTY
artificially
AACFIIIMNORT
ramification
AACFIIINORTT
ratification
AACFIINOSSTT
satisfaction
AACFILLLOSUY
fallaciously
AACFIORSSTTY
satisfactory
AACGHILLOOPT
pathological
AACGIIILNPTZ
capitalizing
AACGIIINNPTT
anticipating
AACGIILMNNTU
calumniating
AACGIILNPTTU
capitulating
AACGIILNRTTU
articulating
AACGIINNNNTU
annunciating
AACGIINNOSTT
antagonistic
AACGIINNRSST
incrassating
AACGILLRRTUU
agricultural
AACHHIIMNPRS
chairmanship

AACHIILMOPRS
parochialism
AACHIMMNNOPY
nymphomaniac
AACHLLNNNOTY
nonchalantly
AACIIINNOPTT
anticipation
AACIILLNOOTZ
localization
AACIILLRSTTY
artistically
AACIILNOPTTU
capitulation
AACIILNORTTU
articulation
AACIINNNNOTU
annunciation
AACIIOPPRRTT
participator
AACILLMNOSTY
monastically
AACILLPRRTUY
particularly
AACILMNOORST
astronomical
AADDDEINRSTZ
standardized
AADDEEIMNRTV
animadverted
AADDGIIILNPT
dilapidating
AADDIILLNOTY
additionally
AADEEEHQRRSTU
headquarters
AADEEIILMRTZ
materialized
AADEEILNQTUY
inadequately
AADEELLLNPRU
unparalleled
AADEEQRRSTUW
quartersawed
AADEFGGILNRT
deflagrating
AADEFHINNOTU
fountainhead
AADEFIIILMRZ
familiarized
AADEGIINPPRS
disappearing
AADEGIINPRST
deaspirating
AADEGIMNQRSU
masquerading
AADEGINNPPRS
sandpapering
AADEGOPRRSTTU
postgraduate
AADEIILLNNOTZ
nationalized
AADEIILNNTUV
antediluvian

AADEIILNORTZ
rationalized
AADEIIMNRSTT
administrate
AADEILNORTTU
adulteration
AADEIMOPPRTX
approximated
AADEIOPPPRRT
appropriated
AADELNNPRSTT
transplanted
AADGIIILNNTV
invalidating
AADIILMNOQRU
quadrinomial
AADLMNNORUWY
laundrywoman
AAEEGGGINRTX
exaggerating
AAEEGGINNRTU
guaranteeing
AAEEGGINORTX
exaggeration
AAEEGINPRSTX
exasperating
AAEEGLMNORTV
galvanometer
AAEEHHIMPRTT
amphitheater
AAEEIIILLRTTV
alliterative
AAEEIINNRRTV
veterinarian
AAEELMMNRTTT
maltreatment
AAEFFQRRSTTU
quarterstaff
AAEFGGILLLNT
flagellating
AAEFILNQRRTU
quarterfinal
AAEGGINNPRRR
prearranging
AAEGHHIKNRST
earthshaking
AAEGHIILNRTX
exhilarating
AAEGHIMNPRST
metaphrasing
AAEGHIMNRRTW
heartwarming
AAEGHLMNRSTU
manslaughter
AAEGIILMNORT
ameliorating
AAEGIINNPPRT
appertaining
AAEGILLNNTTY
tangentially
AAEGIMNNOTTU
augmentation
AAEHIILNORTX
exhilaration

AAEHILMNPSSS
salesmanship
AAEIILLNORTT
alliteration
AAEIILMNOORT
amelioration
AAEIILMNPTUV
manipulative
AAEIILNOQTUZ
equalization
AAEIINQTTTUV
quantitative
AAEILLLMRTTU
multilateral
AAEILMNORSTV
malversation
AAEILNOPSSTY
passionately
AAEIMNOOOOPT
onomatopoeia
AAELNPRRSTUU
supernatural
AAFILMMNOORT
malformation
AAFILMMNORTY
inflammatory
AAGGIIILNPRZ
plagiarizing
AAGGIIINNRTT
ingratiating
AAGGIILLNNTV
gallivanting
AAGGIINNNOTZ
antagonizing
AAGGIINNRTUU
inaugurating
AAGHIIILNNNT
annihilating
AAGHIINPSTXY
asphyxiating
AAGIILMNNSST
assimilating
AAGIIILNPRTZ
partializing
AAGIILMNNPTU
manipulating
AAGIILNNRTUZ
naturalizing
AAGIINNNQRTU
quarantining
AAGIINNOORTZ
organization
AAGIINNORTUU
inauguration
AAHIIILNNNOT
annihilation
AAHIINOPSTXY
asphyxiation
AAHIKMMNPRSS
marksmanship
AAIIILMNOSST
assimilation
AAIIILMPRTTY
impartiality

AAIIIMMNOTXZ
maximization
AAIILLNNOSTT
installation
AAIILMNNOPTT
implantation
AAIILMNNOPTU
manipulation
AAIILMNOORTZ
moralization
AAIILNNORSTT
transitional
AAIILNOOPRTZ
polarization
AAIIMNOORTTZ
amortization
ABBCDEEIKLRR
blackberried
ABBCEEIKLRRS
blackberries
ABBEEEEILLNUV
unbelievable
ABBENNNOORST
nonabsorbent
ABBGHIILOPRY
bibliography
ABCCDEEHKORR
checkerboard
ABCCEEIILNSS
inaccessible
ABCDEEEJNSST
abjectedness
ABCDEEEILNORS
considerable
ABCDEGKNORRU
backgrounder
ABCDEHHLOOOR
bachelorhood
ABCDEILNORSY
considerably
ABCDEOOOORRRT
corroborated
ABCEEFIILLNY
beneficially
ABCEEIILLNPX
inexplicable
ABCEEIILNNNT
bicentennial
ABCEEIILNRTX
inextricable
ABCEENOPRRTU
protuberance
ABCEHIKNRSSS
brackishness
ABCEHKLRSSUW
swashbuckler
ABCEIILMNOPT
incompatible
ABCEIILNRTXY
inextricably
ABCEIINORSTT
obstetrician
ABCGIIKLLNST
blacklisting

ABCGIILLLOOY
biologically
ABCGIINNRRST
transcribing
ABCIILMNOPTY
incompatibly
ABCILLMNOOSY
monosyllabic
ABCILLNNOOSY
inconsolably
ABCIMNORSTUU
rambunctious
ABDDEEEELNNPU
undependable
ABDDEINORSTU
subordinated
ABDEEEERRRTV
reverberated
ABDEEFIIILNT
identifiable
ABDEEGIILNRT
deliberating
ABDEEIILNORT
deliberation
ABDEEIILMNOPR
imponderable
ABDEFFHLORSU
shuffleboard
ABDEGIIILNTT
debilitating
ABDEGIIKMNRS
disembarking
ABDEIIIILSST
disabilities
ABDEIIILMNSS
inadmissible
ABDEIILNPSTU
indisputable
ABDEIMORSTUX
ambidextrous
ABDFGINORRSU
surfboarding
ABDGHINOOSWX
shadowboxing
ABEEEGGILNRU
beleaguering
ABEEEHHIRRST
heathberries
ABEEEEHKORRSU
housebreaker
ABEEEILMNPRT
impenetrable
ABEEEINRRTTV
invertebrate
ABEEFFILNRSU
insufferable
ABEEFGLNORTU
unforgetable
ABEEGINPRSTT
bespattering
ABEEHILPRSST
preestablish
ABEEIIILLRST
liberalities

ABEEIILMNNRT
interminable
ABEEIIPRSSTT
baptisteries
ABEEILLNNRUV
invulnerable
ABEEILMNPRTY
impenetrably
ABEEILNOQSTU
questionable
ABEEINPRRSTY
presbyterian
ABEEKLMORRTU
troublemaker
ABEEKORRSSTT
breaststroke
ABEELNOSSSTU
absoluteness
ABEFFILNRSUY
insufferably
ABEFGILNORUV
unforgivable
ABEFILNOPRTU
unprofitable
ABEGHHKORRTU
breakthrough
ABEGHIILNSST
establishing
ABEGHINNRRTU
heartburning
ABEGIIILLNRZ
liberalizing
ABEGIILMNOTZ
metabolizing
ABEGIILNORTT
obliterating
ABEHIILNOPST
inhospitable
ABEIIILNOSTT
notabilities
ABEILMOSSTUY
abstemiously
ABGGIILNRRUZ
burglarizing
ABHIILNOPSTY
inhospitably
ABIIILLPSTUY
plausibility
ABIIILMNOOST
abolitionism
ABIIILMNOOTZ
mobilization
ABIIILNOOSTT
abolitionist
ACCCEEEEINQSU
acquiescence
ACCCEEIILSST
ecclesiastic
ACCCEEIILLTY
eclectically
ACCCEIMNRSTU
circumstance
ACCCIILNOOST
iconoclastic

ACCDDEEINRTU
unaccredited
ACCDEEILNOPY
encyclopedia
ACCDEEIINNNST
incandescent
ACCDEEIOPRRT
reciprocated
ACCDEFGIILNY
decalcifying
ACCDEGIINNNS
incandescing
ACCDEHILMOPS
accomplished
ACCDEIILNNOT
coincidental
ACCDEIMMNNOTU
communicated
ACCDEMNOSTUU
unaccustomed
ACCDFIIINOOT
codification
ACCDIINOORST
accordionist
ACCEEFGIIMNN
magnificence
ACCEEHIRRTTU
architecture
ACCEEHMNNORT
encroachment
ACCEEIIOPPSS
episcopacies
ACCEEIILLLRTY
electrically
ACCEEIMNNORS
necromancies
ACCEELNNOSTV
convalescent
ACCEEMMNORTTU
accouterment
ACCEFGIIINNS
significance
ACCEGIINRTUX
excruciating
ACCEGILNNOSV
convalescing
ACCEGINNORST
consecrating
ACCEHIILLNST
callisthenic
ACCEHIILNTTY
technicality
ACCEIILMMORT
microclimate
ACCEIINOPRSS
conspiracies
ACCEILLMNOOY
economically
ACCEINNOORST
consecration
ACCFGIINNOST
confiscating
ACCGHHIINTTT
chitchatting

ACCGIIILNNOT
conciliating
ACCGIILLOOOS
sociological
ACCGIILMNOPT
complicating
ACCHIILOPRTY
hypocritical
ACCHILOPPRTY
prophylactic
ACCHIMNOOPPT
phonocamptic
ACCHIOOPRRRT
chiropractor
ACCIIILNNOOT
conciliation
ACCIILOPRSUY
capriciously
ACDDEEEEFNORT
confederated
ACDDEEGHNRRU
undercharged
ACDDEEGKLNOW
acknowledged
ACDDHIMNORYY
hydrodynamic
ACDEEEFFNSST
affectedness
ACDEEEGILNRT
decelerating
ACDEEEHIRTTZ
catheterized
ACDEEEILNRTZ
decentralize
ACDEEEILNSST
delicatessen
ACDEEEINSSTT
necessitated
ACDEEFFLNTUY
unaffectedly
ACDEEFHHIKNR
handkerchief
ACDEEGHINNRT
interchanged
ACDEEGHLLNNU
unchallenged
ACDEEGIINPRT
depreciating
ACDEEGILSTTU
gesticulated
ACDEEHORRSTT
orchestrated
ACDEEIIINNRS
incendiaries
ACDEEIIILLMPY
epidemically
ACDEEIIPPRTT
precipitated
ACDEEIKLOOPS
kaleidoscope
ACDEEILMNPST
displacement
ACDEEINOPRTU
precautioned

ACDEEIPQRSSU
quadricepses
ACDEEIRSSTTU
resuscitated
ACDEELMNNOTT
malcontented
ACDEELMNOPTT
contemplated
ACDEEMMMOORT
commemorated
ACDEENNNRSTT
transcendent
ACDEFIILNNOT
confidential
ACDEFIILNSSU
unclassified
ACDEFIINNSTT
disinfectant
ACDEGIINOTTX
detoxicating
ACDEHIIPRTYY
hyperacidity
ACDEHILLMOTY
methodically
ACDEIIMMNNRT
incriminated
ACDEIIMNNRST
discriminate
ACDEIIINORST
dictionaries
ACDEIIINPPST
appendicitis
ACDEIILLNNTY
incidentally
ACDEIILLNSTT
scintillated
ACDEIILLOPRY
periodically
ACDEIILLOPSY
episodically
ACDEIIMNORTZ
romanticized
ACDEIINNORTT
indoctrinate
ACDEILLRSTYZ
crystallized
ACDEILNOOSST
disconsolate
ACDEINNNOOST
condensation
ACDEINOOPRRT
incorporated
ACDFIIIMNOOT
modification
ACDGGIINORSU
discouraging
ACDGIIINOSST
dissociating
ACDGIINNOORT
coordinating
ACDHHINOOPRY
hypochondria
ACDHIIOPRSTT
dictatorship

ACDIINORSSYY
idiosyncrasy
ACDINOOQRSTU
conquistador
ACEEEEGIKNPP
peacekeeping
ACEEEEHLPSST
steeplechase
ACEEEENPRRSV
perseverance
ACEEEFNNRRST
transference
ACEEEIILLSTZ
celestialize
ACEEEIMNNPRT
intemperance
ACEEEELNNSTVY
evanescently
ACEEEELNRSSSS
carelessness
ACEEEMNNNRRTT
entrancement
ACEEFFGINTTU
effectuating
ACEEFGLNRSSU
gracefulness
ACEEFIKNNNRS
frankincense
ACEEGIINRSTV
eviscerating
ACEEGINNPRRT
carpentering
ACEEGINPRRTU
recuperating
ACEEGLMNOORT
conglomerate
ACEEHHMOPRTY
chemotherapy
ACEEHIILNPST
encephalitis
ACEEHIINORTT
theoretician
ACEEHILLMRTY
hermetically
ACEEHILLSTTY
esthetically
ACEEHOPPRRRS
sharecropper
ACEEIIILPSST
specialities
ACEEIINORSSS
cessionaries
ACEEIJORRSTT
trajectories
ACEEILLLNTTU
intellectual
ACEEILLNRSUV
surveillance
ACEEIMMMNOTT
committeeman
ACEEIMMNORST
commentaries
ACEEINORSTVV
conservative

ACEEJKLLOTWY
yellowjacket
ACEELMNNORTU
nomenclature
ACEEMMNORSTU
commensurate
ACEEMNNNNOTU
announcement
ACEEMNNORRST
remonstrance
ACEEOOPRRTTT
protectorate
ACEFGIIILNTT
felicitating
ACEFIIILNOTT
felicitation
ACEFIIINORTV
verification
ACEFIILNOQTU
liquefaction
ACEFINOPRTTU
putrefaction
ACEFINOPSTTU
stupefaction
ACEGGGINNORT
congregating
ACEGGINNOORT
congregation
ACEGHIILLNYY
hygienically
ACEGHILNNNTY
enchantingly
ACEGHILOORST
archeologist
ACEGIIILLMTY
illegitimacy
ACEGIIILNPSZ
specializing
ACEGIIINNNRT
incinerating
ACEGIILNNRTZ
centralizing
ACEGIILNRSUZ
secularizing
ACEGIINOQTUV
equivocating
ACEGILLNOORU
neurological
ACEGILORSTTU
gesticulator
ACEGIMNNOPSS
encompassing
ACEGIMNNOPST
compensating
ACEGINORSSSU
graciousness
ACEHHILOPTTY
hypothetical
ACEHIINSSTTU
enthusiastic
ACEHIINTTTUY
authenticity
ACEHIIOPSSTT
sophisticate

ACEHIKNQSSSU
quackishness
ACEHILLRSTYY
hysterically
ACEHIMORSTTT
thermostatic
ACEHLMMNOOTW
commonwealth
ACEHLMOORSST
schoolmaster
ACEIIINNNORT
incineration
ACEIIIORSSTV
varicosities
ACEIILMMNRST
mercantilism
ACEIILMNRSTT
mercantilist
ACEIILMOPPSS
episcopalism
ACEIILMOPRST
semitropical
ACEIIMMORSSS
commissaries
ACEIINOOQTUV
equivocation
ACEIINOPRRTT
practitioner
ACEIIOPPRRTT
precipitator
ACEILLRRSTYZ
crystallizer
ACEIMMNNOOPST
compensation
ACEIMNSSTTUY
unsystematic
ACEINNOORSTV
conservation
conversation
ACEINOSSSTUU
cautiousness
ACEOPRRSSSTT
sportscaster
ACFIIILLNOTV
vilification
ACFIIINNOOTT
notification
ACFIIINOPRTU
purification
ACFIIMNNOORT
confirmation
ACGHHOPPRSYY
psychography
ACGHIILNNORT
chlorinating
ACGIIINNOTTX
intoxicating
ACGIIINNNORST
constraining
ACHHIILMNOPR
philharmonic
ACHHIIMNOPPS
championship
ACHIILLORSTY

historically
ACHIILNNOORT
chlorination
ACHIIMNOPRST
misanthropic
ACHIIPRSSTTY
psychiatrist
ACHILLNOPTYY
hypnotically
ACHIOPRSSSTY
astrophysics
ACIIIILNOTVZ
civilization
ACIIILMNPTUY
municipality
ACIIILNOOSTT
coalitionist
solicitation
ACIIILNPPRTY
principality
ACIIINNOOTTX
intoxication
ACIILNOPPSTU
supplication
ACILLMORSUUY
miraculously
ACILMMNNOOTT
noncommittal
ACILMNOOOPST
cosmopolitan
ACIORRRSSTTU
cirrostratus
ACLMOOPRSTUY
compulsatory
ADDEEEIMPRTT
premeditated
ADDEEEOPPRSV
eavesdropped
ADDEEFHLMORY
formaldehyde
ADDEEFHOORSW
foreshadowed
ADDEEIIMNRST
administered
ADDEEIIMNSST
disseminated
ADDEEMNORSTT
demonstrated
ADDEFIIILQSU
disqualified
ADDEFIIISSST
dissatisfied
ADDEGGIINRRS
disregarding
ADDEEIINOPPST
disappointed
ADDIIIILLNUVY
individually
ADEEEFFIINRT
differentiae
ADEEEFGIRRRT
refrigerated
ADEEEGGINNRT
degenerating

ADEEEHINSSSV
adhesiveness
ADEEEHINSTTZ
anesthetized
ADEEEIIMNRTT
intermediate
ADEEEIILLMMOS
mademoiselle
ADEEEIMNRTTX
exterminated
ADEEEELOPPRST
tradespeople
ADEEEEOPPRRSV
eavesdropper
ADEEFFIILNRT
differential
ADEEFOOPRRTW
waterproofed
ADEEGGHIRSTT
straightedge
ADEEGGIRRTTU
regurgitated
ADEEGHINNPPR
apprehending
ADEEGHINNRRT
heartrending
ADEEGHINRSTT
straightened
ADEEGHPRSTTU
stepdaughter
ADEEGIIINRSTT
disintegrate
ADEEGIINSTTV
investigated
ADEEGIKNNRRT
kindergarten
ADEEGILRRRSS
irregardless
ADEEGINORRTT
interrogated
ADEEGNRRSSST
transgressed
ADEEHIMRSSST
headmistress
ADEEHMNNOSSS
handsomeness
ADEEIILMMORZ
memorialized
ADEEIIMNRRTY
intermediary
ADEEIIMNRRRT
intermarried
ADEEIINPRSSS
dispensaries
ADEEILMMORTY
immoderately
ADEEILNOPRSZ
personalized
ADEEILNOPRTT
interpolated
ADEEIMNOPRST
impersonated
ADEEIMNRSTUV
misadventure

ADEEINNRRSTU
unrestrained
ADEFIIILQSSU
disqualifies
ADEFIIISSSST
dissatisfies
ADEFLLNRTUUY
fraudulently
ADEGHIILNNPR
philandering
ADEGHIINRRSS
hairdressing
ADEGIIILNNST
disentailing
ADEGIIJNOPRZ
jeopardizing
ADEGIILMNORZ
demoralizing
ADEGIINNOPRR
preordaining
ADEGILNNPRUY
underplaying
ADEGILNNRUUV
undervaluing
ADEGINNRSTTU
understating
ADEHHOPRRTYY
hydrotherapy
ADEHIILOPSTZ
hospitalized
ADEHIIMNORSS
disharmonies
ADEHINORTUUZ
unauthorized
ADEIILLOSSTY
disloyalties
ADEIILMMORTZ
immortalized
ADEIILNQRTUZ
tranquilized
ADEIIMNNNOOT
denomination
ADEIINORSSTT
dissertation
ADEIINOSTTUV
adventitious
ADEMNOORRSTT
demonstrator
ADFIILNOORTU
fluoridation
ADGGIIMNNORZ
gormandizing
ADGGILNNNOST
longstanding
ADGHIINNSTTW
withstanding
ADGIILLNNOTU
longitudinal
ADGIINOPPRSV
disapproving
ADIIIIMNNOTT
intimidation
AEEEFFILMNTY
effeminately

AEEEGGINNNRRT
regenerating
AEEEGIILNRST
generalities
AEEEGINNSSTV
negativeness
AEEEGLMNNNTT
entanglement
AEEEGMNNRSTT
estrangement
AEEEHILNNSSV
heavenliness
AEEEHINPPRSV
apprehensive
AEEEHLORSTUX
heterosexual
AEEEILMNPRTX
experimental
AEEEIPRRSTVV
preservative
AEEEKLRRSTTW
streetwalker
AEEEMNRSSSST
reassessment
AEEFGIORRRRT
refrigerator
AEEFHOOPRRTW
weatherproof
AEEFIINRRSTT
fraternities
AEEEGGHIINNRS
garnisheeing
AEEGGHILNPRT
telegraphing
AEEGGIILNNRZ
generalizing
AEEGGIILNNVZ
evangelizing
AEEGHHIOPRST
ethographies
AEEGHGNOPRRST
stenographer
AEEGIIILLLST
illegalities
AEEGIIILLMTT
illegitimate
AEEGIIILLMTTY
legitimately
AEEGIIINNNRTT
entertaining
AEEGIIINNRTVW
interweaving
AEEGIJNNRTUV
rejuvenating
AEEGIKLLNPSW
sleepwalking
AEEGIMNNOSTT
segmentation
AEEGIMNNRRTU
remunerating
AEEGINPPRRTT
perpetrating
AEEGINPPRTTU
perpetuating

AEEGLMNNORTV
governmental
AEEHHILNSTTU
unhealthiest
AEEHILLPPRRY
peripherally
AEEHILSTUVXY
exhaustively
AEEHIMMOPRTZ
metamorphize
AEEHINNOPPRS
apprehension
AEEHLMNRSSSS
harmlessness
AEEHLNOPRTUY
polyurethane
AEEHNNORRSTT
northeastern
AEEIIILNQSTU
inequalities
AEEIIKLMNPRS
marlinespike
AEEIILLMRSTU
mitrailleuse
AEEIILMPRTVY
imperatively
AEEIILNRSTTU
neutralities
AEEIINNOPRSS
pensionaries
AEEIINNORTTZ
eternization
AEEIINNPRTTY
penitentiary
AEEIIPRTTUVV
vituperative
AEEIILNRRSTT
interstellar
AEEILMNNNRSS
mannerliness
AEEILNNNOSST
nonessential
AEEIMMNRSTTT
mistreatment
AEEINNOPRSTT
presentation
AEELLLMNOTVY
malevolently
AEELLMNPPSTU
supplemental
AEELMNPRRSTU
premenstrual
AEFFHILNSSTU
faithfulness
AEFGGGILNOPR
leapfrogging
AEFGGHINORRT
forgathering
AEFGHHOOORRTU
thoroughfare
AEFGHHORTTTU
afterthought
AEFGIILRTUVY
figuratively

AEFGIINNRRTZ
fraternizing
AEFGILLNORST
forestalling
AEFGINNRRRST
transferring
AEFHOOPRRSTT
shatterproof
AEFIIILMNSST
semifinalist
AEFILNOOPRSS
professional
AEFIMNNORRST
frontiersman
AEGGHILNRSTU
slaughtering
AEGGHLNOOSTT
snaggletooth
AEGGIIILMNTT
legitimating
AEGGIIILLNNTZ
gelatinizing
AEGGIIMNNPRT
impregnating
AEGGIINNORRZ
reorganizing
AEGHHIINSTWW
whitewashing
AEGHHIPRSUWY
superhighway
AEGHHOOPPRRT
photographer
AEGHIILNSTTY
hesitatingly
AEGHIINNSTTU
unhesitating
AEGHIMNORSUW
housewarming
AEGHINRRSSTT
heartstrings
AEGHLMNNOORS
longshoreman
AEGHOOPRRTUV
photogravure
AEGIIILMNNRZ
mineralizing
AEGIIILNRTVZ
revitalizing
AEGIILMNNRST
streamlining
AEGIILMNORST
mineralogist
AEGIILNNRTUZ
neutralizing
AEGIILNNSSUZ
sensualizing
AEGIILNPRSTT
earsplitting
AEGIILRRRTUY
irregularity
AEGIIMNNOPTT
pigmentation
AEGIINNNRSTT
intransigent

AEGIINNOPTTT
potentiating
AEGIINPRTTUV
vituperating
AEGIMNNRSTTU
menstruating
AEGINNNRRSSTV
transversing
AEGLLNOOOOPTY
paleontology
AEGNORRRSSST
transgressor
AEHHILNOPPRT
philanthrope
AEHHIMNOPRSS
horsemanship
AEHHOOPRRSST
sharpshooter
AEHIIIMNNSTU
inhumanities
AEHIMNNOSSTT
astonishment
AEHIOPRRSTWY
praiseworthy
AEIIIILMRSST
similarities
AEIIIILRSTTV
trivialities
AEIIILMMORST
immoralities
AEIIIMNNNOST
insemination
AEIIIMNORSSS
missionaries
AEIIINNRSTTV
intransitive
AEIIILRSTTUV
illustrative
AEIIMMNNNOORT
renomination
AEIIMNNOSSST
sensationism
AEIINOPPRRST
perspiration
AEIINOPRTTUV
vituperation
AEILLNORRTTY
torrentially
AEILMNNRSTTU
instrumental
AEILMNOOPRTT
metropolitan
AEILMNOSSTUU
simultaneous
AEILNOORTUVY
evolutionary
AEIMNNORSTTU
menstruation
AEIMNOOPRRST
impersonator
AEINOOSSTTTU
ostentatious
AELLMMNNOTUY
monumentally

AFGIIILNNRT
infiltrating
AFGIILNSSTYY
satisfyingly
AFGIMNNNORRST
transforming
AFIIILNNORTT
infiltration
AFIILMORSTUU
multifarious
AFIINOPRSSTU
passionfruit
AGGHIIKNNSTV
thanksgiving
AGGHIMNNOOPR
monographing
AGGHLOPPRTYY
glyptography
AGGIIIMNSTTZ
stigmatizing
AGGIIINNORTV
invigorating
AGHLNOOOPRTY
anthropology
AGIIILLMNNTU
illuminating
AGIIIMNNOPSS
impassioning
AGIIINNOPRTT
partitioning
AGIIINOPPRTT
propitiating
AGIILLNRSTTU
illustrating
AGIILNOORSUV
vainglorious
AGIIMNNRSTTT
transmitting
AGIINNOOPPRT
apportioning
AGINNOPRRSTT
transporting
AHHIILMOPSTT
ophthalmitis
AHHILNOPPRTY
philanthropy
AHILLNOORTYZ
horizontally
AHILMNOORSUY
harmoniously
AHILNOPPRSTY
psilanthropy
AHIMOOPPPSTU
hippopotamus
AIIIIMMNNOTZ
minimization
AIIILLMNNOTU
illumination
AIIILLNNOSTT
instillation
AIIILMPRSSTU
spiritualism
AIIILPRSSTTU
spiritualist

AIIILPRSTTUY
spirituality
AIIIMNNORSTT
ministration
AIILLNORSTTU
illustration
AIILMNNORTTU
malnutrition
AIIMNNORSSST
transmission
AIIMNOOPRSSU
parsimonious
BCCCEIIMRRSU
circumscribe
BCCEEEELNOOSS
obsolescence
BCCEEIIMNNSU
incumbencies
BCCEHORSTTTU
butterscotch
BCCINOOSSSUU
subconscious
BCDEEINPRRSU
unprescribed
BCEEEEGHRRSU
cheeseburger
BCEEEEGILLNR
belligerence
BCEEEGILLNRY
belligerency
BCEEEHIKORRS
chokeberries
BCEEEEINRSSUV
subservience
BCEEIMMOSTTU
subcommittee
BCEGHIILNTWY
bewitchingly
BCEGIIILNORR
incorrigible
BCEGILMNNOUY
unbecomingly
BCEHMOORSSSV
schussboomer
BCEIIJSTTUVY
subjectivity
BCEILORSSTUU
tuberculosis
BCGIILMOOORY
microbiology
BCGIINNORTTU
contributing
BCIINNOORTTU
contribution
BCIINOPRSSTU
subscription
BDDEGIIMNOSY
disembodying
BDDFGIILLNNO
blindfolding
BDEEEEILRRRS
elderberries
BDEEEFIILNNS
indefensible**

BDEEEILMNRTW
bewilderment
BDEEFIILNNSY
indefensibly
BDEEFIILRSTU
filibustered
BDEEGGGIJRTTU
jitterbugged
BDEEGIIILNST
indigestible
BDEEGIIILNSV
disbelieving
BDEEGIIMMNRS
dismembering
BDEEGIIMNORR
embroidering
BDEEIIRRSTTU
redistribute
BDEGHHINOOOR
neighborhood
BDEGHHOORRTU
thoroughbred
BDEGIIILMNOZ
demobilizing
BDEGIIILLNNRU
underbilling
BDEGILLNOOTT
bloodletting
BDGIIINRSTTU
distributing
BDHILOORSTTY
bloodthirsty
BDIIINORSTTU
distribution
BEEEGIOORRSS
gooseberries
BEEEIILRRRSV
irreversible
BEEEEILNNSSSS
sensibleness
BEEEIPRRSSTY
presbyteries
BEEEELMNPTUZZ
bepuzzlement
BEEFIILRRSTU
filibusterer
BEEGHIILLMNS
embellishing
BEEGIIILLLNT
intelligible
BEEIIILRRSST
irresistible
BEEIIKLNSSSU
businesslike
BEELNNOSSSUU
nebulousness
BEEOOPRRSSTU
obstreperous
BEFGHIINRRSU
refurbishing
BEFILLNSSSSU
blissfulness
BEGHILNNORUY
unneighborly

BEIIILRRSSTY
irresistibly
BEILOORSSTUY
boisterously
BGIILMNNOOSW
snowmobiling
BGHILLNNSUUY
unblushingly
BGIIIILMMNOZ
immobilizing
BGIINSSTTTUU
substituting
BIILOQSTUUUY
ubiquitously
BIINOSSTTTUU
substitution
CCCDEEEILNOPY
encyclopedic
CCCEEIINRTTY
eccentricity
CCCIIIMNORSU
circumcision
CCDDEEINNOST
disconnected
CCDDEEINORST
disconcerted
CCDEEEFIIINS
deficiencies
CCDEEEINNOPRV
preconceived
CCDEEEELORTTU
electrocuted
CCDEEIMNRTUV
circumvented
CCDEIORRSSSS
crisscrossed
CCDHHILOORRY
hydrochloric
CCDIINOTTUVY
conductivity
CCEEEEIILLNSX
excellencies
CCEEEFFIIINS
efficiencies
CCEEEFINOORV
foreconceive
CCEEEFLNORSU
fluorescence
CCEEEIMNNOPT
incompetence
CCEEFINNOORT
confectioner
CCEEGILLNORT
recollecting
CCEEHIILNORT
heliocentric
CCEEILLLOTVY
collectively
CCEEIINNNORTT
interconnect
CCEEOOPPRSST
spectroscope
CCEGIJNNORTU
conjecturing

CCEGINOPPRUY
preoccupying
CCEHHIILMOOR
heliochromic
CCEHINOPRSTY
pyrotechnics
CCEIILLMOSTV
collectivism
CCEIILNNOSUV
inconclusive
CCEILLOOOPSS
oscilloscope
CCEINOOPRSSU
preconscious
CCGIINNOPRST
conscripting
CCGIINNORSTT
constricting
CCGINNORSTTU
constructing
CCIINNOOPRST
conscription
CCILMORRSUUU
cirrocumulus
CDDEEEEINNNP
independence
CDDEEEINORRS
reconsidered
CDDEEIIRRSTT
redistricted
CDDEEIJNPRUU
unprejudiced
CDDEEINNORSU
unconsidered
CDDEEINNOSTT
discontented
CDDEEINORSUV
undiscovered
CDDEEKNORSTU
understocked
CDDEELLNOORT
decontrolled
CDDEENOOPRRS
corresponded
CDDEFIMOORST
discomforted
CDDEGIIINRST
discrediting
CDEEEHNRSSTW
wretchedness
CDEEELMMNOPT
complemented
CDEEELNPTUXY
unexpectedly
CDEEGIILNQSU
deliquescing
CDEEGIMMNNOR
recommending
CDEEGINNORUZ
unrecognized
CDEEHLNORSTU
underclothes
CDEEHORSTTTU
outstretched

CDEEIILNRSTY
indiscreetly
CDEEIMOPRTUZ
computerized
CDEENNRRRTUU
undercurrent
CDEFFIIILSTU
difficulties
CDEFGIIINNST
disinfecting
CDEGIIINNRTT
interdicting
CDEGINNRTTUU
undercutting
CDEHIIKNORTY
hydrokinetic
CDEHINNORSYZ
synchronized
CDEIIINNORST
indiscretion
CDEIIINNORTT
interdiction
CDEIINOOPRST
periodontics
CDEIMNORSSTU
misconstrued
CDEINCOPRRTU
reproduction
CDEINOPRTUUV
unproductive
CDEIOORSSTUU
discourteous
CDELLNNOORTU
uncontrolled
CDFGIIMMNOST
discomfiting
CDFHILOORRUY
hydrofluoric
CDGIIIILNNPS
disciplining
CDGIIINNNOOT
conditioning
CDIIIJNORSTU
jurisdiction
CDIINNOORTTU
introduction
CEEEEFFNRSTV
effervescent
CEEEEFINNRRT
interference
CEEEEIINNPRX
inexperience
CEEEFFLNORST
efflorescent
CEEEGIILLNNT
intelligence
CEEEGIINNPRX
experiencing
CEEEIIMNNPRT
impertinence
CEEEIIPRRSTV
irrespective
CEEEIMMMNOTT
committeemen

CEEEINNQSSTU
quintessence
CEEEINRRRSTW
screenwriter
CEEFFGILNORS
efflorescing
CEEFGGILLNNTU
genuflecting
CEEFGIILNRTY
electrifying
CEEFGILNNOTU
genuflection
CEEFIIMNOPRT
imperfection
CEEFIINOPRST
frontispiece
CEEGIIJNNRTT
interjecting
CEEGIIINNPRTT
intercepting
CEEGIIINNRSTT
intersecting
CEEGINNNNORTU
encountering
CEEGINRRRSTU
resurrecting
CEEHHLOORSST
clotheshorse
CEEHHOOPPRSS
phosphoresce
CEEHIIKNPRTY
hyperkinetic
CEEHIKMNOSSS
homesickness
CEEHILNNORTY
incoherently
CEEHINOOPRST
stereophonic
CEEHMORSTTYY
hysterectomy
CEEIIINRSSTU
insecurities
CEEIIJNNORTT
interjection
CEEIILMOPSTX
complexities
CEEIIMNOPPRT
imperception
CEEIIMOPRSSU
semiprecious
CEEIIMORRSTU
meretricious
CEEIINNNNOTV
inconvenient
CEEIINNORSTT
intersection
CEEIINOPRSTT
receptionist
CEEIIOPPRRSTV
prescriptive
CEEIKLMNPPRU
pumpernickel
CEEIILLMNOPTY
incompletely

CEEIILLORSSTY
electrolysis
CEEILNOOPRSS
necropolises
CEEIINNPRTUUV
venipuncture
CEEIINOPRSSTU
counterspies
CEEINORRRSTU
resurrection
CEEINORSTTTU
reconstitute
CEEIOOPRRSTT
protectories
CEFFIIINNSTU
insufficient
CEFIILMNNTUY
munificently
CEFIILNORSST
frictionless
CEFILNNOSSTU
functionless
CEFILOORSUVY
vociferously
CEGHHIILOPRY
hieroglyphic
CEGHIIKNPRSW
shipwrecking
CEGHILOOPSYZ
psychologize
CEGIIKLNNORT
interlocking
CEGIINNOOPRT
precognition
CEGINNPSSTUU
unsuspecting
CEHIILNQSSSU
cliquishness
CEHIIMNOOSTT
monotheistic
CEHILORRTTUU
horticulture
CEIIILOPRSTV
proclivities
CEIILOPRSSUU
supercilious
CEIIMMNOORSS
commissioner
CEIINNNOSSTT
inconsistent
CEIINNORRSTU
insurrection
CEIINOPPRRST
prescription
CEIIPRRRSTTW
scriptwriter
CEIMNNOOPRSU
mispronounce
CEINNOOPRTTU
counterpoint
CGHILOOPSSTY
psychologist
CGHINOOOOPPTY
photocopying

CGIIIILNOPTZ
politicizing
CGIIINNRSTUZ
scrutinizing
CGIIMMNOOPRS
compromising
CIIILLMPTTUY
multiplicity
CIILMNOOOPST
monopolistic
CIINNOOSTTTU
constitution
CIINOPSSSUUU
unsuspicious
CLNOPRSSUUUU
unscrupulous
DDDEEINRSTUU
understudied
DDEEEFGINNRU
underfeeding
DDEEELNRSUVY
undeservedly
DDEEHIIINRST
disinherited
DDEEIOPSSSSS
dispossessed
DDEHILNNOOPR
philodendron
DEEEEIMNPRRT
predetermine
DEEEEIMNPRTX
experimented
DEEEGHINNPRR
reprehending
DEEEGILNOPRV
redeveloping
DEEEIMOPRTXZ
extemporized
DEEEIMPRRTTT
pretermitted
DEEEINNRSTTU
uninterested
DEEFGIIINPRS
presignified
DEEFIIIILNST
infidelities
DEEFIIILNNTY
indefinitely
DEEGGIINPRST
predigesting
DEEGIILMNNRT
intermingled
DEEGIILMOOPY
epidemiology
DEEGIIMNPRST
distempering
DEEGIILLNNRSU
underselling
DEEGINNOPRRV
provendering
DEEGINNOPRSV
overspending

DEEGINNRRRSU
surrendering
DEEHHIOPPRSW
horsewhipped
DEEHIILNQRSU
relinquished
DEEHIIMOPRSV
impoverished
DEEIIILLRSST
distilleries
DEEILOPRSTYZ
proselytized
DEEINNRRTTUW
underwritten
DEELMNORSTUY
tremendously
DEFGIIIMNNNY
indemnifying
DEFGIIINRSVY
diversifying
DEGHILMOOTYZ
mythologized
DEGIIIILNPPSS
sideslipping
DEGIIIINNORST
disorienting
DEGIINNNNPRU
underpinning
DEGIINNRRTUW
underwriting
DEGIINOPPRSS
predisposing
DEHLLOORRTWY
otherworldly
DEHLNORSTUUY
thunderously
DEHMNORRSTTU
thunderstorm
DFGGIIINNNUY
undignifying
DGGIILNNRSTU
disgruntling
EEEEHLNRRSTW
sternwheeler
EEEEHLNRSSTV
nevertheless
EEEENNPRRRTU
entrepreneur
EEEFFINORRST
effronteries
EEEGHIKNOPSU
housekeeping
EEEGHILRTTWW
welterweight
EEEGIINORSST
generosities
EEEGINNPRRST
representing
EEEGINNQRSSTU
sequestering
EEEEHLLNOPTYY
polyethylene
EEEEHLLNPSSSS
helplessness

EEEEHLNOPSSSS
hopelessness
EEEHMNNNORTT
enthronement
EEEIILPPRSTX
perplexities
EEEIIPPRSTTU
perpetuities
EEEIIPQRRSTU
prerequisite
EEEIMNPRRSST
misrepresent
EEELMNNOOSSS
lonesomeness
EEFGILMNPXY
exemplifying
EEFGIKNNOORT
foretokening
EEFILNNQRTUY
infrequently
EEFIMNNORRST
frontiersmen
EEFLLNNTUUVY
uneventfully
EEGGHIILNNNT
enlightening
EEGHIILNNPRS
replenishing
EEGHIINSSTUX
extinguishes
EEGHILMNORVW
overwhelming
EEGHLMNNOORS
longshoremen
EEGIIINNRTVW
interviewing
EEGIILMMNNPT
implementing
EEGIINNPRRST
enterprising
EEGIINNPRRTT
interpreting
EEGIINNPRSTZ
serpentizing
EEGIINNRSTWZ
westernizing
EEGILMOOPSTY
epistemology
EEGILNNORTUV
volunteering
EEGINOOPRRVW
overpowering
EEGINOPRSSSS
repossessing
EEGNORRRSUUY
neurosurgery
EEHIIKNPRSSY
hyperkinesis
EEHIILNQRSSU
relinquishes
EEHILMNORSST
motherliness
EEHMNOORSTUY
heteronymous

EEHNNORRSTTW
northwestern
EEIIINRSSTUV
universities
EEIILMPRSSVY
impressively
EEIIMNNRTTTT
intermittent
EEIIMNPRRSTT
misinterpret
EEIINNNORRTV
intervention
EEIINOPPRSST
propensities
EEIIOOPRRSST
repositories
EEIIOPPRRSST
prosperities
EEILNOQSSSTU
questionless
EEILNPRSSTTY
persistently
EEILOPPRSSVY
oppressively
EELMMNNOPTUY
unemployment
EENNOSSSSSUU
sensuousness
EEOOPPRRSSTU
preposterous
EFFGIINOOPRR
fireproofing
EFFILNRSSTUU
fruitfulness
EFGGGIINOPTT
pettifogging
EFGGIIINNORZ
foreignizing
EFGIIINNNSTY
intensifying
EFGIINNOPRSY
personifying
EFHLNOSSTUUY
youthfulness
EFIILMOPRSVY
oversimplify
EGGHIILNOOTZ
theologizing

EGGHIIMNNOOZ
homogenizing
EGGIILMNNORZ
mongrelizing
EGGIMNOOPRSS
gossipmonger
EGHIILNPRSWY
whisperingly
EGHIILPRSSTT
sprightliest
EGHIINNSSTYZ
synthesizing
EGHIINNSTTYZ
synthetizing
EGHILNOPRSTU
upholstering
EGHIMNNNOOOY
honeymooning
EGHINOOORSTV
overshooting
EGHINORSTTTW
ghostwritten
EGIIILNOPSTZ
epistolizing
EGIIINNNRTTW
intertwining
EGIINNNORTVY
inventorying
EGIINNPRRTTU
interrupting
EGILLNORSTTY
storytelling
EGIMNOOORRTY
trigonometry
EGINOPPRRSSU
presupposing
EHIILMOOPRST
heliotropism
EHMNOORSSTTU
southernmost
EIIIMNNORSST
intermission
EIILMOPRSUVY
imperviously
EIINNOPRRTTU
interruption
EIINOPRSSTTU
superstition

EIMOPRSSSSTT
postmistress
EIOPRRRSSTTW
sportswriter
EMOPPRSSTUUU
presumptuous
FGHHLLOTTUUY
thoughtfully
FGIIIMMNNORS
misinforming
FHILLOPRSUWY
worshipfully
FIILMMORTTUY
multiformity
GGIIILLNNOTU
guillotining
GGIILLNNOTTUZ
gluttonizing
GHIIKLNNNTUY
unthinkingly
GHILMOOOPRST
morphologist
GIIINMNOOPRSV
provisioning
GIILMNNOOOPZ
monopolizing
GIINNOOPPRTU
pourpointing
GIINOPPRSTTU
outstripping
GIINOPRSTTTU
prostituting
HIILLOOPPRWW
whippoorwill
HIMOOOPPRSTT
phototropism
IIINNORSTTTU
nutritionist
IINOOPPRSTUU
unpropitious
IINOOPRSTTTU
prostitution
ILLMNOOSUUVY
voluminously
LMNNOOOOOSTUY
monotonously